Microsoft®
Training &
Certification

D1309621

2273A: Managing and Maintaining a Microsoft® Windows Server™ 2003 Environment

Released: 04/2003

Microsoft®

Course Number: 2273A
Part Number: X10-00817
Released: 04/2003

END-USER LICENSE AGREEMENT FOR MICROSOFT OFFICIAL CURRICULUM COURSEWARE –STUDENT EDITION

PLEASE READ THIS END-USER LICENSE AGREEMENT ("EULA") CAREFULLY. BY USING THE MATERIALS AND/OR USING OR INSTALLING THE SOFTWARE THAT ACCOMPANIES THIS EULA (COLLECTIVELY, THE "LICENSED CONTENT"), YOU AGREE TO THE TERMS OF THIS EULA. IF YOU DO NOT AGREE, DO NOT USE THE LICENSED CONTENT.

1. **GENERAL.** This EULA is a legal agreement between you (either an individual or a single entity) and Microsoft Corporation ("Microsoft"). This EULA governs the Licensed Content, which includes computer software (including online and electronic documentation), training materials, and any other associated media and printed materials. This EULA applies to updates, supplements, add-on components, and Internet-based services components of the Licensed Content that Microsoft may provide or make available to you unless Microsoft provides other terms with the update, supplement, add-on component, or Internet-based services component. Microsoft reserves the right to discontinue any Internet-based services provided to you or made available to you through the use of the Licensed Content. This EULA also governs any product support services relating to the Licensed Content except as may be included in another agreement between you and Microsoft. An amendment or addendum to this EULA may accompany the Licensed Content.

2. **GENERAL GRANT OF LICENSE.** Microsoft grants you the following rights, conditioned on your compliance with all the terms and conditions of this EULA. Microsoft grants you a limited, non-exclusive, royalty-free license to install and use the Licensed Content solely in conjunction with your participation as a student in an Authorized Training Session (as defined below). You may install and use one copy of the software on a single computer, device, workstation, terminal, or other digital electronic or analog device ("Device"). You may make a second copy of the software and install it on a portable Device for the exclusive use of the person who is the primary user of the first copy of the software. A license for the software may not be shared for use by multiple end users. An "Authorized Training Session" means a training session conducted at a Microsoft Certified Technical Education Center, an IT Academy, via a Microsoft Certified Partner, or such other entity as Microsoft may designate from time to time in writing, by a Microsoft Certified Trainer (for more information on these entities, please visit www.microsoft.com). WITHOUT LIMITING THE FOREGOING, COPYING OR REPRODUCTION OF THE LICENSED CONTENT TO ANY SERVER OR LOCATION FOR FURTHER REPRODUCTION OR REDISTRIBUTION IS EXPRESSLY PROHIBITED.

3. **DESCRIPTION OF OTHER RIGHTS AND LICENSE LIMITATIONS**

   3.1 *Use of Documentation and Printed Training Materials.*

   3.1.1 The documents and related graphics included in the Licensed Content may include technical inaccuracies or typographical errors. Changes are periodically made to the content. Microsoft may make improvements and/or changes in any of the components of the Licensed Content at any time without notice. The names of companies, products, people, characters and/or data mentioned in the Licensed Content may be fictitious and are in no way intended to represent any real individual, company, product or event, unless otherwise noted.

   3.1.2 Microsoft grants you the right to reproduce portions of documents (such as student workbooks, white papers, press releases, datasheets and FAQs) (the "Documents") provided with the Licensed Content. You may not print any book (either electronic or print version) in its entirety. If you choose to reproduce Documents, you agree that: (a) use of such printed Documents will be solely in conjunction with your personal training use; (b) the Documents will not republished or posted on any network computer or broadcast in any media; (c) any reproduction will include either the Document's original copyright notice or a copyright notice to Microsoft's benefit substantially in the format provided below; and (d) to comply with all terms and conditions of this EULA. In addition, no modifications may made to any Document.

   Form of Notice:

   © 2003. Reprinted with permission by Microsoft Corporation. All rights reserved.

   Microsoft and Windows are either registered trademarks or trademarks of Microsoft Corporation in the US and/or other countries. Other product and company names mentioned herein may be the trademarks of their respective owners.

   3.2 *Use of Media Elements.* The Licensed Content may include certain photographs, clip art, animations, sounds, music, and video clips (together "Media Elements"). You may not modify these Media Elements.

   3.3 *Use of Sample Code.* In the event that the Licensed Content includes sample code in source or object format ("Sample Code"), Microsoft grants you a limited, non-exclusive, royalty-free license to use, copy and modify the Sample Code; if you elect to exercise the foregoing rights, you agree to comply with all other terms and conditions of this EULA, including without limitation Sections 3.4, 3.5, and 6.

   3.4 *Permitted Modifications.* In the event that you exercise any rights provided under this EULA to create modifications of the Licensed Content, you agree that any such modifications: (a) will not be used for providing training where a fee is charged in public or private classes; (b) indemnify, hold harmless, and defend Microsoft from and against any claims or lawsuits, including attorneys' fees, which arise from or result from your use of any modified version of the Licensed Content; and (c) not to transfer or assign any rights to any modified version of the Licensed Content to any third party without the express written permission of Microsoft.

3.5   *Reproduction/Redistribution Licensed Content.* Except as expressly provided in this EULA, you may not reproduce or distribute the Licensed Content or any portion thereof (including any permitted modifications) to any third parties without the express written permission of Microsoft.

4.   **RESERVATION OF RIGHTS AND OWNERSHIP.** Microsoft reserves all rights not expressly granted to you in this EULA. The Licensed Content is protected by copyright and other intellectual property laws and treaties. Microsoft or its suppliers own the title, copyright, and other intellectual property rights in the Licensed Content. You may not remove or obscure any copyright, trademark or patent notices that appear on the Licensed Content, or any components thereof, as delivered to you. **The Licensed Content is licensed, not sold.**

5.   **LIMITATIONS ON REVERSE ENGINEERING, DECOMPILATION, AND DISASSEMBLY.** You may not reverse engineer, decompile, or disassemble the Software or Media Elements, except and only to the extent that such activity is expressly permitted by applicable law notwithstanding this limitation.

6.   **LIMITATIONS ON SALE, RENTAL, ETC. AND CERTAIN ASSIGNMENTS.** You may not provide commercial hosting services with, sell, rent, lease, lend, sublicense, or assign copies of the Licensed Content, or any portion thereof (including any permitted modifications thereof) on a stand-alone basis or as part of any collection, product or service.

7.   **CONSENT TO USE OF DATA.** You agree that Microsoft and its affiliates may collect and use technical information gathered as part of the product support services provided to you, if any, related to the Licensed Content. Microsoft may use this information solely to improve our products or to provide customized services or technologies to you and will not disclose this information in a form that personally identifies you.

8.   **LINKS TO THIRD PARTY SITES.** You may link to third party sites through the use of the Licensed Content. The third party sites are not under the control of Microsoft, and Microsoft is not responsible for the contents of any third party sites, any links contained in third party sites, or any changes or updates to third party sites. Microsoft is not responsible for webcasting or any other form of transmission received from any third party sites. Microsoft is providing these links to third party sites to you only as a convenience, and the inclusion of any link does not imply an endorsement by Microsoft of the third party site.

9.   **ADDITIONAL LICENSED CONTENT/SERVICES.** This EULA applies to updates, supplements, add-on components, or Internet-based services components, of the Licensed Content that Microsoft may provide to you or make available to you after the date you obtain your initial copy of the Licensed Content, unless we provide other terms along with the update, supplement, add-on component, or Internet-based services component. Microsoft reserves the right to discontinue any Internet-based services provided to you or made available to you through the use of the Licensed Content.

10.   **U.S. GOVERNMENT LICENSE RIGHTS**. All software provided to the U.S. Government pursuant to solicitations issued on or after December 1, 1995 is provided with the commercial license rights and restrictions described elsewhere herein. All software provided to the U.S. Government pursuant to solicitations issued prior to December 1, 1995 is provided with "Restricted Rights" as provided for in FAR, 48 CFR 52.227-14 (JUNE 1987) or DFAR, 48 CFR 252.227-7013 (OCT 1988), as applicable.

11.   **EXPORT RESTRICTIONS**. You acknowledge that the Licensed Content is subject to U.S. export jurisdiction. You agree to comply with all applicable international and national laws that apply to the Licensed Content, including the U.S. Export Administration Regulations, as well as end-user, end-use, and destination restrictions issued by U.S. and other governments. For additional information see <http://www.microsoft.com/exporting/>.

12.   **TRANSFER.** The initial user of the Licensed Content may make a one-time permanent transfer of this EULA and Licensed Content to another end user, provided the initial user retains no copies of the Licensed Content. The transfer may not be an indirect transfer, such as a consignment. Prior to the transfer, the end user receiving the Licensed Content must agree to all the EULA terms.

13.   **"NOT FOR RESALE" LICENSED CONTENT.** Licensed Content identified as "Not For Resale" or "NFR," may not be sold or otherwise transferred for value, or used for any purpose other than demonstration, test or evaluation.

14.   **TERMINATION.** Without prejudice to any other rights, Microsoft may terminate this EULA if you fail to comply with the terms and conditions of this EULA. In such event, you must destroy all copies of the Licensed Content and all of its component parts.

15.   <u>**DISCLAIMER OF WARRANTIES.**</u> **TO THE MAXIMUM EXTENT PERMITTED BY APPLICABLE LAW, MICROSOFT AND ITS SUPPLIERS PROVIDE THE LICENSED CONTENT AND SUPPORT SERVICES (IF ANY)** *AS IS AND WITH ALL FAULTS,* **AND MICROSOFT AND ITS SUPPLIERS HEREBY DISCLAIM ALL OTHER WARRANTIES AND CONDITIONS, WHETHER EXPRESS, IMPLIED OR STATUTORY, INCLUDING, BUT NOT LIMITED TO, ANY (IF ANY) IMPLIED WARRANTIES, DUTIES OR CONDITIONS OF MERCHANTABILITY, OF FITNESS FOR A PARTICULAR PURPOSE, OF RELIABILITY OR AVAILABILITY, OF ACCURACY OR COMPLETENESS OF RESPONSES, OF RESULTS, OF WORKMANLIKE EFFORT, OF LACK OF VIRUSES, AND OF LACK OF NEGLIGENCE, ALL WITH REGARD TO THE LICENSED CONTENT, AND THE PROVISION OF OR FAILURE TO PROVIDE SUPPORT OR OTHER SERVICES, INFORMATION, SOFTWARE, AND RELATED CONTENT THROUGH THE LICENSED CONTENT, OR OTHERWISE ARISING OUT OF THE USE OF THE LICENSED CONTENT. ALSO, THERE IS NO WARRANTY OR CONDITION OF TITLE, QUIET ENJOYMENT, QUIET POSSESSION, CORRESPONDENCE TO DESCRIPTION OR NON-INFRINGEMENT WITH REGARD TO THE LICENSED CONTENT. THE ENTIRE RISK AS TO THE QUALITY, OR ARISING OUT OF THE USE OR PERFORMANCE OF THE LICENSED CONTENT, AND ANY SUPPORT SERVICES, REMAINS WITH YOU.**

16.   <u>**EXCLUSION OF INCIDENTAL, CONSEQUENTIAL AND CERTAIN OTHER DAMAGES.**</u> **TO THE MAXIMUM EXTENT PERMITTED BY APPLICABLE LAW, IN NO EVENT SHALL MICROSOFT OR ITS SUPPLIERS BE LIABLE FOR ANY SPECIAL, INCIDENTAL, PUNITIVE, INDIRECT, OR CONSEQUENTIAL DAMAGES WHATSOEVER (INCLUDING, BUT NOT**

LIMITED TO, DAMAGES FOR LOSS OF PROFITS OR CONFIDENTIAL OR OTHER INFORMATION, FOR BUSINESS INTERRUPTION, FOR PERSONAL INJURY, FOR LOSS OF PRIVACY, FOR FAILURE TO MEET ANY DUTY INCLUDING OF GOOD FAITH OR OF REASONABLE CARE, FOR NEGLIGENCE, AND FOR ANY OTHER PECUNIARY OR OTHER LOSS WHATSOEVER) ARISING OUT OF OR IN ANY WAY RELATED TO THE USE OF OR INABILITY TO USE THE LICENSED CONTENT, THE PROVISION OF OR FAILURE TO PROVIDE SUPPORT OR OTHER SERVICES, INFORMATION, SOFTWARE, AND RELATED CONTENT THROUGH THE LICENSED CONTENT, OR OTHERWISE ARISING OUT OF THE USE OF THE LICENSED CONTENT, OR OTHERWISE UNDER OR IN CONNECTION WITH ANY PROVISION OF THIS EULA, EVEN IN THE EVENT OF THE FAULT, TORT (INCLUDING NEGLIGENCE), MISREPRESENTATION, STRICT LIABILITY, BREACH OF CONTRACT OR BREACH OF WARRANTY OF MICROSOFT OR ANY SUPPLIER, AND EVEN IF MICROSOFT OR ANY SUPPLIER HAS BEEN ADVISED OF THE POSSIBILITY OF SUCH DAMAGES. BECAUSE SOME STATES/JURISDICTIONS DO NOT ALLOW THE EXCLUSION OR LIMITATION OF LIABILITY FOR CONSEQUENTIAL OR INCIDENTAL DAMAGES, THE ABOVE LIMITATION MAY NOT APPLY TO YOU.

17.   LIMITATION OF LIABILITY AND REMEDIES. NOTWITHSTANDING ANY DAMAGES THAT YOU MIGHT INCUR FOR ANY REASON WHATSOEVER (INCLUDING, WITHOUT LIMITATION, ALL DAMAGES REFERENCED HEREIN AND ALL DIRECT OR GENERAL DAMAGES IN CONTRACT OR ANYTHING ELSE), THE ENTIRE LIABILITY OF MICROSOFT AND ANY OF ITS SUPPLIERS UNDER ANY PROVISION OF THIS EULA AND YOUR EXCLUSIVE REMEDY HEREUNDER SHALL BE LIMITED TO THE GREATER OF THE ACTUAL DAMAGES YOU INCUR IN REASONABLE RELIANCE ON THE LICENSED CONTENT UP TO THE AMOUNT ACTUALLY PAID BY YOU FOR THE LICENSED CONTENT OR US$5.00. THE FOREGOING LIMITATIONS, EXCLUSIONS AND DISCLAIMERS SHALL APPLY TO THE MAXIMUM EXTENT PERMITTED BY APPLICABLE LAW, EVEN IF ANY REMEDY FAILS ITS ESSENTIAL PURPOSE.

18.   APPLICABLE LAW. If you acquired this Licensed Content in the United States, this EULA is governed by the laws of the State of Washington. If you acquired this Licensed Content in Canada, unless expressly prohibited by local law, this EULA is governed by the laws in force in the Province of Ontario, Canada; and, in respect of any dispute which may arise hereunder, you consent to the jurisdiction of the federal and provincial courts sitting in Toronto, Ontario. If you acquired this Licensed Content in the European Union, Iceland, Norway, or Switzerland, then local law applies. If you acquired this Licensed Content in any other country, then local law may apply.

19.   ENTIRE AGREEMENT; SEVERABILITY. This EULA (including any addendum or amendment to this EULA which is included with the Licensed Content) are the entire agreement between you and Microsoft relating to the Licensed Content and the support services (if any) and they supersede all prior or contemporaneous oral or written communications, proposals and representations with respect to the Licensed Content or any other subject matter covered by this EULA. To the extent the terms of any Microsoft policies or programs for support services conflict with the terms of this EULA, the terms of this EULA shall control. If any provision of this EULA is held to be void, invalid, unenforceable or illegal, the other provisions shall continue in full force and effect.

Should you have any questions concerning this EULA, or if you desire to contact Microsoft for any reason, please use the address information enclosed in this Licensed Content to contact the Microsoft subsidiary serving your country or visit Microsoft on the World Wide Web at http://www.microsoft.com.

Si vous avez acquis votre Contenu Sous Licence Microsoft au CANADA :

DÉNI DE GARANTIES. Dans la mesure maximale permise par les lois applicables, le Contenu Sous Licence et les services de soutien technique (le cas échéant) sont fournis *TELS QUELS ET AVEC TOUS LES DÉFAUTS* par Microsoft et ses fournisseurs, lesquels par les présentes dénient toutes autres garanties et conditions expresses, implicites ou en vertu de la loi, notamment, mais sans limitation, (le cas échéant) les garanties, devoirs ou conditions implicites de qualité marchande, d'adaptation à une fin usage particulière, de fiabilité ou de disponibilité, d'exactitude ou d'exhaustivité des réponses, des résultats, des efforts déployés selon les règles de l'art, d'absence de virus et d'absence de négligence, le tout à l'égard du Contenu Sous Licence et de la prestation des services de soutien technique ou de l'omission de la 'une telle prestation des services de soutien technique ou à l'égard de la fourniture ou de l'omission de la fourniture de tous autres services, renseignements, Contenus Sous Licence, et contenu qui s'y rapporte grâce au Contenu Sous Licence ou provenant autrement de l'utilisation du Contenu Sous Licence. PAR AILLEURS, IL N'Y A AUCUNE GARANTIE OU CONDITION QUANT AU TITRE DE PROPRIÉTÉ, À LA JOUISSANCE OU LA POSSESSION PAISIBLE, À LA CONCORDANCE À UNE DESCRIPTION NI QUANT À UNE ABSENCE DE CONTREFAÇON CONCERNANT LE CONTENU SOUS LICENCE.

EXCLUSION DES DOMMAGES ACCESSOIRES, INDIRECTS ET DE CERTAINS AUTRES DOMMAGES. DANS LA MESURE MAXIMALE PERMISE PAR LES LOIS APPLICABLES, EN AUCUN CAS MICROSOFT OU SES FOURNISSEURS NE SERONT RESPONSABLES DES DOMMAGES SPÉCIAUX, CONSÉCUTIFS, ACCESSOIRES OU INDIRECTS DE QUELQUE NATURE QUE CE SOIT (NOTAMMENT, LES DOMMAGES À L'ÉGARD DU MANQUE À GAGNER OU DE LA DIVULGATION DE RENSEIGNEMENTS CONFIDENTIELS OU AUTRES, DE LA PERTE D'EXPLOITATION, DE BLESSURES CORPORELLES, DE LA VIOLATION DE LA VIE PRIVÉE, DE L'OMISSION DE REMPLIR TOUT DEVOIR, Y COMPRIS D'AGIR DE BONNE FOI OU D'EXERCER UN SOIN RAISONNABLE, DE LA NÉGLIGENCE ET DE TOUTE AUTRE PERTE PÉCUNIAIRE OU AUTRE PERTE

DE QUELQUE NATURE QUE CE SOIT) SE RAPPORTANT DE QUELQUE MANIÈRE QUE CE SOIT À L'UTILISATION DU CONTENU SOUS LICENCE OU À L'INCAPACITÉ DE S'EN SERVIR, À LA PRESTATION OU À L'OMISSION DE LA 'UNE TELLE PRESTATION DE SERVICES DE SOUTIEN TECHNIQUE OU À LA FOURNITURE OU À L'OMISSION DE LA FOURNITURE DE TOUS AUTRES SERVICES, RENSEIGNEMENTS, CONTENUS SOUS LICENCE, ET CONTENU QUI S'Y RAPPORTE GRÂCE AU CONTENU SOUS LICENCE OU PROVENANT AUTREMENT DE L'UTILISATION DU CONTENU SOUS LICENCE OU AUTREMENT AUX TERMES DE TOUTE DISPOSITION DE LA U PRÉSENTE CONVENTION EULA OU RELATIVEMENT À UNE TELLE DISPOSITION, MÊME EN CAS DE FAUTE, DE DÉLIT CIVIL (Y COMPRIS LA NÉGLIGENCE), DE RESPONSABILITÉ STRICTE, DE VIOLATION DE CONTRAT OU DE VIOLATION DE GARANTIE DE MICROSOFT OU DE TOUT FOURNISSEUR ET MÊME SI MICROSOFT OU TOUT FOURNISSEUR A ÉTÉ AVISÉ DE LA POSSIBILITÉ DE TELS DOMMAGES.

<u>LIMITATION DE RESPONSABILITÉ ET RECOURS.</u>   MALGRÉ LES DOMMAGES QUE VOUS PUISSIEZ SUBIR POUR QUELQUE MOTIF QUE CE SOIT (NOTAMMENT, MAIS SANS LIMITATION, TOUS LES DOMMAGES SUSMENTIONNÉS ET TOUS LES DOMMAGES DIRECTS OU GÉNÉRAUX OU AUTRES), LA SEULE RESPONSABILITÉ 'OBLIGATION INTÉGRALE DE MICROSOFT ET DE L'UN OU L'AUTRE DE SES FOURNISSEURS AUX TERMES DE TOUTE DISPOSITION DEU LA PRÉSENTE CONVENTION EULA ET VOTRE RECOURS EXCLUSIF À L'ÉGARD DE TOUT CE QUI PRÉCÈDE SE LIMITE AU PLUS ÉLEVÉ ENTRE LES MONTANTS SUIVANTS : LE MONTANT QUE VOUS AVEZ RÉELLEMENT PAYÉ POUR LE CONTENU SOUS LICENCE OU 5,00 $US. LES LIMITES, EXCLUSIONS ET DÉNIS QUI PRÉCÈDENT (Y COMPRIS LES CLAUSES CI-DESSUS), S'APPLIQUENT DANS LA MESURE MAXIMALE PERMISE PAR LES LOIS APPLICABLES, MÊME SI TOUT RECOURS N'ATTEINT PAS SON BUT ESSENTIEL.

À moins que cela ne soit prohibé par le droit local applicable, la présente Convention est régie par les lois de la province d'Ontario, Canada. Vous consentez Chacune des parties à la présente reconnaît irrévocablement à la compétence des tribunaux fédéraux et provinciaux siégeant à Toronto, dans de la province d'Ontario et consent à instituer tout litige qui pourrait découler de la présente auprès des tribunaux situés dans le district judiciaire de York, province d'Ontario.

Au cas où vous auriez des questions concernant cette licence ou que vous désiriez vous mettre en rapport avec Microsoft pour quelque raison que ce soit, veuillez utiliser l'information contenue dans le Contenu Sous Licence pour contacter la filiale de succursale Microsoft desservant votre pays, dont l'adresse est fournie dans ce produit, ou visitez écrivez à : Microsoft sur le World Wide Web à http://www.microsoft.com

Contents

Part I, Managing a Microsoft® Windows® Server 2003 Environment

Introduction

Additional Reading from Microsoft Press 3

Prerequisites 4

Course Outline 5

Setup 7

Microsoft Official Curriculum 8

Microsoft Certified Professional Program 9

Multimedia: Job Roles in Today's Information Systems Environment 12

Facilities 13

Module 1: Introduction to Administering Accounts and Resources

Overview 1

Multimedia: Introduction to Managing a Microsoft Windows Server 2003
Environment 2

Lesson: The Windows Server 2003 Environment 3

Lesson: Logging on to Windows Server 2003 12

Lesson: Installing and Configuring Administrative Tools 19

Lesson: Creating an Organizational Unit 29

Lesson: Moving Domain Objects 38

Lab A: Creating Organizational Units 42

Module 2: Managing User and Computer Accounts

Overview 1

Lesson: Creating User Accounts 2

Lesson: Creating Computer Accounts 17

Lesson: Modifying User and Computer Account Properties 26

Lesson: Creating a User Account Template 35

Lesson: Enabling and Unlocking User and Computer Accounts 42

Lesson: Resetting User and Computer Accounts 50

Lesson: Locating User and Computer Accounts in Active Directory 56

Lesson: Saving Queries 66

Lab A: Managing User and Computer Accounts 71

Module 3: Managing Groups

Overview 1

Lesson: Creating Groups 2

Lesson: Managing Group Membership 19

Lesson: Strategies for Using Groups 26

Lesson: Modifying Groups 37

Lesson: Using Default Groups 47

Best Practices for Managing Groups 60

Lab A: Creating and Managing Groups 61

Module 4: Managing Access to Resources

Overview 1
Lesson: Overview of Managing Access to Resources...................................2
Lesson: Managing Access to Shared Folders 7
Lesson: Managing Access to Files and Folders Using NTFS Permissions 22
Lesson: Determining Effective Permissions...38
Lesson: Managing Access to Shared Files Using Offline Caching 51
Lab A: Managing Access to Resources 61

Module 5: Implementing Printing

Overview 1
Lesson: Introduction to Printing in the Windows Server 2003 Family 2
Lesson: Installing and Sharing Printers 8
Lesson: Managing Access to Printers Using Shared Printer Permissions 17
Lesson: Managing Printer Drivers...24
Lesson: Implementing Printer Locations...31
Lab A: Implementing Printing..47

Module 6: Managing Printing

Overview 1
Lesson: Changing the Location of the Print Spooler 2
Lesson: Setting Printer Priorities 10
Lesson: Scheduling Printer Availability 15
Lesson: Configuring a Printing Pool 21
Lab A: Managing Printing..25

Module 7: Managing Access to Objects in Organizational Units

Overview 1
Multimedia: The Organizational Unit Structure 2
Lesson: Modifying Permissions for Active Directory Objects.............................3
Lesson: Delegating Control of Organizational Units....................................18
Lab A: Managing Access to Objects in Organizational Units 27

Module 8: Implementing Group Policy

Overview 1
Multimedia: Introduction to Group Policy 2
Lesson: Implementing Group Policy Objects 3
Lesson: Implementing GPOs on a Domain 10
Lesson: Managing the Deployment of Group Policy 21
Lab A: Implementing Group Policy 33
Course Evaluation..38

Module 9: Managing the User Environment by Using Group Policy

Overview 1
Lesson: Configuring Group Policy Settings 2
Lesson: Assigning Scripts with Group Policy 11
Lesson: Configuring Folder Redirection 18
Lesson: Determining Applied GPOs 30
Lab A: Using Group Policies Reports 50

Module 10: Implementing Administrative Templates and Audit Policy

Overview 1
Lesson: Overview of Security in Windows Server 2003 2
Lesson: Using Security Templates to Secure Computers 12
Lesson: Testing Computer Security Policy 26
Lesson: Configuring Auditing 31
Lesson: Managing Security Logs 49
Lab A: Managing Security Settings..60
Course Evalution 65

Part II, Maintaining a Microsoft® Windows® Server 2003 Environment
Introduction

Course Materials..2
Prerequisites 4
Course Outline..5
Setup...8
Microsoft Official Curriculum...9
Microsoft Certified Professional Program...10
Multimedia: Job Roles in Today's Information Systems Environment.................13
Facilities 14

Module 1: Preparing to Administer a Server

Overview 1
Lesson: Administering a Server 2
Lesson: Configuring Remote Desktop to Administer a Server 18
Lesson: Managing Remote Desktop Connections 34
Lab A: Preparing to Administer a Server 41

Module 2: Preparing to Monitor Server Performance

Overview 1
Lesson: Introduction to Monitoring Server Performance 2
Lesson: Performing Real-Time and Logged Monitoring.......................................7
Lesson: Configuring and Managing Counter Logs...20
Lesson: Configuring Alerts 34
Lab A: Preparing to Monitor Server Performance..42

Module 3: Monitoring Server Performance

Overview 1
Multimedia: The Primary Server Subsystems 2
Lesson: Monitoring Server Memory 3
Lesson: Monitoring Processor Usage 12
Lesson: Monitoring Disks 18
Lesson: Monitoring Network Usage...26
Lab A: Monitoring Server Performance 38

Module 4: Maintaining Device Drivers

Overview 1

Lesson: Configuring Device Driver Signing Options...2

Lesson: Using Device Driver Rollback 17

Lab A: Maintaining Device Drivers 25

Module 5: Managing Disks

Overview 1

Lesson: Preparing Disks 2

Lesson: Managing Disk Properties..17

Lesson: Managing Mounted Drives...24

Lesson: Converting Disks...29

Lesson: Creating Volumes..37

Lesson: Importing a Disk...47

Lab A: Managing Disks..55

Module 6: Managing Data Storage

Overview 1

Lesson: Managing File Compression 2

Lesson: Configuring File Encryption 13

Lesson: Implementing Disk Quotas...21

Lab A: Managing Data Storage 30

Course Evaluation..37

Module 7: Managing Disaster Recovery

Overview 1

Lesson: Preparing for Disaster Recovery 2

Lesson: Backing Up Data 7

Lesson: Scheduling Backup Jobs..25

Lesson: Restoring Data..34

Lesson: Configuring Shadow Copies 44

Lesson: Recovering from Server Failure..60

Lesson: Selecting Disaster Recovery Methods...76

What Are Server Disaster Recovery Tools? 77

Lab A: Managing Disaster Recovery..79

Module 8: Maintaining Software by Using Software Update Services

Overview 1

Lesson: Introduction to Software Update Services..2

Lesson: Installing and Configuring Software Update Services 13

Lesson: Managing a Software Update Services Infrastructure...............................24

Lab A: Maintaining Software by Using Software Update Services 36

Course Evaluation..41

About This Course

This section provides you with a brief description of the course, audience, suggested prerequisites, and course objectives.

Description

This three-day instructor-led course provides students with the knowledge and skills that are needed to effectively maintain server resources, monitor server performance, and safeguard data on a computer running one of the operating systems in the Microsoft® Windows® Server 2003 family.

Audience

This course is intended for individuals who are employed as or seeking employment as a systems administrator or a systems engineer.

Student prerequisites

This course requires that students meet the following prerequisites:

- A+ certification, or equivalent knowledge and skills
- Network+ certification, or equivalent knowledge and skills

Course objectives

After completing this course, the student will be able to:

- Prepare to administer server resources.
- Configure a server to monitor system performance.
- Monitor system performance.
- Manage device drivers by configuring device driver signing and restoring a device driver.
- Manage hard disks.
- Manage data storage.
- Manage disaster recovery.
- Maintain software by using Microsoft Software Update Services.

Student Materials Compact Discs Contents

The Student Materials compact discs contain the following files and folders:

- *Autorun.exe*. When the compact disc is inserted into the CD-ROM drive, or when you double-click the **Autorun.exe** file, this file opens the compact disc and allows you to browse the Student Materials compact disc.

- *Autorun.inf*. When the compact disc is inserted into the compact disc drive, this file opens Autorun.exe.

- *Default.htm*. This file opens the Student Materials Web page. It provides you with resources pertaining to this course, including additional reading, review and lab answers, lab files, multimedia presentations, and course-related Web sites.

- *Readme.txt*. This file explains how to install the software for viewing the Student Materials compact disc and its contents and how to open the Student Materials Web page.

- *Addread*. This folder contains additional reading pertaining to this course.

- *Appendix*. This folder contains appendix files for this course.

- *Flash*. This folder contains the installer for the Macromedia Flash 6.0 browser plug-in.

- *Fonts*. This folder contains fonts that may be required to view the Microsoft Word documents that are included with this course.

- *Labfiles*. This folder contains files that are used in the hands-on labs. These files may be used to prepare the student computers for the hands-on labs.

- *Media*. This folder contains files that are used in multimedia presentations for this course.

- *Mplayer*. This folder contains the setup file to install Microsoft Windows Media® Player.

- *Practices*. This folder contains files that are used in the hands-on practices.

- *Sampcode*. This folder contains sample code that is accessible through the Web pages on the Student Materials compact disc

- *Webfiles*. This folder contains the files that are required to view the course Web page. To open the Web page, open Windows Explorer, and in the root directory of the compact disc, double-click **Default.htm** or **Autorun.exe**.

- *Wordview*. This folder contains the Word Viewer that is used to view any Word document (.doc) files that are included on the compact disc.

Document Conventions

The following conventions are used in course materials to distinguish elements of the text.

Convention	Use
Bold	Represents commands, command options, and syntax that must be typed exactly as shown. It also indicates commands on menus and buttons, dialog box titles and options, and icon and menu names.
Italic	In syntax statements or descriptive text, indicates argument names or placeholders for variable information. Italic is also used for introducing new terms, for book titles, and for emphasis in the text.
Title Capitals	Indicate domain names, user names, computer names, directory names, and folder and file names, except when specifically referring to case-sensitive names. Unless otherwise indicated, you can use lowercase letters when you type a directory name or file name in a dialog box or at a command prompt.
ALL CAPITALS	Indicate the names of keys, key sequences, and key combinations—for example, ALT+SPACEBAR.
`monospace`	Represents code samples or examples of screen text.
[ ]	In syntax statements, enclose optional items. For example, [*filename*] in command syntax indicates that you can choose to type a file name with the command. Type only the information within the brackets, not the brackets themselves.
{ }	In syntax statements, enclose required items. Type only the information within the braces, not the braces themselves.
|	In syntax statements, separates an either/or choice.
▶	Indicates a procedure with sequential steps.
...	In syntax statements, specifies that the preceding item may be repeated.
. . .	Represents an omitted portion of a code sample.

Microsoft®
Training &
Certification

Introduction

Contents

Introduction	1
Course Materials	2
Prerequisites	4
Course Outline	5
Unit 1:	5
Unit 2:	7
2274 Appendixes	10
2275 Appendixes	10
Setup	11
Microsoft Official Curriculum	12
Microsoft Certified Professional Program	13
Multimedia: Job Roles in Today's Information Systems Environment	16
Facilities	17

Introduction

- Name
- Company affiliation
- Title/function
- Job responsibility
- Systems administration experience
- Windows server operating systems experience
- Expectations for the course

Course Materials

- Name card
- Student workbook
- Student Materials compact disc
- Course evaluation

The following materials are included with your kit:

- *Name card*. Write your name on both sides of the name card.

- *Student workbook*. The student workbook contains the material covered in class, in addition to the hands-on lab exercises.

- *Student Materials compact disc*. The Student Materials compact disc contains the Web page that provides you with links to resources pertaining to this course, including additional readings, review and lab answers, lab files, multimedia presentations, and course-related Web sites.

Note To open the Web page, insert the Student Materials compact disc into the CD-ROM drive, and then in the root directory of the compact disc, double-click **Autorun.exe** or **Default.htm**.

- *Assessments*. There are assessments for each lesson, located on the Student Materials compact disc. You can use them as pre-assessments to identify areas of difficulty, or you can use them as post-assessments to validate learning.

- *Course evaluation*. To provide feedback on the course, training facility, and instructor, you will have the opportunity to complete an online evaluation near the end of the course.

To provide additional comments or feedback on the course, send e-mail to support@mscourseware.com. To inquire about the Microsoft® Certified Professional program, send e-mail to mcphelp@microsoft.com.

Additional Reading from Microsoft Press

Microsoft Windows Server™ 2003 books from Microsoft Press can help you do your job—from the planning and evaluation stages through deployment and ongoing support—with solid technical information to help you get the most out of the Windows Server 2003 key features and enhancements. The following titles supplement the skills taught in this course:

Title	ISBN
Microsoft® Windows Server™ 2003 Security Administrator's Companion	0-7356-1574-8
Microsoft® Windows Server™ 2003 Administrator's Companion	0-7356-1367-2
Microsoft® Windows Server™ 2003 Admin Pocket Consultant	0-7356-1354-0

Prerequisites

- A+ Certification, or equivalent knowledge and skills
- Network+ Certification, or equivalent knowledge and skills

This course requires that you meet the following prerequisites:

- A+ Certification, or equivalent knowledge and skills
- Network+ Certification, or equivalent knowledge and skills

Course Outline

- Module 1: Introduction to Administering Accounts and Resources
- Module 2: Managing User and Computer Accounts
- Module 3: Managing Groups
- Module 4: Managing Access to Resources
- Module 5: Implementing Printing

Unit 1:

Module 1, "Introduction to Administering Accounts and Resources," introduces the Microsoft Windows™ Server 2003 family of operating systems and the tasks and tools for administering accounts and resources on computers running Windows Server 2003 in a networked environment.

Module 2, "Managing User and Computer Accounts," explains how to create and modify user and computer accounts on computers running Windows Server 2003 in a networked environment.

Module 3, "Managing Groups," explains how to use groups to simplify domain administration.

Module 4, "Managing Access to Resources," explains how permissions enable resource access. You also learn how to manage access to files and folders by using NTFS permissions, manage access to files and folders by using special permissions, and manage permission inheritance.

Module 5, "Implementing Printing," explains how to install, configure, and manage printers.

Course Outline *(continued)*

- **Module 6: Managing Printing**
- **Module 7: Managing Access to Objects in Organizational Units**
- **Module 8: Implementing Group Policy**
- **Module 9: Managing the User Environment by Using Group Policy**
- **Module 10: Implementing Administrative Templates and Audit Policy**

Module 6, "Managing Printing," explains how to set up a network-wide printing strategy to meet the needs of users and troubleshoot installation or configuration problems.

Module 7, "Managing Access to Objects in Organizational Units," explains the permissions available for managing access to objects in Active Directory® directory service. You also learn how to move objects between organizational units in the same domain and delegate control of an organizational unit.

Module 8, "Implementing Group Policy," explains the purpose and function of Group Policy in a Windows Server 2003 environment. It also explains how to implement and manage Group Policy objects (GPOs).

Module 9, "Managing the User Environment by Using Group Policy," explains how to use Group Policy to configure Folder Redirection, Microsoft Internet Explorer connectivity, and the desktop.

Module 10, "Implementing Administrative Templates and Audit Policy," explains how to manage security in an Active Directory domain and how to audit events to ensure the effectiveness of a security strategy.

Course Outline *(continued)*

- Module 1: Preparing to Administer a Server
- Module 2: Preparing to Monitor Server Performance
- Module 3: Monitoring Server Performance
- Module 4: Maintaining Device Drivers
- Module 5: Managing Disks

Unit 2:

Module 1, "Preparing to Administer a Server," describes the role of a systems administrator in performing server administration locally and remotely, which tools to use, and which permissions are required to administer a server. It also discusses how to administer remote connections and why that is an important aspect of systems administration. This module is the foundation for the rest of the course. After completing this module, you will be able to administer a server to manage all the systems administrator tasks that are discussed in the rest of the course.

Module 2, "Preparing to Monitor Server Performance," is the first of two modules that discuss the concept of performance monitoring, performance objects, and counters, and explain how to create a baseline to compare server performance. After completing this module, you will be able to create a performance baseline.

Module 3, "Monitoring Server Performance," discusses collecting performance data by monitoring the four primary server subsystems and their effect on server performance. It also covers how to identify system bottlenecks by using the Performance console and Task Manager in Microsoft Windows Server 2003. After completing this module, you will be able to monitor server performance.

Module 4, "Maintaining Device Drivers," provides information about device drivers and how they are used with the Windows Server 2003 operating system. This module covers in detail the configuration of device drivers and describes how to use device drivers to prevent startup and stop problems. After completing this module, you will be able to maintain device drivers.

Module 5, "Managing Disks," discusses partitions, describes how to create and use partitions, explains the differences between basic and dynamic disks, and explains how to use each disk type. This module explains how to use Disk Management and a new command-line tool, DiskPart, to manage your disks. This module also covers in detail how to manage volumes. After completing this module, you will be able to manage disks.

Course Outline *(continued)*

- Module 6: Managing Data Storage
- Module 7: Managing Disaster Recovery
- Module 8: Maintaining Software by Using Software Update Services
- Self-Study: Managing Fault Tolerant Disks

Module 6, "Managing Data Storage," discusses file and folder compression and describes how to use it to manage the data that is stored on your network storage devices. This module also covers Encrypting File System, which is a method that helps to make files and folders secure from intruders to your systems. This module also describes disk quotas and explains how a systems administrator uses this tool. After completing this module, you will be able to manage data storage.

Module 7, "Managing Disaster Recovery," provides information about disaster recovery methods. This module explains how to use tools to back up and restore the data that is critical to your systems and describes the tools that you can use to start a server if it cannot be started normally. After completing this module, you will be able to manage disaster recovery.

Module 8, "Maintaining Software by Using Software Update Services," explains what Software Update Services is, how it works, and how it can help keep networks up-to-date with the latest service packs that are available from Microsoft. After completing this module, you will be able to maintain software by using Software Update Services.

2274 Appendixes

Appendix A, "Differences Between the Microsoft Windows 2000 Server Family and the Microsoft Windows Server 2003 Family", explains the differences between the operating systems in the context of the tasks in each module. This appendix is provided for students who are familiar with Microsoft Windows® 2000 Server.

Appendix B, "References for Exam Preparation", provides references for further study for Exam 70-290, *Managing and Maintaining a Microsoft Windows Server 2003 Environment*.

Appendix C, "Administering Microsoft Windows Server 2003 by Using Scripts", provides information on using scripts to perform the administration tasks taught in Unit 1 of this course.

2275 Appendixes

Appendix A, "Differences Between Microsoft Windows 2000 Server and Microsoft Windows Server 2003," explains the differences between the operating systems in the context of the tasks in each module. This appendix is provided for students who are familiar with Windows 2000 Server.

Appendix B, "References for Exam Preparation," provides references for further study for Exam 70-290: *Managing and Maintaining a Microsoft Windows Server 2003 Environment*.

Appendix C, "Administering Microsoft Windows Server 2003 by Using Scripts," provides information about using scripts to perform the administration tasks taught in this course.

Appendix D, "Partition Styles," provides information about the way that information about the partition is stored.

Self-Study (Appendix E), "Managing Fault-Tolerant Disks," explains the types of fault-tolerant disks and how they are used. This lesson also describes how to implement each type of fault-tolerant disk. After completing this lesson, you will be able to manage fault-tolerant disks.

Appendix F, "Foreign Disks Volume Status in Disk Management," describes the types of status that an administrator can encounter when working with foreign disks.

Appendix G, "Using Dynamic Disks," provides more information about tasks that can be performed only on dynamic disks, and describes which operating systems cannot start on dynamic disks.

Appendix H, "Which Recovery Tool Do I Use?" is a job aid that describes which disaster recovery tool or tools to use to recover lost data.

Setup

- The classroom is configured as one Windows Server 2003 domain: nwtraders.msft
- London is a domain controller and the instructor computer
- Glasgow is a member server and is used as a remote computer for student labs
- Student computers are running Windows Server 2003, Enterprise Edition
- Each student computer has an organizational unit
- Students are administrators for their server and organizational unit

Course files

There are files associated with the labs and practices in this course. The lab files for Unit 1 are located in the C:\MOC\2274 folder on the student computers. The lab files for Unit 2 are located in the C:\MOC\2275 folder on the student computers.

Classroom setup

The classroom configuration consists of one domain controller and multiple student computers. Each computer is running Windows Server 2003, Enterprise Edition.

The name of the domain is nwtraders.msft. It is named after Northwind Traders, a fictitious company that has offices worldwide. The names of the computers correspond with the names of the cities where the fictitious offices are located.

The instructor has two computers: the domain controller, which is named London, and the a member server called Glasgow. The student computers are named after various cities, such as Acapulco, Bonn, and Casablanca. The name of each computer corresponds with an organizational unit of the same name. For example, the Acapulco computer is part of the Acapulco organizational unit.

The domain has been prepopulated with users, groups, and computer accounts for each administrator to manage.

Microsoft Official Curriculum

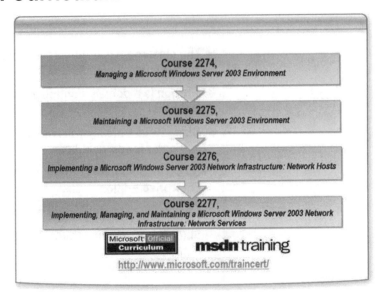

Introduction

Microsoft Training and Certification develops Microsoft Official Curriculum (MOC), including MSDN® Training, for computer professionals who design, develop, support, implement, or manage solutions by using Microsoft products and technologies. These courses provide comprehensive skills-based training in instructor-led and online formats.

Additional recommended courses

Each course relates in some way to another course. A related course may be a prerequisite, a follow-up course in a recommended series, or a course that offers additional training.

It is recommended that you take the following courses in this order:

- Course 2274 *Managing a Microsoft Windows Server 2003 Environment*
- Course 2275, *Maintaining a Microsoft Windows Server 2003 Environment*
- Course 2276, *Implementing a Microsoft Windows Server 2003 Network Infrastructure: Network Hosts*
- Course 2277, *Implementing, Managing, and Maintaining a Microsoft Windows Server 2003 Network Infrastructure: Network Services*
- Course 2278, *Planning and Maintaining a Microsoft Windows Server 2003 Network Infrastructure*
- Course 2279, *Planning, Implementing, and Maintaining a Microsoft Windows Server 2003 Active Directory Infrastructure*

Other related courses may become available in the future, so for up-to-date information about recommended courses, visit the Training and Certification Web site.

Microsoft Training and Certification information

For more information, visit the Microsoft Training and Certification Web site at http://www.microsoft.com/traincert/.

Microsoft Certified Professional Program

Exam number and title	Core exam for the following track	Elective exam for the following track
70-290: *Managing and Maintaining a Microsoft Windows Server 2003 Environment*	MCSA	n/a

Microsoft
C E R T I F I E D
Professional

http://www.microsoft.com/traincert/

Introduction

Microsoft Training and Certification offers a variety of certification credentials for developers and IT professionals. The Microsoft Certified Professional program is the leading certification program for validating your experience and skills, keeping you competitive in today's changing business environment.

Related certification exams

This course, in combination with Course 2275, *Maintaining a Microsoft Windows Server 2003 Environment,* helps students to prepare for Exam 70-290: *Managing and Maintaining a Microsoft Windows Server 2003 Environment.* To prepare for the exam, you should complete both courses and study Course 2274, Appendix B, "References for Exam Preparation", on the Student Materials Web page.

Exam 70-290 is a core exam for the Microsoft Certified Systems Administrator certification.

MCP certifications

The Microsoft Certified Professional program includes the following certifications.

- MCSA on Microsoft Windows Server 2003

  The Microsoft Certified Systems Administrator (MCSA) certification is designed for professionals who implement, manage, and troubleshoot existing network and system environments based on Microsoft Windows 2000 platforms, including the Windows Server 2003 family. Implementation responsibilities include installing and configuring parts of the systems. Management responsibilities include administering and supporting the systems.

- MCSE on Microsoft Windows Server 2003

  The Microsoft Certified Systems Engineer (MCSE) credential is the premier certification for professionals who analyze the business requirements and design and implement the infrastructure for business solutions based on the Microsoft Windows 2000 platform and Microsoft server software, including the Windows Server 2003 family. Implementation responsibilities include installing, configuring, and troubleshooting network systems.

- MCAD

  The Microsoft Certified Application Developer (MCAD) for Microsoft .NET credential is appropriate for professionals who use Microsoft technologies to develop and maintain department-level applications, components, Web or desktop clients, or back-end data services or work in teams developing enterprise applications. The credential covers job tasks ranging from developing to deploying and maintaining these solutions.

- MCSD

  The Microsoft Certified Solution Developer (MCSD) credential is the premier certification for professionals who design and develop leading-edge business solutions with Microsoft development tools, technologies, platforms, and the Microsoft Windows DNA architecture. The types of applications MCSDs can develop include desktop applications and multi-user, Web-based, N-tier, and transaction-based applications. The credential covers job tasks ranging from analyzing business requirements to maintaining solutions.

- MCDBA on Microsoft SQL Server™ 2000

  The Microsoft Certified Database Administrator (MCDBA) credential is the premier certification for professionals who implement and administer Microsoft SQL Server databases. The certification is appropriate for individuals who derive physical database designs, develop logical data models, create physical databases, create data services by using Transact-SQL, manage and maintain databases, configure and manage security, monitor and optimize databases, and install and configure SQL Server.

- MCP

  The Microsoft Certified Professional (MCP) credential is for individuals who have the skills to successfully implement a Microsoft product or technology as part of a business solution in an organization. Hands-on experience with the product is necessary to successfully achieve certification.

- MCT

  Microsoft Certified Trainers (MCTs) demonstrate the instructional and technical skills that qualify them to deliver Microsoft Official Curriculum through Microsoft Certified Technical Education Centers (Microsoft CTECs).

Certification requirements

The certification requirements differ for each certification category and are specific to the products and job functions addressed by the certification. To become a Microsoft Certified Professional, you must pass rigorous certification exams that provide a valid and reliable measure of technical proficiency and expertise.

For More Information   See the Microsoft Training and Certification Web site at http://www.microsoft.com/traincert/.

You can also send e-mail to mcphelp@microsoft.com if you have specific certification questions.

Acquiring the skills tested by an MCP exam

Microsoft Official Curriculum (MOC) and MSDN Training can help you develop the skills that you need to do your job. They also complement the experience that you gain while working with Microsoft products and technologies. However, no one-to-one correlation exists between MOC and MSDN Training courses and MCP exams. Microsoft does not expect or intend for the courses to be the sole preparation method for passing MCP exams. Practical product knowledge and experience is also necessary to pass the MCP exams.

To help prepare for the MCP exams, use the preparation guides that are available for each exam. Each Exam Preparation Guide contains exam-specific information, such as a list of the topics on which you will be tested. These guides are available on the Microsoft Training and Certification Web site at http://www.microsoft.com/traincert/.

Multimedia: Job Roles in Today's Information Systems Environment

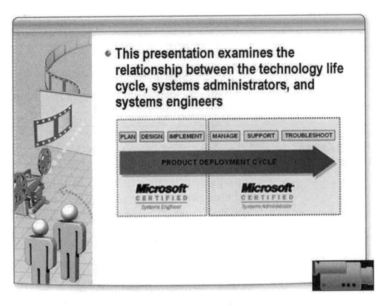

File location

To view the *Job Roles in Today's Information Systems Environment* presentation, open the Web page on the Student Materials compact disc, click **Multimedia**, and then click the title of the presentation. Do not open this presentation unless your instructor tells you to.

Facilities

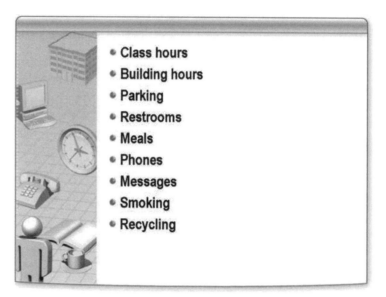

- Class hours
- Building hours
- Parking
- Restrooms
- Meals
- Phones
- Messages
- Smoking
- Recycling

Microsoft®
Training &
Certification

Part I: Managing a Microsoft® Windows® Server 2003 Environment

Microsoft®
Training &
    Certification

Module 1: Introduction to Administering Accounts and Resources

Contents

Overview	1
Multimedia: Introduction to Managing a Microsoft Windows Server 2003 Environment	2
Lesson: The Windows Server 2003 Environment	3
Lesson: Logging on to Windows Server 2003	12
Lesson: Installing and Configuring Administrative Tools	19
Lesson: Creating an Organizational Unit	29
Lesson: Moving Domain Objects	37
Lab A: Creating Organizational Units	41

Microsoft®

Overview

- **Multimedia: Introduction to Managing a Microsoft Windows Server 2003 Environment**
- **The Windows Server 2003 Environment**
- **Logging on to Windows Server 2003**
- **Installing and Configuring Administrative Tools**
- **Creating an Organizational Unit**
- **Moving Domain Objects**

Introduction

In this module, you will learn the skills and knowledge that you need to administer accounts and resources on computers running Microsoft® Windows® Server 2003 software in a networked environment. These lessons provide information and procedures that you will use throughout the course.

Objectives

After completing this module, you will be able to:

- Describe the Windows Server 2003 environment.
- Log on to a computer running Windows Server 2003.
- Install and configure the administrative tools.
- Create an organizational unit.
- Move objects within a domain.

Multimedia: Introduction to Managing a Microsoft Windows Server 2003 Environment

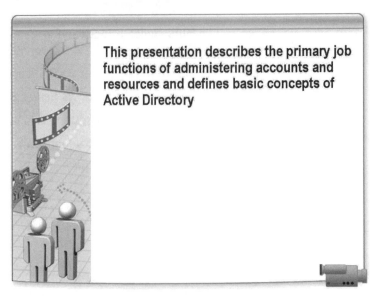

This presentation describes the primary job functions of administering accounts and resources and defines basic concepts of Active Directory

Introduction

In this presentation, you are introduced to the primary job functions of administering accounts and resources in a Windows Server 2003 environment. The tasks and concepts in this presentation are explained in more detail throughout the course.

File location

To view the *Introduction to Administering Accounts and Resources* presentation, open the Web page on the Student Materials compact disc, click **Multimedia**, and then click the title of the presentation. Do not open this presentation unless the instructor tells you to.

Objective

After completing this lesson, you will be able to describe some common tasks for administering accounts and resources.

Lesson: The Windows Server 2003 Environment

- Computer Roles
- The Windows Server 2003 Family
- What Is a Directory Service?
- Active Directory Terms
- Classroom Setup Review

Introduction

To manage a Windows Server 2003 environment, you must understand which operating system edition is appropriate for different computer roles. You must also understand the purpose of a directory service and how Active Directory® directory service provides a structure for the Windows Server 2003 environment.

Lesson objectives

After completing this lesson, you will be able to:

- Describe the different computer roles in a Windows Server 2003 environment.
- Describe the uses of the different editions of Windows Server 2003.
- Explain the purpose of a directory service.
- Differentiate between the components of an Active Directory structure.

Computer Roles

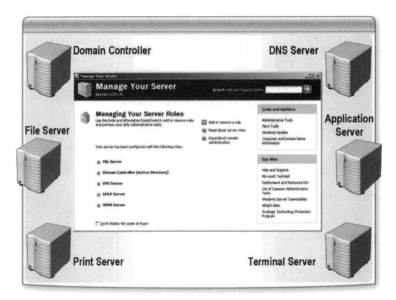

Introduction

Servers play many roles in the client/server networking environment. Some servers are configured to provide authentication, and others are configured to run applications. Some provide network services that enable users to communicate or find other servers and resources in the network. As a systems administrator, you are expected to know the primary types of servers and what functions they perform in your network.

Domain controller (Active Directory)

Domain controllers store directory data and manage communication between users and domains, including user logon processes, authentication, and directory searches. When you install Active Directory on a computer running Windows Server 2003, the computer becomes a domain controller.

Note In a Windows Server 2003 network, all servers in the domain that are not domain controllers are called *member servers*. Servers not associated with a domain are called *workgroup servers*.

File server

A file server provides a central location on your network where you can store and share files with users across your network. When users require an important file such as a project plan, they can access the file on the file server instead of passing the file between their separate computers.

Print server

A print server provides a central location on your network where users can print. The print server provides clients with updated printer drivers and handles all print queuing and security.

DNS server

Domain Name System (DNS) is an Internet and TCP/IP standard name service. The DNS service enables client computers on your network to register and resolve DNS domain names. A computer configured to provide DNS services on a network is a DNS server. You must have a DNS server on your network to implement Active Directory.

Application server

An application server provides key infrastructure and services to applications hosted on a system. Typical application servers include the following services:

- Resource pooling (for example, database connection pooling and object pooling)
- Distributed transaction management
- Asynchronous program communication, typically through message queuing
- A just-in-time object activation model
- Automatic Extensible Markup Language (XML) Web Service interfaces to access business objects
- Failover and application health detection services
- Integrated security

Microsoft Internet Information Services (IIS) provides the tools and features necessary to easily manage a secure Web server. If you plan to host Web and File Transfer Protocol (FTP) sites with IIS, configure the server as an application server.

Terminal server

A terminal server provides remote computers with access to Windows-based programs running on Windows Server 2003, Standard Edition; Windows Server 2003, Enterprise Edition; or Windows Server 2003, Datacenter Edition. With a terminal server, you install an application at a single point on a single server. Multiple users then can access the application without installing it on their computers. Users can run programs, save files, and use network resources all from a remote location, as if these resources were installed on their own computer.

The Manage Your Server tool

When Windows Server 2003 is installed and a user logs on for the first time, the Manage Your Server tool starts automatically. You use this tool to add or remove server roles. When you add a server role to the computer, the Manage Your Server tool adds this server role to the list of available, configured server roles. After the server role is added to the list, you can use various wizards that help you manage the specific server role. The Manage Your Server tool also provides Help files specific to the server role that have checklists and troubleshooting recommendations.

The Windows Server 2003 Family

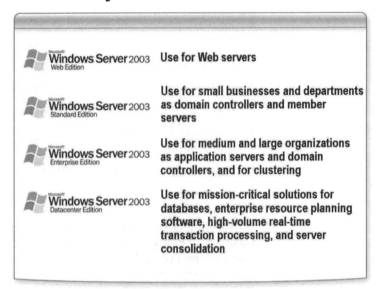

Introduction	Windows Server 2003 is available in five editions. Each edition is developed to be used in a specific server role. This enables you to select the operating system edition that provides only the functions and capabilities that your server needs.
Web Edition	Windows Server 2003, Web Edition, is designed to be used specifically as a Web server. It is available only through selected partner channels and is not available for retail. Although computers running Windows Server 2003, Web Edition, can be members of an Active Directory domain, you cannot run Active Directory on Windows Server 2003, Web Edition.
Standard Edition	Windows Server 2003, Standard Edition, is a reliable network operating system that delivers business solutions quickly and easily. This flexible server is the ideal choice for small businesses and departmental use. Use Windows Server 2003, Standard Edition, when your server does not require the increased hardware support and clustering features of Windows Server 2003, Enterprise Edition.
Enterprise Edition	Windows Server 2003, Enterprise Edition, has all the features in Windows Server 2003, Standard Edition. However, it also has features not included in Standard Edition that enhance availability, scalability, and dependability.

Windows Server 2003, Enterprise Edition, is designed for medium to large businesses. It is the recommended operating system for applications, XML Web services, and infrastructure, because it offers high reliability, performance, and superior business value.

The major difference between Windows Server 2003, Enterprise Edition, and Windows Server 2003, Standard Edition, is that Enterprise Edition supports high-performance servers. Windows Server 2003, Enterprise Edition, is recommended for servers running applications for networking, messaging, inventory and customer service systems, databases, and e-commerce Web sites. Also, you can cluster servers running Enterprise Edition together to handle larger loads. |

Datacenter Edition

Windows Server 2003, Datacenter Edition, is designed for business-critical and mission-critical applications that demand the highest levels of scalability and availability.

The major difference between Windows Server 2003, Datacenter Edition, and Windows Server 2003, Enterprise Edition, is that Datacenter Edition supports more powerful multiprocessing and greater memory. In addition, Windows Server 2003, Datacenter Edition, is available only through the Windows Datacenter Program offered to Original Equipment Manufacturers (OEMs).

Additional reading

For detailed information about each edition's capabilities, see the product overviews on the Windows Server 2003 page at http://www.microsoft.com/windowsserver2003/default.mspx.

What Is a Directory Service?

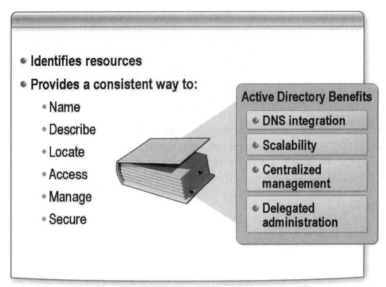

Introduction

As a user logged on to a network, you might need to connect to a shared folder or send a print job to a printer on the network. How do you find that folder and printer and other network resources?

Definition

A directory service is a network service that identifies all resources on a network and makes that information available to users and applications. Directory services are important, because they provide a consistent way to name, describe, locate, access, manage, and secure information about these resources.

When a user searches for a shared folder on the network, it is the directory service that identifies the resource and provides that information to the user.

Active Directory

Active Directory is the directory service in the Windows Server 2003 family. It extends the basic functionality of a directory service to provide the following benefits:

- DNS integration

    Active Directory uses DNS naming conventions to create a hierarchical structure that provides a familiar, orderly, and scalable view of network connections. DNS is also used to map host names, such as microsoft.com, to numeric TCP/IP addresses, such as 192.168.19.2.

- Scalability

    Active Directory is organized into sections that permit storage for a very large number of objects. As a result, Active Directory can expand as an organization grows. An organization that has a single server with a few hundred objects can grow to thousands of servers and millions of objects.

- Centralized management

  Active Directory enables administrators to manage distributed desktops, network services, and applications from a central location, while using a consistent management interface. Active Directory also provides centralized control of access to network resources by enabling users to log on only once to gain full access to resources throughout Active Directory.

- Delegated administration

  The hierarchical structure of Active Directory enables administrative control to be delegated for specific segments of the hierarchy. A user authorized by a higher administrative authority can perform administrative duties in their designated portion of the structure. For example, users may have limited administrative control over their workstation's settings, and a department manager may have the administrative rights to create new users in an organizational unit.

Additional reading

For more information on Active Directory, see *Technical Overview of Windows Server 2003 Active Directory* at http://www.microsoft.com/windowsserver2003/techinfo/overview/activedirectory.mspx.

Active Directory Terms

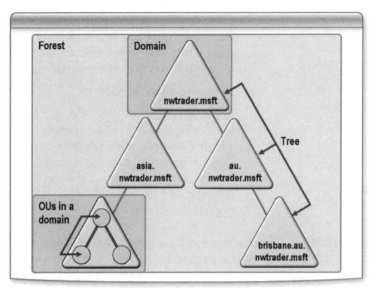

Introduction   The logical structure of Active Directory is flexible and provides a method for designing a hierarchy within Active Directory that is comprehensible to both users and administrators.

Logical components   The logical components of the Active Directory structure include the following:

- *Domain*. The core unit of the logical structure in Active Directory is the domain. A domain is a collection of computers, defined by an administrator, that share a common directory database. A domain has a unique name and provides access to the centralized user accounts and group accounts maintained by the domain administrator.

- *Organizational unit*. An organizational unit is a type of container object that you use to organize objects within a domain. An organizational unit may contain objects, such as user accounts, groups, computers, printers, and other organizational units.

- *Forest*. A forest is one or more domains that share a common configuration, schema, and global catalog.

- *Tree*. A tree consists of domains in a forest that share a contiguous DNS namespace.

Additional reading   For more information about Active Directory domains, see:

- Article 310996, "Active Directory Services and Windows 2000 or Windows Server 2003 Domains (Part 1)" in the Microsoft Knowledge Base at http://support.microsoft.com/?kbid=310996.

- Article 310997, "Active Directory Services and Windows 2000 or Windows Server 2003 Domains (Part 2)" in the Microsoft Knowledge Base at http://support.microsoft.com/?kbid=310997.

Classroom Setup Review

- The classroom is configured as one Windows Server 2003 domain: nwtraders.msft
- London is a domain controller and the instructor computer
- Glasgow is a member server and is used as a remote computer for student labs
- Student computers are running Windows Server 2003, Enterprise Edition
- Each student computer has an organizational unit
- Students are administrators for their server and organizational unit

Introduction

Now that you have been introduced to the basic components of an Active Directory structure, you can understand the setup of the classroom better.

Classroom setup

The classroom configuration consists of one domain controller and multiple student computers. Each computer is running Windows Server 2003, Enterprise Edition.

The name of the domain is nwtraders.msft. It is named after Northwind Traders, a fictitious company that has offices worldwide. The names of the computers correspond with the names of the cities where the fictitious offices are located.

The domain controller is named London, and the instructor also has a member server called Glasgow. The student computers are named after various cities, such as Acapulco, Bonn, and Casablanca. The name of each computer corresponds with an organizational unit of the same name. For example, the Acapulco computer is part of the Acapulco organizational unit.

The domain has been prepopulated with users, groups, and computer accounts for each administrator to manage.

Lesson: Logging on to Windows Server 2003

- **Multimedia: Logon and Authentication**
- **Logon Dialog Box Options**

Introduction

Windows Server 2003 authenticates a user during the logon process to verify the identity of the user. This mandatory process ensures that only valid users can access resources and data on a computer or the network.

Lesson objectives

After completing this lesson, you will be able to:

- Log on locally.
- Log on to a domain.

Practice: Logging on Using a Local Computer Account

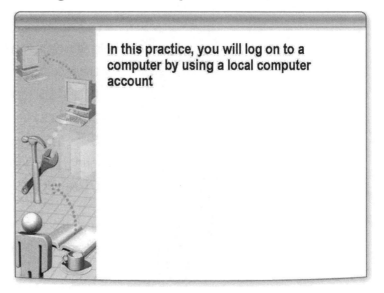

In this practice, you will log on to a computer by using a local computer account

Objective

In this practice, you will log on to a computer by using a local computer account.

Scenario

You have just been hired by Northwind Traders to help with the administration of computers, users, and resources for a city location in the Northwind Traders global network. You will also be responsible for a member server in your city and will occasionally log on with the local Administrator account on the member server.

Practice

▶ **Log on to your member server by using the local Administrator account**

1. Press CTRL+ALT+DEL.

2. In the **Log On to Windows** dialog box, in the **User name** box, type **Administrator**

3. In the **Password** box, type **P@ssw0rd** (The 0 is a zero).

4. In the **Log on to** box, click the name of your computer.

   The name of your computer has **(this computer)** after your computer name.

5. Click **OK**.

6. Log off the computer by doing the following:

   a. On the **Start** menu, click **Log Off**.

   b. In the message box, click **Log Off**.

Multimedia: Logon and Authentication

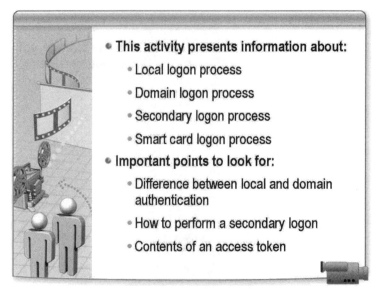

File location

To start the *Logon and Authentication* activity, open the Web page on the Student Materials compact disc, click **Multimedia**, and then click the title of the activity.

Questions

Review the information and processes in *Logon and Authentication*, and then answer the following questions.

1. What is the difference between authentication of a local logon and authentication of a domain logon?

   _____

   _____

   _____

2. How do you perform a secondary logon?

   _____

   _____

   _____

3. What type of information is contained in an access token?

    _____

    _____

    _____

Logon Dialog Box Options

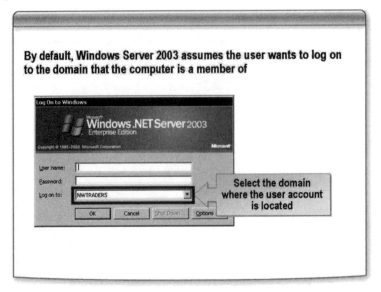

Introduction

Windows Server 2003 provides two options when a user logs on to a domain. Windows Server 2003 enables the user to specify the domain that contains their user account from a computer that is located in a different domain. By default, Windows Server 2003 assumes that the user wants to log on to the domain that the computer is a member of and does not provide a way to specify a domain.

The logon dialog box

The following table describes all the options in the logon dialog box.

Option	Description
User name	A unique user logon name that is assigned by an administrator. To log on to a domain, this user account must reside in the directory database in Active Directory.
Password	The password that is assigned to the user account. Users must enter a password to prove their identity.
	Passwords are case sensitive. The password appears on the screen as asterisks (*) to protect it from onlookers. To prevent unauthorized access to resources and data, users must keep passwords secret.
Log on to	Determines whether a user logs on to a domain or logs on locally. A user can choose one of the following:
	• **Domain name**: The user must select the domain that their user account is in. This list contains all of the domains in a domain tree.
	• **Computer name**: The name of the computer that the user is logging on to. The user must have the Log on Locally user right for the computer. The option to log on locally is not available on a domain controller.
Log on using dial-up connection	Permits a user to connect to a server in the domain by using a dial-up network connection. Dial-up networking enables a user to log on and perform work from a remote location.
Shutdown	Closes all files, saves all operating system data, and prepares the computer so that a user can safely turn it off. On a computer running Windows Server 2003, the **Shutdown** button is not active. This prevents an unauthorized user from using this dialog box to shut down the server. To shut down a server, a user must be able to log on to it.
Options	Switches between the two versions of the **Enter Password** dialog box. One of these two dialog boxes provides the **Log on to** option, which enables the user to select a domain or the local computer.

Practice: Logging on Using a Domain Account

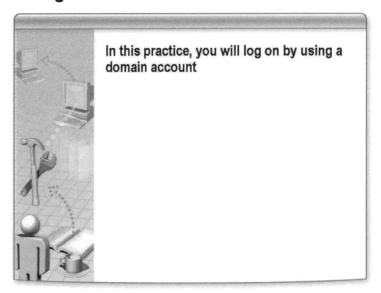

Objective

In this practice, you will log on to a local computer with a domain account.

Scenario

You have just been hired by Northwind Traders to help with the administration of computers, users, and resources for a city location in the Northwind Traders global network. You need to make sure you can successfully log on with your domain Administrator account.

Practice

▶ **Log on to your member server by using your domain Administrator account**

1. Press CTRL+ALT+DEL.

2. In the **Log On to Windows** box, in the **User name** dialog box, type *ComputerName***Admin** (Example: LondonAdmin).

3. In the **Password** box, type **P@ssw0rd** (The 0 is a zero).

4. In the **Log on to** box, click **NWTraders**, and then click **OK**.

5. Log off the computer by doing the following:

   a. On the **Start** menu, click **Log Off**.

   b. In the message box, click **Log Off**.

Lesson: Installing and Configuring Administrative Tools

- • What Are Administrative Tools?
- • How to Install Administrative Tools
- • What Is MMC?
- • How to Create a Custom MMC
- • How to Resolve Problems with Installing and Configuring Administrative Tools

Introduction

In this lesson, you will learn how to install and configure administrative tools. This lesson also introduces the different types of user accounts and how to create them.

Lesson objectives

After completing this lesson, you will be able to:

- ■ List the most commonly used administrative tools.
- ■ Install administrative tools.
- ■ Describe the Microsoft Management Console (MMC).
- ■ Create a custom MMC.
- ■ Resolve problems with installing and configuring administrative tools.

What Are Administrative Tools?

- Commonly used administrative tools:
  - Active Directory Users and Computers
  - Active Directory Sites and Services
  - Active Directory Domains and Trusts
  - Computer Management
  - DNS
  - Remote Desktops
- Install to perform remote administration

Introduction

Administrative tools enable network administrators to add, search, and change computer and network settings and Active Directory objects. You can install the administrative tools for managing a Windows Server 2003 environment on computers running Microsoft Windows XP Professional and Windows Server 2003 to remotely administer Active Directory and network settings.

Administrative tools

Some of the more commonly used tools include the following:

- Active Directory Users and Computers
- Active Directory Sites and Services
- Active Directory Domains and Trusts
- Computer Management
- DNS
- Remote Desktops

Installing administrative tools

You will need to install administrative tools on Windows XP Professional when you want to remotely manage network resources such as Active Directory, or network services such as Windows Internet Name Service (WINS) or Dynamic Host Configuration Protocol (DHCP), from a workstation. If you want to install the administrative tools on a computer running Windows XP Professional, Service Pack 1 and a hot fix from Microsoft Knowledge Base article 329357 must be installed.

Windows Server 2003 includes all the administrative tools as snap-ins that can be added to a custom MMC. This includes all the tools for managing Active Directory, but does not include management tools for services that are not installed on the server, such as WINS or DHCP. If you must remotely manage a network service from a computer running Windows Server 2003, and the service is not installed on the computer, you must install the administrative tools.

Note Uninstall the Windows Server 2003 Administration Tools Pack if someone who is not an administrator is going to use the computer running Windows XP Professional.

How to Install Administrative Tools

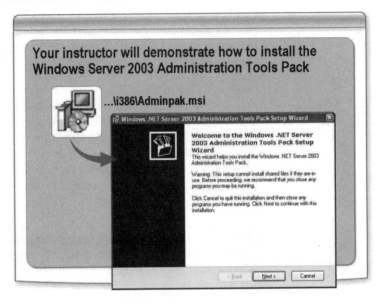

Introduction

To install the Windows Server 2003 Administration Tools Pack on a computer running Windows XP Professional, you must have administrative permissions on the local computer. If the computer is joined to a domain, members of the Domain Administrator group might be able to perform this procedure.

Procedure

To install or reinstall the Windows Server 2003 Administration Tools Pack from the Windows Server 2003 compact disc (CD):

1. Put your Windows Server 2003 CD into the CD tray of a computer running Windows XP Professional.

2. The CD installation setup runs automatically. If it does not:

   a. Click **Start**, and then click **Run**.

   b. In the **Run** dialog box, click **Browse**.

   c. In the **Browse** dialog box, click **My Computer**.

   d. Double-click the CD drive, and then double-click **setup.exe**.

   e. In the **Run** dialog box, click **OK**.

3. In the **Welcome to Microsoft Windows Server 2003** dialog box, click **Perform additional tasks**.

4. In the **What do you want to do?** dialog box, click **Browse this CD**.

5. Double-click the **i386** folder.

6. Double-click the **Adminpak.msi** icon.

7. Specify the installation location or drive where you want to install the Windows Server 2003 Administration Tools Pack.

What Is MMC?

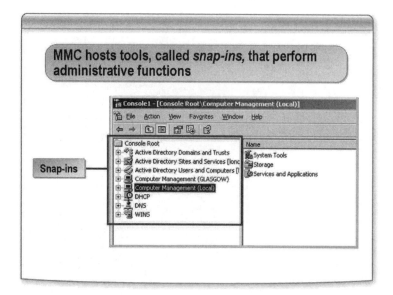

MMC hosts tools, called *snap-ins*, that perform administrative functions

Definition

You use Microsoft Management Console (MMC) to create, save, and open administrative tools, called consoles, which manage the hardware, software, and network components of your Windows operating system. MMC runs on all client operating systems that are currently supported.

What are snap-ins?

A snap-in is a tool that is hosted in MMC. MMC offers a common framework in which various snap-ins can run so that you can manage several services with a single interface. MMC also enables you to customize the console. By picking and choosing specific snap-ins, you can create management consoles that include only the administrative tools that you need. For example, you can add tools to manage your local computer and remote computers.

Additional reading

For more information about MMC, see *Step-by-Step Guide to the Microsoft Management Console* at http://www.microsoft.com/technet/treeview/default.asp?url=/technet/prodtechnol/windows2000serv/howto/mmcsteps.asp.

How to Create a Custom MMC

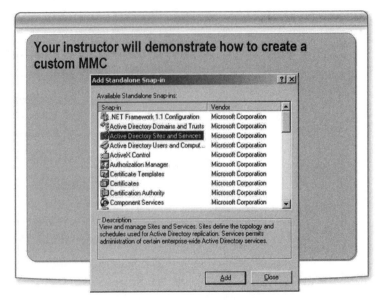

Introduction

You can use MMC to create custom tools and distribute these tools to users. With both Windows XP Professional and Windows Server 2003, you can save these tools so that they are available in the Administrative Tools folder on the Programs menu. To create a custom MMC, you will use the **Run as** command.

Procedure

1. Click **Start**, click **Run**, type **MMC** and then click **OK**.

2. In the console, on the **File** menu, click **Add/Remove Snap-in**.

3. In the **Add/Remove Snap-in** dialog box, click **Add**.

4. In the **Add Standalone Snap-in** dialog box, double-click the item that you want to add.

5. If a wizard appears, follow the instructions in the wizard.

6. To add another item to the console, repeat step 4.

7. In the **Add Standalone Snap-in** dialog box, click **Close**.

8. Click **OK** when you are finished.

9. On the **File** menu, click **Save**.

Practice: Configuring the Administrative Tools

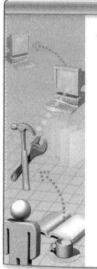

In this practice, you will:

- Create a custom MMC that contains the following:
  - Computer Management (Local)
  - Computer Management (Glasgow)
  - Active Directory Users and Computers
- Save the MMC as C:\MOC\CustomMMC.msc

Objective

In this practice, you will:

- Create a custom MMC.
- Add MMC snap-ins.
- Save a custom MMC.

Instructions

Before you begin this practice:

- Log on to the domain by using the *ComputerName*Admin account.
- Review the procedures in this lesson that describe how to perform this task.

Scenario

Your manager instructs you that you will be adding domain user accounts on the member server that supports your city and an additional server called Glasgow. Configure the support tools so that you have one administrative console that gives you quick access to the tools that you need to do the most common tasks for your job.

Practice

▶ **Configure a custom MMC**

1. Open a blank MMC.

2. Add a Computer Management snap-in for the local computer.

3. Add a Computer Management snap-in for Glasgow.

4. Add the Active Directory Users and Computers snap-in.

5. Save the MMC as C:\MOC\CustomMMC.msc.

Note   This practice focuses on the concepts in this lesson and as a result may not comply with Microsoft security recommendations. For example, this practice does not comply with the recommendation that users log on with domain user account and use the **Run as** command when performing administrative tasks.

How to Resolve Problems with Installing and Configuring Administrative Tools

Symptom	Cause	Resolution
Cannot install the administrative tools	Insufficient permissions	You must have administrative permissions on the local computer
	Incorrect operating system	You can install the Windows Server 2003 Administration Tools Pack only on currently supported operating systems
Broken links in Help files	Both server and client Help systems are required	Use both Help systems for the Windows Server 2003 Administration Tools Pack by installing the server Help on currently supported client operating systems

Introduction

Two common problems you might encounter when installing and configuring administrative tools are that you cannot install the administrative tools properly and that there are broken links in the Help files.

Cannot install

If you have problems installing or configuring administrative tools in Windows Server 2003, verify that you have administrative permissions on the local computer.

Another reason you may not be able to install the administrative tools is that the incorrect operating system is installed. You can only install the Windows Server 2003 Administration Tools Pack on computers running Windows XP Professional or Windows Server 2003.

Broken Help links

When the Windows Server 2003 Administration Tools Pack is installed on Windows XP Professional, some Help links might appear to be broken. The reason this happens is that you must have both server and client Help files for the Windows Server 2003 Administration Tools Pack on Windows XP Professional.

To resolve the problem, you must integrate the server and client Help files for the Windows Server 2003 Administration Tools Pack by installing the server Help files on Windows XP Professional. This is fairly easy to do and should be done after the Windows Server 2003 Administration Tools Pack is installed on Windows XP Professional.

To install Help files from another Windows computer, CD, or disk image:

1. On the **Start** menu, click **Help and Support**.

2. In the Help and Support window, in the navigation bar, click **Options**.

3. In the left pane, click **Install and share Windows Help**.

4. In the right pane, depending on where you want to install Help from, click **Install Help content from another Windows computer** or **Install Help content from a CD or disk image**.

5. Type the location of the computer, CD, or disk image, and then click **Find**.

   If you are installing from a CD or disk image, you can click **Browse** to locate the disk containing Help files.

6. When available Help files appear, click the version of Help you want, and then click **Install**.

   When the installation is complete, you can switch to the new Help files.

Lesson: Creating an Organizational Unit

* What Is an Organizational Unit?
* Organizational Unit Hierarchical Models
* Names Associated with Organizational Units
* How to Create an Organizational Unit

Introduction

In this lesson, you will learn how to create an organizational unit.

Lesson objectives

After completing this lesson, you will be able to create an organizational unit, including:

- Explain the purpose of an organizational unit.
- Describe organizational unit hierarchical models.
- Identify the names associated with organizational units.
- Create an organizational unit.

What Is an Organizational Unit?

* Organizes objects in a domain
* Allows you to delegate administrative control
* Simplifies the management of commonly grouped resources

Definition

An organizational unit is a particularly useful type of Active Directory object contained in a domain. Organizational units are useful, because you can use them to organize hundreds of thousands of objects in the directory into manageable units. You use an organizational unit to group and organize objects for administrative purposes, such as delegating administrative rights and assigning policies to a collection of objects as a single unit.

Benefits of using organizational units

You can use organizational units to:

- Organize objects in a domain.

    Organizational units contain domain objects, such as user and computer accounts and groups. File and printer shares that are published to Active Directory are also found in organizational units.

- Delegate administrative control.

    You can assign either complete administrative control, such as the Full Control permission, over all objects in the organizational unit, or you can assign limited administrative control, such as the ability to modify e-mail information, over user objects in the organizational unit. To delegate administrative control, you assign specific permissions on the organizational unit and the objects that the organizational unit contains for one or more users and groups.

- Simplify the management of commonly grouped resources.

    You can delegate administrative authority over individual attributes on individual objects in Active Directory, but you will usually use organizational units to delegate administrative authority. A user can have administrative authority for all organizational units in a domain or for a single organizational unit. Using organizational units, you can create containers in a domain that represent the hierarchical or logical structures in your organization. You can then manage the configuration and use of accounts and resources based on your organizational model.

Organizational Unit Hierarchical Models

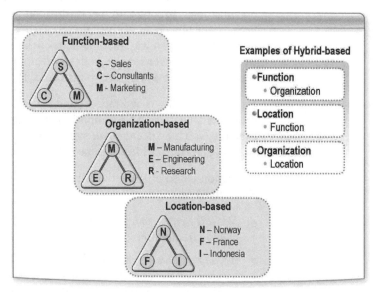

Introduction	As a systems administrator, you do not select the design of the Active Directory structure for your organization. However, it is important to know the characteristics and ramifications of each structure. This knowledge may be critical to you when performing systems administrator tasks within the Active Directory structure. This topic describes the four basic hierarchy designs.
Function-based hierarchy	The function-based hierarchy is based on only the business functions of the organization, without regard to geographical location or departmental or divisional barriers. Choose this approach only if the IT function is not based on location or organization.

When deciding whether to organize the Active Directory structure by function, consider the following characteristics of function-based designs:

- *Not affected by reorganizations*. A function-based hierarchy is not affected by corporate or organizational reorganizations.

- *May require additional layers*. When using this structure, it may be necessary to create additional layers in the organizational unit hierarchy to accommodate the administration of users, printers, servers, and network shares.

- *May impact replication*. Structures that are used to create domains may not result in efficient use of the network, because the domain naming context may replicate across one or more areas of low bandwidth.

This structure is only appropriate in small organizations because functional departments in medium and large organizations are often very diverse and cannot be effectively grouped into broad categories.

Organization-based hierarchy

The organization-based hierarchy is based on the departments or divisions in your organization. If the Active Directory structure is organized to reflect the organizational structure, it may be difficult to delegate administrative authority, because the objects in Active Directory, such as printers and file shares, may not be grouped in a way that facilitates delegation of administrative authority. Because users never see the Active Directory structure, the design should accommodate the administrator instead of the user.

Location-based hierarchy

If the organization is centralized, and network management is geographically distributed, then using a location-based hierarchy is recommended. For example, you may decide to create organizational units for New England, Boston, and Hartford in the same domain, such as contoso.msft.

A location-based organizational units or domain hierarchy has the following characteristics:

- *Not affected by reorganizations*. Although divisions and departments may change frequently, location rarely does change in most organizations.

- *Accommodates mergers and expansions*. If an organization merges with or acquires another company, it is simple to integrate the new locations into the existing organizational units and domain hierarchy structure.

- *Takes advantage of network strengths*. Typically, an organization's physical network topology resembles a location-based hierarchy. If you create domains with a location-based hierarchy, you can take advantage of areas where the network has high bandwidth and limit the amount of data replicated across low bandwidth areas.

- *May cause compromise security*. If a location includes multiple divisions or departments, an individual or group with administrative authority over that domain or over organizational units may also have authority over any child domains or organizational units.

Hybrid-based hierarchy

A hierarchy based on location and then by organization, or any other combination of structure types, is called a hybrid-based hierarchy. The hybrid-based hierarchy combines strengths from several areas to meet the needs of the organization. This type of hierarchy has the following characteristics:

- Accommodates additional growth in geographic, departmental, or divisional areas.

- Creates distinct management boundaries according to department or division.

- Requires cooperation between administrators to ensure the completion of administrative tasks if they are in the same location but in different divisions or departments.

Names Associated with Organizational Units

Name	Example
LDAP relative distinguished name	OU=MyOrganizationalUnit
LDAP distinguished name	OU=MyOrganizationalUnit, DC=microsoft, DC=com
Canonical name	Microsoft.com/MyOrganizationalUnit

Domain Componantes (handwritten annotation)

Introduction

Each object in Active Directory can be referenced by several different types of names that describe the location of the object. Active Directory creates a relative distinguished name, a canonical name, and a relative distinguished name for each object, based on information that is provided when the object is created or modified.

LDAP relative distinguished name

The Lightweight Directory Access Protocol (LDAP) relative distinguished name uniquely identifies the object in its parent container. For example, the LDAP relative distinguished name of an organizational unit named MyOrganizational Unit is OU=MyOrganizationalUnit. Relative distinguished names must be unique in an organizational unit. It is important to understand the syntax of the LDAP relative distinguished name when using scripts to query and manage Active Directory.

LDAP distinguished name

Unlike the LDAP relative distinguished name, the LDAP distinguished name is globally unique. An example of the LDAP distinguished name of an organizational unit named MyOganizationalUnit in the microsoft.com domain is OU=MyOrganizationalUnit, DC=microsoft, DC=com. Systems administrators use the LDAP relative distinguished name and the LDAP distinguished name only when writing administrative scripts or during command-line administration.

Canonical name

The canonical name syntax is constructed in the same way as the LDAP distinguished name, but it is represented by a different notation. The canonical name of the organizational unit named myOrganizationalUnit in the microsoft.com domain is Microsoft.com/MyOrganizationalUnit. Administrators use canonical names through some administrative tools. It is used to represent a hierarchy in the administrative tools.

How to Create an Organizational Unit

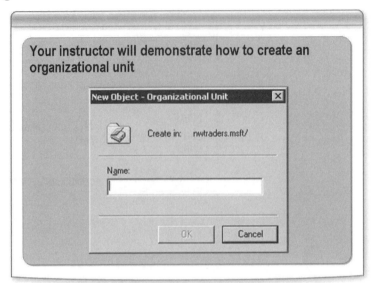

Introduction

You can create organizational units to represent a hierarchy or to manage the objects that go into organizational units.

Procedure

To create a new organizational unit:

1. Open Active Directory Users and Computers.

2. In the console tree, double-click the domain node.

3. Right-click the domain node or the folder in which you want to add the organizational unit, point to **New**, and then click **organizational unit**.

4. In the **New Object – Organizational Unit** dialog box, in the **Name** box, type the name of the organizational unit, and then click **OK**.

Note To perform this procedure, you must be a member of the Domain Admins group or the Enterprise Admins group in Active Directory, or you must be delegated the appropriate authority. As a security best practice, consider using **Run as** to perform this procedure.

Using a command line

To create an organizational unit by using **dsadd**:

1. Open a command prompt.

2. Type **dsadd ou** *OrganizationalUnitDomainName* [**-desc** *Description*] [{**-s** *Server* | **-d** *Domain*}] [**-u** *UserName*] [**-p** {*Password* | *****}] [**-q**] [{**-uc** | **-uco** | **-uci**}]

Practice: Creating an Organizational Unit

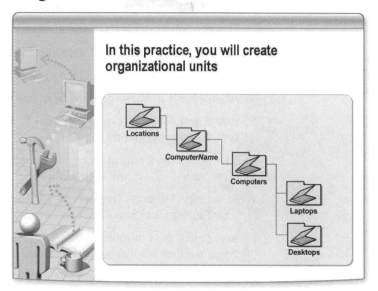

Objective

In this practice, you will create three organizational units.

Instructions

Before you begin this practice:

- Log on to the domain by using the *ComputerName*Admin account.
- Review the procedures in this lesson that describe how to perform this task.

Scenario

As a systems administrator for Northwind Traders, you are given the task of creating an organizational unit hierarchy designed by the Northwind Traders design team. The organizational unit hierarchy will use a location-based design that separates laptop computers from desktop computers. You will create a hierarchy of organizational units in your city organizational unit to separate computer types.

The following graphic is a representation of what you need to create for the NWTraders domain. The Locations organizational unit and the *ComputerName* organizational unit have already been created.

Practice

▶ **Create the computers, laptops, and desktops organizational units**

1. Open CustomMMC with the **Run as** command.

   Use the following user account: *ComputerName*Admin@nwtraders.msft

2. Expand **Active Directory Users and Computers**.

3. Expand **nwtraders.msft**, and then expand **Locations**.

4. Right-click *CityName*, point to **New**, and then click **organizational unit**.

5. In the **New Object – Organizational Unit** dialog box, in the **Name** box, type **Computers** and then click **OK**.

6. Right-click the **Computers** organizational unit that you just created, point to **New**, then click **organizational unit**.

7. In the **New Object – Organizational Unit** dialog box, in the **Name** box, type **Laptops** and then click **OK**.

8. Right-click the **Computer** organizational unit that you just created, point to **New**, and then click **organizational unit**.

9. In the **New Object – Organizational Unit** dialog box, in the **Name** box, type **Desktops** and then click **OK**.

10. Close and save CustomMMC.

    Your organizational unit hierarchy should look like the preceding diagram.

Scenario

The systems engineers want to test some advanced features of Active Directory. They want your team to create some organizational units in the IT Test organizational unit.

The IT Test organizational unit has already been created. You must add an additional organizational unit that matches your city, as shown in the following graphic.

    IT Test
        City

Practice: Using a command line

▶ **Create an organizational unit by using dsadd**

1. Click **Start**, and then click **Run**.

2. In the **Open** box, type **runas /user:nwtraders*ComputerName*Admin cmd** and then click **OK**

3. When prompted for the password, type **P@ssw0rd** and then press ENTER.

4. At the command prompt, type the following command:

   dsadd ou *OrganizationalUnitDomainName*

   Example: dsadd ou "ou=London,ou=IT Test, dc=nwtraders,dc=msft"

   LIMA

Lesson: Moving Domain Objects

- When Do You Move a Domain Object?
- How to Move a Domain Object

Introduction

The information in this lesson presents the skills and knowledge that you need to move domain objects.

Lesson objectives

After completing this lesson, you will be able to:

- List reasons for moving a domain object.
- Move a domain object.

When Do You Move a Domain Object?

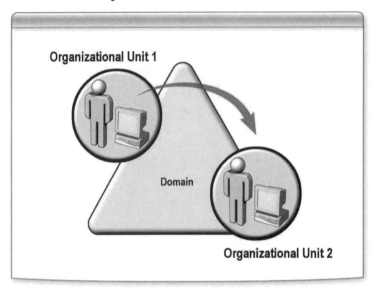

Introduction

You can move objects between organizational units in Active Directory when organizational or administrative functions change, for example, when an employee moves from one department to another. As a systems administrator, it is your task to maintain the Active Directory structure as business needs change.

The following items can be moved within the Active Directory structure:

- User account
- Contact account
- Group
- Shared folder
- Printer
- Computer
- Domain controller
- Organizational unit

Change locations

One reason to move a domain object is when your business physically moves from one location to another. If the Active Directory structure is based on geopolitical boundaries, such as city or country, you may need to move objects from one location to another location as objects are physically moved.

Organizational unit restructuring

Another reason to move a domain object is if your Active Directory structure is based on an organizational chart. You may need to move objects if the organizational structure changes.

For example, suppose the Sales team is represented by an organizational unit, the Marketing team is represented by another organizational unit, and both teams are merged into one Sales and Marketing team. In Active Directory, the objects are merged into one organizational unit. To make this process easier, you can select and move multiple domain objects at the same time.

How to Move a Domain Object

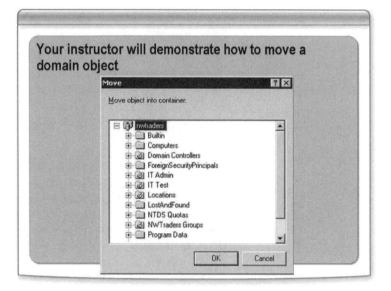

Introduction

You can move domain objects either by using the menu option or by dragging the object from one organizational unit to another.

Procedure

To move a domain object:

1. In Active Directory Users and Computers, right-click the object you want to move, and then click **Move**.

   You can also drag the object to the new location.

2. In the **Move** dialog box, browse to the container that you want to move the object to, and then click **OK**.

Practice: Moving Active Directory Domain Objects

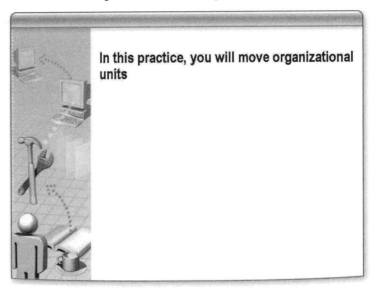

In this practice, you will move organizational units

Objective

In this practice, you will move domain objects from one organizational unit to another.

Instructions

Before you begin this practice:

■ Log on to the domain by using the *ComputerName*User account.

■ Open CustomMMC with the **Run as** command.

Use the user account Nwtraders*ComputerName*Admin (Example: LondonAdmin).

■ Ensure that CustomMMC contains Active Directory Users and Computers.

■ Review the procedures in this lesson that describe how to perform this task.

Scenario

The systems engineers are testing some advanced reporting functionalities in Active Directory. They want you to create some domain objects and move them from the IT Test organizational unit to an organizational unit named IT Test Move.

Practice

▶ **Create and move organizational units**

1. Create the following organizational units in the IT Test organizational unit:

   • OU*ComputerName*1

   • OU*ComputerName*2

2. Move them to the IT Test Move organizational unit.

Lab A: Creating Organizational Units

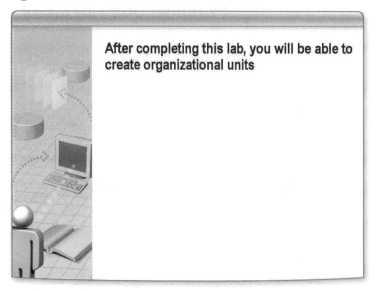

After completing this lab, you will be able to create organizational units

Introduction

After completing this lab, you will be able to create organizational units.

Prerequisites

Before working on this lab, you must have:

- Experience navigating an organizational unit structure in Active Directory Users and Computers.

- Experience creating organizational units.

Lab setup

The Lab Setup section lists the tasks that you must perform before you begin the lab. To complete this lab, you must have reviewed the procedures in the module and successfully completed each practice.

Before you begin this lab:

- Log on to the domain by using the *ComputerName*User account.

- Open CustomMMC with the **Run as** command.

   Use the user account Nwtraders*ComputerName*Admin (Example: LondonAdmin).

- Ensure that CustomMMC contains the following snap-ins:

   - Computer Management (Glasgow)

   - Computer Management (Local)

   - Active Directory Users and Computers

Review the procedures in this lesson that describe how to perform this task.

Estimated time to complete this lab: 30 minutes

Exercise 1
Creating an Organizational Unit Hierarchy

In this exercise, you will create an organizational unit hierarchy.

Scenario

As a systems administrator for Northwind Traders, you have been given the task of creating an organizational unit hierarchy designed by the Northwind Traders design team. The organizational unit hierarchy will use a location-based design that separates user and group accounts. You will create the organizational unit hierarchy in your city organizational unit.

At the end of this lab your organizational unit hierarchy should look like the following diagram:

Note You created the Computers, Laptops, and Desktops organizational units that are shown in the graphic in practices.

Tasks	Specific Instructions
1. Open CustomMMC by using the **Run as** command.	▪ User name: **NWTraders***ComputerName***Admin** ▪ Password: **P@ssw0rd**
2. Find the organizational unit that matches your computer name.	▪ Find the Nwtraders/Locations/*ComputerName* organizational unit.
3. Create an organizational unit in your *ComputerName* organizational unit named Users.	▪ Create the Nwtraders/Locations/*ComputerName*/Users organizational unit.
4. Create an organizational unit in your *ComputerName* organizational unit named Groups.	▪ Create the Nwtraders/Locations/*ComputerName*/Groups organizational unit.

Microsoft® Training & Certification

Module 2: Managing User and Computer Accounts

Contents

Overview	1
Lesson: Creating User Accounts	2
Lesson: Creating Computer Accounts	17
Lesson: Modifying User and Computer Account Properties	26
Lesson: Creating a User Account Template	35
Lesson: Enabling and Unlocking User and Computer Accounts	42
Lesson: Resetting User and Computer Accounts	50
Lesson: Locating User and Computer Accounts in Active Directory	56
Lesson: Saving Queries	66
Lab A: Managing User and Computer Accounts	71

Microsoft®

Overview

- Creating User Accounts
- Creating Computer Accounts
- Modifying User and Computer Account Properties
- Creating a User Account Template
- Enabling and Unlocking User and Computer Accounts
- Resetting User and Computer Accounts
- Locating User and Computer Accounts in Active Directory
- Saving Queries

Introduction

One of your functions as a systems administrator is to manage user and computer accounts. These accounts are Active Directory objects, and you use these accounts to enable individuals to log on to the network and access resources. In this module, you will learn the skills and knowledge that you need to modify user and computer accounts on computers running Microsoft® Windows® Server 2003 in a networked environment.

Objectives

After completing this module, you will be able to:

- Create user accounts.
- Create computer accounts.
- Modify user and computer account properties.
- Create a user account template.
- Enable and unlock user and computer accounts.
- Reset user and computer accounts.
- Locate user and computer accounts in the Active Directory® directory service.
- Save queries.

Lesson: Creating User Accounts

* What Is a User Account?
* Names Associated with Domain User Accounts
* Guidelines for Creating a User Account Naming Convention
* User Account Placement in a Hierarchy
* User Account Password Options
* When to Require Password Changes
* How to Create User Accounts
* Best Practices for Creating User Accounts

Introduction

As a systems administrator, you give users access to various network resources. Therefore, you must create user accounts to identify and authenticate the users so that they can gain access to the network.

Lesson objectives

After completing this lesson, you will be able to:

* Explain the purpose of user accounts.
* Describe the types of names associated with domain user accounts.
* Explain guidelines for creating a convention for naming user accounts.
* Describe user account placement in an Active Directory hierarchy.
* Describe user account password options.
* Determine when to require password changes on domain user accounts.
* Create local and domain user accounts.

What Is a User Account?

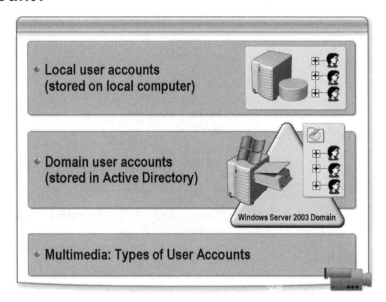

Definition

A user account is an object that consists of all the information that defines a user in Windows Server 2003. The account can be either a local or domain account. A user account includes the user name and password with which the user logs on, the groups that the user account is a member of, and the user rights and permissions the user has for gaining access to computer and network resources.

You can use a user account to:

- Enable someone to log on to a computer based on a user account's identity.

- Enable processes and services to run under a specific security context.

- Manage a user's access to resources such as Active Directory objects and their properties, shared folders, files, directories, and printer queues.

Multimedia: Types of User Accounts

To view the *Types of User Accounts* presentation, open the Web page on the Student Materials compact disc, click **Multimedia**, and then click the title of the presentation.

The *Types of User Accounts* presentation explains how using accounts that grant different levels of access to the network satisfy the needs of network users.

Names Associated with Domain User Accounts

Name	Example
User logon name	Jayadams
Pre-Windows 2000 logon name	Nwtraders\jayadams
User principal logon name	Jayadams@nwtraders.msft
LDAP relative distinguished name	CN=jayadams,CN=users,dc=nwtraders,dc=msft

Introduction

There are four types of names associated with domain user accounts. In Active Directory, each user account consists of a user logon name, a pre-Windows 2000 user logon name (Security Accounts Manager account name), a user principal logon name, and a Lightweight Directory Access Protocol (LDAP) relative distinguished name.

User logon name

When creating a user account, an administrator types a user logon name. The full name must be unique in the container in which you create the user account. It is used as the relative distinguished name. Users use this name only during the logon process. The user enters the user logon name, a password, and the domain name in separate fields on the logon screen.

User logon names can:

- Contain up to 20 uppercase and lowercase characters (the field accepts more than 20 characters, but Windows Server 2003 recognizes only 20).

- Include a combination of special and alphanumeric characters, except the following: " / \ [ ] : ; | = , + * ? < >.

An example of a user logon name is Jayadams or Jadams.

Pre-Windows 2000 logon name

You can use the pre-Windows 2000 network basic input/output system (NetBIOS) user account to log on to a Windows domain from computers running pre-Windows 2000 operating systems by using a name with the *DomainName\UserName* format. You can also use this name to log on to Windows domains from computers running Microsoft Windows 2000 or Microsoft Windows XP or servers running Windows Server 2003. The Pre-Windows 2000 logon name must be unique in the domain. Users can use this logon name with the **Run as** command or on a secondary logon screen.

An example of a Pre-Windows 2000 logon name is nwtraders\jayadams.

User principal logon name

The user principal name (UPN) consists of the user logon name and the user principal name suffix, joined by the at sign (@). The UPN must be unique in the forest.

The second part of the UPN is the user principal name suffix. The user principal name suffix can be the Domain Name System (DNS) domain name, the DNS name of any domain in the forest, or an alternative name that an administrator creates only for logon purposes. Users can use this name to log on with the **Run as** command or on a secondary logon screen.

An example of a UPN is Jayadams@nwtraders.msft.

LDAP relative distinguished name

The LDAP relative distinguished name uniquely identifies the object in its parent container. Users never use this name, but administrators use this name to add users to the network from a script or command line. All objects use the same LDAP naming convention, so all LDAP relative distinguished names must be unique in an organizational unit.

The following are examples of an LDAP relative distinguished name:

- CN=jayadams,CN=users,dc=nwtraders,dc=msft
- CN=computer1,CN=users,dc=nwtraders,dc=msft

Guidelines for Creating a User Account Naming Convention

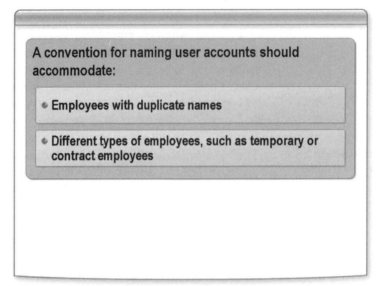

Introduction

A naming convention establishes how user accounts are identified in the domain. A consistent naming convention makes it easier for you to remember user logon names and locate them in lists. It is a good practice to adhere to the naming convention already in use in an existing network that supports a large number of users.

Guidelines

Consider the following guidelines for creating a naming convention:

- If you have a large number of users, your naming convention for user logon names should accommodate employees with duplicate names. A method to accomplish this is to use the first name and the last initial, and then add additional letters from the last name to accommodate duplicate names. For example, for two users named Judy Lew, one user logon name can be Judyl and the other can be Judyle.

- In some organizations, it is useful to identify temporary employees by their user accounts. To do so, you can add a prefix to the user logon name, such as a T and a hyphen. An example is T-Judyl.

- User logon names for domain user accounts must be unique in Active Directory. Full names for domain user accounts must be unique in the domain in which you create the user account.

User Account Placement in a Hierarchy

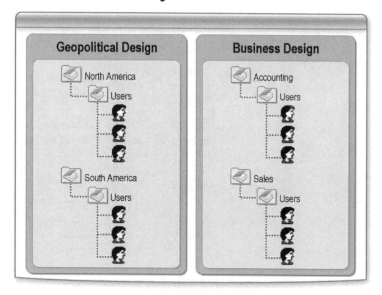

Introduction	You can place domain user accounts in any domain in the forest and any organizational unit in the domain. Typically, account hierarchies are based on geopolitical boundaries or business models. By structuring the Active Directory hierarchy and then managing the permissions on the objects and properties in Active Directory, you can precisely specify the accounts that can access information in Active Directory and the level of permissions that they can have.

Place user accounts in an Active Directory hierarchy based on the way the user accounts are managed.

Geopolitical design	In a geopolitical design, you place users in domains that match their physical location. Geopolitical domain structures place domain controllers that support users of the domain close to the users. This reduces logon times for users and enables users to log on if the wide area network (WAN) is down.

Business design	When the hierarchy of domains is based on business models, you place your sales personnel in a Sales domain and manufacturing personnel in a Manufacturing domain. This model ensures that there are enough domain controllers to support all the users in the WAN.

Note In many cases, one domain will work for a corporate environment. You can still separate administrative control of users by placing them into organizational units.

User Account Password Options

Account options	Description
User must change password at next logon	**Users must change their passwords the next time they log on to the network**
User cannot change password	A user does not have the permissions to change their own password
Password never expires	A user password is prevented from expiring
Account is disabled	A user cannot log on by using the selected account

Introduction

As a systems administrator, you can manage user account password options. These options can be set when the user account is created or in the **Properties** dialog box of a user account.

Password options

The administrator can choose from the following password options to protect access to the domain or a computer:

- **User must change password at the next logon**. This is used when a new user logs on to a system for the first time or when the administrator resets forgotten passwords for users.

- **User cannot change password**. Use this option when you want to control when a user account password can be changed.

- **Password never expires**. This option prevents the password from expiring. As a security best practice, do not use this option.

- **Account is disabled**. This option prevents the user from logging on by using the selected account.

When to Require or Restrict Password Changes

Option	Use this option when you:
Require password changes	• Create new domain accounts • Reset passwords
Restrict password changes	• Create local and domain service accounts • Create new local accounts that will not log on locally

Introduction

To create a more secure environment, require password changes on user accounts and restrict password changes on service accounts. The following table lists when you need to restrict or require password changes.

Password modifications options

Option	Use this option when you:
Require password changes	• Create new domain user accounts. Select the check box that requires the user to change the password the first time the user logs on to the domain. • Reset passwords. This option enables the administrator to reset a password when the password expires or if the user forgets it.
Restrict password changes	• Create local or domain service accounts. Service accounts typically have many dependencies on them. As a result, you may want to restrict the password change policy so that service account passwords are changed by the administrator who is responsible for the applications that depend on the service account. • Create new local accounts that will not log on locally.

Additional Readings

For more information about service accounts, see "Services permissions" at http://www.microsoft.com/technet/treeview/default.asp?url=/technet/prodtechnol/windowsserver2003/proddocs/server/sys_srv_permissions.asp.

Form more information about changing passwords, see:

■ Article 324744, "HOW TO: Prevent Users from Changing a Password Except When Required in Windows Server 2003," in the Microsoft Knowledge Base at http://support.microsoft.com/?kbid=324744.

■ Article 320325, "User May Not Be Able to Change Their Password If You Configure the 'User Must Change Password at Next Logon' Setting," in the Microsoft Knowledge Base at http://support.microsoft.com/?kbid=320325.

For more information about preventing passwords of service accounts from being changed, see article 324744, "HOW TO: Prevent Users from Changing a Password Except When Required in Windows Server 2003," in the Microsoft Knowledge Base at http://support.microsoft.com/?kbid= 324744.

How to Create User Accounts

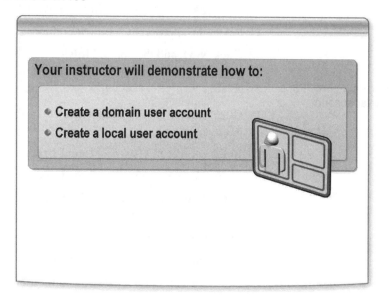

Introduction

Domain user accounts enable users to log on to a domain and access resources anywhere on the network, and local user accounts enable users to log on and access resources only on the computer on which you create the local user account. As a systems administrator, you must create domain and local user accounts to manage your network environment.

Important   You cannot create local user accounts on a domain controller.

Procedure for creating a domain user account

To create a domain user account:

1. Click **Start**, point to **Administrative Tools**, and then click **Active Directory Users and Computers**.

2. In the console tree, double-click the domain node.

3. In the details pane, right-click the organizational unit where you want to add the user, point to **New**, and then click **User**.

4. In the **New Object - User** dialog box, in the **First name** box, type the user's first name.

5. In the **Initials** box, type the user's initials.

6. In the **Last name** box, type the user's last name.

7. In the **User logon name** box, type the name that the user will log on with.

8. From the drop-down list, click the UPN suffix that must be appended to the user logon name after the at sign (@).

9. Click **Next**.

10. In the **Password** and **Confirm password** boxes, type the user's password.

11. Select the appropriate password options.

12. Click **Next**, and then click **Finish**.

Procedure for creating a local user account

To create a local user account:

1. Click **Start**, point to Administrative Tools, and then click **Computer Management**.

2. In the console tree, expand **Local Users and Groups**, and then click **Users**.

3. On the **Action** menu, click **New User**.

4. In the **New User** dialog box, in the **User name** box, type the name that the user will log on with.

5. Modify the full name as desired.

6. In the **Password** and **Confirm password** boxes, type the user's password.

7. Select the appropriate password options.

8. Click **Create**, and then click **Close**.

Note A user name cannot be identical to any other user or group name on the computer being administered. It can contain up to 20 uppercase or lowercase characters, except for the following:

" / \ [ ] : ; | = , + * ? < >

A user name cannot consist solely of periods or spaces.

Using a command line

Another way to create a domain user account is to use the **dsadd** command. The **dsadd user** command adds a single user to the directory from a command prompt or batch file.

To create a user account by using **dsadd user**:

1. Open a command prompt.

2. Type **dsadd user** *UserDomainName* [**-samid** *SAMName*] [**-upn** *UPN*] [**-fn** *FirstName*] [**-ln** *LastName*] [**-display** *DisplayName*] [**-pwd** {*Password*|***}] Use " " if there is a space in any variable.

Note For the complete syntax of the dsadd user command, at a command prompt, type **dsadd user /?**.

Example of **dsadd user**:

```
dsadd user "cn=testuser,cn=users,dc=nwtraders,dc=msft" -samid
testuser -upn testuser@nwtraders.msft -fn test -ln user -
display "test user" -pwd P@ssw0rd
```

Practice: Creating User Accounts

In this practice, you will:

- Create a local user account by using Computer Management
- Create a domain account by using Active Directory Users and Computers
- Create a domain user account by using Run as
- Create a domain user account by using dsadd

Objective

In this practice, you will:

- Create a local user account by using Computer Management.
- Create a domain account by using Active Directory Users and Computers.
- Create a domain user account by using **Run as**.
- Create a domain user account by using **dsadd**.

Instructions

Before you begin this practice:

- Log on to the student computer by using the *ComputerName*User account.
- Open CustomMMC with the **Run as** command.

  Use the user account Nwtraders*ComputerName*Admin (Example: LondonAdmin).

- Ensure that CustomMMC contains the following snap-ins:
  - Computer Management (local)
  - Active Directory Users and Computers
- Review the procedures in this lesson that describe how to perform this task.

Scenario

Your manager asks you to create a local user account that will be used to back up your company's software. Another department in your organization will install the software and give the account the user rights needed to back up the server. You must create a local user account to be used as a service account.

Practice: Creating a local user account

▶ **Create a local user account**

1. Open Computer Management for your local server.

2. Create an account by using the following parameters:

   a. User name: **Service_Backup**

   b. Description: **Service Account for Backup Software**

   c. Password: **P@ssw0rd**

3. Clear the **User must change password at next logon** check box.

Scenario

You will use the Administrator account to perform management tasks. Your company's security practices require that you create a personal user account that you will use to log on to the domain, read and send e-mail, and other nonadministrative tasks.

You must set up a domain user account for yourself. When you need to perform administrative tasks, you will either log on as a different user or use secondary logon credentials. This new account should be created in the nwtraders.msft/IT Admin/IT Users container.

Practice: Creating a domain user account

▶ **Create a domain user account**

1. Open Active Directory Users and Computers.

2. Add a user account to the IT Users container with the following parameters:

   a. First name: Your first name (Example: Misty)

   b. Last name: Your last name (Example: Shock)

   c. Full name: Your full name (Example: Misty Shock)

   d. User logon name: The first three letters of your first name and the first three letters of your last name (Example: MisSho)

   e. Password: Use a password that:

   - Is at least seven characters long.

   - Does not contain your user name, real name, or company name.

   - Does not contain a complete word that is found in the dictionary.

   - Contains characters from each of the following four groups.

Group	Examples
Uppercase letters	A, B, C ..
Lowercase letters	a, b, c ..
Numerals	0, 1, 2, 3, 4, 5, 6, 7, 8, 9
Symbols found on the keyboard (all keyboard characters not defined as letters or numerals)	` ~ ! @ # $ % ^ & * ( ) _ + - = { } | [ ] / : " ; ' < > ? , . \

An example of a strong password is J*p2leO4>F.

3. Log off.

4. Test the user account that you just created by logging on by using the user account.

5. Log off.

Scenario

Northwind Traders is in the process of testing advanced features of Active Directory. Your team has the task of creating user accounts in the IT Test organizational unit. The test team will use these accounts. Each member of your team must create five accounts.

Practice: Creating a domain user account using Run as

▶ **Create a domain user account by using Run as**

1. Log on to the student computer by using the *ComputerName*User account.

2. Open CustomMMC with the **Run as** command.

   - Use the user account Nwtraders*ComputerName*Admin (Example: LondonAdmin).

3. In Active Directory Users and Computers, expand **nwtraders.msft**.

4. Right-click the **IT Test** organizational unit, point to **New**, and then click **User**.

5. Add a user account to the IT Test organizational unit with the following parameters:

   a. First name: **User1**

   b. Last name: Your last name (Example: Shock)

   c. User logon name: **User1** followed by the first three letters of your last name (Example: User1Sho)

   d. Password: **P@ssw0rd**

6. Repeat step 5 and create four more user accounts.

   Example: User2Sho, User3Sho, User4Sho, User5Sho

7. Close all windows.

Scenario

Northwind Traders is in the process of testing advanced features of Active Directory. Your team has the task of creating user accounts in the IT Test organizational unit. The test team will use these accounts. Each member of your team must create five accounts.

Practice: Using a command line

▶ **Create a domain user account by using dsadd**

1. Click **Start**, click **Run**, and then type **runas /user:nwtraders*ComputerName*Admin cmd** and then click **OK**.

2. When prompted for the password, type **P@ssw0rd** and then press **ENTER**.

3. At the command prompt, type the following command:

   dsadd user "cn=User6*FirstThreeLettersOfLastName***,ou=it test,dc=nwtraders,dc=msft" -samid User6***FirstThreeLettersOfLastName* **-pwd** *P@ssw0rd*

Best Practices for Creating User Accounts

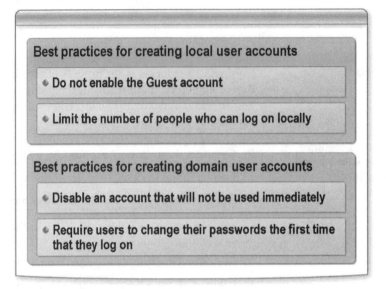

Introduction

There are several best practices for creating user accounts that reduce security risks in the network environment. While software products change, review current best practices at www.microsoft.com/security.

Local user accounts

Consider the following best practices when creating local user accounts:

- Do not enable the Guest account.
- Rename the Administrator account.
- Limit the number of people who can log on locally.
- Use strong passwords.

Domain user accounts

Consider the following best practices when creating domain user accounts:

- Disable any account that will not be used immediately.
- Require users to change their passwords the first time that they log on.
- As a security best practice, it is recommended that you do not log on to your computer with administrative credentials.
- When you are logged on to your computer without administrative credentials, it is recommended that you use the **Run as** command to accomplish administrative tasks.
- Rename or disable the Administrator and Guest accounts in each domain to reduce the attacks on your domain.
- By default, all traffic on Active Directory administrative tools is signed and encrypted while in transit on the network. Do not disable this feature.

Lesson: Creating Computer Accounts

- What Is a Computer Account?
- Why Create a Computer Account?
- Where Computer Accounts Are Created in a Domain
- Computer Account Options
- How to Create a Computer Account

Introduction

The information in this lesson presents the skills and knowledge that you need to create a computer account.

Lesson objectives

After completing this lesson, you will be able to:

- Define computer account.
- Describe the purpose of computer accounts.
- Describe where computer accounts are created in a domain.
- Describe the various computer account options.
- Create a computer account.

What Is a Computer Account?

- Identifies a computer in a domain
- Provides a means for authenticating and auditing computer access to the network and to domain resources
- Is required for every computer running:
  - Windows Server 2003
  - Windows XP Professional
  - Windows 2000
  - Windows NT

Introduction

Every computer running Microsoft Windows NT®, Windows 2000, Windows XP, or Windows Server 2003 that joins a domain has a computer account. Similar to user accounts, computer accounts provide a means for authenticating and auditing computer access to the network and to domain resources.

What does a computer account do?

In Active Directory, computers are security principles, just like users. This means that computers must have accounts and passwords. To be fully authenticated by Active Directory, a user must have a valid user account, and the user must also log on to the domain from a computer that has a valid computer account.

Note You cannot create computer accounts for computers running Microsoft Windows 95, Microsoft Windows 98, Microsoft Windows Millennium Edition, and Windows XP Home Edition, because their operating systems do not adhere to Active Directory security requirements.

Why Create a Computer Account?

- Security
  - Authentication
  - IPSec
  - Auditing
- Management
  - Active Directory features:
    Software deployment
    Desktop management
  - Hardware and software inventory through SMS

Introduction

Computers are responsible for performing key tasks, such as authenticating user logons, distributing Internet Protocol (IP) addresses, maintaining the integrity of Active Directory, and enforcing security policies. To have full access to these network resources, computers must have valid accounts in Active Directory. The two main functions of a computer account are performing security and management activities.

Security

A computer account must be created in Active Directory for users to take full advantage of Active Directory features. When a computer account is created, the computer can use advanced authentication processes such as Kerberos authentication and IP security (IPSec) to encrypt IP traffic. The computer also needs a computer account to dictate how auditing is applied and recorded.

Management

Computer accounts help the systems administrator manage the network structure. The systems administrator uses computer accounts to manage the functionality of the desktop environment, automate the deployment of software by using Active Directory, and maintain a hardware and software inventory by using Microsoft Systems Management Server (SMS). Computer accounts in the domain are also used to control access to resources.

Where Computer Accounts Are Created in a Domain

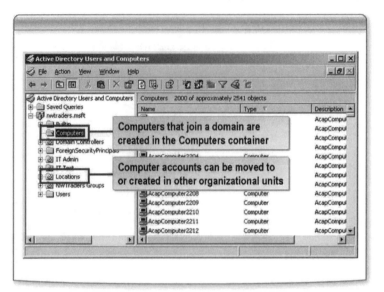

Introduction	When the systems administrator creates a computer account, they can choose the organizational unit in which to create that account. If a computer joins a domain, the computer account is created in the Computers container, and the administrator can move the account to its proper organizational unit as necessary.
Administrators designate the location of computer accounts	By default, Active Directory users can add up to 10 computers to the domain with their user account credentials. This default configuration can be changed. If the systems administrator adds a computer account directly to Active Directory, a user can join a computer to the domain without using any of the 10 allocated computer accounts.
Pre-staged computer accounts	Adding a computer to the domain with a previously created account is called pre-staging, which means that computers are added to any organizational unit where the systems administrator has permissions to add computer accounts. Usually, users do not have the appropriate permissions to pre-stage a computer account, so as an alternative they join a computer to the domain by using a pre-staged account.
Users designate the location of computer accounts	When a user joins a computer to the domain, the computer account is added to the Computers container in Active Directory. This is accomplished through a service that adds the computer account on behalf of the user. The system account also records how many computers each user has added to the domain. By default, any authenticated user has the user right to add workstations to a domain and can create up to 10 computer accounts in the domain.
Additional reading	For more information about users adding computer accounts to a domain, see article 251335, "Domain Users Cannot Join Workstation or Server to a Domain," in the Microsoft Knowledge Base at http://support.microsoft.com/?kbid=251335.

Computer Account Options

Introduction

There are two optional features that you can enable when creating a computer account. You can assign a computer account as a Pre-Windows 2000 computer or as a backup domain controller (BDC).

Pre-Windows 2000

Select the **Assign this computer account as a pre-Windows 2000 computer** check box to assign a password based on the computer name. If you do not select this check box, a random password is assigned as the initial password for the computer account. The password automatically changes every five days between the computer and the domain where the computer account is located. This option guarantees that a pre-Windows 2000 computer will be able to interpret whether the password meets the password requirements.

Backup domain controller

Select the **Assign this computer as a backup domain controller** check box if you intend to use the computer as a backup domain controller. You should use this feature if you are still in a mixed environment with a Window Server 2003 domain controller and Windows NT 4.0 BDC. After the account is created in Active Directory, you can then join the BDC to the domain during the installation of Windows NT 4.0.

Additional Reading

For more information about delegating authentication, see "Delegating authentication" at http://www.microsoft.com/technet/treeview/default.asp?url=/technet/prodtechnol/windowsserver2003/proddocs/server/SE_constrained_delegation.asp.

How to Create a Computer Account

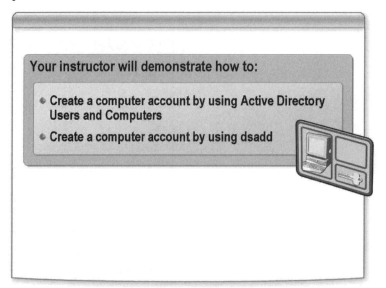

Introduction

By default, members of the Account Operators group can create computer accounts in the Computers container and in new organizational units. However, they cannot create computer accounts in the Builtin, Domain Controllers, ForeignSecurityPrincipals, LostAndFound, Program Data, System, or Users containers.

Procedure

To create a computer account:

1. In Active Directory Users and Computers, in the console tree, right-click **Computers** or the container in which you want to add the computer, point to **New**, and then click **Computer**.

2. In the **New Object – Computer** dialog box, in the **Computer name** box, type the computer name.

3. Select the appropriate options, and then click **Next**.

4. In the **Managed** dialog box, click **Next**.

5. Click **Finish**.

Note To perform this procedure, you must be a member of the Account Operators group, Domain Admins group, or the Enterprise Admins group in Active Directory, or you must be delegated the appropriate authority. As a security best practice, consider using **Run as** to perform this procedure.

Using a command line   To create a computer account by using **dsadd computer**:

1. Open a command prompt.

2. Type **dsadd computer** *ComputerDomainName* [**-samid** *SAMName*] [**-desc** *Description*] [**-loc** *Location*] [**-memberof** *GroupDomainName* ..] [{**-s** *Server* | **-d** *Domain*}] [**-u** *UserName*] [**-p** {*Password* | ***}] [**-q**] [{**-uc** | **-uco** | **-uci**}]

Note   For the complete syntax of the dsadd user command, at a command prompt, type **dsadd computer /?**.

Practice: Creating a Computer Account

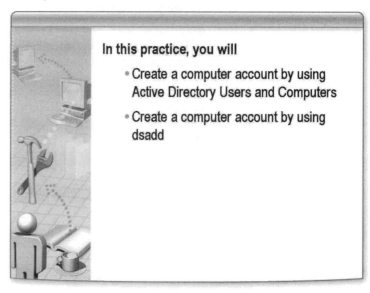

Objective

In this practice, you will create computer accounts.

Instructions

Before you begin this practice:

- Log on to the domain by using the *ComputerName*User account.
- Open CustomMMC with the **Run as** command.

  Use the user account Nwtraders*ComputerName*Admin (Example: LondonAdmin).
- Ensure that CustomMMC contains Active Directory Users and Computers.
- Review the procedures in this lesson that describe how to perform this task.

Scenario

The systems engineers for Northwind Traders are testing some advanced features of Active Directory. Each member of your team must create five computer accounts in the IT Test organizational unit.

Practice: Creating a computer account

▶ **Create a computer account**

1. In Active Directory Users and Computers, expand **nwtraders.msft**, and then click the **IT Test** organizational unit.

2. Create a computer account with the following parameters:

   a. Computer name: *ComputerName***001**

   b. Computer name (pre-Windows 2000): *ComputerName***001**

3. Repeat step 2 for the following computer names: *ComputerName***002**, *ComputerName***003**, *ComputerName***004**

4. Close all windows.

Scenario

The systems engineers for Northwind Traders are testing some advanced features of Active Directory. Each member of your team must create five computer accounts in the IT Test organizational unit.

Practice: Using a command line

▶ **Create a computer account by using dsadd**

1. Click **Start**, click **Run**, and then type **runas /user:nwtraders***ComputerName***Admin cmd**

2. When prompted for the password, type **P@ssw0rd** and then press **ENTER**.

3. At the command prompt, type the following command:

   dsadd computer "cn=*ComputerName***005,ou=IT Test,dc=nwtraders,dc=msft"**

Lesson: Modifying User and Computer Account Properties

- When to Modify User and Computer Account Properties
- Properties Associated with User Accounts
- Properties Associated with Computer Accounts
- How to Modify User and Computer Account Properties

Introduction

This lesson presents the skills and knowledge that you need to modify user and computer accounts.

Lesson objectives

After completing this lesson, you will be able to:

- Determine when to modify user and computer account properties.
- Describe properties associated with user accounts.
- Describe properties associated with computer accounts.
- Modify user and computer account properties.

When to Modify User and Computer Account Properties

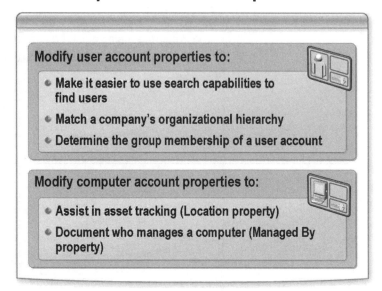

Modify user account properties to:

* Make it easier to use search capabilities to find users
* Match a company's organizational hierarchy
* Determine the group membership of a user account

Modify computer account properties to:

* Assist in asset tracking (Location property)
* Document who manages a computer (Managed By property)

Introduction

As a systems administrator, you may be responsible for creating user and computer accounts in Active Directory. You also may be responsible for maintaining those user and computer accounts. To complete these tasks, you must be very familiar with the various properties for each user and computer account.

User account properties

It is critical that systems administrators are familiar with user account properties so that they can manage the network structure. Users may use the user account properties as a single source of information about users, like a telephone book, or to search for users based on items such as office location, supervisor, or department name. The systems administrator can use the properties of a user account to determine how the user account behaves in a terminal server session or how the user can gain access to the network through a dial-up connection.

Computer account properties

To maintain computer accounts, you must find the physical location of the computer. The most commonly used properties for computer accounts in Active Directory are the **Location** and **Managed by** properties. The **Location** property is useful, because you can document the computer's physical location in your network. The **Managed By** tab lists the individual responsible for the server. This can be useful when you have a data center with servers for different departments and you need to perform maintenance on the server. You can call or send e-mail to the person who is responsible for the server before you perform maintenance on the server.

Properties Associated with User Accounts

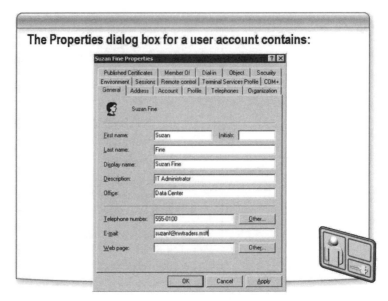

The Properties dialog box for a user account contains:

Introduction

The **Properties** dialog box for a user account contains information about each user account that is stored in Active Directory. The more complete the information in the **Properties** dialog box, the easier it is to search for users in Active Directory.

User account properties

The following table lists the most commonly used property options for user accounts.

Tab	Properties
General	Name, description, office location, telephone number, e-mail address, and home page information
Address	Street address, post office box, city, state or province, postal zip code, and country
Account	Logon name, account options, unlock account, and account expiration
Profile	Profile path and home folder
Telephone	Home, pager, mobile phone, fax, and IP telephone numbers
Organization	Title, department, manager, and direct reports
Member Of	Groups to which the user belongs
Dial-in	Remote access permissions, callback options, and static IP address and routes
Environment	One or more applications to start and the devices to connect to when a Terminal Services user logs on
Sessions	Terminal Services settings
Remote control	Terminal Services remote control settings
Terminal Services Profile	The user's Terminal Services profile

Properties Associated with Computer Accounts

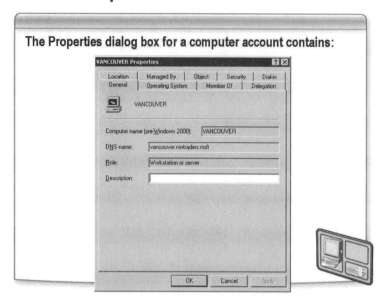

Introduction

The **Properties** dialog box for a computer account contains unique information about each computer account that is stored in Active Directory. The more complete the information in the **Properties** dialog box, the easier it is to search for computers in Active Directory.

Computer account properties

The following table lists the most commonly used property options for computer accounts.

Tab	Properties
General	Computer name, DNS name, description, and role
Operating System	Name and version of the operating system running on the computer and the latest service pack installed
Member Of	The groups in the local domain and any groups to which the computer belongs
Location	The location of the computer
Managed By	Name, office location, street, city, state or province, country or region, telephone number, and fax number of the person that manages the computer
Object	The canonical name of the object, object class, the date it was created, the date it was last modified, and update sequence numbers (USNs)
Security	The users and groups who have permissions for the computer
Dial-in	Remote access permission, callback options, and routing options

How to Modify User and Computer Account Properties

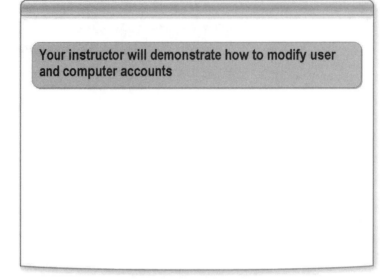

Introduction

As a systems administrator, you must be able to modify user and computer account properties to manage the network efficiently.

Procedure

To modify user and computer accounts:

1. In Active Directory Users and Computers, in the console tree, navigate to the container that contains the user or computer account that you want to modify.

2. In the details pane, select the user or computer account that you want to modify, right-click the selection, and then click **Properties**.

3. In the **Properties** dialog box, modify the properties of the account as necessary.

Note To perform this procedure, you must be a member of the Account Operators, Domain Admins, or Enterprise Admins group in Active Directory, or you must be delegated the appropriate authority. As a security best practice, consider using **Run as** to perform this procedure.

Using a command line

You can use the **dsmod** command to modify attributes of one or more existing users or computers in Active Directory. To modify the attributes of a user account:

1. Open a command prompt.

2. For a user account, type **dsmod user** *UserDN* ... [**-upn** *UPN*] [**-fn** *FirstName*] [**-mi** *Initial*] [**-ln** *LastName*] [**-display** *DisplayName*] [**-empid** *EmployeeID*] [**-pwd** (*Password* | *)*] [**-desc** *Description*] [**-office** *Office*] [**-tel** *PhoneNumber*] [**-email** *E-mailAddress*] [**-hometel** *HomePhoneNumber*] [**-pager** *PagerNumber*] [**-mobile** *CellPhoneNumber*] [**-fax** *FaxNumber*] [**-iptel** *IPPhoneNumber*] [**-webpg** *WebPage*] [**-title** *Title*] [**-dept** *Department*] [**-company** *Company*] [**-mgr** *Manager*] [**-hmdir** *HomeDirectory*] [**-hmdrv** *DriveLetter:*] [**-profile** *ProfilePath*] [**-loscr** *ScriptPath*] [**-mustchpwd** {**yes** | **no**}] [**-canchpwd** {**yes** | **no**}] [**-reversiblepwd** {**yes** | **no**}] [**-pwdneverexpires** {**yes** | **no**}] [**-acctexpires** *NumberOfDays*] [**-disabled** {**yes** | **no**}] [{**-s** *Server* | **-d** *Domain*}] [**-u** *UserName*] [**-p** {*Password* | *}*] [**-c**] [**-q**] [{**-uc** | **-uco** | **-uci**}]

   —or—

   For a computer account, type **dsmod computer** *ComputerDN* ... [**-desc** *Description*] [**-loc** *Location*] [**-disabled** {**yes** | **no**}] [**-reset**] [{**-s** *Server* | **-d** *Domain*}] [**-u** *UserName*] [**-p** {*Password* | *}*] [**-c**] [**-q**] [{**-uc** | **-uco** | **-uci**}]

Note   For the complete syntax of the dsmod command, at a command prompt, type **dsmod user /?** or **dsmod computer /?**.

Practice: Modifying User and Computer Account Properties

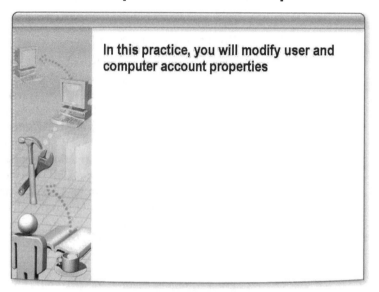

In this practice, you will modify user and computer account properties

Objective

In this practice, you will modify user and computer account properties.

Instructions

Before you begin this practice:

- Log on to the domain by using the *ComputerName*User account.
- Open CustomMMC with the **Run as** command.

  Use the user account Nwtraders*ComputerName*Admin (Example: LondonAdmin).

- Ensure that CustomMMC contains Active Directory Users and Computers.
- Review the procedures in this lesson that describe how to perform this task.

Scenario

The systems engineers for Northwind Traders are working on integrating Active Directory with the payroll system. You must create a user in the IT Test organizational unit and set user account properties that the payroll system will use to identify the user. Because this is a test account, you will not mandate the user to change the password. Also, because the systems engineers will use this account later, you should disable the account.

Practice: Modify user account properties

▶ **Create a user account**

- In Active Directory Users and Computers, create a user account with the following parameters:

  - First name: *ComputerName* (Example: London)
  - Last name: **Payroll**
  - Full name: *ComputerName* **Payroll** (Example: London Payroll)
  - User logon name: *ComputerName***Payroll** (Example: LondonPayroll)
  - User logon name [pre-Windows 2000]: *ComputerName***Payroll** (Example: LondonPayroll)
  - Password: **P@ssw0rd**

▶ **Modify the user account**

- In Active Directory Users and Computers, modify the following parameters of the *ComputerName*Payroll user account:

  - Description: **Account for AD and Payroll Test**

  - Office: **Payroll**

  - Telephone number: **973-555-0198**

  - E-mail: *ComputerName***Payroll@nwtraders.msft**

  - Title: **Payroll Test Account**

  - Department: **Payroll Test**

  - Company: **Payroll Test**

  - Manager: **User0002**

  - Home Telephone number: **555-0101**

Scenario

The systems engineers for Northwind Traders want to test your ability to track and search for computer assets by using the **Location** property of a computer account. You must create a computer account in the IT Test organizational unit and edit the **Location** property to match your city location.

Practice: Modifying computer account properties

▶ **Create a computer account**

- In Active Directory Users and Computers, create a computer account whose computer name is **Server***ComputerName* (Example: ServerLondon).

▶ **Modify the computer account**

- In Active Directory Users and Computers, change the **Location** property of the Server*ComputerName* computer account to *ComputerName*.

Scenario

The systems engineers for Northwind Traders are modifying user accounts with command-line tools. You must create a user and modify its properties.

Practice: Using a command line to modify user accounts

▶ **Add a user account**

- Using **dsadd**, add a user account with a user name of *ComputerName***Dsmod**.

  Example: dsadd user "cn=londonDsmod,ou=it test,dc=nwtraders,dc=msft"

▶ **Modify the user account**

- Using **dsmod**, modify the following parameters of the user account:
  - First name: *ComputerName*
  - Last name: **Dsmod**
  - Full name: *ComputerName* **Dsmod**
  - User logon name: *ComputerName***Dsmod**
  - Password: **P@ssw0rd**
  - Description: **Account for AD and Dsmod Test**
  - Office: **DataCenter**
  - Telephone number: **555-0101**
  - E-mail: *ComputerName***Dsmod@nwtraders.msft**
  - Title: **Dsmod Test Account**
  - Department: **Data Center**
  - Company: **NWTraders**
  - Home Telephone number: **555-0101**

  Example: dsmod user "cn=Londondsmod,ou=it test,dc=nwtraders,dc=msft" -upn Londondsmod@nwtraders.msft -fn London -ln dsmod -display Londondsmod -office DataCenter -tel 555-0101 -title Title ITAdmin -dept DataCenter -company NWTraders -hometel 555-0101

Scenario

The systems engineers for Northwind Traders want to test your ability to track and search for computer assets by using the **Location** property of the Active Directory computer account. You need to create a computer account in the IT Test organizational unit and edit the **Location** property to match your city location.

Practice: Using a command line to modify computer accounts

▶ **Add a computer account**

1. Click **Start**, click **Run**, and then type **runas /user:nwtraders***ComputerName***Admin cmd**

2. When prompted for the password, type **P@ssw0rd** and then press **ENTER**.

3. In the command prompt, using **dsadd**, add a computer account with the following parameters:
   - Computer name: **dsmod***ComputerName*
   - Organizational unit: IT Test

   Example: dsadd computer "cn=dsmodlondon,ou=it test,dc=nwtraders,dc=msft"

▶ **Modify the location attribute for a computer account**

- Using **dsmod**, modify the computer account **dsmod***ComputerName* with the following attribute:
  - Location: *ComputerName*

  Example: dsmod computer "cn=serverlondon,ou=it test,dc=nwtraders,dc=msft" -loc London

Lesson: Creating a User Account Template

- What Is a User Account Template?
- What Properties Are in a Template?
- Guidelines for Creating User Account Templates
- How to Create a User Account Template

Introduction

The information in this lesson presents the skills and knowledge that you need to create a user account template.

Lesson objectives

After completing this lesson, you will be able to:

- Explain the purpose of a user account template.
- Describe the properties of a user account template.
- Create a user account template.

What Is a User Account Template?

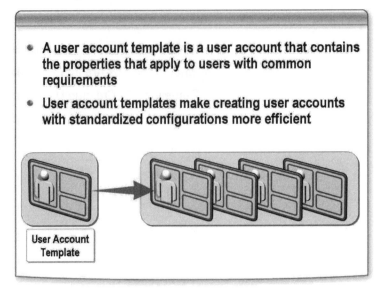

- A user account template is a user account that contains the properties that apply to users with common requirements
- User account templates make creating user accounts with standardized configurations more efficient

User Account Template

Definition

You can simplify the process of creating domain user accounts by creating a user account template. A user account template is an account that has commonly used settings and properties already configured.

Using account templates

For each new user account, you only need to add the information that is unique to that user account. For example, if all sales personnel must be a member of 15 sales groups and have the same manager, you can create a template that includes membership to all the groups and the reporting manager. When the template is copied for a new salesperson, it retains the group memberships and manager that were in the template.

What Properties Are in a Template?

Tab	Properties copied
Address	All properties except **Street Address**
Account	All properties except **Logon Name**
Profile	All properties, except **Profile path** and **Home folder**, reflect new user's logon name
Organization	All properties except **Title**
Member Of	All properties

Properties

There are numerous properties associated with each account. However, only a limited number of properties can be copied in a template. The following table lists the user properties that can be copied from an existing domain user account to a new domain user account.

Properties tab	Properties copied to new domain user account
Address	All properties, except **Street Address**, are copied.
Account	All properties, except **Logon Name**, which is copied from the **Copy Object – User** dialog box, are copied.
Profile	All properties, except the **Profile path** and **Home folder** entries, are modified to reflect the new user's logon name.
Organization	All properties, except **Title**, are copied.
Member Of	All properties are copied.

Additional reading

For more information about profiles, see article 324749, "HOW TO: Create a Roaming User Profile in Windows Server 2003" in the Microsoft Knowledge Base at http://support.microsoft.com/?kbid=324749.

Form more information about home folders, see article 325853, "HOW TO: Use Older Roaming User Profiles with Windows Server 2003" in the Microsoft Knowledge Base at http://support.microsoft.com/?kbid=325853.

Guidelines for Creating User Account Templates

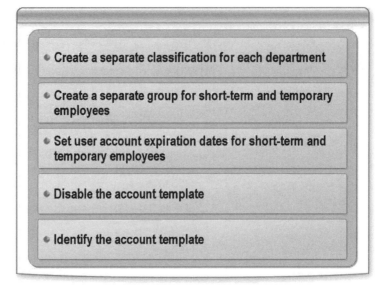

Guidelines

Consider the following best practices for creating user account templates:

- Create a separate classification for each department in your business group.

- Create a separate group for short-term and temporary employees with logon and workstation restrictions.

- Set user account expiration dates for short-term and temporary employees to prevent them from accessing the network when their contracts expire.

- Disable the account template.

- Identify the account template. For example, place a T_ before the name of the account to identify the account as an account template.

How to Create a User Account Template

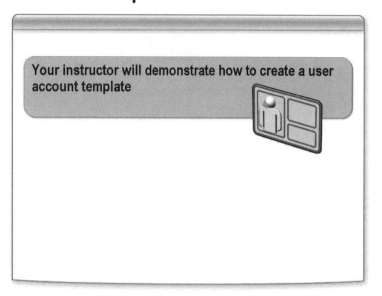

Your instructor will demonstrate how to create a user account template

Introduction

To create an account that you can use as a template, you create a user account, configure the settings that you want, disable the account, and then copy the account when you need to create a new user.

Procedure

To create a new user account template:

1. Create a new domain user account, or copy an existing domain user account.

2. Type the user name and user logon name information for the new user account, and then click **Next**.

3. Type and confirm the password, set the password requirements, select the **Account is disabled** check box, if necessary, and then click **Next**.

4. Verify the new user account information, and then click **Finish**.

Practice: Creating a User Account Template

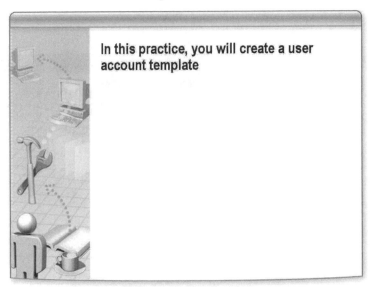

In this practice, you will create a user account template

Objective

In this practice, you will create and copy a user account template.

Instructions

Before you begin this practice:

- Log on to the domain by using the *ComputerName*User account.

- Open CustomMMC with the **Run as** command.

  Use the user account Nwtraders*ComputerName*Admin (Example: LondonAdmin).

- Ensure that CustomMMC contains Active Directory Users and Computers.

- Review the procedures in this lesson that describe how to perform this task.

Scenario

Your manager asks you to research the values to be copied from an account template. You must create an account template with the following parameters, copy the account to a user account, and document the variables that were copied and the variables that were not copied.

Practice: creating a user account template

▶ **Create a user account template**

- Create a user account template with the following parameters.

Parameter	Properties	Example
First name	*ComputerName*	London
Last name	**Template**	
Full name	*ComputerName* **Template**	London Template
User logon name	_*ComputerName***Template**	_LondonTemplate
Password	**P@ssw0rd**	

▶ **Modify the user account template**

- Modify the following parameters of the *ComputerName*Template user account.

Parameter	Properties	Example
Description	**Telemarketing User**	
Office	**Telemarketing**	
Telephone number	**555-1000**	
E-mail	*ComputerName***Template@ nwtraders.msft**	LondonTemplate@ nwtraders.msft
City	**Redmond**	
Street	**One Microsoft Way**	
State	**Washington**	
Zip	**98052**	
Country/region	**United States**	
Home Telephone number	**555-0101**	
Title	**Telemarketing User**	
Department	**Telemarketing**	
Company	**NWTraders**	
Manager	**User 0001**	
Member (group membership)	**G NWTraders Telemarketing Personnel**	
Account is disabled		

Scenario

You must create accounts for the Telemarketing team at Northwind Traders. The Telemarketing team has a high turnover of employees. For security reasons, Northwind Traders does not want to rename and reuse user accounts. You must create a user account template that meets the needs of the Telemarketing team.

Practice: copying a user account template

▶ **Copy the user account template**

- Copy the *ComputerName*Template account that has the following parameters.

Parameter	Properties	Example
First name	*ComputerName*	London
Last name	**User**	
Full name	*ComputerName* **User**	London User
User logon name	*ComputerName***Template**	LondonTemplate
Password	**P@ssw0rd**	

Lesson: Enabling and Unlocking User and Computer Accounts

- Why Enable and Disable User and Computer Accounts?
- How to Enable and Disable User and Computer Accounts
- What Are Locked-out User Accounts?
- How to Unlock User Accounts

Introduction
The information in this lesson presents the skills and knowledge that you need to enable and disable user and computer accounts.

Lesson objectives
After completing this lesson, you will be able to:

- Explain why you enable and disable user and computer accounts.
- Enable and disable user and computer accounts.
- Explain how user accounts can become locked-out.
- Unlock user accounts.

Why Enable or Disable User and Computer Accounts?

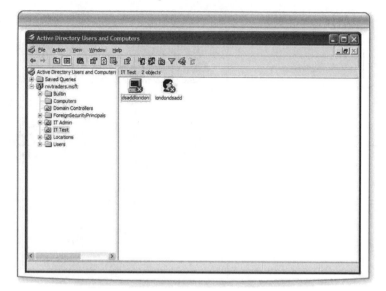

Introduction

After creating user accounts, you perform frequent administrative tasks to ensure that the network continues to meet the organization's needs. These administrative tasks include enabling and disabling user and computer accounts. When you enable or disable an account, you give or restrict access to the account.

Scenarios for enabling and disabling accounts

To provide a secure network environment, a systems administrator must disable user accounts when users do not need their accounts for an extended period, but need to use them later. The following are examples of when you need to enable or disable user accounts:

- If the user takes a two-month leave of absence from work, you disable the account when the user leaves and then enable the account when the user returns.

- When you add accounts in the network that will be used in the future or for security purposes, you disable the accounts until they are needed.

- Disable an account when you do not want users to be authenticated from a shared computer.

How to Enable and Disable User and Computer Accounts

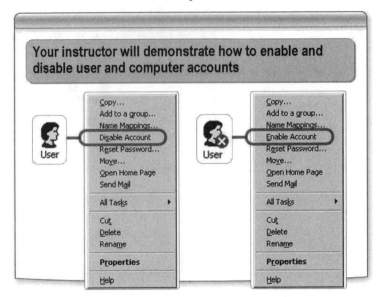

Introduction

When an account is disabled, the user cannot log on. The account appears in the details pane with an X on the account icon.

Procedure

To enable and disable a user or computer account by using Active Directory Users and Computers:

1. In Active Directory Users and Computers, in the console tree, select the container or the user that contains the account to be enabled or disabled.

2. In the details pane, right-click the user account.

3. To disable, click **Disable Account**.

4. To enable, click **Enable Account**.

To disable or enable a local user account by using Computer Management:

1. In Computer Management, expand **System Tools**.

2. In System Tools, expand **Local Users and Groups**, and then click **Users**.

3. Right-click the user account, and then click **Properties**.

4. In the **Properties** dialog box, to disable, select the **Account is Disabled** check box, and then click **OK**.

5. To enable, clear the **Account is Disabled** check box.

Note   To enable and disable user and computer accounts, you must be a member of the Account Operators group, Domain Admins group, or the Enterprise Admins group in Active Directory, or you must be delegated the appropriate authority. As a security best practice, consider using **Run as** to perform this procedure.

Using a command line   You can also enable or disable accounts by using the **dsmod** command. As a security best practice, consider using **runas** to perform this procedure.

To enable or disable accounts by using **dsmod**:

1. Open a command prompt with the **runas** command.

2. Type **dsmod user** *UserDN* **-disabled {yes|no}**

Value	Description
UserDN	Specifies the distinguished name of the user object to be disabled or enabled
{yes|no}	Specifies whether the user account is disabled for log on (**yes**) or enabled (**no**)

What Are Locked-out User Accounts?

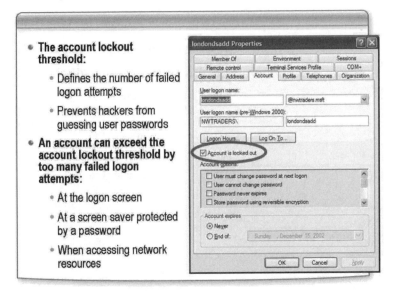

- The account lockout threshold:
  - Defines the number of failed logon attempts
  - Prevents hackers from guessing user passwords
- An account can exceed the account lockout threshold by too many failed logon attempts:
  - At the logon screen
  - At a screen saver protected by a password
  - When accessing network resources

Introduction

A user account is locked out because the account has exceeded the account lockout threshold for a domain. This may be because the user has attempted to access the account with an incorrect password too many times or because a computer hacker has attempted to guess users' passwords and invoked the lockout policy on the account.

Account lockout threshold

Authorized users can lock themselves out of an account by mistyping or forgetting their password or by changing their password on a computer while they are logged on to another computer. The computer with the incorrect password continuously tries to authenticate the user. Because the password it is using to authenticate is incorrect, the user account is eventually locked out.

A security setting in Active Directory determines the number of failed logon attempts that causes a user to be locked out. A user cannot use a locked-out account until an administrator resets the account or until the lockout duration for the account expires. When a user account is locked out, an error message appears, and the user is not allowed any further logon attempts.

What is a failed logon attempt?

A user can be locked out of an account if there are too many failed password attempts. Failed password attempts happen when:

- A user logs on at the logon screen and supplies a bad password.
- A user logs on with a local account and supplies a domain user account and a bad password while accessing network resources.
- A user logs on with a local account and supplies a domain user account and a bad password while accessing resources with the **runas** command.

By default, domain account lockout attempts are not recorded when unlocking a workstation (using a password protected screen saver). You can change this behavior by modifying the **Interactive logon: Require Domain controller authentication to unlock workstation** Group Policy setting.

How to Unlock User Accounts

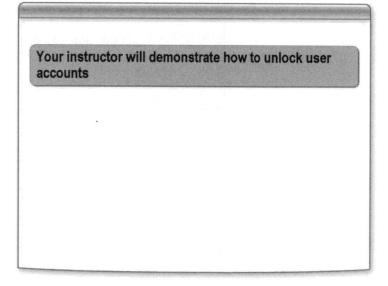

Your instructor will demonstrate how to unlock user accounts

Introduction

After an account is locked out, you must unlock the account to maintain and manage the account.

Procedure

To unlock an account:

1. In Active Directory Users and Computers, in the console tree, select the organizational unit that contains the user account that you want to unlock.

2. In the details pane, select the user account you want to unlock.

3. Right-click the selected account and then click **Unlock**.

Practice: Enabling and Disabling User and Computer Accounts

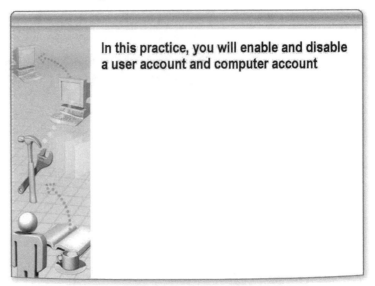

In this practice, you will enable and disable a user account and computer account

Objective

In this exercise, you will disable and enable a user account and a computer account.

Instructions

Before you begin this practice:

- Log on to the domain by using the *ComputerName*User account.
- Open CustomMMC with the **Run as** command.

  Use the user account Nwtraders*ComputerName*Admin (Example: LondonAdmin).

- Ensure that CustomMMC contains Active Directory Users and Computers.
- Review the procedures in this lesson that describe how to perform this task.

Scenario

The security policy of Northwind Traders states that the user accounts of employees going on extended leave must be disabled for the duration of their leave. This is one of your job tasks. You must create an account in the IT Test organizational unit, disable the account, and log on as the user to verify that the account is disabled.

Practice: Disabling a user account

▶ **Create a disabled user account**

- Create a user account with the following parameters:

  - Organizational Unit: **IT Test**
  - User name: *ComputerName***Disabled**
  - Password: **P@ssw0rd**
  - The account is disabled

▶ **Test the disabled user account**

- Try to log on as the new user to verify that you cannot log on.

Scenario

You have just disabled a user account and verified that the user cannot log on. You want to verify that there are no other problems with the account, so you must enable the user account and log on to verify that the user account is activated.

Practice: Enabling a user account

▶ **Enable the user account**

- Enable the user account that has the following parameters:
  - Organizational unit: IT Test
  - User name: *ComputerName*Disabled

▶ **Test the enabled user account**

1. Log on with the *ComputerName*Disabled user account to verify that you can log on.
2. Log on with a password of P@ssw0rd.

Scenario

A systems engineer is concerned that an unauthorized user is attempting to use a kiosk computer after business hours. The systems engineer asks you to disable the computer account until they can look at the log files on the computer. You must disable the computer account.

Practice: Disabling a computer account

▶ **Create a disabled computer account**

- Create a disabled computer account with the following parameters:
  - Organizational unit: IT Test
  - Computer name: *ComputerName***Kiosk**
  - The account is disabled

Scenario

The systems engineer discovers that the nightly security guard was trying to log on to the kiosk computer without a domain account. The security guard has been notified that they should not attempt to log on to the kiosk computer. The systems engineer wants you to enable the kiosk computer for your city location.

Practice: Enabling a computer account

▶ **Enable the computer account**

- Enable the computer account that has the following parameters:
  - Organizational unit: IT Test
  - Computer name: *ComputerName*Kiosk

Practice: Using a command line

▶ **Disable a user account by using dsmod**

- Disable a user account in the IT Test organizational unit by using **dsmod**.

  Example: Dsmod user "cn=London user,ou=it test,dc=nwtraders,dc=msft" -disabled yes

▶ **Enable a user account by using dsmod**

- Enable a user account in the IT Test organizational unit by using **dsmod**.

  Example: Dsmod user "cn=London user,ou=it test,dc=nwtraders,dc=msft" -disabled no

Lesson: Resetting User and Computer Accounts

- When to Reset Passwords
- How to Reset Passwords
- When to Reset Computer Accounts
- How to Reset Computer Accounts

Introduction

Resetting passwords and accounts are common administrative tasks. Be aware of the impact of performing these procedures.

Lesson objectives

After completing this lesson, you will be able to:

- Explain the situations that require you to reset passwords and the potential data loss resulting from resetting passwords.
- Reset passwords for domain and local accounts.
- Determine when to reset computer accounts.
- Reset computer accounts.

When to Reset User Passwords

- **Reset a password when a user forgets his or her password**
- **After resetting a password, a user can no longer access some types of information, including:**
  - E-mail that is encrypted with the user's public key
  - Internet passwords that are saved on the computer
  - Files that the user has encrypted

Introduction

People occasionally forget their passwords. Without their passwords, these people cannot access their user accounts. Administrators can reset users' passwords so that users can access their accounts again. Before attempting to reset local or domain passwords, verify that you have the appropriate level of authority.

Consequences of resetting passwords

After a user's password is reset, some types of information are no longer accessible, including the following:

- E-mail that is encrypted with the user's public key
- Internet passwords that are saved on the computer
- Files that the user has encrypted

Additional reading

For more information about resetting a domain controller account and resetting a computer account with a script, see article 325850, "HOW TO: Use Netdom.exe to Reset Machine Account Passwords of a Windows Server 2003 Domain Controller," in the Microsoft Knowledge Base at: http://support.microsoft.com/?kbid=325850.

For more information about how Windows data protection API handles stored passwords, see "Windows Data Protection" at http://msdn.microsoft.com/library/default.asp?url=/library/en-us/dnsecure/html/windataprotection-dpapi.asp.

How to Reset User Passwords

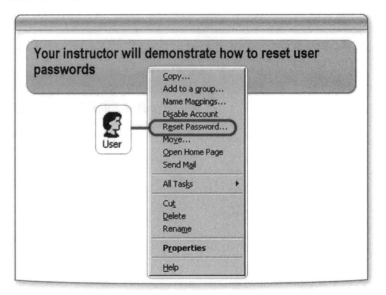

Introduction

When you need to reset a user password, you must remember that only local administrators are authorized to reset local user passwords and that only domain administrators are authorized to reset domain user passwords.

Procedure for resetting local user passwords

To reset local user passwords:

1. In Computer Management, in the console tree, double-click **Local Users and Groups**, and then click **Users**.

2. In the details pane, right-click the user name, and then click **Set Password**.

3. Read the warning message. If you want to continue, click **Proceed**.

4. In the **New password** and **Confirm password** boxes, type the new password, and then click **OK**.

Procedure for resetting domain user passwords

To reset domain user passwords:

1. In Active Directory Users and Computers, in the console tree, click **Users**.

2. In the details pane, right-click the user name, and then click **Reset Password**.

3. In the **New Password** and **Confirm New Password** boxes, type a new password, and then click **OK**.

When to Reset Computer Accounts

Reset computer accounts when:
- Computers fail to authenticate to the domain
- Passwords need to be synchronized

Introduction

As a systems administrator, you occasionally need to reset computer accounts. For example, suppose your network went through a full backup seven days ago. The computer relayed information to the domain controller that changed the password on the computer account. However, the computer's hard drive crashed, and the computer was restored from tape backup. The computer now has an outdated password, and the user cannot log on because the computer cannot authenticate to the domain. You now need to reset the computer account.

Considerations

There are two items that you must consider before resetting the computer account:

- To perform this procedure, you must be a member of the Account Operators group, Domain Admins group, or the Enterprise Admins group in Active Directory, or you must be delegated the appropriate authority. As a security best practice, consider using **Run as** to perform this procedure.

- When you reset a computer account, you break the computer's connection to the domain, and you must rejoin it to the domain.

How to Reset Computer Accounts

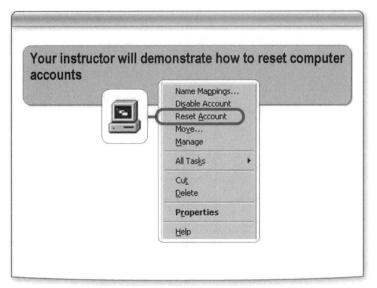

Introduction

To perform this procedure, you must be a member of the Account Operators group, Domain Admins group, or the Enterprise Admins group in Active Directory, or you must be delegated the appropriate authority. As a security best practice, consider using **Run as** to perform this procedure.

Procedure

To reset computer accounts:

1. In Active Directory Users and Computers, in the console tree, click **Computers** or the container that contains the computer that you want to reset.

2. In the details pane, right-click the computer, and then click **Reset Account**.

Using a command line

You can use the **dsmod** command to reset computer accounts. As a security best practice, consider using **runas** to perform this procedure.

1. Open a command prompt by using the **runas** command.

2. Type **dsmod computer** *ComputerDN* **–reset**

Value	Description
ComputerDN	Specifies the distinguished names of one or more computer objects that you want to reset

Practice: Resetting a User Account Password

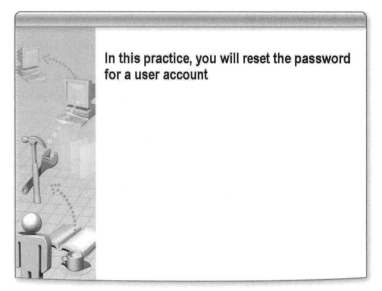

In this practice, you will reset the password for a user account

Objective

In this practice, you will reset a user account so that the user can log on to the domain.

Instructions

Before you begin this practice:

- Log on to the domain by using the *ComputerName*User account.

- Open CustomMMC with the **Run as** command.

  Use the user account Nwtraders*ComputerName*Admin (Example: LondonAdmin).

- Ensure that CustomMMC contains Active Directory Users and Computers.

- Review the procedures in this lesson that describe how to perform this task.

Scenario

You are notified that a user in your city recently forgot their password. You have followed company policy and verified the user is who they say they are. You must reset the password on their account and make them change their password at next logon.

Practice

▶ **Reset the user account**

1. In Active Directory Users and Computer, find the *ComputerName*User account in the Users organizational unit.

2. Reset the password to **P@ssw0rd1** and make the user change the password at next logon.

3. Close all programs and log off.

▶ **Test the new password**

1. Log on as *ComputerName*User with a password of P@ssw0rd1.

2. Change the password to **P@ssword2**

Lesson: Locating User and Computer Accounts in Active Directory

- Multimedia: Introduction to Locating User and Computer Accounts in Active Directory
- Search Types
- How to Search for Active Directory Objects
- How to Search Using Common Queries
- Using a Custom Query

Introduction

The information in this lesson presents the skills and knowledge that you need to use common and custom queries.

Lesson objectives

After completing this lesson, you will be able to:

- Explain the criteria for locating a user or computer account.
- Describe the types of common queries.
- Explain the uses of custom queries.
- Locate user and computer accounts in Active Directory.

Multimedia: Introduction to Locating User and Computer Accounts in Active Directory

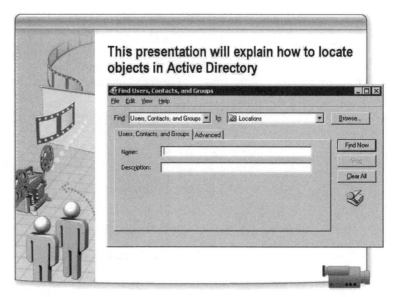

File location

To view the *Introduction to Locating User and Computer Accounts in Active Directory* presentation, open the Web page on the Student Materials compact disc, click **Multimedia**, and then click the title of the presentation. Do not open this presentation unless the instructor tells you to.

Search Types

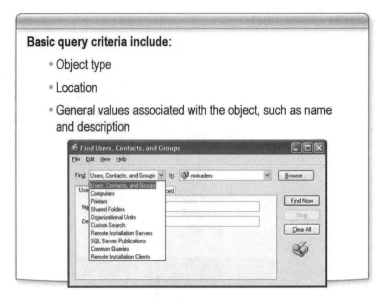

Basic query criteria include:

- Object type
- Location
- General values associated with the object, such as name and description

Introduction

Because all user accounts reside in Active Directory, administrators can search for the user account that they administer. By searching Active Directory for user accounts, you do not need to browse through hundreds or thousands of user accounts in Active Directory Users and Computers.

In addition to searching for user accounts, you can also search for other Active Directory objects, such as computers, printers, and shared folders. After locating these objects, you can administer these objects from the **Search Results** box.

Administering objects from Search Results

After a successful search, the results are displayed, and you can then perform administrative functions on the found objects. The administrative functions that are available depend on the type of object you find. For example, if you search for user accounts, you can rename and delete the user account, disable the user account, reset the password, move the user account to another organizational unit, or modify the user account's properties.

To administer an object from the **Search Results** box, right-click the object and select an action from the menu.

Find Users, Contacts and Groups

Active Directory provides information about all objects on a network, which includes people, groups, computers, printers, shared folders, and organizational units. It is easy to search for users, contacts, and groups by using the **Find Users, Contacts, and Groups** dialog box.

Find Computers

Use **Find Computers** to search for computers in Active Directory by using criteria such as the name assigned to the computer or the operating system on which the computer runs. After you find the computer you want, you can manage it by right-clicking the computer in the **Search Results** box, and then clicking **Manage**.

Find Printers

When a shared printer is published in Active Directory, you can use **Find Printers** to search for it by using criteria such as its asset number, the printer language it uses, or whether it supports double-sided printing. After you find the printer you want, you can easily connect to it by right-clicking the printer in the **Search Results** box, and then clicking **Connect**, or by double-clicking the printer.

Find Shared Folders

When a shared folder is published in Active Directory, you can use **Find Shared Folders** to search for it by using criteria such as keywords assigned to it, the name of the folder, or the name of the person managing the folder. After you find the folder you want, you can open Windows Explorer to view the files located in the folder by right-clicking the folder in the **Search Results** box, and then clicking **Explore**.

Find Custom Search

In Active Directory, you can search for familiar objects such as computers, printers, and users. You can also search for other objects, such as a specific organizational unit or certificate template. Use **Find Custom Search** to build custom search queries by using advanced search options or build advanced search queries by using LDAP, which is the primary access protocol for Active Directory.

Find Common Queries

You can use **Find Common Queries** to perform common administrative queries in Active Directory. For example, you can quickly search for user or computer accounts that have been disabled.

Advanced query options

For each search option except **Find Common Queries**, there is an **Advanced** tab that you can use to create a more detailed search. For example, you can search for all users in a city or zip code from the **Advanced** tab.

Additional reading

For more information about searching Active Directory see "Search Companion overview" at http://www.microsoft.com/technet/treeview/default.asp?url=/technet/prodtechnol/windowsserver2003/proddocs/server/find_overview.asp.

How to Search for Active Directory Objects

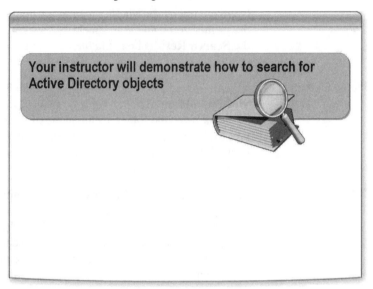

Introduction

To perform administrative tasks on a user or computer account, you must first find the account in Active Directory. This may be difficult if your Active Directory structure is large.

Procedure

To find a user account:

1. Open Active Directory Users and Computers.

2. To search the entire domain, in the console tree, right-click the domain node, and then click **Find**.

   If you know which organizational unit the user is in, right-click the organizational unit, and then click **Find**.

3. In the **Find Users, Contacts, and Groups** dialog box, in the **Name** box, type the name of the user you want to find.

4. Click **Find Now**.

Using a command line   You can use the **dsquery** command to find users and computers in Active Directory that match the specified search criteria. If the predefined search criteria in this command are insufficient, use the more general version of the command, **dsquery ***.

To search for a user by using **dsquery**:

- In a command prompt, type the following:

  dsquery user [{*StartNode* | **forestroot** | **domainroot**}] [**-o** {**dn** | **rdn** | **upn** | **samid**}] [**-scope** {**subtree** | **onelevel** | **base**}] [**-name** *Name*] [**-desc** *Description*] [**-upn** *UPN*] [**-samid** *SAMName*] [**-inactive** *NumberOfWeeks*] [**-stalepwd** *NumberOfDays*] [**-disabled**] [{**-s** *Server* | **-d** *Domain*}] [**-u** *UserName*] [**-p** {*Password* | *****}] [**-q**] [**-r**] [**-gc**] [**-limit** *NumberOfObjects*] [{**-uc** | **-uco** | **-uci**}]

To search for a computer by using **dsquery**:

- In a command prompt, type the following:

  dsquery computer [{*StartNode* | **forestroot** | **domainroot**}] [**-o** {**dn** | **rdn** | **samid**}] [**-scope** {**subtree** | **onelevel** | **base**}] [**-name** *Name*] [**-desc** *Description*] [**-samid** *SAMName*] [**-inactive** *NumberOfWeeks*] [**-stalepwd** *NumberOfDays*] [**-disabled**] [{**-s** *Server* | **-d** *Domain*}] [**-u** *UserName*] [**-p** {*Password* | *****}] [**-q**] [**-r**] [**-gc**] [**-limit** *NumberOfObjects*] [{**-uc** | **-uco** | **-uci**}]

How to Search Using Common Queries

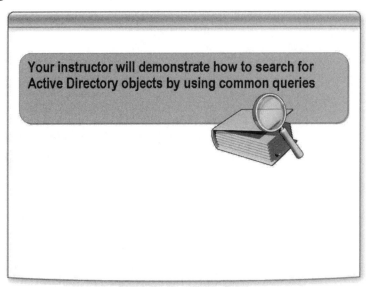

Your instructor will demonstrate how to search for Active Directory objects by using common queries

Introduction

The search functionality is one of the key features of Active Directory. A search operation enables you to find objects in Active Directory based on selection criteria and to retrieve specified properties for the objects that you find.

Procedure

To start a basic search operation:

1. In Active Directory Users and Computers, on the **Action** menu, click **Find**.

2. In the **Find Users, Contacts, and Groups** dialog box, in the **Find** box, select the type of object for which you want to search.

3. Enter the search text in the search criteria boxes.

   The types of search criteria that are available vary depending on the type of object that you selected.

Using a Custom Query

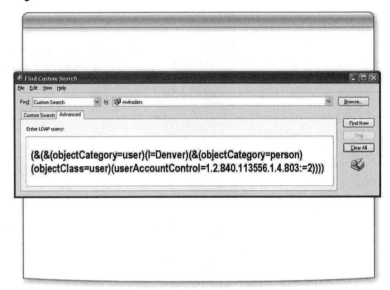

Introduction

In Active Directory, you can search for familiar objects, such as computers, printers, and users, and you can also search for other objects, such as a specific organizational units or certificate templates.

Custom Search

Use the **Find Custom Search** dialog box to build custom search queries using advanced search options and to build advanced search queries by using LDAP, which is the primary access protocol for Active Directory.

The LDAP query on the slide includes the following items:

- **l=Denver**

  The **l** is the city property or location attribute for a user account.

- **(ObjectClass=user)(ObjectCategory=person)**

  To query for a user, the query must contain the **(&(objectClass=user)(objectCategory=person))** search expression. This is because the computer class is a subclass of the user class. A query containing only **(objectClass=user)** returns user objects and computer objects.

- **UserAccountControl:**1.2.840.113556.1.4.803:=2

  This specifies the flags that control the password, lockout option, disable or enable option, script, and home directory behavior for the user. This property also contains a flag that indicates the account type of the object. The flag used here is for disabled accounts.

Additional reading

For more information about LDAP language, see "Listing Properties to Retrieve for Each Object Found" at http://msdn.microsoft.com/library/default.asp?url=/library/en-us/netdir/ad/listing_properties_to_retrieve_for_each_object_found.asp.

Practice: Locating User and Computer Accounts

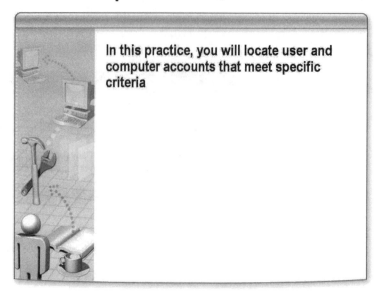

In this practice, you will locate user and computer accounts that meet specific criteria

Objective

In this exercise, you will locate:

- User accounts by name.

- Computer accounts by name.

- Disabled accounts.

- Computer accounts by city.

- User and computer accounts by using **dsquery**.

Instructions

Before you begin this practice:

- Log on to the domain by using the *ComputerName*User account.

- Open CustomMMC with the **Run as** command.

  Use the user account Nwtraders*ComputerName*Admin (Example: LondonAdmin).

- Ensure that CustomMMC contains Active Directory Users and Computers.

- Review the procedures in this lesson that describe how to perform this task.

Scenario

The systems engineers are bulk importing user accounts into the Users container. They need you to verify that all Sales Manager user accounts were successfully imported into Active Directory.

Practice: locating user accounts by name

▶ **Locate user accounts by name**

- Locate user accounts:

  - In the Users container in the NWTraders domain.

  - With a description of Sales Manager.

  Your search should produce approximately 24 Sales Manager user accounts.

Scenario

The systems engineers are bulk importing computer accounts into the Computers container. They need you to verify that all computer accounts from your city location were successfully imported into Active Directory. The naming convention used to bulk import computer accounts is the first three to four letters of the city location, followed by **Computer** and an incremental number, for example, CasaComputer2005.

Practice: locating computer accounts by name

▶ **Locate computer accounts by name**

- Locate a computer account:

    - In the Computers container in the NWTraders domain.

    - With a computer name that is the first three letters of your city location.

    Your search should produce approximately 101 computer accounts.

Scenario

The systems engineers are bulk importing computer accounts into the Computers container. They need you to verify that all computer accounts from your city location have been successfully imported into Active Directory. The naming convention used to bulk import computer accounts is to use the first three to four letters of the city location, followed by **Computer** and an incremental number, for example, CasaComputer2005.

Practice: locating disabled accounts

▶ **Locate disabled accounts**

- Locate user accounts:

    - In the NWTraders domain.

    - With a description that starts with Sales.

    - That are disabled (*Do not enable the accounts*).

    Your search should produce approximately 240 disabled user accounts.

Scenario

The systems engineers are bulk importing computer accounts into the Computers container. They need you to verify that all computer accounts from your city location were successfully imported into Active Directory. The naming convention used to bulk import computer accounts is to use the first three to four letters of the city location, followed by **Computer** and an incremental number, for example, CasaComputer2005.

Practice: locating computer accounts by city

▶ **Locate computer accounts by city**

- Locate computer accounts:

    - In the Computers container in the NWTraders domain.

    - With a computer name that is the first three letters of your city location.

    Your search should produce approximately 101 computer accounts.

Practice: locating user and computer accounts by using dsquery

▶ **Locate all users with the first name of user**

- From a command prompt, type **Dsquery user** –name user*

▶ **Locate all computers with the first 3 letters lon**

- From a command prompt, type **Dsquery computer –name lon***

Lesson: Saving Queries

* What Is a Saved Query?
* How to Create a Saved Query

Introduction

You can use saved queries to quickly and consistently access a common set of Active Directory objects that you want to perform specific tasks on or monitor.

Lesson objectives

After completing this lesson, you will be able to:

- Explain what a saved query is.
- Create a saved query.

What Is a Saved Query?

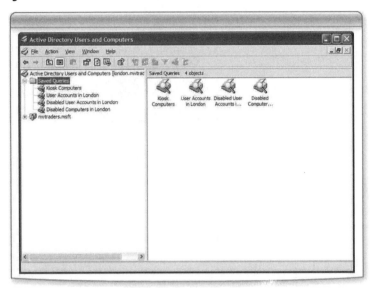

Introduction

Active Directory Users and Computers has a Saved Queries folder in which you can create, edit, save, and organize saved queries. Before saved queries, administrators were required to create custom Active Directory Services Interfaces (ADSI) scripts that performed a query on common objects. This was an often lengthy process that required knowledge of how ADSI uses LDAP search filters to resolve a query.

Definition

Saved queries use predefined LDAP strings to search only the specified domain partition. You can narrow searches to a single container object. You can also create a customized saved query that contains an LDAP search filter.

All queries are located in the Saved Queries folder called dsa.msc, which is stored in Active Directory Users and Computers. After you successfully create your customized set of queries, you can copy the .msc file to other Windows Server 2003 domain controllers that are in the same domain and reuse the same set of saved queries. You can also export saved queries to an Extensible Markup Language (XML) file. You can then import them into other Active Directory Users and Computers consoles located on Windows Server 2003 domain controllers that are in the same domain.

Additional Reading

For more information about saved queries see "Using saved queries" at: http://www.microsoft.com/technet/treeview/default.asp?url=/technet/ prodtechnol/windowsserver2003/proddocs/server/usingsavedqueries.asp.

How to Create a Saved Query

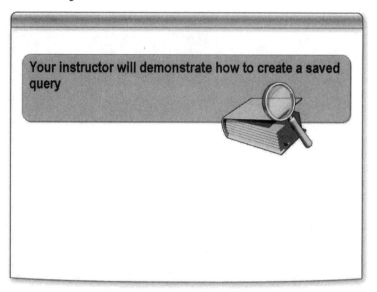

Introduction

You can save queries to search for disabled user or computer accounts, number of days since the last user logon, users with passwords that do not expire, and many other commonly used queries. After a saved query is executed and the desired objects are displayed, you can then modify each object directly in the **Query results** box.

Procedure

To create a saved query:

1. In Active Directory Users and Computers, in the console tree, right-click **Saved Queries** or any of its subfolders in which you want to save a query, point to **New**, and then click **Query**.

2. In the **New Query** dialog box, in the **Name** box , type a query name.

3. In the **Description** box, type a query description.

4. Click **Browse** to define the container from which to begin your search.

5. To search all subcontainers of the selected container, select the **Include subcontainers** check box.

6. Click **Define Query** to define your query.

Practice: Creating Saved Queries

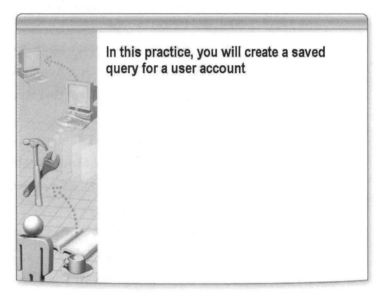

In this practice, you will create a saved query for a user account

Objectives

In this practice, you will create a saved query for a user account.

Instructions

Before you begin this practice:

- Log on to the domain by using the *ComputerName*User account.
- Open CustomMMC with the **Run as** command.

  Use the user account Nwtraders*ComputerName*Admin (Example: LondonAdmin).

- Ensure that CustomMMC contains Active Directory Users and Computers.
- Review the procedures in this lesson that describe how to perform this task.

Scenario

You discover that you often search for the same information. You want to save searches for future use. Create a saved query for a user account. The saved query must have the following properties:

- The saved query is named *ComputerName* User Account.
- The saved query is saved in the Users container in the NWTraders domain.
- The City value equals your computer name that equals your computer name.

Practice

▶ **Create a saved query**

1. In Active Directory Users and Computers, right-click **Saved Queries**, click **New**, and then click **Query**.

2. In the **New Query** dialog box, create a query with the following parameters:

   • Name: *ComputerName* **User Accounts**

   • Description: *ComputerName* **User Accounts**

3. Click **Define Query**.

4. In the **Find** box, click **Users, Contacts, and Groups**.

5. On the **Advanced** tab, click **Field**, point to **User**, and then click **City**.

6. Verify that **Starts with** is in the **Condition** box.

7. In the **Value** box, type *ComputerName* and then click **Add**.

8. Click **OK** to close the **Find Users, Contacts, and Groups** dialog box.

9. Click **OK** to close the **New Query** dialog box.

10. Right-click the query, and then click **Refresh** to refresh the saved query.

Lab A: Managing User and Computer Accounts

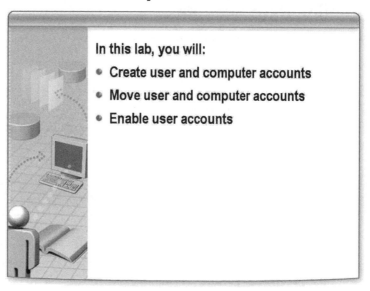

In this lab, you will:
* Create user and computer accounts
* Move user and computer accounts
* Enable user accounts

Objectives

After completing this lab, you will be able to:

■ Create user and computer accounts.

■ Move user and computer accounts to a new organizational unit.

■ Enable user accounts.

Lab setup

This lab requires that your computer has:

■ Log on to the domain by using the *ComputerName*User account.

■ Open CustomMMC with the **Run as** command.

   Use the user account Nwtraders*ComputerName*Admin (Example: LondonAdmin).

■ Ensure that CustomMMC contains Active Directory Users and Computers.

■ Review the procedures in this lesson that describe how to perform this task.

■ An organizational unit called Locations/*ComputerName*/Computers/Desktops.

■ An organizational unit called Locations/*ComputerName*/Computers/Laptops.

Estimated time to complete this lab: 30 minutes

Exercise 1
Creating User Accounts

In this exercise, you will create two user accounts.

Scenario

You have been given a list of users that need to be added to Active Directory. Find the users on the list that have an office in your city location and add them to the appropriate organizational unit in your city organizational unit.

Tasks	Specific Instructions
1. Create user accounts.	▪ Create user accounts in the nwtraders.msft/Locations/*ComputerName*/Users organizational unit. ▪ Create the accounts for the users in the following table that match your organization's city location by using the following parameters: • First name: *FirstName* • Last name: *LastName* • User logon name: The first three letters of the first name and the first three letters of the last name • User logon name (pre-Windows 2000): The first three letters of the first name and the first three letters of the last name • Password: **P@ssw0rd** • Disable the user account
2. Modify the user accounts.	▪ City: *ComputerName* ▪ Telephone number: **555-2469** ▪ Manager: *ComputerName***User**

Last name, First name	City
Brown, Robert	Acapulco
Browne, Kevin F.	Acapulco
Byham, Richard A.	Auckland
Calafato, Ryan	Auckland
Berg, Karen	Bangalore
Berge, Karen	Bangalore
Barnhill, Josh	Bonn
Barr, Adam	Bonn
Altman, Gary E. III	Brisbane
Anderson, Nancy	Brisbane
Chapman, Greg	Caracas
Charles, Mathew	Caracas

(*continued*)

Last name, First name	City
Bonifaz, Luis	Casablanca
Boseman, Randall	Casablanca
Ackerman, Pilar	Denver
Adams, Jay	Denver
Connelly, Peter	Khartoum
Conroy, Stephanie	Khartoum
Barreto de Mattos, Paula	Lima
Bashary, Shay	Lima
Arthur, John	Lisbon
Ashton, Chris	Lisbon
Bankert, Julie	Manila
Clark, Brian	Manila
Burke, Brian	Miami
Burlacu, Ovidiu	Miami
Chor, Anthony	Montevideo
Ciccu, Alice	Montevideo
Casselman, Kevin A.	Moscow
Cavallari, Matthew J.	Moscow
Cornelsen, Ryan	Nairobi
Cox, Brian	Nairobi
Alberts, Amy E.	Perth
Alderson, Gregory F. (Greg)	Perth
Benshoof, Wanida	Santiago
Benson, Max	Santiago
Bezio, Marin	Singapore
Bischoff, Jimmy	Singapore
Carothers, Andy	Stockholm
Carroll, Matthew	Stockholm
Cannon, Chris	Suva
Canuto, Suzana De Abreu A.	Suva
Combel, Craig M.	Tokyo
Con, Aaron	Tokyo
Bradley, David M.	Tunis
Bready, Richard	Tunis
Abolrous, Sam	Vancouver
Acevedo, Humberto	Vancouver

Exercise 2
Creating Computer Accounts

In this exercise, you will create 10 computer accounts.

Scenario

You are expecting to receive four new laptop computers and five new desktop computers in your location. A consultant with a user account in the domain will add these computers to the domain. Northwind Traders policy states that the laptop and desktop computers will be managed by the administrators of the city organizational unit.

Tasks	Special instructions
1. Create five desktop computers.	▪ Create accounts in the nwtraders.msft/Locations/*ComputerName*/Computers/Desktops organizational unit. ▪ Add the following five computer accounts: 01*ComputerName*Desk, 02*ComputerName*Desk, 03*ComputerName*Desk, 04*ComputerName*Desk, 05*ComputerName*Desk
2. Create five laptop computers.	▪ Create accounts in the nwtraders.msft/Locations/*ComputerName*/Computers/Laptops organizational unit. ▪ Add the following five computer accounts: 01*ComputerName*Lap, 02*ComputerName*Lap, C03*omputerName*Lap, 04*ComputerName*Lap, 05*ComputerName*Lap

Exercise 3
Searching for and Moving Users Accounts

In this exercise, you will search for users in your city location and move them to the *ComputerName*/Users organizational unit.

Scenario

The system engineers at NorthWind Traders have imported user accounts for the entire nwtraders domain. The system administrators are responsible for searching for the user accounts that have a city location attribute of their *ComputerName* and move the account to the Users folder in their *ComputerName* organizational unit.

Tasks	Special instructions
1. Search for user accounts by using the following advanced search criteria.	▪ Starting point for the search: nwtraders.msft ▪ Find: **Users, Contacts, and Groups** ▪ Field: **City** ▪ Condition: **Is (exactly)** ▪ Value: *ComputerName*
2. Move user accounts to the following location.	▪ Nwtraders.msft/Locations/*ComputerName*/Users

Exercise 4
Searching for and Moving Computer Accounts

In this exercise, you will search for computer accounts whose names have the first three letters of your computer name and move them to your *ComputerName*/Computers organizational unit.

Scenario

The system engineers at NorthWind Traders have imported computer accounts for the entire nwtraders domain. The system administrators are responsible for searching for the computer accounts that have the first three letters of their *ComputerName* and move the account to the Computers folder in their *ComputerName* organizational unit.

Tasks	Special instructions
1. Search for computer accounts by using the following advanced search criteria.	▪ Starting point for the search: nwtraders.msft ▪ Find: **Computers** ▪ Field: **Computer name (pre-Windows 2000)** ▪ Condition: **Starts with** ▪ Value: The first three letters of your computer name
2. Move computer accounts to the following location.	▪ Nwtraders.msft/Locations/*ComputerName*/Computers

Exercise 5
Searching for and Enabling User Accounts

In this exercise, you will enable user and computer accounts in your city organizational unit.

Scenario

The system engineers at NorthWind Traders have imported user account for the entire nwtraders domain. The system administrators are responsible for searching user accounts that have a city location attribute of their *ComputerName* and then enabling the accounts so that the users can logon.

Tasks	Special instructions
1. Search for disabled user accounts in the following location.	▪ Nwtraders.msft/Locations/*ComputerName*/Users
2. Enable all disabled user accounts.	

Microsoft Official Curriculum

Module 3: Managing Groups

Contents

Overview	1
Lesson: Creating Groups	2
Lesson: Managing Group Membership	19
Lesson: Strategies for Using Groups	26
Lesson: Modifying Groups	37
Lesson: Using Default Groups	47
Best Practices for Managing Groups	60
Lab A: Creating and Managing Groups	61

Overview

- Creating Groups
- Managing Group Membership
- Strategies for Using Groups
- Modifying Groups
- Using Default Groups
- Best Practices for Managing Groups

Introduction

A group is a collection of user accounts. You can use groups to efficiently manage access to domain resources, which helps simplify network maintenance and administration. You can use groups separately, or you can place one group within another to further simplify administration.

Before you can effectively use groups, you must understand the function of groups and the types of groups that you can create. The Active Directory® directory service supports different types of groups and also provides options to determine the group's scope, which is how the group can be used in multiple domains.

Objectives

After completing this module, you will be able to:

- Create groups.
- Manage group membership.
- Apply strategies for using groups.
- Modify groups.
- Manage default groups.

Lesson: Creating Groups

- What Are Groups?
- What Are Domain Functional Levels?
- What Are Global Groups?
- What Are Universal Groups?
- What Are Domain Local Groups?
- What Are Local Groups?
- Where to Create Groups
- Naming Guidelines for Groups
- How to Create a Group

Introduction

The information in this lesson presents the skills and knowledge that you need to create groups.

Lesson objectives

After completing this lesson, you will be able to:

- Explain the purpose of groups, group types, and group scopes.
- Identify the domain functional levels.
- Describe global groups.
- Describe universal groups.
- Describe domain local groups.
- Describe local groups.
- Decide whether to create groups in a domain or organizational unit.
- Determine naming guidelines for groups.
- Create a group.

What Are Groups?

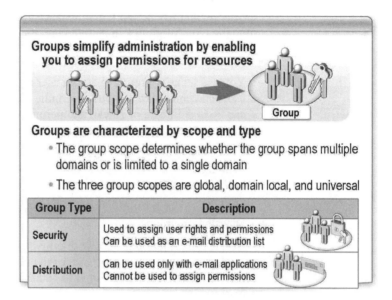

Groups simplify administration by enabling you to assign permissions for resources

Group

Groups are characterized by scope and type
- The group scope determines whether the group spans multiple domains or is limited to a single domain
- The three group scopes are global, domain local, and universal

Group Type	Description
Security	Used to assign user rights and permissions Can be used as an e-mail distribution list
Distribution	Can be used only with e-mail applications Cannot be used to assign permissions

---

Definition

Groups are a collection of user and computer accounts that you can manage as a single unit. Groups:

- Simplify administration by enabling you to grant permissions for resources, once to a group rather than to each user account individually.

- Can be based on Active Directory or local to an individual computer.

- Are characterized by scope and type.

- Can be nested, which means that you can add a group to another group.

Group scopes

The group scope determines whether the group spans multiple domains or is limited to a single domain. Group scopes enable you to use groups to grant permissions. The group scope determines:

- The domains from which you can add members to the group.

- The domains in which you can use the group to grant permissions.

- The domains in which you can nest the group within other groups.

The group scope determines who the members of the group are. Membership rules govern the members that a group can contain and the groups of which a group can be a member. Group members consist of user accounts and other groups.

To assign the correct members to groups and to use nesting, it is important to understand the characteristics of the group scope. There are the following group scopes:

- Global

- Domain local

- Universal

Group types

You use groups to organize user accounts, computer accounts, and other group accounts into manageable units. Working with groups instead of individual users helps simplify network maintenance and administration. There are the following types of groups in Active Directory:

- Security groups

    You use security groups to assign user rights and permissions to groups of users and computers. Rights determine what members of a security group can do in a domain or forest, and permissions determine what resources a member of a group can access on the network.

    You can also use security groups to send e-mail messages to multiple users. Sending an e-mail message to the group sends the message to all members of the group. Therefore, security groups have the capabilities of distribution groups.

- Distribution groups

    You use distribution groups with e-mail applications, such as Microsoft® Exchange, to send e-mail messages to collections of users. The primary purpose of this type of group is to gather related objects, not to grant permissions.

    Distribution groups are not security-enabled, meaning that they cannot be used to assign permissions. If you need a group for controlling access to shared resources, create a security group.

    Even though security groups have all the capabilities of distribution groups, distribution groups are still required, because some applications can use only distribution groups.

Both distribution and security groups support one of the three group scopes.

What Are Domain Functional Levels?

	Windows 2000 mixed (default)	Windows 2000 native	Windows Server 2003
Domain controllers Supported	Windows NT® Server 4.0, Windows 2000, Windows Server 2003	Windows 2000, Windows Server 2003	Windows Server 2003
Group scopes supported	Global, domain local	Global, domain local, universal	Global, domain local, universal

Definition

The characteristics of groups in Active Directory depend on the domain functional level. Domain functionality enables features that will affect the entire domain and that domain only. Three domain functional levels are available: Microsoft Windows® 2000 mixed, Windows 2000 native, and Microsoft Windows Server 2003. By default, domains operate at the Windows 2000 mixed functional level. You can raise the domain functional level to either Windows 2000 native or Windows Server 2003.

The table above lists the domain functional levels and the domain controllers and group scopes they each support.

Note   You can convert a group from a security group to a distribution group, and vice versa, at any time, but only if the domain functional level is set to Windows 2000 native or higher.

Additional Reading

For more information on raising functional levels see KB Article How To: Raise the Domain Functional Level in Windows Server 2003.

What Are Global Groups?

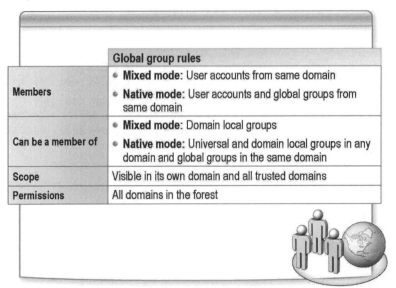

	Global group rules
Members	• **Mixed mode:** User accounts from same domain • **Native mode:** User accounts and global groups from same domain
Can be a member of	• **Mixed mode:** Domain local groups • **Native mode:** Universal and domain local groups in any domain and global groups in the same domain
Scope	Visible in its own domain and all trusted domains
Permissions	All domains in the forest

Definition

A global group is a security or distribution group that can contain users, groups, and computers that are from the same domain as the global group. You can use global security groups to assign user rights and permissions to resources in any domain in the forest.

Characteristics of global groups

The following summarizes the characteristics of global groups:

- Members

  - In domain mixed functional level, global groups can contain user and computer accounts that are from the same domain as the global group.

  - In native functional level, global groups can contain user accounts and global groups that are from the same domain as the global group.

- Can be a member of

  - In mixed mode, a global group can be a member of only domain local groups.

  - In native mode, a global group can be a member of universal and domain local groups in any domain and global groups that are from the same domain as the global group.

- Scope

  A global group is visible within its domain and all trusted domains, which include all of the domains in the forest.

- Permissions

  You can grant permissions to a global group for all domains in the forest.

When to use global groups

Because global groups have a forest-wide visibility, do not create them for domain-specific resource access. Use a global group to organize users who share the same job tasks and have similar network access requirements. A different group type is more appropriate for controlling access to resources within a domain.

What Are Universal Groups?

Universal group rules	
Members	• **Mixed mode:** Not applicable • **Native mode:** User accounts, global groups, and other universal groups from any domain in the forest
Can be a member of	• **Mixed mode:** Not applicable • **Native mode:** Domain local and universal groups in any domain
Scope	Visible in all domains in a forest
Permissions	All domains in a forest

Definition

A universal group is a security or distribution group that can contain users, groups, and computers from any domain in its forest. You can use universal security groups to assign user rights and permissions to resources in any domain in the forest.

Characteristics of universal groups

The following summarizes the characteristics of universal groups:

- Members

  - You cannot create universal groups in mixed mode.

  - In native mode, universal groups can contain user accounts, global groups, and other universal groups from any domain in the forest.

- Can be a member of

  - The universal group is not applicable in mixed mode.

  - In native mode, the universal group can be a member of domain local and universal groups in any domain.

- Scope

  Universal groups are visible in all domains in the forest.

- Permissions

  You can grant permissions to universal groups for all domains in the forest.

When to use universal groups

Use universal groups to nest global groups so that you can assign permissions to related resources in multiple domains. A Windows Server 2003 domain must be in Windows 2000 native mode or higher to use universal groups.

What Are Domain Local Groups?

Domain local group rules	
Members	• **Mixed mode:** User accounts and global groups from any domain • **Native mode:** User accounts, global groups, and universal groups from any domain in the forest, and domain local groups from the same domain
Can be a member of	• **Mixed mode:** None • **Native mode:** Domain local groups in the same domain
Scope	Visible only in its own domain
Permissions	Domain to which the domain local group belongs

Definition

A domain local group is a security or distribution group that can contain universal groups, global groups, other domain local groups that are from its own domain, and accounts from any domain in the forest. You can use domain local security groups to assign user rights and permissions to resources only in the same domain where the domain local group is located.

Characteristics of domain local groups

The following summarizes the characteristics of domain local groups:

- Members

  - In mixed mode, domain local groups can contain user accounts and global groups from any domain. Member servers cannot use domain local group in mixed mode.

  - In native mode, domain local groups can contain user accounts, global groups, and universal groups from any domain in the forest, and domain local groups that are from the same domain as the domain local group.

- Can be a member of

  - In mixed mode, a domain local group cannot be a member of any group.

  - In native mode, a domain local group can be a member of domain local groups that are from the same domain as the domain local group.

- Scope

  A domain local group is visible only in the domain that the domain local group belongs to.

- Permissions

  You can assign permissions to a domain local group for the domain that the domain local group belongs to.

When to use domain local groups

Use a domain local group to assign permissions to resources that are located in the same domain as the domain local group. You can place all global groups that need to share the same resources into the appropriate domain local group.

What Are Local Groups?

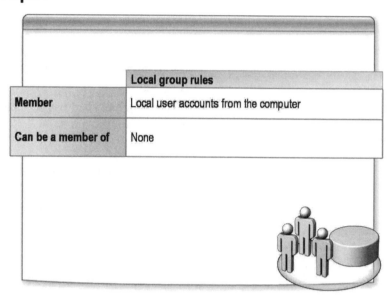

	Local group rules
Member	Local user accounts from the computer
Can be a member of	None

Definition

A local group is a collection of user accounts or domain groups created on a member server or a stand-alone server. You can create local groups to grant permissions for resources residing on the local computer. Windows 2000 or Windows Server 2003 creates local groups in the local security database. Local groups can contain users, computers, global groups, universal groups, and other domain local groups.

Because groups with a domain local scope are sometimes referred to as local groups, it is important to distinguish between a local group and a group with domain local scope. Local groups are sometimes referred to as machine local groups to distinguish them from domain local groups.

Characteristics of local groups

The following summarizes the characteristics of local groups:

- Local groups can contain local user accounts from the computer where you create the local group.

- Local groups cannot be members of any other group.

When to use local groups

The following are guidelines for using local groups:

- You can use local groups only on the computer where you create the local groups. Local group permissions provide access to resources only on the computer where you created the local group.

- You can use local groups on computers running currently supported Microsoft client operating systems and member servers running Windows Server 2003. You cannot create local groups on domain controllers, because domain controllers cannot have a security database that is independent of the database in Active Directory.

- Create local groups to limit the ability of local users and groups to access network resources when you do not want to create domain groups.

Where to Create Groups

- You can create groups in the root domain of the forest, any other domain in the forest, or an organizational unit
- Choose the domain or organizational unit where you create a group based on the administration requirements for the group
  - For example:
    If your directory has multiple organizational units, each of which has a different administrator, you can create global groups in those organizational units

Introduction

In Active Directory, groups are created in domains. You use Active Directory Users and Computers to create groups. If you have the necessary permissions, and by correctly associating users and computers with groups, you can create groups in any other domain in the forest, or an organizational unit.

Besides the domain in which it is created, a group is also characterized by its scope. The scope of a group determines:

- The domain from which members can be added.
- The domain in which the user rights and permissions assigned to the group are valid.

Choosing a domain or organizational unit

Choose the particular domain or organizational unit where you create a group based on the administration requirements for the group.

For example, suppose your directory has multiple organizational units, each of which has a different administrator. You may want to create global groups in those organizational units so that those administrators can manage group membership for users in their respective organizational units.

If groups are required to control access outside the organizational unit, you can nest the groups within the organizational unit into universal groups (or other groups with global scope) that can be used elsewhere in the forest. It may be more efficient to nest global groups if the domain functional level is set to Windows 2000 native or higher, the domain contains a hierarchy of organizational units, and administration is delegated to administrators at each organizational unit.

Naming Guidelines for Groups

> **For security groups:**
>
> * Incorporate the scope in the naming convention of the group name
> * The name should reflect the ownership (division or team name)
> * Place domain names or abbreviations at the beginning of the group name
> * Use a descriptor to identify the maximum permissions a group can have, such as DL IT London OU Admins
>
> **For distribution groups:**
>
> * Use a short alias name
> * Do not include a user's alias name as part of a display name
> * Allow a maximum of five co-owners of a single distribution group

Introduction

In Active Directory, there are many security and distribution groups. The following naming conventions help you manage these groups. Organizations develop their own naming conventions for their security and distribution groups. A group name should identify the scope, type, who the group was created for, and what permissions the group can have.

Security group

Consider the following in defining a naming convention for security groups:

- Scope of security groups

    Although the group type and scope are displayed as the group type in Active Directory Users and Computers, organizations often incorporate the scope in the naming convention of the group name.

    For example, Northwind Traders identifies the scope of security groups by adding a first letter to the group name:

    - **G** IT Admins

        G for global groups

    - **U** All IT Admins

        U for universal groups

    - **DL** IT Admins Full Control

        DL for domain local groups

- Ownership of the security group

  The name for any domain-level security group, whether universal, global, or domain local, should clearly identify ownership by including the name of the division or team that owns the group.

  The following is an example of a naming convention that Northwind Traders might use to identify group ownership:

  - G **Marketing** Managers
  - DL **IT Admins** Full Control

- Domain name

  Upon client request, the domain name or abbreviation is placed at the beginning of the group name. For example:

  - G **NWTraders** Marketing
  - DL **S.N.MSFT** IT Admins Read

- Purpose of the security group

  Finally, in a name, you can include the business purpose of the group and maximum permissions the group should ever have on the network. This naming convention is more applicable to domain local or local groups.

  The following is an example of a naming convention that Northwind Traders might use to identify the purpose of the security group. Northwind Traders uses a descriptor to identify the maximum permissions a group should ever have on the network. For example:

  - DL IT London **OU Admins**
  - DL IT Admins **Full Control**

Distribution groups

Because security groups are mostly used for network administration, only the personnel administering the network must use the naming convention. End users use distribution groups, so the naming convention must be relevant to an end user.

When defining a naming convention for distribution groups consider the following:

- E-mail names

  - *Length*. Use a short alias name. To conform to current downstream data standards, the minimum length of this field is three characters, and the maximum length is eight characters.

  - *Offensive words*. Do not create distribution groups with words that may be considered offensive. If in doubt, do not use the word.

  - *Allowed characters*. You can use all ASCII characters. The only allowed special characters are the hyphen (-) and underscore (_).

  - *Special designations*. Do not use the following character combinations for distributions groups:

    - An underscore (_) as the beginning character of the group name of the alias name

    - A first name or combination of first name and last name that may easily be confused with a user account name

- Display names

  - *User alias names*. For standardization purposes, do not include a user's alias name as part of a display name (for example, Sfine Direct Reports). Include the full name (for example, Suzan Fine's Direct Reports).

  - *Offensive words*. Do not create distribution groups with words that may be considered offensive.

  - *Social discussions*. Distribution groups for social discussions should not be allowed, because public folders are a more efficient means of transmitting and storing high-volume communications associated with social discussions. Because a post is visible to multiple users, both network traffic and data storage are minimized if you use public folders instead of corporate distribution groups.

  - *Length*. The maximum length of this field is 40 characters. Abbreviations are acceptable as long as the meaning is clear.

  - *Style*. Do not capitalize the entire description, but capitalize the first letter in the display name. Use proper punctuation and spelling.

  - *Top of the address book*. Do not use the word *A*, numbers, special characters (especially quotes), or a space to begin a description. This makes it appear at the top of the address book. The address book should begin with individual user names starting with A.

  - *Special characters*. Slashes (/) are acceptable in display names, but do not use them in front of server names. Do not use more than one apostrophe (') and do not use the following special characters: " * @ # $ % | [ ] ; < > =

- Ownership

  There can be a maximum of five co-owners of a single distribution group.

Local groups

A local group name cannot be identical to any other group or user name on the local computer being administered. A local group name cannot consist solely of periods (.) or spaces. It can contain up to 256 uppercase or lowercase characters, except the following: " / \ [ ] : ; | = , + * ? < >

Note   Your environment may not use these guidelines but will most likely use some group naming conventions.

How to Create a Group

Your instructor will demonstrate how to:

- Create a group in a domain
- Create a local group on a member server
- Create a group by using the command line
- Delete a group
- Delete a group by using the command line

Introduction

In most corporate environments, you will create groups in domains. Active Directory has security and tracking features that limit the addition of users to groups. Active Directory also gives corporations the flexibility to use groups on member servers. Corporations often have servers that are exposed to the Internet and want to use local groups on member servers rather than domain local groups to limit the exposure of internal groups and group members.

Procedure for creating a group in a domain

To create a group in an Active Directory domain:

1. In Active Directory Users and Computers, in the console tree, right-click the folder to which you want to add the group, point to **New**, and then click **Group**.

2. In the **New Object – Group** dialog box, in the **Group name** box, type the name of the new group.

3. Under **Group scope**, click the group scope for the new group.

4. Under **Group type**, click the group type for the new group.

Note   To perform this procedure, you must be a member of the Account Operators group, Domain Admins group, or the Enterprise Admins group in Active Directory, or you must be delegated the appropriate authority. As a security best practice, consider using **Run as** to perform this procedure.

Important   If the domain in which you are creating the group is set to the domain functional level of Windows 2000 mixed, you can select only security groups with domain local or global scope.

Procedure for creating a local group on a member server

To create a local group on a member server:

1. In Computer Management, in the console tree, click **Groups**.

2. On the **Action** menu, click **New Group**.

3. In the **New Group** dialog box, in the **Group name** box, type a name for the new group.

4. In the **Description** box, type a description for the new group.

5. To add one or more users to a new group, click **Add**.

6. Click **Create**, and then click **Close**.

Note   To perform this procedure, you must be a member of the Power Users group or the Administrators group on the local computer, or you must be delegated the appropriate authority. If the computer is joined to a domain, members of the Domain Admins group might be able to perform this procedure. As a security best practice, consider using **Run as** to perform this procedure.

Using a command line

To create a group in an Active Directory domain by using **dsadd**:

1. Open a command prompt.

2. Type **dsadd group** *GroupDN* **-samid** *SAMName* **-secgrp** *yes* | *no* **-scope** *l* | *g* | *u*

Value	Description
GroupDN	Specifies the distinguished name of the group object that you want to add
SAMName	Specifies the Security Accounts Manager (SAM) name as the unique SAM account name for this group (for example, operators)
yes	*no*	Specifies whether the group you want to add is a security group (yes) or a distribution group (no)
l	*g*	*u*	Specifies whether the scope of the group you want to add is domain local (l), global (g), or universal (u)

Note   To view the complete syntax for this command, at a command prompt, type **dsadd group /?**

Procedure for deleting a group

To delete a group:

1. In Active Directory Users and Computers, in the console tree, click the folder that contains the group.

2. In the details pane, right-click the group, and then click **Delete**.

Note   To perform this procedure, you must be a member of the Account Operators group, Domain Admins group, or the Enterprise Admins group in Active Directory, or you must be delegated the appropriate authority. As a security best practice, consider using **Run as** to perform this procedure.

Using a command line

To delete a group by using **dsrm**:

1. Open a command prompt.

2. Type **dsrm** *GroupDN*

Value	Description
GroupDN	Specifies the distinguished name of the group object to be deleted.

Note   To view the complete syntax for this command, at a command prompt, type **dsrm /?**

Practice: Creating Groups

In this practice, you will:

- Create groups by using Active Directory Users and Computers

- Create groups by using the dsadd command-line tool

Objective

In this practice, you will create global and local groups by using Active Directory Users and Computers. You will also create global groups by using the **dsadd** command-line tool.

Instructions

Before you begin this practice:

- Log on to the domain by using the *ComputerName*User account.

- Open CustomMMC with the **Run as** command.

  Use the user account Nwtraders*ComputerName*Admin (Example: LondonAdmin).

- Ensure that CustomMMC contains Active Directory Users and Computers.

- Review the procedures in this lesson that describe how to perform this task.

Scenario

As a systems administrator, you must create multiple groups for the Accounting department. These groups will eventually be used for grouping accounts and assigning groups to resources.

Practice

▶ **Create groups by using Active Directory Users and Computers**

1. Create the following global groups in the organizational unit Locations/*ComputerName*/Groups:

   - G *ComputerName* Accounting Managers

   - G *ComputerName* Accounting Personnel

2. Create the following domain local groups in the organizational unit Locations/*ComputerName*/Groups:

   - DL *ComputerName* Accounting Managers Full Control

   - DL *ComputerName* Accounting Managers Read

   - DL *ComputerName* Accounting Personnel Full Control

   - DL *ComputerName* Accounting Personnel Read

Practice: Using the command line

▶ **Create groups by using the dsadd command-line tool**

1. Create the following global group in the IT Test organizational unit:

   - G *ComputerName*Test

   Example: C:\>dsadd group "cn=G London Test,ou=it test,dc=nwtraders,dc=msft" -secgrp yes -scope g -samid "G London Test"

2. Create the following domain local group in the IT Test organizational unit:

   - DL *ComputerName*Test

   Example: C:\>dsadd group "cn=DL London Test,ou=it test,dc=nwtraders,dc=msft" -secgrp yes -scope L -samid "DL London Test"

Lesson: Managing Group Membership

- **The Members and Member Of Properties**
- **Demonstration: Members and Member Of**
- **How to Determine the Groups That a User Account Is a Member Of**
- **How to Add and Remove Members from a Group**

Introduction

Because many users often require access to different resources throughout an organization, administrators may have to grant membership to groups that reside in Active Directory or on local computers.

When adding members to or removing members from groups in Active Directory, an administrator can open Active Directory Users and Computers, click on a user account, drag it to the desired group, and drop the user account onto the group. This action quickly adds the user account to the group.

When adding members to or removing members from groups on a local computer, an administrator can use Computer Management to change group membership on the local computer.

Lesson objectives

After completing this lesson, you will be able to:

- Distinguish between the **Members** and **Member Of** properties.
- Use the **Members** and **Member Of** properties by using the interface.
- Determine the groups that a user account is a member of.
- Add members to and remove members from a group.

The Members and Member Of Properties

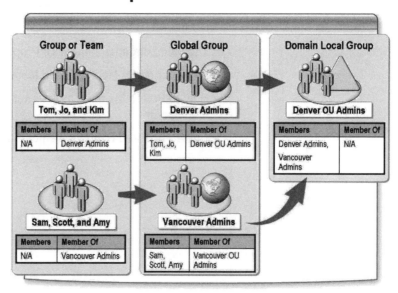

Introduction

The illustration in the slide describes the **Members** and **Member Of** properties.

Definition of Members and Member Of

Tom, Jo, and Kim are *members of* the Denver Admins global group. The global group Denver Admins is a *member of* the domain local group Denver OU Admins.

Sam, Scott, and Amy are *members of* the Vancouver Admins global group. The global group Vancouver Admins is a *member of* the domain local group Denver OU Admins.

The following table summarizes the information in the slide.

User or Group	Members	Members Of
Tom, Jo, Kim		Denver Admins
Denver Admins	Tom, Jo, Kim	Denver OU Admins
Sam, Scott, Amy		Vancouver Admins
Vancouver Admins	Sam, Scott, Amy	Denver OU Admins
Denver OU Admins	Denver Admins	
	Vancouver Admins	

By using the **Members** and **Member Of** properties, you can determine groups that the user belongs to and what groups that group belongs to.

Demonstration: Members and Member Of

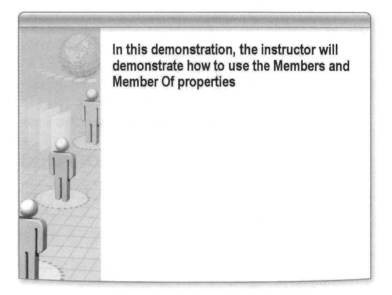

In this demonstration, the instructor will demonstrate how to use the Members and Member Of properties

Objective

In this demonstration, the instructor will demonstrate how to use the **Members** and **Member Of** properties.

Demonstration

To demonstrate how to use **Members** and **Member Of**:

1. Open Active Directory Users and Computers.

2. In the console tree, expand **NWTraders.msft**, and then expand the **IT Admin** organizational unit.

3. Click the **IT Users** organizational unit.

4. In the details pane double-click the **AcapulcoAdmin** user account.

5. In the **Properties** dialog box, on the **Member Of** tab, notice that the AcapulcoAdmin user account is a member of the following groups:

   - Domain Users

   - G Acapulco Admins

   - G IT Admins

6. Double-click the **G IT Admins** group.

7. In the **Properties** dialog box, on the **Members** tab, notice that the G IT Admins group has many members.

8. On the **Member Of** tab, notice the G IT Admins group is a member of the DL IT OU Administrators group.

9. Double-click the **DL IT OU Administrators** group.

10. In the **Properties** dialog box, on the **Members** tab, notice that the G IT Admins group is a member.

How to Determine the Groups That a User Account Is a Member Of

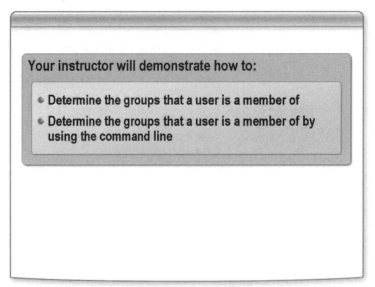

Introduction

After you add users to groups, Active Directory updates the **Member Of** property of their user accounts.

Procedure

To determine the groups that a user is a member of:

1. In Active Directory Users and Computers, in the console tree, click **Users** or click the folder that contains the user account.

2. In the details pane, right-click a user account, and then click **Properties**.

3. In the **Properties** dialog box, click the **Member Of** tab.

Note You do not need administrative credentials to perform this task. Therefore, as a security best practice, consider performing this task as a user without administrative credentials.

Using a command line

To determine the groups a user is a member of by using **dsget**:

1. Open a command prompt.

2. Type **dsget user** *UserDN* **-memberof**

Value	Description
UserDN	Specifies the distinguished name of the user object for which you want to display group membership

---

Note To view the complete syntax for this command, at the command prompt, type **dsget user /?**

How to Add and Remove Members from a Group

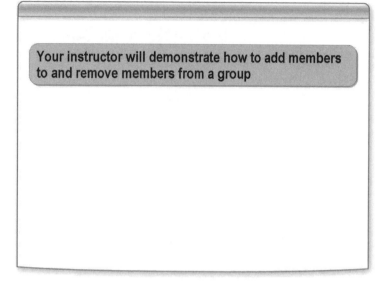

Introduction

After creating a group, you add members by using Active Directory Users and Computers. Members of groups can include user accounts, other groups, and computers.

Procedure

To add members to or remove members from a group:

1. In Active Directory Users and Computers, in the console tree, click the folder that contains the group to which you want to add a member.

2. In the details pane, right-click the group, and then click **Properties**.

3. In the **Properties** dialog box, on the **Members** tab, click **Add**.

   If you want to remove a member from the group, click the member, and then click **Remove**.

4. In the **Select Users, Contact, Computers, or Groups** dialog box, in the **Enter the object names to select** box, type the name of the user, group, or computer that you want to add to the group, and then click **OK**.

Tip   You can also add a user account or group by using the **Member Of** tab in the **Properties** dialog box for that user account or group. Use this method to quickly add the same user or group to multiple groups.

Practice: Managing Group Membership

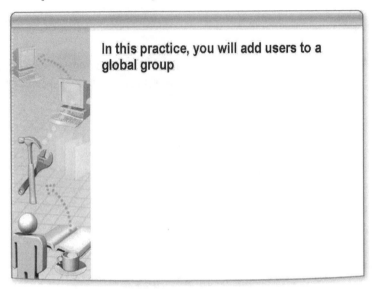

In this practice, you will add users to a
global group

Objectives

In this practice, you will add users to a global group.

Instructions

Before you begin this practice:

- Log on to the domain by using the *ComputerName*User account.

- Open CustomMMC with the **Run as** command.

  Use the user account Nwtraders\ComputerNameAdmin (Example: LondonAdmin).

- Ensure that CustomMMC contains Active Directory Users and Computers.

- Ensure that the following groups are in the Locations/*ComputerName*/Groups organizational unit:

  - Global groups:

    - G *ComputerName* Accounting Managers

    - G *ComputerName* Accounting Personnel

- Review the procedures in this lesson that describe how to perform this task.

Scenario

Northwind Traders is starting to implement global groups. You will need to find all Accounting personnel in your city organizational unit and add them to the G *ComputerName* Accounting Personnel group.

Practice

▶ **Perform a custom search for Accounting personnel**

- Search for users with the City search attribute of *ComputerName* (Example: London) and the Department search attribute of Accounting.

  This search should produce approximately 10 users. One of the users is the Accounting manager.

▶ **Add the users to G *ComputerName* Accounting Personnel**

1. Select all users produced by the preceding search.

2. Right-click the selection, and then click **Add to a group**.

3. Add the users to G *ComputerName* Accounting Personnel.

Lesson: Strategies for Using Groups

- Multimedia: Strategy for Using Groups in a Single Domain
- What Is Group Nesting?
- Group Strategies

Introduction

To use groups effectively, you need strategies for applying different group scopes. This lesson covers skills and knowledge that you need to use groups optimally by employing different strategies with groups.

Lesson objectives

After completing this lesson, you will be able to:

- Explain the AGDLP strategy for using groups in a single domain.
- Describe group nesting.
- Describe the following strategies for using groups:
  - A G P
  - A DL P
  - A G DL P
  - A G U DL P
  - A G L P

Multimedia: Strategy for Using Groups in a Single Domain

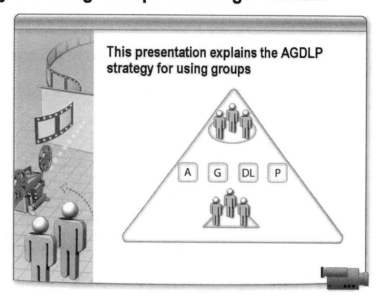

File location

To view the *Strategy for Using Groups in a Single Domain* presentation, open the Web page on the Student Materials compact disc, click **Multimedia**, and then click the title of the presentation. Do not open this presentation unless the instructor tells you to.

Key points

User accounts → Global groups → Domain Local groups ← Permissions

     (A)   (G)   (DL)   (P)

What Is Group Nesting?

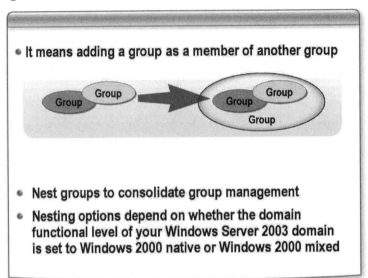

Introduction

Using nesting, you can add a group as a member of another group. You can nest groups to consolidate group management. Nesting increases the member accounts that are affected by a single action and reduces replication traffic caused by the replication of changes in group membership.

Nesting options

Your nesting options depend on whether the domain functional level of your Windows Server 2003 domain is set to Windows 2000 native or Windows 2000 mixed. In domains where the domain functional level is set to Windows 2000 native, group membership is determined as follows:

- Universal groups can have as their members: user accounts, computer accounts, universal groups, and global groups from any domain.

- Global groups can have as their members: user accounts from the same domain and global groups from the same domain.

- Domain local groups can have as their members: user accounts, universal groups, and global groups, all from any domain. They can also have as members domain local groups from within the same domain.

You cannot create security groups with universal scope in domains where the domain functional level is set to Windows 2000 mixed. Universal scope is supported only in domains where the domain functional level is set to Windows 2000 native or Windows Server 2003.

Note   Minimize the levels of nesting. A single level of nesting is the most effective method, because tracking permissions is more complex with multiple levels.

Also, troubleshooting becomes difficult if you must trace permissions through multiple levels of nesting. Therefore, document group membership to keep track of permissions.

Group Strategies

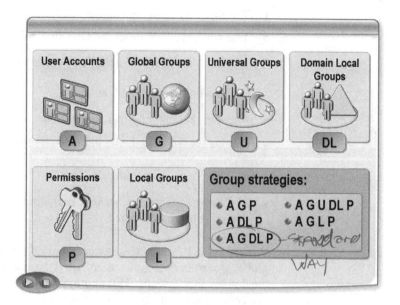

Introduction

To use groups effectively, you need strategies for applying the different group scopes. The strategy you choose depends on the Windows network environment of your organization. In a single domain, the common practice is to use global and domain local groups to grant permissions for network resources. In a network with multiple domains, you can incorporate global and universal groups into your strategy.

A G P

With A G P, you place user accounts (A) in global groups (G), and you grant permissions (P) to the global groups. The limitation of this strategy is that it complicates administration when you use multiple domains. If global groups from multiple domains require the same permissions, you must grant permissions to each global group individually.

When to use the A G P strategy

Use A G P for forests with one domain and very few users and to which you will never add other domains.

A G P has the following advantages:

- Groups are not nested and therefore troubleshooting may be easier.

- Accounts belong to a single group scope.

A G P has the following disadvantages:

- Every time a user authenticates with a resource, the server must check the global group membership to determine if the user is still a member of the group.

- Performance degrades, because a global group is not cached.

A DL P

With A DL P, you place user accounts (A) in domain local groups (DL), and you grant permissions (P) to the domain local groups. One limitation of this strategy is that it does not allow you to grant permissions for resources outside of the domain. Therefore, it reduces flexibility as your network grows.

When to use the A DL P strategy

Use A DL P for a forest where all of the following are true:

- The forest has only one domain and very few users.
- You will never add other domains to the forest.
- There are no Microsoft Windows NT 4.0 member servers in the domain.

A DL P has the following advantages:

- Accounts belong only to a single group scope.
- Groups are not nested, and therefore troubleshooting may be easier.

A DL P has the following disadvantage:

- Performance degrades, because each domain local group has many members that must be authenticated.

A G DL P

With A G DL P, you place user accounts (A) in global groups (G), place the global groups in domain local groups (DL), and then grant permissions (P) to the domain local groups. This strategy creates flexibility for network growth and reduces the number of times you must set permissions.

When to use the A G DL P strategy

Use A G DL P for a forest consisting of one or more domains and to which you might have to add future domains.

A G DL P has the following advantages:

- Domains are flexible.
- Resource owners require less access to Active Directory to flexibly secure their resources.

A G DL P has the following disadvantage:

- A tiered management structure is more complex to set up initially, but easier to manage over time.

A G U DL P

With A G U DL P, you place user accounts (A) in global groups (G), place the global groups in universal groups (U), place the universal groups in domain local groups (DL), and then grant permissions (P) to the domain local groups.

When to use the A G U DL P strategy

Use A G U DL P for a forest with more than one domain where administrators require centralized administration for many global groups.

A G U DL P has the following advantages:

- There is flexibility across the forest.
- It enables centralized administration.

Note Domain Local groups should not be used to assign Active Directory object permissions in a Forest with more than one Domain. For more information see Microsoft Knowledge Base Article 231273, Group Type and Scope Usage in Windows at http://support.microsoft.com/ default.aspx?scid=kb%3Ben-us%3B231273.

A G U DL P has the following disadvantage:

- The membership of universal groups is stored in the global catalog.

    Note The global catalog is a domain controller that stores a copy of all Active Directory objects in a forest. The global catalog stores a full copy of all objects in Active Directory for its host domain and a partial copy of all objects for all other domains in the forest.

- It may be necessary to add more global catalog servers.
- There may be global catalog replication latency. When referring to the global catalog, *latency* is the time it takes to replicate a change to each global catalog server in the forest.

There is a disadvantage to using universal groups only if the universal groups have a very dynamic membership with a lot of global catalog replication traffic as the membership changes) in a multidomain forest. With A G U DL P, this is less of an issue, because the membership of universal groups is relatively static (that is, the universal group has global groups, not individual users, as members).

A G L P

Use the A G L P strategy to place user accounts in a global group and grant permissions to the local group. One limitation of this strategy is that you cannot grant permissions for resources outside the local computer.

Therefore, place user accounts in a global group, add the global group to the local group, and then grant permissions to the local group. With this strategy, you can use the same global group on multiple local computers.

Note Use domain local groups whenever possible. Use local groups only when a domain local group has not been created for this purpose.

When to use the A G L P strategy

Use the A G L P strategy when your domain has the following characteristics:

- Upgrade from Windows NT 4.0 to Windows Server 2003
- Contain one domain
- Have few users
- Will never add other domains
- To maintain a Windows NT 4.0 group strategy
- To maintain centralized user management and decentralized resource management

It is recommended that you use A G L P with Windows Server 2003 Active Directory and Windows NT 4.0 member servers.

A G L P has the following advantages:

- It maintains the Windows NT 4.0 group strategy.
- Resource owners own membership to every group that needs access.

A G L P has the following disadvantages:

- Active Directory does not control access.
- You must create redundant groups across member servers.
- It does not enable centralized administration.

Class Discussion: Using Groups in a Single Domain

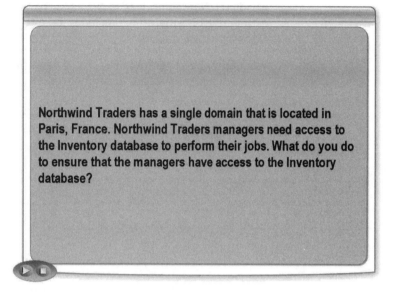

Northwind Traders has a single domain that is located in Paris, France. Northwind Traders managers need access to the Inventory database to perform their jobs. What do you do to ensure that the managers have access to the Inventory database?

Example 1

Northwind Traders has a single domain that is located in Paris, France. Northwind Traders managers need access to the Inventory database to perform their jobs.

What do you do to ensure that the managers have access to the Inventory database?

_____

_____

_____

_____

Example 2

Northwind Traders wants to react more quickly to market demands. It is determined that the accounting data must be available to all Accounting personnel. Northwind Traders wants to create the group structure for the entire Accounting division, which includes the Accounts Payable and Accounts Receivable departments.

What do you do to ensure that the managers have the required access and that there is a minimum of administration?

_____

_____

_____

_____

Practice: Adding Global Groups to Domain Local Groups

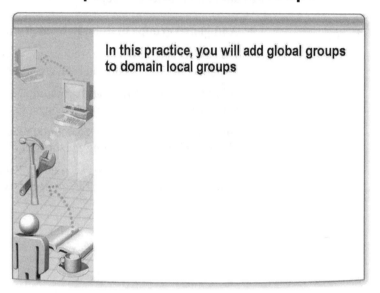

In this practice, you will add global groups to domain local groups

Objective

In this exercise, you will add a global group to a domain local group.

Instructions

Before you begin this practice:

- Log on to the domain by using the *ComputerName*User account.

- Open CustomMMC with the **Run as** command.

  Use the user account Nwtraders\ComputerNameAdmin (Example: LondonAdmin).

- Ensure that CustomMMC contains Active Directory Users and Computers.

- Ensure that the following groups are in the Locations/*ComputerName*/Groups organizational unit:

  - Global groups:

    - G *ComputerName* Accounting Managers

    - G *ComputerName* Accounting Personnel

  - Domain local groups:

    - DL *ComputerName* Accounting Managers Full Control

    - DL *ComputerName* Accounting Managers Read

    - DL *ComputerName* Accounting Personnel Full Control

    - DL *ComputerName* Accounting Personnel Read

- Review the procedures in this lesson that describe how to perform this task.

Scenario   Northwind Traders is implementing A G DL P and needs you to add global groups to domain local groups.

Practice   ▶ **Add global groups to domain local groups**

1. Add the G *ComputerName* Accounting Managers global group to DL *ComputerName* Accounting Managers Full Control.

2. Add the G *ComputerName* Accounting Managers global group to DL *ComputerName* Accounting Managers Read.

3. Add the G *ComputerName* Accounting Personnel global group to DL *ComputerName* Accounting Personnel Full Control.

4. Add the G *ComputerName* Accounting Personnel global group to DL *ComputerName* Accounting Personnel Read.

Lesson: Modifying Groups

- What Is Modifying the Scope or Type of a Group?
- How to Change the Scope or Type of a Group
- Why Assign a Manager to a Group?
- How to Assign a Manager to a Group

Introduction

This lesson introduces you to the skills and knowledge that you need to modify groups.

Lesson objectives

After completing this lesson, you will be able to:

- Explain what it means to modify the scope or type of a group.
- Change the scope or type of a group.
- Explain why you assign a manager to a group.
- Assign a manager to a group.

What Is Modifying the Scope or Type of a Group?

```
• Changing group scope
    • Global to universal
    • Domain local to universal
    • Universal to global
    • Universal to domain local
• Changing group type
    • Security to distribution
    • Distribution to security
```

Introduction

When creating a new group, by default, the new group is configured as a security group with global scope, regardless of the current domain functional level.

Changing group scope

Although you cannot change group scope in domains with a domain functional level set to Windows 2000 mixed, you can make the following scope changes in domains with the domain functional level set to Windows 2000 native or Windows Server 2003:

- *Global to universal*. This is allowed only if the group you want to change is not a member of another global group.

  Note You cannot change a group's scope from global to domain local directly. To do that, you must change the group's scope from global to universal and then from universal to domain local.

- *Domain local to universal*. This is allowed only if the group you want to change does not have another domain local group as a member.

- *Universal to global*. This is allowed only if the group you want to change does not have another universal group as a member.

- *Universal to domain local*. There are no restrictions for this change.

Changing group type

You can convert a group from a security group to a distribution group, and vice versa, at any time, but only if the domain functional level is set to Windows 2000 native or higher. You cannot convert a group while the domain functional level is set to Windows 2000 mixed.

You may convert groups from one type to the other in the following scenarios:

- Security to distribution

   A company splits into two companies. Users migrate from one domain to another domain, but they keep their old e-mail addresses. You want to send them e-mail messages by using old security groups, but you want to remove security context from the group.

- Distribution to security

   A distribution group gets very large, and the users want to use this group for security-related tasks. However, they still want to use the group for e-mail.

Note Although you can add a contact to a security group and to a distribution group, you cannot grant permissions to contacts. You can send contacts e-mail messages.

How to Change the Scope or Type of a Group

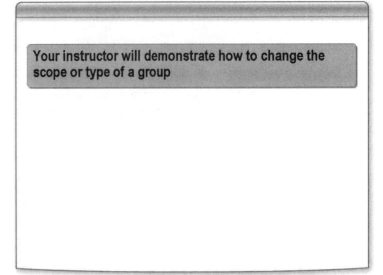

Your instructor will demonstrate how to change the scope or type of a group

Introduction

To change the scope or type of a group, the domain functional level must be set to Windows 2000 native or higher. You cannot change the scope or type of groups if the domain functional level is set to Windows 2000 mixed.

Procedure

To change the scope or type of a group:

1. In Active Directory Users and Computers, in the console tree, click the folder that contains the group.

2. In the details pane, right-click the group, and then click **Properties**.

3. In the **Properties** dialog box, on the **General** tab, under **Group type**, click the group type to change it.

4. Under **Group scope**, click the group scope to change it.

Note   To perform this procedure, you must be a member of the Account Operators group, Domain Admins group, or Enterprise Admins group in Active Directory, or you must be delegated the appropriate authority. As a security best practice, consider using **Run as** to perform this procedure.

Practice: Changing the Scope and Type of a Group

In this practice, you will:

- Change the group scope from global to domain local
- Convert a security group into a distribution group

Objective

In this practice, you will:

- Change the group scope from global to a domain local.
- Convert a security group into a distribution group.

Instructions

Before you begin this practice:

- Log on to the domain by using the *ComputerName*User account.
- Open CustomMMC with the **Run as** command.

  Use the user account Nwtraders\ComputerNameAdmin (Example: LondonAdmin).

- Ensure that CustomMMC contains Active Directory Users and Computers.

Scenario

The IT managers at Northwind Traders want you to write a procedure for changing the scope of a security group from global to domain local. You must create all test groups in the IT Test organizational unit.

Practice: Changing group scope

▶ **Create a global security group**

- In the IT Test organizational unit, create a global security group named *ComputerName* Group Scope Test.

▶ **Document the procedure for converting the global group into a domain local group**

_____

_____

_____

_____

_____

_____

_____

Scenario

The IT managers at Northwind Traders want you to test the Active Directory feature that enables you to convert a security group into a distribution group. They want you to convert the security group you created into a distribution group.

Practice: Changing group type

▶ **Convert a global security group into a distribution group**

- Change the _ComputerName_ Group Scope group from a security group to a distribution group.

Why Assign a Manager to a Group?

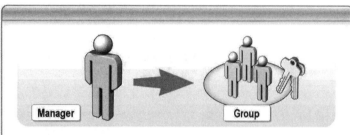

* To enable you to:
  * Track who is responsible for groups
  * Delegate to the manager of the group the authority to add users to and remove users from the group
* To distribute the administrative responsibility of adding users to groups to the people who request the group

Advantages of assigning a manager to a group

Active Directory in Windows Server 2003 allows you to assign a manager to a group as a property of the group. This enables you to:

- Track who is responsible for groups.

- Delegate to the manager of the group the authority to add users to and remove users from the group.

Because people in large organizations are added to and removed from groups so often, some organizations distribute the administrative responsibility of adding users to groups to the people who request the group.

If you document who the manager of the group is, the contact information for that user account is recorded. If the group ever needs to be migrated to another domain or needs to be deleted, the network administrator has a record of who owns the group and their contact information. Therefore, the network administrator can call or send an e-mail message to the manager to notify the manager about the change that needs to be made to the group.

How to Assign a Manager to a Group

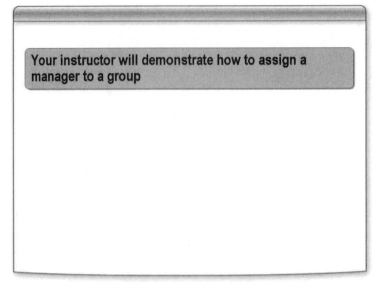

Your instructor will demonstrate how to assign a manager to a group

Introduction

Use the following procedure to assign a manager to a group.

Procedure

To assign a manager to a group:

1. In Active Directory Users and Computers, in the console tree, double-click the group that needs a manager.

2. In the **Properties** dialog box, on the **Managed By** tab, click **Change** to add a manager to a group or to change the manager of a group.

3. In the **Select User or Contact** dialog box, in the **Enter the object name to select** box, type the user name of the user who you want to manage the group, and then click **OK**.

4. Select the **Manager can update membership list** check box if you want the manager to add and remove users and groups.

5. In the **Properties** dialog box, click **OK**.

Practice: Assigning a Manager to a Group

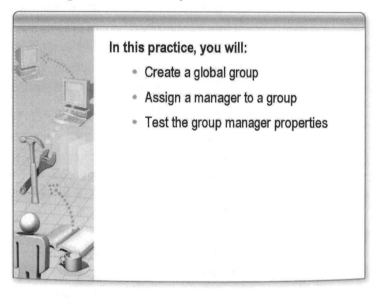

In this practice, you will:

- Create a global group
- Assign a manager to a group
- Test the group manager properties

Objective

In this practice, you will:

- Create a global group.
- Assign a manager to the group who can modify group membership.
- Test the group manager properties.

Instructions

Before you begin this practice:

- Log on to the domain by using the *ComputerName*User account.
- Open CustomMMC with the **Run as** command.

  Use the user account Nwtraders\ComputerNameAdmin (Example: LondonAdmin).

- Ensure that CustomMMC contains Active Directory Users and Computers.

Scenario

You have been asked to create a group for the Sales department called G *ComputerName* Sales Strategy. The owner of the group will be the Sales manager for your city organizational unit.

Practice

▶ **Create a global group in your city organizational unit**

1. Create a global group called G *ComputerName* Sales Strategy in the organizational unit Locations/*ComputerName*

2. Log off.

▶ **Test the group manager properties**

1. Log on by using the *ComputerName*User account.

2. Open CustomMMC and try to add a user to G *ComputerName* Sales Strategy.

   You should not be able to add any users to this group.

3. Close CustomMMC.

4. Open CustomMMC (do not use the **Run as** command).

5. In Active Directory Users and Computers, navigate to your city organizational unit, and then double-click **G** *ComputerName***Sales Strategy**.

6. In the **Properties** dialog box, click the **Members** tab, and notice that you cannot add any users, because the **Add** button is unavailable.

7. Close CustomMMC.

▶ **Make *ComputerName*User a manager of G *ComputerName* Sales Strategy**

1. Open CustomMMC with the **Run as** command.

   Use the Nwtraders*ComputerName*Admin account.

2. In Active Directory Users and Computers, navigate to your city organizational unit, and then double-click **G** *ComputerName* **Sales Strategy**.

3. In the **Properties** dialog box, on the **Managed By** tab, add the *ComputerName*User user account.

4. Select the **Manager can update membership list** check box.

5. Close CustomMMC.

▶ **Test the group manager properties**

1. In Active Directory Users and Computers, navigate to your city organizational unit, and then double-click **G** *ComputerName* **Sales Strategy**.

2. In the **Properties** dialog box, on the **Members** tab, add the User0001 user account.

3. Close all windows and CustomMMC.

Lesson: Using Default Groups

- Default Groups on Member Servers
- Default Groups in Active Directory
- When to Use Default Groups
- Security Considerations for Default Groups
- System Groups

Introduction

This lesson introduces how default groups are used.

Lesson objectives

After completing this lesson, you will be able to:

- Explain how default groups are used on member servers.
- Explain how default groups are used in Active Directory.
- Identify when to use default groups.
- Identify the security considerations for default groups.
- Explain how system groups are used.

Default Groups on Member Servers

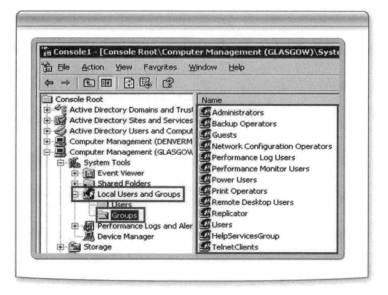

Definition

The Groups folder is located on a member server in the Local Users and Groups console, which displays all built-in default local groups and any local groups you create. The default local groups are created automatically when you install Windows Server 2003. The local groups can contain local user accounts, domain user accounts, computer accounts, and global groups.

Default local groups on member server

The following table describes some of the default local groups on a member or stand-alone server running Windows Server 2003.

Group	Description
Administrators	• Members have full control of the server and can assign user rights and access control permissions to users as necessary.
	• Administrators is a default member account and has full control of the server.
	• Users should be added with caution.
	• When joined to a domain, the Domain Admins group is automatically added to this group.
Guests	• A temporary profile is created for a member when the member logs on.
	• When the guest member logs off, the profile is deleted.
	• The Guest account is disabled by default.
Performance Log Users	• Members can manage performance counters, logs, and alerts on the server locally and from remote clients without being a member of the Administrators group.

(continued)

Group	Description
Performance Monitor Users	• Members can monitor performance counters on the server locally and from remote clients without being a member of the Administrators or Performance Log Users groups.
Power Users	• Members can create user accounts and then modify and delete the accounts they have created.
	• Members can create local groups and then add or remove users from the local groups they have created.
	• Members can add or remove users from the Power Users, Users, and Guests groups.
	• Members can create shared resources and administer the shared resources they have created.
	• Members cannot take ownership of files, back up or restore directories, load or unload device drivers, or manage security and auditing logs.
Print Operators	• Members can manage printers and print queues.
Users	• Members perform common tasks, such as running applications, using local and network printers, and locking the server.
	• Users cannot share directories or create local printers.
	• The Domain Users, Authenticated Users, and Interactive groups are members of this group. Therefore, any user account created in the domain becomes a member of this group.

The following additional groups are also default groups on a member server which are not commonly used.

- Network Configuration Operators
- Remote Desktop Users
- Replicator
- HelpServicesGroup
- Terminal Server Users

Note   For more information about default groups on member servers, search for "default local groups" in Windows Server 2003 Help.

Default groups used by network services

The following table describes the default groups used by network services and installed only with the Dynamic Host Configuration Protocol (DHCP) service.

Group	Membership
DHCP Administrators	• Members have administrative access to the DHCP service. • The DHCP Administrators group provides security to assign limited administrative access to the DHCP server only, while not providing full access to the server. • Members can administer DHCP on a server by using the DHCP console or the **Netsh** command, but they cannot perform other administrative actions on the server.
DHCP Users	• Members have read-only access to the DHCP service. • Members can view information and properties stored at a specified DHCP server. This information is useful to support staff when they need to obtain DHCP status reports.
WINS Users	• Members are permitted read-only access to the Windows Internet Name Service (WINS). • Members can view information and properties stored at a specified WINS server. This information is useful to support staff when they need to obtain WINS status reports.

Default Groups in Active Directory

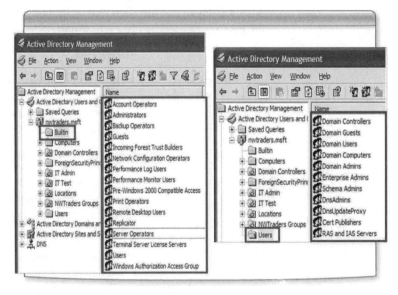

Definition

Default groups are security groups automatically created when you install an Active Directory domain. You can use these predefined groups to manage shared resources and delegate specific domain-wide administrative roles.

Many default groups are automatically assigned a set of user rights that determine what each group and their members can do within the scope of a domain or forest. User rights authorize members of a group to perform specific actions, such as log on to a local system or back up files and folders. For example, a member of the Backup Operators group has the right to perform backup operations for all domain controllers in the domain.

Several default groups are available in the Users and Builtin containers of Active Directory. The Builtin container contains domain local groups. The Users container contains global groups and domain local groups. You can move groups in the Users and Builtin containers to other group or organizational unit folders in the domain, but you cannot move them to other domains.

Groups in the Builtin container

The following table describes each default group in the Builtin container that is added to the default groups on a stand-alone or member server when Active Directory is installed. All of these default groups are added along with the user rights assigned to each group.

Group	Description
Account Operators	• Members can create, modify, and delete accounts for users, groups, and computers located in the Users or Computers containers and organizational units in the domain, except the Domain Controllers organizational unit.
	• Members do not have permission to modify the Administrators or the Domain Admins groups or accounts for members of those groups.
	• Members can log on locally to domain controllers in the domain and shut them down.
	• Because this group has significant power in the domain, add users with caution.
Incoming Forest Trust Builders	• Members can create one-way, incoming forest trusts to the forest root domain.
	• This group has no default members.
Pre-Windows 2000 Compatible Access	• Members have read access on all users and groups in the domain.
	• This group is provided for backward compatibility for computers running Windows NT 4.0 and earlier.
	• Add users to this group only if they are using Remote Access Service (RAS) on a computer running Windows NT 4.0 or earlier.
Server Operators	• Members can log on interactively, create and delete shared resources, start and stop some services, back up and restore files, format the hard disk, and shut down the computer.
	• This group has no default members.
	• Because this group has significant power on domain controllers, add users with caution.

Groups in the Users container

The following table describes each default group in the Users container and the user rights assigned to each group.

Group	Description
Domain Controllers	• This group contains all domain controllers in the domain.
Domain Guests	• This group contains all domain guests.
Domain Users	• This group contains all domain users.
	• Any user account created in the domain is a member of this group automatically.
Domain Computers	• This group contains all workstations and servers joined to the domain.
	• Any computer account created becomes a member of this group automatically.
Domain Admins	• Members have full control of the domain.
	• This group is a member of the Administrators group on all domain controllers, all domain workstations, and all domain member servers at the time they are joined to the domain.
	• The Administrator account is a member of this group. Because the group has full power in the domain, add users with caution.
Enterprise Admins	• Members have full control of all domains in the forest.
	• This group is a member of the Administrators group on all domain controllers in the forest.
	• The Administrator account is a member of this group. Because this group has full control of all domains in the forest, add users with caution.
Group Policy Creator Owners	• Members can modify Group Policy in the domain.
	• The Administrator account is a member of this group. Because this group has significant power in the domain, add users with caution.

The following list contains the additional Default groups that Systems Engineers would use to manage groups:

- Schema Admins

- DnsAdmins

- DnsUpdateProxy

- Cert Publishers

- RAS and IAS Servers

Note For more information about other groups in the Users container, search for "Active Directory default groups" in Windows Server 2003 Help.

When to Use Default Groups

- **Default groups are:**
  - Created during the installation of the operating system or when services are added such as Active Directory or DHCP
  - Automatically assigned a set of user rights
- **Use Default groups to:**
  - Control access to shared resources
  - Delegate specific domain-wide administration

Using default groups

Predefined groups help you to control access to shared resources and delegate specific domain-wide administrative roles. Many default groups are automatically assigned a set of user rights that authorize members of the group to perform specific actions in a domain, such as log on to a local system or back up files and folders.

When you add a user to a group, the user receives all the user rights assigned to the group and all the permissions assigned to the group for any shared resources.

As a security best practice, it is recommended that members of default groups with broad administrative access use **Run as** to perform administrative tasks.

Security Considerations for Default Groups

- Place a user in a default group only when you are sure you want to give the user all the user rights and permissions assigned to that group in Active Directory; otherwise, create a new security group

- As a security best practice, members of default groups should use Run as

Security considerations for default groups

Only place a user in a default group when you are sure you want to give the user:

- All the user rights assigned to that group in Active Directory.

- All of the permissions assigned to that group for any shared resources associated with that default group.

Otherwise, create a new security group and assign the group only those user rights or permissions that the user absolutely requires.

As a security best practice, members of default groups that have broad administrative access should not perform an interactive logon by using administrative credentials. Instead, users with this level of access should use **Run as**.

Warning Only add members to default groups when members need all rights associated with the group. For example, if you need to add a service account to back up and restore files on a member server, you add the service account to the Backup Operators group. The Backup Operators group has the user rights to back up and restore files on the computer.

However, if your service account only needs to back up files and not restore them, it is better to create a new group. You can then grant the group the user right to back up files and not grant the group the right to restore files.

System Groups

- System groups represent different users at different times
- You can grant user rights and permissions to system groups, but you cannot modify or view the memberships
- Group scopes do not apply to system groups
- Users are automatically assigned to system groups whenever they log on or access a particular resource

Introduction

You cannot change the membership of system groups. The operating system creates them, and you cannot change or manage them. It is important to understand the system groups, because you can use them for security purposes.

Definition

Servers running Windows Server 2003 include several special identities in addition to the groups in the Users and Builtin containers. For convenience, these identities are generally referred to as system groups.

System groups represent different users at different times, depending on the circumstances. Although you can grant user rights and permissions to the system groups, you cannot modify or view their memberships.

Group scopes do not apply to system groups. Users are automatically assigned to system groups whenever they log on or access a particular resource.

System groups

The following table describes the system groups.

System group	Description
Anonymous Logon	The Anonymous Logon system group represents users and services that access a computer and its resources through the network without using an account name, password, or domain name.
	On computers running Windows NT and earlier, the Anonymous Logon group is a member of the Everyone group by default.
	On computers running a member of the Windows Server 2003 family, the Anonymous Logon group is not a member of the Everyone group by default. If you want to create a file share for an anonymous user, you grant permissions to the Anonymous Logon group.
Everyone	The Everyone system group represents all current network users, including guests and users from other domains. Whenever a user logs on to the network, the user is automatically added to the Everyone group.
	If security is not a concern for a specific group in your domain, you can grant permissions to the Everyone group. However, because the Anonymous Logon group can become a member of the Everyone group, it is not recommended that you use this group for permissions above read-only.
Network	The Network system group represents users currently accessing a given resource over the network, as opposed to users who access a resource by logging on locally at the computer where the resource is located. Whenever a user accesses a given resource over the network, the user is automatically added to the Network group.
Interactive	The Interactive system group represents all users currently logged on to a particular computer and accessing a given resource located on that computer, as opposed to users who access the resource over the network. Whenever a user accesses a resource on the computer to which they are currently logged on, the user is automatically added to the Interactive group.
Authenticated Users	The Authenticated Users system group represents all users within Active Directory. Always use the Authenticated Users group when granting permissions for a resource instead of using the Everyone group to prevent guests from accessing resources.
Creator Owner	The Creator Owner system group includes the user account for the user who created or took ownership of a resource. If a member of the Administrators group creates a resource, the Administrators group is the owner of the resource.

Class Discussion: Using Default Groups vs. Creating New Groups

Northwind Traders has over 100 servers across the world. You are attending a meeting to discuss the current tasks that administrators must perform and what minimum level of access the users need to perform specific tasks. You also must determine if you can use default groups or if you must create groups and assign specific user rights and permissions to the groups to perform the tasks.

Scenario

Northwind Traders has over 100 servers across the world. You are attending a meeting to discuss the current tasks that administrators must perform and what minimum level of access the users need to perform specific tasks. You also must determine if you can use default groups or if you must create groups and assign specific user rights and permissions to the groups to perform the tasks.

Discussion

You must assign default groups or create new groups for the following tasks. List the group that has the most restrictive user rights for performing the following actions or determine if you must create a new group.

1. Backing up and restoring domain controllers

   _____

   _____

   _____

2. Backing up member servers

   _____

   _____

   _____

3. Creating groups in the NWTraders Groups organizational unit

   _____

   _____

   _____

4. Logging on to the domain

    _____

    _____

    _____

5. Determining who needs read-only access to the DHCP servers

    _____

    _____

    _____

6. Determining what help desk employees need access to control the desktop remotely

    _____

    _____

    _____

7. Determining who needs administrative access to all computers in the entire domain

    _____

    _____

    _____

8. Determining who need access to a shared folder called Sales on a server called LonSrv2

    _____

    _____

    _____

Best Practices for Managing Groups

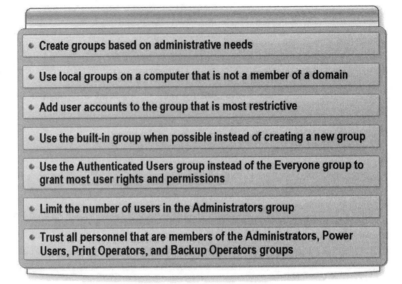

- Create groups based on administrative needs
- Use local groups on a computer that is not a member of a domain
- Add user accounts to the group that is most restrictive
- Use the built-in group when possible instead of creating a new group
- Use the Authenticated Users group instead of the Everyone group to grant most user rights and permissions
- Limit the number of users in the Administrators group
- Trust all personnel that are members of the Administrators, Power Users, Print Operators, and Backup Operators groups

Best practices

Consider the following best practices for managing groups:

- Create groups based on administrative needs. When you create a group based on a job function and another person takes over that job, you only need to change the group membership. You do not need to change all permissions that are granted to the individual user account. Because of this, it is sometimes advantageous to create a group that has only one member.

- Use local groups to give users access to resources on local computers when the computer is not a member of a domain.

- If you have multiple groups to which you can add user accounts, add user accounts to the group that is most restrictive. However, ensure that you grant the appropriate user rights and permissions so that users can accomplish any required task.

- Whenever a default group enables users to accomplish a task, use the default group instead of creating a new group. Create groups only when there are no default groups that provide the required user rights and permissions.

- Use the Authenticated Users group instead of the Everyone group to grant most user rights and permissions. Using this group minimizes the risk of unauthorized access, because Windows Server 2003 adds only valid user accounts to members of the Authenticated Users system group.

- Limit the number of users in the Administrators group. Members of the Administrators group on a local computer have Full Control permissions for that computer. Add a user to the Administrators group if the user will perform only administrative tasks.

- Your organization must equally trust all personnel that are members of the Administrators, Power Users, Print Operators, and Backup Operators groups. Some default user rights assigned to specific default local groups may allow members of those groups to gain additional rights on your computer, including administrative rights.

Lab A: Creating and Managing Groups

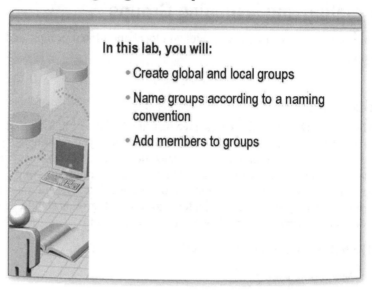

In this lab, you will:
- Create global and local groups
- Name groups according to a naming convention
- Add members to groups

Objectives

After completing this lab, you will be able to:

- Create global and domain local groups.
- Name groups according to a naming convention.
- Add members to groups.

Prerequisites

Before working on this lab, you must have knowledge of Active Directory, organizational units, organizational unit hierarchy, and accounts in Active Directory.

Before you begin this lab:

- Log on to the domain by using the *ComputerName*User account.
- Open CustomMMC with the **Run as** command.

  Use the user account Nwtraders\ComputerNameAdmin (Example: LondonAdmin).

- Ensure that CustomMMC contains Active Directory Users and Computers.

Estimated time to complete this lab: 60 minutes

Exercise 1
Creating and Managing Groups

In this exercise, you will create domain local and global groups, add members to groups, and nest groups.

Scenario

The Active Directory designers have just finished creating the group naming convention. They have given you a list of teams in Northwind Traders that you must create groups for. Some groups have already been created in your city organizational unit, so you must determine if the existing groups meet the naming convention and contain the appropriate users and groups. You then must add the appropriate user to the appropriate global groups. Finally, you must add the appropriate global groups to the appropriate domain local groups. All groups should be created in the Locations/*ComputerName*/Groups organizational unit.

The following teams in Northwind Traders need groups:

- Marketing Managers

- Marketing Personnel

- HR Managers

- HR Personnel

The Active Directory designers have created the following naming convention for groups:

- The first part of the group name defines the scope of the group (Example: **G** for global group and **DL** for domain local group).

- The second part of the group name defines the city organizational unit that the group belongs to (Example: London).

- The third part of the group name defines who the group is created for (Example: Sales Managers or Sales Personnel).

- If the group is a domain local group, the last part of the group name defines the maximum permissions the group will be used for (Example: Read or Full Control).

Tasks	Specific instructions
1. Create global groups for the following teams in the Locations/*ComputerName*/G roups organizational unit.	**a.** Marketing Managers (Example: G London Marketing Managers) **b.** Marketing Personnel **c.** HR Managers **d.** HR Personnel
2. Search for users who are managers and add them to the manager global groups.	**a.** Search for all Marketing Managers in the city called *ComputerName* and add them to the G *ComputerName* Marketing Managers group. **b.** Do the preceding step for the following groups: • G ComputerName Marketing Personnel • G ComputerName HR Managers • G ComputerName HR Personnel
3. Search for users who are personnel and add them to the personnel global groups.	**a.** Search for all users in the city called *ComputerName* and in the Marketing department and add them to the G Marketing Personnel group. **b.** Do the preceding step for each global personnel group.
4. Create domain local groups that will be used for Read and Modify permissions for the following teams in the Locations/*ComputerName*/G roups organizational unit.	■ Create the following Domain Local groups: • DL ComputerName Marketing Managers Read • DL ComputerName Marketing Personnel Read • DL ComputerName HR Managers Read • DL ComputerName HR Personnel Read • DL ComputerName Marketing Managers Modify • DL Co*mputerName* Marketing Personnel Modify • DL ComputerName HR Managers Modify • DL ComputerName HR Personnel Modify
5. Add members to the domain local groups for managers.	**a.** For each manager domain local group that was created, add the appropriate managers global group. For example: add G *ComputerName* Marketing Managers to DL ComputerName Marketing Managers Read and DL ComputerName Marketing Managers Modify. **b.** Do the preceding step for every manager's domain local group.
6. Add members to the domain local groups for personnel.	**a.** For each personnel domain local group that was created, add the appropriate global group for personnel. For example: add G *ComputerName* Marketing Personnel to DL *ComputerName* Marketing Personnel Read and DL *ComputerName* Marketing Personnel Modify. **b.** Do the preceding step for every personnel's domain local group.

Microsoft®
Training &
Certification

Module 4: Managing Access to Resources

Contents

Overview	1
Lesson: Overview of Managing Access to Resources	2
Lesson: Managing Access to Shared Folders	7
Lesson: Managing Access to Files and Folders Using NTFS Permissions	22
Lesson: Determining Effective Permissions	38
Lesson: Managing Access to Shared Files Using Offline Caching	51
Lab A: Managing Access to Resources	61

Overview

- Overview of Managing Access to Resources
- Managing Access to Shared Folders
- Managing Access to Files and Folders Using NTFS Permissions
- Determining Effective Permissions
- Managing Access to Shared Files Using Offline Caching

Introduction

This module introduces the job function of managing access to resources. Specifically, the module provides the skills and knowledge that you need to explain; manage access to files and folders by using shared folder permissions, NTFS permissions, or effective permissions; and manage access to shared files using offline caching.

Objectives

After completing this module, you will be able to:

- Manage access to resources.
- Manage access to shared folders.
- Manage access to files and folders by using NTFS permissions.
- Determine effective permissions.
- Managing access to shared files by using offline caching.

Lesson: Overview of Managing Access to Resources

- Multimedia: Access Control in Microsoft Windows Server 2003
- What Are Permissions?
- What Are Standard and Special Permissions?
- Multimedia: Permission States

Introduction

The information in this lesson presents the knowledge that you need to manage access to resources.

Lesson objectives

After completing this lesson, you will be able to:

- Describe the components of access control in Microsoft® Windows® Server 2003.
- Define permissions.
- Explain the differences between standard and special permissions.
- Explain the characteristics of implicit and explicit permission states.

Multimedia: Access Control in Microsoft Windows Server 2003

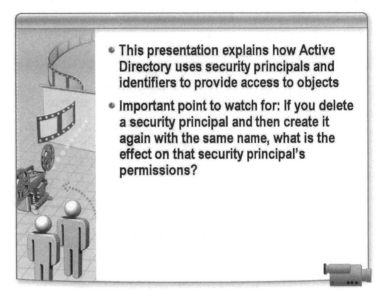

File location

To view the *Access Control in Microsoft Windows Server 2003* presentation, open the Web page on the Student Materials compact disc, click **Multimedia**, and then click the title of the presentation.

Key points

Key points from the presentation are summarized in the following list:

- Security principal

  A security principal is an account that can be authenticated.

- Security identifier (SID)

  A SID is an alphanumeric structure that is issued when an account is created and that uniquely identifies a security principal.

- Discretionary access control list (DACL)

  Each resource is associated with a DACL, which identifies the users and groups that are allowed or denied access to that resource.

- Access control entry (ACE)

  A DACL contains multiple ACEs. Each ACE specifies a SID, special permissions, inheritance information, and an Allow or Deny permission.

Additional reading

For more information about access control, see "Access Control Components" at http://msdn.microsoft.com/library/default.asp?url=/ library/en-us/security/security/access_control_components.asp.

What Are Permissions?

- Permissions define the type of access granted to a user, group, or computer for an object
- You apply permissions to objects such as files, folders, shared folders, and printers
- You assign permissions to users and groups in Active Directory or on a local computer

Definition

Permissions define the type of access granted to a user, group, or computer for an object. For example, you can let one user read the contents of a file, let another user make changes to the file, and prevent all other users from accessing the file. You can set similar permissions on printers so that certain users can configure the printer and other users can only print from it.

Permissions are also applied to any secured objects, such as files, objects in the Active Directory® directory service, and registry objects. Permissions can be granted to any user, group, or computer.

You can grant permissions for objects to:

- Groups, users, and special identities in the domain.
- Groups and users in any trusted domains.
- Local groups and users on the computer where the object resides.

Permission types

When you set permissions, you specify the level of access for groups and users. The permissions attached to an object depend on the type of object. For example, the permissions that are attached to a file are different from those that are attached to a registry key. Some permissions, however, are common to most types of objects. The following permissions are common permissions:

- Read permissions
- Write permissions
- Delete permissions

What Are Standard and Special Permissions?

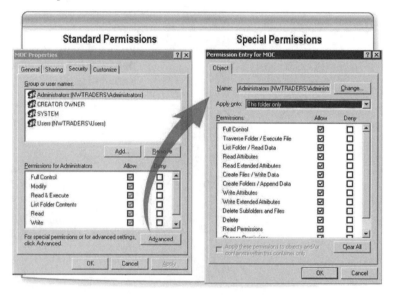

Introduction	You can grant standard and special permissions for objects. Standard permissions are the most frequently assigned permissions. Special permissions provide you with a finer degree of control for assigning access to objects.
Standard permissions	The system has a default level of security settings for a specific object. These are the most common set of permissions that a systems administrator uses on a daily basis. The list of standard permissions that are available varies depending on what type of object you are modifying the security for.
Special permissions	Special permissions are a more detailed list of permissions. A standard NFTS permission of Read is related to the following special permissions:

- List Folder/Read Data
- Read Attributes
- Read Extended Attributed
- Read Permissions

If the systems administrator removes a special permission that relates to a standard permission, the check box for the standard permission is no longer selected. The check box for the special permission under the standard permission list is selected.

Multimedia: Permission States

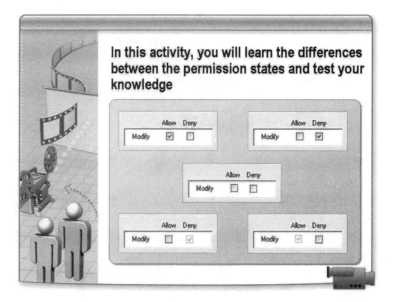

File location

To start the *Permission States* activity, open the Web page on the Student Materials compact disc, click **Multimedia**, and then click the title of the activity.

Lesson: Managing Access to Shared Folders

- What Are Shared Folders?
- What Are Administrative Shared Folders?
- Who Can Access Shared Folders?
- How to Create a Shared Folder
- What Are Published Shared Folders?
- How to Publish a Shared Folder
- Shared Folder Permissions
- How to Set Permissions on a Shared Folder
- How to Connect to Shared Folders

Introduction

The Windows Server 2003 family organizes files into directories that are graphically represented as folders. These folders contain all types of files and can contain subfolders. Some of these folders are reserved for operating system files and program files. Users should never place any data into the operating system folders or program file folders.

Shared folders give users access to files and folders over a network. Users can connect to the shared folder over the network to access the folders and files they contain. Shared folders can contain applications, public data, or a user's personal data. Using shared application folders centralizes administration by enabling you to install and maintain applications on a server instead of client computers. Using shared data folders provides a central location for users to access common files and makes it easier to back up data contained in those files.

Lesson objectives

After completing this lesson, you will be able to:

- Explain what shared folders are.
- Explain what administrative shared folders are.
- Identify the requirements for sharing folders.
- Create a shared folder.
- Explain what published shared folders are.
- Publish a shared folder.
- Explain what shared folder permissions are.
- Set permissions on a shared folder.
- Connect to shared folders.

What Are Shared Folders?

- **Copy a shared folder**
  - The original shared folder is still shared, but the copy of the folder is not shared
- **Move a shared folder**
  - The folder is no longer shared
- **Hide a shared folder**
  - Include a $ after the name of the shared folder
  - Users can access a hidden shared folder by typing the UNC, for example, \\server\secrets$

Introduction

Sharing a folder is when a folder is made accessible to multiple users simultaneously over the network. After a folder is shared, users can access all of the files and subfolders in the shared folder if they are granted permission.

You can place shared folders on a file server and also place them on any computer on the network. You can store files in shared folders according to categories or functions. For example, you can place shared data files in one shared folder and shared application files in another.

Characteristics of shared folders

Some of the most common characteristics of shared folders are as follows:

- A shared folder appears in Windows Explorer as an icon of a hand holding the folder.

- You can only share folders, not individual files. If multiple users need access to the same file, you must place the file in a folder and then share the folder.

- When a folder is shared, the Read permission is granted to the Everyone group as the default permission. Remove the default permission and grant the Change permission or Read permission to groups as needed.

- When users or groups are added to a shared folder, the default permission is Read.

- When you copy a shared folder, the original shared folder is still shared, but the copy is not shared. When a shared folder is moved to another location, the folder is no longer shared.

- You can hide a shared folder if you put a dollar sign ($) after the name of the shared folder. The user cannot see the shared folder in the user interface, but a user can access the shared folder by typing the Universal Naming Convention (UNC) name, for example, \\server\secrets$.

What Are Administrative Shared Folders?

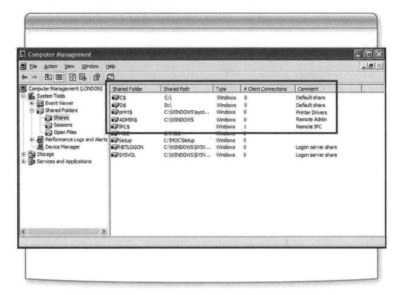

Introduction

Windows Server 2003 automatically shares folders that enable you to perform administrative tasks. They are designated by an appended dollar sign ($) at the end of the folder name. The dollar sign hides the shared folder from users who browse to the computer in My Network Places. Administrators can quickly administer files and folders on remote servers by using these hidden shared folders.

Types of administrative shared folders

By default, members of the Administrators group have the Full Control permission for administrative shared folders. You cannot modify the permissions for administrative shared folders. The following table describes the purpose of the administrative shared folders that Windows Server 2003 automatically provides.

Shared folder	Purpose
C$, D$, E$	You use these shared folders to remotely connect to a computer and perform administrative tasks. The root of each partition (that has a drive letter assigned to it) on a hard disk is automatically shared. When you connect to this folder, you have access to the entire partition.
Admin$	This is the systemroot folder, which is C:\Winnt by default. Administrators can access this shared folder to administer Windows Server 2003 without knowing the folder in which it is installed.
Print$	This folder provides access to printer driver files for client computers. When you install the first shared printer, the *Systemroot*\System32\ Spool\Drivers folder is shared as Print$. Only members of the Administrators, Server Operators, and Print Operators groups have Full Control permission for this folder. The Everyone group has Read permission for this folder.
IPC$	This folder is used during remote administration of a computer and when viewing a computer's shared resources.
FAX$	This shared folder is used to temporarily cache files and access cover pages on the server.

Additional reading   For more information on IPC$, see article 101150, "Operating Characteristics and Restrictions of Named Pipes" in the Microsoft Knowledge Base at http://support.microsoft.com/?kbid=101150.

Who Can Access Shared Folders?

- **Windows Server 2003 domain controller**
  - Administrators Group
  - Server Operators Group
- **A member server or stand-alone server running Windows Server 2003**
  - Administrators Group
  - Power Users Group

Introduction

In Windows Server 2003, the only groups that can access shared folders are the Administrators, Server Operators, and Power Users groups. These groups are built-in groups that are placed in the Group folder in Computer Management or the built-in folder in Active Directory Users and Groups.

Groups that can access shared folders

The following table describes who can access shared folders.

To share folders:	You must be a member of:
On a Windows Server 2003 domain controller	The Administrators or Server Operators group.
	Note that the Power Users group can share folders on a member server in a Windows Server 2003 domain.
On a stand-alone or member server running Windows Server 2003	The Administrators or Power Users group.

How to Create a Shared Folder

Your instructor will demonstrate how to:

- Create a shared folder by using Computer Management
- Create a shared folder by using Windows Explorer
- Create a shared folder by using net share

Introduction

When you create a shared folder, you give it a shared folder name and provide a comment that describes the folder and its contents. You can also limit the number of users who can access the folder, grant permissions, and share the same folder multiple times.

Procedure using Computer Management

To create a shared folder by using Computer Management:

1. In Computer Management, in the console tree, expand **Shared Folders** and then click **Shares**.

2. On the **Action** menu, click **New Share**.

3. Follow the steps in the Share a Folder Wizard.

Procedure using Windows Explorer

To create a shared folder by using Windows Explorer:

1. In Windows Explorer, right-click the folder, and then click **Sharing and Security**.

2. In the **Properties** dialog box, on the **Sharing** tab, configure the options described in the following table.

Option	Description
Share this folder	Click to share the folder.
Share name	Enter the name that users from remote locations use to connect to the shared folder. The default shared folder name is the folder name. This option is required.
	Note: Some client computers that connect to a shared folder only see a limited number of characters.
Description	Enter an optional description for the shared folder. You can use this comment to identify the contents of the shared folder.
User Limit	Enter the number of users who can concurrently connect to the shared folder. This option is not required if you click **Maximum Allowed**, current Windows client operating systems supports up to 10 concurrent connections.
Permissions	Click to set the shared folder permissions that apply only when the folder is accessed over the network. This option is not required. By default, the Everyone group is granted the Read permission for all new shared folders.

Using a command line

The **net share** command creates, deletes, or displays shared folders. To create a shared folder by using **net share**:

1. Open a command prompt.

2. Type **net share** *SharedFolderName=Drive:Path*

Value	Description
SharedFolderName=Drive:Path	This is the network name of the shared folder and the absolute path of its location.

What Are Published Shared Folders?

- A published shared folder is a shared folder object in Active Directory
- Clients can search Active Directory for shared folders that are published
- Clients do not need to know the name of the server to connect to a shared folder

Definition

Publishing resources and shared folders in Active Directory enables users to search Active Directory and locate resources on the network even if the physical location of the resources changes.

For example, if you move a shared folder to another computer, all shortcuts pointing to the Active Directory object that represents the published shared folder continue to work, as long as you update the reference to the physical location. Users do not have to update their connections.

Publishing the folder

You can publish any shared folder in Active Directory that can be accessed by using a UNC name. After a shared folder is published, a user at a computer running Windows Server 2003 can use Active Directory to locate the object representing the shared folder and then connect to the shared folder.

When the shared folder is published to Active Directory, the shared folder becomes a child object of the computer account. To view shared folders as an object, in Active Directory Users and Computers, on the **View** menu, click **Users, Group, and Computers as containers**. Then, in the console tree, click the computer account. On the details pane, you will see all the published shared folders that are associated with the computer account.

How to Publish a Shared Folder

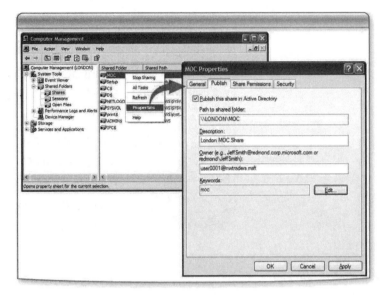

Introduction

Publishing information about network resources in Active Directory makes it easy for users to find them on the network. You can publish information about printers and shared folders by using Computer Management or Active Directory Users and Computers.

Procedure for publishing a shared folder as a server object

To publish a shared folder as a server object:

1. In Computer Management, in the console tree, expand **Shared Folders** and then click **Shares**.

2. Right-click a shared folder, and then click **Properties**.

3. In the **Properties** dialog box, on the **Publish** tab, select the **Publish this share in Active Directory** check box, and then click **OK**.

Procedure for publishing a shared folder to an organizational unit

To publish a shared folder to an organizational unit:

1. In Active Directory Users and Computers, in the console tree, right-click the folder in which you want to add the shared folder, point to **New**, and then click **Shared Folder**.

2. In the **New Object – Shared Folder** dialog box, in the **Name** box, type the name of the folder you want clients to use.

3. In the **Network path** box, type the UNC name that you want to publish in Active Directory, and then click **OK**.

Shared Folder Permissions

Permission	Allows the user to:
Read (Default, applied to the Everyone group)	• View data in files and attributes • View file names and subfolder names • Run program files
Change (Includes all Read permissions)	• Add files and subfolders • Change data in files • Delete subfolders and files
Full Control	• Includes all Read and Change permissions • Enables you to change NTFS files and folders permissions

Introduction

Shared folder permissions only apply to users who connect to the folder over the network. They do not restrict access to users who access the folder at the computer where the folder is stored. You can grant shared folder permissions to user accounts, groups, and computer accounts.

Permissions

Shared folder permissions include the following:

- Read

  Read is the default shared folder permission and is applied to the Everyone group. Read permission enables you to:

  - View file names and subfolder names.

  - View data in files and attributes.

  - Run program files.

- Change

  The Change permission includes all Read permissions and also enables you to:

  - Add files and subfolders.

  - Change data in files.

  - Delete subfolders and files.

- Full Control

  Full Control includes all Read and Change permissions and also enables you to change permissions for NTFS files and folders.

How to Set Permissions on a Shared Folder

Your instructor will demonstrate how to:

- Set permissions on a shared folder by using Computer Management
- Set permissions on a shared folder by using Windows Explorer

Introduction

Use the following procedure to set permissions on a shared folder.

Procedure using Computer Management

To set permissions on a shared folder by using Computer Management:

1. In Computer Management, in the console tree, expand **Shared Folders**, and then click **Shares**.

2. In the details pane, right-click the shared folder for which you want to set permissions, and then click **Properties**.

3. In the **Properties** dialog box, on the **Share Permissions** tab, do one of the following:

   - Click **Add** to grant a user or group permission for a shared folder. In the **Select Users, Computers, or Groups** dialog box, select or type the user or group name, and then click **OK**.

   - Click **Remove** to revoke access to a shared folder.

4. In the **Permissions** box, select the **Allow** or **Deny** check boxes to set individual permissions for the selected user or group, and then click **OK**.

Procedures using Windows Explorer

To set permissions on a shared folder by using Windows Explorer:

1. In Windows Explorer, right-click the shared folder for which you want to set permissions, and then click **Sharing and Security**.

2. In the **Properties** dialog box, on the **Sharing** tab, click **Permissions**.

3. In the **Permissions** dialog box, do one of the following:

   - Click **Add** to grant a user or group permission for a shared folder. In the **Select Users, Computers, or Groups** dialog box, select or type the user or group name, and then click **OK**.

   - Click **Remove** to revoke access to a shared resource.

4. In the **Permissions** box, select the **Allow** or **Deny** check boxes to set individual permissions for the selected user or group.

How to Connect to Shared Folders

Introduction

After you create a shared folder, users can access the folder across the network. Users can access a shared folder on another computer by using My Network Places, the **Map Network Drive** feature, or the **Run** command on the **Start** menu.

Procedure using My Network Places

To connect to a shared folder by using My Network Places:

1. Open My Network Places and double-click **Add a network place**.

2. In the Add Network Place Wizard, on the **Welcome** page, click **Next**.

3. On the **Where do you want to create this network place** page, click **Choose another network location**, and then click **Next**.

4. On the **What is the address of this network place** page, type the UNC path of the shared folder or click **Browse**.

   a. If you click **Browse**, expand **Entire Network**.

   b. Expand **Microsoft Windows Network**.

   c. Expand the domain and server you want to connect to.

   d. Click the shared folder that you want to add, and then click **OK**.

5. Click **Next**.

6. On the **What do you want to name this place** page, type the name of the network place, and then click **Next**.

7. On the **Completing the Add Network Place Wizard** page, click **Finish**.

Note When you open a shared folder over the network, Windows Server 2003 automatically adds it to My Network Places.

Procedure using Map Network Drive

When you want a drive letter and icon associated with a specific shared folder, you must map to a network drive. This makes it easier to refer to the location of a file in a shared folder. You can also use drive letters to access shared folders for which you cannot use a UNC path, such as a folder for an older application.

To connect to a shared folder by using My Network Places:

1. Right-click **My Network Places**, and then click **Map Network Drive**.

2. In the **Map Network Drive** dialog box, in the **Drive** box, select the drive that you want to use.

3. In the **Folder** box, type the name of the shared folder you want to connect to or click **Browse**.

4. For a shared folder that you will use on a recurring basis, select the **Reconnect at logon** check box to connect automatically to the shared folder each time you log on.

Procedure using the Run command

When you use the **Run** command on the **Start** menu to connect to a network resource, a drive letter is not required. This enables you to connect to the shared folder an unlimited number of times, independent of available drive letters.

1. Click **Start**, and then click **Run**.

2. In the **Run** dialog box, enter a UNC path, and then click **OK**.

   When you enter the server name, a list of available shared folders appears. Windows Server 2003 gives you the option to choose one of the entries based on the shared folders that are available to you.

Practice: Managing Access to Shared Folders

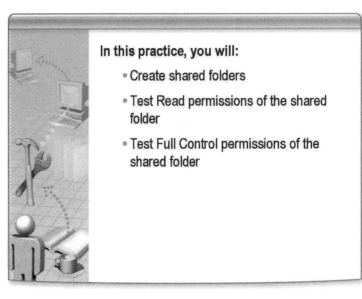

Objective

In this practice, you will create a shared folder, grant Read and Full Control permissions to two separate groups, and test the permissions.

Instructions

Before you begin this practice:

■ Log on to the domain as *ComputerName*Admin.

> **Note** You cannot use the **Run as** command with Windows Explorer, so you must log on as *ComputerName*Admin to have the permissions that you need to complete this practice.

■ Ensure that CustomMMC contains Computer Management (Local).

■ Review the procedures in this lesson that describe how to perform this task.

Scenario

You have been asked to create a shared folder for the Human Resources department. The Human Resources department needs a shared folder for which Human Resources personnel will have Full Control permissions and all Accounting managers will have read access. You must create the shared folder with the proper permissions to meet the needs of the Human Resources personnel and Accounting managers.

Practice

▶ **Create a shared folder**

Adminstrative Tools

- Using Computer Management, create a shared folder on your student computer with the following parameters:

    - Folder location: D:\

    - Folder name: **HR Reports**

    - Security:

        - Grant Full Control permissions to DL NWTraders HR Personnel Full Control

        - Grant Read permissions to DL NWTraders Accounting Managers Read

        - Remove the Everyone group

▶ **Test Read permissions of the shared folder**

1. Log on as **AccountingManager** with a password of **P@ssw0rd**.

2. Connect to the shared folder *ComputerName*\HR Reports.

3. Try to create a text file in the HR Reports folder.

   You *should not* be able to create a text file in the shared folder.

▶ **Test Full Control permissions of the shared folder**

1. Log on as **HRUser** with a password of **P@ssw0rd**.

2. Connect to the shared folder *ComputerName*\HR Reports.

3. Try to create a text file in the HR Reports folder.

   You *should* be able to access the shared folder.

Lesson: Managing Access to Files and Folders Using NTFS Permissions

- What Is NTFS?
- NTFS File and Folder Permissions
- Effects on NTFS Permissions When Copying and Moving Files and Folders
- What Is NTFS Permissions Inheritance?
- How to Copy or Remove Inherited Permissions
- Best Practices for Managing Access to Files and Folders Using NTFS Permissions
- How to Manage Access to Files and Folders Using NTFS Permissions

Introduction

The information in this lesson presents the skills and knowledge that you need to manage access to files and folders by using NTFS permissions.

Lesson objectives

After completing this lesson, you will be able to:

- Explain what NTFS is.
- Explain what NTFS file and folder permissions are.
- Explain the effects on NTFS permissions of copying and moving files and folders.
- Explain what NTFS permissions inheritance is.
- Explain best practices for managing access to files and folders by using NTFS permissions.
- Copy or remove inherited permissions.
- Manage access to files and folders by using NTFS permissions.

What Is NTFS?

NTFS is a file system that provides:

- Reliability

- Security at the file level and folder level

- Improved management of storage growth

- Multiple user permissions

Introduction

NTFS is a file system that is available on Windows Server 2003. NTFS provides performance and features that are not found in either FAT (file allocation table) or FAT32.

Benefits of NTFS

NTFS provides the following benefits:

- Reliability

  NTFS uses log file and checkpoint information to restore the integrity of the file system when the computer is restarted. If there is a bad-sector error, NTFS dynamically remaps the cluster containing the bad sector and allocates a new cluster for the data. NTFS also marks the cluster as unusable.

- Greater security

  NTFS files use the Encrypting File System (EFS) to secure files and folders. If EFS is enabled, files and folders can be encrypted for use by single or multiple users. The benefits of encryption are data confidentiality and data integrity, which means that data is protected against malicious or accidental modification. NTFS also enables you to set access permissions on a file or folder. Permissions can be set to Read, Read and Write, or Deny.

  NTFS also stores an access control list (ACL) with every file and folder on an NTFS partition. The ACL contains a list of all user accounts, groups, and computers that are granted access for the file or folder and the type of access that they are granted. For a user to access a file or folder, the ACL must contain an entry, called an ACE, for the user account, group, or computer that the user is associated with. The ACE must specifically allow the type of access the user is requesting for the user to access the file or folder. If no ACE exists in the ACL, Windows Server 2003 denies the user access to the resource.

■ Improved management of storage growth

NTFS supports disk quotas, which enable you to specify the amount of disk space that is available to a user. By using disk quotas, you can track and control disk space usage and configure whether users are allowed to exceed a warning level or storage quota limit.

NTFS supports larger files and a larger number of files per volume than FAT or FAT32. NTFS also manages disk space efficiently by using smaller cluster sizes. For example, a 30-gigabyte (GB) NTFS volume uses four-kilobyte (KB) clusters. The same volume formatted with FAT32 uses 16-KB clusters. Using smaller clusters reduces wasted space on hard disks.

■ Multiple user permissions

If you grant NTFS permissions to an individual user account and to a group to which the user belongs, then you grant multiple permissions to the user. There are rules for how NTFS combines these multiple permissions to produce the user's effective permissions.

Additional reading

For more information on NTFS, see "NTFS" at http://www.microsoft.com/technet/treeview/default.asp?url=/technet/prodtechnol/windowsserver2003/proddocs/server/ntfs.asp.

For more information on FAT and NTFS, see "Choosing Between FAT and NTFS" at http://www.microsoft.com/technet/treeview/default.asp?url=/technet/ittasks/deploy/fat.asp.

NTFS File and Folder Permissions

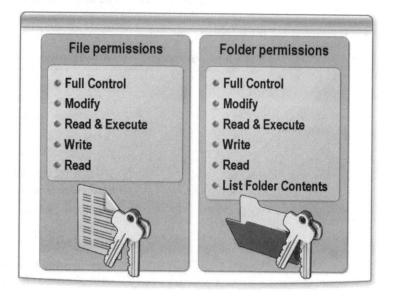

Introduction

NTFS permissions are used to specify which users, groups, and computers can access files and folders. NTFS permissions also dictate what users, groups, and computers can do with the contents of the file or folder.

NTFS file permissions

The following table lists the standard NTFS file permissions that you can grant and the type of access that each permission provides.

NTFS file permission	Allows the user to:
Full Control	Change permissions, take ownership, and perform the actions permitted by all other NTFS file permissions
Modify	Modify and delete the file and perform the actions permitted by the Write permission and the Read & Execute permission
Read & Execute	Run applications and perform the actions permitted by the Read permission
Write	Overwrite the file, change file attributes, and view file ownership and permissions
Read	Read the file and view file attributes, ownership, and permissions

NTFS folder permissions   Permissions control access to folders and the files and subfolders that are contained in those folders. The following table lists the standard NTFS folder permissions that you can grant and the type of access that each permission provides.

NTFS folder permission	Allows the user to:
Full Control	Change permissions, take ownership, delete subfolders and files, and perform actions permitted by all other NTFS folder permissions
Modify	Delete the folder and perform actions permitted by the Write permission and the Read & Execute permission
Read & Execute	Traverse folders and perform actions permitted by the Read permission and the List Folder Contents permission
Write	Create new files and subfolders in the folder, change folder attributes, and view folder ownership and permissions
Read	View files and subfolders in the folder, folder attributes, ownership, and permissions
List Folder Contents	View the names of files and subfolders in the folder

Additional reading   For more information about permissions, see "Permissions" at http://www.microsoft.com/technet/treeview/default.asp?url=/technet/ prodtechnol/windowsserver2003/proddocs/server/sag_sfmhowworks_13.asp.

Effects on NTFS Permissions When Copying and Moving Files and Folders

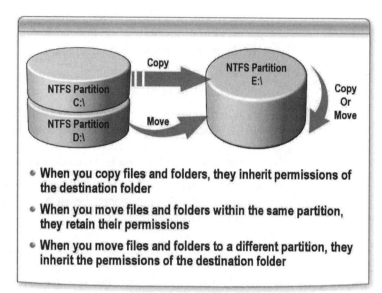

- **When you copy files and folders, they inherit permissions of the destination folder**
- **When you move files and folders within the same partition, they retain their permissions**
- **When you move files and folders to a different partition, they inherit the permissions of the destination folder**

Introduction

When you copy or move a file or folder, the permissions may change depending on where you move the file or folder. It is important to understand the changes that the permissions undergo when being copied or moved.

Effects of copying files and folders

When you copy files or folders from one folder to another folder, or from one partition to another partition, permissions for the files or folders may change. Copying a file or folder has the following effects on NTFS permissions:

- When you copy a folder or file within a single NTFS partition, the copy of the folder or file inherits the permissions of the destination folder.

- When you copy a folder or file to a different NTFS partition, the copy of the folder or file inherits the permissions of the destination folder.

- When you copy a folder or file to a non-NTFS partition, such as a FAT partition, the copy of the folder or file loses its NTFS permissions, because non-NTFS partitions do not support NTFS permissions.

Effects of moving files and folders

To copy files and folders within a single NTFS partition or between NTFS partitions, you must have Read permission for the source folder and Write permission for the destination folder.

When you move a file or folder, permissions may change, depending on the permissions of the destination folder. Moving a file or folder has the following effects on NTFS permissions:

- When you move a folder or file within an NTFS partition, the folder or file retains its original permissions.

- When you move a folder or file to a different NTFS partition, the folder or file inherits the permissions of the destination folder. When you move a folder or file between partitions, Windows Server 2003 copies the folder or file to the new location and then deletes it from the old location.

- When you move a folder or a file to a non-NTFS partition, the folder or file loses its NTFS permissions, because non-NTFS partitions do not support NTFS permissions.

To move files and folders within an NTFS partition or between NTFS partitions, you must have both Write permission for the destination folder and Modify permission for the source folder or file. The Modify permission is required to move a folder or file, because Windows Server 2003 removes the folder or file from the source folder after it copies it to the destination folder.

Effects of copying and moving within volumes

The following table lists the possible copy and move options and describes how Windows Server 2003 treats the compression state of a file or folder.

Action	Result
Copy a file or folder within a volume	Inherits compression state of the destination folder
Move a file or folder within a volume	Retains original compression state of the source
Copy a file or folder between volumes	Inherits compression state of the destination folder
Move a file or folder between volumes	Inherits compression state of source file or folder

What Is NTFS Permissions Inheritance?

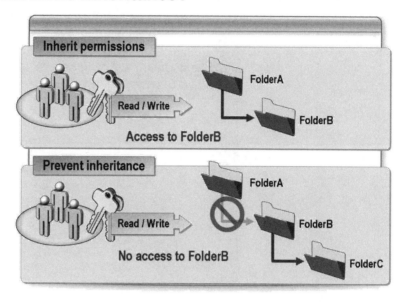

Definition

By default, permissions that you grant to a parent folder are inherited by the subfolders and files that are contained in the parent folder. When you create files and folders, and when you format a partition with NTFS, Windows Server 2003 automatically assigns default NTFS permissions.

Controlling permissions inheritance

You can prevent subfolders and files from inheriting permissions that are assigned to the parent folder. When you prevent permissions inheritance, you can either:

- Copy inherited permissions from the parent folder.

   - or -

- Remove the inherited permissions and retain only the permissions that were explicitly assigned.

The folder at which you prevent permissions inheritance becomes the new parent folder, and the subfolders and files that are contained in it inherit the permissions assigned to it.

Why prevent propagating permissions?

Permissions inheritance simplifies how permissions for parent folders, subfolders, and resources are assigned. However, you may want to prevent inheritance so that permissions do not propagate from a parent folder to subfolders and files.

For example, you may need to keep all Sales department files in one Sales folder for which everyone in the Sales department has Write permission. However, for a few files in the folder, you may need to limit the permissions to Read. To do so, prevent inheritance so that the Write permission does not propagate to the files contained in the folder.

How to Copy or Remove Inherited Permissions

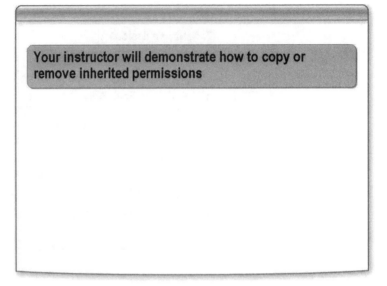

Your instructor will demonstrate how to copy or remove inherited permissions

Introduction   Use the following procedure to copy or remove inherited permissions.

Procedure   To copy or remove inherited permissions:

1. In Windows Explorer, right-click the file or folder you want to change inherited permissions on, and then click **Properties**.

2. In the **Properties** dialog box, on the **Security** tab, click **Advanced**.

3. In the **Advanced Security Settings** dialog box, clear the check box labeled **Allow inheritable permissions from the parent to propagate to this object and all child objects. Include these with entries explicitly defined here**.

4. In the **Security** dialog box, click one of the following:

    • Click **Copy** to copy the permission entries that were previously applied from the parent to this object.

    • Click **Remove** to remove permission entries that were previously applied from the parent and keep only those permissions explicitly assigned.

5. In the **Advanced Security Settings** dialog box, click **OK**.

6. In the **Properties** dialog box, click **OK**.

Best Practices for Managing Access to Files and Folders Using NTFS Permissions

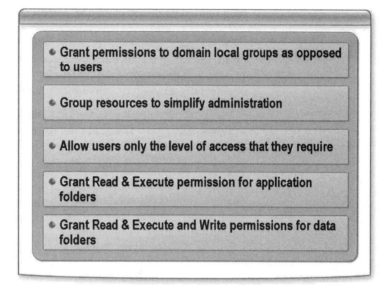

Best practices

When managing access to files and folders, consider the following best practices when granting NTFS permissions:

- Grant permissions to groups instead of users. Because it is inefficient to maintain user accounts directly, avoid granting permissions to individual users.

- Use Deny permissions in the following situations:

    - To exclude a subset of a group that has Allow permissions

    - To exclude one permission when you have already granted Full Control permissions to a user or group

- If possible, do not change the default permission entries for file system objects, particularly on system folders and root folders. Changing default permissions can cause unexpected access problems or reduce security.

- Never deny the Everyone group access to an object. If you deny everyone access to an object, you deny administrators access. Instead, it is recommended that you remove the Everyone group, as long as you grant permissions for the object to other users, groups, or computers.

- Grant permissions to an object that is as high on the tree as possible so that the security settings are propagated throughout the tree. You can quickly and effectively grant permissions to all children or a subtree of a parent object. By doing this, you affect the most objects with the least effort. Grant permissions that are adequate for the majority of users, groups, and computers.

- To simplify administration, group files according to function, for example:
  - Group program files into folders where commonly used applications are kept.
  - Group data folders containing home folders into one folder.
  - Group data files that are shared by multiple users into one folder.
- Grant the Read & Execute permission to the Users and Administrators groups for application folders. This prevents users or viruses from accidentally deleting or damaging data and application files.
- Only allow users the level of access that they require. For example, if a user only needs to read a file, grant the Read permission for the file to the user or group to which the user belongs.
- Grant the Read & Execute and Write permissions to the Users group and the Modify permission to the Creator Owner group for data folders. This enables users to read and modify documents that other users create and to read, modify, and delete the files and folders that they themselves create.

How to Manage Access to Files and Folders Using NTFS Permissions

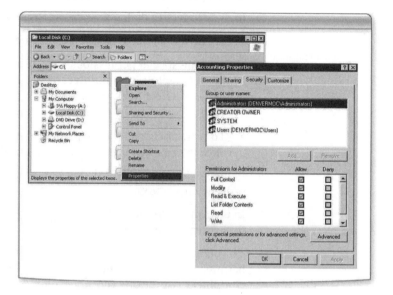

Introduction

Use the follow procedure to change standard and special permissions for files and folders.

Procedure for changing standard permissions

To change standard permissions:

1. In Windows Explorer, right-click the file or folder for which you want to grant permissions, and then click **Properties**.

2. In the **Properties** dialog box, on the **Security** tab, do one of the following:

   - To grant permissions to a group or user that does not appear in the **Group or user names** box, click **Add**. In the **Select users, computers, or groups** dialog box, in the **Enter object names to select** box, type the name of the group or user you want to grant permissions to, and then click **OK**.

   - To change or remove permissions from an existing group or user, in the **Group or user names** box, click the name of the group or user, and then do one of the following:

     - To allow or deny permission, in the **Permissions for** box, select the **Allow** or **Deny** check box.

     - To remove the group or user from the **Group or user names** box, click **Remove**.

Procedure for changing special permissions

To change special permissions:

1. In Windows Explorer, right-click the object for which you want to grant special permissions, and then click **Properties**.

2. In the **Properties** dialog box, on the **Security** tab, click **Advanced**.

3. In the **Advanced Security Settings** dialog box, do one of the following:

    - To grant special permissions to an additional group or user, click **Add**. In the **Select user, computer, or group** dialog box, in the **Enter object name to select** box, type the name of the user or group, and then click **OK**.

    - To view or change special permissions for an existing group or user, click the name of the group or user, and then click **Edit**.

4. In the **Permissions Entry** dialog box, select or clear the appropriate **Allow** or **Deny** check box.

5. In the **Apply onto** drop down list, click the folders or subfolders you want these permissions to be applied to.

6. To configure security so that the subfolders and files do not inherit these permissions, clear the **Apply these permissions to objects and/or containers within this container only** check box.

7. Click **OK** and then, in the **Advanced Security Settings** dialog box, click **OK**.

Note To remove an existing group or user and its special permissions, click the name of the group or user, and then click **Remove**. If the **Remove** button is unavailable, clear the **Allow inheritable permissions from the parent to propagate to this object and all child objects. Include these with entries explicitly defined here** check box, and then click **Copy** or **Remove**.

Practice: Managing Access to Files and Folders Using NTFS Permissions

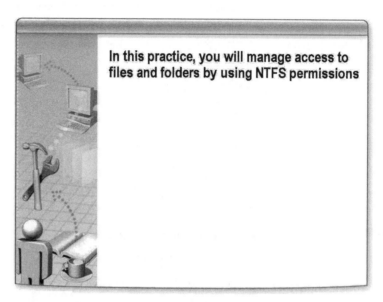

In this practice, you will manage access to files and folders by using NTFS permissions

Objective

In this practice, you will manage access to files and folders by using NTFS permissions.

Instructions

Before you begin this practice:

- Log on to the domain as *ComputerName*Admin.

  Note You cannot use the **Run as** command with Windows Explorer, so you must log on as *ComputerName*Admin to have the permissions that you need to complete this practice.

- Review the procedures in this lesson that describe how to perform this task.

Scenario

Northwind Traders wants you to create a shared folder called Public that is accessible to the Accounting department and the Human Resources department. All employees will need to access the same shared folder and will then navigate to the appropriate folder for their job tasks. You must create the folders represented in the following diagram and configure the shared folder and NTFS permissions:

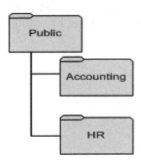

Practice

▶ **Share the Public folder**

1. Create and share the folder D:\Public.

2. Configure the Authenticated Users group to have Change permission for the D:\Public folder.

3. Remove the Everyone group.

▶ **Create folders according to the diagram**

1. Create the folder D:\Public\Accounting.

2. Create the folder D:\Public\HR.

▶ **Configure NTFS permissions**

- Remove all inherited permissions in the following folders and apply the permissions only to the folder. Do not let subfolders inherit permissions.

Folder	Group	NTFS Special Permissions
D:\Public	Authenticated Users	Traverse Folder / Execute File List Folder / Read Data Read Permissions
	ComputerName\Administrators	Full Control
D:\Public\Accounting	DL NWTraders Accounting Personnel Full Control	Full Control
	ComputerName\Administrator	Full Control
D:\Public\HR	DL NWTraders HR Personnel Full Control	Full Control
	ComputerName\Administrators	Full Control

▶ **Test the NTFS permissions**

1. Log on as **HRUser** with a password of **P@ssw0rd**.

2. Attempt to access *ComputerName*\Public\Accounting.

   You should *not* be able to access the Accounting folder. If you can access the folder, check that there are no NTFS permissions granted to Authenticated Users for the Accounting folder.

3. Attempt to Connect to D:\Public\Accounting.

   You should *not* be able to access the Accounting folder. If you can access the folder, check that there are no NTFS permissions granted to Authenticated Users for the Accounting folder.

4. Connect to *ComputerName*\Public\HR.

   You *should* be able to access the HR folder. If you cannot access the folder, check that the DL NWTraders HR Personnel Full Control group has NTFS Full Control permissions granted to the HR folder.

5. Connect to D:\Public\HR.

   You *should* be able to access the HR folder. If you cannot access the folder, check that the DL NWTraders HR Personnel Full Control group has NTFS Full Control permissions granted to the HR folder.

Lesson: Determining Effective Permissions

- What Are Effective Permissions on NTFS Files and Folders?
- How to Determine Effective Permissions on NTFS Files and Folders
- Effects of Combined Shared Folder and NTFS Permissions
- How to Determine the Effective Permissions on Combined Shared Folder and NTFS Permissions

Introduction

If you grant NTFS permissions to an individual user account and a group to which the user belongs, then you grant multiple permissions to the user. There are rules for how NTFS combines these multiple permissions to produce the user's effective permissions.

Lesson objectives

After completing this lesson, you will be able to:

- Explain what effective permissions on NTFS files and folders are.
- Determine effective permissions on NTFS files and folders.
- Explain the effects of combined shared folder and NTFS permissions.
- Determine effective permissions on combined shared folder and NTFS permissions.

What Are Effective Permissions on NTFS Files and Folders?

- Permissions are cumulative
- File permissions are separate from folder permissions
- Deny overrides all permissions
- Take ownership

Introduction

Windows Server 2003 provides a tool that shows effective permissions, which are cumulative permissions based on group membership. The information is calculated from the existing permissions entries and is displayed in a read-only format.

Characteristics

Effective permissions have the following characteristics:

- Cumulative permissions are the combination of the highest NTFS permissions granted to the user and all the groups the user is a member of.

- NTFS file permissions take priority over folder permissions.

- Deny permissions override all permissions.

- Every object is owned in an NTFS volume or Active Directory. The owner controls how permissions are set on the object and to whom permissions are granted.

Important An administrator who needs to repair or change permissions on a file must take ownership of the file.

Ownership

By default, in the Windows Server 2003 family, the owner is the Administrators group. The owner can always change permissions on an object, even when denied all access to the object.

Ownership can be taken by:

- An administrator. By default, the Administrators group is given the **Take ownership of files or other objects** user right.

- Anyone or any group who has the **Take ownership** permission for the object in question.

- A user who has the **Restore files and directories** privilege.

Ownership can be transferred in the following ways:

- The current owner can grant the **Take ownership** permission to another user. The user must actually take ownership to complete the transfer.

- An administrator can take ownership.

- A user who has the **Restore files and directories** privilege can double-click **Other users and groups** and choose any user or group to assign ownership to.

Important Permissions on a shared folder are not part of the effective permissions calculation. Access to shared folders can be denied though shared folder permissions even when access is allowed through NTFS permissions.

Class Discussion: Applying NTFS Permissions

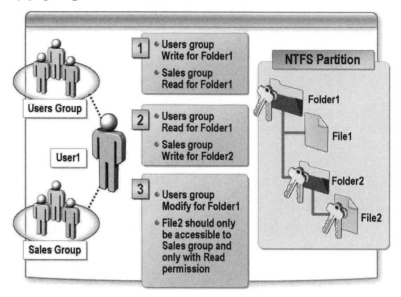

Introduction	In this exercise, you are presented with a scenario where you are asked to apply NTFS permissions. You and your classmates will discuss possible solutions to the scenario.
Discussion	User1 is a member of the Users group and the Sales group.

1. The Users group has Write permission and the Sales group has Read permission for Folder1. What permissions does User1 have for Folder1?

    _____

    _____

2. The Users group has Read permission for Folder1. The Sales group has Write permission for Folder2. What permissions does User1 have for File2?

    _____

    _____

3. The Users group has Modify permission for Folder1. File2 should only be accessible to the Sales group, and they should only be able to read File2. What do you do to ensure that the Sales group has only Read permission for File2?

_____

_____

How to Determine Effective Permissions on NTFS Files and Folders

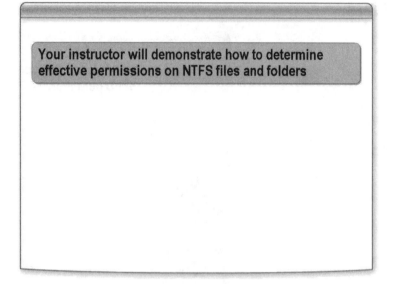

Your instructor will demonstrate how to determine effective permissions on NTFS files and folders

Introduction

Use the following procedure to view the effective permissions for files and folders.

Procedure

To view the effective permissions for files and folders:

1. In Windows Explorer, right-click the file or folder for which you want to view effective permissions, and then click **Properties**.

2. In the **Properties** dialog box, on the **Security** tab, click **Advanced**.

3. In the **Advanced Security Settings** dialog box, on the **Effective Permissions** tab, click **Select**.

4. In the **Select, User, Computer or Group** dialog box, in the **Enter the object name to select** box, type the name of a user or group, and then click **OK**.

   The selected check boxes in the **Advanced Security Settings** dialog box indicate the effective permissions of the user or group for that file or folder.

Additional reading

For more information about effective permissions, see "Effective Permission tool" at http://www.microsoft.com/technet/treeview/default.asp?url=/ technet/prodtechnol/windowsserver2003/proddocs/server/ acl_effective_perm.asp.

Practice: Determining Effective Permissions on NTFS Files and Folders

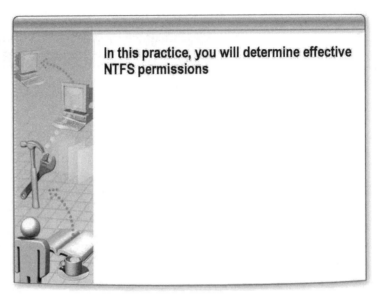

In this practice, you will determine effective NTFS permissions

Objective

In this practice, you will determine the effective NTFS permissions.

Instructions

Before you begin this practice:

- Log on to the domain as *ComputerName*Admin.

  Note You cannot use the **Run as** command with Windows Explorer, so you must log on as *ComputerName*Admin to have the permissions that you need to complete this practice.

- Review the procedures in this lesson that describe how to perform this task.

Scenario

The HR Manager for your city calls you and wants to know if they have the permissions to create documents in the *ComputerName*\Public\HR folder and what permissions a user called TelemarketingUser has for the HR folder.

Practice

▶ **Determine effective permissions for HRManager**

1. Navigate to *ComputerName*\Public\HR.

2. Determine effective permissions for the HRManager user account.

3. Write the highest permissions granted to HRManager

_____

_____

▶ **Determine effective permissions for TelemarketingUser**

1. Navigate to *ComputerName*\Public\HR.

2. Determine effective permissions for the Telemarketing user account.

3. Write the highest permissions granted to TelemarketingUser.

_____

_____

Effects of Combined Shared Folder and NTFS Permissions

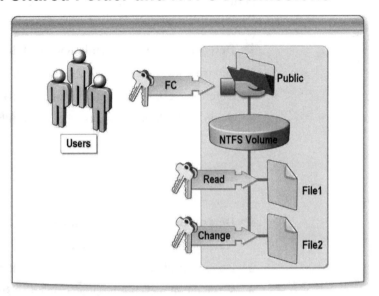

Introduction

When allowing access to network resources on an NTFS volume, it is recommended that you use the most restrictive NTFS permissions to control access to folders and files, combined with the most restrictive shared folder permissions that control network access.

What are combined permissions?

When you create a shared folder on a partition formatted with NTFS, both the shared folder permissions and the NTFS permissions combine to secure file resources. NTFS permissions apply whether the resource is accessed locally or over a network.

When you grant shared folder permissions on an NTFS volume, the following rules apply:

- NTFS permissions are required on NTFS volumes. By default, the Everyone groups has Read permission.

- Users must have the appropriate NTFS permissions for each file and subfolder in a shared folder, in addition to the appropriate shared folder permissions, to access those resources.

- When you combine NTFS permissions and shared folder permissions, the resulting permission is the most restrictive permission of the combined shared folder permissions or the combined NTFS permissions.

How to Determine the Effective Permissions on Combined Shared Folder and NTFS Permissions

> Your instructor will demonstrate how to determine effective permissions on combined shared folder and NTFS permissions

Introduction

Use Windows Explorer to view effective permissions on shared folders. To determine effective permissions, you need to first determine the maximum NTFS and the shared folder permissions and then compare the permissions.

Procedure for determining maximum NTFS permissions

To determine the maximum permissions a user has for a file on an NTFS volume:

1. In Windows Explorer, locate the file or folder for which you want to view effective permissions.

2. Right-click the file or folder, and then click **Properties**.

3. In the **Properties** dialog box, on the **Security** tab, click **Advanced**.

4. In the **Advanced Security Settings** dialog box, on the **Effective Permissions** tab, click **Select**.

5. In the **Select User, Computer, or Group** dialog box, in the **Enter the object name to select (examples)** box, enter the name of a user or group, and then click **OK**.

   The selected check boxes indicate the maximum NTFS permissions that a user or group has for a file or folder.

Procedure for determining maximum shared folder permissions

To determine the maximum permissions a user has for a shared folder:

1. Open the **Properties** dialog box for the shared folder.

2. Find the maximum permissions the user has to the share by determining what groups the user belongs to.

Procedure for determining effective permissions

To determine the effective permissions for a shared folder:

1. Compare the maximum NTFS permissions with the maximum shared folder permissions.

2. The most restrictive permission for the user between the maximum NTFS and shared folder permissions is the effective permissions.

Practice: Determining Effective NTFS and Shared Folder Permissions

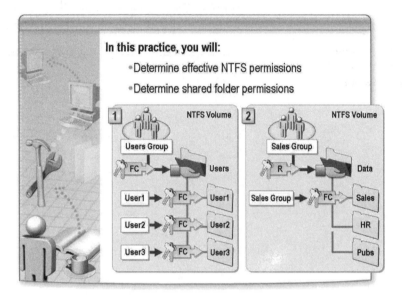

In this practice, you will:

- Determine effective NTFS permissions
- Determine shared folder permissions

Objective

In this practice, you will determine the effective NTFS and shared folder permissions.

Class discussion

The graphic on this page illustrates two shared folders that contain folders or files that have been assigned NTFS permissions. Look at each example and determine a user's *effective* permissions.

1. In the first example, the Users folder has been shared, and the Users group has the shared folder permission Full Control. User1, User2, and User3 have been granted the NTFS permission Full Control to *only* their folder. These users are all members of the Users group.

    Do members of the Users group have Full Control to *all* home folders in the Users folder once they connect to the Users shared folder?

    _____

    _____

2. In the second example, the Data folder has been shared. The Sales group has been granted the shared folder permission Read for the Data shared folder and the NTFS permission Full Control for the Sales folder.

What are the Sales group's effective permissions when they access the Sales folder by connecting to the Data shared folder?

_____

_____

Lesson: Managing Access to Shared Files Using Offline Caching

- What Is Offline Files?
- How Offline Files Are Synchronized
- Offline File Caching Options
- How to Use Offline Caching

Introduction

The information in this lesson presents the skills and knowledge that you need to manage access to shared files by using offline caching.

Lesson objectives

After completing this lesson, you will be able to:

- Explain what Offline Files is.
- Explain how offline files are synchronized.
- Explain the offline file caching modes.
- Use offline caching.

What Is Offline Files?

> • Offline Files is a document-management feature that
>   provides the user with consistent online and offline
>   access to files
>
> • Advantages of using Offline Files:
>   • Support for mobile users
>   • Automatic synchronization
>   • Performance advantages
>   • Backup advantages

Definition

Offline Files is an important document-management feature that provides the user with consistent online and offline access to files. When the client disconnects from the network, anything that has been downloaded to the local cache remains available. Users can continue working as though they were still connected to the network. They can continue editing, copying, deleting, and so forth.

From the user's perspective, the workspaces appear identical, whether they are on or off the network. Visual cues, such as icons, menus, and Active Directory, remain the same, including the view of the mapped network drives. Network files appear in the same network drive directory and can be accessed, copied, edited, printed, or deleted precisely as they are when they are online. When you reconnect to the network, client and server files are automatically resynchronized.

Advantages of using Offline Files

Using Offline Files has the following advantages:

■ Support for mobile users

When a mobile user views the shared folder while disconnected, the user can still browse, read, and edit files, because they have been cached on the client computer. When the user later connects to the server, the system reconciles the changes with the server.

■ Automatic synchronization

You can configure synchronization policy and behavior based on the time of day and network connection type by using Synchronization Manager. For example, you can configure synchronization so that it occurs automatically when the user logs on to a direct local area network (LAN) connection, but only at a user's request when he or she uses a dial-up connection.

■ Performance advantages

Offline Files provides performance advantages for networks. While connected to the network, clients can still read files from the local cache, reducing the amount of data transferred over the network.

- Backup advantages

  Offline Files solves a dilemma facing most enterprise organizations today. Many organizations implement a backup policy that requires all user data to be stored on managed servers. The organization's IT department often does not back up data stored on local disks. This becomes a problem for mobile users of portable computers.

  If you want to access data when offline, a mechanism is needed to replicate data between the portable computer and the servers. Some organizations use the Briefcase tool. Others use batch files or replicate data manually. With Windows Server 2003, replication between client and server is managed automatically. Files can be accessed while offline and are automatically synchronized with the managed server.

Additional reading

For more information about offline file security, see "Securing Offline Files" at http://www.microsoft.com/technet/treeview/default.asp?url=/technet/prodtechnol/winxppro/reskit/prdc_mcc_lvvu.asp.

How Offline Files Are Synchronized

- **Disconnected from the network**
  - Windows Server 2003 synchronizes the network files with a locally cached copy of the file
  - The user works with the locally cached copy
- **Logged on to the network**
  - Windows Server 2003 synchronizes offline files that the user has modified with the network version of the files
- **If a file has been modified in both locations**
  - The user is prompted to choose which version of the file to keep or to rename one file and keep both versions

Introduction

A user can configure a file on a network to be available offline, provided that Offline Files is enabled for the folder in which the file resides. When users configure files to be available offline, the users work with the network version of the files while they are connected to the network and then with a locally cached version of the files when they are not connected to the network.

Synchronization events

When a user configures a file to be available offline, the following synchronization events occur when the user disconnects from the network:

- When the user logs off the network, the Windows client operating system synchronizes the network files with a locally cached copy of the file.

- While the computer is disconnected from the network, the user works with the locally cached copy of the file.

- When the user again logs on to the network, the Windows client operating system synchronizes any offline file that the user has modified with the network version of the file. If the file has been modified on both the network and the user's computer, the Windows client operating system prompts the user to choose which version of the file to keep, or the user can rename one file and keep both versions.

Important   Using offline files is not a substitute for document version control. If two users work with the same offline file at the same time, and then synchronize the file with the network version, one of the versions may be lost.

Additional reading

For more information about how clients synchronize offline files, see "Offline Files overview" at http://www.microsoft.com/technet/treeview/default.asp?url=/technet/prodtechnol/windowsserver2003/proddocs/datacenter/csc_overview.asp.

Offline File Caching Options

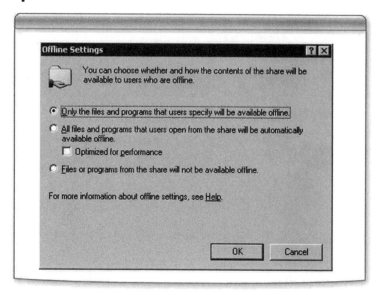

Introduction	Offline Files caches files that are often accessed from a shared folder. This is similar to the way in which a Web browser keeps a cache of recently visited Web sites. When you create shared folders on the network, you can specify the caching option for the files and programs in that folder. There are three different caching options.
Manual caching of documents	Manual caching of documents provides offline access for only the files and programs that the user specifies will be available. This caching option is ideal for a shared network folder containing files that several people will access and modify. This is the default option when you configure a shared folder to be available offline.
Automatic caching of documents	With automatic caching of documents, all files and programs that users open from the shared folder are automatically available offline. Files that the user does not open are not available offline. Older copies are automatically overwritten by newer versions of files.
Automatic caching of programs	When the **Optimized for performance** check box is selected, it provides automatic caching of programs, which provides offline access to shared folders containing files that are not to be changed. Automatic caching of programs reduces network traffic, because offline files are opened directly. The network versions are not accessed in any way, and the offline files generally start and run faster than the network versions.
	When you use automatic caching of programs, be sure to restrict permissions for the files contained in the shared folders to Read access.

How to Use Offline Caching

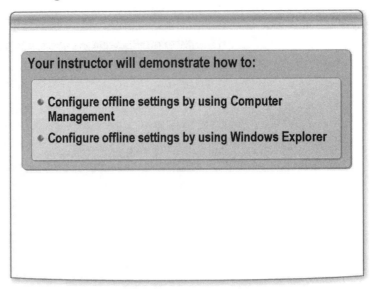

Your instructor will demonstrate how to:

- Configure offline settings by using Computer Management
- Configure offline settings by using Windows Explorer

Introduction

Use the following procedures to manage access to shared files by using offline caching.

Procedure using Computer Management

To configure offline settings by using Computer Management:

1. In Computer Management, in the console tree, expand **Shared Folders**, and then click **Shares**.

2. In the details pane, right-click the shared resource for which you want to configure offline settings, and then click **Properties**.

3. In the **Properties** dialog box, on the **General** tab, click **Offline Settings**.

4. In the **Offline Settings** dialog box, select the option that you want, and then click **OK**.

Procedure using Windows Explorer

To configure offline settings by using Windows Explorer:

1. In Windows Explorer, right-click the shared folder or drive for which you want to configure offline access, and then click **Sharing and Security**.

2. In the **Properties** dialog box, on the **Sharing** tab, click **Offline Settings**.

3. In the **Offline Settings** dialog box, select the option that you want, and then click **OK**.

Using a command line

To configure offline settings by using **net share**:

1. Open a command prompt.

2. To configure manual caching, type
   net share *SharedFolderName* **/cache:manual**

3. To configure caching of documents, type
   net share *SharedFolderName* **/cache:documents**

4. To configure caching of programs, type
   net share *SharedFolderName* **/cache:programs**

5. To configure a shared folder to not cache, type
   net share *SharedFolderName* **/cache:none**

Practice: Using Offline Caching

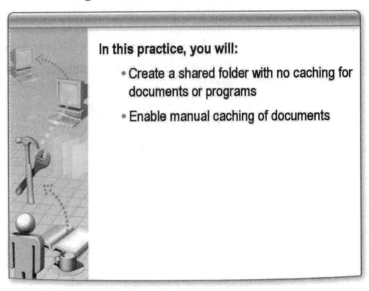

In this practice, you will:

- Create a shared folder with no caching for documents or programs
- Enable manual caching of documents

Objective

In this practice, you will create a shared folder and use different caching options.

Instructions

Before you begin this practice:

- Log on to the domain as *ComputerName*Admin.

   Note   You cannot use the **Run as** command with Windows Explorer, so you must log on as *ComputerName*Admin to have the permissions that you need to complete this practice.

- Review the procedures in this lesson that describe how to perform this task.

Scenario

The Human Resources department wants you to configure a shared folder that contains sensitive human resources data. Northwind Traders does not want this data to be cached on any desktop and laptop computer of Human Resources personnel.

Practice: Creating a shared folder with no caching

▶ **Create a shared folder with no caching for documents of programs**

1. Create a shared folder on the your student computer by using the following parameters:

   - Folder location: D:\

   - Folder name: **HR Confidential**

   - Share name: **HR Confidential**

2. Configure shared folder permissions as follows:

   - Grant Full Control permissions to DL NWTraders HR Personnel Full Control.

   - Remove the Everyone group.

3. Configure NTFS permissions as follows:

   - Remove all inherited NTFS permissions.

   - Grant Full Control permission to DL NWTraders HR Personnel Full Control.

   - Grant Full Control permission to *ComputerName*\Administrators.

4. Set the offline settings to **Files or programs from the share will not be available offline**.

Scenario

Corporate policy has changed and now states that all desktop and laptop computers must have only NTFS partitions, and all laptops of Human Resources personnel must use the EFS feature of NTFS. Your IT security team notifies the Human Resources department that they are now allowed to copy all sensitive Human Resources information for offline use.

Practice: Enabling manual caching of documents

▶ **Enable manual caching of documents**

- Enable manual caching of documents in the HR Confidential folder by changing the offline settings to **Only the files and programs that users specify will be available offline**.

Scenario

The Human Resources department uses a custom application based on Microsoft Visual Basic® that has a single executable file. For performance reasons, you want this file to run from the local hard drive. However, sometimes this application is updated, and you want this application to be automatically redeployed after it is updated. You decide to put this application on the server in your city organizational unit and use automatic caching for programs that is optimized for performance.

Practice: Enabling automatic caching of programs

▶ **Create a shared folder for the Human Resources department**

1. Create a share by using the following parameters:

   • Folder location: D:\

   • Folder name: **HR App**

   • Share name: **HR App**

2. Configure shared folder permissions as follows:

   • Grant Change permission to DL NWTraders HR Personnel Change.

   • Remove the Everyone group.

3. Configure NTFS permissions as follows:

   • Grant Change permission to DL NWTraders HR Personnel Change.

   • Grant Full Control permission to *ComputerName*\Administrators.

4. Set offline settings to **All files and programs that users open from the share will be automatically available offline** and **Optimized for performance**.

Lab A: Managing Access to Resources

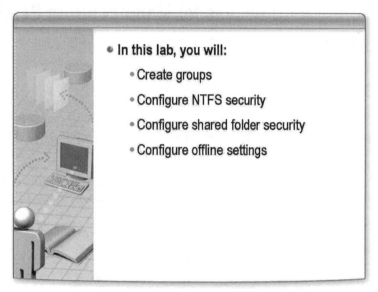

Objectives

After completing this lab, you will be able to:

- Create groups.
- Configure NTFS security.
- Configure shared folder security.
- Configure offline settings.

Instructions

Before you begin this practice:

- Log on to the domain as *ComputerName*Admin.

  Note   You cannot use the **Run as** command with Windows Explorer, so you must log on as *ComputerName*Admin to have the permissions that you need to complete this practice.

- Ensure that CustomMMC contains Computer Management (Glasgow).
- Review the procedures in this lesson that describe how to perform this task.

Estimated time to complete this lab: 30 minutes

Exercise 1
Configuring Access for Manufacturing Personnel

In this exercise, you will configure access for Manufacturing personnel.

Scenario

The Manufacturing managers in your city organizational unit need a shared folder for thousands of specification documents. These documents do not often change, but the managers need to be able to add, change, and delete documents. They want the Manufacturing personnel to only read the documents, without changing or deleting the files, and they want to have Change permission. Manufacturing personnel do not have any laptops and do require offline access to the documents. You must configure security, offline settings, and permissions for the Manufacturing personnel.

Tasks	Detailed Information

1. Create a shared folder.	▪ Tool: Computer Management (Glasgow)
	▪ Server name: Glasgow
	▪ Folder path: D:*ComputerName* Manufacturing
	▪ Share name: *ComputerName* Manufacturing
	▪ Shared folder permissions:
	  • Grant Full Control to DL NWTraders Manufacturing Managers Full Control
	  • Grant Read to DL NWTraders Manufacturing Personnel Read
	  • Remove Everyone

2. Set the NTFS permissions.	▪ Grant Modify to DL Manufacturing Managers Full Control ▪ Grant Read to DL Manufacturing Personnel Read ▪ Grant Full Control to GLASGOW\\Administrators ▪ Copy all NTFS permissions inheritance
3. Set the offline caching settings.	▪ Clear the offline caching settings

Exercise 2
Configuring Access for Marketing Personnel

In this exercise, you will configure access for Marketing personnel.

Scenario

The Marketing department at Northwind Traders needs you to create a shared folder that will contain electronic catalog files. There will be hundreds of electronic catalog files that change quarterly, and the Marketing personnel need offline access to all catalog files. You must create a shared folder, configure security, offline settings, and permissions for Marketing personnel.

Tasks	Detailed Information

1. Create a shared folder.	▪ Tool: Computer Management (Glasgow)
	▪ Server name: Glasgow
	▪ Folder path: D:*ComputerName* Marketing
	▪ Share name: *ComputerName* Marketing
	▪ Shared folder permissions:
	  • Grant Full Control to DL NWTraders Marketing Personnel Full Control
	  • Grant Full Control GLASGOW\Administrators

2. Set the NTFS permissions.	▪ Grant Modify to DL Marketing Personnel Full Control ▪ Grant Full Control to GLASGOW\Administrators ▪ Copy all NTFS permissions inheritance
3. Set the offline caching settings.	▪ Enable automatic caching for documents

Exercise 3
Configure Access for Accounting Personnel

In this exercise, you will configure access for Accounting personnel.

Scenario

The Accounting department at Northwind Traders needs a shared folder for accounting policies and procedures so that everyone in the department can change the shared documents. Most of the Accounting personnel use laptops. They only need offline access to the policy and procedures that they open from the shared folder. You must create groups and configure security, offline settings, and permissions for the Accounting personnel.

Tasks	Detailed Information

1. Create a shared folder.	▪ Tool: Computer Management (Glasgow)
	▪ Server name: Glasgow
	▪ Folder path: D:\ComputerName Accounting
	▪ Share name: ComputerName Accounting
	▪ Shared folder permissions:
	   • Grant Full Control to DL NWTraders Accounting Personnel Full Control
	   • Grant Full Control to GLASGOW\Administrators

2. Set NTFS permissions.	▪ Grant Modify to DL ComputerName Accounting Personnel Full Control ▪ Grant Full Control to GLASGOW\Administrators ▪ Copy all NTFS permissions inheritance
3. Set the offline caching settings.	▪ Enable caching for files that the users opens from the shared folder

Module 5: Implementing Printing

Contents

Overview	1
Lesson: Introduction to Printing in the Windows Server 2003 Family	2
Lesson: Installing and Sharing Printers	8
Lesson: Managing Access to Printers Using Shared Printer Permissions	17
Lesson: Managing Printer Drivers	24
Lesson: Implementing Printer Locations	31
Lab A: Implementing Printing	47

Overview

- Introduction to Printing in the Windows Server 2003 Family
- Installing and Sharing Printers
- Managing Access to Printers Using Shared Printer Permissions
- Managing Printer Drivers
- Implementing Printer Locations

Introduction

Printers are common resources that are shared by multiple users on a network. As a systems administrator, you should set up a network-wide printing strategy that meets the needs of users. To set up an efficient network of printers, you must know how to install and share network printers and how to mange printer drivers and printer locations. The Microsoft® Windows® Server 2003 family helps you to perform these tasks efficiently though an easy-to-use interface.

Objectives

After completing this module, you will be able to:

- Explain the printing process in the Windows Server 2003 family.
- Install and share printers.
- Manage access to printers by using shared printer permissions.
- Manage printer drivers.
- Implement printer locations.

Lesson: Introduction to Printing in the Windows Server 2003 Family

* Multimedia: Printing Terminology

* Types of Clients That Can Print to Servers Running Windows Server 2003

* How Printing Works in a Windows Server 2003 Environment

Introduction

The Windows Server 2003 family makes it easy for an administrator to set up network printing and configure the print resources from a central location. You can also configure client computers running Microsoft Windows 95, Microsoft Windows 98, or Microsoft Windows NT® to print from the network print devices.

Before you set up printing in Windows Server 2003, you should be aware of the terms used and how printing works in a Windows Server 2003 environment.

Lesson objectives

After completing this lesson, you will be able to:

■ Explain printing terminology.

■ Describe the client computers that can print to servers running Windows Server 2003.

■ Explain how printing works in a Windows Server 2003 environment.

Multimedia: Printing Terminology

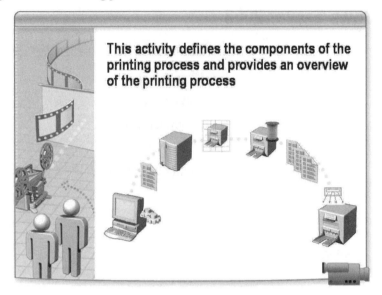

File location

To start the *Printing Terminology* activity, open the Web page on the Student Materials compact disc, click **Multimedia**, and then click the title of the activity.

Component definitions

In the first part of the activity, you drag labels to components of the printing process. When you drop a label on the correct component, the definition of that component is displayed. You can also click **Show me** to have all definitions displayed.

Printing process

After all component definitions are displayed, click **Play** to view an animation of the basic printing process.

Types of Clients That Can Print to Servers Running Windows Server 2003

* **Microsoft clients**
* **NetWare clients**
* **Macintosh clients**
* **UNIX clients**
* **Clients that supports IPP 1.0**

Introduction

Client computers can access a printer immediately after a systems administrator adds the printer to a print server running Windows Server 2003.

Client computers that can print to Windows Server 2003

A print server running Windows Server 2003 supports the following clients:

■ Microsoft clients

All 16-bit clients running Windows and clients running Microsoft MS-DOS® require 16-bit printer drivers on each client. Necessary drivers are downloaded to 32- and 64-bit Windows clients.

■ NetWare clients

NetWare clients require that Microsoft File and Print Services for NetWare is installed on the print server running Windows Server 2003. They also require that transport compatible with Internetwork Packet Exchange/ Sequenced Packed Exchange (IPX/SPX) is installed on the print server and on each client.

■ Macintosh clients

Macintosh clients require that Microsoft Print Services for Macintosh is installed on the print server running Windows Server 2003. They also require that the Appletalk networking protocol transport is installed on the print server and on each client.

- UNIX clients

  UNIX clients require that Microsoft Print Services for UNIX is installed on the print server running Windows Server 2003. UNIX clients that support the Line Printer Remote (LPR) specification connect to a print server by using the Line Printer Daemon (LPD) service.

- Client that support Internet Printing Protocol (IPP) 1.0

  Any client that supports IPP 1.0 can print to a print server running Windows Server 2003 by using Hypertext Transfer Protocol (HTTP). The clients that support IPP are clients running Windows 95, Windows 98, or Windows Server 2003. You must first install Microsoft Internet Information Services (IIS) or Microsoft Peer Web Services (PWS) on the computer running Windows Server 2003.

Additional reading

For more information about IPP, see article 323428 "How To: Configure Internet Printing in Windows Server 2003" in the Microsoft Knowledge Base at http://support.microsoft.com/?kbid=323428.

How Printing Works in a Windows Server 2003 Environment

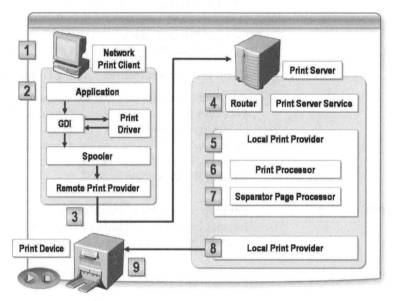

Introduction	When you add a printer that is connected to a network through a network adapter, you can implement printing in the following ways:

- Add a printer directly to each user's computer without using a print server computer.

- Add the printer once to a print server computer and then connect each user to the printer through the print server computer.

Printing without using a print server

Suppose that a small workgroup has only a few computers and a printer that is connected directly to the network. Each user on the network adds the printer to their Printers and Faxes folder without sharing the printer and sets their own driver setting.

This configuration has the following disadvantages:

- The users do not know the actual state of the printer.

- Each computer has its own print queue that displays only those print jobs sent from that computer.

- You cannot determine where your print job is in relation to all the print jobs from other computers.

- Error messages, such as paper jams or empty paper trays, appear only on the print queue for the current print job.

- All the processes on a document submitted for printing are done on that one computer.

Printing with a print server

A computer running Windows Server 2003 functions as a print server. The computer adds the printer and shares it with the other users. A computer running Microsoft Windows XP Professional can also function as a print server. However, it cannot support Macintosh or NetWare services, and it is limited to only 10 connections in the same local area network (LAN).

Printing with a print server has the following advantages:

- The print server manages the printer driver settings.

- A single print queue appears on every computer connected to the printer, enabling each user to see where their print job is in relation to others waiting to print.

- Because error messages appear on all computers, everyone knows the actual state of the printer.

- Some processing is passed from the client computer to the print server.

- You can have a single log for administrators wanting to audit the printer events.

Note Typically, print servers are implemented on servers that also perform other functions.

Additional reading

For more information about the printing process, see:

- "Printing overview" at http://www.microsoft.com/technet/treeview/ default.asp?url=/technet/prodtechnol/windowsserver2003/proddocs/ entserver/sag_PRINTconcepts_01.asp?frame=true.

- "Printing and print servers" at http://www.microsoft.com/technet/treeview/ default.asp?url=/technet/prodtechnol/windowsserver2003/proddocs/ entserver/sag_PRINTconcepts_ps_queue_spooler.asp?frame=true.

Lesson: Installing and Sharing Printers

- **What Is a Local Printer and a Network Printer?**
- **Hardware Requirements for Configuring a Print Server**
- **How to Install and Share a Local Printer**
- **How to Install and Share a Network Printer**

Introduction

Users in a home environment mostly print to a local printer attached to their client computer. In a businesses environment, client computers print to a centralized print server that redistributes the print jobs to a print device. By using a print server, the network administrators can centrally manage all printers and print devices.

Lesson objectives

After completing this lesson, you will be able to:

- Explain the differences between printing to a local printer and printing to a network printer.
- Explain the requirements for configuring a print server.
- Install and share local printers.
- Install and share network printers.

What Is a Local Printer and a Network Printer?

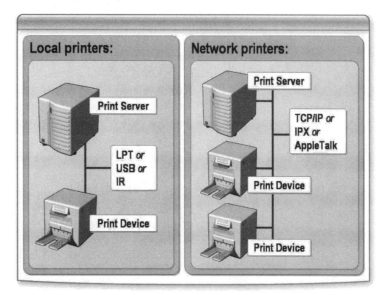

Introduction

As a systems administrator, you will be asked to create two types of printers: a local printer and a network printer. You must create both types of printers before sharing them for others to use.

Definition

Local printers are created to print to a locally attached print device by using parallel (LPT), Universal Serial Bus (USB), or infrared (IR). Local printers also print to a network print device that uses Internet Protocol (IP) or IPX. They also support Plug and Play.

Network printers print to a network printer by using IP, IPX or Appletalk. Network printers also print to a printer that redirects the print job to a print device.

Advantages and disadvantages

The following table lists the advantages and disadvantages of printing to a local printer or a network printer.

	Local printer	Network printer
Advantages	• The print device is in close proximity to the user's computer • Plug and Play can detect local printers and automatically install drivers	• Many users can access print devices
Disadvantages	• A print device is needed for every computer • Drivers must be manually installed to every local printer • A local printer takes more processor clock cycles to print	• Security is limited on the physical security of the print device • Network printers support distributing updated printer drivers to multiple clients • The local computer takes more processor clock cycles to print

Hardware Requirements for Configuring a Print Server

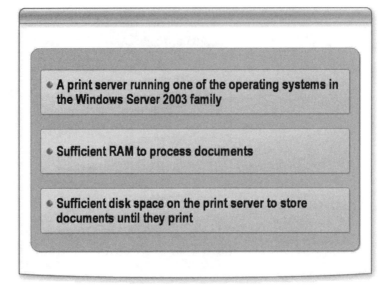

Introduction

There are certain hardware requirements for setting up an efficient printing environment. Whether you are using a local printer or a network printer, if the minimum hardware requirements are not met, network printing may be highly inefficient.

Hardware requirements

Setting up printing on a Windows Server 2003 network requires the following:

- At least one computer to function as the print server that is running one of the operating systems in the Windows Server 2003 family

  If the print server is expected to manage many print jobs, it is recommended that you dedicate a server for printing. The print server can run any operating system in the Windows Server 2003 family. Use one of these products when you need to support a large number of connections in addition to Macintosh, UNIX, and NetWare clients.

- Sufficient RAM to process documents

  If a print server manages many printers or many large documents, the server may require additional RAM beyond what Windows Server 2003 requires for other tasks. If a print server does not have sufficient RAM for its workload, printing performance may decline.

- Sufficient disk space on the print server to store documents

  You must have enough disk space to ensure that Windows Server 2003 can store documents that are sent to the print server until the print server sends the documents to the print device. This is critical when documents are large or when documents accumulate. For example, if 10 users each send one large document to print at the same time, the print server must have enough disk space to hold all of the documents until the print server sends them to the print device.

How to Install and Share a Local Printer

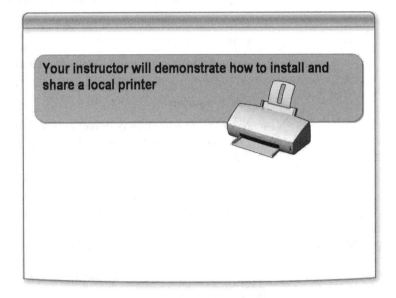

Introduction

To install and share a local printer, you use the Add Printer Wizard, located in the Printers and Faxes folder. You can also add and configure printer ports in the Add Printer Wizard. The Add Printer Wizard prompts you to install a printer driver if one is needed or to replace the existing driver.

The Add Printer Wizard also enables you to connect to a remote shared printer and install its software interface on your computer, assuming that you want local control and have the correct permissions. If you do this, the printing process bypasses the print server for the remote printer by processing print jobs locally and redirecting the output to a remote printer.

Install a printer attached to your computer with a parallel port (LPT):

Connect the printer to the appropriate port on your computer according to the printer manufacturer's documentation, and verify that it is ready to print.

1. Connect the printer to your computer.

2. In Control Panel, in the Printers and Faxes folder, double-click **Add Printer**.

3. In the Add Printer Wizard, on the **Welcome** page, click **Next**.

4. On the **Local or Network Printer** page, click **Local printer attached to this computer**.

5. Select the **Automatically detect and install my Plug and Play printer** check box, and then click **Next**.

6. Depending on the printer you are installing, a Found New Hardware message or the Found New Hardware Wizard appears to notify you that the printer has been detected and that installation has begun.

7. Follow the instructions on the screen to complete the printer installation.

8. The printer icon is added to your Printers and Faxes folder.

Installation without using Plug and Play

If you could not install your printer by using Plug and Play, or if the printer is attached to your computer with a serial (COM) port:

1. In Control Panel, in the Printers and Faxes folder, double-click **Add Printer**.

2. In the Add Printer Wizard, on the **Welcome** page, click **Next**.

3. On the **Local or Network Printer** page, click **Local printer attached to this computer**.

4. Clear the **Automatically detect and install my Plug and Play printer** check box to avoid waiting for the completion of another printer search, and then click **Next**.

5. Follow the instructions on the screen to finish installing the printer by selecting a printer port, selecting the manufacturer and model of your printer, and typing a name for your printer.

Sharing a local printer

In Windows Server 2003, the Add Printer Wizard shares the printer and publishes it in the Active Directory® directory service by default, unless you select the **Do not share this printer** check box on the **Printer Sharing** page of the Add Printer Wizard.

How to Install and Share a Network Printer

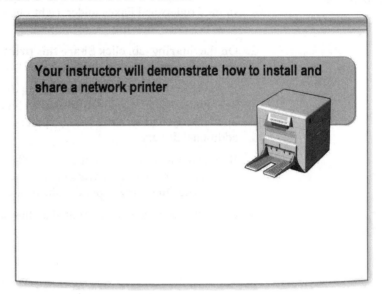

Your instructor will demonstrate how to install and share a network printer

Introduction

In larger organizations, most print devices have a network interface. Using these print devices has several advantages. There is greater flexibility in where you locate your printers. In addition, network connections transfer data quicker than printer cable connections.

Procedure for installing a network printer

To install a network printer:

1. In the Printers and Faxes folder, double-click **Add Printer**.

2. In the Add Printer Wizard, on the **Welcome** page, click **Next**.

3. On the **Local or Network Printer** page, click **Local printer attached to this computer**.

4. Clear the **Automatically detect and install my Plug and Play printer** check box, and then click **Next**.

5. When the Add Printer Wizard prompts you to select the printer port, click **Create a new port**.

6. From the list, click the appropriate port type and follow the instructions.

   By default, only **Local Port** and **Standard TCP/IP Port** appear in the list.

Procedure for sharing a network printer

To share a network printer:

1. In the Printers and Faxes folder, right-click the printer you want to share, and then click **Sharing**.

2. On the **Sharing** tab, click **Share this printer**, and then type a name for the shared printer.

   If you share the printer with users using different hardware or different operating systems, click **Additional Drivers**. Click the environment and operating system for the other computers, and then click **OK** to install the additional drivers.

   If you are logged on to a Windows 2000 or Windows Server 2003 domain, you can make the printer available to other users on the domain by clicking **List in the Directory** to publish the printer in Active Directory.

3. Click **OK**, or if you have installed additional drivers, click **Close**.

Practice: Installing and Sharing Printers

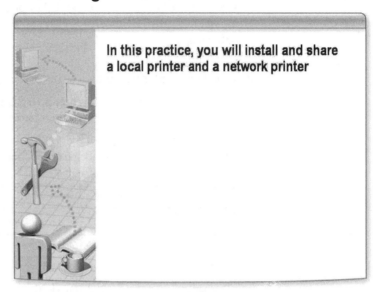

In this practice, you will install and share a local printer and a network printer

Objective

In this practice, you will install and share a local printer and a network printer.

Instructions

Before you begin this practice:

- Log on to the domain as *ComputerName*Admin.

Note This practice focuses on the concepts in this lesson and as a result may not comply with Microsoft security recommendations. For example, this practice does not comply with the recommendation that users log on with domain user account and use the **Run as** command when performing administrative tasks. When using the Printers and Faxes interface, you cannot use the **Run as** command.

- Review the procedures in this lesson that describe how to perform this task.

Scenario

As a network administrator, you must configure your server running Windows Server 2003 Server as a print server for a print device attached locally and a print device attached to the network. The Sales department in your city organizational unit is located in Building 1 on the first floor and has a network print device that must be configured. The IT department has a print device attached to the local LPT1 port of your server.

Note Your student computer is not actually attached to a print server. This practice simulates the creation of a print server. A test page will not print, so you will receive a test page print error if you attempt to print a test page.

Practice

▶ **Create a printer attached to an LPT1 port**

- Create an HP LaserJet 5si on an LPT1 port, name the printer *ComputerName* IT Datacenter Printer, and then share the printer with the same name.

▶ **Create a printer based on a print device on a subnet**

- Create a local LaserJet 5si printer on a Standard TCP/IP port. Find the name of your computer in the following table and use the port and shared printer name next to it.

  The LaserJet 5si print device uses a Generic Network Card and a LaserJet 5si driver.

City	IP address	Shared printer name
Vancouver	192.168.11.50	Vancouver Sales Printer
Denver	192.168.21.50	Denver Sales Printer
Perth	192.168.31.50	Perth Sales Printer
Brisbane	192.168.41.50	Brisbane Sales Printer
Lisbon	192.168.51.50	Lisbon Sales Printer
Bonn	192.168.61.50	Bonn Sales Printer
Lima	192.168.71.50	Lima Sales Printer
Santiago	192.168.169.50	Santiago Sales Printer
Bangalore	192.168.179.50	Bangalore Sales Printer
Singapore	192.168.189.50	Singapore Sales Printer
Casablanca	192.168.199.50	Casablanca Sales Printer
Tunis	192.168.209.50	Tunis Sales Printer
Acapulco	192.168.219.50	Acapulco Sales Printer
Miami	192.168.229.50	Miami Sales Printer
Auckland	192.168.239.50	Auckland Sales Printer
Suva	192.168.9.50	Suva Sales Printer
Stockholm	192.168.19.50	Stockholm Sales Printer
Moscow	192.168.29.50	Moscow Sales Printer
Caracas	192.168.39.50	Caracas Sales Printer
Montevideo	192.168.49.50	Montevideo Sales Printer
Manila	192.168.59.50	Manila Sales Printer
Tokyo	192.168.69.50	Tokyo Sales Printer
Khartoum	192.168.79.50	Khartoum Sales Printer
Nairobi	192.168.89.50	Nairobi Sales Printer

Lesson: Managing Access to Printers Using Shared Printer Permissions

- What Are Shared Printer Permissions?
- Why Modify Shared Printer Permissions?
- How to Manage Access to Printers

Introduction

Most corporate printers do not enforce security on printers, because limiting who can print to a printer may be counterproductive in a work environment. However, strict security should be enabled for some printers, such as printers that print payroll checks or high-capacity printers that print bound booklets or photo-quality print jobs. You must configure printer security to enable the correct people to use the printers with the level of access they need to do their job.

Lesson objectives

After completing this lesson, you will be able to:

- Explain the different types of shared printer permissions.
- Explain why you modify shared printer permissions.
- Manage access to printers by setting and removing permissions for a printer.

What Are Shared Printer Permissions?

Permission	Allows the user to:
Print	Connect to a printer and send documents to the printer.
Manage Printers	Perform the tasks associated with the Print permission. The user also has complete administrative control of the printer. The user can pause and restart the printer, change spooler settings, share a printer, adjust printer permissions, and change printer properties.
Manage Documents	Pause, resume, restart, cancel, and rearrange the order of documents that all other users submit. The user cannot send documents to the printer or control the status of the printer.

Introduction

Windows provides the following levels of shared printer permissions:

- Print
- Manage Printers
- Manage Documents

When multiple permissions are granted to a group of users, the least restrictive permission applies. However, when a Deny permission is applied, it takes precedence over any permission.

Tasks that can be performed at each permission level

The following is a brief explanation of the types of tasks a user can perform at each permission level:

- Print

  The user can connect to a printer and send documents to the printer. By default, the Print permission is granted to all members of the Everyone group.

- Manage Printers

  The user can perform the tasks associated with the Print permission and has complete administrative control of the printer. The user can pause and restart the printer, change spooler settings, share a printer, adjust printer permissions, and change printer properties. By default, the Manage Printers permission is granted to members of the Administrators and Power Users groups.

  By default, members of the Administrators and Power Users groups have full access, which means that the users are granted the Print, Manage Documents, and Manage Printers permissions.

- Manage Documents

  The user can pause, resume, restart, cancel, and rearrange the order of documents submitted by all other users. The user cannot, however, send documents to the printer or control the status of the printer. By default, the Manage Documents permission is granted to members of the Creator Owner group.

  When a user is granted the Manage Documents permission, the user cannot access existing documents currently waiting to be printed. They can only access documents sent to the printer after they are granted the permission.

Printer permissions assigned to default groups

Windows assigns printer permissions to six groups of users. These groups include Administrators, Creator Owner, Everyone, Power Users, Print Operators, and Server Operators. By default, each group is granted a combination of the Print, Manage Documents, and Manage Printers permissions, as shown in the following table.

Group	Print	Manage Documents	Manage Printers
Administrators	X	X	X
Creator Owner		X	
Everyone	X		
Power Users	X	X	X
Print Operators	X	X	X
Server Operators	X	X	X

Caution Add a minimum number of trusted users to the Administrators, Power Users, Print Operators, and Server Operators groups.

Why Modify Shared Printer Permissions?

- Limit access to a printer for selected users

  - Example: Give all nonadministrative users in a department a low-level permission and give all managers a higher-level permission. This enables both users and managers to print documents, but managers can change the print status of any document sent to the printer.

- Deny access to a printer for selected users

  - Example: Give selected members of a group the ability to print documents, and deny other group members access to the printer to force them to use another printer.

Introduction

When a shared printer is installed on a network, default printer permissions are assigned that enable all users to print. You can also enable selected groups to manage documents sent to the printer and enable selected groups to mange the printer. You can explicitly deny access to the printer through user or group membership.

Limit access to a printer for selected users

You might want to limit access for some users by granting specific printer permissions. For example, you can grant the Print permission to all nonadministrative users in a department and grant the Print and Manage Documents permissions to all managers. As a result, all users and managers can print documents, but managers can also change the print status of any document sent to the printer.

Deny access to a printer for selected users

In some cases, you may need to give access to a printer to a group of users. However, there may be a few users in the group whom you do not want to access the printer. In this case, you can grant permissions to the group and deny permission to specific users in the group. For example, you can give selected members of a group the ability to print documents and deny other group members access to the printer to force them to use another printer.

How to Manage Access to Printers

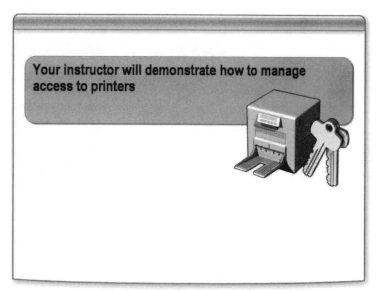

Introduction

You must change shared printer permissions as your networking environment changes.

Procedure

To manage access to printers by allowing or denying permissions for a printer:

1. In the Printers and Faxes folder, right-click the printer for which you want to set permissions, and then click **Properties**.

2. In the **Properties** dialog box, on the **Security** tab, do one of the following:

   - To change or remove permissions of an existing user or group, under **Group or User names**, click the name of the user or group.

   - To grant permissions to a new user or group, click **Add**. In the **Select Users, Computers, or Groups** dialog box, type the name of the user or group you want to grant permissions to, and then click **OK**.

3. Under **Permissions for Administrators**, select the **Allow** or **Deny** check box for each permission you want to allow or deny.

Note   To view or change the underlying permissions that make up the Print, Manage Printers, and Manage Documents permissions, click **Advanced**.

Practice: Managing Access to Printers Using Shared Printer Permissions

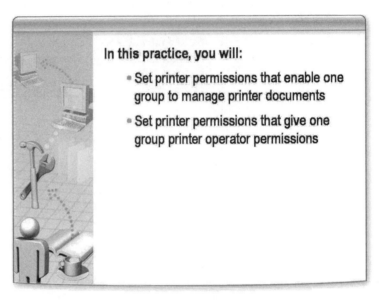

In this practice, you will:

- Set printer permissions that enable one group to manage printer documents

- Set printer permissions that give one group printer operator permissions

Objective

In this practice, you will:

- Set printer permissions that enable one group to manage printer documents.

- Set printer permissions that give one group printer operator permissions.

Instructions

Before you begin this practice:

- Log on to the domain by using the *ComputerName*Admin account.

Note This practice focuses on the concepts in this lesson and as a result may not comply with Microsoft security recommendations. For example, this practice does not comply with the recommendation that users log on with domain user account and use the **Run as** command when performing administrative tasks. When using the Printers and Faxes interface, you cannot use the **Run as** command.

- Ensure that you have a printer called *ComputerName* Sales Printer.

- Review the procedures in this lesson that describe how to perform this task.

Scenario

A systems engineer asks you to modify printer permissions for the printer used by the Sales department. You must configure printer permissions so that only users in the Sales department can print to the printer and that IT personnel can manage the printer.

Practice

▶ **Modify printer permissions**

- Configure permissions for *ComputerName* Sales Printer as follows:

  - Grant Print permission to the group DL NWTraders Sales Personnel Print.

  - Grant Manage Printers permissions to the group DL NWTraders IT Personnel Print.

  - Remove the Everyone group.

Lesson: Managing Printer Drivers

- **What Is a Printer Driver?**
- **How to Install Printer Drivers**
- **How to Add Printer Drivers for Other Client Operating Systems**

Introduction

This lesson introduces you to the skills and knowledge that you need to manage printer drivers.

Lesson objectives

After completing this lesson, you will be able to:

- Explain what a printer driver is.
- Install new or updated printer drivers.
- Add printer drivers for other client operating systems.

What Is a Printer Driver?

- **Software that computer programs use to communicate with printers and plotters**
- **Translates the information you send from the computer into commands that the printer understands**
- **Consists of the following types of files:**

Configuration or printer interface file	• Displays the Properties and Preferences dialog boxes when you configure a printer • Has a .dll extension
Data file	• Provides information about the capabilities of a specific printer • Can have a .dll, .pcd, .gpd, or .ppd extension
Printer graphics driver file	• Translates DDI commands into commands that a printer can understand • Has a .dll extension

Definition

A printer driver is software used by computer programs to communicate with printers and plotters.

What is the purpose of printer drivers?

Printer drivers translate the information you send from the computer into commands that the printer understands. Usually, printer drivers are not compatible across platforms, so various drivers must be installed on the print server to support different hardware and operating systems. For example, if your computer is running Windows XP and you share a printer with users with computers running Microsoft Windows 3.1, you might need to install multiple printer drivers.

Printer driver files

Printer drivers consist of the following three types of files:

- Configuration or printer interface file

  - This file displays the **Properties** and **Preferences** dialog boxes when you configure a printer.

  - This file has a .dll extension.

- Data file

  - This file provides information about the capabilities of a specific printer, including its resolution capability, whether it can print on both sides of the page, and what size paper it can accept.

  - This file can have a .dll, .pcd, .gpd, or .ppd extension.

- Printer graphics driver file

  - This file translates device driver interface (DDI) commands into commands that a printer can understand. Each driver translates a different printer language. For example, the file Pscript.dll translates the PostScript printer language.

  - This file has a .dll extension.

Example of how printer driver files works

Printer driver files, which are usually accompanied by a Help file, work together to make printing possible. For example, when you install a new printer, the configuration file reads the data file and displays the available printer options. When you print, the printer graphics driver file queries the configuration file about your selections so that it can create the proper printer commands.

Signed print drivers

It is strongly recommended that you use only device drivers with the **Designed for Microsoft Windows XP** or **Designed for Microsoft Windows 2003 Server** logos. Installing device drivers that Microsoft has not digitally signed might disable the system, allow viruses on to your computer, or otherwise impair the correct operation of your computer either immediately or in the future.

How to Install Printer Drivers

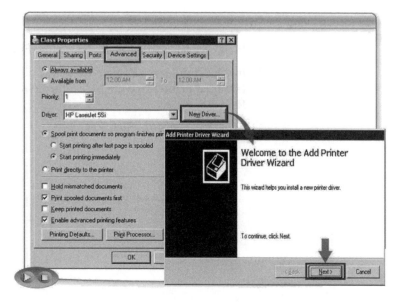

Introduction

If you are managing a print server, you occasionally receive updated printer drivers from print device manufacturers. These updated drivers often have hot fixes, but they should be thoroughly tested before you install them on your print server.

Procedure for installing new or updated printer drivers

To install new or updated printer drivers:

1. In the Printers and Faxes folder, right-click the printer for which you want to change drivers, and then click **Properties**.

2. In the **Properties** dialog box, on the **Advanced** tab, click **New Driver**.

3. In the Add Printer Driver Wizard, on the **Welcome** page, click **Next**.

4. Do one of the following:

   - Select the appropriate printer manufacturer and printer model if the new or updated driver is in the list.

   - Click **Have Disk** if the printer driver is not included in the list or if you have received a new or updated driver on CD or diskette from the printer manufacturer. Type the path where the driver is located, and then click **OK**.

5. Click **Next**, and then follow the instructions on the screen to finish installing the printer driver.

Note To install new or updated printer drivers, you must be logged on to your computer as a member of the Administrators group. When using Windows 2000 Professional, you may be able to install new or updated printer drivers when you are logged on as a member of the Power Users group, depending on the components required by the printer driver.

If the printer driver you want to use already exists on the print server, you can install it by selecting it in the **Driver** list.

Procedure for removing printer drivers

To remove printer drivers:

1. In the Printers and Faxes folder, on the **File** menu, click **Server Properties**.

2. In the **Print Server Properties** dialog box, on the **Drivers** tab, under **Installed printer drivers**, select the driver you want to remove, click **Remove**.

3. In the message box, click **Yes**.

How to Add Printer Drivers for Other Client Operating Systems

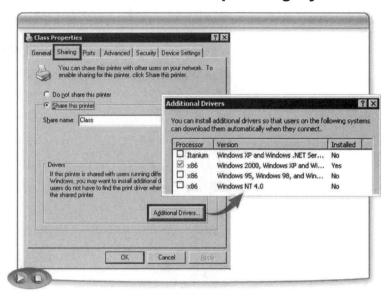

Introduction

If you share a printer with users running Windows 95, Windows 98, or Windows NT 4.0, you can install additional printer drivers on your computer so that those users can connect to your printer without being prompted to install the drivers missing from their systems. The drivers are located on the Windows Server 2003 Support CD. Printer drivers for Microsoft Windows NT version 3.1 and Microsoft Windows NT version 3.5 are not included but might be available from the print device manufacturer.

Procedure

To add printer drivers for other versions of Windows:

1. In the Printers and Faxes folder, right-click the printer for which you want to install additional drivers, and then click **Properties**.

2. In the **Properties** dialog box, on the **Sharing** tab, click **Additional Drivers**.

3. In the **Additional Drivers** dialog box, select the check boxes for the additional environments and operating systems, and then click **OK**.

Additional reading

For more information about downloading print drivers to clients, see "Managing printer drivers" at http://www.microsoft.com/technet/treeview/default.asp?url=/technet/prodtechnol/windowsserver2003/proddocs/entserver/sag_printconcepts_20.asp?frame=true.

Practice: Managing Printer Drivers

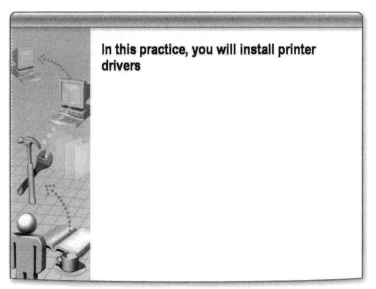

Objective

In this practice, you will install printer drivers.

Instructions

Before you begin this practice:

- Log on to the domain by using the *ComputerName*Admin account.
- Ensure that you have a printer called *ComputerName* Sales Printer.
- Review the procedures in this lesson that describe how to perform this task.

Note This practice focuses on the concepts in this lesson and as a result may not comply with Microsoft security recommendations. For example, this practice does not comply with the recommendation that users log on with domain user account and use the **Run as** command when performing administrative tasks. When using the Printers and Faxes interface, you cannot use the **Run as** command.

Scenario

You have discovered that the Sales department for your city organizational unit uses clients running Windows 98 and Windows NT 4.0. The Sales manager informs you that the Sales staff keeps asking for printer drivers when they connect to printers on your print server. You must add Windows 98 and Windows NT 4.0 drivers to the *ComputerName* Sales Printer so that clients can automatically install the appropriate drivers.

Practice

▶ **Install printer drivers for other client operating systems**

- Install printer drivers for *ComputerName* Sales Printer for the following operating systems:
  - Windows 98
  - Windows NT 4.0

Lesson: Implementing Printer Locations

- What Are Printer Locations?
- Requirements for Implementing Printer Locations
- Naming Conventions for Printer Locations
- How Printer Locations Are Configured
- How to Set the Location of Printers
- How to Locate Printers

Introduction

This lesson introduces you to skills and knowledge that you need to implement printer locations.

Lesson objectives

After completing this lesson, you will be able to:

- Explain the purpose of printer locations.
- Explain the requirements for implementing printer locations.
- Explain the naming conventions for printer locations.
- Explain the tasks involved in configuring printer locations.
- Set the location of the printers.
- Locate printers.

What Are Printer Locations?

* Printer locations enable users to search and connect to print devices that they are in close physical proximity to

* In Active Directory, an IP subnet is represented by a subnet object, which contains a Location attribute that is used during a search for printers

* Active Directory uses the value of the Location attribute as the text string to display printer location

Definition

Printer locations enable users to search and connect to print devices that they are in close physical proximity to.

Why implement printer locations?

Implementing printer locations:

■ Enables you to install printers easily in a prepopulated query.

■ Enables users to use a hierarchy to find printers in other locations by clicking **Browse**.

Active Directory and printer locations

When you implement printer locations, a search for published printers in Active Directory returns a list of printers that are located in the same physical location (for example, in the same building or on the same floor) as the client computer the user is using to perform the search.

This printer location tracking capability is based on the assumption that print devices that are physically located near a user reside on the same Internet IP subnet as the user's client computer. Subnets are subdivisions of an IP network. Each subnet possesses its own unique network address.

In Active Directory, an IP subnet is represented by a subnet object, which contains a Location attribute that is used during a search for printers. Active Directory uses the value of the Location attribute as the text string to display printer location. Therefore, when a user searches for a printer and a printer location is implemented, Active Directory:

- Finds the subnet object that corresponds to the subnet on which the user's computer is located.

- Uses the value in the Location attribute of the subnet object as the text string for a search for all published printers that have the same Location attribute value.

- Returns to the user a list of printers whose Location attribute value matches the one that is defined for the subnet object. The user can then connect to the nearest printer.

Additionally, users can also search for printers in any location. This is useful if they need to find and connect to a printer in a physical location different from the one in which they normally work.

Requirements for Implementing Printer Locations

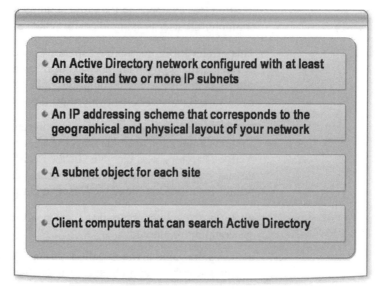

Requirements

Before you can implement printer locations, your Windows Server 2003 network must have the following:

- An Active Directory network configured with at least one site and two or more IP subnets

  Networks with one subnet do not need printer location tracking. Because IP subnets are used to identify the physical location of a printer, a network with only one subnet will generally have all printers in close proximity to users.

- An IP addressing scheme that corresponds to the geographical and physical layout of your network

  Computers and printers that reside on the same IP subnet must also reside in approximately the same physical location. If this is not the case with your network, you cannot implement printer locations.

- A subnet object for each site

  The subnet object, which represents an IP subnet in Active Directory, contains a Location attribute that is used during a search for printers. The value of this Location attribute is used during a search in Active Directory to locate printers that reside near the physical location of the user's client computer.

- Client computers that can search Active Directory

  Users with client computers running Windows 2000 Professional, or previous versions of Windows on which Active Directory client software is installed, can use printer locations when searching for printers.

When printer location is disabled

You can add information to the **Location** box on the **General** tab of the printer's **Properties** dialog box even if printer location is disabled. However, this may make printers difficult for users to locate. When users search for printers on the tenth floor and printer location is disabled, they need to know exactly what to type in the **Find Printers** dialog box. When printer location is enabled, the **Location** box in the **Find Printers** dialog box is filled in automatically.

Naming Conventions for Printer Locations

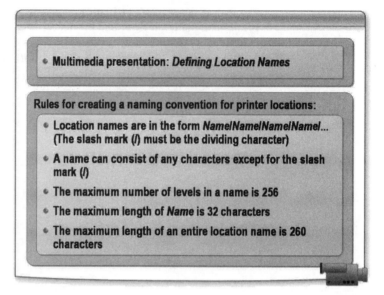

Introduction

The key to implementing printer locations is developing a naming convention for printer locations that corresponds to the physical layout of your network. Printer location names must correspond to an IP subnet. You use a naming convention to determine the values of the Location attributes for both the subnet object and the printer object.

Multimedia: Defining Location Names

The *Defining Location Names* presentation explains the relationship between the Location attributes of subnets and printers. To start the presentation, open the Web page on the Student Materials compact disc, click **Multimedia**, and then click **Defining Location Names**. Do not open the presentation unless the instructor tells you to.

Rules for creating a naming convention for printer locations

To enable printer locations, create a naming convention for printer locations by using the following rules:

- Location names are in the form *Name/Name/Name/Name/*... (The slash mark (/) must be the dividing character).

- A name can consist of any characters except for the slash mark (/).

- The maximum number of levels in a name is 256.

- The maximum length of *Name* is 32 characters.

- The maximum length of an entire location name is 260 characters.

Because location names are used by end users, they should be simple and easy to recognize. Avoid using special names that only facilities management knows. To make the name easier to read, avoid using special characters in a name, and keep names to a maximum of 32 characters so that the whole name string is visible in the user interface.

Example

Note that the tree varies in depth depending on the complexity of the organization and the amount of detail available in the IP network. The naming convention for this example includes more levels than for a smaller organization located in a single city or a single building. The full name for Floor1 of Building1 in London is London/Building1/Floor1, and the full name for RemoteOffice1 in Vancouver is Vancouver/RemoteOffice1.

How Printer Locations Are Configured

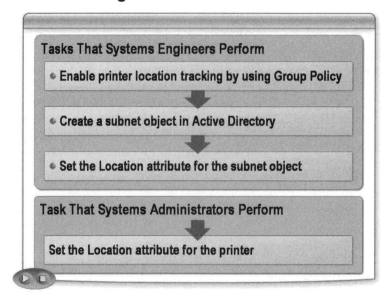

Introduction

To initially set up printer locations, you must have read/write access to Active Directory Sites and Subnet Objects so that you can create subnet objects, give the subnet object a location, and associate the subnet object with a site. When assigning locations to a printer, you must match the location for the printer with the location for the subnet object.

Tasks that systems engineers perform

After a systems engineer ensures that the network meets the requirements for implementing printer locations and a naming convention is created, the systems engineer performs the following tasks to configure printer locations:

1. Enable printer location tracking by using Group Policy. Printer location tracking prepopulates the Location search field when a user searches for a printer in Active Directory. The value used to prepopulate the search field is the same value that is specified in the Location attribute of the subnet object that corresponds to the IP subnet in which the user's computer is located.

2. Create a subnet object in Active Directory. If a subnet object does not already exist, use Active Directory Sites and Services to create a subnet object.

3. Set the Location attribute of the subnet object. Use the naming convention that you developed for printer location names as the value of this attribute.

Note To set the Location attribute for the subnet object, in Active Directory Sites and Services, right-click the subnet object, and then click **Properties**. On the **Location** tab, type the location name that corresponds to the subnet object, and then click **OK**.

Tasks that systems administrators perform

The following task is the only task that a systems administrator performs to configure printer locations:

- Set the Location attribute of printers. For each printer, add the Location attribute of the IP subnet in which the printer resides to the printer's properties. Use the same printer location name that you used for the location of the subnet object.

  When installing a new printer, you can specify the Location attribute by using the Add Printer Wizard.

How to Set the Location of Printers

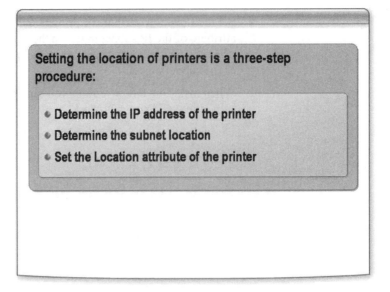

Setting the location of printers is a three-step procedure:

- Determine the IP address of the printer
- Determine the subnet location
- Set the Location attribute of the printer

Introduction

Before setting the Location attribute of a printer, you must determine the following two things:

- The IP address of the printer to determine the Location attribute of the subnet object

  After you determine the proper location name, you can then add the name to the Location attribute of the printer. If you are configuring a new printer, the systems engineer gives you a printout from the print device that tells you the IP address and the appropriate driver to use. If you are adding the location name to an existing printer, you can determine the IP address of the print device by looking at the TCP/IP port that the printer is printing to.

- Subnet location

Procedure for determining the IP address of an existing printer

To determine the IP address of an existing printer:

1. In the Printers and Faxes folder, right-click the printer whose Location attribute you want to set, and then click **Properties**.

2. In the **Properties** dialog box, on the **Ports** tab, click the TCP/IP port used for the printer, and then click **Configure Port**.

3. In the **Configure Standard TCP/IP Port Monitor** dialog box, write down the IP address found in the Printer Name or IP Address, and then click **OK**.

4. In the **Properties** dialog box, click **Close**.

Procedure for determining the subnet location

To determine the subnet location:

1. In Active Directory Sites and Services, in the console tree, expand **Sites**, and then expand **Subnets**.

2. Right-click the network that matches the IP address of the print device, and then click **Properties**.

3. Look on the **Location** tab, and then write down the Location attribute of the subnet object.

4. Click **OK**.

Procedure for setting the Location attribute of the printer

To set the Location attribute of the printer:

1. In the Printers and Faxes folder, right-click the printer whose Location attribute you want to set, and then click **Properties**.

2. In the **Properties** dialog box, on the **General** tab, in the **Location** box, type the printer location, or click **Browse** to find it.

    It is recommended that you are more precise when you describe the printer location than the subnet location. For example, for the subnet location US/NYC, you might enter the printer location as US/NYC/Floor42/Room4207.

How to Locate Printers

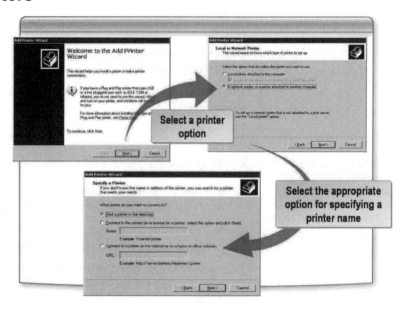

Introduction

Location tracking is used whenever a user queries Active Directory. To start the query, a user clicks **Start**, clicks **Search**, and then clicks **Find Printers**. Users can also click **Find a printer in the directory** in the Add Printer Wizard to launch the **Find Printers** dialog box.

If location tracking is enabled, the system first determines where the client computer is physically located in the organization. While this is in progress, the **Location** box of the **Find Printers** dialog box displays **Checking**. After the location is determined, it is entered into **Location** box. If the location cannot be determined, the **Location** box is left blank.

When the user clicks **Find Now**, Active Directory lists all printers matching the user's query that are located in the location of the user. Users can change the value in the **Location** box by clicking **Browse**.

For example, suppose an organization is located in a building with several floors, and each floor is configured as a subnet. If a user located on the first floor fails to locate a color printer on Floor 1, then the user can change the location to **Organization 1/Floor 2** or even to **Organization 1** to increase the scope of the search.

Note   The **Location** box is not automatically available for users running Windows 95, Windows 98, or Windows NT 4.0 without a directory service client.

Procedure

To locate a printer:

1. In the Printers and Faxes folder, double-click **Add Printer**.

2. In the Add Printer Wizard, on the **Welcome** page, click **Next**.

3. On the **Local or Network Printer** page, click **A network printer, or a printer attached to another computer**, and then click **Next**.

4. On the **Specify a Printer** page, connect to the desired printer by using one of the following three methods:

    - Search for it in Active Directory by doing the following:

    Note   If the user is not logged on to a domain running Active Directory, this method is not available.

    ---

        i.   Click **Find a printer in the directory**, and then click **Next**.

             If needed, change the default printer location listed in the **Location** box by clicking **Browse** and then choosing the appropriate location.

        ii. In the **Find Printers** dialog box, click **Find Now**.

        iii. In the list that appears, click the printer you want to connect to, and then click **OK**.

    - Type the printer name or browse for it by doing the following:

        i.   Click **Connect to this printer**.

        ii. In the **Name** box, type the printer name by using the *\\PrintServerName\SharedPrinterName* format, and then click **Next**.

             - or -

             Browse for it on the network by clicking **Next**. On the **Browse for Printer** page, in the **Shared printers** box, locate the printer, and then click **Next**.

    - Connecting to a printer on the Internet or intranet by doing the following:

        i.   Click **Connect to a printer on the Internet or on a home or office network**.

        ii. In the **URL** box, type the URL to the printer by using the **http://***PrintServerName***/Printers** format, and then click **Next**.

5. Follow the instructions on the screen to finish connecting to the printer.

   The icon for the printer appears in your Printers and Faxes folder.

Practice: Implementing Printer Locations

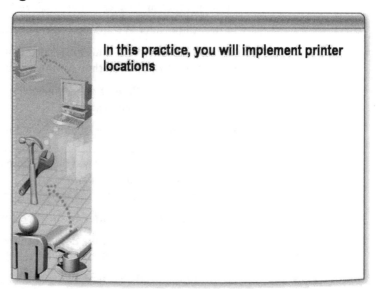

In this practice, you will implement printer locations

Objective

In this practice, you will implement printer locations.

Instructions

Before you begin this practice:

- Log on to the domain by using the *ComputerName*Admin account.
- Ensure that you have a printer called *ComputerName* Sales Printer.
- Ensure that you have a printer called *ComputerName* IT Datacenter Printer.
- Review the procedures in this lesson that describe how to perform this task.

Note This practice focuses on the concepts in this lesson and as a result may not comply with Microsoft security recommendations. For example, this practice does not comply with the recommendation that users log on with domain user account and use the **Run as** command when performing administrative tasks. When using the Printers and Faxes interface, you cannot use the **Run as** command.

Scenario

You have learned that the Northwind Traders systems administrators have finished testing printer location tracking. They want you to set the value of the Location attributes for the printers in your city.

Practice

▶ **Determine the Location attribute of your printers**

1. In the Printer Subnet table below, write down the printer share name and the subnet number for each printer in your city. (Example: Bonn Sales Printer, 192.168.61.0/24)

Printer Share Name	Subnet

2. Open Active Directory Sites and Services.

3. In the console tree, expand **Sites**, and then click **Subnets**.

4. Take the subnet number from step 1. Write down the Location attribute for each subnet in your city by using the Location attribute of the subnet object for each printer in your city.

Printer Share Name	Subnet	Location

5. Close Active Directory Sites and Services.

▶ **Set the location of the printers on your student computer**

- Set the Location attribute of the Sales and IT Datacenter Printer on your student computer found in step 4.

Printer Subnet Table

City	Printer Share Name	Subnet
Acapulco	Acapulco Sales Printer	192.168.131.0/24
Acapulco	Acapulco IT Datacenter Printer	192.168.129.0/24
Auckland	Auckland Sales Printer	192.168.151.0/24
Auckland	Auckland IT Datacenter Printer	192.168.149.0/24
Bangalore	Bangalore Sales Printer	192.168.91.0/24
Bangalore	Bangalore IT Datacenter Printer	192.168.89.0/24
Bonn	Bonn Sales Printer	192.168.61.0/24
Bonn	Bonn IT Datacenter Printer	192.168.59.0/24
Brisbane	Brisbane Sales Printer	192.168.41.0/24
Brisbane	Brisbane IT Datacenter Printer	192.168.39.0/24
Caracas	Caracas Sales Printer	192.168.191.0/24
Caracas	Caracas IT Datacenter Printer	192.168.189.0/24
Casablanca	Casablanca Sales Printer	192.168.111.0/24
Casablanca	Casablanca IT Datacenter Printer	192.168.109.0/24
Denver	Denver Sales Printer	192.168.21.0/24
Denver	Denver IT Datacenter Printer	192.168.19.0/24
Khartoum	Khartoum Sales Printer	192.168.231.0/24

(continued)

City	Printer Share Name	Subnet
Khartoum	Khartoum IT Datacenter Printer	192.168.229.0/24
Lima	Lima Sales Printer	192.168.71.0/24
Lima	Lima IT Datacenter Printer	192.168.69.0/24
Lisbon	Lisbon Sales Printer	192.168.51.0/24
Lisbon	Lisbon IT Datacenter Printer	192.168.49.0/24
Manila	Manila Sales Printer	192.168.59.0/24
Manila	Manila IT Datacenter Printer	192.168.211.0/24
Miami	Miami Sales Printer	192.168.141.0/24
Miami	Miami IT Datacenter Printer	192.168.139.0/24
Montevideo	Montevideo Sales Printer	192.168.201.0/24
Montevideo	Montevideo IT Datacenter Printer	192.168.199.0/24
Moscow	Moscow Sales Printer	192.168.181.0/24
Moscow	Moscow IT Datacenter Printer	192.168.179.0/24
Nairobi	Nairobi Sales Printer	192.168.241.0/24
Nairobi	Nairobi IT Datacenter Printer	192.168.239.0/24
Perth	Perth Sales Printer	192.168.31.0/24
Perth	Perth IT Datacenter Printer	192.168.29.0/24
Santiago	Santiago Sales Printer	192.168.81.0/24
Santiago	Santiago IT Datacenter Printer	192.168.79.0/24
Singapore	Singapore Sales Printer	192.168.101.0/24
Singapore	Singapore IT Datacenter Printer	192.168.99.0/24
Stockholm	Stockholm Sales Printer	192.168.171.0/24
Stockholm	Stockholm IT Datacenter Printer	192.168.169.0/24
Suva	Suva Sales Printer	192.168.161.0/24
Suva	Suva IT Datacenter Printer	192.168.159.0/24
Tokyo	Tokyo Sales Printer	192.168.221.0/24
Tokyo	Tokyo IT Datacenter Printer	192.168.219.0/24
Tunis	Tunis Sales Printer	192.168.121.0/24
Tunis	Tunis IT Datacenter Printer	192.168.119.0/24
Vancouver	Vancouver Sales Printer	192.168.11.0/24
Vancouver	Vancouver IT Datacenter Printer	192.168.9.0/24

Lab A: Implementing Printing

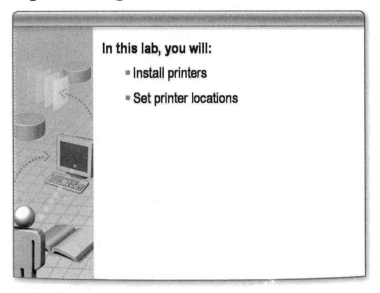

In this lab, you will:
- Install printers
- Set printer locations

Objectives

After completing this lab, you will be able to:

- Install printers.
- Set printer locations.

Instructions

Before you begin this lab, log on to the domain by using the *ComputerName*Admin account.

Note This practice focuses on the concepts in this lesson and as a result may not comply with Microsoft security recommendations. For example, this practice does not comply with the recommendation that users log on with domain user account and use the **Run as** command when performing administrative tasks. When using the Printers and Faxes interface, you cannot use the **Run as** command.

**Estimated time to complete this lab:
10 minutes**

Exercise 1
Installing Printers

In this exercise, you will install printers.

Scenario

The home office in London needs the help of all systems administrators. Northwind Traders just upgraded all print devices in the offices in London and needs your help to configure them on a print server called Glasgow. To help you create these new printers, the systems engineers have provided a table that lists the printers each systems administrator must create and specific information about the printers.

All print devices are HP LaserJet 5si, and all printers are located on the remote computer named Glasgow. Printer permissions should be configured so that:

- DL NWTraders Legal Personnel Print has Print permission for the Legal printer.
- The group Authenticated Users has Print permissions for the Exec printer.
- DL NWTraders IT Print has Manage Printer permission for both printers.

Tasks	Specific Instructions
1. Connect to the print server named Glasgow.	a. In the **Run** box, type **glasgow** and then click **OK**. b. From \\glasgow, double-click **Printers and Faxes**.
2. Create two printers on Glasgow.	▪ In the table at the end of the lab, find your student account, and then create two network printers on Glasgow with the print device port, location, and share name values in the table.
3. Configure printer permissions for the Legal printer.	a. Grant Print permission to the group DL NWTraders Legal Personnel Print. b. Grant Manage Printers permission to the group DL NWTraders IT Personnel Print. c. Remove the Everyone group.
4. Configure printer permissions for the Exec printer.	a. Grant Print permission to the group Authenticated Users. b. Grant Manage Printers permission to the group DL NWTraders IT Personnel Print. c. Remove the Everyone group.

Exercise 2
Searching for Network Printers with Locations

In this exercise, you will set printer locations.

Scenario

Your team has just installed many printers for the corporate office. You must confirm that the printers have been successfully configured for printer location tracking.

Tasks	Specific Instructions
1. Open Active Directory Users and Computers.	▪ Open Active Directory Users and Computers.
2. Search for printers in the London location. (The results of your search may vary depending on the number of students in the classroom.)	a. From the root of nwtraders.msft, search for printers in the **London/Build 2** location. b. How many printers are in the **London/Build 2/FL 1/** location? _____ Your answer may vary depending on the number of students in the classroom. c. From the root of nwtraders.msft, search for printers in the **London** location. d. How many printers are in the **London** location? _____ Your answer may vary depending on the number of students in the classroom. e. From the root of nwtraders.msft, search for printers in the **Entire Directory** (Click **Browse**, and then click **Entire Directory**). f. How many printers are in the entire directory? _____ Your answer may vary depending on the number of students in the classroom.
3. Close all windows and log off.	

Student Account Table

Student account	Print device port	Location	Printer name & Share name
AcapulcoAdmin	192.168.5.13	London/Build 3	Exec Printer 13
AcapulcoAdmin	192.168.3.13	London/Build 2/Fl 1	Legal Printer 13
AucklandAdmin	192.168.5.15	London/Build 3	Exec Printer 15
AucklandAdmin	192.168.3.15	London/Build 2/Fl 1	Legal Printer 15
BangaloreAdmin	192.168.5.9	London/Build 3	Exec Printer 09
BangaloreAdmin	192.168.3.9	London/Build 2/Fl 1	Legal Printer 09
BonnAdmin	192.168.5.6	London/Build 3	Exec Printer 06
BonnAdmin	192.168.3.6	London/Build 2/Fl 1	Legal Printer 06
BrisbaneAdmin	192.168.5.4	London/Build 3	Exec Printer 04
BrisbaneAdmin	192.168.3.4	London/Build 2/Fl 1	Legal Printer 04
CaracasAdmin	192.168.5.19	London/Build 3	Exec Printer 19
CaracasAdmin	192.168.3.19	London/Build 2/Fl 1	Legal Printer 19
CasablancaAdmin	192.168.5.11	London/Build 3	Exec Printer 11
CasablancaAdmin	192.168.3.11	London/Build 2/Fl 1	Legal Printer 11
DenverAdmin	192.168.5.25	London/Build 3	Exec Printer 25
DenverAdmin	192.168.3.25	London/Build 2/Fl 1	Legal Printer 25
KhartoumAdmin	192.168.5.23	London/Build 3	Exec Printer 23
KhartoumAdmin	192.168.3.23	London/Build 2/Fl 1	Legal Printer 23
LimaAdmin	192.168.5.7	London/Build 3	Exec Printer 07
LimaAdmin	192.168.3.7	London/Build 2/Fl 1	Legal Printer 07
LisbonAdmin	192.168.5.5	London/Build 3	Exec Printer 05
LisbonAdmin	192.168.3.5	London/Build 2/Fl 1	Legal Printer 05
ManilaAdmin	192.168.5.21	London/Build 3	Exec Printer 21
ManilaAdmin	192.168.3.21	London/Build 2/Fl 1	Legal Printer 21
MiamiAdmin	192.168.5.14	London/Build 3	Exec Printer 14
MiamiAdmin	192.168.3.14	London/Build 2/Fl 1	Legal Printer 14
MontevideoAdmin	192.168.5.20	London/Build 3	Exec Printer 20
MontevideoAdmin	192.168.3.20	London/Build 2/Fl 1	Legal Printer 20
MoscowAdmin	192.168.5.18	London/Build 3	Exec Printer 18
MoscowAdmin	192.168.3.18	London/Build 2/Fl 1	Legal Printer 18
NairobiAdmin	192.168.5.24	London/Build 3	Exec Printer 24
NairobiAdmin	192.168.3.24	London/Build 2/Fl 1	Legal Printer 24
PerthAdmin	192.168.5.03	London/Build 3	Exec Printer 03
PerthAdmin	192.168.3.3	London/Build 2/Fl 1	Legal Printer 03
SantiagoAdmin	192.168.5.8	London/Build 3	Exec Printer 08
SantiagoAdmin	192.168.3.8	London/Build 2/Fl 1	Legal Printer 08

(continued)

Student account	Print device port	Location	Printer name & Share name
SingaporeAdmin	192.168.5.10	London/Build 3	Exec Printer 10
SingaporeAdmin	192.168.3.10	London/Build 2/Fl 1	Legal Printer 10
StockholmAdmin	192.168.5.17	London/Build 3	Exec Printer 17
StockholmAdmin	192.168.3.17	London/Build 2/Fl 1	Legal Printer 17
SuvaAdmin	192.168.5.16	London/Build 3	Exec Printer 16
SuvaAdmin	192.168.3.16	London/Build 2/Fl 1	Legal Printer 16
TokyoAdmin	192.168.5.22	London/Build 3	Exec Printer 22
TokyoAdmin	192.168.3.22	London/Build 2/Fl 1	Legal Printer 22
TunisAdmin	192.168.5.12	London/Build 3	Exec Printer 12
TunisAdmin	192.168.3.12	London/Build 2/Fl 1	Legal Printer 12
VancouverAdmin	192.168.5.2	London/Build 3	Exec Printer 02
VancouverAdmin	192.168.3.2	London/Build 2/Fl 1	Legal Printer 02

Microsoft®
Training &
   Certification

Module 6: Managing Printing

Contents

Overview	1
Lesson: Changing the Location of the Print Spooler	2
Lesson: Setting Printer Priorities	10
Lesson: Scheduling Printer Availability	15
Lesson: Configuring a Printing Pool	21
Lab A: Managing Printing	25

Overview

- **Changing the Location of the Print Spooler**
- **Setting Printer Priorities**
- **Scheduling Printer Availability**
- **Configuring a Printing Pool**

Introduction

As a systems administrator, you should set up a network-wide printing strategy that will meet the needs of users. To set up an efficient network of printers, you must know how to troubleshoot installation and configuration problems. Microsoft® Windows® Server 2003 helps you to perform these tasks efficiently.

Objectives

After completing this module, you will be able to:

- Change the location of the print spooler.

- Set printing priorities.

- Schedule printer availability.

- Configure a printing pool.

Additional reading

For more information about printer management, see "Print and Output Management Operations Guide" at http://www.microsoft.com/technet/ treeview/default.asp?url=/technet/prodtechnol/windows2000serv/maintain/ opsguide/pomgmtog.asp.

Lesson: Changing the Location of the Print Spooler

- What Is a Print Spooler?
- Why Change the Location of the Print Spooler?
- How to Change the Location of the Print Spooler

Introduction

This lesson introduces you to the skills and knowledge that you need to change the location of the print spooler.

Lesson objectives

After completing this lesson, you will be able to:

- Explain the purpose of the print spooler.
- Explain situations that require you to change the location of the print spooler.
- Change the location of the print spooler.

What Is a Print Spooler?

* An executable file that manages the printing process, which involves:
  * Retrieving the location of the correct printer driver
  * Loading that driver
  * Spooling high-level function calls into a print job
  * Scheduling the print job for printing
* Takes files to be printed, stores them on the hard disk, and then sends them to the printer when the printer is ready

Definition

The primary component of the printing interface is the print spooler. The print spooler is an executable file that manages the printing process. Management of the printing process involves:

- Retrieving the location of the correct printer driver.
- Loading that driver.
- Spooling high-level function calls into a print job.
- Scheduling the print job for printing.

The print spooler is loaded at system startup and continues to run until the operating system shuts down. The print spooler takes files to be printed, stores them on the hard disk, and then sends them to the printer when the printer is ready. Additionally, you can log events during this process, or you can turn off logging during high-demand periods to minimize disk space and improve the performance of the print spooler service.

Location of the spool folder

Files that are waiting to be printed are collected in a spool folder that is located on the print server's hard drive. By default, the spool folder is located at *SystemRoot*\System32\Spool\Printers. However, this hard drive also holds the Windows system files. Because the operating system frequently accesses these files, performance of both Windows and the printing functions might be slowed.

If your print server serves only one or two printers with low traffic volumes, the default location of the spool folder is sufficient. However, to support high traffic volumes, large numbers of printers, or large print jobs, you should relocate the spool folder. For best results, move the spool folder to a drive that has its own input/output (I/O) controller, which reduces printing's impact on the rest of the operating system.

Situations in which spooling should be used

The spooling solution should enable the following types of output to be delivered in a manner that is consistent with the needs of the organization:

- *Real-time business critical*. These are jobs that are typically short, but must be printed within a certain time period, with implicit financial penalties if they fail. An example is loading dock pick lists.

  Note A pick list is a printout that an employee uses to go into a warehouse and get items that are going to be shipped out.

- *Scheduled business critical*. Examples include large financial statements that print overnight. No one is at the printer waiting for them, but if they are not there by morning, it is a problem.

- *On-demand*. This category includes most typical desktop printing. The output may not be critical, but the user needs the output within a certain time period.

Why Change the Location of the Print Spooler?

- Change the location of the print spooler to:
    - Improve performance
    - Resolve disk space problems
    - Reduce fragmentation of the boot partition
    - Ensure security
    - Manage disk quotas
    - Improve reliability

Reasons to change the location of the print spooler

Change the location of the print spooler to do the following:

- Improve performance

    Print servers must have sufficient disk space and RAM to manage print jobs. Ideally, plan to have a minimum of two disks, one for the operating system, the startup files, and the paging file, and another one that holds the spool folder. This isolates the spool folder from the operating system, which improves performance and stability. To improve efficiency, add one or more drives for the paging file.

- Resolve disk space problems

    Print servers create a print queue to manage print requests. Documents may be 20 megabytes (MB) in size if they include embedded graphics. As a result, you should use disk space on a drive other than the one being used for the operating system. This helps ensure that you do not use all the free disk space on the system or boot partitions, which can cause difficulties with the swap file. If you configure the print queue on the same disk as the operating system, Windows does not have sufficient disk space to write the swap file, which can lead to problems with the overall performance of the printer.

- Reduce fragmentation of the boot partition

    When a file prints to a network printer, a spool file is created and almost immediately deleted. This process alone is repeated hundreds or thousands of times during a normal working day. If the spool folder is on a volume that is shared with other data, the volume may become fragmented. You can eliminate fragmentation if you locate the spool folder on a volume that is dedicated to the printer. After all spool files are printed, they are deleted from the volume, and new print jobs can start on a clean disk.

- Ensure security

  If print jobs are configured to not be deleted after they are printed, it is advantageous to have the print jobs on a different disk or volume so that the spool folder does not inherit any changes in the security of any parent folders. It is also advantageous to move the spool folder for printers that print sensitive data, such as payroll checks or financial reports, so that you can audit all transactions on the disk that contains the spool folder.

- Manage disk quotas

  On the disks that contain the operating system, quotas are not usually configured to increase performance. However, you may want to limit the amount of print jobs that users or groups print to the print server so that no user can fill all the available free space on a server. If this occurs, others cannot print until the print queue releases some documents.

- Improve reliability

  Typically, a boot partition is on a mirrored disk (RAID 1). For performance and recoverability, you may want to move the spool folder to a volume that has RAID 5 on it to decrease the odds of a single point of failure of a disk subsystem.

How to Change the Location of the Print Spooler

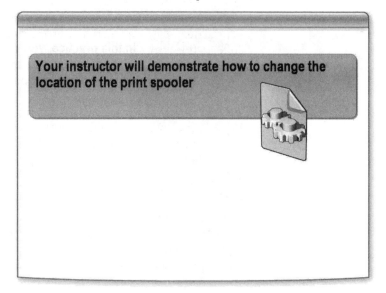

Introduction

You may want to move the location of the spool folder to increase server performance by causing less fragmentation on the boot partition or to move the spool files to another partition with greater disk space.

Procedure

To change the location of the spool folder:

1. In Printers and Faxes, on the **File** menu, click **Server Properties**.

2. In the **Print Server Properties** dialog box, on the **Advanced** tab, in the **Spool folder** box, type the path and the name of the new default spool folder for the print server, and then click **OK**.

3. Stop and restart the spooler service.

Note   The location of the spool folder will be changed immediately and any documents waiting to be printed will not print. It is recommended that you wait for all documents to complete printing before changing the spool folder.

Practice: Changing the Location of the Print Spooler

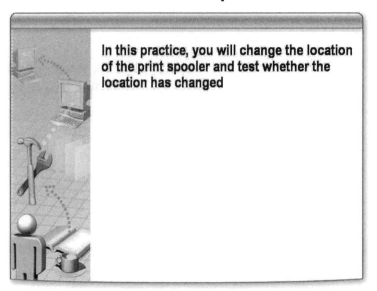

In this practice, you will change the location of the print spooler and test whether the location has changed

Objective

In this practice, you will change the location of the print spooler and test whether the location has changed.

Instructions

Before you begin this practice:

- Log on to the domain as *ComputerName*Admin.

- Ensure that you have a local printer named *ComputerName* IT Datacenter Printer.

- Review the procedures in this lesson that describe how to perform this task.

Scenario

The systems engineers at Northwind Traders have noticed that the C drive on your print server (which has the operating system on it) has been getting fragmented by the printers configured on your member server. The systems engineers have asked you to move the spool folder to the D partition so that the operating system partition will not become fragmented by the print server. You must document the current location of the spool folder and move the spooler to the D partition.

Practice

▶ **Document the current location of the spool folder**

1. In Printers and Faxes, on the **File** menu, click **Server Properties**.

2. In the **Print Server Properties** dialog box, click the **Advanced** tab.

3. Document the current location of the spool folder:

_____

▶ **Create a spool folder on the D drive**

1. Create a folder on the D drive named **Spool** (Example: D:\Spool).

2. Create a subfolder in the D:\Spool folder, named **Printers** (Example: D:\Spool\Printers).

▶ **Change the location of the spool folder**

- Change the spool folder location to D:\Spool\Printers.

▶ **Stop and start the spooler service**

1. Click **Start**, click **Run**, type **cmd** and then click **OK**.

2. From a command prompt, type **net stop spooler**

3. From a command prompt, type **net start spooler**

▶ **Test to see if the spool files are being directed to the D:\Spool\Printers folder**

1. In Printers and Faxes, right-click *ComputerName* **IT Datacenter Printer**, and then click **Pause Printing**.

   If the printer is already paused, you will not see **Pause Printing** in the list. Continue to the next step.

2. Right-click *ComputerName* **IT Datacenter Printer**, and then click **Properties**.

3. In the **Properties** dialog box, click **Print Test Page**.

4. In the message box, click **OK**.

5. In the **Properties** dialog box, click **OK**.

6. Click **Start**, click **Run**, type **D:\Spool\Printers** and then click **OK**.

7. Verify that there are two files created and close all windows.

Lesson: Setting Printer Priorities

- What Are Printer Priorities?
- How to Set Printer Priorities

Introduction

You may want to configure printer priorities for two printers that print to the same print device. This configuration guarantees that the printer with the highest priority prints to the print device before the printer with the lower priority.

This is a good strategy if the printer with the lower priority is only available to print during nonbusiness hours and has many documents waiting to print. If you must print to the print device, you can select the printer with the higher print priority, and your print job will move to the top of the print queue.

The information in this lesson presents the skills and knowledge that you need to set printer priorities.

Lesson objectives

After completing this lesson, you will be able to:

- Explain the purpose of printer priorities.
- Set printing priorities.

What Are Printer Priorities?

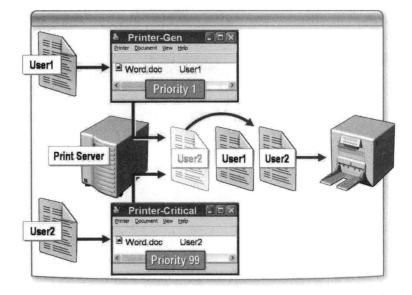

Introduction

Set priorities between printers to prioritize documents that print to the same print device. To do this, create multiple printers pointing to the same print device. Users can then send critical documents to a high-priority printer and documents that are not critical to a low-priority printer. The documents sent to the high-priority printer will print first.

Key tasks

To set priorities between printers, perform the following tasks:

- Point two or more printers to the same print device (the same port). The port can be either a physical port on the print server or a port that points to a network-interface print device.

- Set a different priority for each printer that is connected to the print device, and then have different groups of users print to different printers. You can also have users send high-priority documents to the printer with higher priority and low-priority documents to the printer with lower priority.

How to use priorities

In the illustration on the slide, User1 sends documents to a printer with the lowest priority of 1, and User2 sends documents to a printer with the highest priority of 99. In this example, User2's documents will print before User1's documents.

You can expedite documents that must be printed immediately. Documents sent by users with high priority levels can bypass a queue of lower-priority documents waiting to be printed. If two logical printers are associated with the same printer, Windows Server 2003 routes documents with the highest priority level to the printer first.

To use printer priorities, create multiple logical printers for the same printer. Assign each a different priority level, and then create a group of users that corresponds to each printer. For example, users in Group1 might have access rights to a priority 1 printer, users in Group2 might have access rights to a printer with priority 2, and so on.

How to Set Printer Priorities

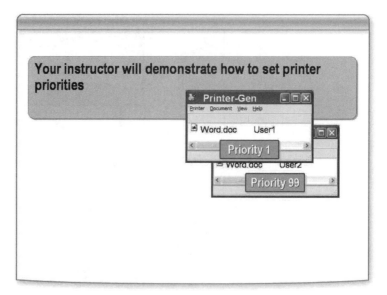

Introduction

Printer priorities are often used if two or more printers print to the same print device. Use the following procedure to set printer priorities.

Procedure

To set different print priorities for different groups:

1. In Printers and Faxes, right-click the printer you want to set, and then click **Properties**.

2. In the **Properties** dialog box, on the **Advanced** tab, in the **Priority** box, enter a priority level, where 1 is the lowest level and 99 is the highest.

3. Click **OK**.

4. Click **Add Printer** to add a second logical printer for the same physical printer.

5. On the **Advanced** tab, in the **Priority** box, set a priority higher than that of the first logical printer.

Practice: Setting Printer Priorities

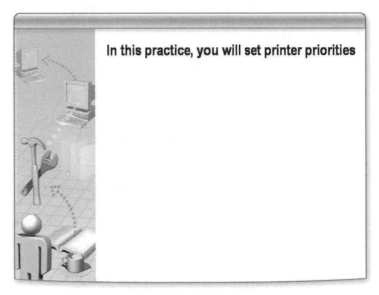

In this practice, you will set printer priorities

Objective

In this practice, you will set printer priorities.

Instructions

Before you begin this practice:

- Log on to the domain as *ComputerName*Admin.
- Review the procedures in this lesson that describe how to perform this task.

Scenario

Northwind Traders is testing printer priorities that will later be used for scheduling printer availability. You must create two printers that print to LPT2. You will name these printers Printer1 and Printer2. Printer1 will have a priority of 1, and Printer2 will have a priority of 99. You will use the default security for Printer1. You will then remove the Everyone group for Printer2 and grant Print permission to the group DL NWTraders IT Personnel Print for Printer2.

Practice

▶ **Set the priority for Printer1**

- Open Printers and Faxes, and create a printer by using the following information:
  - Port: LPT2
  - Driver: HP LaserJet 5si
  - Printer name: **Printer1**
  - Share name: **Printer1**
  - Shared printer permissions: Grant Print permission to the Authenticated Users group
  - Printer priority: 1

▶ **Set the priority for Printer2**

- Open Printers and Faxes, and create a printer by using the following information:

  - Port: LPT2

  - Driver: HP LaserJet 5si

  - Printer name: **Printer2**

  - Share name: **Printer2**

  - Shared printer permissions:

    - Remove the Everyone group

    - Grant Print permission to DL NWTraders IT Personnel Print

  - Printer priority: 99

Lesson: Scheduling Printer Availability

* When to Schedule Printer Availability
* Guidelines for Scheduling Printer Availability
* How to Schedule Printer Availability

Introduction

This lesson introduces you to skills and knowledge that you need to schedule printer availability.

Lesson objectives

After completing this lesson, you will be able to:

* Explain when to schedule printer availability.
* Describe the guidelines for scheduling printer availability.
* Schedule printer availability.

When to Schedule Printer Availability

- Schedule printer availability to print long documents or certain types of documents
- Consider scheduling printer availability:
  - To postpone printing long documents during the day by routing them to a printer that prints only during off-hours
  - To set different printers for the same print device and configure each printer to be available at different times
    For example, one printer is available from 6:00 P.M. to 6:00 A.M., and the other is available 24 hours a day

Situations in which you schedule printer availability

One way to efficiently use printers is to schedule alternate printing times for long documents or certain types of documents. Consider scheduling printer availability in the following situations:

- Schedule printer availability if printer traffic is heavy during the day, and you can postpone printing long documents by routing them to a printer that prints only during off-hours. The print spooler continues to accept documents, but it does not send them to the destination printer until the designated start time.

- Instead of dedicating an actual print device for only off-hour printing, which is not an efficient use of resources, you can set different logical printers for the same print device. You can then configure each with different times. One printer might be available from 6:00 P.M. to 6:00 A.M, and the other might be available 24 hours a day. You can then tell users to send long documents to the printer available only during off hours and all other documents to the printer available all the time.

Guidelines for Scheduling Printer Availability

- Use security to limit who can use the printer during available hours

- Educate users about when printers are available to reduce support calls when the printer is not available

- Configure two printers with different schedules to print to the same print device

- Maintain enough disk space to hold spooled print jobs that are waiting to print

Introduction

If you schedule the availability of a printer, users and systems administrators must be aware of the security requirements and the additional support the print server needs.

Guidelines

Consider the following guidelines when scheduling printer availability:

- Use security to limit who can use the printer during available hours.

  You may want to limit when one group can use a print device, and give another group access to the same print device at all times. To do this, you must configure two printers to print to the same print device. You also must configure additional security to isolate the group that needs access to the printer at all times.

- Educate users about when printers are available to reduce support calls when the printer is not available.

  Many users are accustomed to having a printer available all the time. When they print to a printer that has a scheduling limitation, those users may try to reprint their job and then call help desk to see why their print job did not print. Educate these users that the print job is at the print server waiting to be delivered to the print device and that they should not try to reprint their job.

■ Configure two printers with different schedules to print to the same print device.

If a print device must be available to one group of people all the time and to other groups only during specific hours, configure two printers to print to the same print device.

■ Maintain enough disk space to hold spooled print jobs that are waiting to print.

When you schedule a printer to be available only for certain hours, be aware that users can still print to the printer during off hours and that the printer holds the print jobs until the available hours. Because the printer holds the print jobs during off hours, you must have enough free disk space for the printer to hold the print jobs. If this becomes a problem and you cannot get more disk space, you can set quotas on the volume that holds the print queue.

How to Schedule Printer Availability

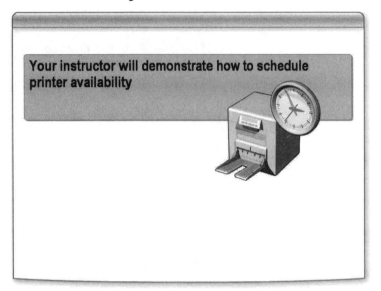

Introduction

Use the following procedure to schedule printer availability.

Procedure

To schedule printer availability:

1. In Printers and Faxes, right-click the printer you want to configure, and then click **Properties**.

2. In the **Properties** dialog box, on the **Advanced** tab, click **Available from**.

3. In the two boxes to the right of **Available from**, enter a start and end time, such as **6:00 PM** and **6:00 AM**, and then click **OK**.

Practice: Scheduling Printer Availability

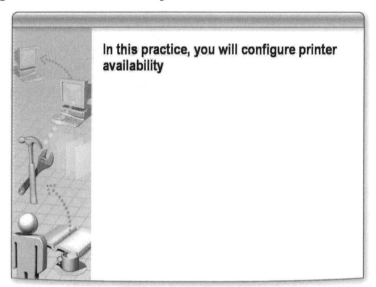

In this practice, you will configure printer availability

Objective

In this practice, you will configure printer availability.

Instructions

Before you begin this practice:

■ Log on to the domain as *ComputerName*Admin.

■ Ensure that you have two printers named Printer1 and Printer2 set to print to LPT2.

■ Review the procedures in this lesson that describe how to perform this task.

Note You will not be able to test this practice, because there are no classroom print devices.

Scenario

Northwind Traders is testing printer priorities that will later be used for scheduling printer availability. You must configure printer availability for Printer1 and Printer2. Printer1 will have a printing schedule of 12:00 A.M. to 6:00 A.M., and Printer2 will have the default printing schedule.

Practice

▶ **Configure the printing schedule for Printer1**

● Configure Printer1 to be available from 12:00 A.M. to 6:00 A.M.

▶ **Verify that Printer2 is available 24 hours a day**

● Open the **Properties** dialog box for Printer2, and verify that the printer is always available.

Lesson: Configuring a Printing Pool

- Multimedia: How Printing Pools Work
- How to Configure a Printing Pool

Introduction

The information in this lesson presents the skills and knowledge that you need to configure a printing pool.

Lesson objectives

After completing this lesson, you will be able to:

- Explain the purpose of a printing pool.
- Explain when to configure a printing pool.
- Explain the process for configuring a printing pool.
- Configure a printing pool.

Multimedia: How Printing Pools Work

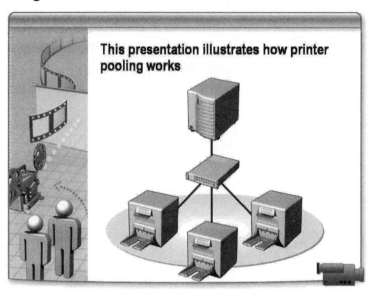

File location

To view the *How Printing Pools Work* presentation, open the Web page on the Student Materials compact disc, click **Multimedia**, and then click the title of the presentation. Do not open this presentation unless the instructor tells you to.

How to Configure a Printing Pool

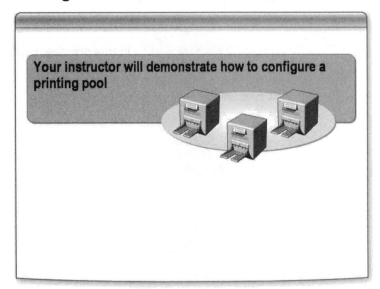

Introduction

Printing pools are very common in high volume printing areas. Use the following procedure to configure a printing pool.

Procedure

To configure a printing pool:

1. In Printers and Faxes, right-click the printer you are using, and then click **Properties**.

2. In the **Properties** dialog box, on the **Ports** tab, select the **Enable printer pooling** check box.

3. Select the check box for each port that the printers you want to pool are connected to, and then click **OK**.

Note   With printer pooling, the printers must be the same type of printer using the same printer driver.

Practice: Configuring a Printing Pool

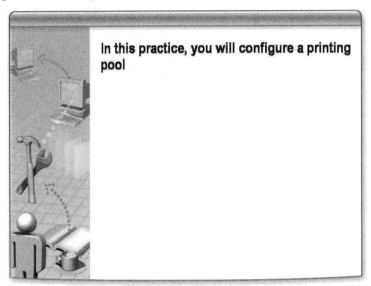

Objective

In this practice, you will configure a printing pool.

Instructions

Before you begin this practice:

- Log on to the domain as *ComputerName*Admin.

- Review the procedures in this lesson that describe how to perform this task.

Note You will not be able to test this practice, because there are no classroom print devices.

Scenario

Northwind Traders is testing the implementation of printing pools. You must create a printer that prints to LPT1 or LPT2 and configure it to be used in a printing pool. The printer will be called PrntPool1 and will use a HP LaserJet 5si printer driver.

Practice

▶ **Create a printer to be used in a printing pool**

1. Open Printers and Faxes, and create a printer by using the following information:

   - Port: LPT1

   - Driver: HP LaserJet 5si

   - Printer name: **PrntPool1**

   - Share name: **PrntPool1**

   - Shared printer permissions: Grant the Print permission to Authenticated Users

2. Configure PrntPool1 for printer pooling with the following ports:

   - LPT1

   - LPT2

Lab A: Managing Printing

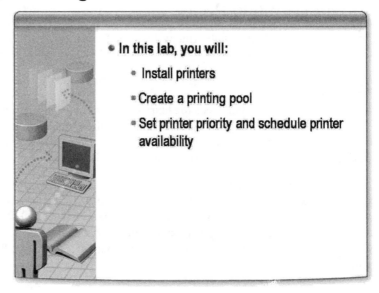

Objectives

After completing this lab, you will be able to:

- Install printers.
- Create a printing pool.
- Set printer priority and schedule printer availability.

Instructions

Before working on this lab:

- Log on to the domain as *ComputerName*Admin.
- Ensure that you have a local printer created on LPT1 called *ComputerName* Datacenter IT Printer.

Estimated time to complete this lab: 20 minutes

Exercise 1
Creating Printing Pools

In this exercise, you will install printers and create a printing pool.

Scenario

The home office in London needs the help of all systems administrators. Northwind Traders is merging with Contoso, Ltd. Because of this acquisition, many new printers must be configured as printing pools in the London corporate office. The corporate office in London needs your help to configure the new printers on a print server called Glasgow.

To help you create these new printers, the systems engineers have provided a table that lists the printers that each systems administrator must create and specific information about the printers. You must log on as *ComputerName*Admin. All print devices are HP LaserJet 5si, and all printers are located on the remote computer named Glasgow. The domain local group called DL NWTraders Legal Personnel Print should be the only group to have Print permission for these printers.

Tasks	Specific Instructions
1. Connect to the print server named Glasgow.	a. From the **Run** box, type **glasgow** and then click **OK**. b. From \\glasgow, double-click **Printers and Faxes**.
2. Create print device ports.	▪ In the student account table, find your administrator account and create two print device ports according to the table.
3. Create a printer to be used as a printing pool.	a. In the Printers and Faxes folder on Glasgow, double-click **Add Printer**. b. In the student account table, find your student account, and then create a network printer on Glasgow with the print device port, location, and shared printer name in the table.
4. Enable printer pooling and add a port to a printer.	a. Enable printer pooling. b. In the student account table, find your student account in the list, and then click the second print device port listed in the table.
5. Configure security.	a. Configure the group DL NWTraders Legal Personnel Print to have Print permission. b. Remove the Everyone group.

Student Account Table

Student account	Print device port	Location	Printer name and share name
AcapulcoAdmin	192.168.3.26 192.168.3.27	London/Build 2/Fl 1/Room 01	Legal Pool 1
BangaloreAdmin	192.168.3.28 192.168.3.29	London/Build 2/Fl 1/Room 02	Legal Pool 2
BonnAdmin	192.168.3.30 192.168.3.31	London/Build 2/Fl 1/Room 03	Legal Pool 3
BrisbaneAdmin	192.168.3.32 192.168.3.33	London/Build 2/Fl 1/Room 04	Legal Pool 4
CaracasAdmin	192.168.3.34 192.168.3.35	London/Build 2/Fl 1/Room 05	Legal Pool 5
CasablancaAdmin	192.168.3.36 192.168.3.37	London/Build 2/Fl 1/Room 06	Legal Pool 6
DenverAdmin	192.168.3.38 192.168.3.39	London/Build 2/Fl 1/Room 07	Legal Pool 7
KhartoumAdmin	192.168.3.40 192.168.3.41	London/Build 2/Fl 1/Room 08	Legal Pool 8
LimaAdmin	192.168.3.42 192.168.3.43	London/Build 2/Fl 1/Room 09	Legal Pool 9
LisbonAdmin	192.168.3.44 192.168.3.45	London/Build 2/Fl 1/Room 10	Legal Pool 10
ManilaAdmin	192.168.3.46 192.168.3.47	London/Build 2/Fl 1/Room 11	Legal Pool 11
MiamiAdmin	192.168.3.48 192.168.3.49	London/Build 2/Fl 1 Room 12	Legal Pool 12
MontevideoAdmin	192.168.3.50 192.168.3.51	London/Build 2/Fl 1 Room 13	Legal Pool 13
MoscowAdmin	192.168.3.52 192.168.3.53	London/Build 2/Fl 1 Room 14	Legal Pool 14
NairobiAdmin	192.168.3.54 192.168.3.55	London/Build 2/Fl 1 Room 15	Legal Pool 15
PerthAdmin	192.168.3.56 192.168.3.57	London/Build 2/Fl 1 Room 16	Legal Pool 16
SantiagoAdmin	192.168.3.58 192.168.3.59	London/Build 2/Fl 1 Room 17	Legal Pool 17

(continued)

Student account	Print device port	Location	Printer name and share name
SingaporeAdmin	192.168.3.60 192.168.3.61	London/Build 2/Fl 1 Room 18	Legal Pool 18
StockholmAdmin	192.168.3.62 192.168.3.63	London/Build 2/Fl 1 Room 19	Legal Pool 19
SuvaAdmin	192.168.3.64 192.168.3.65	London/Build 2/Fl 2 Room 20	Legal Pool 20
TokyoAdmin	192.168.3.66 192.168.3.67	London/Build 2/Fl 1 Room 21	Legal Pool 21
TunisAdmin	192.168.3.68 192.168.3.69	London/Build 2/Fl 1 Room 22	Legal Pool 22
VancouverAdmin	192.168.3.70 192.168.3.71	London/Build 2/Fl 1 Room 23	Legal Pool 23

Exercise 2
Setting Printer Priorities and Availability

In this exercise, you will set printer priority and availability.

Scenario

The data center in your city has been printing event logs to the printer on your member server, which is named *ComputerName* Datacenter IT Printer. These event logs are archived and are not needed on the same day that the reports are generated. You must create another printer so that the reports can print between 6:00 P.M. and 6:00 A.M. on the new printer and your IT staff can still print to the existing printer.

You will name and share the new printer as *ComputerName* Report. *ComputerName* Report will also print to LPT1. Configure *ComputerName* Datacenter IT Printer to have a priority of 50 and *ComputerName* Report to have a priority of 10. You can keep all default security settings for the new and existing printers. Because *ComputerName* Report is a printer that will be used for reports only, you do not need to implement a printer location.

Tasks	Specific Instructions
1. Create a local printer.	■ Printer name: *ComputerName* **Report** ■ Share name: *ComputerName* **Report** ■ Port: LPT1 ■ Manufacturer and model: HP LaserJet 5si
2. Configure a printer schedule for *ComputerName* Report.	■ Print from 6:00 P.M. to 6:00 A.M.
3. Configure printer priority for *ComputerName* Report.	■ Priority: 10
4. Configure printer priority for *ComputerName* Datacenter IT Printer.	■ Priority: 50

Microsoft®
Training &
  Certification

Microsoft Official
Curriculum

Module 7: Managing Access to Objects in Organizational Units

Contents

Overview	1
Multimedia: The Organizational Unit Structure	2
Lesson: Modifying Permissions for Active Directory Objects	3
Lesson: Delegating Control of Organizational Units	18
Lab A: Managing Access to Objects in Organizational Units	27

Microsoft®

Overview

- Multimedia: The Organizational Unit Structure
- Modifying Permissions for Active Directory Objects
- Delegating Control of Organizational Units

Introduction

The information in this module introduces the job function of managing access to objects in organizational units. Specifically, the module provides the skills and knowledge that you need to explain the permissions available for managing access to objects in the Active Directory® directory service, move objects between organizational units in the same domain, and delegate control of an organizational unit.

Objectives

After completing this module, you will be able to:

- Identify the role of the organizational unit.
- Modify permissions for Active Directory objects.
- Delegate control of organizational units.

Multimedia: The Organizational Unit Structure

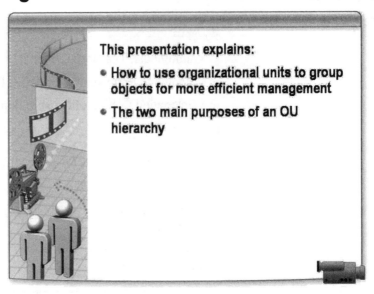

File location

To view the *The Organizational Unit Structure* presentation, open the Web page on the Student Materials compact disc, click **Multimedia**, and then click the title of the presentation. Do not open this presentation unless the instructor tells you to.

Objectives

After completing this lesson, you will be able to explain how to use organizational units to manage objects.

Lesson: Modifying Permissions for Active Directory Objects

- **What Are Active Directory Object Permissions?**
- **Characteristics of Active Directory Object Permissions**
- **Permissions Inheritance for Active Directory Object Permissions**
- **Effects of Modifying Objects on Permissions Inheritance**
- **How to Modify Permissions on Active Directory Objects**
- **What Are Effective Permissions for Active Directory Objects?**
- **How to Determine Effective Permissions for Active Directory Objects**

Introduction

Every object in Active Directory has a security descriptor that defines which accounts have permission to access the object and what type of access is allowed. The Microsoft® Windows® Server 2003 family uses these security descriptors to control access to objects.

Lesson objectives

After completing this lesson, you will be able to:

- Explain what Active Directory object permissions are.
- Describe the characteristics of Active Directory object permissions.
- Describe permissions inheritance for Active Directory object permissions.
- Describe the effects of modifying objects on permission inheritance.
- Modify permissions for Active Directory objects.
- Explain what effective permissions are for Active Directory objects.
- Determine effective permissions for Active Directory objects.

What Are Active Directory Object Permissions?

Permission	Allows the user to:
Full Control	Change permissions, take ownership, and perform the tasks that are allowed by all other standard permissions
Write	Change object attributes
Read	View objects, object attributes, the object owner, and Active Directory permissions
Create All Child Objects	Add any type of object to an organizational unit
Delete All Child Objects	Remove any type of child object from an organizational unit

Introduction

Active Directory object permissions provide security for resources by enabling you to control which administrators or users can access individual objects or object attributes and the type of access allowed. You use permissions to assign administrative privileges for an organizational unit or a hierarchy of organizational units to manage network access. You can also use permissions to assign administrative privileges for a single object to a specific user or group.

Standard and special permissions

Standard permissions are the most frequently granted permissions and consist of a collection of special permissions. Special permissions give you a higher degree of control over the type of access you can grant for objects. The standard permissions include the following:

- Full Control
- Write
- Read
- Create All Child Objects
- Delete All Child Objects

Access authorized by permissions

An administrator or the owner of the object must grant permissions for the object before users can access it. The Windows Server 2003 family stores a list of user access permissions, called the discretionary access control list (DACL), for every object in Active Directory. The DACL for an object lists who can access the object and the specific actions that each user can perform on the object.

Additional reading

For more information about Active Directory permissions, see "Best practices for assigning permissions on Active Directory objects" at http://www.microsoft.com/technet/treeview/default.asp?url=/technet/ prodtechnol/windowsserver2003/proddocs/datacenter/ACLUI_acl_BP.asp.

Characteristics of Active Directory Object Permissions

Active Directory object permissions can be:

- Allowed or denied

- Implicitly or explicitly denied

- Set as standard or special permissions

  Standard permissions are the most frequently assigned permissions

  Special permissions provide a finer degree of control for assigning access to objects

- Set at the object level or inherited from its parent object

---

Introduction

Although NTFS permissions and Active Directory object permissions are similar, certain characteristics are specific to Active Directory object permissions. Active Directory object permissions can be allowed or denied, implicitly or explicitly denied, set as standard or special permissions, and set at the object level or inherited from its parent object.

Allowing and denying permissions

You can allow or deny permissions. Denied permissions take precedence over any permission that you otherwise allow to user accounts and groups. Deny permissions only when it is necessary to remove a permission that a user is granted by being a member of a group.

Implicit or explicit permissions

You can implicitly or explicitly deny permissions as follows:

- When permission to perform an operation is not explicitly allowed, it is *implicitly denied*.

  For example, if the Marketing group is granted Read permission for a user object, and no other security principal is listed in the DACL for that object, users who are not members of the Marketing group are implicitly denied access. The operating system does not allow users who are not members of the Marketing group to read the properties of the user object.

- You *explicitly deny* a permission when you want to exclude a subset within a larger group from performing a task that the larger group has permissions to perform.

  For example, it may be necessary to prevent a user named Don from viewing the properties of a user object. However, Don is a member of the Marketing group, which has permissions to view the properties of the user object. You can prevent Don from viewing the properties of the user object by explicitly denying Read permission to him.

Standard and special permissions

Most Active Directory object permissions tasks can be configured through standard permissions. These permissions are the most commonly used, however if you need to grant a finer level of permissions, you will use special permissions.

Inherited permissions

When permissions are set on a parent object, new objects inherit the permissions of the parent. You can remove inherited permissions, but you can also re-enable them if you want to.

Permissions Inheritance for Active Directory Object Permissions

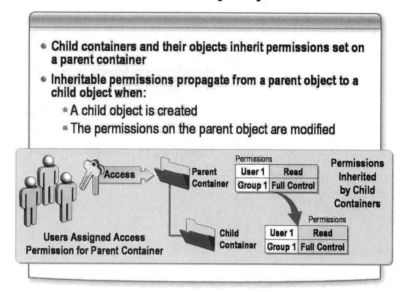

- Child containers and their objects inherit permissions set on a parent container
- Inheritable permissions propagate from a parent object to a child object when:
  - A child object is created
  - The permissions on the parent object are modified

Benefits of permissions inheritance

A parent object is any object that has a relationship with another object called a child. A child object inherits permissions from the parent object. Permissions inheritance in Active Directory minimizes the number of times that you need to grant permissions for objects.

Permissions inheritance in Windows Server 2003 simplifies the task of managing permissions in the following ways:

- You do not need to apply permissions manually to child objects while they are created.

- The permissions applied to a parent object are applied consistently to all child objects.

- When you need to modify permissions for all objects in a container, you only need to modify the permissions for the parent object. The child objects automatically inherit those changes.

Effects of Modifying Objects on Permissions Inheritance

* Permissions that are set explicitly remain the same
* Moved objects inherit permissions from the new parent organizational unit
* Moved object no longer inherit permissions from the previous parent organizational unit
* Preventing permission Inheritance

Introduction

Modifying Active Directory objects affects permissions inheritance. As a systems administrator, you will be asked to move objects between organizational units in Active Directory when organizational or administrative functions change. When you do this, the inherited permissions will change. It is imperative that you are aware of these consequences prior to modifying Active Directory objects.

Effects of moving objects

When you move objects between organizational units, the following conditions apply:

- Permissions that are set explicitly remain the same.

- An object inherits permissions from the organizational unit that it is moved to.

- An object no longer inherits permissions from the organizational unit that it is moved from.

Note   When modifying Active Directory objects, you can move multiple objects at the same time.

Preventing permissions inheritance

You can prevent permissions inheritance so that a child object does not inherit permissions from its parent object. When you prevent inheritance, only the permissions that you set explicitly apply.

When you prevent permissions inheritance, the Windows Server 2003 family enables you to:

- Copy inherited permissions to the object. The new permissions are explicit permissions for the object. They are a copy of the permissions that the object previously inherited from its parent object. After the inherited permissions are copied, you can make any necessary changes to the permissions.

- Remove inherited permissions from the object. By removing these permissions, you eliminate all permissions for the object. Then, you can grant any new permission that you want for the object.

How to Modify Permissions for Active Directory Objects

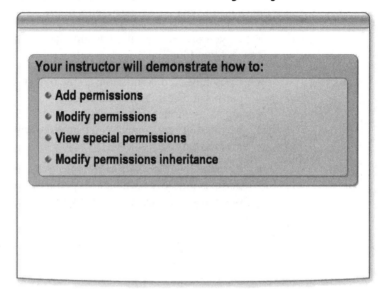

Your instructor will demonstrate how to:

- Add permissions
- Modify permissions
- View special permissions
- Modify permissions inheritance

Introduction

Windows Server 2003 determines if a user is authorized to use an object by checking the permissions granted to the user for that object, which are listed in the DACL. When you allow or deny permissions for an object, those settings override permissions inherited from a parent object.

Procedure for adding permissions

To add permissions for an object:

1. If Advanced Features is not already checked, in Active Directory Users and Computers, on the **View** menu, click **Advanced Features**.

2. In the console tree, right-click the object, and then click **Properties**.

3. In the **Properties** dialog box, on the **Security** tab, click **Add**.

4. In the **Select Users, Computers, or Groups** dialog box, in the **Name** box, type the name of the user or group to which you want to grant permissions, and then click **OK**.

Procedure for modifying permissions

To modify an existing permission:

1. If Advanced Features is not already checked, in Active Directory Users and Computers, on the **View** menu, click **Advanced Features**.

2. In the console tree, right-click the object, and then click **Properties**.

3. In the **Properties** dialog box, on the **Security** tab, in the **Permissions** box, select the **Allow** or **Deny** check box for each permission that you want to allow or deny.

Procedure for viewing special permissions

Standard permissions are sufficient for most administrative tasks. However, you may need to view the special permissions that constitute a standard permission.

To view special permissions:

1. In the **Properties** dialog box for the object, on the **Security** tab, click **Advanced**.

2. In the **Advanced Security Settings** dialog box, on the **Permissions** tab, click the entry that you want to view, and then click **Edit**.

3. To view the permissions for specific attributes, in the **Permission Entry** dialog box, click the **Properties** tab.

Procedure for modifying permission inheritance

To modify permissions inheritance:

1. In the **Properties** dialog box for the object, on the **Security** tab, click **Advanced**.

2. In the **Advanced Security Settings** dialog box, on the **Permissions** tab, click the entry that you want to view, and then click **Edit**.

3. In the **Permission Entry** dialog box, on the **Object** tab, in the **Apply onto** box, select the option that you want.

What Are Effective Permissions for Active Directory Objects?

- **Permissions are cumulative**
- **Deny permissions override all other permissions**
- **Object owners can always change permissions**
- **Retrieving effective permissions**

Introduction

You can use the Effective Permissions tool to determine what the permissions for an Active Directory object are. The tool calculates the permissions that are granted to the specified user or group and takes into account the permissions that are in effect from group memberships and any permissions inherited from parent objects.

Characteristics

Effective permissions for Active Directory objects have the following characteristics:

- Cumulative permissions are the combination of Active Directory permissions granted to the user and group accounts.

- Deny permissions override all inherited permissions. Permissions explicitly assigned take priority.

- Every object has an owner, whether in an NTFS volume or Active Directory. The owner controls how permissions are set on the object and to whom permissions are granted.

  By default, in Windows Server 2003, the owner is the Administrators group. The owner can always change permissions for an object, even when the owner is denied all access to the object.

  The current owner can grant the Take ownership permission to another user, which enables that user to take ownership of that object at any time. The user must actually take ownership to complete the transfer of ownership.

Retrieving effective permissions

To retrieve information about effective permissions in Active Directory, you need the permission to read membership information. If the specified user or group is a domain object, you must have permission to read the object's membership information on the domain. The following users have relevant default domain permissions:

- Domain administrators have permission to read membership information on all objects.

- Local administrators on a workstation or stand-alone server cannot read membership information for a domain user.

- Authenticated domain users can read membership information only when the domain is in pre-Windows 2000 compatibility mode.

How to Determine Effective Permissions for Active Directory Objects

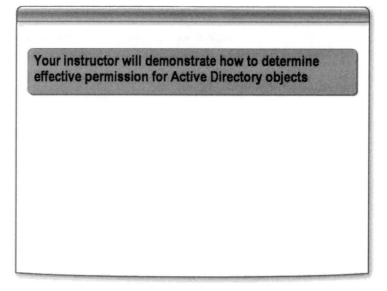

Introduction

Use the following procedure to view the effective permissions log for Active Directory objects.

Procedure

To view the effective permissions log:

1. In Active Directory Users and Computers, in the console tree, browse to the organizational unit or object for which you want to view effective permissions.

2. Right-click the organizational unit or object, and then click **Properties**.

3. In the **Properties** dialog box, on the **Security** tab, click **Advanced**.

4. In the **Advanced Security Settings** dialog box, on the **Effective Permissions** tab, click **Select**.

5. In the **Select User, Computer, or Group** dialog box, in the **Enter the object name to select** box, enter the name of a user or group, and then click **OK**.

   The selected check boxes indicate the effective permissions of the user or group for that object.

Additional reading

For more information about effective permissions, see "Effective Permissions tool" at http://www.microsoft.com/technet/treeview/default.asp?url=/technet/prodtechnol/windowsserver2003/proddocs/datacenter/acl_effective_perm.asp.

Practice: Modifying Permissions for Active Directory Objects

In this practice, you will:

- Remove the inherited permissions for your city organizational unit

- Document the security changes made to your city organizational unit

Objective

In this practice, you will:

- Remove the inherited permissions for your city organizational unit.

- Document the security changes made to your city organizational unit.

Instructions

Before you begin this practice:

- Log on to the domain by using the *ComputerName*User account.

- Open CustomMMC with the **Run as** command.

  Use the user account Nwtraders*ComputerName*Admin (Example: LondonAdmin).

- Ensure that CustomMMC contains Active Directory Users and Computers.

- Ensure that you are viewing the advanced features of Active Directory Users and Computers.

- Review the procedures in this lesson that describe how to perform this task.

Scenario

The system engineer for Northwind Traders has delegated administrative control to administrators or each *ComputerName* location. You need to determine what permissions are being inherited to your *ComputerName* organizational unit, and then remove all inherited permissions. Document the results of each step of the removal of inherited permissions.

Practice

▶ **Document the security for your city organizational unit**

1. Open Active Directory Users and Computers.

2. View the security settings for your *ComputerName* organizational unit by doing the following:

   a. Right-click your *ComputerName* organizational unit, and then click **Properties**.

   b. In the **Properties** dialog box, click the **Security** tab.

3. Document the group or users names that have inherited or explicit permissions in the following table. Write a Y for yes under Inherited or Explicit for each item in the Group or user names column.

   An explicit permission has a selected check box under **Allow** or **Deny**. Unchangeable and inherited permissions have a shaded selected check box under **Allow** or **Deny**.

Group or user names	Inherited	Explicit
Example: Account Operators	Y	
Account Operators	Y	
Administrators	Y	
Authenticated Users		Y
DL *ComputerName* OU Administrators		Y
Domain Admins		Y
Enterprise Admins	Y	
ENTERPRISE DOMAIN CONTROLLERS		Y
Pre-Windows 2000 Compatible Access	Y	
Printer Operators	Y	
System		Y

▶ **Remove inherited permissions**

1. In **Properties** dialog box for your city organizational unit, click **Advanced**.

2. In the **Advanced Security Settings** dialog box, on the **Permissions** tab, clear the **Allow inheritable permissions from the parent to propagate to this object and all child objects. Include these with entries explicitly defined here.** check box.

3. In the security dialog box, click **Remove**.

4. In the **Advanced Security Settings** dialog box, click **OK**.

▶ **Document the security changes for your city organizational unit**

1. Open Active Directory Users and Computers.

2. View the security settings for your *ComputerName* organizational unit by doing the following:

   a. Right-click your *ComputerName* organizational unit, and then click **Properties**.

   b. In the **Properties** dialog box, click the **Security** tab.

3. Document the group or users names that have inherited or explicit permissions in the following table. Write a Y for yes under Inherited or Explicit for each item in the Group or user names column.

   An explicit permission has a selected check box under **Allow** or **Deny**. Unchangeable and inherited permissions have a shaded selected check box under **Allow** or **Deny**.

Group or user names	Inherited	Explicit
Example: Account Operators	Y	
Account Operators	Y	
Administrators		
Authenticated Users		Y
DL *ComputerName* OU Administrators		Y
Domain Admins		Y
Enterprise Admins		
ENTERPRISE DOMAIN CONTROLLERS		Y
Pre-Windows 2000 Compatible Access		
Printer Operators	Y	
System		Y

Lesson: Delegating Control of Organizational Units

- **What Is Delegation of Control of an Organizational Unit?**
- **The Delegation of Control Wizard**
- **How to Delegate Control of an Organizational Unit**

Introduction

Active Directory enables you to efficiently manage objects by delegating administrative control of the objects. You can use the Delegation of Control Wizard and customized consoles in Microsoft Management Console (MMC) to grant specific users the permissions to perform various administrative and management tasks.

Lesson objectives

After completing this lesson, you will be able to:

- Describe what it means to delegate control of an organizational unit.

- Describe the purpose and function of the Delegation of Control Wizard.

- Delegate control of an organizational unit by using the Delegation of Control Wizard.

What Is Delegation of Control of an Organizational Unit?

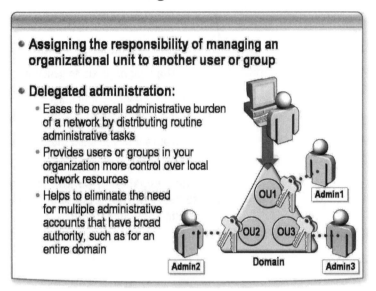

Definition

Delegation of control is the ability to assign the responsibility of managing Active Directory objects to another user, group, or organization. By delegating control, you can eliminate the need for multiple administrative accounts that have broad authority.

You can delegate the following types of control:

- Permissions to create or modify objects in a specific organizational unit
- Permissions to modify specific attributes of an object, such as granting the permission to reset passwords on a user account

Why delegate administrative control?

Delegated administration in Active Directory helps ease the administrative burden of managing your network by distributing routine administrative tasks to multiple users. With delegated administration, you can assign basic administrative tasks to regular users or groups and assign domain-wide and forest-wide administrative tasks to trusted users in your Domain Admins and Enterprise Admins groups.

By delegating administration, you give groups in your organization more control of their local network resources. You also help secure your network from accidental or malicious damage by limiting the membership of administrator groups.

Ways to define the delegation of administrative control

You define the delegation of administrative control in the following three ways:

- Change properties for a particular container.
- Create and delete objects of a specific type under an organizational unit, such as users, groups, or printers.
- Update specific properties on objects of a specific type under an organizational unit. For example, you can delegate the permission to set a password on a user object or all objects in an organizational unit.

The Delegation of Control Wizard

- Use the Delegation of Control Wizard to specify:
  - The user or group to which you want to delegate control
  - The organizational units and objects you want to grant the user or group the permission to control
  - Tasks that you want the user or group to be able to perform
- The Delegation of Control Wizard automatically assigns to users the appropriate permissions to access and modify specified objects

Introduction

You use the Delegation of Control Wizard to select the user or group to which you want to delegate control. You also use the wizard to grant users permissions to control organizational units and objects and to access and modify objects.

Delegate permissions

You can use the Delegation of Control Wizard to grant permissions at the organizational unit level. You must manually grant additional specialized permissions at the object level.

In Active Directory Users and Computers, right-click the organizational units that you want to delegate control for, and then click **Delegate control** to start the wizard. You can also select the organizational unit and then click Delegate control on the Action menu.

Options

The following table describes the options in the Delegation of Control Wizard.

Option	Description
Users or Groups	The user accounts or groups to which you want to delegate control.
Tasks to Delegate	A list of common tasks, or the option to customize a task. When you select a common task, the wizard summarizes your selections to complete the delegation process. When you choose to customize a task, the wizard presents Active Directory object types and permissions for you to choose from.
Active Directory Object Type	Either all objects or only specific types of objects in the specified organizational unit.
Permissions	The permissions to grant for the object or objects.

Note The Delegation of Control Wizard can append permissions to an organizational unit if it is run more than once. However, you must manually remove delegated permissions.

How to Delegate Control of an Organizational Unit

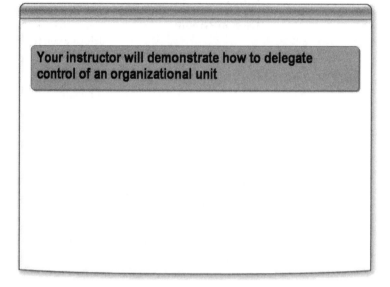

Your instructor will demonstrate how to delegate control of an organizational unit

Introduction

To grant permissions at the organizational unit level, use the Delegation of Control Wizard. You can grant permissions for managing objects, or you can grant permissions for managing specific attributes of those objects. Using the Delegation of Control Wizard is the preferred method for delegating control, because it reduces the possibility of unwanted effects from permission assignments.

Procedure for delegating control for common tasks

To delegate administrative control for common tasks:

1. Start the Delegation of Control Wizard, by performing the following steps:

   a. In Active Directory Users and Computers, click the organizational unit for which you want to delegate control.

   b. On the **Action** menu, click **Delegate control**.

2. In the Delegation of Control Wizard, on the **Welcome** page, click **Next**.

3. On the **Users or Groups** page, select a user or group to which you want to grant permissions, and then click **Next**. If there are not Users or Groups displayed to select from, do the following:

   a. Click Add.

   b. In the Select Users, Computers or Groups dialog box, in the Enter the object names to select box, type the name of a user or group, and then click OK.

4. On the **Tasks to Delegate** page, specify one or more of the following tasks to delegate:

   - Create, delete, and manage user accounts

   - Reset user passwords and force password change at next logon

   - Read all user information

   - Create, delete, and manage groups

   - Modify the membership of a group

   - Manage Group Policy links

   Note   You can delegate a custom task to users or groups by clicking **Create a custom task to delegate**.

   ---

5. Click **Next**.

6. On the **Completing the Delegation of Control Wizard** page, click **Finish**.

Procedure for delegating control for a custom task

To delegate administrative control for a custom task:

1. Start the Delegation of Control Wizard, by performing the following steps:

   a. In Active Directory Users and Computers, click the organizational unit for which you want to delegate control.

   b. On the **Action** menu, click **Delegate control**.

2. In the Delegation of Control Wizard, on the **Welcome** page, click **Next**.

3. On the **Users or Groups** page, select a user or group to which you want to grant permissions, and then click **Next**.

4. On the **Tasks to Delegate** page, click **Create a custom task to delegate**, and then click **Next**.

5. On the **Active Directory Object Type** page, click **Next**.

6. On the **Permissions** page, specify the permissions that you want to grant to the organizational unit or its objects.

   You can select the following types of permissions:

   - *General*. Displays the most commonly used permissions that are available for the selected organizational unit or the objects in the organizational unit.

   - *Property specific*. Displays all attribute permissions applicable to the type of object.

   - *Creation/deletion of specific child object*. Displays permissions that you need to create new objects in the organizational unit.

7. Click **Next**.

8. On the **Completing the Delegation of Control Wizard** page, click **Finish**.

Practice: Delegating Control of an Organizational Unit

In this practice, you will:

- Delegate control of the Computers organizational unit
- Test delegated permissions for your Computers organizational unit
- Delegate control of the Users organizational unit
- Test delegated permissions for your Users organizational unit

Objective

In this practice, you will:

- Delegate control of the Computers organizational unit.
- Test delegated permissions for your Computers organizational unit.
- Delegate control of the Users organizational unit.
- Test delegated permissions for your Users organizational unit.

Instructions

Before you begin this practice:

- Log on to the domain by using the *ComputerName*User account.
- Open CustomMMC with the **Run as** command.

  Use the user account Nwtraders*ComputerName*Admin (Example: LondonAdmin).

- Ensure that CustomMMC contains Active Directory Users and Computers.
- Review the procedures in this lesson that describe how to perform this task.

Scenario

To distribute the workload among administrators, Northwind Traders wants administrators to be able to do specific tasks in their designated organizational units. The following tasks must be delegated in the following organizational units:

- Organizational unit: Locations/*ComputerName*/Computers

  Task: Create and delete computer accounts in the organizational unit

- Organizational unit: Locations/*ComputerName*/Users

  Task: Reset user passwords and force password change at next logon

  Task: Read all user information

Practice

▶ **Delegate control of the Computers organizational unit**

1. In Active Directory Users and Computers, in the console tree, navigate to your *ComputerName* organizational unit, right-click **Computers**, and then click **Delegate Control**.

2. In the Delegation of Control Wizard, on the **Welcome** page, click **Next**.

3. On the **Users or Groups** page, add *ComputerName*User, and then click **Next**.

4. On the **Tasks to Delegate** page, click **Create a custom task to delegate**, and click **Next**.

5. On the **Active Directory Object Type** page, click **Only the Following Objects in the Folder**, and then select the **Computer objects** check box.

6. Select the **Create selected objects in this folder** and **Delete selected objects in this folder** check boxes, and then click **Next**.

7. On the **Permissions** page, select the **General** check box.

8. Under **Permissions**, select the **Read** and **Write** check boxes, and then click **Next**.

9. On the **Completing the Delegation of Control Wizard**, click **Finish**.

▶ **Test permissions for the Computers organizational unit**

1. Close CustomMMC, and then open it again without using the **Run as** command.

2. In Active Directory Users and Computers, create a computer account by using the following parameters:

   • Location: Locations/*ComputerName*/Computers

   • Computer account name: First three letters of the city and **Test** (Example: LonTest)

   You should be able to create a computer account in the Locations/*ComputerName*/Computers organizational unit.

3. Close Active Directory Users and Computers.

▶ **Delegate control of the Users organizational unit**

1. Open Active Directory Users and Computers with the **Run As** command by using the *ComputerName*Admin account.

2. Navigate to your *ComputerName* organizational unit, right-click **Users**, and then click **Delegate Control**.

3. In the **Delegation of Control Wizard**, on the Welcome page, click **Next**.

4. On the **Users of Groups** page, add *ComputerName*User and then click **Next**.

5. Delegate the following common tasks:

   • Reset user passwords and force password change at next logon

   • Read all user information

6. Click **Next**, and then click **Finish**.

▶ **Test your permissions for the Users organizational unit**

1. Close CustomMMC, and then open it again without using the **Run as** command.

2. In Active Directory Users and Computers, navigate to the Locations/ComputerName/Users organizational unit.

3. Try to delete a user account.

   You should be unsuccessful.

4. Try to enable or disable any user account.

   You should be unsuccessful.

5. Reset any user's password.

   You should be able to reset any user accounts password in the Locations/*ComputerName*/Users organizational unit.

Lab A: Managing Access to Objects in Organizational Units

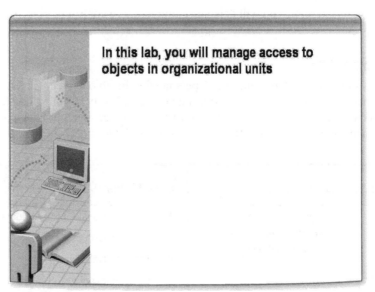

In this lab, you will manage access to objects in organizational units

Objectives

After completing this lab, you will be able to manage access to objects in organizational units.

Instructions

Before you begin this lab:

- Log on to the domain by using the *ComputerName*User account.

- Open CustomMMC with the **Run as** command.

  Use the user account Nwtraders*ComputerName*Admin (Example: LondonAdmin).

- Ensure that CustomMMC contains Active Directory Users and Computers.

Estimated time to complete this lab: 15 minutes

Exercise 1
Delegating Administrative Control

In this exercise, you will delegate administrative control of objects in an organizational unit.

Scenario

Northwind Traders wants all IT personnel to be able to create, delete, and modify groups in every city organizational unit. You must delegate authority in your *ComputerName* organizational unit to enable a global group named G NWTraders IT Personnel to have permissions to Create, delete and manage groups and to Modify membership of a group.

Tasks	Specific instructions
1. Delegate control of the *ComputerName*/Groups organizational unit.	▪ Organizational unit: nwtraders.msft/Locations/*ComputerName*/Groups ▪ Users or Groups: G NWTraders IT Personnel ▪ Tasks to Delegate: • Create, delete, and manage groups • Modify the membership of a group

Exercise 2
Documenting Security of an Active Directory Object

In this exercise, you will document the security settings of the object created in the delegated organizational unit.

Scenario

You have just created many groups in a delegated organizational unit, and you have been asked to document what permissions one of those groups has inherited. Enter information in the following table to document the permissions of the group.

Tasks	Detailed steps
1. Document the special permissions for a group created in a delegated organizational unit.	▪ Document the special permissions for the group G NWTraders IT Personnel.

Module 8: Implementing Group Policy

Contents

Overview	1
Multimedia: Introduction to Group Policy	2
Lesson: Implementing Group Policy Objects	3
Lesson: Implementing GPOs on a Domain	10
Lesson: Managing the Deployment of Group Policy	21
Lab A: Implementing Group Policy	33
Course Evaluation	38

Overview

- **Multimedia: Introduction to Group Policy**
- **Implementing Group Policy Objects**
- **Implementing GPOs on a Domain**
- **Managing the Deployment of Group Policy**

Introduction

The information in this module introduces the job function of implementing Group Policy. Specifically, the module provides the skills and knowledge that you need to explain the purpose and function of Group Policy in a Microsoft® Windows® Server 2003 environment, implement Group Policy objects (GPOs), and manage GPOs.

Objectives

After completing this module, you will be able to:

- Implement a Group Policy objects.

- Implement GPOs on a domain.

- Manage the deployment of Group Policy.

Multimedia: Introduction to Group Policy

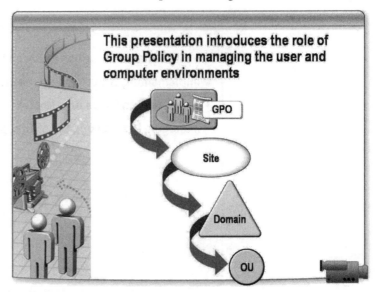

File location	To view the *Introduction to Group Policy* presentation, open the Web page on the Student Materials compact disc, click **Multimedia**, and then click the title of the presentation.
Objectives	After completing this lesson, you will be able to:

- Describe the types of settings that you can define in Group Policy.
- Describe how Group Policy is applied.

Additional reading	For more information about how clients apply Group Policy, see "Order of events in startup and logon" at http://www.microsoft.com/technet/treeview/ default.asp?url=/technet/prodtechnol/winxppro/proddocs/orderofevents.asp.

Lesson: Implementing Group Policy Objects

- What Is Group Policy?
- What Are User and Computer Configuration Settings?
- How to Set Local Computer Policy Settings

Introduction

After completing this lesson, students will be able to implement GPOs.

Lesson objectives

After completing this lesson, you will be able to:

- Explain what Group Policy is.
- Describe users and computer configuration settings.
- Set local computer policy settings.

What Is Group Policy?

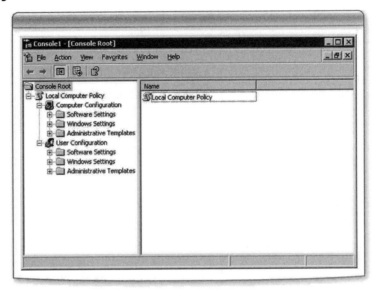

Definition

The Active Directory® directory service uses Group Policy to manage users and computers in your network. When using Group Policy, you can define the state of a user's work environment once, and then rely on the Windows Server 2003 family to continually enforce the Group Policy settings that you defined. You can apply Group Policy settings across an entire organization, or you can apply Group Policy settings to specific groups of users and computers.

Additional reading

For more information about Group Policy, see:

- "Microsoft IntelliMirror®" at http://www.microsoft.com/technet/treeview/ default.asp?url=/technet/prodtechnol/windowsserver2003/proddocs/server/ sag_IMirror_top_node.asp.

- "Group Policy settings overview" at http://www.microsoft.com/technet/ treeview/default.asp?url=/technet/prodtechnol/windowsserver2003/ proddocs/server/gpsettings.asp.

What Are User and Computer Configuration Settings?

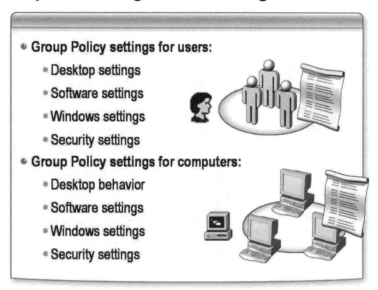

Group Policy settings for users:
- Desktop settings
- Software settings
- Windows settings
- Security settings

Group Policy settings for computers:
- Desktop behavior
- Software settings
- Windows settings
- Security settings

Introduction

You can enforce Group Policy settings for computers and users by using the Computer Configuration and User Configuration features in Group Policy.

User configuration

Group Policy settings for users include specific operating system behavior, desktop settings, security settings, assigned and published application options, application settings, folder redirection options, and user logon and logoff scripts. User-related Group Policy settings are applied when users log on to the computer and during the periodic refresh cycle.

Group Policy settings that customize the user's desktop environment, or enforce lockdown policies on users, are contained under User Configuration in Group Policy Object Editor.

Software settings for user configuration

The Software Settings folder under User Configuration contains software settings that apply to users regardless of which computer they log on to. This folder also contains software installation settings, and it might contain other settings that are placed there by independent software vendors (ISVs).

Windows settings for user configuration

The Windows Settings folder under User Configuration contains Windows settings that apply to users regardless of which computer they log on to. This folder also contains the following items: Folder Redirection, Security Settings, and Scripts.

Computer configuration

Group Policy settings for computers include how the operating system behaves, desktop behavior, security settings, computer startup and shutdown scripts, computer-assigned application options, and application settings. Computer-related Group Policy settings are applied when the operating system initializes and during the periodic refresh cycle. In general, computer-related Group Policy settings takes precedence over conflicting user-related Group Policy settings.

Group Policy settings that customize the desktop environment for all users of a computer, or enforce security policies on a network's computers, are contained under Computer Configuration in Group Policy Object Editor.

Software Settings for computer configuration

The Software Settings folder under Computer Configuration contains software settings that apply to all users who log on to the computer. This folder contains software installation settings, and it may contain other settings that are placed there by ISVs.

Windows settings for computer configuration

The Windows Settings folder under Computer Configuration contains Windows settings that apply to all users who log on to the computer. This folder also contains the following items: Security Settings and Scripts.

Security settings for user and computer configuration

Security settings are available under the Windows Settings folder under Computer Configuration and User Configuration in Group Policy Object Editor. Security settings or security policies are rules that you configure on a computer or multiple computers that protect resources on a computer or network. With security settings, you can specify the security policy of an organizational unit, domain, or site.

Additional reading

For more information about extending Group Policy, see "Advanced methods of extending Group Policy" at http://www.microsoft.com/technet/treeview/ default.asp?url=/technet/prodtechnol/windowsserver2003/proddocs/server/ sag_SPconcepts_30.asp.

How to Set Local Computer Policy Settings

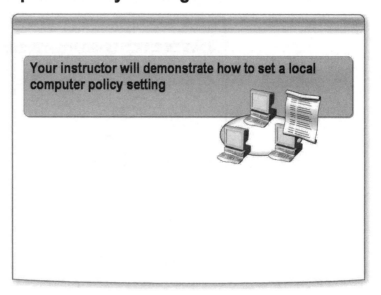

Introduction

To edit a local GPO, you must be logged on as a member of the Domain Admins group, the Enterprise Admins group, or the Group Policy Creator Owners group.

Note You can access Group Policy Object Editor from Administrative Tools or through a Microsoft Management Console (MMC) snap-in.

Procedure

To set local computer policy settings:

1. Open Group Policy Object Editor.

2. In the console tree, double-click the folders to view the policy settings in the details pane.

3. In the details pane, double-click a policy setting to open the **Properties** dialog box, and then change the policy setting.

Practice: Setting Local Computer Policy Settings

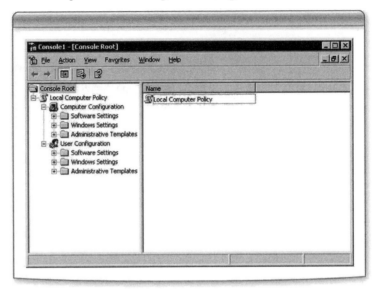

Objective

In this exercise, you will set a local computer policy setting by using Group Policy Object Editor.

Instruction

Before you begin this practice:

- Log on to the domain by using the *ComputerName*User account.

- Open CustomMMC with the **Run as** command.

  Use the user account Nwtraders*ComputerName*Admin (Example: LondonAdmin).

- Review the procedures in this lesson that describe how to perform this task.

Scenario

The systems administrators team has asked you to test some local policy settings before they deploy the policy settings to production servers. You will set some local computer policy settings on your server and test the policy settings to make sure they work.

Practice

▶ **Add Group Policy Object Editor to CustomMMC**

1. Open CustomMMC.

2. Add the snap-in Group Policy Object Editor.

3. Save CustomMMC.

► **Prevent users from shutting down the server by using a local policy setting**

1. In CustomMMC, expand the snap-in, **Local Computer Policy**.

2. In the console tree, expand **User Configuration**, expand **Administrative Templates**, and then click **Start Menu and Taskbar**.

3. In the details pane, double-click **Remove and prevent access to the Shut Down command**.

4. In the **Remove and prevent access to the Shut Down command Properties** dialog box, click **Enabled**, and then click **OK**.

5. Close and save all programs and log off.

► **Test the policy setting that prevents users from shutting down the server**

1. Log on as *ComputerName***User** with a password of **P@ssw0rd** in the NWTraders domain.

2. Click **Start** and verify that the **Shut Down** button has been removed from the **Start** menu.

3. Close and save all programs and log off.

► **Enable the Shut Down button on the server by using a local policy setting**

1. Log on as *ComputerName***User** with a password of **P@ssw0rd** in the NWTraders domain.

2. Open CustomMMC with the **Run as** command with the Nwtraders*ComputerName*Admin user account.

3. In CustomMMC, expand the snap-in, **Local Computer Policy**.

4. In the console tree, expand **User Configuration**, expand **Administrative Templates**, and then click **Start Menu and Taskbar**.

5. In the details pane, double-click **Remove and prevent access to the Shut Down command**.

6. In the **Remove and prevent access to the Shut Down command Properties** dialog box, click **Not configured**, and then click **OK**.

7. Close and save all programs and log off.

► **Test the local policy that enables the shut down option on the server**

1. Log on as *ComputerName***User** with a password of **P@ssw0rd** in the NWTraders domain.

2. Click **Start** and verify that the **Shut Down** button on the **Start** menu had been enabled.

3. Close all programs and log off.

Lesson: Implementing GPOs on a Domain

- Tools Used to Create GPOs
- What Is GPO Management on a Domain?
- How to Create a GPO
- What Is a GPO Link?
- How to Create a GPO Link
- How Group Policy Permission Is Inherited in Active Directory

Introduction

Implementing Group Policy on a domain provides the network administrator with greater control over computer configurations throughout the network structure. Also, by using Group Policy in Windows Server 2003, you can create a managed desktop environment that is tailored to the user's job responsibilities and experience level, which can decrease the amount of network support needed.

Lesson objectives

After completing this lesson, you will be able to:

- Understand the tools used to create GPOs.
- Explain what GPO management on a domain is.
- Create a GPO.
- Explain what a GPO link is.
- Explain how to configure attributes of GPO links.
- Explain how Group Policy permission is inherited in Active Directory.

Tools Used to Create GPOs

- **Default Group Policy tools**
    - **Active Directory Users and Computers**
      Domain and organizational unit GPOs
    - **Active Directory Sites and Services**
      Site GPOs
    - **Local Security Policy**
      Local computer security settings
- **Add-in tools**
    - **Group Policy Management**
      Domain, organizational unit, and site GPOs

Introduction

You can open Group Policy Object Editor from other tools to edit GPOs.

Active Directory Users and Computers

You can open Group Policy Object Editor from Active Directory Users and Computers to manage GPOs for domains and organizational units. In the **Properties** dialog box for a domain or an organizational unit, there is a **Group Policy** tab. On this tab, you can manage GPOs for the domain or organizational units.

Active Directory Sites and Services

You can open Group Policy Object Editor from Active Directory Sites and Services to manage GPOs for sites. In the **Properties** dialog box for a site, there is a **Group Policy** tab. On this tab, you can manage GPOs for the site.

Note If the Group Policy Management console is installed, the ADUC and ADSS are replaced by a button to launch the Group Policy Management console.

Group Policy Management console

The Group Policy Management console is a set of programmable interfaces for managing Group Policy, as well as an MMC snap-in that is built on those programmable interfaces. Together, the components of Group Policy Management consolidate the management of Group Policy across the enterprise.

The Group Policy Management console combines the functionality of multiple components in a single user interface (UI). The UI is structured to match the way you use and manage Group Policy. It incorporates functionality related to Group Policy from the following tools into a single MMC snap-in:

- Active Directory Users and Computers

- Active Directory Sites and Services

- Resultant Set of Policy (RSoP)

Group Policy Management also provides the following extended capabilities that were not available in previous Group Policy tools. With Group Policy Management, you can:

- Back up and restore GPOs.

- Copy and import GPOs.

- Use Windows Management Instrumentation (WMI) filters.

- Report GPO and RSoP data.

- Search for GPOs.

Group Policy Management vs. default Group Policy tools

Prior to Group Policy Management, you managed Group Policy by using a variety of Windows-based tools, including Active Directory Users and Computers, Active Directory Sites and Services, and RSoP. Group Policy Management consolidates management of all core Group Policy tasks into a single tool. Because of this consolidated management, Group Policy functionality is no longer required in these other tools.

After installing Group Policy Management, you still use each of the Active Directory tools for their intended directory management purposes, such as creating user, computer, and group objects. However, you can use Group Policy Management to perform all tasks related to Group Policy. Group Policy functionality is no longer available through the Active Directory tools when Group Policy Management is installed.

Group Policy Management does not replace Group Policy Object Editor. You still must edit GPOs by using Group Policy Object Editor. Group Policy Management integrates editing functionality by providing direct access to Group Policy Object Editor.

Note The Group Policy Management console does not come with Windows Server 2003. You must download it from http://www.microsoft.com.

Administrative Templates

There are several template files with an .adm extension that are included with Windows. These files, called Administrative Templates, provide policy information for the items that are under the Administrative Templates folder in the console tree of Group Policy Object Editor. Administrative Templates include Registry-based settings, which are available under Computer Configuration and User Configuration in Group Policy Object Editor.

An .adm file consists of a hierarchy of categories and subcategories that define how the policy settings appear. It also contains the following information:

- Registry locations that correspond to each setting

- Options or restrictions in values that are associated with each setting

- For many settings, a default value

- Explanation of what each setting does

- The versions of Windows that support each setting

What Is GPO Management on a Domain?

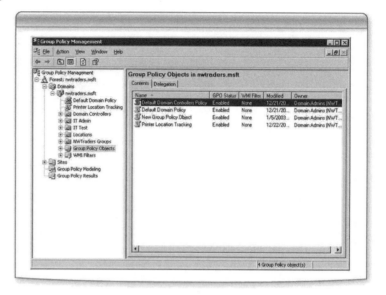

Introduction

After you create a GPO, you then configure the settings for that specific GPO. By grouping collections of settings into separate GPOs, you can specify different configurations for each GPO so that each GPO affects only the computers and users that you specify. When you place GPOs on a domain, you can manage the configuration settings on a domain-wide basis.

Group Policy container

The Group Policy container is an Active Directory object that contains GPO attributes. It includes subcontainers for Group Policy information about computers and users. The Group Policy container includes the following information:

- *Version information*. Ensures that the information in the Group Policy container is synchronized across all domain controllers.

- *Status information*. Indicates whether the GPO is enabled or disabled.

- *List of extensions*. Lists any of the Group Policy extensions that are used in the GPO.

Additional reading

For more information about Group Policy Management, see:

- "Introducing the Group Policy Management Console" at http://www.microsoft.com/windowsserver2003/gpmc/gpmcintro.mspx.

- "Enterprise Management with the Group Policy Management Console" at http://www.microsoft.com/windowsserver2003/gpmc/default.mspx.

How to Create a GPO

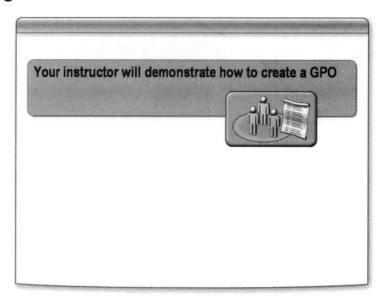

Introduction

Use the following procedures to create a new GPO or link an existing GPO by using Active Directory Users and Computers and to create a GPO in a site, domain, or organizational unit.

Procedure using Active Directory Users and Computers

To create a new GPO or link an existing GPO by using Active Directory Users and Computers:

1. In Active Directory Users and Computers, right-click the Active Directory container (domain or organizational unit) for which you want to create a GPO, and then click **Properties**.

2. In the **Properties** dialog box, on the **Group Policy** tab, choose one of the following options:

   • To create a new GPO, click **New**, type a name for the new GPO, and then press ENTER.

   • To link an existing GPO, click **Add**, and then select the GPO from the list.

   The GPO that you create or link is displayed in the list of GPOs that are linked to the Active Directory container.

Procedure using Group Policy Management

To create a GPO for a site, a domain, or an organizational unit:

1. Click **Start**, point to **Administrative Tools**, and then click **Group Policy Management**.

2. In Group Policy Management, in the console tree, expand the forest containing the domain in which you want to create a new GPO, expand **Domains**, and then expand the domain.

3. Right-click **Group Policy Objects**, and then click **New**.

4. In the **New GPO** dialog box, type a name for the new Group Policy object, and then click **OK**.

Practice: Creating a GPO

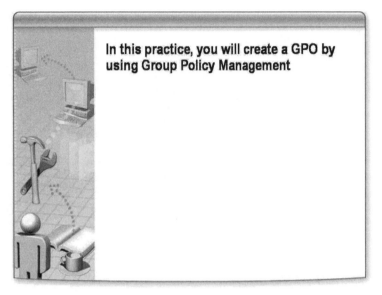

In this practice, you will create a GPO by using Group Policy Management

Objective

In this practice, you will create a GPO by using Group Policy Management.

Instructions

Before you begin this practice:

- Log on to the domain by using the *ComputerName*User account.
- Open CustomMMC with the **Run as** command.

  Use the user account Nwtraders*ComputerName*Admin (Example: LondonAdmin).

- Ensure that Custom MMC contains Group Policy Management.
- Review the procedures in this lesson that describe how to perform this task.

Scenario

The systems engineers at Northwind Traders are going to test Group Policy settings in a test environment. These Group Policy settings will be used later for scalability testing. The systems engineers need your team of systems administrators to create a GPO called *ComputerName*GP in the Group Policy Objects container.

Practice

▶ **Create a GPO by using Group Policy Management**

1. In Group Policy Management, expand **nwtraders.msft**.
2. Create a GPO called *ComputerName***GP** in the Group Policy Objects container.

Additional reading

For more information about migrating GPOs, see "Migrating GPOs Across Domains with GPMC" at http://www.microsoft.com/windowsserver2003/gpmc/migrgpo.mspx.

What Is a GPO Link?

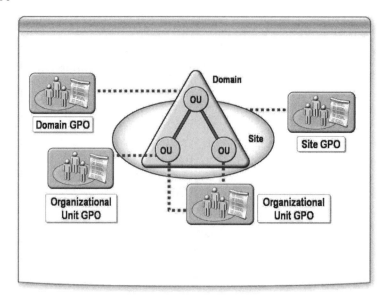

Introduction

All GPOs are stored in a container in Active Directory called Group Policy Objects. When a GPO is used by a site, domain, or organizational unit, the GPO is linked to the Group Policy Objects container. As a result, you can centrally administer and deploy the GPOs to many domains or organizational units.

Creating a linked GPO

When you create a GPO linked to a site, domain, or organizational unit, you actually perform two separate operations: creating the new GPO, and then linking it to the site, domain, or organizational unit. When delegating permissions to link a GPO to a domain, organizational unit, or site, you must have Modify permission for the domain, organizational unit, or site that you want to delegate.

By default, only members of the Domain Admins and Enterprise Admins groups have the necessary permissions to link GPOs to domains and organizational units. Only members of the Enterprise Admins group have the permissions to link GPOs to sites. Members of the Group Policy Creator Owners group can create GPOs but cannot link them.

Creating an unlinked GPO

When you create a GPO in the Group Policy Objects container, the GPO is not deployed to any users or computers until a GPO link is created. You can create an unlinked GPO by using Group Policy Management. You might create unlinked GPOs in a large organization where one group creates GPOs, and another group links the GPOs to the required site, domain, or organizational unit.

How to Create a GPO Link

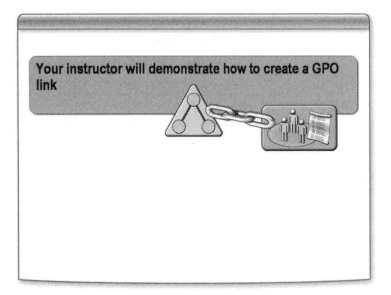

Introduction

Use the following procedures to create and link GPOs, link existing GPOs, unlink a GPO, delete a GPO link, delete a GPO, and disable a GPO.

Procedure for creating and linking a GPO

To link a GPO when you create it:

1. In Group Policy Management, in the console tree, expand the forest containing the domain in which you want to create and link a GPO, expand **Domains**, and then do one of the following:

   - To create a GPO and link it to a domain, right-click the domain, and then click **Create and Link a GPO Here**.

   - To create a GPO and link it to an organizational unit, expand the domain containing the organizational unit, right-click the organizational unit, and then click **Create and Link a GPO Here**.

2. In the **New GPO** dialog box, type a name for the new GPO, and then click **OK**.

Procedure for linking an existing GPO

To link an existing GPO to a site, domain, or organizational unit:

1. In Group Policy Management, in the console tree, expand the forest containing the domain in which you want to link an existing GPO, expand **Domains**, and then expand the domain.

2. Right-click the domain, site, or organizational unit, and then click **Link an Existing GPO**.

3. In the **Select GPO** dialog box, click the GPO that you want to link, and then click **OK**.

Important You cannot link a GPO to containers in Active Directory like the Users and Computers containers. However, any GPO linked to the domain applies to users and computers in these containers.

Procedure for unlinking a GPO

To unlink a GPO from a site, domain, or organizational unit:

1. In Group Policy Management, in the console tree, expand the forest containing the domain from which you want to unlink an existing GPO, expand **Domains**, and then expand the domain.

2. Right-click a linked GPO, and then clear the **Link Enabled** option.

Note Unlinking a GPO and deleting a GPO have the same effect. However, if you want to temporarily remove the GPO, you unlink it, which disables it. If you want to completely remove the GPO, then delete the link.

Procedure for deleting a GPO link

To delete a GPO link to a site, domain, or organizational unit:

1. In Group Policy Management, in the console tree, expand the forest containing the domain in which you want to delete an existing GPO link, expand **Domains**, and then expand the domain.

2. Right-click a linked GPO, and then click **Delete**.

   This deletes only the GPO link and not the GPO.

3. In the message box, click **OK**.

Procedure for deleting a GPO

To delete a GPO:

1. In Group Policy Management, in the console tree, expand the forest containing the domain in which you want to delete a GPO, expand **Domains**, expand the domain, and then expand **Group Policy Objects**.

2. Right-click the GPO that you want to delete, and then click **Delete**.

   This does not delete the link to the GPO from other domains.

3. In the message box, click **OK**.

Procedure for disabling a GPO

To disable a GPO:

1. In Group Policy Management, in the console tree, expand the forest containing the domain in which you want to disable a GPO, expand **Domains**, expand the domain, and then expand **Group Policy Objects**.

2. Click the GPO that you want to disable.

3. In the details pane, on the **Details** tab, in the **GPO status** box, click one of the following:

   - **All settings disabled**

   - **Computer configuration settings disabled**

   - **Users configuration settings disabled**

How Group Policy Permission Is Inherited in Active Directory

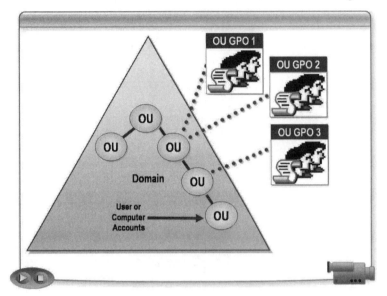

Introduction	The order in which Windows Server 2003 applies GPOs depends on the Active Directory container to which the GPOs are linked. The GPOs are applied first to the site, then to domains, and then to organizational units in the domains.
Flow of inheritance	A child container inherits GPOs from the parent container. This means that the child container can have many Group Policy settings applied to its users and computers without having a GPO linked to it. However, there is no hierarchy of domains like there is for organizational units, such as parent organizational units and child organizational units.
Order of inheritance	GPOs are cumulative, meaning that they are inherited. Group Policy inheritance is the order in which Windows Server 2003 applies GPOs. The order in which GPOs are applied and how GPOs are inherited ultimately determines which settings affect users and computers. If there are multiple GPOs that are set at the same value, by default the GPO applied last takes precedence.
	You can also have multiple GPOs linked to the same containers. For example, you can have three GPOs linked to a single domain. Because the order in which the GPOs are applied may affect the resultant Group Policy settings, there is also an order, or priority of Group Policy settings, of GPOs for each container.
Multimedia activity	The *Implementing Group Policy* activity includes multiple choice and drag-and-drop exercises that test your knowledge. To start the activity, open the Web page on the Student Materials compact disc, click **Multimedia**, and then click **Implementing Group Policy**. Read the instructions, and then click the **Effects of Group Policy Settings** tab to begin the activity.

Practice: Creating a GPO Link

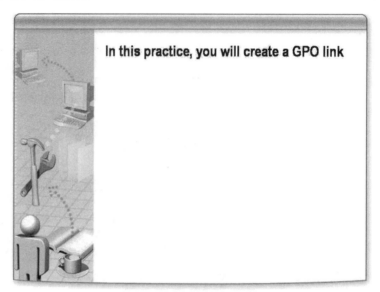

Objective

In this practice, you will create a GPO link.

Instructions

Before you begin this practice:

- Log on to the domain by using the *ComputerName*User account.
- Open CustomMMC with the **Run as** command.

  Use the user account Nwtraders*ComputerName*Admin (Example: LondonAdmin).

- Ensure that CustomMMC contains Group Policy Management and Active Directory Users and Computers.
- Review the procedures in this lesson that describe how to perform this task.

Scenario

The systems engineers at Northwind Traders are going test Group Policy settings in a test environment. These Group Policy settings will be used later for scalability testing. The systems engineers need your team of systems administrators to create GPOs for these tests.

Practice

▶ **Create an organizational unit in the IT Test organizational unit**

1. In Active Directory Users and Computers, expand **nwtraders.msft**, and then expand the **IT Test** organizational unit.

2. Create an organizational unit called *ComputerName*.

▶ **Create a GPO link to the IT Test/*ComputerName* organizational unit**

- In Group Policy Management, create a GPO called *ComputerName* **GP** and link it to the IT Test/*ComputerName* organizational unit.

Lesson: Managing the Deployment of Group Policy

- What Happens When GPOs Conflict
- Blocking the Deployment of a GPO
- How to Block the deployment of a GPO
- Attributes of a GPO Link
- How to Configure Group Policy Enforcement
- Filtering the Deployment of a GPO
- How to Configure Group Policy Filtering

Introduction

After completing this lesson, students will be able to manage the deployment of Group Policy.

Lesson objectives

After completing this lesson, you will be able to:

- Explain what happens when GPOs conflict.
- Explain what it means to block the deployment of a GPO.
- Block the deployment of a GPO.
- Describe attributes of a GPO link.
- Configure Group Policy enforcement.
- Explain what it means to filter the deployment of a GPO.
- Configure Group Policy filtering.

What Happens When GPOs Conflict

- **How conflicts are resolved**
  - When Group Policy settings in the Active Directory hierarchy conflict, the settings for the child container GPO apply
- **Options for modifying inheritance**
  - No Override
  - Block Policy inheritance

Introduction

Complex combinations of GPOs may create conflicts, which may require you to modify default inheritance behavior. When a Group Policy setting is configured for a parent organizational unit, and the same Group Policy setting is not configured for a child organizational unit, the objects in the child organizational unit inherit the Group Policy setting from the parent organizational unit.

How conflicts are resolved

When Group Policy settings are configured for both the parent organizational unit and the child organizational units, the settings for both organizational units apply. If the settings are incompatible, the child organizational unit retains its own Group Policy setting. For example, a Group Policy setting for the organizational unit that was last applied to the computer or user overwrites a conflicting Group Policy setting for a container that is higher up in the Active Directory hierarchy.

Options for modifying inheritance

If the default inheritance order does not meet your organization's needs, you can modify the inheritance rules for specific GPOs. Windows Server 2003 provides the following two options for changing the default inheritance order:

- **No Override**

  Use this option to prevent child containers from overriding a GPO with a higher priority setting. This option is useful for enforcing GPOs that represent organization-wide business rules. The **No Override** option is set on an individual GPO basis.

  You can set this option on one or more GPOs as required. When more than one GPO is set to **No Override**, the GPO set to **No Override** that is highest in the Active Directory hierarchy takes precedence.

- **Block Policy inheritance**

  Use this option to force a child container to block inheritance from all parent containers. This option is useful when an organizational unit requires unique Group Policy settings. **Block Policy inheritance** is set on a per-container basis. In the case of a conflict, the **No Override** option always takes precedence over the **Block Policy inheritance** option.

Blocking the Deployment of a GPO

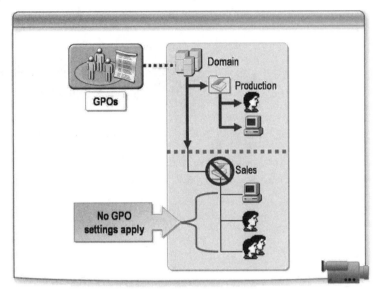

Introduction

You can prevent a child container from inheriting any GPOs from parent containers by enabling **Block Policy inheritance** on the child container.

Why use Block Policy inheritance?

Enabling **Block Policy inheritance** on a child container prevents the container from inheriting all Group Policy settings, not just selected Group Policy settings. This is useful when an Active Directory container requires unique Group Policy settings, and you want to ensure that Group Policy settings are not inherited. For example, you can use **Block Policy inheritance** when the administrator of an organizational unit must control all GPOs for that container.

Considerations

Consider the following when using **Block Policy inheritance**:

- You cannot selectively choose which GPOs are blocked. **Block Policy inheritance** affects all GPOs from all parent containers, except GPOs configured with the **No Override** option with out GPMC installed and **Enforced** with GPMC installed.

- **Block Policy inheritance** does not block the inheritance of a GPO linked to a parent container if the link is configured with the **No Override** option.

Multimedia activity

The *Implementing Group Policy* activity includes multiple choice and drag-and-drop exercises that test your knowledge. To start the activity, open the Web page on the Student Materials compact disc, click **Multimedia**, and then click **Implementing Group Policy**. Read the instructions, and then click the **Managing the Deployment of Group Policy** tab to begin the activity.

How to Block the Deployment of a GPO

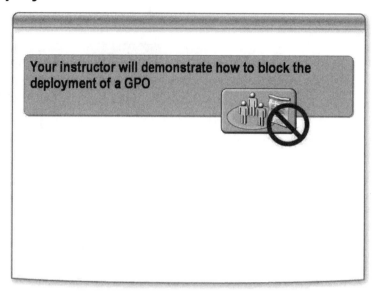

Introduction

Use the following procedure to enable **Block Policy inheritance**.

Procedure

To enable **Block Policy inheritance**:

1. In Group Policy Management, in the console tree, expand the forest in which you want to block inheritance, and then do one of the following:

   - To block inheritance of the GPO links for an entire domain, expand **Domains**, and then right-click the domain.

   - To block inheritance of the GPO links for an organizational unit, expand **Domains**, expand the domain containing the organizational unit, and then right-click the organizational unit.

2. Click **Block Inheritance**.

Attributes of a GPO Link

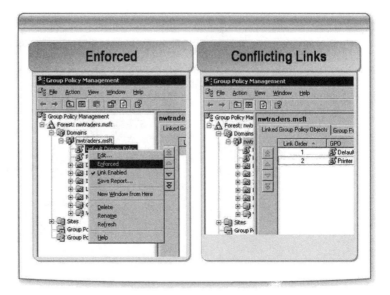

Introduction

You can enable, disable, enforce, and group GPO links. These options significantly affect the user and computers accounts in the organizational unit that the GPO is linked to.

The Enforced option

The **Enforced** option is an attribute of the GPO link, *not* the GPO itself. If you have a GPO that is linked to multiple containers, you configure the **Enforced** option on each individual container. Furthermore, if the same GPO is linked elsewhere, the **Enforced** option does not apply to that link unless you also modify that link.

All Group Policy settings contained in the GPO whose link is configured with **Enforced** apply, even if they conflict with Group Policy settings processed after them or if inheritance is blocked lower in the Active Directory tree. You should enable the **Enforced** option only for the links to the GPO that represents critical organization-wide rules. Link the GPO high in the Active Directory tree so that it affects multiple organizational units. For example, you will want to link a GPO with network security settings to a domain or site.

Important   The **Enforced** option is called **No Override** in Active Directory Users and Computers before Group Policy Management is installed.

Enabling and disabling a link

Link Enabled is another attribute that you may use when you are troubleshooting a GPO. You can disable the GPO link by clearing the **Link Enabled** option, instead of deleting the GPO link. By disabling the link, you only change the effect on the user and computer accounts in the organizational unit and all child organizational units. You do not affect other links to the GPO may have.

Conflicting links

When multiple GPOs are linked to an organizational unit, the GPO with the highest link order is applied last. If Group Policy settings in the GPO conflict, the last one applied takes precedence.

How to Configure Group Policy Enforcement

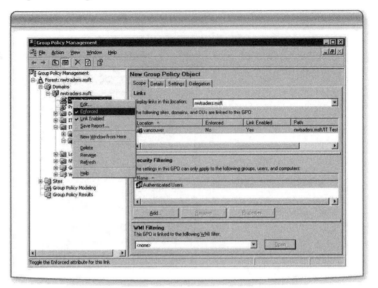

Introduction

Use the following procedure to configure the enforcement of a GPO link.

Procedure

To configure the enforcement of a GPO link:

1. In Group Policy Management, in the console tree, expand the forest with the link for which you want to configure enforcement, and then do one of the following:

   • To configure enforcement for a GPO link to a domain, expand **Domains**, and then expand the domain containing the GPO link.

   • To configure enforcement for a GPO link to an organizational unit, expand **Domains**, expand the domain containing the organizational unit, and then expand the organizational unit, which may include any parent or child organizational unit containing the GPO link.

   • To configure enforcement for a GPO link to a site, expand **Sites**, and then expand the site containing the GPO link.

2. Right-click the GPO link, and then click **Enforced** to enable or disable enforcement.

Note   Include only critical Group Policy settings in linked GPOs that are set to **Enforced**, because they take effect regardless of how other GPOs are configured. You want to be sure that you are not overriding important GPOs.

Filtering the Deployment of a GPO

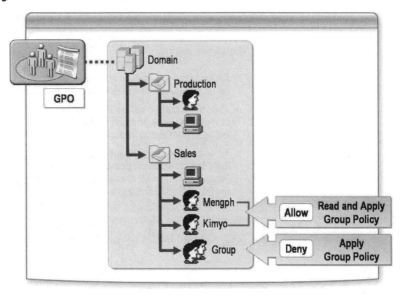

Introduction

By default, all Group Policy settings contained in the GPOs that affect the container are applied to all users and computers in that container, which may not produce the results that you desire. By using the filtering feature, you can determine which settings are applied to the users and computers in the specific container.

Permissions for GPOs

You can filter the deployment of a GPO by setting permissions on the GPO Link to determine the access of the read or deny permission on the GPO. For Group Policy settings to apply to a user or computer account, the account must have at least Read permission for a GPO. The default permissions for a new GPO have the following access control entries (ACEs):

■ Authenticated Users—Allow Read and Allow Apply Group Policy

■ Domain Admins, Enterprise Admins and SYSTEM—Allow Read, Allow Write, Allow Create All Child objects, Allow Delete All Child objects

Filtering methods

You can use the following filtering methods:

■ Explicitly deny

This method is used when denying access to the Group Policy. For example, you could explicitly deny permission to the administrators security group, which would prevent administrators in the organizational unit from receiving the GPO settings.

■ Remove Authenticated Users

You can omit the organizational unit administrators from the security group, which means that they have no explicit permissions for the GPO.

Class Discussion: Modifying Group Policy Inheritance

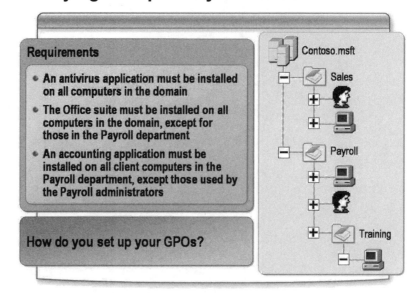

Class discussion

You have determined that the following conditions must exist in your network:

- An antivirus application must be installed on all computers in the domain.

- The Microsoft Office suite must be installed on computers in the domain, except those in the Payroll department.

- A line-of-business accounting application must be installed on all computers in the Payroll department, except those that are used by administrators of the Payroll organizational unit.

How do you set up GPOs so that the above conditions are met?

_____

_____

_____

_____

_____

How to Configure Group Policy Filtering

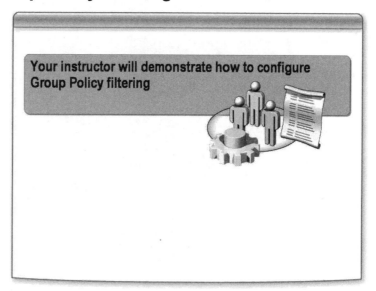

Your instructor will demonstrate how to configure Group Policy filtering

Introduction

Use the following procedure to configure Group Policy filtering.

Procedure

To filter the scope of a GPO by using security groups:

1. In Group Policy Management, in the console tree, expand the forest and domain with the GPO, expand **Group Policy objects**, and then click the GPO.

2. In the details pane, on the **Scope** tab, click **Add**.

3. In the **Select User, Computer, or Group** dialog box, in the **Enter the object name to select** box, enter the name of the security principal, and then click **OK**.

Practice: Managing the Deployment of Group Policy

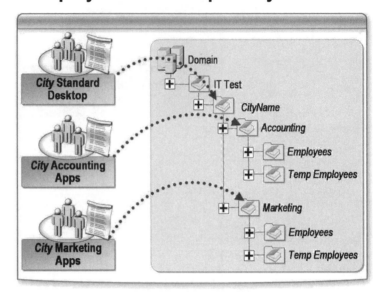

Objective	In this practice, you will manage the deployment of Group Policy.
Instructions	Before you begin this practice:

- Log on to the domain by using the *ComputerName*User account.

- Open CustomMMC with the **Run as** command.

  Use the user account Nwtraders*ComputerName*Admin (Example: LondonAdmin).

- Ensure that CustomMMC contains the following snap-ins:

  - Active Directory Users and Computers

  - Group Policy Management

- Review the procedures in this lesson that describe how to perform this task.

Scenario

Northwind Traders is testing the effect of multiple Group Policy settings on users and computers. Northwind Traders wants to implement an organizational unit that gives all users a standard desktop, except managers whose accounts are in the Employees organizational unit.

Management has asked the systems administrators team to create an organizational unit hierarchy in the IT Test organizational unit. The organizational unit hierarchy must contain an Accounting organizational unit and a Marketing organizational unit like in the diagram on the slide.

Management has also asked you to create a GPO to be used to install an Accounting and a separate Marketing application. The Accounting and Marketing applications are to be eventually installed to all Accounting and Marketing personnel; however, management wants to wait to deploy the application for the temporary employees. Management wants to maintain flexibility so when the temporary employees are ready for the applications, it can easily be enabled for them.

Practice

▶ **Create three GPOs for testing purposes**

- In Group Policy Management, create three GPOs in the Group Policy Objects container with the following names:

  - *ComputerName* Standard Desktop

  - *ComputerName* Accounting Apps

  - *ComputerName* Marketing Apps

▶ **Create an organizational unit structure that matches the slide**

- In Active Directory Users and Computers, create the organizational unit structure that appears on the slide.

▶ **Create an enforced GPO link**

1. Link the *ComputerName* Standard Desktop GPO to the IT Test/*ComputerName* organizational unit.

2. In the IT Test/*ComputerName* organizational unit, right-click the *ComputerName* **Standard Desktop** link, and click **Enforced**.

▶ **Configure a GPO security filter**

1. In Group Policy Management, in the **Group Policy Objects** container, double-click the *ComputerName* **Standard Desktop GPO** link.

2. In the details pane, on the **Scope** tab, add the following groups:

   - G NWTraders Accounting Managers

   - G NWTraders Accounting Personnel

   - G NWTraders Marketing Managers

   - G NWTraders Marketing Personnel

3. Remove Authenticated Users.

4. On the **Delegation** tab, click **Advanced**.

5. In the **Security Settings** dialog box, configure the following advanced security settings:

   - For the G NWTraders Accounting Managers group, set the Apply Group Policy permissions to Deny.

   - For the G NWTraders Marketing Managers group, set the Apply Group Policy permissions to Deny.

▶ **Configure GPOs to block inheritance**

1. Link the *ComputerName* Accounting Apps GPO to the IT
   Test/*ComputerName*/Accounting organizational unit.

2. Click the **Temp Employees** organizational unit in the IT
   Test/*ComputerName*/Accounting organizational unit.

3. List the GPOs that the IT Test/*ComputerName*/Accounting organizational
   unit inherits.

   _____

   _____

   _____

4. Right-click the **Temp Employees** organizational unit in the IT
   Test/*ComputerName*/Accounting organizational unit, and then click **Block
   Inheritance**.

5. List the GPOs that the IT Test/*ComputerName*/Accounting organizational
   unit inherits.

   _____

   _____

Lab A: Implementing Group Policy

- In this lab, you will:
  - Link a GPO to an organizational unit
  - Identify the effects of inheritance when multiple GPOs are assigned
  - Block Group Policy inheritance
  - Force a GPO to be applied to child organizational units
  - Filter a GPO so that it is applied to selected users and groups in an organizational unit

Objectives

After completing this lab, you will be able to:

- Link a GPO to an organizational unit.
- Identify the effects of inheritance when multiple GPOs are assigned.
- Block Group Policy inheritance.
- Force a GPO to be applied to child organizational units.
- Filter a GPO so that it is applied to selected users and groups in an organizational unit.

Instructions

Before you begin this lab:

- Log on to the domain by using the *ComputerName*User account.
- Open CustomMMC with the **Run as** command.

  Use the user account Nwtraders*ComputerName*Admin (Example: LondonAdmin).

- Ensure that CustomMMC contains the following snap-ins:
  - Active Directory Users and Computers
  - Group Policy Management

Estimated time to complete this lab: 25 minutes

Scenario

Northwind Traders is preparing to implement GPOs to the users and computers throughout all cities on their network. The systems engineers want the systems administrators team to create all the necessary GPOs and then link the GPOs to the appropriate organizational units. After the GPOs are created and deployed to the workstations, you must then configure the GPOs to perform the intended functions.

The systems administrators have provided you with a list of GPOs, along with their properties, that need to be created and configured. You should reuse GPOs that have already been created if you can. You also must make sure that no computer-related Group Policy settings affect laptops in your city, so you must block any GPOs from affecting the Laptops organizational unit.

GPO name	Location	Filtering	Enforcement
ComputerName Standard Desktop	Location/*ComputerName*	Default	Enforced
ComputerName Folder Redirection	Location/*ComputerName*/Users	DL Temp Employees = Deny	
ComputerName Scripts	Location/*ComputerName*/Users	Default	
ComputerName Proxy Settings	Location/*ComputerName*/Computers/ Desktops	Default	Enforced

Exercise 1
Creating and Linking GPOs

In this exercise, you will create and link GPOs to your *ComputerName* organizational unit.

Tasks	Detailed Steps
1. Link a Standard Desktop GPO.	a. Location: nwtraders.msft/Locations/*ComputerName* b. GPO Name: *ComputerName* **Standard Desktop**
2. Create and link a Folder Redirection GPO.	a. Location: nwtraders.msft/Locations/*ComputerName*/Users b. GPO Name: *ComputerName* **Folder Redirection**
3. Create and link a Scripts GPO.	a. Location: nwtraders.msft/Locations/*ComputerName*/Users b. GPO Name: *ComputerName* **Scripts**
4. Create and link a Proxy Settings GPO.	a. Location: nwtraders.msft/Locations/*ComputerName*/Computers/ Desktops b. GPO Name: *ComputerName* **Proxy Settings**

Exercise 2
Filtering the Deployment of a GPO

In this exercise, you will set Deny permissions for all temporary employees of Northwind Traders so that the *ComputerName* Folder Redirection GPO is not applied to them.

Tasks	Detailed Steps
1. Configure filtering of a GPO for a group.	a. Location: nwtraders.msft/Locations/*ComputerName*/Users
	b. GPO: *ComputerName* Folder Redirection
	c. Group: DL Temp Employees
	d. Permissions: Set the Apply Group Policy permission to Deny

Exercise 3
Configuring the Enforcement of GPOs

In this exercise, you will configure GPOs to be enforced throughout your organizational unit hierarchy.

Tasks	Detailed Steps
1. Set the **Enforced** option on a GPO link.	a. Location: nwtraders.msft/Locations/*ComputerName*. b. GPO: *ComputerName* Standard Desktop link c. Option: **Enforced**
2. Set the **Enforced** option on a GPO link.	a. Location: nwtraders.msft/Locations/*ComputerName*/Computers/ Desktops b. GPO: *ComputerName* Proxy Settings c. Option: **Enforced**

Exercise 4
Configuring the Blocking of GPOs

In this exercise, you will block inheritance of GPOs throughout your organizational unit hierarchy.

Tasks	Detailed Steps
1. Set the **Block Policy inheritance** option on an organizational unit.	a. Location: nwtraders.msft/Locations/*ComputerName*/Computers/ Laptops b. Option: **Block Policy inheritance**

Course Evaluation

Your evaluation of this course will help Microsoft understand the quality of your learning experience.

At a convenient time before the end of the course, please complete a course evaluation, which is available at http://www.CourseSurvey.com.

Microsoft will keep your evaluation strictly confidential and will use your responses to improve your future learning experience.

Microsoft®
Training &
Certification

Module 9: Managing the User Environment by Using Group Policy

Contents

Overview	1
Lesson: Configuring Group Policy Settings	2
Lesson: Assigning Scripts with Group Policy	11
Lesson: Configuring Folder Redirection	18
Lesson: Determining Applied GPOs	30
Lab A: Using Group Policies Reports	50

Overview

- Configuring Group Policy Settings
- Assigning Scripts with Group Policy
- Configuring Folder Redirection
- Determining Applied GPOs

Introduction

This module introduces the job function of managing the user environment by using Group Policy. Specifically, the module provides the skills and knowledge that you need to use Group Policy to configure Folder Redirection, Microsoft® Internet Explorer connectivity, and the desktop.

Objectives

After completing this module, you will be able to:

- Configure Group Policy settings.
- Assign scripts with Group Policy.
- Configure Folder Redirection.
- Determine Applied Group Policy objects (GPOs).

Lesson: Configuring Group Policy Settings

- Why Use Group Policy?
- What Are Disabled and Enabled Group Policy Settings?
- How to Edit a Group Policy Setting

Introduction

After completing this lesson, you will be able to configure Group Policy settings.

Lesson objectives

After completing this lesson, you will be able to:

- Explain why you use Group Policy.
- Explain what disabled and enabled Group Policy settings are.
- Edit a Group Policy setting.

Why Use Group Policy?

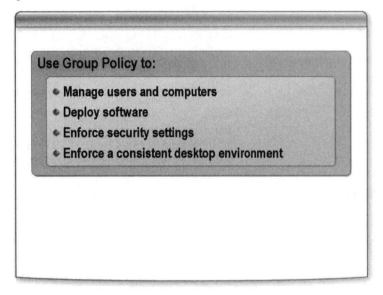

Use Group Policy to:

- Manage users and computers
- Deploy software
- Enforce security settings
- Enforce a consistent desktop environment

Introduction

Managing user environments means controlling what users can do when logged on to the network. You do this by controlling their desktops, network connections, and user interfaces through Group Policy. You manage user environments to ensure that users have what they need to perform their jobs, but that they cannot corrupt or incorrectly configure their environments.

Tasks you can perform with Group Policy

When you centrally configure and manage user environments, you can perform the following tasks:

- Manage users and computers

   By managing user desktop settings with registry-based policies, you ensure that users have the same computing environments even if they log on from different computers. You can control how Microsoft Windows® Server 2003 manages user profiles, which includes how a user's personal data is made available. By redirecting user folders from the user's local hard disks to a central location on a server, you can ensure that the user's data is available to them regardless of the computer they log on to.

- Deploy software

   Software is deployed to computers or users through the Active Directory® directory service. With software deployment, you can ensure that users have their required programs, service packs, and hotfixes.

- Enforce security settings

   By using Group Policy in Active Directory, the systems administrator can centrally apply the security settings required to protect the user environment. In Windows Server 2003, you can use the Security Settings extension in Group Policy to define the security settings for local and domain security policies.

- Enforce a consistent desktop environment

   Group Policy settings provide an efficient way to enforce standards, such as logon scripts and password settings. For example, you can prevent users from making changes to their desktops that may make their user environments more complex than necessary.

Additional reading

For more information about desktop management, see:

- "Windows 2000 Desktop Management Overview" at http://www.microsoft.com/windows2000/techinfo/howitworks/ management/ccmintro.asp.

- "Introduction to Windows 2000 Group Policy" at http://www.microsoft.com/windows2000/techinfo/howitworks/ management/grouppolicyintro.asp.

- The Group Policy newsgroup at http://www.microsoft.com/ windows2000/community/newsgroups/.

What Are Disabled and Enabled Group Policy Settings?

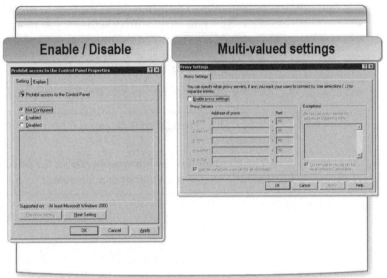

Disable a policy setting	If you disable a policy setting, you are disabling the action of the policy setting. For example, users by default can access Control Panel. You do not need to disable the policy setting **Prohibit access to the Control Panel** to allow a user to access Control Panel unless a previously applied policy setting enabled it. In this situation, you set another policy setting that disables the previously applied policy setting.
	This is helpful when you have inherited policy settings, and you do not want to use filtering to apply policy settings to one group and not to another group. You can apply a GPO that enables one policy setting on the parent organizational unit and another policy setting that disables the GPO on a child organizational unit.
Enable a policy setting	If you enable a policy setting, you are enabling the action of the policy setting. For example, to revoke someone's access to Control Panel, you enable the policy setting **Prohibit access to the Control Panel**.
Not Configured	A GPO holds the values that change the registry for users and computers that are subject to the GPO. The default configuration for a policy setting is **Not Configured**. If you want to set a computer or user policy setting back to the default value or back to the local policy, select the **Not Configured** option.
	For example, you may enable a policy setting for some clients, and when using the not Configured option, the policy will revert to the default, local policy setting.

Multi-valued policy settings

Some GPOs require you to provide some additional information after you enable the object. Sometimes you may need to select a group or computer if the policy setting needs to redirect the user to some information. Other times, as the slide shows, to enable proxy settings, you must provide the name or Internet Protocol (IP) address of the proxy server and the port number. If a policy setting is multi-valued and the settings are in conflict with another policy setting, the conflicting multi-valued settings are replaced with the last conflicting policy setting that was applied.

Note The **Settings** tab indicates the operating systems that support the policy setting.

The **Explain** tab has information about the effects of the **Enabled** and **Disabled** options on a user and computer account.

How to Edit a Group Policy Setting

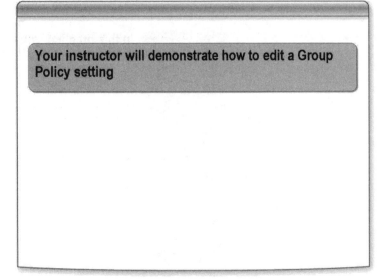

Your instructor will demonstrate how to edit a Group Policy setting

Introduction

As a systems administrator, you must edit Group Policy settings. Use the following procedure to perform this task.

Procedure

To edit Group Policy settings:

1. In Group Policy Management, in the console tree, navigate to **Group Policy Objects**.

2. Right-click a GPO, and then click **Edit**.

3. In Group Policy Object Editor, navigate to the Group Policy setting that you want to edit, and then double-click the setting.

4. In the **Properties** dialog box, configure the Group Policy setting, and then click **OK**.

Practice: Editing Group Policy Settings

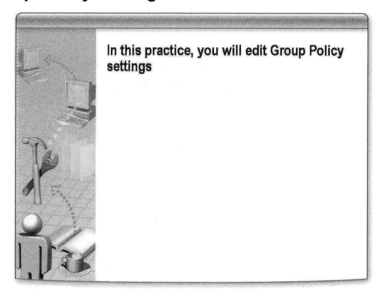

In this practice, you will edit Group Policy settings

Objective

In this practice, you will edit Group Policy settings.

Instructions

Before you begin this practice:

- Log on to the domain by using the *ComputerName*User account.

- Open CustomMMC with the **Run as** command.

  Use the user account Nwtraders*ComputerName*Admin (Example: LondonAdmin).

- Ensure that CustomMMC contains the following snap-ins:

  - Active Directory Users and Computers

  - Group Policy Management

- Review the procedures in this lesson that describe how to perform this task.

Scenario

Northwind Traders must implement the *ComputerName* Standard Desktop GPO. This GPO is linked to the IT Test/*ComputerName* organizational unit for the test environment and the Locations/*ComputerName* organizational unit for the production environment. You must disable the link for the production environment first. When that is done, Northwind Traders wants to implement the following Group Policy settings in the *ComputerName* Standard Desktop GPO:

- **Remove Run menu from the Start Menu**

- **Prohibit access to the Control Panel**

- **Hide My Network Places icon on desktop**

- **Remove Network Connections from Start Menu**

- **Remove "Map Network Drive" and "Disconnect Network Drive"**

Practice

▶ **Verify that the GPO links are configured**

- Verify that the *ComputerName* Standard Desktop GPO is linked to the Locations/*ComputerName* organizational unit.

▶ **Configure security filtering**

- Location: Locations/*ComputerName*
- GPO link: *ComputerName* Standard Desktop
- Security filtering:
  - Remove all security group filtering
  - Add the Everyone group

▶ **Disable a GPO link**

- Location: Locations/*ComputerName*
- GPO link: *ComputerName* Standard Desktop

▶ **Edit a GPO**

- GPO: *ComputerName* Standard Desktop

▶ **Remove Run from the Start menu**

- Location: User Configuration/Administrative Templates/Start Menu and Taskbar
- Group Policy setting: **Remove Run menu from Start Menu Properties**
- Option: **Enabled**

▶ **Disable access to Control Panel**

- Location: User Configuration/Administrative Templates/Control Panel
- Group Policy setting: **Prohibit access to the Control Panel**
- Option: **Enabled**

▶ **Hide My Network Places icon on desktop**

- Location: User Configuration/Administrative Templates/Desktop
- Group Policy setting: **Hide My Network Places icon on desktop**
- Option: **Enabled**

▶ **Remove Network Connections from the Start menu**

- Location: User Configuration/Administrative Templates/Start Menu and Taskbar
- Group Policy setting: **Remove Network Connections from Start Menu**
- Option: **Enabled**

▶ **Enable Remove "Map Network Drive" and "Disconnect Network Drive"**

- Location: User Configuration/Administrative Templates/ Windows Components/Windows Explorer

- Group Policy setting: **Remove "Map Network Drive" and "Disconnect Network Drive"**

- Option: **Enabled**

▶ **Enable a GPO link**   *Group Policy Management*

- Location: Locations/*ComputerName*

- GPO link: *ComputerName* Standard Desktop

▶ **Create a user account**   *Activate Directentive Directory*

1. Create a user account (if the user account does not already exist) with the following properties:

   - First name: *ComputerName*

   - Last name: **Test**

   - User logon name: *ComputerName***Test**

   - Password: **P@ssw0rd**

   - Organizational unit: Locations/*ComputerName*/User

2. Log off.

Log off then ▶ **Log on**

1. Log on as *ComputerName***Test** with a password of **P@ssw0rd**.

2. Verify that the following is true:

   - **Run** has been removed menu from the **Start** menu.

   - **Control Panel** has been removed from the **Start** menu.

   - The **My Network Places** icon is hidden on the desktop.

   - **Network Connections** has been removed from the **Start** menu.

   - **Map Network Drive** and **Disconnect Network Drive** have been removed from Windows Explorer.

3. Log off.

Lesson: Assigning Scripts with Group Policy

- What Are Group Policy Script Settings?
- How to Assign Scripts with Group Policy

Introduction

You can use Group Policy to deploy scripts to users and computers. A script is a batch file or a Microsoft Visual Basic® script that can execute code or perform management tasks. You can use Group Policy script settings to automate the process of running scripts.

There are script settings under both Computer Configuration and User Configuration in Group Policy. You can use Group Policy to run scripts when a computer starts and shuts down and when a user logs on and logs off. As with all Group Policy settings, you configure a Group Policy script setting once, and Windows Server 2003 continually implements and enforces it throughout your network.

Lesson objectives

After completing this lesson, you will be able to:

- Explain what Group Policy script settings are.
- Assign scripts with Group Policy.

What Are Group Policy Script Settings?

```
Set objNetwork = Wscript.CreateObject("WScript.Network")
objNetwork.MapNetworkDrive"G:", "\\ComputerName\ComputerName Data"
msgbox "Your Script worked!!!!!"
```

Introduction

You can use Group Policy script settings to centrally configure scripts to run automatically when the computer starts and shuts down and when users log on and log off. You can specify any script that runs in Windows Server 2003, including batch files, executable programs, and scripts supported by Windows Script Host (WSH).

Benefits of Group Policy script settings

To help you manage and configure user environments, you can:

- Run scripts that perform tasks that you cannot perform through other Group Policy settings. For example, you can populate user environments with network connections, printer connections, shortcuts to applications, and corporate documents.

- Clean up desktops when users log off and shut down computers. You can remove connections that you added with logon or startup scripts so that the computer is in the same state as when the user started the computer.

- Run pre-existing scripts already set up to manage user environments until you configure other Group Policy settings to replace these scripts.

Note From Active Directory Users and Computers, you can assign logon scripts individually to user accounts in the **Properties** dialog box for each user account. However, Group Policy is the preferred method for running scripts, because you can manage these scripts centrally, along with startup, shutdown, and logoff scripts.

Additional reading

For more information about scripting, see the TechNet Script Center at http://www.microsoft.com/technet/treeview/default.asp?url=/technet/scriptcenter/default.asp.

How to Assign Scripts with Group Policy

Your instructor will demonstrate how to assign scripts by using Group Policy

Introduction

To implement a script, you use Group Policy to add that script to the appropriate setting in the Group Policy template. This indicates that the script will run during startup, shutdown, logon, or logoff.

Procedure

To add a script to a GPO:

1. In Group Policy Management, edit a GPO.

2. In Group Policy Object Editor, in the console tree, navigate to User Configuration/Windows Settings/Scripts (Logon/Logoff).

3. In the details pane, double-click **Logon**.

4. In the **Logon Properties** dialog box, click **Add**.

5. In the **Add a Script** dialog box, configure any of the following settings that you want to use, and then click **OK**:

   - **Script Name**. Type the path to the script or click **Browse** to locate the script file in the Netlogon share of the domain controller.

   - **Script Parameters**. Type any parameters that you want to use in the same way that you type them on the command line.

6. In the **Logon Properties** dialog box, configure any of the following settings that you want to use:

- **Logon Scripts for**. This box lists all of the scripts that are currently assigned to the selected GPO. If you assign multiple scripts, the scripts are processed in the order that you specify. To move a script in the list, click the script, and then click either **Up** or **Down**.

- **Add**. Click **Add** to specify any additional scripts that you want to use.

- **Edit**. Click **Edit** to modify script information such as the name and parameters.

- **Remove**. Click **Remove** to remove the selected script from the **Logon Scripts** list.

- **Show Files**. Click **Show Files** to view the script files that are stored in the selected GPO.

Note Logon scripts are run in the context of the user account and not in the context of the administrator account.

Practice: Assigning Scripts with Group Policy

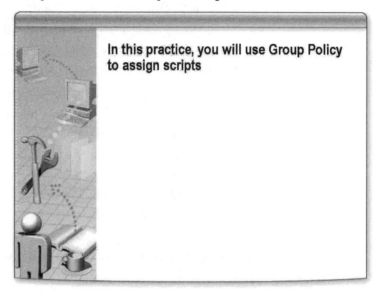

In this practice, you will use Group Policy to assign scripts

Objective

In this practice, you will use Group Policy to assign scripts.

Instructions

Before you begin this practice:

- Log on to the domain by using the *ComputerName*Admin account.

Note This practice focuses on the concepts in this lesson and as a result may not comply with Microsoft security recommendations. For example, this practice does not comply with the recommendation that users log on with domain user account and use the **Run as** command when performing administrative tasks. When using the Windows Explorer, you cannot use the **Run as** command.

- Open CustomMMC.
- Ensure that CustomMMC contains the following snap-ins:
  - Active Directory Users and Computers
  - Group Policy Management
- Review the procedures in this lesson that describe how to perform this task.

Scenario

Northwind Traders wants drive S on the computers of all personnel to be mapped to a shared folder called *ComputerName* Public on your member server. You must link a GPO named *ComputerName* Logon Scripts to the called IT Test/*ComputerName* organizational unit. You then must test the logon script.

Practice

▶ **Create a shared folder on your computer**

- Folder path: D:*ComputerName* Public

- Shared folder name: *ComputerName* **Public**

- Permissions: Grant Full Control permission to Administrators and grant Read and Write permissions to other users

▶ **Create and link a GPO**   /Group Policy Management   ···s

- Location: IT Test/*ComputerName*

- GPO name: **Group** *ComputerName* **Logon Script**

▶ **Edit a GPO**

- GPO: *ComputerName* Scripts

▶ **Configure a logon script Group Policy setting**

- Location: User Configuration/Windows Settings/Scripts

- Group Policy setting: Logon

- Options:

1. In the **Logon Properties** dialog box, click **Show Files**.

2. In Windows Explorer, on the **Tools** menu, click **Folder Options**.

3. In the **Folder Options** dialog box, on the **View** tab, under **Advanced settings**, clear the **Hide extensions for known file types** check box, and then click **OK**.

4. In Windows Explorer, on the **File** menu, point to **New**, and then click **Text Document**.

5. Change the name of the file called New Text Document.txt to **Logon.vbs**.

6. In the message box, click **Yes**.

7. Right-click **Logon.vbs**, and then click **Edit**.

8. On the **File Download** dialog box, click **Open**.

9. In Microsoft Notepad, type the following:

```
Set objNetwork = Wscript.CreateObject("WScript.Network")
objNetwork.MapNetworkDrive "S:","\\ComputerName\ComputerName Public"
msgbox "Your Script worked!!!!!"
```

10. On the **File** menu, click **Save**.

11. Close Notepad, and then close Windows Explorer.

12. In the **Logon Properties** dialog box, click **Add**.

13. In the **Add a Script** dialog box, click **Browse**.

14. In the **Browse** dialog box, click **logon.vbs**, and then click **Open**.

15. In the **Add a Script** dialog box, click **OK**.

16. In the **Logon Properties** dialog box, click **OK**.

17. Close all windows and log off.

▶ **Test the logon script**

1. Log on as *ComputerName***Test** with a password of **P@ssw0rd**.

2. In the **Your Script worked!!!!!** box, click **OK**.

3. Close all windows and log off.

▶ **Delete a GPO Link**

- Location: Locations/*ComputerName*

- GPO: *ComputerName* Standard Desktop

- Action: Delete the GPO Link

Lesson: Configuring Folder Redirection

- **What Is Folder Redirection?**
- **Folders That Can Be Redirected**
- **Settings Required to Configure Folder Redirection**
- **Security Considerations for Configuring Folder Redirection**
- **How to Configure Folder Redirection**

Introduction

Windows Server 2003 enables you to redirect folders that are part of the user profile from users' local hard disks to a central location on a server. By redirecting these folders, you can ensure that users' data is located in a central location and that users' data is available to them regardless of the computers to which they log on.

Folder Redirection makes it easier for you to manage and back up centralized data. The folders that you can redirect are My Documents, Application Data, Desktop, and Start Menu. Windows Server 2003 automatically creates these folders and makes them part of the user profile for each user account.

Lesson objectives

After completing this lesson, you will be able to:

- Explain what Folder Redirection is.
- Explain which folders can be redirected.
- Determine which settings are required to configure Folder Redirection.
- Explain security considerations for configuring Folder Redirection.
- Configure Folder Redirection.

What Is Folder Redirection?

- **Folder Redirection enables users and administrators to redirect the folders to a new location**
  - The new location can be a folder on the local computer or a shared folder on the network
  - Users can work with documents on a server as if the documents are located on the local drive

Introduction

When you redirect folders, you change the storage location of folders from the local hard disk on the user's computer to a shared folder on a network file server. After you redirect a folder to a file server, it still appears to the user as if it is stored on the local hard disk. You can redirect four folders that are part of the user profile: My Documents, Application Data, Desktop, and Start Menu.

Benefits of Folder Redirection

By storing data on the network, users benefit from increased availability and frequent backup of their data. Redirecting folders has the following benefits:

- The data in the folders is available to the user regardless of the client computer that the user logs on to.

- The data in the folders is centrally stored so that the files that they contain are easier to manage and back up.

- Files that are located in redirected folders, unlike files that are part of a roaming user profile, are not copied and saved on the computer that the user logs on to. This means that when a user logs on to a client computer, no storage space is used to store these files, and that data that might be confidential does not remain on a client computer.

- Data that is stored in a shared network folder can be backed up as part of routine system administration. This is safer because it requires no action on the part of the user.

- As an administrator, you can use Group Policy to set disk quotas, limiting the amount of space that is taken by users' special folders.

- Data specific to a user can be redirected to a different hard disk on the user's local computer rather than to the hard disk holding the operating system files. This protects the user's data if the operating system must be reinstalled.

Folders That Can Be Redirected

- • My Documents
- • Application Data
- • Desktop
- • Start Menu

Introduction

You can redirect the My Documents, Application Data, Desktop, and Start Menu folders. An organization should redirect these folders to preserve important user data and settings. There are several advantages to redirecting each of these folders. The advantages vary according to your organization's needs.

Redirected folders

You can use Folder Redirection to redirect any of the following folders in a user profile:

- ■ My Documents

  Redirecting My Documents is particularly advantageous because the folder tends to become large over time.

  Offline Files technology gives users access to My Documents even when the users are not connected to the network. This is particularly useful for people who use portable computers.

- ■ Application Data

  A Group Policy setting controls the behavior of Application Data when client-side caching is enabled. This setting synchronizes application data that is centralized on a server with the local computer. As a result, the user can work online or offline. If any changes are made to the application data, synchronization updates the application data on the client and server.

- ■ Desktop

  You can redirect Desktop and all the files, shortcuts, and folders to a centralized server.

- ■ Start Menu

  When you redirect Start Menu, its subfolders are also redirected.

Settings Required to Configure Folder Redirection

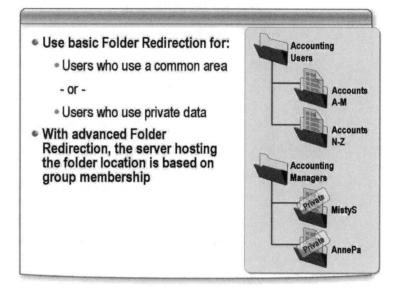

* **Use basic Folder Redirection for:**
    * Users who use a common area
    * or -
    * Users who use private data
* **With advanced Folder Redirection, the server hosting the folder location is based on group membership**

Introduction

There are three available settings for Folder Redirection: none, basic, and advanced. Basic Folder Redirection is for users who must redirect their folders to a common area or users that need their data to be private.

Basic Folder Redirection

You have the following basic options for Folder Redirection:

- **Redirect folder to the following location**

    All users who redirect their folders to a common area can see or use each other's data in the redirected folder. To do this, choose a **Basic** setting and set **Target folder location** to **Redirect folder to the following location**. Use this option for all redirected folders that contain data that is not private. An example of this is redirecting My Documents for a team of Accounts Receivable personnel who all share the same data.

- **Create a folder for each user under the root path**

    For users who need their redirected folders to be private, choose a **Basic** setting and set **Target folder location** to **Create a folder for each user under the root path**. Use this option for users who need their data to be private, like managers who keep personal data about employees.

Advanced Folder Redirection

When you select **Advanced – specify locations for various user groups**, folders are redirected to different locations based on the security group membership of the users.

You have the following advanced options for Folder Redirection:

- **Select a group(s)**. This is where you specify who you want to deploy redirection to.

- **Target Folder Location**. You can choose any of the following options:

  - **Create a folder for each user under the root path**. Use this for private data.

  - **Redirect to the following location**. Use this for shared data.

  - **Redirect to the local userprofile location**. Use this for users who use a mixture of legacy client computers that are not Active Directory enabled and computers that are Active Directory enabled.

- **Root Path**. In this box, specify the server and shared folder name that you want to redirect the folders to.

Security Considerations for Configuring Folder Redirection

- NTFS permissions for folder redirection root folder
- Shared folder permissions for folder redirection root folder
- NTFS permissions for each user's redirected folder

Introduction

Folder Redirection can create folders for you, which is the recommended option. When you use this option, the correct permissions are set automatically. Usually, you do need to know what the permissions are. However, if you manually create folders, you will need to know what the permissions are. The following tables show which permissions to set for Folder Redirection.

Note Although it is not recommended, administrators can create the redirected folders before Folder Redirection creates them.

NTFS permissions required for the root folder

Set the following NTFS permissions for the root folder.

User account	Folder Redirection defaults	Minimum permissions needed
Creator/owner	Full Control, this folder, subfolders, and files	Full Control, this folder, subfolders, and files
Administrators	No permissions	No permissions
Everyone	No permissions	No permissions
Local System	Full Control, this folder, subfolders, and files	Full Control, this folder, subfolders, and files
Security group of users who need to put data on the shared network server	N/A	List Folder/Read Data, Create Folders/Append Data - This folder only

Shared folder permissions required for the root folder

Set the following shared folder permissions for the root folder.

User account	Folder Redirection defaults	Minimum permissions needed
Everyone	Full Control	No permissions (use security group)
Security group of users who need to put data on the shared network server	N/A	Full Control

NTFS permissions required for each user's redirected folder

Set the following NTFS permissions for each user's redirected folder.

User account	Folder Redirection defaults	Minimum permissions needed
UserName	Full Control, owner of folder	Full Control, owner of folder
Local System	Full Control	Full Control
Administrators	No permissions	No permissions
Everyone	No permissions	No permissions

Note When offline folders are synchronized over the network, the data is transmitted in plain text format. The data is then susceptible to interception by network monitoring tools.

Additional reading

For more information about Folder Redirection, see "Best practices for Folder Redirection," at http://www.microsoft.com/technet/treeview/default.asp?url=/ technet/prodtechnol/windowsserver2003/proddocs/server/ sag_sp_bestprac_foldred.asp

How to Configure Folder Redirection

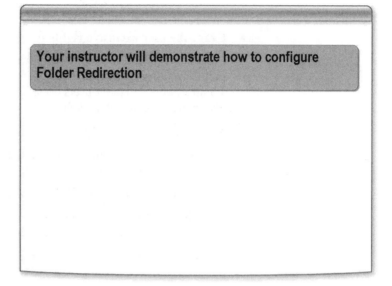

Your instructor will demonstrate how to configure Folder Redirection

Introduction

You configure Folder Redirection settings by using Group Policy Object Editor.

Procedure

To configure Folder Redirection:

1. In Group Policy Management, edit or create a GPO.

2. In Group Policy Object Editor, in the console tree, expand **User Configuration**, expand **Windows Settings**, and then expand **Folder Redirection**.

   Icons for the four folders that can be redirected are displayed.

3. Right-click the folder that you want to redirect, and then click **Properties**.

4. In the **Properties** dialog box, in the **Setting** tab, click one of the following options:

   - **Basic - Redirect everyone's folder to the same network share point.**

     All folders affected by this GPO are stored in the same shared network folder.

   - **Advanced - Redirect personal folders based on the user's membership in a Windows Server 2003 security group.**

     Folders are redirected to different shared network folders based on security group membership. For example, folders belonging to users in the Accounting group are redirected to the Accounting server, and folders belonging to users in the Marketing group are redirected to the Marketing server.

5. In the **Properties** dialog box, Click **Add**.

6. Under **Target folder location**, in the **Root path** box, type the name of the shared network folder to use, or click **Browse** to locate it.

7. On the **Settings** tab, configure the options you want to use, and then click **OK**.

The following options for settings are available:

- **Grant the user exclusive rights to My Documents.**

  Sets the NTFS security descriptor for the usernames unique folder to Full Control for the user and local system *only*. This means that administrators and other users do *not* have access rights to the folder. This option is enabled by default.

- **Move the contents of My Documents to the new location.**

  Moves any document the user has in the local My Documents folder to the shared network folder. This option is enabled by default.

- **Leave the folder in the new location when policy is removed.**

  Specifies that files remain in the new location if the GPO no longer applies. This option is enabled by default.

- **Redirect the folder back to the local user profile location when policy is removed.**

  Specifies that the folder is moved back to the local profile location if the GPO no longer applies.

The **My Documents Properties** dialog box has the following additional options for the My Pictures folder:

- **Make My Pictures a subfolder of My Documents.**

  When the My Documents folder is redirected, My Pictures remains as a subfolder of My Documents. This option is enabled by default.

- **Do not specify administrative policy for My Pictures.**

  Group Policy does not control the location of My Pictures. The location of My Pictures is determined by the user profile.

Note You should allow the operating system to create the directory and security for Folder Redirection. Do not manually create the directory defined by username. Folder Redirection sets the appropriate permissions on the folder. If you choose to manually create folders for each user, be sure to set the permissions correctly.

Practice: Configuring Folder Redirection

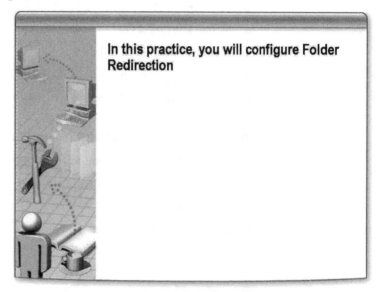

In this practice, you will configure Folder Redirection

Objective

In this practice, you will configure Folder Redirection.

Instructions

Before you begin this practice:

- Log on to the domain by using the *ComputerName*User account.
- Open CustomMMC with the **Run as** command.

  Use the user account Nwtraders*ComputerName*Admin (Example: LondonAdmin).

- Ensure that CustomMMC contains the following snap-ins:

  - Active Directory Users and Computers

  - Group Policy Management

  - Computer Management (Local)

- Review the procedures in this lesson that describe how to perform this task.

Scenario

Northwind Traders is setting up a test environment to test Folder Redirection of the My Documents folder for each city in Northwind Traders. You must create a folder called D:\\UserDataTest and share it as UserDataTest$ on your *ComputerName* server.   *[handwritten: $ means Hidden]*

You also must create a GPO, linked to the IT Test/*ComputerName* organizational unit, called *ComputerName* Folder Redirection Test. This GPO should redirect the My Documents folder to *ComputerName*\\UserDataTest$. Do not give users exclusive rights to the redirected folder so that administrators can see if documents are added to it.

Practice

▶ **Create a shared folder**   *Explorer*

- Folder path: D:\
- Name: **UserDataTest**
- Share name: **UserDataTest$**
- Shared folder permissions: Authenticated Users = Full Control
- NTFS permissions: Default

▶ **Create a user account for the test (If one does not already exist)**

- Organizational unit: Locations/*ComputerName*
- First name: *ComputerName*   *Activate Directory Users/Admins*
- Last name: **Test**
- User logon name: *ComputerName***Test**
- Password: **P@ssw0rd**

▶ **Link a GPO**   *Group Policy Management*

- Organizational unit: Locations/*ComputerName*
- GPO name: *ComputerName* **Folder Redirection**
- Security filtering: Authenticated Users

▶ **Edit a GPO**

- GPO: *ComputerName* Folder Redirection

▶ **Configure Folder Redirection**

- Location: /User Configuration/Windows Settings/Folder Redirection
- Group Policy setting: My Documents
- Options:
  - Target folder setting: **Basic – Redirect everyone's folder to the same location**
  - Target folder location: **Create a folder for each user under the root path**
  - Root path: *ComputerName*\UserDataTest$
  - Redirect settings: Clear the **Grant the user exclusive rights to My Documents** check box
  - Policy Removal: **Redirect the folder back to the local userprofile location when policy is removed**
  - My Pictures Preferences: **Make My Pictures a subfolder of My Documents**

▶ **Test the Folder Redirection of My Documents**

1. Log off.

2. Log on as *ComputerName***Test** with a password of **P@ssw0rd**.

3. In the message box, click **OK**.

4. Click **Start**.

5. Right-click **My Documents**, and then click **Properties**.

6. In the **My Document Properties** dialog box, verify that the following is in the **Target** box:

   *ComputerName***userdatatest$***ComputerName*test**My Documents**

7. Click **OK**.

8. Click **Start**, and then click **My Documents**.

9. In My Documents, on the **File** menu, point to **New**, and then click **Text Document**.

10. Close all windows and log off.

▶ **Test the permissions of redirected folders**

1. Log on as *ComputerName***Admin** with a password of **P@ssw0rd**.

2. Go to: **D:\UserDataTest**.

3. In D:\UserDataTest*ComputerName*Test, double-click *ComputerName***Test's Documents**.

4. In D:\UserDataTest*ComputerName*Test*ComputerName*Test's Documents, verify that the file called New Text Document.txt was created.

5. Close all windows and log off.

Lesson: Determining Applied GPOs

- What Is Gpupdate?
- What Is Gpresult?
- What Is Group Policy Reporting?
- How to Use Group Policy Reporting
- What Is Group Policy Modeling?
- How to Use Group Policy Modeling
- What Is Group Policy Results?
- How to Use Group Policy Results

Introduction

Group Policy is the primary administrative tool for defining and controlling how programs, network resources, and the operating system operate for users and computers in an organization. In an Active Directory environment, Group Policy is applied to users or computers on the basis of their membership in sites, domains, or organizational units.

Lesson objectives

After completing this lesson, you will be able to:

- Explain what **gpupdate** is.
- Explain what **gpresult** is.
- Explain what is group policy reporting.
- Use group policy reporting.
- Explain what is group policy modeling.
- Use group policy modeling.
- Explain what is group policy results.
- Use group policy results.

What Is Gpupdate?

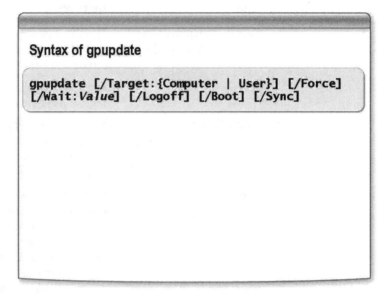

Syntax of gpupdate

```
gpupdate [/Target:{Computer | User}] [/Force]
[/Wait:Value] [/Logoff] [/Boot] [/Sync]
```

Introduction

Gpupdate is a command-line tool that refreshes local Group Policy settings and Group Policy settings that are stored in Active Directory, including security settings. By default, security settings are refreshed every 90 minutes on a workstation or server and every five minutes on a domain controller. You can run **gpupdate** to test a Group Policy setting or to force a Group Policy setting.

Examples of gpupdate

The following examples show how you can use the **gpupdate** command:

- C:\gpupdate

- C:\gpupdate /target:computer

- C:\gpupdate /force /wait:100

- C:\gpupdate /boot

Parameters of gpupdate

Gpupdate has the following parameters.

Value	Description
/Target:{**Computer** | **User**}	Specifies that only user or only computer policy settings are refreshed. By default, both user and computer policy settings are refreshed.
/Force	Reapplies all policy settings. By default, only policy settings that have changed are reapplied.
/Wait:{*Value*}	Sets the number of seconds to wait for policy processing to finish. The default is 600 seconds. The value '0' means not to wait. The value '-1' means to wait indefinitely.
/Logoff	Causes a logoff after the Group Policy settings are refreshed. This is required for those Group Policy client-side extensions that do not process policy settings during a background refresh cycle but do process policy settings when a user logs on. Examples include user-targeted Software Installation and Folder Redirection. This option has no effect if there are no extensions called that require a logoff.
/Boot	Causes the computer to restart after the Group Policy settings are refreshed. This is required for those Group Policy client-side extensions that do not process policy during a background refresh cycle but do process policy when the computer starts. Examples include computer-targeted Software Installation. This option has no effect if there are no extensions called that require the computer to restart.
/Sync	Causes the next foreground policy setting to be applied synchronously. Foreground policy settings are applied when the computer starts and when the user logs on. You can specify this for the user, computer, or both by using the **/Target** parameter. The **/Force** and **/Wait** parameters are ignored.

What Is Gpresult?

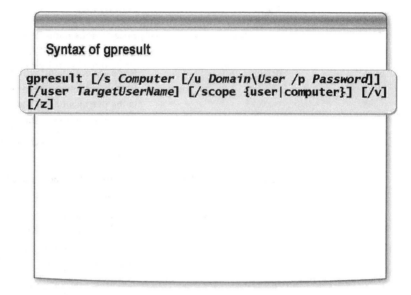

Syntax of gpresult

```
gpresult [/s Computer [/u Domain\User /p Password]]
[/user TargetUserName] [/scope {user|computer}] [/v]
[/z]
```

Introduction

Because you can apply overlapping levels of policy settings to any computer or user, Group Policy generates a resulting set of policies at logon. **Gpresult** displays the resulting set of policies that are enforced on the computer for the specified user at logon.

The **gpresult** command displays Group Policy settings and Resultant Set of Policy (RSoP) data for a user or a computer. You can use **gpresult** to see what policy setting is in effect and to troubleshoot problems.

Examples of gpresult

The following examples show how you can use the **gpresult** command:

- C:\gpresult /user targetusername /scope computer

- C:\gpresult /s srvmain /u maindom/hiropln /p p@ssW23 /user targetusername /scope USER

- C:\gpresult /s srvmain /u maindom/hiropln /p p@ssW23 /user targetusername /z >policy.txt

- C:\gpresult /s srvmain /u maindom/hiropln /p p@ssW23

Parameters of gpresult

Gpresult has the following parameters.

Value	Description
/s *Computer*	Specifies the name or IP address of a remote computer. Do not use backslashes. The default is the local computer.
/u *Domain/User*	Runs the command with the account permissions of the user that is specified by *User* or *Domain/User*. The default is the permissions of the user who is currently logged on to the computer that issues the command.
/p *Password*	Specifies the password of the user account that is specified in the /u parameter.
/user *TargetUserName*	Specifies the user name of the user whose RSoP data is to be displayed.
/scope {user|computer}	Displays either user or computer policy settings. Valid values for the /scope parameter are **user** or **computer**. If you omit the /scope parameter, **gpresult** displays both user and computer policy settings.
/v	Specifies that the output will display verbose policy information.
/z	Specifies that the output will display all available information about Group Policy. Because this parameter produces more information than the /v parameter, redirect output to a text file when you use this parameter (for example, you can type **gpresult /z >policy.txt**).
/?	Displays help in the command prompt window.

Practice: Using Gpupdate and Gpresult

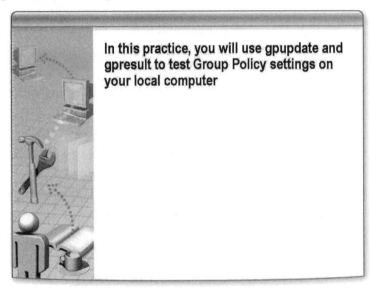

In this practice, you will use gpupdate and gpresult to test Group Policy settings on your local computer

Objective

In this practice, you will use **gpupdate** and **gpresult** to test policy settings on your local computer.

Instructions

Before you begin this practice:

- Log on to the domain by using the *ComputerName*User account.
- Open CustomMMC with the **Run as** command.

  Use the user account Nwtraders*ComputerName*Admin (example: LondonAdmin).

- Ensure that CustomMMC contains Group Policy Management.
- Open a command prompt with the Run as command.

  From Run type **runas /user:nwtraders***ComputerName***Admin cmd** and click **OK**. When prompted for a password type **P@ssw0rd**, and press **ENTER**.

- Ensure that you have a user account created named *ComputerName*Test.
- Review the procedures in this lesson that describe how to perform this task.

Scenario

You are testing some Group Policy settings on your local computer. You do not want to wait for the refresh interval to see the Group Policy update, so you must run the **gpupdate** command.

Gpupdate with no switches

▶ **Use gpupdate with no switches**

- From a command prompt, type **gpupdate**

▶ **Use gpupdate with the /force switch**

- From a command prompt, type **gpupdate /force**. If prompted to logoff, type **N** and press **ENTER**.

Scenario

You must use **gpresult** to see which Group Policy settings are in effect on your server so that you can help troubleshoot remote computers.

Gpresult with no switches

▶ **Use gpresult with no switches**

1. From a command prompt, type **gpresult**

2. Scroll up the command prompt window to see the results of the Group Policy settings that have been applied to your computer.

▶ **Use gpresult with the /scope switch**

1. From a command prompt, type **gpresult /scope computer**

2. Scroll up the command prompt window to see the results of the Group Policy settings that have been applied to your computer.

3. From a command prompt, type **gpresult /scope user**

4. Scroll up the command prompt window to see the results of the Group Policy settings that have been applied to your computer.

▶ **Send the gpresult data to a text file with the /z switch**

1. From a command prompt, type **gpresult /z >gp.txt**

2. From a command prompt, type **notepad gp.txt**

3. In Notepad, scroll through the results, and then close Notepad.

Scenario

Your boss wants you to test a Group Policy setting. The Group Policy setting removes the **Search** option from the **Start** menu and only affects your local computer. When you are done, your boss needs a report to see that the changes were applied correctly.

Testing group policy settings

▶ **Log on as *ComputerName*Test and run CustomMMC**

1. Log on as *ComputerName*Test with a password of **P@ssw0rd**.

2. Open C:\MOC\CustomMMC with the **Run as** command by using the user account nwtraders*ComputerName*Admin.

3. Type your password, and then click **OK**.

▶ **Create and link a GPO**

- Location: Locations/*ComputerName*

- GPO name: *ComputerName* **gpresult**

▶ **Edit a GPO**

- GPO: *ComputerName* gpresult

▶ **Remove Search menu from Start Menu Properties**

- Location: User Configuration/Administrative Templates/Start Menu and Taskbar

- Group Policy setting: **Remove Search menu from Start Menu Properties**

- Option: **Enabled**

▶ **Test to see if the Group Policy setting has been applied**

1. From a command prompt, type **gpresult /z >1.txt**

2. From a command prompt, type **notepad 1.txt**

3. In Notepad, on the **Edit** menu, click **Find**.

4. In the **Find** dialog box, in the **Find what** box, type *ComputerName* **gpresult** and then click **Find Now**.

5. In Notepad, verify that the message says **Cannot find "***ComputerName* **gpresult"** and then click **OK**.

6. In the **Find** dialog box, click **Cancel**, and then close Notepad.

7. From a command prompt, type **gpupdate**

▶ **Test again to see if the Group Policy setting has been applied**

1. From a command prompt, type **gpresult /z >2.txt**

2. From a command prompt, type **notepad 2.txt**

3. In Notepad, on the **Edit** menu, click **Find**.

4. In the **Find** dialog box, in the **Find what** box, type *ComputerName* **gpresult** and then click **Find Now**.

5. In Notepad, verify that *ComputerName* **gpresult** is highlighted under **Applied Group Policy Object**.

6. In the **Find** dialog box, click **Find Next**.

7. In Notepad, verify that *ComputerName* **gpresult** is highlighted under **Administrative Templates**.

8. In the **Find** dialog box, click **Cancel**, and then close Notepad.

9. Close all windows and log off.

What Is Group Policy Reporting?

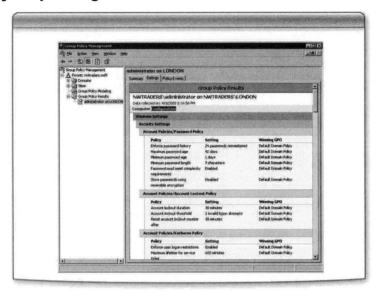

Definition	A systems administrator can make hundreds of changes to a GPO. To verify changes made to a GPO without actually opening the GPO and expanding every folder, you can generate a Hypertext Markup Language (HTML) report that lists the items in the GPO that are configured.
Settings tab	The **Settings** tab of the details pane for a GPO or GPO link in Group Policy Management shows an HTML report that displays all the defined settings in the GPO. Any user with read access to the GPO can generate this report. If you click **show all** at the top of the report, the report is fully expanded, and all settings are shown. Also, using a context menu, you can print the reports or save them to a file as either HTML or Extensible Markup Language (XML).

How to Use Group Policy Reporting

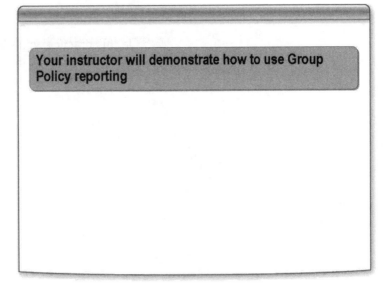

Your instructor will demonstrate how to use Group Policy reporting

Introduction

Use the following procedure to determine applied Group Policy settings by using Group Policy reporting.

Procedure

To use Group Policy reporting:

1. In Group Policy Management, in the console tree, click the GPO that you want to generate a report for.

   You must expand the forest, domain, and domain name to locate the GPO that you want to generate a report for.

2. In the details pane, click the **Settings** tab.

Practice: Using Group Policy Reporting

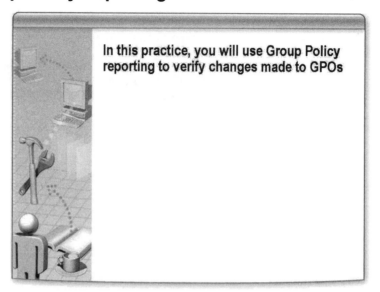

Objective

In this practice, you will use Group Policy reporting to verify changes made to GPOs.

Instructions

Before you begin this practice:

- Log on to the domain by using the *ComputerName*User account.
- Open CustomMMC with the **Run as** command.

  Use the user account Nwtraders*ComputerName*Admin (example: LondonAdmin).
- Ensure that CustomMMC contains Group Policy Management.
- Review the procedures in this lesson that describe how to perform this task.

Scenario

You have been asked to document the Group Policy settings for the Default Domain Policy GPO.

Practice

▶ **View the report for Default Domain Policy**

1. In Group Policy Management, in the console tree, expand **Group Policy Objects**.
2. Click **Default Domain Policy**.
3. In the details pane, click the **Settings** tab.
4. From the **Internet Explorer** box, click **Close**.
5. Review the Group Policy settings for Default Domain Policy.
6. Right-click anywhere in the report, and then click **Save Report**.
7. In the **Save GPO Report** dialog box, click **Save**.

What Is Group Policy Modeling?

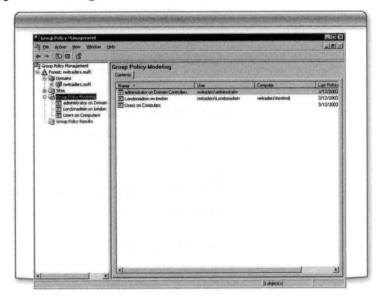

Introduction

Windows Server 2003 enables you to simulate a GPO deployment that is applied to users and computers before you actually deploy the GPO. The simulation creates a report that takes into account the user's organizational unit, the computer's organizational unit, and any group membership or Windows Management Instrumentation (WMI) filtering. It also takes into account any Group Policy inheritance issues or conflicts.

Requirements

If you want to use Group Policy modeling, there must be a Windows Server 2003 domain controller in the forest. This is because the simulation is performed by a service that is only present on Windows Server 2003 domain controllers.

Results of Group Policy Modeling

To perform a Group Policy Modeling query, the user uses the Group Policy Modeling Wizard. After the user completes the Group Policy Modeling Wizard, a new node in the console tree of Group Policy Management appears under **Group Policy Modeling** to display the results. The **Contents** tab in the details pane for Group Policy Modeling displays a summary of all Group Policy Modeling queries that the user has performed.

For each query, Group Policy Management shows the following data:

- **Name**. This is the user-supplied name of the modeling results.

- **User**. This is the user object (or the organizational unit where the user object is located) that the modeling query is based on.

- **Computer**. This is the computer object (or the organizational unit where the computer object is located) that the modeling query is based on.

- **Last refresh time**. This is the last time the modeling query was refreshed.

For each query, the details pane for the node contains the following three tabs:

- **Summary**. This contains an HTML report of the summary information, including the list of GPOs, security group membership, and WMI filters.

- **Settings**. This contains an HTML report of the policy settings that were applied in this simulation.

- **Query**. This lists the parameters that were used to generate the query.

How to Use Group Policy Modeling

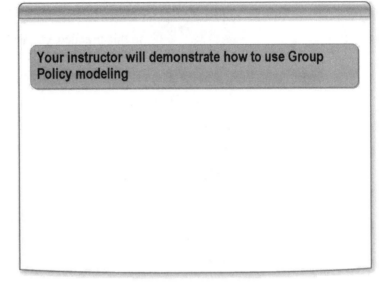

Your instructor will demonstrate how to use Group Policy modeling

Introduction

To determine the applied Group Policy settings, you use the Group Policy Modeling Wizard. This enables you to simulate the results of applying a new GPO before actually applying it.

Procedure

To use Group Policy Modeling:

1. In Group Policy Management, in the console tree, double-click the forest in which you want to create a Group Policy Modeling query, right-click **Group Policy Modeling**, and then click **Group Policy Modeling Wizard**.

2. In the Group Policy Modeling Wizard, click **Next** and then enter the following information:

   - If you want to model what the effect of a new GPO is for a user or computer, enter the name of the container for the user or computer.

   - If you want to model what the effect of a new GPO is for a specific user or computer account that will be migrated to a different organizational unit, enter the user or computer name. The wizard then prompts you for the destination of that user or computer.

3. When finished, click **Finish**.

Practice: Using Group Policy Modeling Wizard

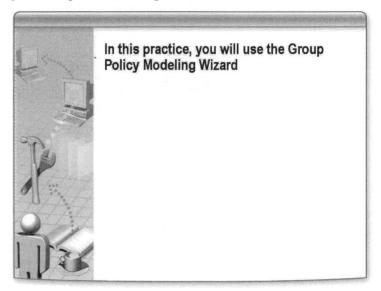

In this practice, you will use the Group Policy Modeling Wizard

Objective

In this practice, you will use the Group Policy Modeling Wizard.

Instructions

Before you begin this practice:

- Log on to the domain by using the *ComputerName*User account.
- Open CustomMMC with the **Run as** command.

  Use the user account Nwtraders*ComputerName*Admin (example: LondonAdmin).

- Ensure that CustomMMC contains Group Policy Management.
- Review the procedures in this lesson that describe how to perform this task.

Scenario

Your manager needs to know how Group Policy will be applied if your *ComputerName* computer account is moved to the IT Test/*ComputerName* organizational unit.

Practice

▶ **Generate a Group Policy Modeling report**

1. In Group Policy Management, in the console tree, right-click **Group Policy Modeling**, and then click **Group Policy Modeling Wizard**.

2. In the Group Policy Modeling Wizard, on the **Welcome** page, click **Next**.

3. On the **Domain Controller Selection** page, click **Next**.

4. On the **User and Computer Selection** page, under **Computer information**, click **Computer**, type **nwtraders**_ComputerName_ and then click **Next**.

5. On the **Advanced Simulation Options** page, click **Next**.

6. On the **Alternative Active Directory Paths** page, in the **Computer location** box, type **OU=**_ComputerName_**,OU=IT Test,DC=nwtraders, DC=msft** and then click **Next**.

7. On the **Computer Security Groups** page, click **Next**.

8. On the **WMI Filters for Computers** page, click **Next**.

9. On the **Summary of Selections** page, click **Next**.

10. Click **Finish**.

11. From the **Internet Explorer** box, click **Close**.

▶ **View the Group Policy Modeling report**

1. On the **Summary** tab, look through the report.

2. From the _ComputerName_ details pane, click the **Settings** tab.

3. From the **Internet Explorer** box, click **Close**.

4. Look through the report.

5. Click the **Query** tab.

6. Look through the report.

What Is Group Policy Results?

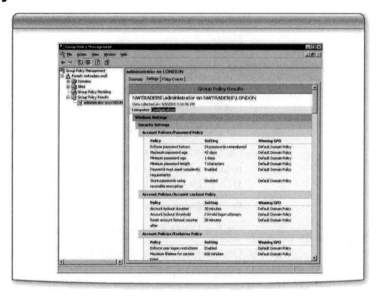

Introduction

The data that is presented in Group Policy Results is similar to Group Policy Modeling data. However, unlike Group Policy Modeling data, this data is not a simulation. It is the actual RSoP data obtained from the target computer. By default, this access is granted to all users on Microsoft Windows XP, but not on Windows Server 2003.

Requirements

Unlike Group Policy Modeling, the data in Group Policy Results is obtained from the client and is not simulated on the domain controller. Technically, a Windows Server 2003 domain controller is not required to be in the forest if you want to access Group Policy Results. However, the client must be running Windows XP or Windows Server 2003. It is not possible to get Group Policy Results data for a client running Microsoft Windows 2000.

Note By default, only users with local administrator privileges on the target computer can remotely access Group Policy Results data. To gather this data, the user performing the query must have access to remotely view the event log.

Results of Group Policy Results

Each Group Policy Results query is represented by a node under the Group Policy Results container in the console tree of Group Policy Management. The details pane for each node has the following three tabs:

- **Summary**. This contains an HTML report of the summary information including the list of GPOs, security group membership, and WMI filters.

- **Settings**. This contains an HTML report of the policy settings that were applied.

- **Events**. This shows all policy-related events from the target computer.

How to Use Group Policy Results

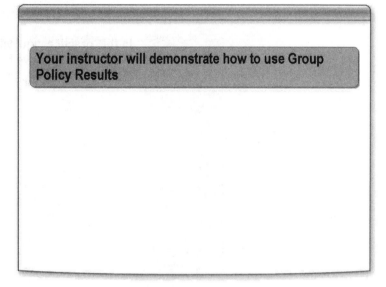

Your instructor will demonstrate how to use Group Policy Results

Introduction

Use the following procedure to use Group Policy Results.

Procedure

To use Group Policy Results:

1. In Group Policy Management, in the console tree, double-click the forest in which you want to create a Group Policy Results query, right-click **Group Policy Results**, and then click **Group Policy Results Wizard**.

2. In the Group Policy Results Wizard, click **Next** and then enter the appropriate information.

3. After completing the wizard, click **Finish**.

Practice: Using Group Policy Results Wizard

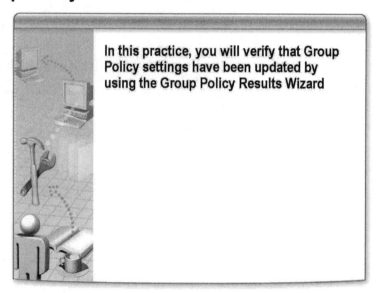

In this practice, you will verify that Group Policy settings have been updated by using the Group Policy Results Wizard

Introduction

In this practice, you will verify that policy settings have been updated by using the Group Policy Results Wizard.

Instructions

Before you begin this practice:

- Log on to the domain by using the *ComputerName*User account.
- Open CustomMMC with the **Run as** command.

  Use the user account Nwtraders*ComputerName*Admin (example: LondonAdmin).

- Ensure that CustomMMC contains Group Policy Management.
- Review the procedures in this lesson that describe how to perform this task.

Scenario

You want to verify that policy settings are being updated on your student computer. You want to look at the computer policy setting being applied to your computer with the *ComputerName*Admin account.

Practice

▶ **Generate a Group Policy Results report**

1. In Group Policy Management, right-click **Group Policy Results**, and then click **Group Policy Results Wizard**.

2. In the Group Policy Results Wizard, on the **Welcome** page, click **Next**.

3. On the **Computer Selection** page, click **Next**.

4. On the **User Selection** page, click **Select a specific user**, click **NWTRADERS**_ComputerName_**Admin**, and then click **Next**.

5. On the **Summary of Selections** page, click **Next**.

6. On the **Completing the Group Policy Results Wizard** page, click **Finish**.

7. From the **Internet Explorer** dialog box, click **Close**.

▶ **View a Group Policy Results report**

1. On the **Summary** tab look through the report.

2. On the **Policy Events** tab, double-click **Source**.

3. Scroll down to see the source labeled SceCli.

4. Double-click the first event with the source labeled SceCli.

5. In the **Event Properties** dialog box, notice the date and time the security policy setting was applied successfully.

6. Click the down arrow to see the next event, notice the date and time the security policy setting was applied successfully, and then click **OK**.

Lab A: Using Group Policies Reports

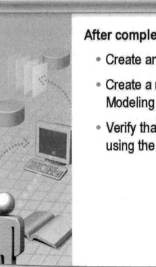

After completing this lab, you will be able to:

- Create and apply GPOs
- Create a report by using the Group Policy Modeling Wizard
- Verify that policy setting were applied by using the Group Policy Results Wizard

Objectives

After completing this lab, you will be able to:

- Create and apply GPOs.
- Create a report by using the Group Policy Modeling Wizard.
- Verify that policy settings were applied by using the Group Policy Results Wizard.

Instructions

Before you begin this lab:

- Log on to the domain by using the *ComputerName*User account.
- Open CustomMMC with the **Run as** command.

  Use the user account Nwtraders*ComputerName*Admin (example: LondonAdmin).

- Ensure that CustomMMC contains the following snap-ins:
  - Active Directory Users and Computers
  - Computer Management (Local)
  - Group Policy Management
- Ensure that you have organizational units named Laptops and Desktops in the Locations/*ComputerName*/Computers organizational unit.

Scenario

Northwind Traders has finished testing GPOs and must configure multiple GPOs that will affect many users and computers in your city. You must create and apply GPOs by using all of the properties in the following tables. After you configure all of the GPOs, you must create reports to show that the appropriate groups are not affected by certain policy settings and that the proper policy settings are applied.

Estimated time to complete this lab: 50 minutes

Exercise 1
Creating a GPO for Standard Desktop Computers

In this exercise, you will create a GPO.

Scenario

Northwind Traders has finished testing a GPO that enables the Marketing personnel to use a standard desktop computer. Create a GPO with the following properties.

Properties	Special Instructions
1. Create a GPO.	■ GPO name: *ComputerName* **Standard Desktop 2**
2. Create a GPO link.	■ Location: Locations/*ComputerName* ■ GPO name: *ComputerName* Standard Desktop 2
3. Configure security filtering.	■ Location: Locations/*ComputerName* ■ GPO: *ComputerName* Standard Desktop 2 ■ Security Filtering: • Remove Authenticated Users • Add G NWTraders Marketing Personnel • Deny the Apply Group Policy permission to G NWTraders Marketing Managers
4. Set the following Group Policy settings to **Enabled**.	■ GPO: *ComputerName* Standard Desktop 2 ■ Location of Group Policy setting: User Configuration/Administrative Templates/Windows Components/Application Compatibility/Prevent access to 16-bit applications ■ Location of Group Policy setting: User Configuration/Administrative Templates/Windows Components/Windows Explorer/Remove Search button from Windows Explorer ■ Location of Group Policy setting: User Configuration/Administrative Templates/Windows Components/ Windows Explorer/Remove Hardware tab ■ Location of Group Policy setting: User Configuration/Administrative Templates/Start Menu and Taskbar/Remove links and access to Windows Update ■ Location of Group Policy setting: User Configuration/Administrative Templates/Start Menu and Taskbar/Remove Network Connections from Start Menu ■ Location of Group Policy setting: User Configuration/Administrative Templates/Start Menu and Taskbar/Remove Run from Start Menu

Exercise 2
Creating a GPO for Folder Redirection

In this exercise, you will set Deny permissions for all temporary employees of Northwind Traders so that they do not receive the *ComputerName* Folder Redirection GPO.

Scenario

Northwind Traders has finished testing a GPO for Folder Redirection. You must create a GPO that redirects folders of Accounting personnel only.

Tasks	Special instructions
1. Create a GPO.	▪ GPO name: *ComputerName* **Accounting Folder Redirection**
2. Create a GPO link.	▪ Location: Locations/*ComputerName*/Users ▪ GPO name: *ComputerName* Accounting Folder Redirection
3. Configure security filtering.	▪ Location: Locations/*ComputerName* ▪ GPO: *ComputerName* Accounting Folder Redirection ▪ Security Filtering: • Remove Everyone • Add DL NWTraders Accounting Personnel Full Control
4. Create a shared folder.	▪ Folder Path: D:\Accounting Data ▪ Share Name: *ComputerName***Accounting Data$** ▪ Permissions: Grant Full Control permission to DL NWTraders Accounting Personnel Full Control
5. Configure Group Policy settings.	▪ Location: Locations/*ComputerName*/Users ▪ GPO: *ComputerName* Accounting Folder Redirection ▪ Location of Group Policy setting: User Configuration/Windows Settings/Folder Redirection/My Documents ▪ Options: • Target folder setting: **Basic – Redirect everyone's folder to the same location** • Target folder location: **Create a folder for each user under the root path** • Root Path: *ComputerName*\Accounting Data$ • Redirection settings: • **Grant the user exclusive user rights to My Documents** • **Redirect the folder back to the local userprofile when the policy is removed**

Exercise 3
Creating a GPO for Laptop Computers

In this exercise, you will configure a GPO for laptop computers.

Scenario

Northwind Traders has finished testing a GPO for laptop computers. Create a GPO with the following properties that will be enforced on all laptop computers.

Tasks	Special instructions
1. Create a GPO	▪ GPO name: *ComputerName* **Laptop Settings**
2. Create a GPO link.	▪ Location: Locations/*ComputerName*/Computers/Laptops ▪ GPO name: *ComputerName* Laptop Settings
3. Set the following Group Policy settings to **Enabled**.	▪ GPO: *ComputerName* Laptop Settings ▪ Location of Group Policy setting: User Configuration/ Administrative Templates/System/Power Management/Prompt for password on resume from hibernation / suspend ▪ Location of Group Policy setting: User Configuration/ Administrative Templates/Network/Offline Files/Synchronize all offline files when logging on ▪ Location of Group Policy setting: User Configuration/ Administrative Templates/Network/Offline Files/Synchronize all offline files before logging off

Exercise 4
Creating a GPO for Desktop Computers

In this exercise, you will configure a GPO for desktop computers.

Scenario

Northwind Traders has finished testing a GPO for desktop computers. Create a GPO with the following properties that will be enforced on all desktop computers.

Tasks	Special instructions
1. Create a GPO.	▪ GPO name: *ComputerName* **Desktop Settings**
2. Create a GPO link.	▪ Location: Locations/*ComputerName*/Computers/Desktop
	▪ GPO name: *ComputerName* Desktop Settings
3. Set the following Group Policy settings to **Enabled**.	▪ GPO: *ComputerName* Desktop Settings
	▪ Location of Group Policy setting: User Configuration/Administrative Templates/Network/Offline Files/Prevent use of offline folders

Exercise 5
Generating a Group Policy Modeling Report

In this exercise, you will generate two Group Policy Modeling reports. You will generate one report for Accounting managers with laptop computers and another report for Accounting personnel with desktop computers.

Report name	Special instructions
1. Create a Group Policy Modeling report for laptop computers.	▪ User Container: OU=Users,OU=*ComputerName*,OU=Locations,DC=nwtraders, DC=msft ▪ Computer Container: OU=Laptops,OU=Computers,OU=*ComputerName*,OU=Locations, DC=nwtraders,DC=msft ▪ User Security Groups: Authenticated Users, Everyone, NWTRADERS\G NWTraders Accounting Managers
2. Create a Group Policy Modeling report for desktop computers.	▪ User Container: OU=Users,OU=*ComputerName*,OU=Locations,DC=nwtraders, DC=msft ▪ Computer Container: OU=Desktops,OU=Computers,OU=*ComputerName*,OU=Locations, DC=nwtraders,DC=msft ▪ User Security Groups: Authenticated Users, Everyone, NWTRADES\G NWTraders Accounting Personnel

Exercise 6
Generating a Group Policy Results Report

In this exercise, you will generate a Group Policy Results report to see what policy settings have been applied to the nwtraders\administrator account on the server named Glasgow.

Task	Special instructions
1. Create a Group Policy Results report.	▪ Computer Selection: Glasgow ▪ User Selection: NWTRADERS\administrator
2. View a Group Policy Results report.	▪ Determine when policy settings were last refreshed

Microsoft®
Training &
Certification

Module 10: Implementing Administrative Templates and Audit Policy

Contents

Overview	1
Lesson: Overview of Security in Windows Server 2003	2
Lesson: Using Security Templates to Secure Computers	12
Lesson: Testing Computer Security Policy	26
Lesson: Configuring Auditing	31
Lesson: Managing Security Logs	49
Lab A: Managing Security Settings	60
Course Evaluation	65

Overview

- Overview of Security in Windows Server 2003
- Using Security Templates to Secure Computers
- Testing Computer Security Policy
- Configuring Auditing
- Managing Security Logs

Introduction

This module will provide a broad overview of security in Microsoft® Windows® Server 2003. You will learn how to use security templates and test computer security policy. You will also learn how to configure auditing and manage security logs.

Objectives

After completing this module, you will be able to:

- Describe administrative templates and audit policy in Windows Server 2003.
- Use security templates to secure computers.
- Test computer security policy.
- Configure auditing.
- Manage security logs.

Lesson: Overview of Security in Windows Server 2003

* What Are User Rights?
* User Rights vs. Permissions
* User Rights Assigned to Built-in Groups
* How to Assign User Rights

Introduction

In this lesson, you will learn about user rights, permissions, and user rights assigned to built-in groups. You will also learn how to assign user rights.

Lesson objectives

After completing this lesson, you will be able to:

- Describe user rights.

- Distinguish between rights and permissions.

- Describe the user rights assigned to built-in groups.

- Assign user rights.

What Are User Rights?

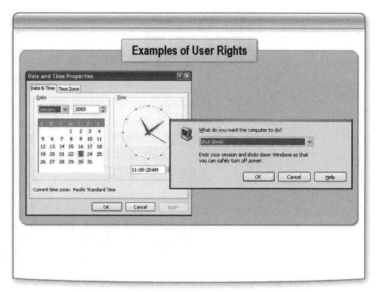

Definition

When a user logs on, the user receives an access token that includes user rights. A user right authorizes a user who is logged on to a computer or a network to perform certain actions on the system. If a user does not have the appropriate rights to perform an action, attempts to perform the action are blocked.

Who do rights apply to?

User rights can apply both to individual users and to groups. However, user rights are best administered when they are assigned to groups. This ensures that a user who logs on as a member of a group automatically receives the rights associated with that group. Windows Server 2003 enables an administrator to assign rights to users and groups.

Common user rights

Common user rights include the following:

- *Log on locally*. Enables a user to log on to the local computer or to the domain from a local computer.

- *Change the system time*. Enables a user to set the time of the internal clock of a computer.

- *Shut down the system*. Enables a user to shut down a local computer.

- *Access this computer from a network*. Enables a user to access a computer running Windows Server 2003 from any other computer on the network.

User Rights vs. Permissions

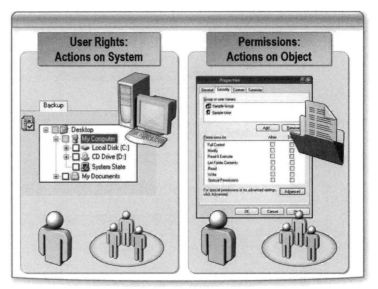

Introduction

Administrators can assign specific user rights to group accounts or to individual user accounts. These rights authorize users to perform specific actions, such as log on to a system interactively or back up files and directories. User rights are different from permissions, because user rights are attached to user accounts, and permissions are attached to objects.

What are user rights?

User rights determine which users can perform a specific task on a computer or in a domain. Although you can assign user rights to individual user accounts, user rights are best administered if they are assigned to group accounts. A user logging on as a member of a group automatically inherits the rights assigned to that group. By assigning user rights to groups rather than individual users, you simplify the task of administering user accounts. When users in a group all require the same user rights, you can assign the set of user rights once to the group, rather than repeatedly assigning the same set of user rights to each individual user account.

User rights that are assigned to a group are applied to all members of the group while they are members. If a user is a member of multiple groups, the user's rights are cumulative, which means that the user has more than one set of rights. The only time that rights assigned to one group might conflict with those assigned to another is in the case of certain logon rights. In general, user rights assigned to one group do not conflict with the rights assigned to another group. To remove rights from a user, the administrator simply removes the user from the group. The user no longer has the rights assigned to that group.

Rights apply to the entire system, rather than to a specific resource, and affect the overall operation of the computer or domain. All users accessing network resources must have certain common rights on the computers they use, such as the right to log on to the computer or change the system time of the computer. Administrators can assign specific common user rights to groups or to individual users. Additionally, Windows Server 2003 assigns certain rights to built-in groups by default.

What are permissions?

Permissions define the type of access granted to a user or group for an object or object property. For example, you can grant the Read and Write permissions to the Finance group for a file named Payroll.dat.

You can grant permissions for any secured objects such as files, objects in the Active Directory® directory service, or registry objects. You can grant permissions to any user, group, or computer. It is a good practice to grant permissions to groups.

You can grant permissions for objects to:

- Groups, users, and special identities in the domain.
- Groups and users in that domain and any trusted domains.
- Local groups and users on the computer where the object resides.

When you provide access to file resources on a computer running Windows Server 2003, you can control who has access to resources and the nature of their access by granting the appropriate permissions. Permissions define the type of access assigned to a user or group for any resource.

For example, users in the Human Resources department of an organization might need to modify the organization's document describing Human Resources policies. To facilitate this, the administrator must grant the appropriate permission to the members of the Human Resources department.

To grant permissions for individual files and folders, Windows Server 2003 uses the NTFS file system. You can also control the permissions for accessing shared folder resources and network printers.

User Rights Assigned to Built-in Groups

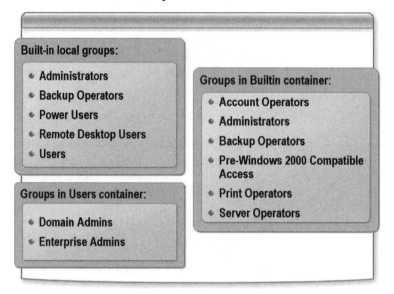

Introduction

By default, Windows Server 2003 assigns certain rights to built-in groups. The built-in groups include local groups, groups in the Builtin container, and groups in the Users container.

User rights assigned to local groups

The following user rights are assigned to local groups:

- Administrators

  Access this computer from the network; Adjust memory quotas for a process; Allow log on locally; Allow log on through Terminal Services; Back up files and directories; Bypass traverse checking; Change the system time; Create a pagefile; Debug programs; Force shutdown from a remote system; Increase scheduling priority; Load and unload device drivers; Manage auditing and security log; Modify firmware environment variables; Perform volume maintenance tasks; Profile single process; Profile system performance; Remove computer from docking station; Restore files and directories; Shut down the system; Take ownership of files or other objects

- Backup Operators

  Access this computer from the network; Allow log on locally; Back up files and directories; Bypass traverse checking; Restore files and directories; Shut down the system

- Power Users

  Access this computer from the network; Allow log on locally; Bypass traverse checking; Change the system time; Profile single process; Remove computer from docking station; Shut down the system

  Caution Members of the Power Users group can elevate their privileges to administrator.

- Remote Desktop Users

  Allow log on through Terminal Services

- Users

  Access this computer from the network; Allow log on locally; Bypass traverse checking

User rights assigned to the Builtin container

The following user rights are assigned to groups in the Builtin container:

- Account Operators

  Allow log on locally; Shut down the system

- Administrators

  Access this computer from the network; Adjust memory quotas for a process; Back up files and directories; Bypass traverse checking; Change the system time; Create a pagefile; Debug programs; Enable computer and user accounts to be trusted for delegation; Force a shutdown from a remote system; Increase scheduling priority; Load and unload device drivers; Allow log on locally; Manage auditing and security log; Modify firmware environment values; Profile single process; Profile system performance; Remove computer from docking station; Restore files and directories; Shut down the system; Take ownership of files or other objects

- Backup Operators

  Back up files and directories; Allow log on locally; Restore files and directories; Shut down the system

- Pre-Windows 2000 Compatible Access

  Access this computer from the network; Bypass traverse checking

- Print Operators

  Allow log on locally; Shut down the system

- Server Operators

  Back up files and directories; Change the system time; Force shutdown from a remote system; Allow log on locally; Restore files and directories; Shut down the system

User rights assigned to the Users container

The following user rights are assigned to groups in the Users container:

■ Domain Admins

Access this computer from the network; Adjust memory quotas for a process; Back up files and directories; Bypass traverse checking; Change the system time; Create a pagefile; Debug programs; Enable computer and user accounts to be trusted for delegation; Force a shutdown from a remote system; Increase scheduling priority; Load and unload device drivers; Allow log on locally; Manage auditing and security log; Modify firmware environment values; Profile single process; Profile system performance; Remove computer from docking station; Restore files and directories; Shut down the system; Take ownership of files or other objects

■ Enterprise Admins (only appears in the forest root domain)

Access this computer from the network; Adjust memory quotas for a process; Back up files and directories; Bypass traverse checking; Change the system time; Create a pagefile; Debug programs; Enable computer and user accounts to be trusted for delegation; Force shutdown from a remote system; Increase scheduling priority; Load and unload device drivers; Allow log on locally; Manage auditing and security log; Modify firmware environment values; Profile single process; Profile system performance; Remove computer from docking station; Restore files and directories; Shut down the system; Take ownership of files or other objects

Additional reading

For more information about user rights and upgrading operating systems, see article 323042, "Required User Rights for the Upgrade from Windows 2000 to Windows Server 2003" in the Microsoft Knowledge Base at http://support.microsoft.com/?kbid=323042.

For more information about user rights and service accounts, see article 325349, "HOW TO: Grant Users Rights to Manage Services in Windows Server 2003" in the Microsoft Knowledge Base at http://support.microsoft.com/?kbid=325349.

How to Assign User Rights

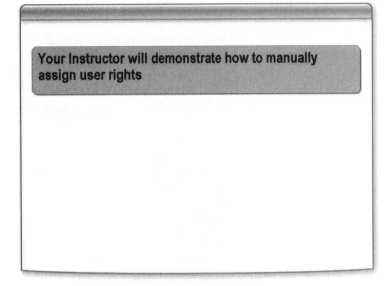

Introduction

Typically, administrators add users or groups to built-in groups that already have rights. In some circumstances, a built-in group might give too much or too little rights to a user, so you must assign rights manually.

Procedure

To assign user rights:

1. Click **Start**, click **Run**, type **mmc** and then press ENTER.

2. Click **Console**.

3. On the **File** menu, click **Add/Remove Snap-in**.

4. In the **Add/Remove Snap-in** dialog box, click **Add**.

5. In the **Add Standalone Snap-in** dialog box, double-click **Group Policy Object Editor**.

6. Click **Finish** to close the Welcome to Group Policy Wizard.

7. Click **Close** to close the **Add Standalone Snap-in** dialog box.

8. Click **OK** to close the **Add/Remove Snap-in** dialog box.

9. Expand **Local Computer Policy**, expand **Computer Configuration**, expand **Windows Settings**, expand **Security Settings**, and then expand **Local Policies**.

10. Click **User Rights Assignment**.

11. Add or remove a group to a user right as needed.

Practice: Assigning User Rights

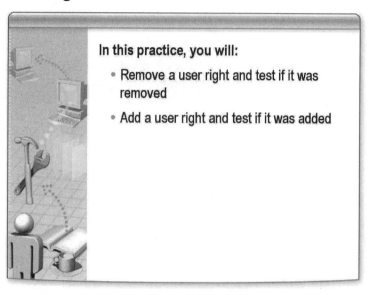

Objective

In this practice, you will:

- Remove the right to log on locally from the Users group and test if the user right is removed.

- Assign the Users group the right to log on locally and test if the user right is assigned.

Instructions

Before you begin this practice:

- Log on to the domain by using the *ComputerName*Admin account.

- Open CustomMMC

Note This practice focuses on the concepts in this lesson and as a result may not comply with Microsoft security recommendations. For example, this practice does not comply with the recommendation that users log on with domain user account and use the **Run as** command when performing administrative tasks.

- Review the procedures in this lesson that describe how to perform this task.

Scenario

The systems engineers want to test user rights by preventing users from logging on locally to your computer. After the test is successful, you will assign users the right to log on locally.

Practice

▶ **Remove the right to log on locally from the Users group**

1. Remove the group Users from the following local computer policy:

   Computer Configuration/Windows Settings/Security Settings/
   Local Policies/User Rights Assignment/Allow log on locally

2. Close all programs and log off.

▶ **Test if the right was removed**

- Log on as *ComputerName*User.

  You should *not* be able to log on.

▶ **Assign the right to log on locally to the Users group**

1. Log on as *ComputerName*Admin.

2. Add the group Users to the following local computer policy:

   Computer Configuration/Windows Settings/Security Settings/
   Local Policies/User Rights Assignment/Allow log on locally

3. Close all programs and log off.

▶ **Test if the right was assigned**

- Log on as *ComputerName*User.

  You should be able to log on.

Lesson: Using Security Templates to Secure Computers

- What Is a Security Policy?
- What Are Security Templates?
- What Are Security Template Settings?
- How to Create a Custom Security Template
- How to Import a Security Template

Introduction

You can create security templates to create a security policy and alter a security policy to meet the security needs of your company. You can implement security policies in several different ways. The method you use depends on your organization's size and security needs. Smaller organizations, or those not using Active Directory, can configure security manually on an individual basis. If your organization is large or requires a high level of security, consider using Group Policy objects (GPOs) to deploy security policy.

Lesson objectives

After completing this lesson, you will be able to:

- Describe a security policy.
- Describe security templates.
- Describe security template settings.
- Create a custom security template.
- Import a security template.

What Is a Security Policy?

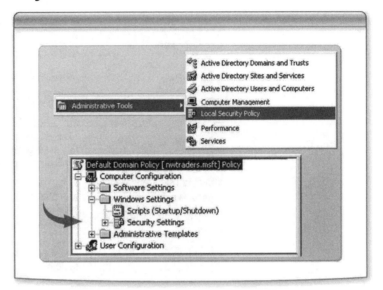

Introduction

A security policy is a combination of security settings that affect the security on a computer. You can use security policy to establish account policies and local policies on your local computer and in Active Directory.

Security policy on a local computer

You can use the security policy on a local computer to directly modify account and local policies, public key policies, and Internet Protocol security (IPSec) policies for your local computer.

With local security policy, you can control:

- Who accesses your computer.

- What resources users are authorized to use on your computer.

- Whether a user or group's actions are recorded in the event log.

If your network does not use Active Directory, you can configure security policy by using Local Security Policy, which is found on the **Administrative Tools** menu on computers running Windows Server 2003.

Security policies in Active Directory

Security policies in Active Directory have the same security settings as a security policy on local computers. However, administrators of Active Directory–based networks can save considerable administrative time by using Group Policy to deploy the security policy. You can edit or import security settings in a GPO for any site, domain, or organizational unit, and the security settings are automatically deployed to the computers when the computers start. When editing a GPO, expand **Computer Configuration** or **User Configuration** and then expand **Windows Settings** to find security policy settings.

Additional reading

For more information about default domain user rights, see article 324800, "HOW TO: Reset User Rights in the Default Domain Group Policy in Windows Server 2003" in the Microsoft Knowledge Base at http://support.microsoft.com/?kbid=324800.

What Are Security Templates?

Template	Description
Default Security (Setup security.inf)	Specifies default security settings
Domain Controller Default Security (DC security.inf)	Specifies default security settings updated from Setup security.inf for a domain controller
Compatible (Compatws.inf)	Modifies permissions and registry settings for the Users group to enable maximum application compatibility
Secure (Securedc.inf and Securews.inf)	Enhances security settings that are least likely to impact application compatibility
Highly Secure (Hisecdc.inf and Hisecws.inf)	Increases the restrictions on security settings
System Root Security (Rootsec.inf)	Specifies permissions for the root of the system drive

Definition

A security template is a collection of configured security settings. Windows Server 2003 provides predefined security templates that contain the recommended security settings for different situations.

You can use predefined security templates to create security policies that are customized to meet different organizational requirements. You customize the templates with the Security Templates snap-in. After you customize the predefined security templates, you can use them to configure security on an individual computer or thousands of computers.

How security templates are applied

You can configure individual computers with the Security Configuration and Analysis snap-in or the **secedit** command-line tool or by importing the template into Local Security Policy. You can configure multiple computers by importing a template into Security Settings, which is an extension of Group Policy.

You can also use a security template as a baseline for analyzing a system for potential security holes or policy violations by using the Security Configuration and Analysis snap-in. By default, the predefined security templates are stored in *systemroot*/Security/Templates.

Predefined templates

Windows Server 2003 provides the following predefined templates:

- Default security (Setup security.inf)

  The Setup security.inf template is created during installation of the operating system for each computer and represents default security settings that are applied during installation, including the file permissions for the root of the system drive. It can vary from computer to computer, based on whether the installation was a clean installation or an upgrade. You can use this template on servers and client computers, but not on domain controllers. You can apply portions of this template for disaster recovery.

  Default security settings are applied only to clean installations of Windows Server 2003 on an NTFS partition. When computers are upgraded from Microsoft Windows NT® version 4.0, security is not modified. Also, when you install Windows Server 2003 on a FAT (file allocation table) file system, security is not applied to the file system.

- Domain controller default security (DC security.inf)

  The DC security.inf template is created when a server is promoted to a domain controller. It reflects default security settings on files, registry keys, and system services. Reapplying it resets these settings to the default values, but it may overwrite permissions on new files, registry keys, and system services created by other applications. You can apply it by using the Security Configuration and Analysis snap-in or the **secedit** command-line tool.

- Compatible (Compatws.inf)

  Default permissions for workstations and servers are primarily granted to three local groups: Administrators, Power Users, and Users. Administrators have the most privileges, and Users have the least.

  Members of the Users group can successfully run applications that take part in the Windows Logo Program for Software. However, they may not be able to run applications that do not meet the requirements of the program. If other applications are to be supported, the Compatws.inf template changes the default file and registry permissions that are granted to the Users group. The new permissions are consistent with the requirements of most applications that do not belong to the Windows Logo Program for Software.

- Secure (Secure*.inf)

  The Secure templates define enhanced security settings that are least likely to affect application compatibility. For example, the Secure templates define stronger password, lockout, and audit settings.

- Highly Secure (hisec*.inf)

  The Highly Secure templates are supersets of the Secure templates. They impose further restrictions on the levels of encryption and signing that are required for authentication and for the data that flows over secure channels and between server message block (SMB) clients and servers.

- System root security (Rootsec.inf)

  By default, Rootsec.inf defines the permissions for the root of the system drive. You can use this template to reapply the root directory permissions if they are inadvertently changed, or you can modify the template to apply the same root permissions to other volumes. As specified, the template does not overwrite explicit permissions that are defined on child objects. It propagates only the permissions that are inherited by child objects.

Additional reading

For more information about applying security policies, see article 325351, "HOW TO: Apply Local Policies to All Users Except Administrators on Windows Server 2003 in a Workgroup Setting" in the Microsoft Knowledge Base at http://support.microsoft.com/?kbid=325351.

For more information on **secedit**, see "Secedit" at http://www.microsoft.com/ technet/treeview/default.asp?url=/technet/prodtechnol/windowsserver2003/ proddocs/datacenter/secedit_cmds.asp?frame=true.

What Are Security Template Settings?

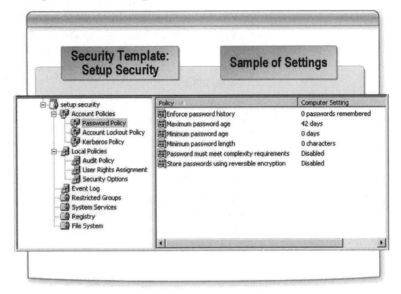

Introduction

Security templates contain security settings for all security areas. You can apply templates to individual computers or deploy them to groups of computers by using Group Policy. When you apply a template to existing security settings, the settings in the template are merged into the computer's security settings.

You can configure and analyze security settings for computers by using the Security Settings Group Policy extension or Security Configuration and Analysis.

Types of security template settings

The following list describes each of the security template settings:

- Account Policies

  You can use account policy settings to configure password policies, account lockout policies, and Kerberos version 5 (V5) protocol policies for the domain. A domain's account policy defines the password history, the lifetime of the Kerberos V5 tickets, account lockouts, and more.

- Local Policies

  Local policy settings, by definition, are local to computers. Local policies include audit policies, the assignment of user rights and permissions, and various security options that can be configured locally.

  It is important not to confuse local policy settings with setting policies locally. As with all of these security settings, you can configure these settings by using Local Security Policy and Group Policy.

- Event Log

  You use event log settings to configure the size, access, and retention parameters for application logs, system logs, and security logs.

■ Restricted Group

You use restricted group settings to manage the membership of built-in groups that have certain predefined capabilities, such as Administrators and Power Users, in addition to domain groups, such as Domain Admins. You can add other groups to the restricted group, along with their membership information. This enables you to track and manage these groups as part of security policy.

You can also use restricted group settings to track and control the reverse membership of each restricted group. Reverse membership is listed in the **Members Of** column, which displays other groups to which the restricted group must belong.

■ System Services

You use system services settings to configure security and startup settings for services running on a computer. System services settings include critical functionality, such as network services, file and print services, telephony and fax services, and Internet or intranet services. The general settings include the service startup mode (automatic, manual, or disabled) and security on the service.

■ Registry

You use registry settings to configure security on registry keys.

■ File System

You use file system settings to configure security on specific file paths.

■ Public Key Policies

You use public key policy settings to configure encrypted data recovery agents, domain roots, trusted certificate authorities, and so on.

Note Public Key Policies are the only settings available under User Configuration.

■ IP Security Policies on Active Directory

You use IP security policy settings to configure IPSec.

Important Only the Account Policies, Local Policies, Public Key Policies, and IP Security Policies on Active Directory areas are available when you use Local Security Policy.

Also, you can assign password settings, account lockout settings, and Kerberos settings at the domain or organizational unit level. However, if you configure the policy at the organizational unit level, the settings affect only the local Security Accounts Manager (SAM) databases of computer objects in the organizational unit, not the domain password policies. Windows Server 2003 does not process any changes that you make to these three settings in a GPO at the site level.

Additional reading

For more information about security template best practices, see the TechNet article "Best practices for Security Templates" at http://www.microsoft.com/technet/treeview/default.asp?url=/technet/prodtechnol/windowsserver2003/proddocs/datacenter/sag_SCEbp.asp.

How to Create a Custom Security Template

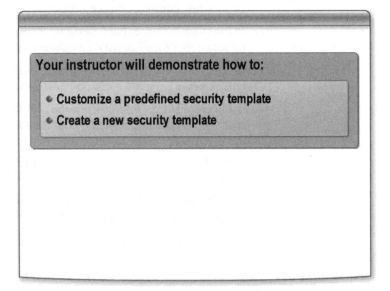

Your instructor will demonstrate how to:

● Customize a predefined security template
● Create a new security template

Introduction

If the predefined templates are insufficient for your security needs, you must create custom templates.

Procedure for customizing a predefined template

To customize a predefined security template:

1. In a Microsoft Management Console (MMC), add the Security Templates snap-in.

2. In the console tree, expand **Security Templates**, and then double-click the default path folder (*systemroot*/Security/Templates).

3. In the details pane, right-click the predefined template you want to modify, and then click **Save As**.

4. In the **Save As** dialog box, type a new file name for the security template, and then click **Save**.

5. In the console tree, double-click the new security template to display the security policies, and navigate until the security attribute you want to modify appears in the details pane.

6. In the details pane, right-click the security attribute, and then click **Properties**.

7. In the **Properties** dialog box, select the **Define this policy setting in the template** check box, make your changes, and then click **OK**.

8. In the console tree, right-click the new security template, and then click **Save**.

Procedure for creating a new security template

To create a new security template:

1. In an MMC console, add the Security Templates snap-in.

2. In the console tree, expand **Security Templates**, right-click the default path folder (*systemroot*/Security/Templates), and then click **New Template**.

3. In the *systemroot*/**security**/**templates** dialog box, in the **Template Name** box, type the template name and description and then click **OK**.

4. In the console tree, double-click the new security template to display the security policies, and navigate until the security attribute you want to modify appears in the details pane.

5. In the details pane, right-click the security attribute, and then click **Properties**.

6. In the **Properties** dialog box, select the **Define this policy setting in the template** check box, make your changes, and then click **OK**.

7. In the console tree, right-click the new security template, and then click **Save**.

How to Import a Security Template

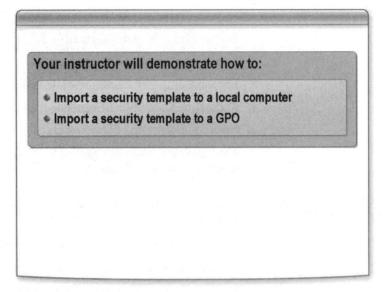

Introduction

When you import a security template to a local computer, you can apply the template settings to the local computer. When you import a security template into a GPO, the settings in the template are applied to computers in the containers to which the GPO is linked.

Procedure for importing a template to a local computer

To import a security template to a local computer:

1. Open Security Configuration and Analysis.

2. In the console tree, right-click **Security Configuration and Analysis**, and then click **Import Template**.

3. (Optional) To clear the database of any template, select the **Clear this database before importing** check box.

4. In the **Import Template** dialog box, click a template file, and then click **Open**.

5. Repeat these steps for each template that you want to merge into the database.

Procedure for importing a template to a GPO without GPMC installed

To import a security template into a GPO when Group Policy Management is not installed:

1. Open Active Directory Users and Computers or Active Directory Sites and Services from the **Administrative Tools** menu.

2. Edit the appropriate GPO.

3. Expand **Computer Configuration**, and then expand **Windows Settings**.

4. Right-click **Security Settings**, and then click **Import Policy**.

5. Click a template, and then click **Open**.

   The template settings are applied to the GPO and will be applied the next time the computer is started.

Procedure for importing a template to a GPO with GPMC

To import a security template into a GPO when Group Policy Management is installed:

1. In Group Policy Management, edit the appropriate GPO.

2. Expand **Computer Configuration**, and then expand **Windows Settings**.

3. Right-click **Security Settings**, and then click **Import Policy**.

4. Click a template, and then click **Open**.

   The template settings are applied to the GPO and will be applied the next time the computer is started.

Practice: Using Security Templates to Secure Computers

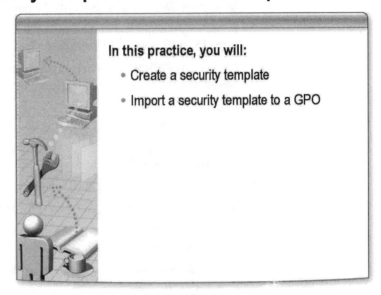

In this practice, you will:
- Create a security template
- Import a security template to a GPO

Objective

In this practice, you will:

- Create a security template.
- Import a security template to a GPO.

Instructions

Before you begin this practice:

- Log on to the domain by using the *ComputerName*User account.
- Open CustomMMC with the **Run as** command.

  Use the user account Nwtraders*ComputerName*Admin (Example: LondonAdmin).

- Open a command prompt with the Run as command.

  From the **Start** menu click **Run**, and then type **runas /user:nwtraders*ComputerName*Admin cmd** and click **OK**. When prompted for a password, type **P@ssw0rd** and press **ENTER**.

- Review the procedures in this lesson that describe how to perform this task.

Practice: Creating a custom template on a local computer

▶ **Check the local group membership of the Power Users local group**

1. To verify that NWTraders\G IT Admins is not a member of the Power Users group from a command prompt type **net localgroup "power users"**

2. There should be no members listed under Members.

3. With a default installation of the operating system, the Power Users group should not contain any members.

4. Leave the command prompt open.

▶ **Create a new security template called *ComputerName***

1. In CustomMMC, add the Security Templates snap-in.

2. In Security Templates, in the console tree, right-click **C:\WINDOWS\cecurity\templates**, and then click **New Template**.

3. In the **C:\WINDOWS\security\templates** dialog box, in the **Template Name** box, type *ComputerName* and then click **OK**.

▶ **Edit the *ComputerName* custom security template**

1. In Security Templates, in the console tree, expand *ComputerName*, and then click **Restricted Groups**.

2. Right-click **Restricted Groups**, and then click **Add Group**.

3. In the **Add Group** dialog box, type **Power Users** and then click **OK**.

4. In the **Power Users Properties** dialog box, under **Members of this group**, click **Add Members**.

5. In the **Add Member** dialog box, type **NWTRADERS\G IT Admins** and then click **OK**.

6. In the **Power Users Properties** dialog box, click **OK**.

7. In the console tree, right-click *ComputerName*, and then click **Save**.

▶ **Import and apply the *ComputerName* custom security template**

1. In CustomMMC, add the Security Configuration and Analysis snap-in.

2. Right-click **Security Configuration and Analysis**, and then click **Open Database**.

3. In the **Open database** box, type *ComputerName* and then click **Open**.

4. In the **Import Template** dialog box, click *ComputerName*.**inf**, and then click **Open**.

5. Right-click **Security Configuration and Analysis**, and then click **Configure Computer Now**.

6. In the message box, click **OK**.

7. Right-click **Security Configuration and Analysis**, and then click **View Log File**.

8. In the details pane for **Security Configuration and Analysis**, verify that the NWTRADERS\G IT Admins group was added to the Power Users group by looking for the following log file entry:

   ----Configure Group Membership...
   Configure Power Users.
   add NWTRADERS\G IT Admins.

▶ **Check the local group membership of the Power Users local group**

1. To verify that NWTraders\G IT Admins is a member of the Power Users group, from a command prompt type **net localgroup "Power Users"**

2. NWTraders\G IT Admins should be listed under Members.

3. Leave the command prompt open.

▶ **Remove the imported custom security template**

1. From a Command prompt type **net localgroup "power users" /delete "g it admins"**

2. Leave the command prompt open.

▶ **Check the local group membership of the Power Users local group**

1. To verify that NWTraders\G IT Admins is not a member of the Power Users group from a command prompt type **net localgroup "power users"**

2. There should be no members listed under Members.

3. Leave the command prompt open.

Practice: Importing a custom template to a GPO

▶ **Import a security template to a GPO**

1. In Group Policy Management, create a GPO called *ComputerName* **Restricted Users**.

2. Link the *ComputerName* Restricted Users GPO to the Locations/*ComputerName*/Computers organizational unit.

3. Edit the *ComputerName* Restricted Users GPO.

4. Import the custom security policy named *ComputerName*.inf.

▶ **Move your *ComputerName* computer account**

1. Search for your *ComputerName* computer account in the nwtraders.msft domain.

2. Move your *ComputerName* computer account to the Locations/*ComputerName*/Computers organizational unit.

3. From a command prompt, type **gpupdate /force**

4. If prompted to logoff, type **N** and then press **ENTER**.

▶ **Check the local group membership of the Power Users local group**

1. To verify that NWTraders\G IT Admins is a member of the Power Users group, from a command prompt type **net localgroup "power users"**

2. NWTraders\G IT Admins should be listed under Members.

3. Close the command prompt

Lesson: Testing Computer Security Policy

* What is the Security Configuration and Analysis tool?
* How to Test Computer Security

Introduction

Before deploying a security template to large groups of computers, it is important to analyze the results of applying a configuration to ensure there are no adverse effects on applications, connectivity, or security. A thorough analysis also helps you identify security holes and deviations from standard configurations. You can use the Security Configuration and Analysis snap-in to create and review possible scenarios and adjust a configuration.

Lesson objectives

After completing this lesson, you will be able to:

- What is the Security Configuration and Analysis tool?
- Test computer security with the Security Configuration and Analysis tool.

What is the Security Configuration and Analysis tool?

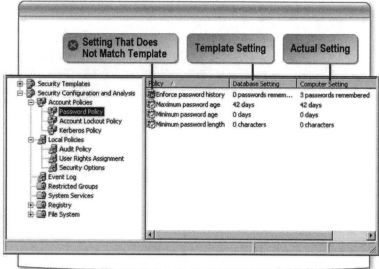

| | Introduction | The most common tool that is used to analyze computer security is the Security Configuration and Analysis tool. |

Introduction

The most common tool that is used to analyze computer security is the Security Configuration and Analysis tool.

Security Configuration and Analysis tool

The Security Configuration and Analysis tool compares the security configuration of the local computer to an alternate configuration that is imported from a template (an .inf file) and stored in a separate database (an .sdb file). When analysis is complete, you can browse the security settings in the console tree to see the results. Discrepancies are marked with a red flag. Consistencies are marked with a green check mark. Settings that are not marked with either a red flag or a green check mark are not configured in the database.

Why use Security Configuration and Analysis tool?

After analyzing the results by using the Security Configuration and Analysis tool, you can perform various tasks, including:

- Eliminate discrepancies by configuring the settings in the database to match the current computer settings. To configure database settings, double-click the setting in the details pane.

- Import another template file, merging its settings and overwriting settings where there is a conflict. To import another template file, right-click **Security Configuration and Analysis**, and then click **Import Template**.

- Export the current database settings to a template file. To export another template file, right-click **Security Configuration and Analysis**, and then click **Export Template**.

Additional reading

For more information about the security tools, see:

- "Security Configuration Manager" at http://www.microsoft.com/technet/ treeview/default.asp?url=/technet/prodtechnol/windowsserver2003/ proddocs/server/SEconcepts_SCM.asp.

- "Best Practices for Security Configuration and Analysis" at http://www.microsoft.com/technet/treeview/default.asp?url=/technet/ prodtechnol/windowsserver2003/proddocs/server/sag_SCMbp.asp.

How to Test Computer Security

> Your instructor will demonstrate how to analyze security settings on a computer by using Security Configuration and Analysis

Introduction

Sometimes you must analyze a computer to see what security settings on a server are different from the settings in a base security template. To do this, you run the Security Configuration and Analysis tool.

Procedure

To analyze security by using Security Configuration and Analysis:

1. Add the Security Configuration and Analysis snap-in to an MMC console.

2. Right-click **Security Configuration and Analysis**, and then click **Open database**.

3. In the **Open database** dialog box, select an existing database file or type a unique name to create a new database, and then click **Open**.

   Existing databases already contain imported settings. If you are creating a new database, the **Import Template** dialog box appears. Select a database, and then click **Open**.

4. Right-click **Security Configuration and Analysis**, and then click **Analyze Computer Now**.

5. In the **Perform Analysis** dialog box, choose a location for the analysis log file, and then click **OK**.

6. In the console tree, expand **Security Configuration and Analysis**.

7. Navigate through the security settings in the console tree, and compare the **Database Setting** and the **Computer Setting** columns in the details pane.

Practice: Testing Computer Security

In this practice, you will:

- Create a custom security template
- Analyze the security settings on your computer with the security settings in the custom security template

Objective

In this practice, you will:

- Create a custom security template.
- Compare the security settings on your computer to the settings in the custom security template.

Instructions

Before you begin this practice:

- Log on to the domain by using the *ComputerName*User account.
- Open CustomMMC with the **Run as** command.

  Use the user account Nwtraders*ComputerName*Admin (Example: LondonAdmin).

- Review the procedures in this lesson that describe how to perform this task.

Scenario

You are a systems administrator for Northwind Traders. You must implement the following security settings on your member servers:

- Passwords must be at least 10 characters.
- A dialog box must be displayed during the logon process, informing users that unauthorized access is not allowed.
- The alerter service, which is set to start manually, must be disabled.

Practice: Creating security templates

▶ **Create a custom security template**

1. In the Security Template snap-in, change the following policies in the securews template:

    - Set **Account Policies/Password Policy/Minimum password length** to 10 characters.

    - Set **Local Policies/Security Options/Interactive Logon/Message text for users attempting to log on** to **Authorized Access Only**.

    - Set **Local Policies/Security Options/Interactive Logon/Message title for users attempting to log on** to *ComputerName*.

    - Set **System Services/Alerter** to **Disabled**.

2. Save the custom security template as *ComputerName***Secure**.

Scenario

Now that you have configured the template and the appropriate policy settings, you want to perform a security analysis to create a baseline for future security analysis and to verify the current configuration.

Practice: Testing computer security

▶ **Import and clear the current security configuration and analysis baseline database**

- In Security Configuration and Analysis, import the *ComputerName*Secure template and clear the database.

▶ **Perform the security analysis**

1. Right-click **Security Configuration and Analysis**, and then click **Analyze Computer Now**.

2. From **Perform Analysis** dialog box, click **OK**.

3. In Security Configuration and Analysis, expand **Local Policies**, and then click **Security Options**.

4. Notice the **Interactive logon: Message text for users attempting to log on** and the **Interactive logon: Message title for users attempting to log on** policies.

5. In the details pane, notice the system settings that have a red flag.

    A red flag indicates that the security template is different than the current computer settings.

Lesson: Configuring Auditing

- What Is Auditing?
- What Is Audit Policy?
- Types of Events to Audit
- Guidelines for Planning an Audit Policy
- How to Enable an Audit Policy
- How to Enable Auditing for Files and Folders
- How to Enable Auditing for Active Directory Objects
- Best Practices for Configuring Auditing

Introduction

No security strategy is complete without a comprehensive auditing strategy. More often than not, organizations learn this only after they experience a security incident. Without an audit trail of actions, it is almost impossible to successfully investigate a security incident. You must determine as part of your overall security strategy what events you need to audit, the level of auditing appropriate for your environment, how the audited events and collected, and how they are reviewed.

Lesson objectives

After completing this lesson, you will be able to:

- Describe auditing.
- Describe what an audit policy is.
- Describe types of events to audit.
- Identify the guidelines for planning an audit policy.
- Enable an audit policy.
- Enable auditing for files and folders.
- Enable auditing for an organizational unit.
- Apply best practices while configuring auditing.

What Is Auditing?

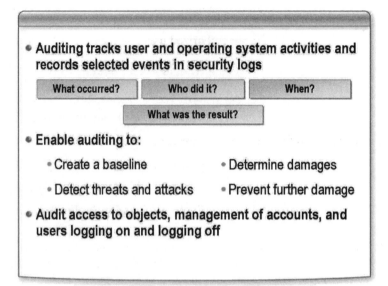

Definition

Auditing is the process that tracks user and operating system activities by recording selected types of events in the security log of a server or a workstation. Security logs contain various audit entries, which contain the following information:

- The action that was performed

- The user who performed the action

- The success or failure of the event and when the event occurred

- Additional information, such as the computer where the event occurred

Why perform auditing?

Enable auditing and monitor audit logs to:

- Create a baseline of normal network and computer operations.

- Detect attempts to penetrate the network or computer.

- Determine what systems and data have been compromised during or after a security incident.

- Prevent further damage to networks or computers after an attacker has penetrated the network.

The security needs of an organization help determine the amount of auditing used. For example, a minimum-security network may choose to audit failed logon attempts to monitor against potential brute force attacks. A high-security network may choose to audit both successful and failed logon attempts to track any unauthorized users who successfully gain access to the network.

Although auditing may provide valuable information, excessive auditing fills the audit log with unnecessary information. This can potentially affect the performance of your system and make it extremely difficult to find relevant information.

Types of events to audit   The most common types of events to audit are when:

■ Objects, such as files and folders, are accessed

■ Managing user accounts and group accounts

■ Users log on to and log off from the system

Additional reading   For more information about auditing, see the TechNet article "Auditing overview" at http://www.microsoft.com/technet/treeview/default.asp?url=/ technet/prodtechnol/windowsserver2003/proddocs/server/ sag_SEconceptsAudit.asp.

What Is Audit Policy?

- An audit policy determines the security events that will be reported to the network administrator

- Set up an audit policy to:

    - Track success or failure of events

    - Minimize unauthorized use of resources

    - Maintain a record of activity

- Security events are stored in security logs

Introduction

Establishing an audit policy is an important part of security. Monitoring the creation or modification of objects gives you a way to track potential security problems, helps to ensure user accountability, and provides evidence in the event of a security breach.

Definition

An audit policy defines the types of security events that Windows Server 2003 records in the security log on each computer. Windows Server 2003 writes events to the security log on the specific computer where the event occurs.

Why set up an audit policy?

Set up an audit policy for a computer to:

- Track the success and failure of events, such as attempts to log on, attempts by a particular user to read a specific file, changes to a user account or group membership, and changes to security settings.

- Minimize the risk of unauthorized use of resources.

- Maintain a record of user and administrator activity.

Use Event Viewer to view events that Windows Server 2003 records in the security log. You can also archive log files to track trends over time. This is useful to determine trends in the use of printers, access to files, and attempts at unauthorized use of resources.

How can you implement an audit policy?

You can set up an audit policy on any single computer, either directly by using the Local Policy snap-in or indirectly by using Group Policy, which is more commonly used in large organizations. After an audit policy is designed and implemented, information begins to appear in the security logs. Each computer in the organization has a separate security log that records local events.

When you implement an audit policy:

- Specify the categories of events that you want to audit. Examples of event categories are user logon, user logoff, and account management. The event categories that you specify constitute your audit policy. There is no default audit policy.

- Set the size and behavior of the security log. You can view the security log with Event Viewer.

- Determine which objects you want to monitor access of and what type of access you want to monitor, if you want to audit directory service access or object access. For example, if you want to audit attempts by users to open a particular file, you can configure audit policy settings in the object access event category so that successful and failed attempts to read a file are recorded.

Default audit policies

The default auditing settings for servers are configured by administrative templates. The following security templates configure default auditing settings:

- Setup security.inf

- Hisecdc.inf

- Hisecws.inf

- Secuerdc.inf

- Securews.inf

To view the policy settings that each security template configures, in the Security Templates snap-in, navigate to Local Policies\Audit Policy for each administrative template.

Additional reading

For more information about audit policies, see the TechNet article "Auditing policy" at http://www.microsoft.com/technet/treeview/default.asp?url=/ technet/prodtechnol/windowsserver2003/proddocs/server/APtopnode.asp.

Types of Events to Audit

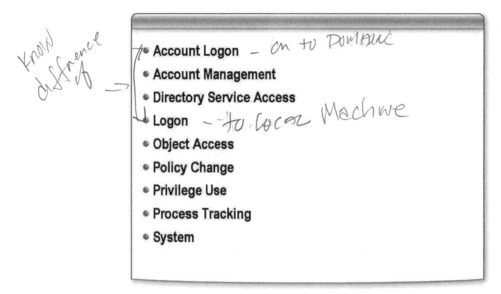

Introduction

The first step in creating a strategy for auditing the operating system is to determine what type of actions or operations that you need to record.

Determining what events to audit

What operating system events should you audit? You do not want to audit every event, because auditing all operating system events requires enormous system resources and may negatively affect system performance. You should work with other security specialists to determine what operating system events to audit. Only audit events that you believe will be useful for later reference.

An effective way to begin determining what events to audit is to gather the relevant group of people and discuss:

- What actions or operations you want to track.

- On what systems you want to track these events.

For example, you may decide to track:

- All domain and local logon events on all computers.

- The use of all files in the Payroll folder on the HR server.

The success and failure events

In Windows Server 2003, audit events can be split into two categories:

- Success events

  A success event indicates that the operating system has successfully completed the action or operation. Success events are indicated by a key icon.

- Failure events

  A failure event indicates that an action or operation was attempted, but did not succeed. Failure events are indicated by a padlock icon.

Failure events are very useful for tracking attempted attacks on your environment, but success events are much more difficult to interpret. The vast majority of success events are indications of normal activity, and an attacker who accesses a system also generates a success event.

Often, a pattern of events is as important as the events themselves. For example, a series of failures followed by a success may indicate an attempted attack that was eventually successful.

Similarly, the deviation from a pattern may also indicate suspicious activity. For example, suppose the security logs show that a user at your organization logs on every workday between 8 A.M. and 10 A.M., but suddenly the user is logging on to the network at 3 A.M. Although this behavior may be innocent, it should be investigated.

Events that Windows Server 2003 can audit

The first step in implementing an audit policy is to select the types of events that you want Windows Server 2003 to audit. The following table describes the events that Windows Server 2003 can audit.

Event	Example
Account Logon	An account is authenticated by a security database. When a user logs on to the local computer, the computer records the AccountLogon event. When a user logs on to a domain, the authenticating domain controller records the Account Logon event.
Account Management	An administrator creates, changes, or deletes a user account or group; a user account is renamed, disabled, or enabled; or a password is set or changed.
Directory Service Access	A user accesses an Active Directory object. To log this type of access, you must configure specific Active Directory objects for auditing.
Logon	A user logs on to or off of a local computer, or a user makes or cancels a network connection to the computer. The event is recorded on the computer that the user accesses, regardless of whether a local account or a domain account is used.
Object Access	A user accesses a file, folder, or printer. The administrator must configure specific files, folders, or printers for auditing.
Policy Change	A change is made to the user security options (for example, password options or account logon settings), user rights, or audit policies.
Privilege Use	A user exercises a user right, such as changing the system time (this does not include rights that are related to logging on and logging off) or taking ownership of a file.
Process Tracking	An application performs an action. This information is generally only useful for programmers who want to track details about application execution.
System	A user restarts or shuts down the computer, or an event occurs that affects Windows Server 2003 security or the security log.

Events edited by default

The Setup security.inf template includes default settings that enable auditing of successful account logon events and successful logon events. No other events are audited by default.

Guidelines for Planning an Audit Policy

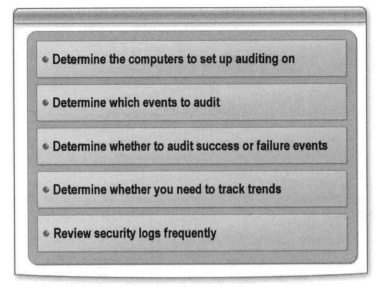

- Determine the computers to set up auditing on
- Determine which events to audit
- Determine whether to audit success or failure events
- Determine whether you need to track trends
- Review security logs frequently

Introduction

Auditing too many types of events may create excess overhead, which may result in diminished system performance.

Guidelines

Use the following guidelines when planning an audit policy:

- Determine the computers to set up auditing on. Plan what to audit for each computer, because Windows Server 2003 audits events on each computer separately. For example, you may frequently audit computers used to store sensitive or critical data, but you may infrequently audit client computers that are used solely for running productivity applications.

- Determine the types of events to audit, such as the following:

  - Access to files and folders

  - Users logging on and off

  - Shutting down and restarting a computer running Windows Server 2003

  - Changes to user accounts and groups

- Determine whether to audit success or failure events, or both. Tracking success events can tell you how often Windows Server 2003 or users access specific files or printers. You can use this information for resource planning. Tracking failure events can alert you to possible security breaches.

- Determine whether you need to track trends of system usage. If so, plan to archive event logs. Some organizations are required to maintain a record of resource and data access.

- Review security logs frequently and regularly according to a schedule. Configuring auditing alone does not alert you to security breaches.

How to Enable an Audit Policy

Your instructor will demonstrate how to:

- Configure an audit policy on a local computer
- Configure an audit policy on a domain or organizational unit

Introduction

There are two procedures for enabling an audit policy, depending on whether the computer is in a workgroup or a domain.

Procedure for an audit policy on a local computer

To enable an audit policy on a local computer:

1. From the **Administrative tools** menu, click **Local Security Policy**.

2. In the console tree, expand **Local Policies**, and then double-click **Audit Policy**.

3. In the details pane, double-click the policy that you want to enable or disable.

4. Do one or both of the following, and then click **OK**:

    - To audit success events, select the **Success** check box.

    - To audit failure events, select the **Failure** check box.

    For example, suppose you select the **Success** and **Fail** check boxes for logon and logoff events. If a user successfully logs on to the system, it is logged as a success audit event. If a user tries to access a network drive and fails, the attempt is logged as a failure audit event.

Note If you are a member of a domain, and a domain-level policy is defined, domain-level settings override the local policy settings.

Procedure for an audit policy on a domain or organizational unit

To enable an audit policy on a domain or an organizational unit:

1. In Group Policy Management, create or browse to a GPO linked to an organizational unit, and then edit it.

2. In the console tree, navigate to Computer Configuration/Windows Settings/ Security Settings/Local Policies/Audit Policy.

3. In the details pane, double-click the policy that you want to enable or disable.

4. Do one or both of the following, and then click **OK**:

   • To audit success events, select the **Success** check box.

   • To audit failure events, select the **Failure** check box.

How to Enable Auditing for Files and Folders

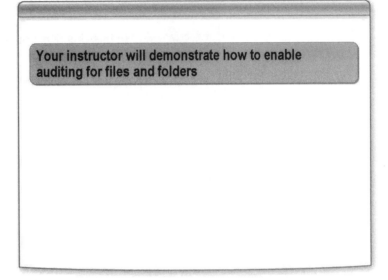

Your instructor will demonstrate how to enable auditing for files and folders

Introduction

You enable auditing to detect and record security-related events, such as when a user attempts to access a confidential file or folder. When you audit an object, an entry is written to the security log whenever the object is accessed in a certain way.

After you enable auditing, you can keep track of users who access certain objects and analyze security breaches. The audit trail shows who performed the actions and who tried to perform actions that are not permitted.

Procedure

To enable auditing for files and folders:

1. In Windows Explorer, locate the file or folder that you want to audit.

2. Right-click the file or folder, and then click **Properties**.

3. In the **Properties** dialog box, on the **Security** tab, click **Advanced**.

4. In the **Advanced Security Settings** dialog box, on the **Auditing** tab, do one of the following:

   - To enable auditing for a new user or group, click **Add**. In the **Enter the object name to select** box, type the name of the user or group, and then click **OK**.

   - To view or change auditing for an existing group or user, click the name, and then click **Edit**.

   - To disable auditing for an existing group or user, click the name, and then click **Remove**.

5. Under **Access**, click **Successful**, **Failed**, or both **Successful** and **Failed**, depending on the type of access that you want to audit.

6. If you want to prevent child objects from inheriting these audit entries, select the **Apply these auditing entries to objects and/or containers within this container only** check box.

Practice: Enabling Auditing for Files and Folders

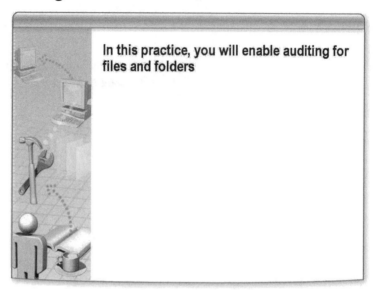

In this practice, you will enable auditing for files and folders

Objective

In this practice, you will enable auditing for files and folders.

Instructions

Before you begin this practice:

- Log on to the domain by using the *ComputerName*User account.
- Open CustomMMC with the **Run as** command.

  Use the user account Nwtraders*ComputerName*Admin (Example: LondonAdmin).

- Ensure that the D:\HR Reports folder is created and shared from a previous practice or lab.
- Review the procedures in this lesson that describe how to perform this task.

Scenario

You get a call from the Human Resources manager, who tells you that files are being deleted. The Sales manager wants to know which user is deleting files. You must enable auditing on your server for the HR-Reports folder.

Practice

▶ **Create a GPO that enables an audit policy**

- Tool: Group Policy Management
- GPO name: *ComputerName* **Audit Policy**
- GPO link to the following location: Locations/*ComputerName*/Computers
- Enable auditing of the success and failure of the following security policy:
  Computer Configuration/Windows Settings/Security Settings/
  Local Policies/Audit Policy/Audit object access

▶ **Verify the location of the computer account**

1. Ensure your computer is in the Locations/*ComputerName*/Computers organizational unit.

   If your computer is not in this organizational unit, search for it and move it.

2. From a command prompt, type **gpupdate /force**

3. If prompted to logoff, type **N** and press **ENTER**.

▶ **Audit the HR-Reports folder**

- Enable auditing for the folder D:\HR Reports by using the following criteria:

  - Audit the group G NWTraders HR Personnel.

  - Audit **Successful - Delete of Subfolders and Files**.

  - Audit **This folder, subfolders and files**.

  - Prevent child objects from inheriting these audit entries.

How to Enable Auditing for Active Directory Objects

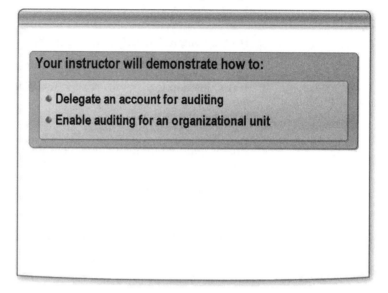

Your instructor will demonstrate how to:

- Delegate an account for auditing
- Enable auditing for an organizational unit

Introduction

When you enable auditing for an organizational unit, you audit the event generated when a user accesses an Active Directory object that has permissions. By default, auditing is set to Success in the Default Domain Controller GPO, and it remains undefined for workstations and servers where it does not apply.

Note By default, only members of the Administrators group have privileges to configure auditing. You can delegate the task of configuring auditing for server events to another user account by assigning the Manage auditing and security log user right in Group Policy.

Procedure for delegating an account to enable auditing

To enable nonadministrators to manage and view audit logs on a member server, you must first delegate the authority to a user or group. To do this:

1. In Group Policy Object Editor, in the console tree, navigate to the following:

   Computer Configuration/Windows Settings/Security Settings/
   Local Polices/User Rights Assignment

2. Click **Manage auditing and security log**.

3. On the **Action** menu, click **Properties**.

4. In the **Manage auditing and security log** dialog box, select the check box, **Define these policy settings**, and then click **Add User or Group**.

5. Type the name of the appropriate user or user group from the list, and then click **OK**.

6. Click **OK**.

Procedure for enabling auditing for an organizational unit

To enable auditing for an organizational unit:

1. In Active Directory Users and Computers, right-click the organizational unit that you want to audit, and then click **Properties**.

2. In the **Properties** dialog box, on the **Security** tab, click **Advanced**.

   To view the security properties, you must click **Advanced Features** on the **View** menu of Active Directory Users and Computers.

3. In the **Advanced Security Settings** dialog box, on the **Auditing** tab, do one of the following:

   - To enable auditing for a new user or group, click **Add**. In the **Enter the object name to select** box, type the name of the user or group, and then click **OK**.

   - To remove auditing for an existing group or user, click the group or user name, click **Remove**, and click **OK**. Skip the rest of this procedure.

   - To view or change auditing for an existing group or user, click the group or user name, and then click **Edit**.

4. In the **Apply onto** box, click the location where you want auditing to take place.

5. Under **Access**, indicate what actions you want to audit by selecting the appropriate check boxes:

   - To audit success events, select the **Successful** check box.

   - To stop auditing success events, clear the **Successful** check box.

   - To audit failure events, select the **Failed** check box.

   - To stop auditing failure events, clear the **Failed** check box.

   - To stop auditing all events, click **Clear All**.

6. If you want to prevent child objects from inheriting these audit entries, select the **Apply these auditing entries to objects and/or containers within this container only** check box.

Practice: Enabling Auditing for an Organizational Unit

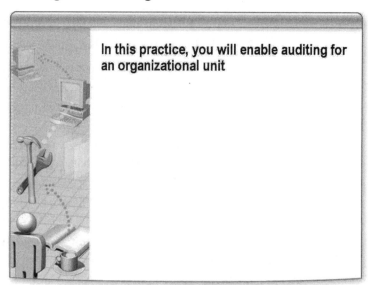

In this practice, you will enable auditing for an organizational unit

Objectives

After completing this practice, you will be able to configure an audit policy that audits the creation and deletion of objects in an organizational unit.

Instructions

Before you begin this practice:

- Log on to the domain by using the *ComputerName*User account.

- Open CustomMMC with the **Run as** command using Nwtraders*ComputerName*Admin (Example: LondonAdmin).

- Review the procedures in this lesson that describe how to perform this task.

Scenario

You are concerned that someone is adding and removing user, computer, and group objects in your *ComputerName* organizational unit. You want to configure an audit policy that audits the successful and unsuccessful creation and deletion of those objects in your *ComputerName* organizational unit.

Practice

▶ **Enable auditing for the organizational unit *ComputerName***

- Enable auditing by using the following criteria:

  - Audit the Everyone group.

  - Audit the *ComputerName* organizational unit and all child objects.

  - Audit the following access properties for success and failure events:

    - Create Account Objects

    - Delete Account Objects

    - Create Computer Objects

    - Delete Computer Objects

    - Create Group Objects

    - Delete Group Objects

Best Practices for Configuring Auditing

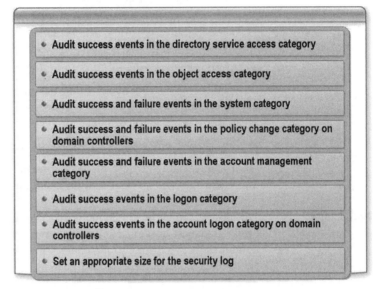

- Audit success events in the directory service access category
- Audit success events in the object access category
- Audit success and failure events in the system category
- Audit success and failure events in the policy change category on domain controllers
- Audit success and failure events in the account management category
- Audit success events in the logon category
- Audit success events in the account logon category on domain controllers
- Set an appropriate size for the security log

Best practices

Apply the following best practices while performing auditing:

- Audit success events in the directory service access category.

  By auditing success events in the directory service access category, you can find out who accessed an object in Active Directory and what operations were performed.

- Audit success events in the object access category.

  By auditing success events in the object access category, you can ensure that users are not misusing their access to secured objects.

- Audit success and failure events in the system category.

  By auditing success and failure events in the system category, you can detect unusual activity that indicates that an attacker is attempting to gain access to your computer or network.

- Audit success and failure events in the policy change category on domain controllers.

  If an event is logged in the policy change category, someone has changed the Local Security Authority (LSA) security policy configuration. If you use Group Policy to edit your audit policy settings, you do not need to audit events in the policy change category on member servers.

- Audit success and failure events in the account management category.

  By auditing success events in the account management category, you can verify changes that are made to account properties and group properties. By auditing failure events in the account management category, you can see if unauthorized users or attackers are trying to change account properties or group properties.

- Audit success events in the logon category.

  By auditing success events in the logon category, you have a record of when each user logs on to or logs off from a computer. If an unauthorized person steals a user's password and logs on, you can find out when the security breach occurred.

- Audit success events in the account logon category on domain controllers.

  By auditing success events in the account logon category, you can see when users log on to or log off from the domain. You do not need to audit events in the account logon category on member servers.

- Set an appropriate size for the security log.

  It is important to configure the size of the security log appropriately, based on the number of events that your audit policy settings generate.

Additional reading

For more information about audit policy best practices, see the TechNet article "Best practices" at http://www.microsoft.com/technet/treeview/ default.asp?url=/technet/prodtechnol/windowsserver2003/proddocs/ server/sag_SEconceptsImpAudBP.asp.

For more information about managing audit logs see:

- TechNet article "Microsoft Operations Manager 2000" at http://www.microsoft.com/technet/treeview/default.asp?url=/technet/ prodtechnol/mom/evaluate/mom2k.asp.

- Article 325898, "HOW TO: Set Up and Manage Operation-Based Auditing for Windows Server 2003, Enterprise Edition" in the Microsoft Knowledge Base at http://support.microsoft.com/?kbid=325898.

Lesson: Managing Security Logs

- What Are Log Files?
- Common Security Events
- Tasks Associated with Managing the Security Log Files
- How to Manage Security Log File Information
- How to View Security Log Events

Introduction

You can configure the security logs to record information about Active Directory and server events. These events are recorded in the Windows security log. The security log can record security events, such as valid and invalid logon attempts, as well as events that are related to resource use, such as creating, opening, or deleting files. You must log on as an administrator to control what events are audited and displayed in the security log.

Lesson objectives

After completing this lesson, you will be able to:

- Describe the types of security log files and the information contained in each log file.

- Identify common security events.

- Describe tasks associated with managing the security log files.

- Manage security log file information.

- View security log events.

What Are Log Files?

The following logs are available in Event Viewer:

- Application
- Security
- System
- Directory service
- File Replication service

Introduction

The security log records events, such as valid and invalid logon attempts, and events related to resource use, such as creating, opening, or deleting files or other objects. For example, if logon auditing is enabled, attempts to log on to the system are recorded in the security log. After an audit policy is designed and implemented, information begins to appear in the security log.

Each computer in the organization has a separate security log that records local events. Domain controllers hold the security log information about Active Directory.

Logs available in Event Viewer

You can view the following logs in Event Viewer, depending on the type of computer that you are using and the services that are installed on that computer:

- Application

  Contains events generated by applications installed on the computer, including server applications, such as Microsoft Exchange Server or Microsoft SQL Server™, and desktop applications, such as Microsoft Office.

- Security

  Contains events generated by auditing. These events include logons and logoffs, access to resources, and changes in policy.

- System

  Contains events generated by components and services in Windows Server 2003.

- Directory service

  Appears only on domain controllers. The directory service event log contains, for example, Active Directory replication.

- File Replication service

  Appears only on domain controllers. The file replication service event log contains, for example, events that are related to the replication of Group Policy.

Tip If you decide to use auditing extensively, increase the size of the security log in the Event Log section of the security policy for the Default Domain Controllers GPO.

Security log files format   Security log files are also stored in the *systemroot*/system32/config directory. Security logs can be exported and archived in the following file formats:

- Event log files (.evt) (Default)

- Comma delimited (.csv)

- Text file (.txt)

Common Security Events

Logon	Event Description
Event ID 528	Successful logon
Event ID 529	Unsuccessful logon attempt
Event ID 539	Attempts to log on to a locked out account
File Ownership	**Event Description**
Event ID 578	Change in file ownership
Security Log	**Event Description**
Event ID 517	Security log cleared
Shutdown	**Event Description**
Event ID 513	System is shut down

Introduction

Many events appear in the security log. The following are some common scenarios that may be cause for concern and suggestions for diagnosing problems by using the event log.

Invalid logon attempts and account lockout

A successful logon generates an Event ID 528. When a user attempts to guess another user's password, they will likely make several incorrect guesses. Each incorrect guess generates an Event ID 529, which is also generated by a misspelled user name. If an account becomes locked out, subsequent attempts generate an Event ID 539.

Notice that one or two of these events might occur when a user types incorrectly, does not realize that the CAPS LOCK key is on, or forgets a password.

Change of file ownership

The owner of a file in the NTFS file system can modify the file's permissions to read and modify the file. A user who has the user right to take ownership can access any file by first taking ownership of that file. This change of ownership constitutes the use of a user right and generates an Event ID 578.

Clearing the security log

An unscrupulous administrator with the user right to clear the security log from Event Viewer can clear the log to hide his or her security-sensitive activities.

The security log must always be cleared according to a well-planned schedule and only immediately after a full copy of the log is archived. If the log is cleared under any other circumstances, the administrator must justify his or her actions. Clearing the security log generates an Event ID 517, which is the first event generated in the new log.

System shutdown

Ordinarily, mission-critical servers must be shut down only by administrators. You can prevent others from shutting down a server by assigning or denying the Shut down the system user right in the local security policy or by using Group Policy.

To identify if the **Shut down the system** right was mistakenly assigned, audit the system Event ID 513, which indicates who shut down the computer.

Additional reading

For more information about security events, see:

- Article 299475, "Windows 2000 Security Event Description (Part 1 of 2)" in the Microsoft Knowledge Base at http://support.microsoft.com/ ?kbid=299475.

- Article 301677, "Windows 2000 Security Event Description (Part 2 of 2)" in the Microsoft Knowledge Base at http://support.microsoft.com/ ?kbid=301677.

- The TechNet article "Security Operations Guide for Windows 2000 Server" at http://www.microsoft.com/technet/treeview/default.asp?url=/ TechNet/security/prodtech/windows/windows2000/staysecure/ DEFAULT.asp.

Tasks Associated with Managing the Security Log Files

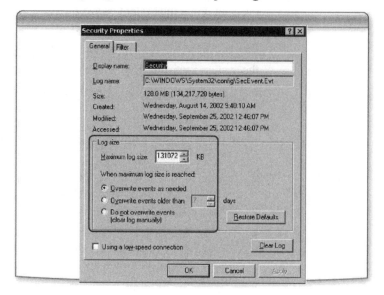

Introduction

All events related to operating system security in Windows NT, Windows Server 2003, and Microsoft Windows XP are recorded in the security log in Event Viewer. Security-related events may also be recorded in the application and system logs.

Evaluate the configuration of the log file

Before you enable audit policies, you must evaluate whether the default configuration of the log files in Event Viewer is appropriate for your organization.

To view the log files settings in Event Viewer:

1. From the **Administrative Tools** menu, open Event Viewer.

2. Right-click the security event log, and then click **Properties**.

Log file location

By default, the security log is stored in the *systemroot*/System32/config directory in a file named SecEvent.evt. In Windows Server 2003, you can change the log file location in the security log properties. In Windows NT 4.0 and Windows Server 2000, you must edit the registry to change the location of each log file.

By default, only the System account and the Administrators group have access to the security log. This ensures that nonadministrators cannot read, write, or delete security events. If you move the log to a new location, ensure that the new file has the correct NTFS permissions. Because the Event Viewer service cannot be stopped, changes to this setting are not applied until the server is restarted.

Maximum log file size

By default, the maximum size that the security log can grow to before the overwrite behavior is initiated is 512 KB. Because hard disk space is much more readily available now than it was in the past, you will likely want to increase this setting. The amount by which you increase this setting depends on the overwrite behavior configured for the log file, but a good general guideline is to set the maximum size to at least 50 MB. You can change the maximum size of the log file on individual computers in the security log properties or on many computers by using security templates or editing the registry.

The maximum size that you should set for the combined total size of all event logs is 300 MB. Each security event is 350 to 500 bytes, so a 10-MB event log contains approximately 20,000 to 25,000 security events.

Log file overwrite behavior

When you configure the security log settings, you must define the overwrite behavior when the maximum log file size is reached. The following list describes the overwrite event options.

- **Overwrite events as needed**

    New events continue to be written when the log is full. Each new event replaces the oldest event in the log.

- **Overwrite events older than [x] days**

    Events are retained in the log for the number of days you specify before they are overwritten. The default is seven days.

- **Do not overwrite events**

    New events are not recorded, and the event log must be cleared manually.

Delegate the right to manage the file

To delegate the rights to manage the security log file, configure the Group Policy setting **Manage auditing and security log**. This is found in Computer Configuration/Windows Settings/Security Settings/Local Policies/User Rights Assignment.

How to Manage Security Log File Information

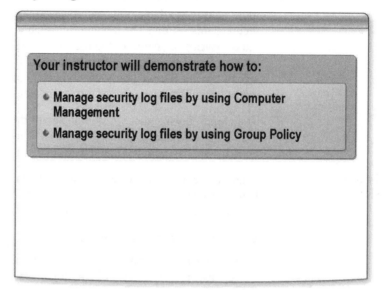

Introduction

The more security information you capture, the bigger the security log file you need. You want a log file to track what security events have occurred since the last archival of the events.

Procedure for using Computer Management

To manage security log file information through Computer Management:

1. In Computer Management, in the console tree, expand **System Tools and Event Viewer**.

2. Right-click a log file, and then click **Properties**.

3. In the **Properties** dialog box, you can do the following:

   - Configure the maximum log file size

   - Configure overwrite behavior

   - Clear the log file

Procedure for using a GPO

To manage security log file information through a GPO:

1. Edit a GPO.

2. In Group Policy Object Editor, in the console tree, expand **Computer Configuration**, expand **Windows Settings**, expand **Security Settings**, and then expand **Event Log**.

3. Define a parameter for the following Group Policy settings:

   - **Log size**

   - **Prevent local guest from accessing logs**

   - **Retain Log**

   - **Retention method for Log**

How to View Security Log Events

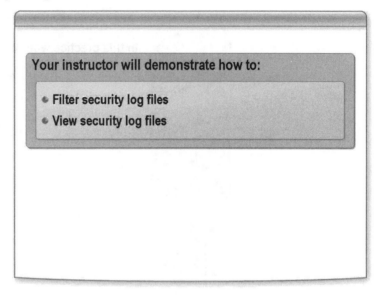

Your instructor will demonstrate how to:
- Filter security log files
- View security log files

Introduction

Security logs can get rather large, and viewing large logs or finding specific types of events in the log may be difficult. You can set a filter on the log to view specific types of events or events from specific users or groups.

Procedure for filtering the security logs

To filter the security logs:

1. In Event Viewer, in the console tree, right-click **Security**, click **View**, and then click **Filter**.

2. In the **Security Properties** dialog box, define your filter criteria, and then click **OK**.

Procedure for viewing security logs

To view security logs:

1. In Event Viewer, in the console tree, click **Security**.

2. The details pane lists individual security events.

   If you want to see more details about a specific event, in the details pane, double-click the event.

Practice: Managing Log File Information

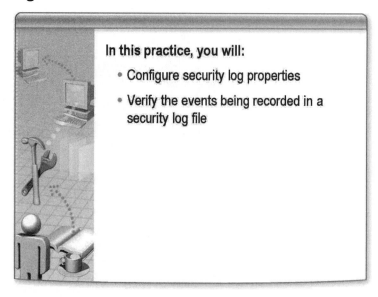

In this practice, you will:
- Configure security log properties
- Verify the events being recorded in a security log file

Objective

In this practice, you will:

- Configure security log properties.
- View security log events.

Instructions

Before you begin this practice:

- Log on to the domain by using the *ComputerName*User account.
- Open CustomMMC with the **Run as** command.

  Use the user account Nwtraders*ComputerName*Admin (Example: LondonAdmin).

- Review the procedures in this lesson that describe how to perform this task.

Scenario

The network security team at Northwind Traders tells you that the security log file must have the following properties on your *ComputerName* server:

- The maximum log size must be 30,016 KB.

- The overwrite behavior is **Do not overwrite events (clear log manually)**.

They also ask you to review your security log file to determine if the security events are being logged for the folder D:\HR Reports.

Practice

▶ **Configure the security log properties**

1. Change the maximum log size to 30,016 KB.

2. Change the overwrite behavior to **Do not overwrite events (clear log manually)**.

▶ **Verify that security events are being logged for D:\HR Reports**

1. Create a security log filter that filters the following types of events:

   - Success events and failure events

   - Security

   - Object access

2. Browse through the security log to see success and failure events for D:\HR Reports.

Lab A: Managing Security Settings

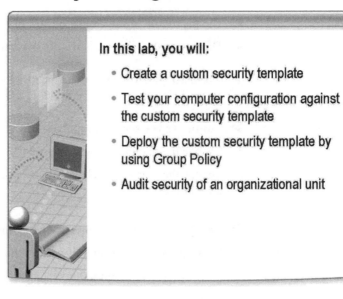

In this lab, you will:

- Create a custom security template
- Test your computer configuration against the custom security template
- Deploy the custom security template by using Group Policy
- Audit security of an organizational unit

Objectives

After completing this lab, you will be able to:

- Create a custom security template.
- Test your computer configuration against the custom security template.
- Deploy a custom template by using a GPO.
- Configure and test security auditing of organizational units.

Instructions

Before you begin this practice:

- Log on to the domain by using the *ComputerName*User account.
- Open CustomMMC with **Run as** command.

  Use the user account NWTraders*ComptuerName*Admin (Example: LondonAdmin).

- Ensure the CustomMMC has the following snap-ins:

  - Security Templates
  - Group Policy Management
  - Security Configuration and Analysis
  - Active Directory Users and Computers
  - Computer Management (Local)
  - Computer Management (London)

Estimated time to complete this lab: 35 minutes

Exercise 1
Creating a Custom Template

In this exercise, you will create a custom security template.

Scenario

The security team has finished testing the security requirements for Northwind Traders. They have given you security requirements that you must use to create a custom security template called *ComputerName* Server Policy.

Tasks	Special instructions
1. Create a new custom security template.	▪ Security template name: *ComputerName* **Server Policy**
2. Enable audit policies.	▪ Enable the following audit policies for failure: • **Audit account logon events** • **Audit logon events** ▪ Enable the following audit policies for success and failure: • **Audit account management events** • **Audit object access events** • **Audit policy change events** • **Audit privilege use events** • **Audit system events**
3. Set event log properties.	▪ Set the following event log properties: • Set maximum application log size to 99,840 KB • Set maximum security log size to 99,840 KB • Retain security log for 7 days • Retain system log for 7 days
4. Save the template.	▪ Save the template *ComputerName* Server Policy.

Exercise 2
Testing a Custom Template

In this exercise, you will compare a custom security template to your server's current security policy.

Tasks	Special instructions
1. Create a new configuration and analysis baseline database.	▪ Database name: *ComputerName* **Security Test** ▪ Template: *ComputerName* **Server Policy Settings.inf**
2. Analyze your server.	▪ Analysis log name: *ComputerName* **Security Test.log**
3. Review the results of the audit policy analysis.	▪ Circle Y if your computer setting matches the database. Circle N if your computer setting differs from the database. • **Audit account logon events** (Y / N) • **Audit account management events** (Y / N) • **Audit logon events** (Y / N) • **Audit object access events** (Y / N) • **Audit policy change events** (Y / N) • **Audit privilege use events** (Y / N) • **Audit system events** (Y / N)
4. Review the results of the event log analysis.	▪ Circle Y if your computer setting matches the database. Circle N if your computer setting differs from the database. • **Maximum application log size** (Y / N) • **Maximum security log size** (Y / N) • **Retain security log** (Y / N) • **Retain system log** (Y / N)

Exercise 3
Deploying a Custom Template Using a GPO

In this exercise, you will import a custom template to a GPO and deploy the template to your computer. You will then test your computer to determine if you received the GPO.

Tasks	Special instructions
1. Create and link a GPO.	■ Organizational unit to link to GPO: Locations/*ComputerName*/Computers ■ GPO name: *ComputerName* **Security Settings**
2. Import a security template to a GPO.	■ Template name: *ComputerName* Server Policy.inf
3. Disable **Block Policy inheritance**.	■ Expand all organizational units of **Locations/*ComputerName*** and remove any blocking of inheritance of all sub organizational units.
4. Verify that the computer account is in the proper organizational unit.	■ Verify that the computer named *ComputerName* is in the organizational unit Locations/*ComputerName*/Computers. ■ If *ComputerName* is not in the Locations/*ComputerName*/Computers organizational unit, move it there.
5. Update your Group Policy settings.	■ Run **gpupdate /force**.
6. Analyze the local computer security policy.	■ Run **Analyze Computer Now** in Security Configuration and Analysis.

7. Review the results of the audit policy analysis.	■ Circle Y if your computer setting matches the database. Circle N if your computer setting differs from the database.
	
	  • **Audit account logon events** (Y / N)
	  • **Audit account management events** (Y / N)
	  • **Audit logon events** (Y / N)
	  • **Audit object access events** (Y / N)
	  • **Audit policy change events** (Y / N)
	  • **Audit privilege use events** (Y / N)
	  • **Audit system events** (Y / N)

8. Review the results of the event log analysis.	■ Circle Y if your computer setting matches the database. Circle N if your computer setting differs from the database.
	
	  • **Maximum application log size** (Y / N)
	  • **Maximum security log size** (Y / N)
	  • **Retain security log** (Y / N)
	  • **Retain system log** (Y / N)

Exercise 4
Configuring and Testing Security Audits of Organizational Units

In this exercise, you will configure and test security audits of organizational units.

Scenario

Northwind Traders wants to configure security on the Location/*ComputerName* organizational units to monitor the G IT Admins group. You must configure and test auditing for failed attempts to delete user and computer accounts.

Tasks	Special instructions
1. Enable auditing for an organizational unit.	▪ Audit the organizational unit Locations/*ComputerName* ▪ Remove inheritable auditing entries ▪ Remove all noninherited auditing entries ▪ Audit the Everyone group ▪ Audit the access of **Delete Computer Objects** for **Failed** access ▪ Apply policy to **This object and all child objects**

2. Try to delete computer account with an unauthorized account.	▪ Tool: DSRM
	   a. Open a command prompt with runas
	   b. runas /user:nwtraders*ComputerName*User cmd
	   c. Password: P@ssw0rd
	 ▪ Use DSRM to try and delete the computer *ComputerName*
	   • Dsrm CN=*ComputerName*,OU=Computers,OU=*ComputerName*,OU=Locations,DC=nwtraders,DC=msft
	 ▪ You should get an access is denied error message

3. Filter the London security log.	▪ Tool: Computer Management (London)
	 ▪ Filter security policy for:
	   • Event types: **Failure audit**
	   • Event source: **Security**
	   • Category: **Directory Service Access**
	   • User: *ComputerName*User

❓	What was *ComputerName*User trying to do? _____ _____

Course Evaluation

Your evaluation of this course will help Microsoft understand the quality of your learning experience.

To complete a course evaluation, go to http://www.CourseSurvey.com.

Microsoft will keep your evaluation strictly confidential and will use your responses to improve your future learning experience.

Microsoft®
Training &
Certification

Part II: Maintaining a Microsoft® Windows® Server 2003 Environment

Microsoft®

Microsoft®
Training &
 Certification

Module 1: Preparing to Administer a Server

Contents

Overview	1
Lesson: Administering a Server	2
Lesson: Configuring Remote Desktop to Administer a Server	18
Lesson: Managing Remote Desktop Connections	34
Lab A: Preparing to Administer a Server	41

Overview

- Administering a Server
- Configuring Remote Desktop to Administer a Server
- Managing Remote Desktop Connections

Introduction

A major responsibility of a systems administrator is to administer the servers in an organization. Because most systems administrators are not located in the same room as the servers they manage, it is important to understand how to manage servers remotely.

This module describes how to use Microsoft® Windows® Server 2003 to administer servers remotely, what tools to use, and what permissions are required to administer a server. It also discusses how to administer remote connections and why that is an important aspect of system administration.

Objectives

After completing this module, you will be able to:

- Explain the tasks, tools, and rights that are required to administer a server.
- Configure Remote Desktop for Administration and client preferences.
- Manage remote desktop connections.

Lesson: Administering a Server

- Multimedia: Introduction to Maintaining a Microsoft Windows Server 2003 Environment
- Group Memberships Used to Administer a Server
- What Is the Run As Command?
- How to Set Up Run As Shortcuts
- How to Use the Run As Command
- What Is Computer Management?
- How to Administer a Server Remotely by Using Computer Management
- Role of MMC in Remote Administration
- How to Configure MMC to Manage a Server Remotely

Introduction

This lesson introduces the tasks, tools, and rights that are required to administer a server. This information is the foundation that you need to perform your job as a systems administrator. This lesson describes the proper use and function of the tools that you use to administer a server and explains the concepts of remote and local server administration.

Lesson objectives

After completing this lesson, you will be able to:

- Explain the tasks that are involved in server administration.
- Explain the group memberships that are used to administer a server.
- Explain the purpose and function of the **Run as** command.
- Configure **Run as** desktop shortcuts.
- Configure a server remotely by using the **Run as** command.
- Explain the role of the Computer Management tool in remote administration.
- Administer a server remotely by using the Computer Management tool.
- Explain the role of Microsoft Management Console (MMC) in remote administration.
- Configure MMC to manage a server remotely.

Multimedia: Introduction to Maintaining a Microsoft Windows Server 2003 Environment

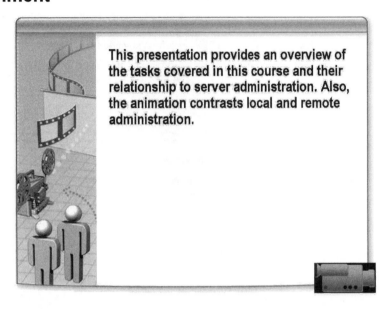

This presentation provides an overview of the tasks covered in this course and their relationship to server administration. Also, the animation contrasts local and remote administration.

File location

To view the *Introduction to Maintaining a Microsoft Windows Server 2003 Environment* presentation, open the Web page on the Student Materials compact disc, click **Multimedia**, and then click the title of the presentation.

Do not start this presentation unless the instructor tells you to.

Group Memberships Used to Administer a Server

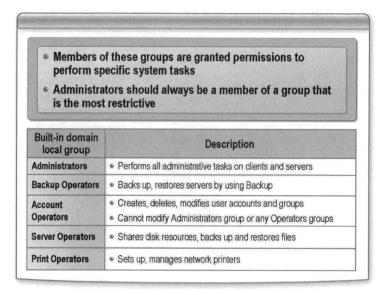

Built-in domain local group	Description
Administrators	• Performs all administrative tasks on clients and servers
Backup Operators	• Backs up, restores servers by using Backup
Account Operators	• Creates, deletes, modifies user accounts and groups • Cannot modify Administrators group or any Operators groups
Server Operators	• Shares disk resources, backs up and restores files
Print Operators	• Sets up, manages network printers

Introduction

To administer a server, you must have appropriate permissions to do the job. It is important to be familiar with the permissions that are assigned to domain local groups that allow their members to perform specific functions, because you can use these groups to perform common administrative tasks.

Built-in domain local groups

When a computer becomes a domain controller, built-in groups are created in the Active Directory® directory service. By default, these groups have predetermined permissions that determine the system tasks that members of a built-in or predefined group can perform. These groups cannot be deleted.

The following list describes the built-in domain local groups and their pre-determined level of permissions.

- *Administrators*. Members of the Administrators group can perform all functions that the operating system supports. Administrators can assign themselves any user rights that they do not have by default. Administrator local group membership should be restricted to only users who require full system access. Log on as an administrator only when necessary.

  Also be very cautious about adding other users to the Administrators group. For example, if a help desk technician is responsible for the printers in your organization, add the technician to the Print Operators group instead of the Administrators group.

- *Backup Operators*. Members of the Backup Operators group can back up and restore files by using the Backup tool.

- *Account Operators*. Members of the Account Operators group can manage user accounts and groups. The exception is that only a member of the Administrators group can modify an Administrators group or any operator group.

- *Server Operators.* Members of the Server Operators group can share disk resources, log on to a server interactively, create and delete network shares, start and stop services, format the hard disk of the server, and shut down the computer. They can also back up and restore files by using the Backup tool.

- *Print Operators.* Member of the Print Operators group can set up local and network printers to ensure that users can easily connect to and use printer resources.

Domain local groups can protect resources

Using a variety of domain local groups and their associated permission levels can protect resources from security breaches. A systems administrator should always be a member of a group that is the most restricted but that provides the appropriate rights and the permissions that are required to accomplish the task. For example, a systems administrator who manages only printers and backup server data should be a member of the printer operators group and should have authority to back up server data.

Domain local group permissions

Members of domain local groups are assigned permissions to perform system tasks, such as backing up files, restoring files, and changing the system time. You can use these groups for administering resources, such as file systems or printers that are located on any computer in the domain where common access permissions are required.

When you run your computer as a member of the Administrators group, the system is vulnerable to Trojan horse attacks and other security risks. The simple act of visiting an Internet site or opening an e-mail attachment can damage the system, because an unfamiliar Internet site or e-mail attachment may contain Trojan horse code that can be downloaded to the system and executed.

What Is the Run As Command?

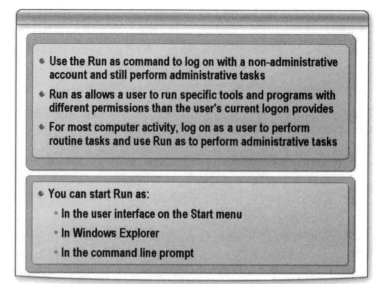

Introduction

By using the **Run as** command, also known as a secondary logon, administrators can log on with a non-administrative account and, without logging off, perform tasks by running trusted programs to perform administrative tasks.

Requires two user accounts

To use **Run as** to perform administrative tasks, systems administrators require two user accounts: a regular account with basic privileges and an administrative account. Each administrator can have a different administrative account, or all administrators can share one administrative account.

Use the **Run as** command for most computer activity. When you run your computer while you are logged on as a member of the Administrators group, security is an issue. Also, some items, such as Windows Explorer, the Printers folder, and desktop items, are launched indirectly by Windows. These items cannot be started with **Run as**.

For tasks that cannot be performed by using the **Run as** command, such as upgrading the operating system or configuring system parameters, log off your user account and then log on as an administrator.

Use Run as to open MMC custom consoles

To administer local or remote computers, you can use the **Run as** command to open custom consoles you have created in the Microsoft Management Console (MMC). Using the **Run as** command offers you access to the services and administrative tools that are included in the console, while providing you with the appropriate permissions on the system for the components that are administered by the console.

Any user can use Run as

Although the **Run as** command is primarily intended for systems administrators, any user with multiple accounts can use **Run as** to start programs under different account contexts without logging off.

Three ways to use Run as

There are three ways to use the **Run as** command:

- You can right-click a program located on the **Start** menu, and then click **Run as**.

- You can right-click a program in Windows Explorer, and then click **Run as**.

- You can also use the **Run as** command from a command prompt. This method is typically used for scripting administrative tasks or to start a command shell in the local administrative context. To run **Run as** from a command prompt, type **runas /user:***domain_name\user_name program_name*

For example, to run the Computer Management tool from the command line as an administrator, open a command prompt and then type **runas /user:nwtraders\admininistrator "mmc %windir%\system32 \compmgmt.msc"**

Set up Run as shortcuts

You can also set up **Run as** shortcuts to the services and administrative tools that you use most often, including Performance, Computer Management, Device Manager, and Disk Manager.

How to Set Up Run As Shortcuts

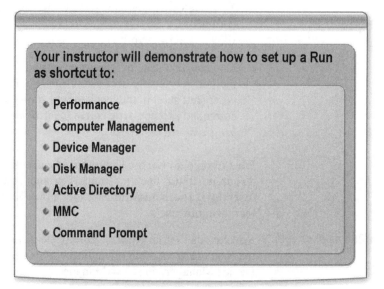

Your instructor will demonstrate how to set up a Run as shortcut to:

- Performance
- Computer Management
- Device Manager
- Disk Manager
- Active Directory
- MMC
- Command Prompt

Introduction

To save time, you can configure **Run as** desktop shortcuts to the administrative tools you use most often.

Procedure

To set up a **Run as** shortcut to Performance:

1. Right-click the desktop, point to **New**, and then click **Shortcut**.

2. On the **Create Shortcut** page, in the **Type the location of the item** box, type **runas /user:Nwtraders\administrator "mmc %windir%\system32\perfmon.msc"** and then click **Next**.

3. On the **Select a Title for the program** page, in the **Type a name for this shortcut** box, type **Performance** and then click **Finish**.

See the following table for additional commands.

Tool	Command line
Computer Management	**runas /user:nwtraders\administrator "mmc %windir%\system32\ compmgmt.msc"**
Device Manager	**runas /user:nwtraders\administrator "mmc %windir%\system32\ devmgmt.msc"**
Disk Manager	**runas /user:nwtraders\administrator "mmc %windir%\system32\ diskmgmt.msc"**
Active Directory	**runas /user:nwtraders\administrator "mmc %windir%\system32\dsa.msc"**
MMC	**runas /user:nwtraders\administrator mmc**
Command Prompt	**runas /user:nwtraders\administrator cmd**

How to Use the Run As Command

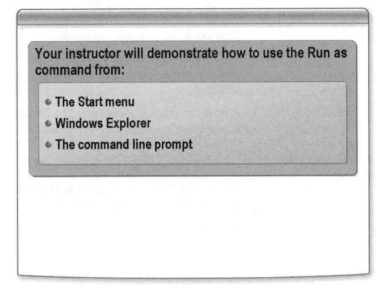

Your instructor will demonstrate how to use the Run as command from:

* The Start menu
* Windows Explorer
* The command line prompt

Introduction

Use the **Run as** command to launch an MMC console in the context of an account that has the appropriate rights to perform the task. For example, if you are logged on a server as a user and you want to install a new software package, you can log off, log on as an administrator, open Control Panel, use **Add/Remove Programs** to install the new software, log off as administrator, and then log on with your user account. With **Run as**, however, you can open Control Panel, press the SHIFT key, right-click **Add/Remove Programs,** and then use **Run as** to start Add/Remove Programs as an administrator.

Procedure for using the Run as command from the Start menu

To use the **Run as** command from the **Start** menu:

1. On the **Start** menu, right-click the program executable file (or shortcut).

2. Click **Run as**.

3. Click **The following user**.

4. In the **User name** and **Password** boxes, type the account name and password.

5. Click **OK**.

Procedure for using the Run as command from Windows Explorer

To use the **Run as** command from Windows Explorer:

1. Open Windows Explorer, and then right-click the program executable file.

2. Click **Run as**.

3. Click **The following user**.

4. In the **User name** and **Password** boxes, type the account name and password.

5. Click **OK**.

Procedure for using the Run as command from the command line prompt

To use the **Run as** command using the command line prompt:

1. On the **Start** menu, click **Run**, type **runas /user:** *domain_name***administrator cmd** (where *domain_name* is the name of your domain), and then click **OK**.

2. A console window appears, prompting for a password for the *domain_name*\administrator account. Type the password for the administrator account, and then press ENTER.

3. A new console appears running in the administrative context. The title of the console displays "running as *domain_ name*\administrator."

Procedure for using Run as shortcuts

To use a **Run as** desktop shortcut to open an administrative tool:

1. On the desktop, double-click the **Performance**, **Computer Manager**, **Device Manager**, or **Disk Manager** icon.

2. Type **P@ssw0rd**

What Is Computer Management?

- A collection of administrative tools
- Use to manage remote and local computers

Tool	Description
System tools	• Monitor system events • Create and manages shared resources • View a list of users who are connected to a local or remote computer • View device configurations and adds new device drivers
Storage tools	• Set properties for storage devices • Update disk information
Services and applications tools	• Manage applications and services • Start and stop system services, such as Task Scheduler and Indexing Service

Definition

Computer Management is a collection of administrative tools that you can use to administer a local or remote computer.

Use Computer Management to manage computers

You can use Computer Management to:

- Monitor system events, such as logon times and application errors.

- Create and manage shared resources.

- View the list of users who are connected to a local or remote computer.

- Start and stop system services, such as Task Scheduler and Indexing Service.

- Set properties for storage devices.

- View device configurations and add new device drivers.

- Manage applications and services.

Computer Management console

The Computer Management console organizes the administrative tools into the following three categories:

- System Tools

- Storage

- Services and Applications

The following sections describe the tools in these categories and explain how to use them to perform administrative tasks.

System Tools

You use the tools in System Tools to manage system events and performance on the computer you are managing.

- *Event Viewer*. Use Event Viewer to manage and view events that are recorded in the application, security, and system logs. You can monitor the logs to track security events and to identify possible software, hardware, and system problems.

- *Shared Folders*. Use Shared Folders to view connections and resources that are in use on the computer. You can create, view, and manage shared resources; view open files and sessions; and close files and disconnect sessions.

- *Local Users and Groups*. Use Local Users and Groups to create and manage your local user accounts and groups.

- *Performance Logs and Alerts*. Use Performance Logs and Alerts to monitor and collect data about your computer's performance.

- *Device Manager*. Use Device Manager to view the hardware devices that are installed in your computer, update device drivers, modify hardware settings, and troubleshoot device conflicts.

Storage

You use the tools in Storage to manage the properties of storage devices.

- *Removable Storage*. Use Removable Storage to track your removable storage media and to manage the libraries or data-storage systems that contain them.

- *Disk Defragmenter*. Use Disk Defragmenter to analyze and defragment volumes on your hard disks.

- *Disk Management*. Use Disk Management to perform disk-related tasks, such as converting disks or creating and formatting volumes. Disk Management helps you manage your hard disks and the partitions or volumes they contain.

Services and Applications

The tools in Services and Applications help you manage services and applications on the specified computer.

- *Services*. Use Services to manage services on local and remote computers. You can start, stop, pause, resume, or disable a service. For example, you can use Services to stop a service on a remote computer.

- *WMI Control*. Use WMI Control to configure and manage the Windows Management Service.

- *Indexing Service*. Use Indexing Service to manage the Indexing service and to create and configure additional catalogs to store index information.

How to Administer a Server Remotely by Using Computer Management

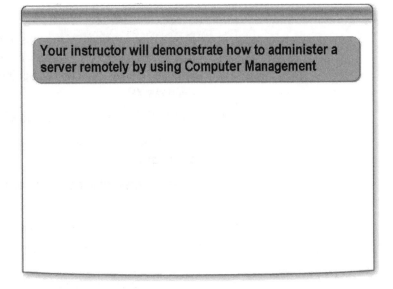

Introduction

You can use Computer Management tools when you are off-site from the server that you need to manage. The remote management tools that are provided with Windows Server 2003 help you identify and solve problems that users encounter without sending support personnel to the users' work sites. For example, if you are working in your office and you must modify a disk partition on a server that is located in another building, you can use Computer Management to complete the task.

Procedure

To use Computer Management to administer a computer remotely:

1. Log on as an administrator with a password of **P@ssw0rd**

2. On the **Start** menu, right-click **My Computer**, and then click **Manage**.

3. Right-click **Computer Management (local)**, and then click **Connect to another computer**.

4. Click **Another Computer**, type the name of the computer that you want to manage remotely, or click **Browse** to locate the computer, and then click **OK**.

5. In Computer Management, in the console tree, expand either **System Tools**, or **Storage**, or **Services and Applications**.

6. Click the item, and then select the tools that you want to use.

Role of MMC in Remote Administration

- **Microsoft Management Console**
  - Provides an interface to snap-ins that manage hardware, software, and network services for servers running Windows Server 2003 and computers running Windows XP
- **Why Use MMC in remote administration?**
  - Use for tasks frequently accomplished on remote computers
  - Use to manage similar tasks on many remote computers

Introduction	Microsoft Management Console (MMC) provides an interface that you can use to create, save, and open administrative tools, called snap-ins, that manage the hardware, software, and network components of Windows Server 2003. When you open an administrative tool in MMC, you can specify whether to apply the tool on the local computer or on a remote computer.
Use MMC for remote and local administration	To perform similar tasks on many servers, use MMC snap-ins. Most of the administrative tools that are provided with Windows Server 2003 family operating systems are MMC snap-ins that you can use to administer remote servers as well as your local computer.
Advantages of MMC snap-ins	The advantages of using MMC snap-ins are that you can:

- Create a console that contains the tools you use for the tasks you perform most often. For example, you use Computer Management to administer a remote server.

- Set the focus for a tool to any of the servers that you administer, and switch between servers and tools within a single MMC console. For example, you can use the Computer Management snap-in to view the performance of multiple remote servers.

How to Configure MMC to Manage a Server Remotely

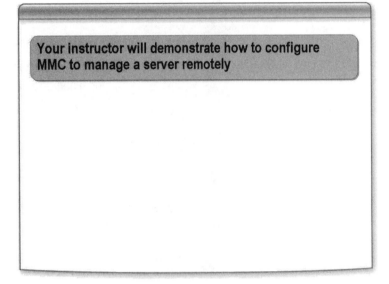

Your instructor will demonstrate how to configure MMC to manage a server remotely

Introduction

Systems administrators are often required to work off-site. As a systems administrator, you may be located at one site but must perform maintenance on a server at a second site. In this case, you can use an MMC console to remotely manage a server. For example, you can start or stop services on a remote server, review the event log, manage shares, or manage disks.

Procedure

To configure MMC to manage a server remotely:

1. Open Microsoft Management Console.

2. On the **File** menu, click **Add/Remove Snap-in**, and then click **Add**.

3. In the snap-in list, click **Computer Management**, and then click **Add**.

4. When prompted, select the local computer or remote computer that you want to manage by using this snap-in, and then click **Finish**.

5. Click **Close** and then click **OK**.

Practice: Configuring MMC to Manage Files on a Remote Server

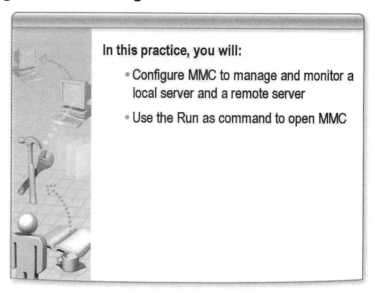

Objective

In this practice, you will:

- Configure MMC to manage and monitor a local server and a remote server.
- Use the **Run as** command to open MMC.

Scenario

You are the systems administrator for an organizational unit on a network. You are responsible for managing and monitoring the shared folders on your server and on a remote server. You will create an MMC snap-in that allows you to manage and monitor shared folders on both servers simultaneously. You will also create a shared folder on the remote server by using the same tool. You will use this tool frequently, so you will save it on your desktop. Because you do not have file privileges on the remote server, you will use the **Run as** command to use the tool.

Practice: Creating a custom MMC console

▶ **Create a custom MMC console to manage and monitor shared folders on multiple servers**

1. Log on to the domain with your *Computer***User** account (where *Computer* is the name of your computer) and with a password of **P@ssw0rd**.

2. On the **Start** menu, click **Run**.

3. In the **Run** dialog box, type **mmc** and then click **OK**.

4. On the **File** menu, click **Add/Remove snap-in**, click **Add**, and then add a Computer Management snap-in for your computer.

5. On the **File** menu, click **Add/Remove snap-in**, click **Add**, and then add a Computer Management snap-in for the Glasgow computer.

6. In the Computer Management (Local) tree, expand **System Tools**, expand **Shared Folders**, and then click **Shares**.

7. Determine whether you can monitor shared folders on your computer.

8. In the Computer Management (Glasgow) tree, expand **System Tools**, expand **Shared Folders**, and then click **Shares**.

9. Determine whether you can monitor shared folders on the Glasgow computer.

10. Save the console on the desktop as **MMC1**.

11. Close MMC1.

12. Using **Run as**, open MMC1 as the domain administrator.

13. Verify that you can monitor shares on your computer and the Glasgow computer.

Practice: Creating a shared folder

▶ **Create a shared folder on a remote computer using MMC1**

1. In the MMC1 window, open the **Computer Management (Glasgow)** tree, expand **System Tools**, expand **Shared Folders**, and then click **Shares**.

2. Right-click **Shares**, and then click **New Share**.

3. Create a shared folder on \\Glasgow with the following parameters:

Parameter	Entries
Share name	*ComputerName* (where *ComputerName* is the name of your computer, such as Vancouver, Denver, and so on)
Location	**C:\MOC\Shares***ComputerName*
Permissions	Administrator: **Full** Users: **Read-only**

4. Close the MMC1 window and do not save console settings.

5. Verify that the administrators have full control and that users have read-only permissions.

6. Close all windows and log off.

Lesson: Configuring Remote Desktop to Administer a Server

- **What Is Remote Desktop for Administration?**
- **Why Use Remote Desktop for Administration?**
- **What Are the Requirements for Remote Desktop Service?**
- **How to Enable Remote Desktop**
- **What Are Client Preferences for Remote Desktop Connection?**
- **Remote Desktop Connection vs. Remote Desktops**
- **How to Connect to a Remote Server**
- **Guidelines for Using Remote Administration Tools**

Introduction

This lesson explains how to configure Remote Desktop for Administration and how to configure the client to allow access to the servers by using Remote Desktop for Administration. This lesson also describes how to establish the connection between the administrator's computer and the server.

Lesson objectives

After completing this lesson, you will be able to:

- Describe Remote Desktop for Administration and explain how it works.
- Explain the uses of Remote Desktop for Administration.
- Describe the requirements for Remote Desktop Service.
- Enable Remote Desktop.
- Explain client preferences for Remote Desktop.
- Describe the differences between Remote Desktops and Remote Desktop Connections.
- Connect to a remote server.
- Explain the guidelines for using Remote Administration tools.

What Is Remote Desktop for Administration?

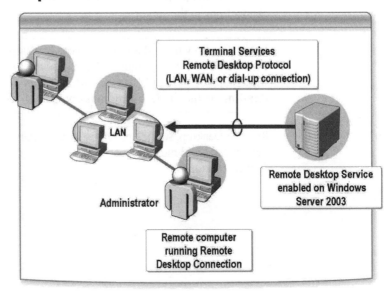

Introduction

By using Remote Desktop for Administration, you can manage one or more remote computers from a single location. In a large organization, you can use remote administration to centrally manage many computers that are located in other buildings or even in other cities. In a small organization, you can use remote administration to manage a single server that is located in an adjacent office.

Remote access to servers

Remote Desktop for Administration provides access to a server from a computer at another location by using Remote Desktop Protocol (RDP). RDP transmits the user interface to the client session, and it also transmits the keyboard and mouse clicks from the client to the server.

You can create up to two simultaneous remote connections. Each session that you log on to is independent of other client sessions and the server console session. When you use Remote Desktop for Administration to log on to the remote server, it is as if you are logged on to the server locally.

Remote Desktop Connection and Remote Desktops snap-in

Remote Desktop for Administration provides two tools that you can use to administer a remote server: Remote Desktop Connection and the Remote Desktops snap-in.

Each instance of the Remote Desktop Connection tool creates its own window and allows you to administer one remote server per window. It always starts a new session on the server.

The Remote Desktops snap-in is useful for administrators who remotely administer multiple servers or for administrators who must connect to the console session remotely. The Remote Desktops snap-in displays a split window with a console tree on the left and remote connection information in the details pane on the right.

The maximum number of remote desktop connections to a server is two. After you reach this limit, Remote Desktops allows no other remote desktop connections to the server.

Note To allow more than two Remote Desktop connections, you must install Terminal Services. For more information about Terminal Services, see the white paper, *Technical Overview of Terminal Services*, under **Additional Reading** on the Student Materials compact disc.

Remote Desktop Service

Remote Desktop Service provides server access. It is installed with Windows Server 2003 and must be enabled before you can configure Remote Desktop Administration.

Why Use Remote Desktop for Administration?

- Provide remote access to most configuration settings
- Diagnose a problem and test multiple solutions quickly
- Allow access to servers from anywhere in the world
- Perform time-consuming batch administrative jobs, such as tape backups
- Upgrade server applications and operating systems remotely

Introduction

Remote Desktop for Administration is a convenient and efficient service that can greatly reduce the overhead that is associated with remote administration. For example, Remote Desktop for Administration allows multiple systems administrators to manage remote servers.

Remote sessions

Remote Desktop for Administration allows you either to start a new remote session on a server or to remotely take over the console session on a server. However, there can be only one console session running on a server at one time. If you log on to the console remotely while another administrator is logged on to the console session, the first administrator is locked out.

Note   System messages that are sent to the console are displayed at the console session and not at the other remote sessions.

Run earlier versions of Windows

By using Remote Desktop Connection, systems administrators can also fully manage computers that are running Windows Server 2003 family operating systems from computers that are running earlier versions of Windows.

Access to configuration settings

Remote Desktop for Administration is useful because it provides remote access to most configuration settings, including Control Panel, which usually cannot be configured remotely.

By using a Remote Desktop session, you can access MMC, Active Directory, Microsoft Systems Management Server, network configuration tools, and most other administrative tools.

Multiple uses

Using Remote Desktop for Administration can help you diagnose a problem and test multiple solutions quickly.

You can access the servers from anywhere in the world by using a wide area network (WAN), a virtual private network (VPN), or a dial-up connection. When you run a time-consuming batch administrative job, such as a tape backup, you can start the job, disconnect from the corporate network, and later reconnect to check progress.

You can use Remote Desktop for Administration to upgrade server applications remotely and to perform tasks that are not usually possible unless you are working at the console.

Administrative tasks are quicker and more intuitive than using command line utilities, although it is still possible to open a command prompt.

What Are the Requirements for Remote Desktop Service?

- **Remote Desktop Service must be enabled locally on the remote server**
- **Remote Desktop Service must be configured to allow users to connect remotely to the server**
  - Systems administrators must have the appropriate permissions to administer the server
  - By default, the administrator has remote connection privileges to the remote server

Introduction

Before you can administer a server remotely, the remote server must be enabled for remote administration.

Remote Desktop Service configuration

Remote Desktop Service must be enabled locally on the remote server by a systems administrator who is working at the console. The systems administrator must have the appropriate permissions to administer the computer. By default, an administrator has remote connection privileges to the remote server.

How to Enable Remote Desktop

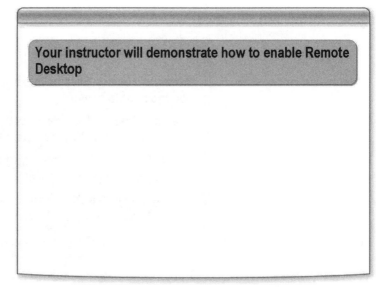

Your instructor will demonstrate how to enable Remote Desktop

Introduction

A systems administrator can use Remote Desktop to perform remote tasks such as adding software and installing service packs on a remote server.

Procedure

To configure the server connections to remotely administer a server:

1. Log on as Administrator.

2. On the **Start** menu, right-click **My Computer**.

3. Click **Properties**.

4. Click **Remote**.

5. Select the **Allow users to connect remotely to this computer** check box.

What Are Client Preferences for Remote Desktop Connection?

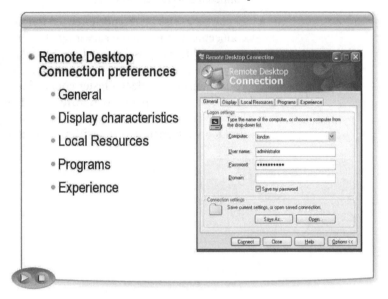

Introduction

Remote Desktop Connection is a client-side application that allows you to connect to a server after Remote Desktop for Administration is enabled on the server.

Client preferences configuration

To configure your remote desktop connection, you must set up client preferences. To do this, use the Remote Desktop Connection interface to configure the information about the connection and the client computer.

To complete your configuration, set the client preferences on the following tabs:

- *General*. Use the **General** tab to provide information that is required for automatic logon to the remote server. This information includes the name of the server, the user name and password, and the domain name. You can also save your password, save your connection settings, and open a saved connection.

- *Display*. Use the **Display** tab to change the screen size and color settings of the remote desktop and to hide or display the connection bar in full-screen mode.

- *Local Resources*. Use the **Local Resources** tab to choose whether to allow a remote desktop to have access to the disk drives, serial ports, printers, or smart card on your local computer. Allowing access from the remote desktop is called *resource redirection*. When you allow the remote desktop to have access to these resources, the remote desktop can use the resources for the duration of the session.

  For example, you choose to make your local disk drive available to the remote desktop. Although this access allows you to easily copy files to or from the remote desktop, it also means that the remote desktop has access to the contents of your local disk drive. If this access is not appropriate, you can clear the appropriate check box to keep your local disk drive or any other local resource from being redirected to the remote desktop.

- *Programs*. Use the **Programs** tab to specify that a program starts upon connection to the remote server.

- *Experience*. Use the **Experience** tab to improve the performance of your connection to the remote server by allowing certain characteristics of the remote Windows session, such as the Desktop background, to appear as if they are enabled on the remote computer. To improve the performance of your connection, select a faster connection speed. The default connection speed, 56 kilobits per second, offers good performance for most networks. Use the faster speed settings to enable richer graphical features, such as desktop wallpaper or menu sliding and fading.

Remote Desktop Connection vs. Remote Desktops

Service	Functions

Remote Desktop Connection	• Connects to one server (running Remote Desktop) per session
	   • You can run multiple connections if you run multiple copies of Remote Desktop Connection
	   • Console tree displays name of server
	• Each connection can be displayed full screen or in a window
	• Opens a remote session to a server by default

Remote Desktops	• Connects to multiple servers simultaneously
	• Each connection is displayed in the MMC console:
	   • Console tree displays name of server
	   • Details pane displays remote session
	• Opens the console session by default

Introduction

Windows Server 2003 comes with two clients that allow administrators to connect to the remote desktop:

- Remote Desktop Connection
- Remote Desktops snap-in

Remote Desktop Connection

Using Remote Desktop Connection, you can connect to one server. You can run multiple copies of Remote Desktop Connection to connect to multiple servers, but you must switch between Remote Desktop Connection sessions to manage each server. Each connection can be displayed full screen or in a window.

When you connect to a server using Remote Desktop Connection, you will open a remote session by default.

Remote Desktops

You can use the Remote Desktops snap-in to connect to multiple servers simultaneously. Each connection is displayed in an MMC console. The console tree displays the name of the server and the details pane displays the remote session.

When you connect to a server by using Remote Desktops, the console session opens by default.

Use the command line tool

You can also connect to the console session on a remote server by using the **Run** command and the **mstsc** command line tool.

How to Connect to a Remote Server

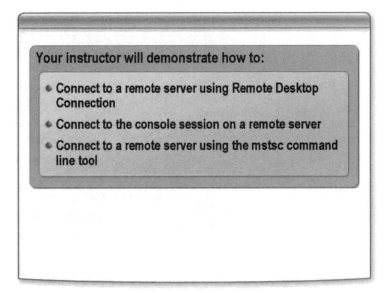

Your instructor will demonstrate how to:

- Connect to a remote server using Remote Desktop Connection
- Connect to the console session on a remote server
- Connect to a remote server using the mstsc command line tool

---

Introduction

As a systems administrator, you may often waste time traveling to remote servers to perform administrative tasks. By using the Remote Desktop Connection tool to remotely administer servers in your organization, you can spend less time commuting and have more time to do your job.

Procedure for connecting to a remote desktop

To connect to a remote server by using Remote Desktop Connection:

1. On the client computer, click **Start**.

2. Point to **All Programs**, point to **Accessories**, point to **Communications**, and then click **Remote Desktop Connection**.

3. In the **Computer** box, type a computer name or the IP address of the server that is running Windows Server 2003 with Remote Desktop Service installed.

4. When finished with the remote session, on the **Start** menu, click **Log off**.

Procedure for connecting to the console session on a remote server

As a systems administrator, you may be required to connect to the console session so that you can see the system messages that are sent to the console. You may also be required to simultaneously manage multiple servers. Use the Remote Desktops snap-in to connect to the console session of a remote server or to manage multiple servers simultaneously.

To connect to a server or servers by using the Remote Desktops snap-in:

1. On the **Start** menu, point to **Administrative Tools**, and then click **Remote Desktops**.

2. In the console tree, right-click **Remote Desktops**, and then click **Add New Connection**.

3. In the **Add New Connection** dialog box, enter the name of the server, a connection name, a user name and password, and the name of the domain.

4. If you want to connect to the console session, verify that the **Connect to console** check box is selected.

5. To manage multiple servers, repeat steps 2 and 3.

6. When finished with the remote session, on the **Start** menu, click **Log off**.

Procedure for connecting to a remote desktop using the mstsc command line tool

To connect to the console session on a remote server by using the **mstsc** command line tool.

1. On the **Start** menu, click **Run**.

2. In the **Run** dialog box, type **cmd** and then click **OK**.

3. At the command prompt, type the following command and then press ENTER:

   mstsc /v:*server* **/console**

   where *server* is the name of the remote server.

4. Log on to the remote server.

For the complete syntax of the **mstsc** command, type **mstsc /?** at the command prompt.

Practice: Configuring Remote Desktop

In this practice, you will:

- Enable Remote Desktop on your server
- Log on to a remote server as a domain administrator
- Allow your partner to log on to your server as a remote administrator

Objective

In this practice, you will:

- Configure your server to allow your partner to gain access to it remotely.
- Connect to your partner's server by using Remote Desktop Connection.
- Allow your partner to log on to your computer as a domain administrator by using Remote Desktop Connection.

Scenario

You are the systems administrator for an organizational unit on a network. Management has asked you to configure your server so that the domain administrator can manage your server remotely.

Practice: Enabling Remote Desktop

▶ **Enable Remote Desktop on your server**

1. Log on to the domain with your *Computer*User account (where *Computer* is the name of your computer) with the password of **P@ssw0rd**.

2. In Control Panel, hold down the SHIFT key, right-click **System**, and then click **Run as**.

3. In the **Run as** dialog box, in the **User name** box, type **nwtraders\administrator** and then in the **Password** box, type **P@ssw0rd** and press ENTER.

4. On the **Remote** tab, in the **Remote Desktop** box, select the **Allow users to connect remotely to this computer** check box.

5. Click **OK** to close all dialog boxes.

6. Wait until your partner has finished this procedure before continuing.

Practice: Verifying that Remote Desktop is enabled

▶ **Verify that Remote Desktop is enabled on your partner's computer**

1. On the **Start** menu, point to **All Programs**, point to **Accessories**, point to **Communications**, and then click **Remote Desktop Connection**.

   Alternatively, you can open a command prompt and use the **mstsc** command to connect to your partner's computer:

   mstsc /v:*PartnerComputer* **/f**

2. Connect to your partner's computer using the following parameters:

Computer	*PartnerComputer* (where Partner*Computer* is the name of your partner's computer)
User name	Administrator
Password	P@ssw0rd
Domain	NWTRADERS

3. Verify that the name of your partner's computer appears at the top of the screen.

4. Log off the remote computer.

5. Close all windows and log off.

Guidelines for Using Remote Administration Tools

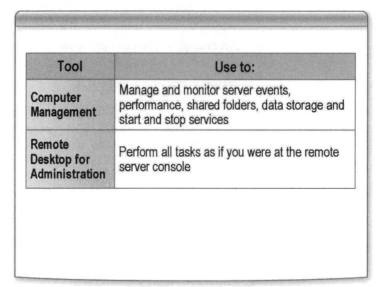

Tool	Use to:
Computer Management	Manage and monitor server events, performance, shared folders, data storage and start and stop services
Remote Desktop for Administration	Perform all tasks as if you were at the remote server console

Introduction

Windows Server 2003 operating systems provide several tools that you can use to manage servers from a remote location. These tools expand your flexibility because you can work as though you are physically present at each server in your organization. By understanding the functions of each tool, you can choose the most appropriate one for your remote administration tasks.

Computer Management tool tasks

The tasks that you can perform by using the Computer Management tool in remote administration are described in the following table.

Application	Task
Server configuration	Manage and monitor shared folders
Accounts	Modify users and groups
Network connectivity	Monitor events
	Manage and monitor performance logs and alerts
	Start and stop services
Data storage	Manage data storage

Remote Desktop for Administration tasks

The uses of the Remote Desktop for Administration tool in remote administration are described in the following table.

Application	Task
Software applications	Install software applications
Server configuration	Defragment a disk
	Domain controller promotion/demotion
	Modify Microsoft .NET Framework configuration
	Modify folder options
Device drivers	Modify device drivers
Update software	Install service packs
	Install hotfixes
	Update system management properties
Desktop options	Modify date and time
	Modify display settings
	Modify fonts
	Modify regional and language settings
	Modify Distributed File System (DFS) services
Hardware configurations	Modify keyboard options
	Modify mouse options
	Modify modem options
	Modify power options
	Modify printer options
	Add and remove printers
Network connectivity	Modify Internet options
	Modify network connection configuration
	Monitor network connections
	Modify accessibility options
	Modify Internet Information Services (IIS) settings
Schedule tasks	Modify scheduled tasks
Accounts	Modify system options
	Modify user and group accounts
Licensing and certificate	Modify licensing
	Modify certificates
Remote services	Modify Component Services
	Modify Data Sources Open Database Connectivity (ODBC)
	Configure and enable Routing and Remote Access
	Modify Terminal Services
Data storage	Manage data storage

Lesson: Managing Remote Desktop Connections

- **What Are Timeout Settings for Remote Desktop Connections?**
- **How to Configure Timeout Settings for Remote Connections**
- **What Is Terminal Services Manager?**
- **How to Manage and Monitor Sessions Using Terminal Services Manager**

Introduction

As a systems administrator, you must monitor users, sessions, and applications on the remote server and perform various tasks to manage the server connection. In this lesson, you will learn the importance of managing Remote Desktop Connection and learn how to terminate sessions that are no longer in use.

Lesson objectives

After completing this lesson, you will be able to:

- Explain timeout settings in Terminal Services Configuration.
- Configure timeout settings for remote connections.
- Explain Terminal Services Manager and when it is used.
- Manage and monitor remote desktop connection sessions.

What Are Timeout Settings for Remote Desktop Connections?

- **Specifies how long client sessions can remain active on the server**
  - Connection sessions remain open after the Remote Desktop window is closed on the client computer
  - Configure timeout settings to reset the session or log off the user
- **Use timeout settings to prevent a remote connection from consuming valuable server resources**

Timeout Settings	Description
End a disconnected session	Forces a user to log off after disconnecting
Active session limit	Disconnects the user after the time limit is exceeded
Idle session limit	Disconnects the user after the amount of idle time is exceeded

Introduction

Each session that you log on to has its own desktop session as well as the server console session. You can configure the amount of time that client sessions can remain active on the server by using Terminal Services Configuration.

Establish timeout sessions

You must establish timeout sessions for these connections because as long as a session is active, it continues to consume valuable server resources. When a session is disconnected but not logged off, that session is using one of two available connections to the server.

Log off a session

Logging off from a session ends the session that is running on the server. Any applications that are running in the session are closed, and unsaved data is lost.

Disconnect a session

After you establish a connection with a remote server, the connection remains open until you log off. When you log off from a session, the session continues to run on the server. The user can log on to the server and resume the session. The session remains open until the user logs off, until an administrator closes it, or until the timeout setting is reached.

Timeout options

Use Terminal Services Configuration to set the appropriate timeouts. The following timeout options are available:

- *End a disconnected session.* Allows you to set the maximum amount of time that a disconnected session remains open on a server.

- *Active session limit.* Allows you to set the maximum amount of time that a user's session can remain active on the server.

- *Idle session limit.* Allows you to set the length of time that a session can be idle before it is logged off.

How to Configure Timeout Settings for Remote Connections

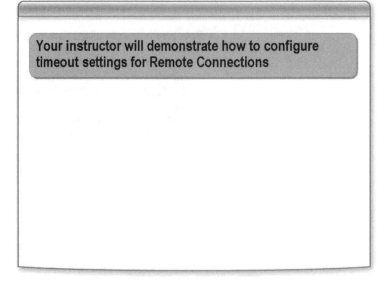

Your instructor will demonstrate how to configure timeout settings for Remote Connections

Introduction

Using timeout settings can help you manage server resources. After you set up session connection limits, you can run server administration more efficiently.

Timeout settings example

For example, another administrator left for a two-week vacation and forgot to log off a remote connection. If you configured the timeout settings, that connection is automatically logged off after a predetermined time.

Procedure

To configure a timeout setting for a remote connection:

1. Click **Start**.

2. On the **Administrative Tools** menu, click **Terminal Services Configuration**.

3. In the details pane, right-click **RDP-Tcp**, and then click **Properties**.

4. On the **Sessions** tab, select the first **Override user settings** check box.

5. Adjust the appropriate settings:

   • End a disconnected session

   • Active session limit

   • Idle session limit

What Is Terminal Services Manager?

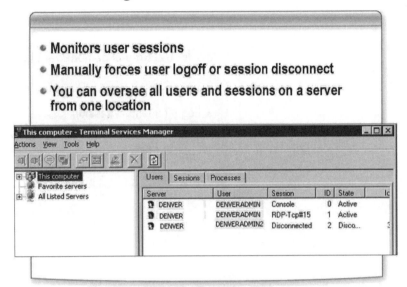

Introduction	You can use Terminal Services Manager to view information about Remote Desktop sessions on your server. Use this tool to monitor users and sessions on each server and to manage disconnected sessions from the remote server.
Obtain administrative information	Use Terminal Services Manager to obtain administrative information about the established Remote Desktop sessions. You can oversee all users and sessions on a terminal server from one location.
Monitor disconnected sessions	Using Terminal Services Manager, you can view the disconnected sessions on the server. Disconnected sessions display the word "Disconnected" under the **Session** and the **State** columns.

Important A disconnected session must be logged off in order to terminate it. It is important to log off all sessions when they are no longer in use, so that the limited number of remote connections can be used most efficiently.

Log off disconnected sessions The **Log Off** command enables you to log off a user from a session on the server. Be aware that logging off a user without warning can result in loss of data at the user's session. When you log off a user, all processes end, and the session is deleted from the server.

How to Manage Sessions by Using Terminal Services Manager

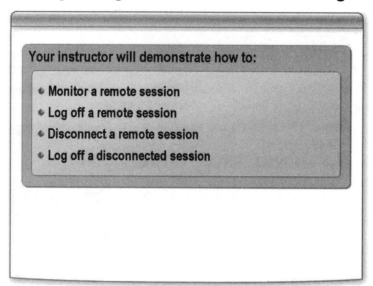

Your instructor will demonstrate how to:

• Monitor a remote session
• Log off a remote session
• Disconnect a remote session
• Log off a disconnected session

Introduction

By monitoring a remote session, you can find out who has established a remote connection and determine the status of that connection. If the connection has been idle, and you suspect that the administrator has disconnected and forgotten to log off, you can manually log off that session remotely.

Procedure for monitoring a remote session

To monitor a remote session by using Terminal Services Manager:

1. On the remote server, click **Start**.

2. On the **Administrative Tools** menu, click **Terminal Services Manager**.

3. Click the **Sessions** tab to view the current sessions.

Procedure for logging off a remote session

To log off a remote session by using Remote Desktop:

1. On the client computer, in the Remote Desktop window, click **Start**.

2. Click **Log Off**, and then click **Log Off**.

Procedure for disconnecting a remote session

To disconnect a remote session by using Remote Desktop:

■ On the client computer, close the Remote Desktop window.

Procedure for logging off a disconnected session

To log off a disconnected session by using Terminal Services Manager:

■ On the remote server, on the **Sessions** tab, right-click the disconnected session, and then click **Reset**.

Practice: Configuring Remote Desktop Sessions

In this practice, you will:

- Monitor the number of remote sessions on your server and log off any disconnected sessions

- Configure your server to log off a disconnected session automatically after the disconnected session exceeds a time limit

Objective

In this practice, you will:

- Monitor the number of remote sessions on the server, and log off any disconnected sessions.

- Configure the server to log off a disconnected session automatically after the disconnected session exceeds a time limit.

Scenario

You are the systems administrator for an organizational unit on a network. You notice that the domain administrator often accesses your server by using Remote Desktop but fails to log off when finished. You often must log off the disconnected sessions manually. You decide to enable the timeout setting to close disconnected sessions after they are idle for more than one minute.

Practice: Logging off disconnected sessions manually

▶ **Manually log off disconnected sessions**

1. Log on to the domain with your *Computer*User account (where *Computer* is the name of your computer) and with a password of **P@ssw0rd**.

2. Open Control Panel, open Administrative Tools, right-click **Terminal Services Manager**, and then click **Run as**.

3. In the **Run As** dialog box, type **nwtraders\administrator** in the **User name** box, type **P@ssw0rd** in the **Password** box, and then press ENTER.

4. If a **Terminal Services Manager** message box appears, click **In the future, do not show this message**, and then click **OK**.

5. Right-click the disconnected session, and then click **Log Off**.

6. Close Terminal Services Manager.

Practice: Configuring a session

▶ **Configure a one-minute time limit for disconnected sessions**

1. In Administrative Tools, open Terminal Services Configuration by using **Run as**.

2. In the **Run As** dialog box, type **nwtraders\administrator** in the **User name** box, type **P@ssw0rd** in the **Password** box, and then press ENTER.

3. Open the **RDP-Tcp Properties** dialog box.

4. On the **Sessions** tab, configure a one-minute time limit for disconnected sessions.

5. Close all windows and log off.

Lab A: Preparing to Administer a Server

In this lab, you will:

- Create a shared folder on a remote computer
- Defragment a disk on a remote computer
- Connect to a remote console session
- Create shortcuts for administrative tools

Objectives

After completing this lab, you will be able to:

- Create a shared folder on a remote computer.
- Defragment a disk on a remote computer.
- Connect to a remote console session.
- Create shortcuts for administrative tools.

Scenario

You are the systems administrator for an organizational unit on a network. Another systems administrator, who is off-site, has sent you an urgent e-mail message asking you to create a new shared folder on her server and to defragment the D drive on her server. You also receive a phone call from a third systems administrator who wants you to review the paging graph that he is viewing on the console at the Glasgow server.

Systems administrator notes

Using Computer Management, share the C:\MOC\Shares\MeetingNotes folder on your partner's computer.

Remotely connect to your partner's computer, and use Computer Management to defragment the D drive.

Connect to the console of the Glasgow computer, and then view the paging graph.

Prerequisites

None.

Estimated time to complete this lab: 40 minutes

Exercise 0
Configuring Folder Permissions

You must run a script to configure the folder permissions on your computer.

▶ **To configure the folder permissions on your computer**

1. Log on to the domain as Administrator with a password of **P@ssw0rd**.

2. On the **Start** menu, click **Run**.

3. In the **Run** dialog box, type **C:\MOC\2275\Labfiles\Setperm.cmd** and then press ENTER.

4. Log off.

Exercise 1
Creating a Shared Folder on a Remote Computer

Using Computer Management, you will create shared folders on your partner's computer. To do this, you will use the **Run as** command to run Computer Management with administrative credentials.

Tasks	Specific instructions
1. Log on to your domain user account.	▪ Log on to your domain user account, *Computer***User** with a password of **P@ssw0rd**.
2. Open an MMC window.	▪ Use the **Run as** command to open an MMC window with administrative credentials.
3. Build a tool by using the Computer Management snap-in for your partner's computer.	▪ On the **File** menu, select **Add/Remove Snap-in** to open the Computer Management snap-in for your partner's computer.
4. Share the folder.	▪ In Computer Management, share the C:\MOC\2275\Labfiles\Test folder as **Test** with the following share permissions: Administrators: **Full** Everyone: **Read-only**
5. Verify that the shared folder exists on the computer.	▪ Use the **Run** command to connect to your partner's computer by using the Universal Naming Convention (UNC) *Partner'sComputer**Test*.

Exercise 2
Defragmenting a Disk on a Remote Computer

In this exercise, you will defragment a disk on a remote computer by using Computer Management and Remote Desktop Connection.

Tasks	Specific instructions
1. In the Console1 window, open Disk Defragmenter.	▪ In the Console1 window, expand **Storage**, and then click **Disk Defragmenter**.
? What happens when you try to defragment a disk on a remote computer by using a local copy of Disk Defragmenter?	
2. Connect to your partner's computer by using Remote Desktop Connection.	▪ Open Remote Desktop Connection and connect to your partner's computer as an administrator.
3. Defragment the D drive on the remote computer.	▪ Open Computer Management on the remote computer, and then open Disk Defragmenter.
4. Log off from the remote connection.	▪ Log off from the remote connection.

Exercise 3
Connecting to a Remote Console Session

In this exercise, you will connect to a remote console session by using Remote Desktops.

Tasks	Specific instructions

1. Connect to a remote computer using Remote Desktops.	a. Open Control Panel, and then open Administrative Tools.
	
	b. Open Remote Desktops.
	
	c. Maximize the Remote Desktops window, and then maximize the Console Root\Remote Desktops window.
	
	d. Right-click **Remote Desktops**, and then click **Add New Connection**.
	
	e. Connect to Glasgow using the following data:
	
	  • Server name or IP Address: **Glasgow**
	
	  • Connection name: **Glasgow**
	
	  • User name: **Administrator**
	
	  • Password: **P@ssw0rd**
	
	  • Domain: **nwtraders**
	
	f. In the console tree, expand **Remote Desktops**, and then click **Glasgow**.

2. Open Task Manager and view remote computer performance.	a. Start Task Manager by opening the **Run** dialog box and typing **taskmgr.exe** b. View Performance.
❓ What happens when another user connects to the Glasgow console session while you are viewing the console session?	
3. Close all windows.	• Close all windows.

Exercise 4
Creating Shortcuts to Administration Tools

In this exercise, you will create shortcuts to commonly used administrative tools.

Tasks	Specific instructions
1. Create a shortcut to Computer Management.	a. Create a shortcut to Computer Management by right-clicking the desktop, clicking **New**, and then clicking **Shortcut**. b. In the **Type the location of the item** box, type **runas /user:nwtraders \administrator "mmc %windir%\system32\compmgmt.msc"** and then click **Next**. c. In the **Type a name for this shortcut** box, type **Computer Management** and then click **Finish**.
2. Create a shortcut to Active Directory Users and Computers.	▪ Use **runas /user:nwtraders\administrator "mmc %windir%\system32\dsa.msc"**
3. Create a shortcut to Performance.	▪ Use **runas /user:nwtraders\administrator "mmc %windir%\system32\perfmon.msc"**
4. Create a shortcut to Device Manager.	▪ Use **runas /user:nwtraders\administrator "mmc %windir%\system32\devmgmt.msc"**
5. Create a shortcut to Disk Manager.	▪ Use **runas /user:nwtraders\administrator "mmc %windir%\system32\diskmgmt.msc"**
6. Create a shortcut to Command Prompt.	▪ Use **runas /user:nwtraders\administrator cmd**
7. Create a shortcut to Microsoft Management Console.	▪ Use **runas /user:nwtraders\administrator mmc**
8. Test each shortcut.	▪ Test each shortcut and verify that the correct tool appears.
9. Close all windows.	▪ Close all windows.

Microsoft®
Training &
Certification

Module 2: Preparing to Monitor Server Performance

Contents

Overview	1
Lesson: Introduction to Monitoring Server Performance	2
Lesson: Performing Real-Time and Logged Monitoring	7
Lesson: Configuring and Managing Counter Logs	20
Lesson: Configuring Alerts	34
Lab A: Preparing to Monitor Server Performance	42

Overview

- Introduction to Monitoring Server Performance
- Performing Real-Time and Logged Monitoring
- Configuring and Managing Counter Logs
- Configuring Alerts

Introduction

Monitoring server performance is an important part of maintaining and administering your operating system. Routine performance monitoring ensures that you have up-to-date information about how your computer is operating. Performance monitoring also provides you with data that you can use to predict future growth and to plan for how changes to your system configurations may affect future operation.

Objectives

After completing this module, you will be able to:

- Establish a performance baseline.
- Perform real-time and logged monitoring.
- Configure and manage counter logs.
- Configure alerts.

Lesson: Introduction to Monitoring Server Performance

- Why Monitor Performance?
- Multimedia: Creating a Performance Baseline
- Guidelines for Establishing a Baseline

Introduction

This lesson explains the concept of performance monitoring, a baseline, performance objects, and counters. It also describes how to establish a performance baseline.

Lesson objectives

After completing this lesson, you will be able to:

- Explain the reason for monitoring performance.
- Explain what a baseline is and when to create one.
- Describe a performance object.
- Explain a counter.
- Explain the guidelines for establishing a baseline.

Why Monitor Performance?

- By monitoring performance, you obtain data that you can use to:
  - Understand your workload and the corresponding effect on your system's resources
  - Observe changes and trends in workloads and resource usage so you can plan for future upgrades
  - Test configuration changes or other tuning efforts by monitoring the results
  - Diagnose system problems and identify components or processes for optimization
- Analyze performance data to uncover bottlenecks

Introduction

Monitoring performance is a necessary part of preventive maintenance for your server. By routinely monitoring the performance of your server over periods ranging from days to weeks to months, you can establish a baseline for server performance. Through monitoring, you obtain performance data that is useful in diagnosing server problems.

Why monitor performance?

You use performance data to:

- Understand your workload characteristics and the corresponding effect on your system's resources.

- Observe changes and trends in workload characteristics and resource usage so you can plan for future upgrades.

- Test configuration changes or other performance tuning efforts by monitoring the results.

- Diagnose problems and identify components or processes for optimization.

Analysis of performance data and bottlenecks

Analysis of performance data can reveal problems, such as excessive demand on certain resources that results in bottlenecks. A bottleneck exists when a single resource adversely affects the performance of the whole system. Demand on the single resource may become excessive enough to cause a bottleneck of the four subsystems: memory, processor, disk, and network.

Some of the reasons that bottlenecks occur are:

- Subsystems are insufficient, so additional or upgraded components are required. For example, lack of memory is a major cause of bottlenecks.

- Subsystems are not sharing workloads evenly and need to be balanced. For example, an older network card that is installed on a new server may cause a bottleneck.

- A subsystem is malfunctioning and needs to be replaced. For example, a hard disk often has minor problems before it fails.

- A program is monopolizing a particular resource. For example, a custom program that was written by a consultant may not be sharing memory correctly. Solutions to this problem include substituting another program, asking a developer to rewrite the program, adding or upgrading resources, or running the program during periods of low demand.

- A subsystem is incorrectly configured, so configuration settings must be changed. For example, an older multispeed network card may be configured for 10 megabits per second (Mbps) when it should be set to 100 Mbps.

Multimedia: Creating a Performance Baseline

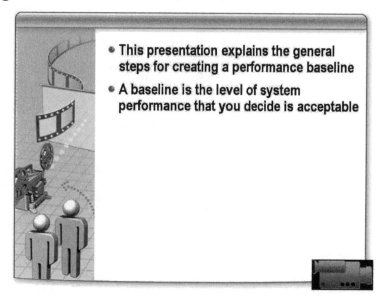

File location	To view the *Creating a Performance Baseline* presentation, open the Web page on the Student Materials compact disc, click **Multimedia**, and then click the title of the presentation.
Objectives	After completing this presentation you will be able to:

- Explain the purpose of a baseline.
- Describe how to use the Performance console.

Key points

Key points from the presentation are summarized in the following list:

- Baseline

  Take samples of counter values every 30 to 45 minutes for a week, during peak, low, and normal operations.

- General steps for creating a baseline

  a. Identify resources

  b. Capture data

  c. Store data

- Four major system resources for performance baselines

  - Memory
  - Processor
  - Physical disk
  - Network

- Performance object

  A performance object is the data generated by a system component or resource. Each performance object provides counters, which represent data about specific aspects of system performance. Performance objects can have multiple instances.

Guidelines for Establishing a Baseline

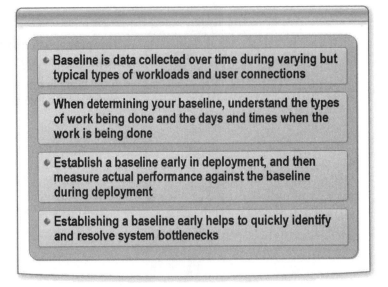

- Baseline is data collected over time during varying but typical types of workloads and user connections
- When determining your baseline, understand the types of work being done and the days and times when the work is being done
- Establish a baseline early in deployment, and then measure actual performance against the baseline during deployment
- Establishing a baseline early helps to quickly identify and resolve system bottlenecks

Introduction

You derive a baseline measurement from a collection of data over an extended period, during varying but typical types of workloads and user connections. The baseline is an indicator of how individual system resources or a group of resources are used during periods of normal activity.

Factors to consider when determining a baseline

You should consider the following factors when determining a baseline:

- When you determine your baseline, it is important to know what type of work is being performed and when it is being performed. That information helps you to associate specific work with specific resource usage and to determine whether the level of performance during those intervals is reasonable. After you gather performance data over an extended period of low, average, and peak usage, you can determine what constitutes acceptable performance for your system. That determination is your baseline.

  For example, if performance diminishes briefly at a certain time of day, and you find that many users log on or off at that time, the slowdown may be acceptable. Similarly, if performance is poor every evening at a certain time when no users are logged on to the system but nightly backups are being performed, the diminished performance may be acceptable. You can determine what performance level is acceptable only when you know the degree of performance loss and its cause.

- Establish a baseline early in the deployment phase. Then, during deployment, you can measure the baseline against actual performance.

- Establishing a baseline early helps you to quickly identify and resolve system bottlenecks.

- Use your baseline to watch for long-term changes in usage patterns that require increased capacity.

Lesson: Performing Real-Time and Logged Monitoring

- What Is Real-Time and Logged Monitoring?
- What Is Task Manager?
- What Is the Performance Console?
- How to Perform Real-Time Monitoring
- How to Perform Logged Monitoring
- Why Monitor Servers Remotely
- How to Monitor a Remote Server

Introduction

The primary monitoring tools in Microsoft® Windows® Server 2003 are the Performance console and Task Manager.

This lesson describes how to perform monitoring by using Performance and Task Manager.

Lesson objectives

After completing this lesson, you will be able to:

- Explain real-time monitoring and logged monitoring.
- Describe the Task Manager tool.
- Describe the Performance console.
- Perform real-time monitoring by using Task Manager and Performance.
- Perform logged monitoring by using Performance.
- Explain the reasons for monitoring remote servers from a workstation.
- Use Performance to monitor a remote computer.

What Is Real-Time and Logged Monitoring?

Real-Time Monitoring

- Involves processing and updating data counters as soon as data is received from the operating system
- Establishes the current state of the four subsystems: memory, processor, disk, and network
- Tool used is System Monitor

Logged Monitoring

- Involves collecting and storing data over time for analysis later
- Detects bottlenecks and determines whether the system changes
- Use Performance Logs and Alerts

Introduction

Administrators can use logged monitoring to monitor servers on a continuous basis. By configuring logged monitoring, you can establish a performance baseline and use trend analysis to identify server problems. For example, if users complain that an application server is gradually slowing down, you can check the log files for that server to investigate the cause of the problem.

Administrators also must investigate problems caused by specific events. For this type of problem, you must enable real-time monitoring. For example, if a help desk technician tells you that the printers attached to the print server are printing intermittently, you use a real-time monitor, such as Task Manager or System Monitor, to investigate the cause of the problem.

Real-time monitoring

In real-time monitoring, System Monitor processes and updates data counters as soon as the data is received from the operating system. You use real-time monitoring to establish the current state of the four subsystems: memory, processor, disk, and network. For example, if users complain about the slow response time of a client/server application in a situation that caused no previous problems, you can use System Monitor to diagnose and troubleshoot the problem.

Logged monitoring

Logged monitoring involves collecting and storing data over time for analysis later. Use logged monitoring to establish a baseline, detect bottlenecks and determine whether the system changed over time. Use the Performance Logs and Alerts tool for logged monitoring.

Example of logged monitoring

For example, when your organization acquires a new server, to understand its capabilities, you can configure several counters to determine memory usage, CPU usage, disk usage, and network usage. You can use the data that you collect to determine the range of counter values that are normal for your environment.

You can also set up multiple logs to monitor several events at various times. This way, you can determine whether events such as backup, domain replication, or users who connect remotely on evenings and weekends cause bottlenecks on the server.

What Is Task Manager?

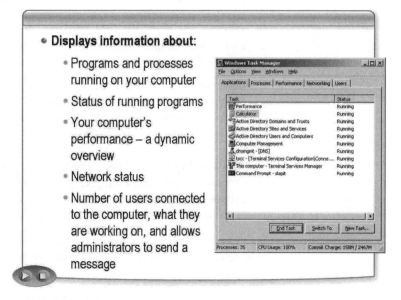

Introduction

Task Manager provides an overview of system activity and performance. It provides information about programs and processes that are running on your computer. It also displays the most commonly used performance measures for processes. You can use Task Manager to perform real-time monitoring.

Task Manager functions

You can use Task Manager to monitor key indicators of your computer's performance:

- You can see the status of the programs that are running and end programs that are not responding.

- You can also assess the activity of running processes by using up to fifteen parameters, and view graphs and data about CPU and memory usage.

- If you are connected to a network, you can view network status.

- If more than one user is connected to your computer, you can see who is connected, see what files they are working on, and send them a message.

Task Manager has five tabs that allow you to perform all these functions.

Applications tab

The **Applications** tab displays the status of the programs that are running on the computer. On this tab, you can end, switch to, or start a program.

Processes tab

The **Processes** tab displays information about the processes that are running on the computer. For example, you can display information about CPU and memory usage, page faults, handle count, and other parameters.

Performance tab

The **Performance** tab displays a dynamic overview of your computer's performance, including:

- Graphs of CPU and memory usage.
- The number of handles, threads, and processes that are running on your computer.
- The amount, in kilobytes, of physical, kernel, and commit memory. Physical memory is total memory, kernel memory is the memory that the system kernel and device drivers use, and commit memory is the amount of memory that is allocated to programs and the operating system.

Networking tab

The **Networking** tab displays a graphical representation of network performance. It provides a simple, qualitative indicator that shows the status of the network or networks that are running on your computer. The **Networking** tab is displayed only if a network card is present.

On this tab, you can view the quality and availability of your network connection, whether you are connected to one or more networks.

Users tab

The **Users** tab displays the names of users who can access the computer, along with session status and names. **Client Name** specifies the name of the client computer that is using the session, if applicable. **Session** provides a name for you to use when you perform such tasks as sending another user a message or connecting to another user's session.

The **Users** tab is displayed only if Fast User Switching is enabled on the computer you are working on. The computer must also be either a member of a workgroup or a standalone computer. The **Users** tab is unavailable on computers that are members of a network domain.

What Is the Performance Console?

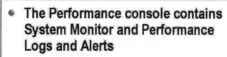

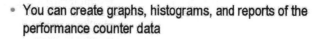

- The Performance console contains System Monitor and Performance Logs and Alerts
- With System Monitor:
  - You can collect and view real-time data of a local computer or several remote computers
  - You can create graphs, histograms, and reports of the performance counter data
- Performance Logs and Alerts:
  - Provides logging and alert capabilities
  - Defines settings for counter logs, trace logs, and alerts

Introduction

Windows Server 2003 provides the following tools as part of the Performance console for monitoring resource usage on your computer:

- System Monitor
- Performance Logs and Alerts

System Monitor capabilities

By using System Monitor, you can collect and view extensive data about the use of hardware resources and the activity of system services on computers that you administer.

With System Monitor you can collect and view the real-time performance data of a local computer or several remote computers.

To select the data to be collected, specify performance objects, performance counters, and performance object instances.

- A *performance object* is a logical collection of counters that is associated with a resource or service that can be monitored.

- A *performance counter* is a data item that is associated with a performance object. For each counter that you select, System Monitor displays a value that corresponds to a specific aspect of the performance that is defined for the performance object.

- *Performance object instances* are multiples of the same object type. For example, if a system has multiple processors, the Processor object type has multiple instances.

View logged counter data

You can view logged counter data by using System Monitor, or you can export the data to spreadsheet programs or databases for analysis and report generation.

By using System Monitor, you can create graphs, histograms, and reports of the performance counter data. The graph view, the default view, offers the widest variety of optional settings.

View	Description
Graph	Useful for real-time analysis of all the processes in a system
	Displays counter data over a given time in line graph format
Histogram	Useful for detecting processor bottlenecks
	Displays counter data in a bar chart, showing only one value per counter instance
Report	Useful for monitoring numerical values from each counter
	Displays counter data in a table, showing only one value per counter instance

Performance Logs and Alerts capabilities

Performance Logs and Alerts provide logging and alert capabilities for both local and remote computers. You use logging for detailed analysis and record-keeping. Retaining and analyzing log data that is collected over time can be helpful for capacity and upgrade planning.

Collect performance data

With Performance Logs and Alerts you can collect performance data by using two types of logs—counter logs and trace logs. You can also set an alert on a counter that sends a message, runs a program, or starts a log when the counter's value exceeds or falls below a specified setting.

Define settings

In Performance Logs and Alerts, you define settings for counter logs, trace logs, and alerts. The details pane of the console window shows counter logs and alerts that you have created. You can define multiple counter logs or alerts to run simultaneously. Each counter log or alert is a saved configuration that you define.

If you configure the log for automatic starting and stopping, a single log can generate many individual log data files. For example, if you generate a log file for each day's activity, one file closes at 11:59 P.M. one day, and a new file opens at midnight the next day.

Other functions

Data that Performance Logs and Alerts collects can be viewed during collection as well as after collection has stopped. Data collection occurs regardless of whether any user is logged on to the computer that is being monitored.

You can define start and stop times, file names, file sizes, and other parameters for automatic log generation, and you can manage multiple logging sessions from a single console window.

How to Perform Real-Time Monitoring

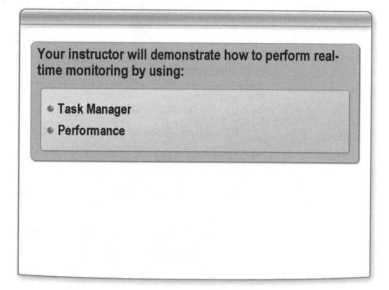

Your instructor will demonstrate how to perform real-time monitoring by using:

- Task Manager
- Performance

Introduction

Administrators often must perform situational real-time monitoring to answer questions about server performance from users, management, other systems administrators, and systems engineers. Task Manager is valuable when you must quickly evaluate processor usage, page file usage, and network usage. Performance monitor provides you with additional counters that can you can use to analyze problems as you view interrupts per second, queue lengths, pages per second, and so on.

Procedure for performing real-time monitoring by using Task Manager

To perform real-time monitoring by using Task Manager, press CTRL+ALT+DEL, and then click **Task Manager**.

To be monitored	Action
Applications	Click the **Applications** tab to monitor running applications
Processes	Click the **Processes** tab to monitor the running processes.
	On the **Processes** tab, click a column name to sort by that column. Click the column name a second time to reverse sort by that column.
	On the **View** menu, click **Select Columns** to add counters to the **Processes** tab.
Performance	Click the **Performance** tab to monitor CPU and memory usage.
Networking	Click the **Networking** tab to monitor network traffic to this computer.
Users	Click the **Users** tab to monitor the names of users who are connected to the computer.

Procedure for performing real-time monitoring by using Performance

To perform real-time monitoring by using Performance:

1. To start Performance, click **Start**, point to **Administrative Tools**, and then click **Performance**.

Note   You can also start Performance by opening a command prompt window and typing **perfmon.msc**

---

2. Click **System Monitor**.

3. Right-click in the details pane, and then click **Add Counters**.

4. For each counter or group of counters that you want to add to the log, perform the following steps:

   a. Under **Performance object**, select the type of performance object to monitor.

   b. Select one of the following options to add counters:

      • **All counters**. Specifies that you want to include all counters for the selected performance object.

      • **Select Counters from list**. Specifies that you want to select individual counters for the selected performance object.

Note   For a description of a counter, select the counter, and then click **Explain**.

---

   c. Select one of the following options to monitor the instances of the selected counters:

      • **All Instances**. Specifies that you want to monitor all instances of the selected counters.

      • **Select Instances From List**. Specifies that you want to monitor particular instances selected from the list of the selected counters.

Note   Some object types have several instances. For example, if a system has multiple processors, the Processor object type has multiple instances. If a system has two disks, the **PhysicalDisk** object type has two instances. Some object types, such as **Memory** and **Server**, have only one instance. If an object type has multiple instances, you can add counters to track statistics for each instance, or in many cases, for all instances at once.

---

5. Click **Add**.

6. Click **Close**.

How to Perform Logged Monitoring

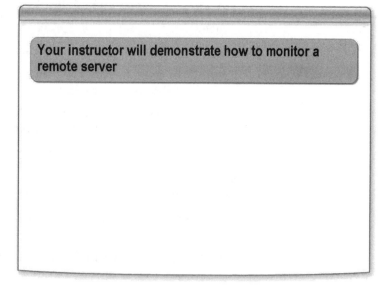

Your instructor will demonstrate how to monitor a remote server

Introduction

Administrators use logged monitoring to:

- Establish a performance baseline.
- Automate monitoring.
- Capture data from multiple servers simultaneously.

Procedure

To perform logged monitoring by using Performance:

1. To start Performance, click **Start**, point to **Administrative Tools**, and then click **Performance**.
2. Double-click **Performance Logs and Alerts**.
3. Right-click **Counter Logs**, and then click **New Log Settings**.
4. In the **New Log Settings** dialog box, specify an appropriate name for the log, and then click **OK**.

5. On the **General** tab, click **Add Counters**. For each counter or group of counters that you want to add to the log, perform the following steps:

    a. Under **Performance object**, select the type of performance object to monitor.

    b. Select one of the following options to add counters:

        - **All counters**. Specifies that you want to include all counters for the selected performance object.

        - **Select Counters from list**. Specifies that you want to select individual counters for the selected performance object.

Note For a description of a counter, click the counter, and then click **Explain**.

---

    c. Select one of the following options to monitor the instances of the selected counters:

        - **All Instances**. Specifies that you want to monitor all instances of the selected counters.

        - **Select Instances From List**. Specifies that you want to monitor particular instances selected from the list of the selected counters.

Note Some object types have several instances. For example, if a system has multiple processors, the **Processor** object type has multiple instances. The **PhysicalDisk** object type has two instances if a system has two disks. Some object types, such as **Memory** and **Server**, have only one instance. If an object type has multiple instances, you can add counters to track statistics for each instance or for all instances at once.

---

6. Click **Add**, and then click **Close**.

7. On the **General** tab, change the **Interval** to an appropriate time.

8. On the **Schedule** tab, change the **Start log** to begin at a specific time and day, change the **Stop log** to a specific time and day, and then click **OK**.

9. If prompted to create a log folder, click **Yes**.

Why Monitor Servers Remotely?

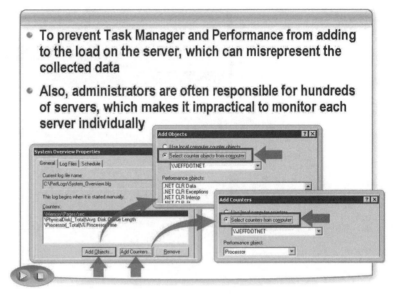

Introduction

You are monitoring a network server that is running Microsoft SQL Server™ 2000. When you monitor the server at the console, you notice that many counters are available that do not appear when you monitor the server remotely from your workstation. This problem occurs because SQL Server is not installed on the workstation. To solve this problem, you may need to install the Management and Client tools that are available on the SQL Server compact disc on the workstation and then monitor the server remotely.

Why monitor a remote server from a workstation?

The additional load that Task Manager and Performance put on the server can cause misrepresentation of the data that you are collecting. By monitoring the server from a remote location, you reduce the likelihood of this occurring.

Also, administrators are often responsible for hundreds of servers, which makes it impractical to monitor each server individually.

Options in the Performance console for monitoring a remote server

The Performance console provides the following options that you can use to monitor a remote server:

- You can add objects or counters to a remote server. On the **General** tab, click **Add Objects** or **Add Counters**, respectively.

- You can log objects or counters from a specific computer regardless of where the service is run. Click **Select counter objects from computer** or **Select counters from computer** respectively. Specify the name of the computer that you want to monitor remotely, such as *MyLogServer*.

Important   If you plan to monitor remote computers, you must have been delegated the appropriate authority to gain access to them.

How to Monitor a Remote Server

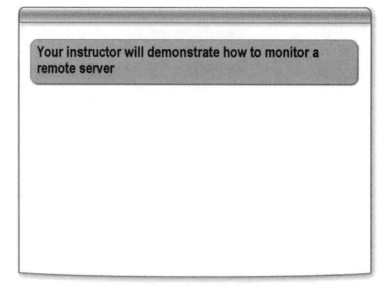

Introduction

Use the following procedure to monitor a remote server.

Procedure

1. To start Performance, click **Start**, point to **Administrative Tools**, and then click **Performance**.

2. Right-click in the right pane of System Monitor, and then click **Add counters**.

3. Click **Select counters from computer**, and then type the name of the remote computer.

4. Under **Performance Object**, in the list, select the objects that you want to monitor. For each performance object, select the appropriate counters in the list. Click **Add** each time you select a counter, and then click **Close**.

Practice: Performing Real-Time and Logged Monitoring

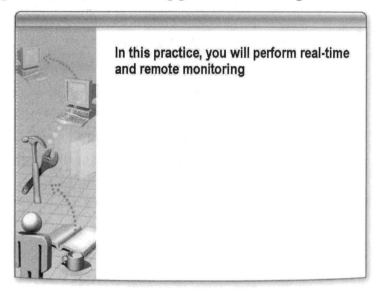

In this practice, you will perform real-time and remote monitoring

Objective

In this practice, you will perform real-time and remote monitoring of a server.

Scenario

Your organization recently acquired two new servers. One of the servers is local and the second server is remote. You want to monitor both servers simultaneously from your local server by using a real-time monitoring tool.

Practice

▶ **Perform real-time and remote monitoring on a local and a remote computer**

1. Log on to the domain as *Computer*User (where *Computer* is the name of your computer) with a password of **P@ssw0rd**.

2. Open the **Run** dialog box, type **runas /env /user:nwtraders\administrator** ∧ *Cmd* **cmd** and then click **OK**.   ∧ ∧

3. When prompted for a password, type **P@ssw0rd** and press ENTER.

4. In the Command Prompt window, start **perfmon.msc**.

5. Open the **Add Counters** dialog box by clicking + and then in the **Add Counters** dialog box, select the counters from **GLASGOW**.

6. Add the following counters:

   • Processor\% Processor Time

   • Memory\Pages/sec

   • PhysicalDisk\Avg. Disk Queue Length

7. Close the **Add Counters** dialog box.

8. Verify that you are monitoring three counters from your server and three counters from the Glasgow server.

9. Close all windows and log off.

Lesson: Configuring and Managing Counter Logs

- What Is a Counter Log?
- How to Create a Counter Log
- Counter Log File Formats
- How to Set File Parameters for a Counter Log
- Why Schedule Counter Logs?
- How to Schedule a Counter Log

Introduction

You use counter logs to gather data about various aspects of performance objects. For example, for the **Memory** object, counter logs gather data about available memory, cache memory, and virtual memory. Counter logs are built into the operating system and continually capture data.

Lesson objectives

After completing this lesson, you will be able to:

- Explain a counter, counter log, and counter log data.
- Create a counter log.
- Explain the counter log file formats.
- Set file parameters for a counter log.
- Explain the reasons for scheduling a counter log.
- Schedule a counter log.

What Is a Counter Log?

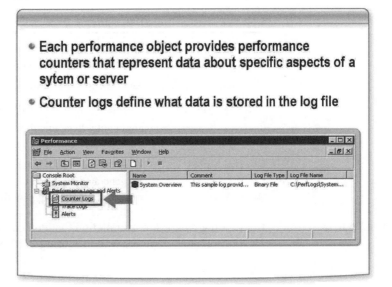

Introduction

Windows Server 2003 collects data about system resources, such as disks, memory, processors, and network components. Also, applications and services that you run on your system, such as Microsoft Exchange Server, can also collect data. This data is described as a performance object and is typically named for the component that generates the data. For example, the Processor object is a collection of performance data about the processors on your system.

Performance counter

A variety of performance objects are built into the operating system. Each performance object provides performance counters that represent data about specific aspects of a system or service. Counters are used to measure various aspects of performance. For example, the Pages/sec counter provided by the **Memory** object tracks the rate of memory paging.

Counter logs

Counter logs are counters that specify what data is stored in the log file. You use counter logs to select counters to collect performance data. You can use the Performance Logs and Alerts to create counter logs. In the interface, you select counter logs by using the **Counter Logs** option. The right pane of the Performance console window shows counter logs that you have created. You can define multiple counter logs to run simultaneously. Each counter log is a saved configuration that you define.

Counter log information in the Performance console

The following table describes the information about the counter logs that is provided by the columns in the right pane of the Performance console.

Column	Description
Name	The name of the counter log. It describes the type of data you are collecting or the condition you are monitoring.
Comment	Any descriptive information about the counter log.
Log File Type	The log file format that you define.
	For counter logs, this format can be binary, binary circular, text file (comma delimited), text file (tab delimited), or SQL.
Log File Name	The path and base file name that you defined for the files that are generated by this counter log. The base file name is used for automatically naming new files.

Counter log data

Counter log data is the information that you can collect automatically from local or remote computers by configuring Performance Logs and Alerts.

Counter log data:

- Can be viewed by using System Monitor.
- Can be exported to spreadsheet programs or databases for analysis and generating reports.
- Is used to compare the values against the counter thresholds to verify that resource usage or other system activity is within acceptable limits.

How to Create a Counter Log

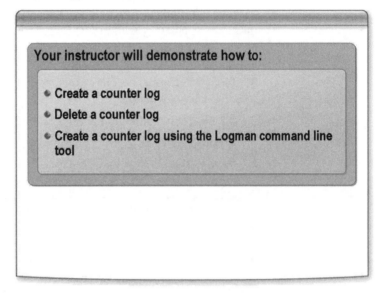

Your instructor will demonstrate how to:

- Create a counter log
- Delete a counter log
- Create a counter log using the Logman command line tool

Introduction

Counter logs record samples of data about hardware resources and system services based on performance objects, counters, and scheduled interval time.

When you create a counter log, Performance Logs and Alerts obtains data from the system when the update interval elapses. For example, when you set the counter data interval to 15 minutes, the data is collected every 15 minutes.

Procedure for creating a counter log

To create a counter log:

1. To start Performance, click **Start**, point to **Administrative Tools**, and then click **Performance**.

2. Double-click **Performance Logs and Alerts**, and then click **Counter Logs**.

   Any existing counter logs are listed in the details pane. A green icon indicates that a log is running; a red icon indicates that a log is stopped.

3. Right-click a blank area of the details pane, and then click **New Log Settings**.

4. In the **Name** box, type the name of the log, and then click **OK**.

5. On the **General** tab, click **Add Counters** to select the counters that you want to log.

6. If you want to change the default file and schedule information, make the changes on the **Log Files** tab and the **Schedule** tab.

Note   To save the settings for a counter log, right-click the counter log in the right pane of the Performance console, and then click **Save Settings As**. You can then specify an .htm file in which to save the settings. To reuse the saved settings for a new counter log, right-click the right pane, and then click **New Log Settings From**. This is an easy way to generate new settings from a counter log configuration. You can also open the HTML file in Microsoft Internet Explorer to display a System Monitor graph.

Procedure for deleting counter logs

Because counter logs can quickly consume a lot of storage space, delete logs when you no longer need them, usually after a baseline is established and the baseline information is recorded. A general guideline is to establish a baseline once a week and delete logs older than 30 days.

To delete a counter log:

1. To start Performance, click **Start**, point to **Administrative Tools**, and then click **Performance**.

2. Double-click **Performance Logs and Alerts**, and then click **Counter Logs**.

3. In the details pane, right-click the counter log that you want to delete.

4. Click **Delete**.

Important   To perform the preceding two procedures, you must be a member of the Administrators group on the local computer, or you must have been delegated the appropriate authority. If the computer is connected to a domain, members of the Domain Admins group can perform this procedure.

As a security best practice, consider using **Run as** to perform this procedure.

Procedure for creating counter logs using the logman command line tool

You can also create counter logs using the **logman** command line tool. Logman allows you to manage and schedule performance counter log collections on local and remote servers.

To create daily performance counter queries with begin and end times, repeat collections, version control numbers, counter paths and sample intervals using logman:

1. On the **Start** menu, click **Run**, type **cmd** and then click **OK**.

2. At the command prompt, type:

   Logman create counter daily_perf_log –b 7/27/2003 13:00:00 –e 7/27/2003 15:00:00 –r –v mmddhhmm –c "\Processor(_Total)\% Processor Time" "\Memory\Available Bytes" –si 00:15 –o "C:\perflogs\daily_log"

   where:

   -b Specifies begin-time for collections in a 24-hour format.

   -e Specifies end-time for collections in a 24-hour format.

   -r Repeats the collection every day at the time periods specified by the **-b** and **-e** options. This command is valid only for begin- and end-times specified on the same day, month, and year.

   -v Attaches the version control information to the end of the output file and path name. Use date format *mmddhhmm* (month, day, 24-hour, minute) for version control.

   -c Specifies the name of the counter

   -si Specifies sample intervals for performance counter collection in hours, minutes, and seconds. Default is 15 seconds.

   -o Specifies the pathname of the output file.

   Additional information can be found on the **Start** menu by clicking **Help and Support** and then searching for **logman**.

Counter Log File Formats

Log File Format	Description	When to use
Text File (Comma delimited)	Comma-delimited log file (with a .csv extension)	To export log data into a spreadsheet program
Text File (Tab delimited)	Tab-delimited log file (with a .tsv extension)	To export log data into a spreadsheet program
Binary File	Sequential, binary-format log file (with a .blg extension)	To record data instances that are intermittent
Binary Circular File	Circular, binary-format log file (with a .blg extension)	To record data continuously to same log file
SQL Database	Name of an existing SQL database and log set within the database where performance data will be read or written	To collect performance data at an enterprise level rather than a per-computer basis

The following table describes the log file formats that you can use to set file parameters for a counter log.

Log file format	Description	When to use
Text File (Comma delimited)	Defines a comma-delimited log file, with a .csv extension.	Use this format, for example, to export the log data into a spreadsheet program.
Text File (Tab delimited)	Defines a tab-delimited log file, with a .tsv extension.	Use this format, for example, to export the log data into a spreadsheet program.
Binary File	Defines a sequential, binary-format log file, with a .blg extension. Only binary file formats can accommodate instances that are not persistent throughout the duration of the log.	Use this file format to record data instances that are intermittent—that is, stopping and resuming after the log begins to run. Use the **tracerpt** command line tool to convert binary files into a comma-delimited log file.
Binary Circular File	Defines a circular, binary-format log file, with a .blg extension.	Use this file format to record data continuously to the same log file, overwriting previous records with new data when the file reaches its maximum size. Use the **tracerpt** command line tool to convert binary files into a comma-delimited log file.
SQL Database	Defines the name of an existing SQL database and log set within the database where the performance data will be read or written.	Use this file format to collect performance data at an enterprise level rather than on a per-computer basis.

Use the text file format or the binary file format if you must export the data to a spreadsheet program later. The binary file format is more compact than the text file format, but you must convert it to the text file format before you export it to a spreadsheet. Use the **tracerpt** command line tool to convert binary files into a comma-delimited log file. For example, type **tracerpt logfile.blg –o logfile.csv**

How to Set File Parameters for a Counter Log

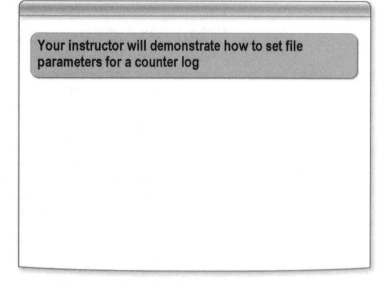

Your instructor will demonstrate how to set file parameters for a counter log

Introduction

When you set file parameters for a counter log, you must select a log file format. Select the log file format that is most appropriate for your environment. For example, if you are responsible for a few servers, the text file or the binary file format is best choice. If you are responsible for a hundred servers, logging your data to a SQL database is the best choice.

Procedure

To set file parameters for a counter log:

1. To start Performance, click **Start**, point to **Administrative Tools**, and then click **Performance**.

2. Double-click **Performance Logs and Alerts**.

3. To set file properties for a counter log, double-click **Counter Logs**.

4. In the details pane, double-click the log.

5. On the **Log Files** tab, complete the following options:

   a. **Log file type**. In the list, select the format you want for this log file, complete the options, and then click the **Configure** button.

   b. **Configure**. Select the configuration parameters using the following options for either **Configure Log Files** or **Configure SQL Logs**, based on the log file type that you selected in the **Log File type** list.

   c. **End file names with**. Select this check box, and then, in the list, click the suffix style that you want to use. Use **End file names with** to distinguish between log files with the same log file name that are in a group of automatically generated logs.

d. **Start numbering at**. Set this option to the start number for automatic file numbering, when you select **nnnnnn** as the **End file names with**.

e. **Comment**. If appropriate, type a comment or description for the log file.

Option	Description	Applies to
Location	Type the name of the folder in which you want to create the log file, or click **Browse** to search for the folder.	Configure Log Files
File name	Type a partial or base name for the log file. You can use File name in conjunction with End file names if appropriate.	Configure Log Files
Repository name	Select the System DSN (Data Source Name) from the drop-down list, and then type the Log set name. The Log set name will be stored in the database within the System DSN.	Configure SQL Logs

6. In the **Configure Log files** dialog box, under **Log file size**, use the following options:

a. **Maximum limit**. When you select this option, data is continuously collected in a log file until it reaches limits that are set by disk quotas or the operating system. For SQL logs, data is collected in a database until it reaches limits that are set by the number of records that are written.

b. **Limit of**. To define a size limit for the log file, specify the size. For counter and trace logs, specify the maximum size in megabytes. For SQL logs, specify the maximum size in records.

Note   In the **Configure SQL Logs** dialog box, instead of **Log file size**, the option is called **Log set size**.

Why Schedule Counter Logs?

Schedule counter logs to:

- Create a performance baseline
- Determine the overall system impact when replication occurs between domain controllers
- Determine whether a bottleneck occurs when users log on in the morning or when users connect remotely in the evening
- Determine whether backup causes a bottleneck when it runs in the evening
- Determine whether a bottleneck is causing the network to slow down during certain times of the day

Introduction

It is impractical for one person to monitor a network server 24 hours a day. You must automate this process so that you have time to perform your other tasks. You can schedule counter logs to create a performance baseline, look for bottlenecks, monitor system events, and collect information about how system events affect the server.

Why schedule counter logs?

You can schedule counter logs to:

- Create a performance baseline.
- Determine the effect on the overall system when replication occurs between domain controllers.
- Determine whether a bottleneck occurs when users log on in the morning.
- Determine whether a bottleneck occurs when users connect remotely in the evening.
- Determine whether Backup causes a bottleneck when it runs in the evening.
- Determine whether a bottleneck occurs during certain times of the day when users complain that the network slows down.

How to Schedule a Counter Log

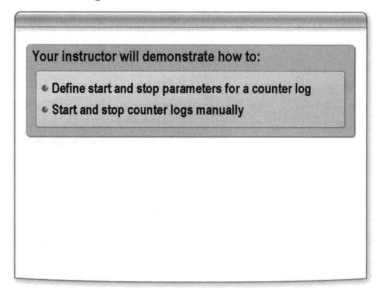

Your instructor will demonstrate how to:

- Define start and stop parameters for a counter log
- Start and stop counter logs manually

Introduction

You typically schedule logging to occur during normal hours of operation. For most organizations, this period is between 8 A.M. and 5 P.M. For organizations that operate 24 hours a day and 7 days a week, logging should be turned on constantly. If logging is turned on constantly, you can create a log file for each shift (typically 8 hours), for the entire day (24 hours), or by size. A log file that is limited by size continues to grow to the size that you specify, and then a new log is started.

To schedule a counter log, you must define its start and stop parameters.

Procedure for defining start and stop parameters for a counter log

To define start and stop parameters for a counter log:

1. To start Performance, click **Start**, point to **Administrative Tools**, and then click **Performance**.

2. Double-click **Performance Logs and Alerts**, and then click **Counter Logs**.

3. In the details pane, double-click the name of the counter log.

4. On the **Schedule** tab, under **Start log**, click **At**, and then specify the time and date.

5. Under **Stop log**, select one of the following options:

   a. To stop the log after a specified duration, click **After**, and then specify the number of intervals and the type of interval (days, hours, and so on).

   b. To stop the log at a specific time and date, click **At**, and then specify the time and date. The year box accepts four characters; the others accept two characters.

c. To stop a counter log when the log file becomes full, click **When the log file is full**. The file will continue to accumulate data according to the file-size limit that you set on the **Log Files** tab (in kilobytes up to two gigabytes).

Note Set the limit in the **Configure Log Files** dialog box before clicking **When the log file is full**. Otherwise, this option is deactivated.

Important When setting this option, take into consideration your available disk space and any disk quotas that are in place. An error can occur if your disk runs out of disk space due to logging.

6. Under **When a log file closes**, select the appropriate option:

a. If you want to configure a circular (continuous, automated) counter logging, select **Start a new log file**.

b. If you want to run a program after the log file stops, such as a copy command for transferring completed logs to an archive site), select **Run this command**. Also, type the path and file name of the program to run, or click **Browse** to locate the program.

Procedure for starting and stopping counter logs manually

In general, all logging should be automated and should follow a schedule. Logging should track usage of the servers during the period of greatest activity. There are times, however, when logging is not necessary, for example during periods of inactivity such as mandatory vacation times, holidays, system maintenance, and so on. During these times, you can stop logging manually.

Likewise, logging may be needed outside of normal hours of operation, for example during periods of increased activity such as mandatory overtime during evenings and weekends. During these times, you can start logging manually.

To start and stop counter logs manually:

1. Open Performance, and then double-click **Performance Logs and Alerts**.

2. Click **Counter Logs**.

3. In the details pane, right-click the counter log that you want to stop or start.

4. Click **Start** or **Stop**.

Note You cannot check a counter log while it is running. You must stop a counter log to view it.

Practice: Configuring and Managing Counter Logs

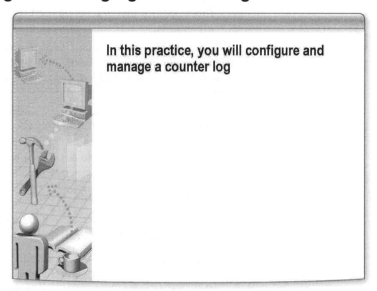

In this practice, you will configure and manage a counter log

Objective

In this practice, you will configure and manage a counter log.

Scenario

You are the systems administrator for a network. Your duties include monitoring servers at a remote data center. Recently, some users at your site complained about the speed of the Glasgow server in the data center. You monitor Glasgow by using System Monitor, but you do not detect any problems. To identify the problem, you decide to monitor Glasgow remotely by scheduling counter logs.

Practice

▶ **Enable counter logs for a remote server**

1. Log on to the domain as *Computer*User with a password of **P@ssw0rd**.

2. Open the **Run** dialog box and type **runas /user:nwtraders\administrator "mmc %windir%\system32\perfmon.msc"** and then click **OK**.

3. When prompted for a password, type **P@ssw0rd** and press ENTER.

4. In the Performance console, expand **Performance Logs and Alerts**, open **Counter Logs**, and then create a new counter log named **Glasgow**.

5. In the **Glasgow** dialog box, open the **Add Counters** dialog box, and then in the **Select counters from computer** box, type **\\Glasgow**

6. Add the following counters, and then close the **Add Counters** dialog box:

   • Processor\% Processor Time

   • Memory\Pages/sec

   • PhysicalDisk\Avg. Disk Queue Length

7. Set the interval to 1 second.

8. In the **Run as** box, type **nwtraders\Administrator** and then click **Set Password**.

9. In the **Password** and **Confirm Password** boxes, type **P@ssw0rd** and then click **OK**.

10. On the **Schedule** tab, set the **Start log** to begin two minutes from now.

11. Set the **Stop log** to stop three minutes from now, change the date to today's date, and then click **OK**.

12. If prompted to create a log folder, click **Yes**.

13. Wait until the time has elapsed.

14. Open the **Run** dialog box, type **runas /user:nwtraders\administrator cmd** and then press ENTER.

15. When prompted for a password, type **P@ssw0rd** and press ENTER.

16. Verify the existence of the performance log by typing the following command: **dir C:\Perflogs**

17. To view the log file, click **System Monitor**, and then right-click the graph and select **Properties**.

18. On the **Source** tab, select **Log files**, click **Add**, select the log file, and then click **Open**.

19. Click **Time Range,** adjust the time range for one minute, and then click **OK**.

20. Close all windows and log off.

Lesson: Configuring Alerts

- What Is an Alert?
- How to Create an Alert
- How to Configure an Alert

Introduction

Use alerts to notify a user or an administrator when a predefined counter value exceeds or falls below a specified setting. In addition, you can use Performance Logs and Alerts to collect data about hardware resources, system services, and performance.

Lesson objectives

After completing this lesson, you will be able to:

- Explain an alert.
- Create an alert.
- Configure an alert.

What Is an Alert?

- **Feature that detects when a predefined counter value rises above or falls below a specified setting**
- **Specified setting on the counter is called alert threshold**
- **Set an alert on a counter when:**
  - Entry is made in application event log
  - Selected counter's value exceeds or falls below alert threshold
  - Message is sent
  - Program runs
- **Set alerts based on established performance baseline values**
- **Use alerts to be notified when a counter threshold value exceeds or falls below a specified value**

Definition

An *alert* is a feature that detects when a predefined counter value exceeds or falls below a specified setting. The specified setting on the counter is called the *alert threshold*.

Why use alerts?

By using the alert feature, you can define a counter value that triggers actions, such as sending a network message, running a program, or starting a log.

Alerts are useful if you are not actively monitoring a particular counter threshold value but want to be notified when it exceeds or falls below a specified setting so that you can investigate and determine the cause of the change. For example, you can set an alert to notify you when the number of failed logon attempts exceeds a specified number.

You may want to set alerts based on established performance baseline values for your system.

Functions of an alert

You can set an alert on a counter to perform the following functions:

- Make an entry in the application event log.

  For example, enable this option if you want a record of all the events that cause an alert.

- Start a log when the selected counter's value exceeds or falls below the alert threshold.

  For example, you can use this option to notify you if the processor usage time exceeds 85 percent.

- Send a message.

  For example, enable this if you want to be alerted when a specific event occurs.

- Run a program.

  Enable this option if you want a program to run when an event occurs. For example, you may want to shut down the server when the hard disk is full.

How to Create an Alert

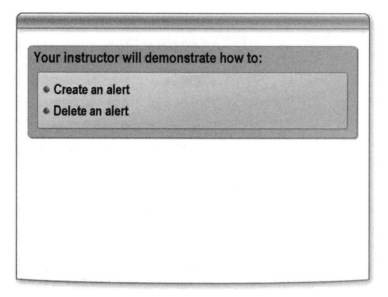

Introduction

Use the following procedure to create an alert.

Procedure for creating an alert

To create an alert:

1. To open Performance, click **Start**, point to **Administrative Tools**, and then click **Performance**.

2. Double-click **Performance Logs and Alerts**, and then click **Alerts**.

   Any existing alerts are listed in the details pane. A green icon indicates that the alerts are running; a red icon indicates alerts are stopped.

3. Right-click a blank area of the details pane, and then click **New Alert Settings**.

4. In the **Name** box, type the name of the alert, and then click **OK**.

   On the **General** tab, you can define a comment for your alert, along with counters, alert thresholds, and the sample interval.

   On the **Action** tab, you can define the actions that occur when counter data triggers an alert.

   On the **Schedule** tab, you can define when the service begins to scan for alerts.

Note To save the settings for an alert, right-click the alert in the right pane of the **Performance** console, and then click **Save Settings As**. You can then specify an .htm file in which to save the settings. To reuse the saved settings for a new alert, right-click the right pane, and then click **New Alert Settings From**. This is an easy way to generate new settings from an alert configuration. You can also open the HTML file in Internet Explorer to display a System Monitor graph.

Procedure for deleting an alert

To delete an alert:

1. To start Performance, click **Start**, point to **Administrative Tools**, and then click **Performance**.

2. Double-click **Performance Logs and Alerts**.

3. In the details pane, right-click the alert that you want to delete.

4. Click **Delete**.

Important   To perform the preceding procedures, you must be a member of the Administrators group, or you must have been delegated the appropriate authority. If the computer is connected to a domain, members of the **Domain Admins** group might be able to perform this procedure.

As a security best practice, consider using **Run as** to perform this procedure.

How to Configure an Alert

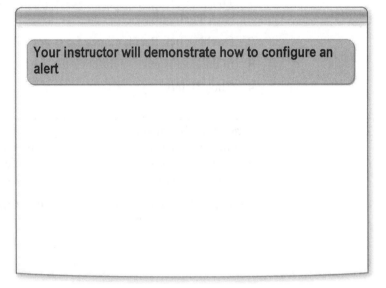

Your instructor will demonstrate how to configure an alert

Introduction

Use the following procedure to configure an alert.

Procedure

1. To open Performance, click **Start**, point to **Administrative Tools**, and then click **Performance**.

2. Double-click **Performance Logs and Alerts**, and then click **Alerts**.

3. In the details pane, double-click the alert.

4. On the **General** tab, in the **Comment** box, type a comment to describe the alert as needed, and then click **Add**.

5. For each counter or group of counters that you want to add to the log, perform the following steps:

   a. To monitor counters from the computer on which Performance Logs and Alerts will run, click **Use local computer counters**.

   Or, to monitor counters from a specific computer regardless of where the service is run, click **Select counters from computer**, and then type the name of the computer that you want to monitor.

   b. Under **Performance object**, click a performance object to monitor.

   c. Under **Select counters from list**, click one or more counters to monitor.

   d. To monitor all instances of the selected counters, click **All Instances**. Binary logs can include instances that are not available at log startup but subsequently become available.

   Or, to monitor particular instances of the selected counters, click **Select instances from list**, and then click an instance or instances to monitor.

   e. Click **Add**, and then click **Close**.

6. Under **Alert when the value is**, specify **Under** or **Over**, and in **Limit**, specify the value that triggers the alert. Perform this step for each counter or group of counters that you added to the log.

   In **Sample data every**, specify the amount and the unit of measure for the update interval.

7. On the **Schedule** tab, under **Start Scan**, click one of the following options:

- To start alert manually, click **Manually**. When this option is selected, to start the log or alert, right-click the log name in the details pane, and then click **Start**.

- To start alert at a specific time and date, click **At**, and then specify the time and date.

- Under **Stop Scan**, select one of the following options:

  - To stop the alert manually, click **Manually**. When this option is selected, to stop the log or alert, right-click the log or alert name in the details pane, and then click **Stop**.

  - To stop the alert after a specified duration, click **After**, and then specify the number of intervals and the type of interval (days, hours, and so on).

  - To stop the alert at a specific time and date, click **At**, and then specify the time and date. (The year box accepts four characters; the others accept two characters.)

8. Under **When an alert scan finishes**, select **Start a new scan** if you want to configure continuous alert scanning.

Practice: Configuring an Alert

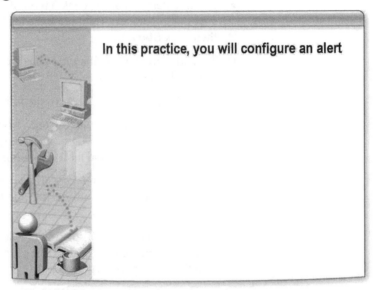

In this practice, you will configure an alert

Objective

In this practice, you will configure an alert.

Scenario

You are the systems administrator for an organizational unit on a network. The organizational unit recently acquired a new file server. You determine that the processor on this server should never exceed 50 percent usage. You want to configure an alert to warn you when the processor exceeds this figure, and you also must test the alert.

Practice

▶ **Configure an alert**

1. Log on as *Computer*User with a password of **P@ssw0rd**.

2. Open the **Run** dialog box, type **runas /env /user:nwtraders\administrator** ∧ *Cmd* **cmd** and then click **OK**.

3. When prompted for a password, type **P@ssw0rd** and then press ENTER.

4. In the Command Prompt window, start **compmgmt.msc**.

5. In the Command Prompt window, start **perfmon.msc**.

6. In the Performance console, open **Alerts** and then create a new alert named **CPU Alert**.

7. Add the Processor\% Processor Time counter, and then close the **Add Counters** dialog box.

8. Change the **Limit** to **50** and then close the **CPU Alert** dialog box.

9. In the Cmd window, change to the **C:\MOC\2275\Labfiles** folder.

10. In the command line, run the **CPULoop** batch file.

11. Stop **CPULoop** by closing the Cmd window.

12. In Computer Management, expand **System Tools**, expand **Event Viewer**, and then open **Application**.

13. Open the first entry and in the **Event Properties** dialog box, read the entry under **Description**.

14. Close all windows and log off.

Lab A: Preparing to Monitor Server Performance

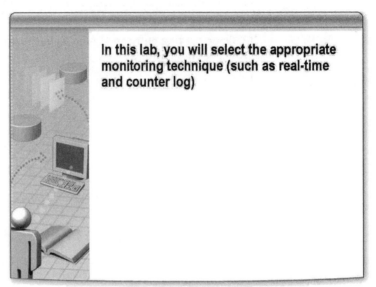

In this lab, you will select the appropriate monitoring technique (such as real-time and counter log)

Objectives

After completing this lab, you will be able to examine various scenarios and select the appropriate monitoring technique.

Prerequisites

None.

Estimated time to complete this lab: 20 minutes

Exercise 1
Selecting the Appropriate Monitoring Technique

In this exercise, you will select the appropriate monitoring technique based on the following scenarios. R=Real Time, L=Logging, A=Alerts. If more than one technique will work, put your selections in order of preference.

Scenario	Monitoring technique(s)
1. Determine when the hard disk is running out of free space.	
2. Provide management with information that can be used for budgeting purposes.	
3. Determine the number of users that a specific server configuration should support.	
4. Analyze a trend.	
5. Monitor multiple servers.	
6. Determine when to increase capacity.	
7. Find intermittent performance problems.	
8. Investigate why a computer application is slow or inefficient.	
9. Determine when to add additional system resources.	
10. Determine when to upgrade the system.	
11. Determine how a server should be used.	
12. Determine expected response times for specific numbers of users and system use.	
13. Analyze data to find and resolve abnormalities in the system use.	
14. Monitor use over time.	
15. Determine a preventive maintenance schedule for your servers.	
16. Create a baseline for a server.	
17. Monitor the effects of replication.	
18. Troubleshoot a server.	
19. Plan for growth.	
20. Find a slow memory leak.	

(continued)

Scenario	Monitoring technique(s)
21. Find a fast memory leak.	
22. Monitor intermittent disk thrashing.	
23. Monitor continuous disk thrashing	
24. Monitor a remote computer.	
25. Respond to user complaints that a server seems to be running slowly.	
26. Monitor a computer 24 hours a day, 7 days a week.	

Microsoft®
Training &
Certification

Module 3: Monitoring Server Performance

Contents

Overview	1
Multimedia: The Primary Server Subsystems	2
Lesson: Monitoring Server Memory	3
Lesson: Monitoring Processor Usage	12
Lesson: Monitoring Disks	18
Lesson: Monitoring Network Usage	26
Lab A: Monitoring Server Performance	38

Overview

- **Multimedia: The Primary Server Subsystems**
- **Monitoring Server Memory**
- **Monitoring Processor Usage**
- **Monitoring Disks**
- **Monitoring Network Usage**

Introduction

Today's business environment demands that systems administrators ensure that their servers are efficient and reliable. To optimize your server's performance, you must collect performance data that helps you to identify system bottlenecks.

This module covers how to collect performance data by monitoring primary server subsystems. It also covers how to identify system bottlenecks by using the Performance console and Task Manager in Microsoft® Windows® Server 2003.

Objectives

After completing this module, you will be able to:

- Explain how the four primary server subsystems affect server performance.
- Monitor server memory.
- Monitor processor usage.
- Monitor disks.
- Monitor network usage.
- Identify the guidelines for using counters and thresholds.
- Describe the best practices for monitoring server performance.

Multimedia: The Primary Server Subsystems

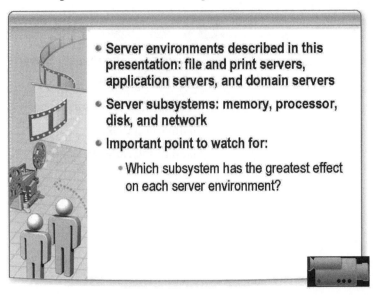

File location

To view the *The Primary Server Subsystems* presentation, open the Web page on the Student Materials compact disc, click **Multimedia**, and then click the title of the presentation. Do not open this presentation unless the instructor tells you to.

Objective

After completing this lesson, you will be able to describe the effect of each primary subsystem on server performance.

Server subsystems

The four primary subsystems are:

- Memory

    Server memory is the subsystem that is most important to general server performance. If the server does not have enough random access memory (RAM) to hold the data that it needs, it must temporarily store the data on the disk. Disk access is much slower than RAM, so storing data on the disk can significantly degrade server performance.

- Processor

    The most important aspect of processor performance is its level of usage. When an application or other software uses more than its share of the processor's cycles, all the other software that is running operates much more slowly.

- Disk

    The access speed of the physical disk drive can greatly affect the speed at which applications operate and data is loaded. Also, the disk storage space must be sufficient for you to install applications, store data, and have enough space for the paging file.

- Network

    The performance of your network is affected by the speed of both the hardware in your network infrastructure and the software that is running on your servers and clients.

Lesson: Monitoring Server Memory

- Why Monitor Server Memory?
- How to Identify and Resolve Memory Bottlenecks
- How to Monitor Memory

Introduction

Memory significantly affects server performance. Low memory conditions can slow the operation of applications and services on your server and can also affect the performance of other resources on your server. Therefore, monitoring and analyzing memory usage is one of the first steps to take when you assess the performance of your server.

Lesson objectives

After completing this lesson, you will be able to:

- Explain the purpose of monitoring server memory.
- Identify and resolve memory bottlenecks.
- Monitor memory by using server monitoring tools.

Why Monitor Server Memory?

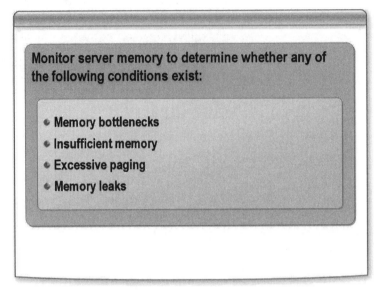

Monitor server memory to determine whether any of the following conditions exist:

- Memory bottlenecks
- Insufficient memory
- Excessive paging
- Memory leaks

Introduction

Lack of memory is the most common cause of serious performance problems in computer systems. Even if you suspect other problems, check memory counters to rule out a memory shortage.

Conditions to look for

Monitor server memory to assess the amount of available memory and the level of paging, and to observe the effects of a memory shortage. Monitoring server memory can help you determine whether any of the following conditions exist:

- Memory bottleneck

    Low memory conditions can slow the operation of applications and services on your server and can impact the performance of other resources on your server. For example, when your server is low on memory, paging can be prolonged, resulting in more work for your disks. Because it involves reading and writing to disk, this paging activity may compete with other disk transactions, thereby intensifying a disk bottleneck.

    In turn, all this work by the disk can mean that the processor is used less or is doing unnecessary work, such as processing numerous interrupts due to repeated page faults. *Page faults* occur when the server cannot locate requested code or data in the physical memory that is available to the requesting process. As a result, applications and services become less responsive. Therefore, it is important to monitor memory regularly to detect memory bottlenecks.

- Insufficient memory

    Insufficient memory is the reason for the symptoms we encounter with low memory, and excessive paging. By monitoring server memory, you can use the baseline established to predict when you will need additional memory, and avoid some of these problems.

- Excessive paging

  The indication of memory shortage is frequent paging. *Paging* is the process of moving fixed-size blocks of code and data from RAM to disk by using units called *pages* to free memory for other uses.

  Although some paging is acceptable, because it enables you to use more memory than actually exists, constant paging slows server performance. Reducing paging significantly improves server responsiveness.

- Memory leak

  A memory leak occurs when applications allocate memory for use but do not free allocated memory when finished. As a result, available memory is used up over time, often causing the server to stop functioning properly.

How to Identify and Resolve Memory Bottlenecks

Memory counter	Acceptable average range	Desired value	Action
Pages/sec	0–20	Low	Find the process that is causing paging Add RAM
Available Bytes	Minimum of 5% of total memory	High	Find the process that is using RAM Add RAM
Committed Bytes	Less than physical RAM	Low	Find the process that is using RAM Add RAM
Pool Nonpaged Bytes	Remain steady, no increase	Not applicable	Check for memory leak in application
Page Faults/sec	Below 5	Low	Find the process that is causing paging Add RAM

Introduction

The most common resource bottleneck in servers is caused by lack of memory. Adding memory is the most effective way to improve server performance.

Paged and nonpaged RAM

In Microsoft Windows Server 2003, RAM is divided into two categories: paged and nonpaged. Paged RAM is virtual memory, where it appears that a full range of memory addresses is available to all applications. Windows Server 2003 does this by giving each application a private memory range called a *virtual memory space* and by mapping that virtual memory to physical memory.

Nonpaged RAM cannot use this configuration. Data that is placed into nonpaged RAM must remain in memory and cannot be written to or retrieved from disk. For example, data structures that are used by interrupt routines or those that prevent multiprocessor conflicts within the operating system use nonpaged RAM.

Virtual memory system

The virtual memory system in Windows Server 2003 combines physical memory, the file system cache, and disk into an information storage and retrieval system. The system stores program code and data on disk until it is needed, and then moves it into physical memory. Code and data that are no longer in active use are written to disk. However, when a computer does not have enough memory, code and data must be written to and retrieved from the disk more frequently—a slow, resource-intensive process that can become a system bottleneck.

Hard page faults

The best indicator of a memory bottleneck is a sustained, high rate of hard page faults. *Hard page faults* occur when the data that a program requires is not found in its working set (the physical memory visible to the program) or elsewhere in physical memory, and must be retrieved from disk. Sustained hard page fault rates—over five per second—indicate a memory bottleneck.

Counters used to determine whether memory is a bottleneck

Use the following Performance memory counters to determine whether memory is causing a bottleneck in the system.

The following list includes two types of counters. The first type of counter is a rate counter, such as Pages/sec and Page Faults/sec. A rate counter samples an increasing count of events over time. To display the rate of activity, the rate counter divides the cache in count values by the change in time. Therefore, to obtain an accurate result, you must monitor rate counters over time—typically for 30 to 60 seconds.

The second type of counter is an instantaneous counter, such as Available Bytes and Committed Bytes. Instantaneous counters display the most recent measurement.

- *Pages/sec.* Number of requested pages that were not immediately available in RAM, and thus were accessed from the disk or were written to the disk to make room in RAM for other pages. Generally, if the value of this counter is over five for extended periods, memory may be a bottleneck in the system.

- *Available Bytes.* Amount of available physical memory. It is normally low, because Windows Disk Cache Manager uses extra memory for caching and then returns it when requests for memory occur. However, if this value is consistently below 5 percent of the total memory on a server, it is an indication that excessive paging is occurring.

- *Committed Bytes.* Amount of virtual memory that is committed to either physical RAM for storage or to pagefile space. If the amount of committed bytes is larger than the amount of physical memory, more RAM may be required.

- *Pool Nonpaged Bytes.* Amount of RAM in the Nonpaged pool system memory area where space is acquired by operating system components as they accomplish their tasks. If the Pool Nonpaged Bytes value shows a steady increase without a corresponding increase in activity on the server, it may indicate that a process with a memory leak is running, and you should monitor it closely.

- *Page Faults/sec.* Number of times a virtual page was not found in memory. If this number is consistently above five, too much memory has been allocated to an application and not enough to the server that you are running.

In Task Manager, to determine whether memory is causing a bottleneck in the system, use the PF Usage memory counter. This counter displays the amount of paging used by the system. A steady increase may indicate that a running process has a memory leak.

How to Monitor Memory

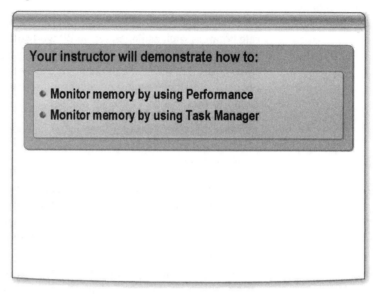

Your instructor will demonstrate how to:

• Monitor memory by using Performance

• Monitor memory by using Task Manager

Introduction

This topic covers the procedure for monitoring memory by using Performance and Task Manager.

Procedure for monitoring memory by using Performance

To monitor memory by using the Performance console:

1. Click **Start**, click **Control Panel**, double-click **Administrative Tools**, and then double-click **Performance**.

2. Right-click in the right pane of System Monitor, and then click **Add Counters**.

   a. Under **Performance object**, click **Memory**, select the following counters one at a time, and then click **Add**.

      • Pages/sec

      • Available Bytes

      • Committed Bytes

      • Pool Nonpaged Bytes

      • Page Faults/sec

   Note Every time you click **Add** to add a counter, that counter is added to the list of counters in the right pane of System Monitor.

   b. Although not specifically memory object counters, the following counters are also useful for memory analysis:

      • Paging File\% Usage

      • Cache\Data Map Hits %

      • Server\Pool Paged Bytes and Server\Pool Nonpaged Bytes

3. In the right pane of System Monitor, view the counters, and then take the appropriate action to resolve any memory problem.

Tip The appropriate action to resolve a memory problem can involve finding the process that is causing paging or using RAM, checking for a memory leak in an application, and adding RAM.

Procedure for monitoring memory by using Task Manager

You can also monitor memory by using Task Manager.

1. Press CTRL+ALT+DEL, and then click **Task Manager**.

2. On the **Performance** tab, monitor the data under Page File, Physical Memory, Kernel Memory, and Commit Charge.

Practice: Monitoring Server Memory

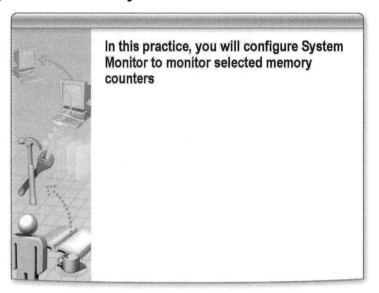

In this practice, you will configure System Monitor to monitor selected memory counters

Objective

In this practice, you will configure System Monitor to monitor selected memory counters.

Scenario

You are the systems administrator for an organizational unit on a large network. Recently, you installed an application on a server. Since you installed the application, users are complaining that the system appears to slow down gradually. You want to monitor memory to determine whether a memory leak is causing the problem.

Practice

▶ **Check for a memory leak**

1. Log on to nwtraders domain as *Computer*User using your password.

2. Open the Performance console by using the Performance shortcut or by using **Run As**.

3. In System Monitor, add the following memory counters: Available MBytes, Committed Bytes, Pooled Nonpaged bytes, and Page Faults/sec.

4. Open the **System Monitor Properties** dialog box and change the sampling rate to 60 seconds.

5. To allow time for the averaging mechanism of the counters to stabilize, wait for a minimum of two minutes before proceeding.

   Switch to the report view (press CTRL+R), and then fill in the following information as your baseline:

   a. Available MBytes _____

   b. Page Faults/sec _____

   c. Pool Nonpaged Bytes _____

   d. Committed Bytes _____

   e. Pages/sec _____

6. Start Task Manager, click the **Performance** tab, and then record the PF Usage value:

   PF Usage _____

7. Open the C:\MOC\2275\Practices\Mod03 folder, start **leakyapp.exe**, and then click **Start Leaking**.

   Wait for a minimum of two minutes before proceeding to allow the averaging mechanism of the counters to stabilize.

8. Fill in the current information for the following counters:

   a. Available MBytes _____

   b. Page Faults/sec _____

   c. Pool Nonpaged Bytes _____

   d. Committed Bytes _____

   e. Pages/sec _____

9. Start Task Manager, click the **Performance** tab, and then record the PF Usage value:

   PF Usage _____

10. Notice that the Page Faults/sec counter has increased by a factor of 50 or more.

11. Switch to **My Leaky App**, click **Stop Leaking**, and then click **Exit**.

    Wait for a minimum of two minutes before proceeding to allow the averaging mechanism of the counters to stabilize.

12. Fill in the current information:

    a. Available MBytes _____

    b. Page Faults/sec _____

    c. Pool Nonpaged Bytes _____

    d. Committed Bytes _____

    e. Pages/sec _____

13. Start Task Manager and record the PF Usage:

    PF Usage _____

14. Verify that your counters are back to their baseline levels.

15. Close all windows.

Lesson: Monitoring Processor Usage

- What Is Processor Usage?
- How to Identify and Resolve Processor Bottlenecks
- How to Monitor Processor Usage

Introduction

After memory consumption, processor activity is the most important data to monitor on your server. To determine whether a busy processor is efficiently handling all the work on your computer or whether it is overwhelmed, you must examine the processor usage.

Lesson objectives

After completing this lesson, you will be able to:

- Explain processor usage.
- Identify and resolve processor bottlenecks.
- Monitor processor usage by using server monitoring tools.

What Is Processor Usage?

- Percentage of time that the processor is working
- Monitor to detect processor bottlenecks

Tool	Counter	Display
Task Manager	CPU Usage	Graph
Performance	%Processor Time	Percentage of elapsed time to run non-idle thread

Definition

Processor usage, also called CPU usage, is the percentage of time that the processor is working. You must monitor processor usage to detect processor bottlenecks.

In Windows Server 2003, you can use Task Manager as well as Performance to monitor processor activity and usage. The counter that defines processor usage in each of these tools is named:

- CPU Usage in Task Manager.
- % Processor Time in Performance.

CPU Usage

In Task Manager, CPU Usage displays a graph indicating the percentage of time the processor is working. This counter is a primary indicator of processor activity. View this graph to see how much processing time you are using. If your computer seems to be running slowly, this graph may display a high percentage.

% Processor Time

In Performance, % Processor Time is the percentage of elapsed time that the processor spends to execute a non-idle thread. Each processor has an idle thread that consumes cycles when no other threads are ready to run.

This counter is the primary indicator of processor activity. It displays the average percentage of busy time observed during the sample interval. It calculates this value by monitoring the time that the idle process is active and subtracting that value from 100%.

It is important to monitor this counter on symmetric multiprocessing (SMP) systems just as it is on single-processor systems. SMP enables any one of the multiple processors in a computer to run any operating system or application thread simultaneously with other processors in the system. Observe processor usage patterns for individual processors and for all processors over an extended period. Also, consider the number of threads in the system's processor queue to determine whether high processor usage is limiting the system's ability to accomplish work.

How to Identify and Resolve Processor Bottlenecks

Processor counter	Acceptable average range	Desired value	Action
% Processor Time	Less than 85%	Low	Find process using excessive processor time Upgrade or add another processor
System: Processor Queue Length	Less than 10	Low	Upgrade or add additional processor
Server Work Queues: Queue Length	Less than four	Low	Find process using excessive processor time Upgrade or add another processor
Interrupts/sec	Depends on processor	Low	Find controller card generating interrupts

Introduction

Just about every activity that occurs on a server involves the processor. The processor on an application server is generally busier than the processor on a file and print server. As a result, the level of processor activity, and what is considered normal, is different between the two types of servers.

Two of the most common causes of processor bottlenecks are CPU-bound applications and drivers, and excessive interrupts that are generated by inadequate disk or network subsystem components.

Determine a bottleneck

Monitor processor counters to help determine whether the processor is causing a bottleneck:

- *% Processor Time*. Measures the amount of time that the processor is busy. When processor usage consistently runs over 85 percent, the processor is a system bottleneck. Analyze processor usage by monitoring individual processes to determine what is causing the processor activity.

- *System: Processor Queue Length*. Number of requests in the queue for the processor. It indicates the number of threads that are ready to be executed and are waiting for processor time. Generally, a processor queue length that is consistently higher than two may indicate congestion. To determine the cause of the congestion, you must further analyze the individual processes that are making requests on the processor.

- *Server Work Queues: Queue Length.* Number of requests in the queue for the selected processor. A consistent queue of over two indicates processor congestion.

- *Interrupts/sec.* Number of interrupts that the processor is servicing from applications or from hardware devices. Windows Server 2003 can handle thousands of interrupts per second. A dramatic increase in this counter value without a corresponding increase in system activity indicates a hardware problem. The problem could be a device that is unable to keep up with the rest of the system, like a disk controller or network interface card (NIC).

  For example, if a conflict occurs between a hard disk controller and a network adapter card, monitor the disk controller and network adapter card. Determine whether excessive requests are being generated by monitoring the queue lengths for the physical disk and network interface. Generally, if the queue length is greater than two requests, check for slow disk drives or network adapters that could be causing the queue length backlog.

Actions to resolve processor bottleneck

If you determined that the processor is a system bottleneck, you can perform the following actions to improve performance:

- Add a faster processor if the system is a file and print server.

- Add multiple processors for application servers, especially if the application is multithreaded.

- Offload processing to another system on the network, such as users, applications, or services.

- Upgrade your network card, disk adapter card, or controller cards. In general, 32-bit intelligent adapters are recommended. Intelligent adapters provide better overall system performance because they allow interrupts to be processed on the adapter itself, thereby relieving the processor of this work.

How to Monitor Processor Usage

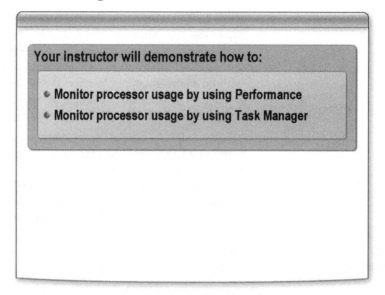

Introduction

To keep your system running efficiently, you must monitor the system's processor to detect any bottlenecks from time to time. Bottlenecks occur only when the processor is so busy that it cannot respond to requests on time. These situations are indicated, in part, by high rates of processor activity, but mainly by long, sustained queues and poor application response.

Procedure for monitoring processor usage by using Performance

To monitor processor usage by using Performance:

- To open Performance, click **Start**, click **Control Panel**, double-click **Administrative Tools**, and then double-click **Performance**.

  In the Performance window, System Monitor is selected by default. In the right pane of System Monitor, the % Processor Time counter is displayed.

Procedure for monitoring processor usage by using Task Manager

To monitor CPU usage by using Task Manager:

1. Press CTRL+ALT+DEL, and then click **Task Manager**.

Note   You can also open Task Manager by right-clicking the taskbar or by pressing CTRL+SH+ESC.

---

2. On the **Performance** tab, view the **CPU Usage** and the **CPU Usage History** counters.

Practice: Monitoring Processor Usage

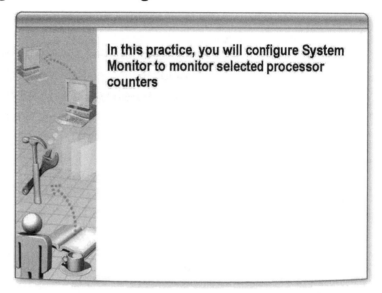

Objective

In this practice, you will configure System Monitor to monitor selected processor counters.

Scenario

You are the systems administrator for an organizational unit on a large network. Recently, you installed an application on a server. Since you installed the application, users are complaining that the system is slow and you want to monitor the processor to determine whether the application is causing a bottleneck.

Practice

▶ **Determine whether an application is causing a processor bottleneck**

1. Log on to **nwtraders** as *Computer*User using your password.

2. Open the Performance console by using the Performance shortcut or by using Run As.

3. Click **System Monitor**, and then add the **System\Processor Queue Length** counter.

4. Record the information for the following counters:

    a. Processor\% Processor Time _____

    b. System\Processor Queue Length _____

5. Open C:\Moc\2275\Practices\Mod03, and then start the **cpustres.exe** application.

6. Set the **Activity** level for Thread 1 to **Maximum**.

7. Record the information for the following counters:

    a. Processor\% Processor Time _____

    b. System\Processor Queue Length _____

8. Is **cpustres.exe** causing a bottleneck? How can you tell?

    _____

9. Close all windows.

Lesson: Monitoring Disks

- Why Monitor Disks?
- How to Identify and Resolve Disk Bottlenecks
- How to Monitor Disks

Introduction

The disk subsystem handles the storage and movement of programs and data on your server, giving it a powerful influence on the overall responsiveness of your server. The Performance console provides disk-specific counters that enable you to measure disk activity and throughput.

Lesson objectives

After completing this lesson, you will be able to:

- Explain the purpose of monitoring disks.
- Identify and resolve disk bottlenecks.
- Monitor disks by using System Monitor.

Why Monitor Disks?

> **Monitor disks to determine:**
>
> - Presence of disk bottlenecks
> - Need for disk defragmentation
> - Need for additional or faster disks
> - Presence of excessive paging
> - Disk efficiency

Introduction

Monitor disks to keep your systems working efficiently. You can also use the data that you collect when you monitor disks to plan for future hardware and software upgrades.

Disk bottlenecks

The existence of a disk bottleneck is indicated by the presence of all of the following conditions:

- Sustained rate of disk activity well above your baseline
- Persistent disk queues that are longer than two per disk
- Absence of a significant amount of paging

Without this combination of factors, it is unlikely that a disk bottleneck exists.

Monitoring disk efficiency

Consider disk capacity and disk throughput when evaluating your starting configuration. Use the bus, controller, cabling, and disk technologies that produce the best throughput that is practical and affordable. Most computers perform adequately with moderately priced disk components. However, if you want to obtain the best performance, you may want to evaluate the latest disk components that are available.

If your configuration contains various types of disks, controllers, and buses, the differences in their designs can affect throughput rates. You might want to test throughput by using these various disk systems to determine whether some components produce less favorable results overall or only for certain types of activity, and then replace those components as needed.

Also, certain kinds of volume-set configurations can offer performance benefits. For example, striped volumes can provide better performance because they increase throughput by enabling multiple disks to service sequential or clustered I/O requests. A *striped volume* is a volume whose data is interleaved across two or more physical disks. The data on this type of volume is allocated alternately and evenly to each of the physical disks. A striped volume cannot be mirrored or extended.

Note   For more information about striped volumes, see Module 5, "Managing Disks," in Course 2275, *Maintaining a Microsoft Windows Server 2003 Environment.*

System Monitor supports monitoring volume sets with the same performance objects and counters that are provided for individual disks. Notice that hardware-based RAID (Redundant Array of Independent Disks) devices report all activity to a single physical disk and do not show distribution of disk operations among the individual disks in the array. RAID is a category of disk drives that combine two or more drives into one volume for fault tolerance and performance.

Note   For more information about RAID, see Appendix E "Managing Fault-Tolerant Disks," in Course 2275, *Maintaining a Microsoft Windows Server 2003 Environment.*

Be aware of the seek time, rotational speed, access time, and data transfer rate of your disks by consulting manufacturer documentation. Also consider the bandwidth of cabling and controllers. The slowest component determines the maximum possible throughput, so be sure to monitor each component.

To compare the performance of different disks, monitor the same counters and activity on the disks. If you find differences in performance, you might want to distribute workload to the disk that performs better, or replace slower performing components.

How to Identify and Resolve Disk Bottlenecks

Physical disk counter	Acceptable average range	Desired high or low value	Action
% Disk Time	Under 50%	Low	Monitor to see if paging is occurring Upgrade disk subsystem
Current Disk Queue Length	0–2	Low	Upgrade disk subsystem
Avg. Disk Bytes/Transfer	Baseline or higher	High	Upgrade disk subsystem
Disk Bytes/sec	Baseline or higher	High	Upgrade disk subsystem

Introduction

Disks store programs and the data that programs process. While waiting for a computer to respond, it is frequently the disk that is the bottleneck. In this case, the disk subsystem can be the most important aspect of I/O performance. However, problems can be hidden by other factors, such as the lack of memory.

Performance disk counters are available with both the **LogicalDisk** and **PhysicalDisk** performance objects. **LogicalDisk** monitors logical partitions of physical drives. It is useful to determine which partition is causing the disk activity, which may indicate the application or service that is generating the requests. **PhysicalDisk** monitors individual hard disk drives and is useful for monitoring disk drives as a whole.

Important Both **LogicalDisk** and **PhysicalDisk** objects are automatically enabled on demand. Therefore, you do not have to enable them manually with the **diskperf – y** command.

Counters used to determine whether the disk is a bottleneck

When analyzing disk subsystem performance and capacity, monitor the following Performance disk subsystem counters for bottlenecks:

- *% Disk Time*. Indicates the amount of time that the disk drive is busy servicing read and write requests. If this is consistently close to 100 percent, the disk is being used very heavily. Monitoring individual processes helps determine which process or processes are making the majority of the disk requests.

- *Current Disk Queue Length*. Indicates the number of pending disk I/O requests for the disk drive. If this value is consistently over two, it indicates congestion.

- *Avg. Disk Bytes/Transfer.* The average number of bytes transferred to or from the disk during write or read operations. The larger the transfer size, the more efficient the system is running.

- *Disk Bytes/sec.* This is the rate at which bytes are transferred to or from the disk during write or read operations. The higher the average, the more efficient the system is running.

- *LogicalDisk\% Free Space.* This is the amount of disk space available.

Actions to resolve disk bottleneck

If you determine that the disk subsystem is a system bottleneck, a number of solutions are possible, including the following:

- Defragment the disk by using Disk Defragmenter.

- Rule out a memory shortage. When memory is scarce, the Virtual Memory Manager writes more pages to disk, resulting in increased disk activity. Before you add hardware, make sure that memory shortage is not the source of the problem because low memory is a common cause of bottlenecks.

- Add a faster controller, such as Fast SCSI-2, or an on-board caching controller.

- Add more disk drives in a RAID environment. This solution spreads the data across multiple physical disks and improves performance, especially during read operations.

- Offload processing to another system on the network, such as users, applications, or services.

How to Monitor Disks

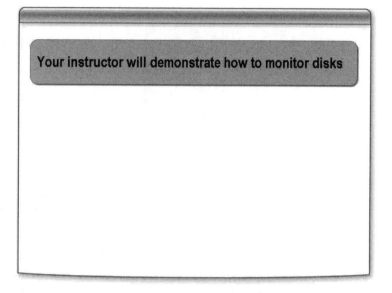

Introduction

A disk bottleneck occurs when disk performance decreases to the extent that it affects overall system performance. You need to observe many factors to determine the level of disk performance.

Monitor disks to detect performance issues before they cause problems.

Procedure

To monitor disks:

1. Click **Start**, click **Control Panel**, double-click **Administrative Tools**, and then double-click **Performance**.

2. Right-click in the right pane of System Monitor, and then click **Add Counters**.

3. In the **Add Counters** dialog box, under **Performance object**, select **PhysicalDisk**, select the following counters, and then click **Add**.

   - % Disk Time

   - Avg. Disk Bytes/Transfer

   - Current Disk Queue Length

   - Disk Bytes/Sec

4. View the counters in the right pane of System Monitor and take the appropriate action to resolve any disk issue.

Tip To resolve a disk bottleneck, you may need to determine whether paging is occurring and, if so, upgrade the disk.

Practice: Monitoring Disks

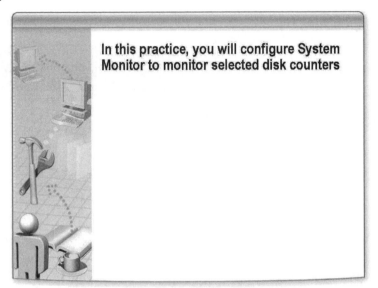

Objective

In this practice, you will configure System Monitor to monitor selected disk counters.

Scenario

You are the systems administrator for an organizational unit on a large network. Recently, you installed an application on a server. Since you installed the application, users are complaining that the system is slow. You want to monitor the disk to determine whether the application is causing the problem.

Practice

▶ **Monitor disk counters**

1. Log on to **nwtraders** as *Computer*User using your password.

2. Open the Performance console by using the Performance shortcut or by using **Run As**.

3. On the **Start** menu, click **Help and Support**. Record how long it takes to start Help.

---

4. Close Help and Support Center.

5. Click **System Monitor**, and then add the following counters:

    a. Memory\Page Faults/sec

    b. PhysicalDisk\% Disk Time

    c. PhysicalDisk\Current Disk Queue Length

    d. System\Processor Queue Length

6. Record the information for the following counters:

    a. Memory\Pages/sec _____

    b. Memory\Page Faults/sec _____

    c. PhysicalDisk\%Disk Time _____

    d. PhysicalDisk\Current Disk Queue Length _____

    e. Processor\% Processor Time _____

7. Open C:\Moc\2275\Practices\Mod03 and start the **disk.bat** application.

8. Switch to report view, and then record the information for the following counters:

    a. Memory\Pages/sec _____

    b. Memory\Page Faults/sec _____

    c. PhysicalDisk\%Disk Time _____

    d. PhysicalDisk\Current Disk Queue Length _____

    e. Processor\% Processor Time _____

9. On the **Start** menu, click **Help and Support** and record how long it takes to start Help.

    _____

10. Is disk.bat causing a disk bottleneck? How can you tell?

    _____

11. Close all windows.

Lesson: Monitoring Network Usage

- What Is Network Usage?
- How to Identify and Resolve Network Bottlenecks
- How to Monitor Network Usage

Introduction

Communications across a network is increasingly important in any work environment. Similar to the processor or disks on your system, the behavior of the network affects the operation of your system. Optimize your system's performance by regularly monitoring network usage, such as network traffic and resource usage.

Lesson objectives

After completing this lesson, you will be able to:

- Explain network usage.
- Identify and resolve network bottlenecks.
- Monitor network usage by using server monitoring tools.

What Is Network Usage?

* Percentage of network bandwidth in use on the segment being monitored
* Monitoring network usage helps you detect network bottlenecks
* Bottlenecks in network communications directly affect the experience of the user at the client workstation and the entire network
* Typical causes of network bottlenecks are:
  * Overloaded server
  * Overloaded network
  * Loss of network integrity

Definition

Network usage is the percentage of network bandwidth that is in use on the segment that is being monitored.

Network bandwidth

Network bandwidth is measured in several different ways:

- The rate at which bytes are transferred to and from the server.

- The rate at which data packages are sent by the server. Data packages include frames, packets, segments, and datagrams.

- The rate at which files are sent and received by the server.

Effective network bandwidth varies widely depending upon the transmission capacity of the link, the server configuration, and the server workload.

Why monitor network usage?

You monitor network usage to detect network bottlenecks. Network bottlenecks directly affect the experience of the user at the client workstation and the entire network. A network bottleneck limits the number of clients that can simultaneously access your server.

Typical causes for network bottlenecks are:

- An overloaded server.

- An overloaded network.

- Loss of network integrity.

How to Identify and Resolve Network Bottlenecks

Network interface counter	Acceptable average range	Desire high or low value	Action
Network Utilization (in Task Manager)	Generally lower than 30%	Low	Low
Network Interface: Bytes Sent/sec	Baseline or higher	High	Upgrade network adapter or physical network
Network Interface: Bytes Total/sec	Baseline or higher	High	Perform further analysis to determine cause of problem Upgrade or add another adapter.
Server: Bytes Received/Sec	Less than 50% of the capacity of the bandwidth of the network card	NA	Upgrade network adapter or physical network

Introduction

Network bottlenecks are difficult to monitor because most networks are complex. Also, many elements can affect the performance of the network. You can monitor various objects and counters on the network, such as server, redirector, network segment, and protocols. Determining which ones to monitor depends upon the environment.

Counters used to determine whether the network is a bottleneck

Use the following commonly monitored counters to form an overall picture of how the network is being used and to help uncover network bottlenecks:

- *Task Manager: % Network utilization.* The percentage of the network bandwidth in use for the local network segment. You can use this counter to monitor the effect of various network operations on the network, such as user logon validation and domain account synchronization.

- *Network Interface: Bytes Sent/sec.* The number of bytes that are sent by using this network adapter card.

- *Network Interface: Bytes Total/sec.* The number of bytes that are sent and received by using this network adapter card. Use this counter to determine how the network adapter is performing. The Bytes Total/sec counter should report high values, to indicate a large number of successful transmissions.

- *Server: Bytes Received/sec.* Compares the bytes received per second counter to the total bandwidth of your network adapter card to determine whether your network connection is creating a bottleneck. To allow room for spikes in traffic, you should usually use no more than 50 percent of capacity. If this number is very close to the capacity of the connection, and processor and memory use are moderate, the connection might be causing a problem.

Actions to resolve network bottleneck

By viewing the preceding counters, you can view the amount of activity on the server for logon requests and data access. If you determine that the network subsystem is causing a bottleneck, you can perform various actions to alleviate the bottleneck. These actions include the following:

- Add servers to the network, thereby distributing the processing load.

- Check and improve the physical layer components, such as routers, switches, and cabling.

- Divide your network into multiple subnets or segments, attaching the server to each segment with a separate adapter. This method reduces congestion at the server by spreading server requests.

- Divide your network traffic into appropriate segments. For example, configure your network so that systems that are shared by the same group of people are on the same subnet.

- Unbind network adapters that are used infrequently.

- For best performance, use adapters with the highest bandwidth that is available. Note, however, that increasing bandwidth increases the number of transmissions and in turn creates more work for your system. For example, the system must generate more interrupts. Remove unused network adapters to reduce overhead.

- Use offline folders to work on network applications without being connected to a network. Offline folders make use of client-side caching, thereby reducing network traffic.

How to Monitor Network Usage

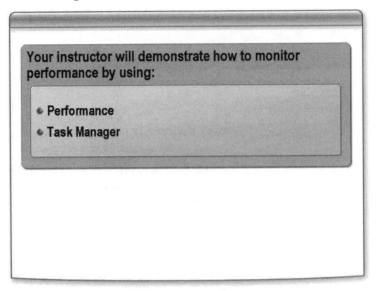

Introduction

It is important to monitor the network usage of your servers so that you can detect network bottlenecks. You can monitor network usage by using either the Performance console or Task Manager.

Procedure for monitoring network usage by using Performance

To monitor network usage by using Performance:

1. Click **Start**, click **Control Panel**, double-click **Administrative Tools**, and then double-click **Performance**.

2. Right-click in the right pane of System Monitor, and then click **Add Counters**.

    a. Under **Performance object**, select **Network Interface**, select the following counters, and then click **Add**.

      • Network Interface\Bytes Sent/sec

      • Network Interface\Bytes Total/sec

    b. Under **Performance object**, select **Server**, select the following counter, click **Add**, and then click **Close**.

      • Server\Bytes Received/sec

3. View the counters in the right pane of System Monitor and take the appropriate action to resolve any network problem.

Tip The appropriate action to resolve a network problem can involve upgrading or adding another adapter. You can also segment the network or limit the protocols that are in use.

Procedure for monitoring network usage by using Task Manager

To monitor network usage by using Task Manager:

- Press CTRL+ALT+DEL, and then click **Task Manager**.

  On the **Networking** tab, in the bottom pane of Windows Task Manager, the Network Utilization counter is displayed.

Practice: Monitoring Network Usage

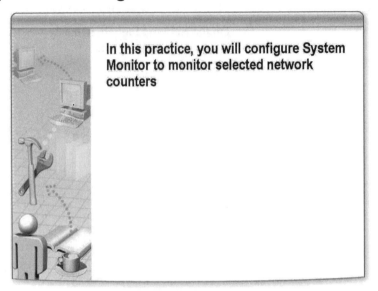

In this practice, you will configure System Monitor to monitor selected network counters

Objective

In this practice, you will configure System Monitor to monitor selected network counters.

Scenario

You are the systems administrator for an organizational unit on a large network. Recently, you installed an application on a server. Since you installed the application, users are complaining that the system is slow. You want to monitor the network connection to determine whether it is causing the bottleneck.

Practice

▶ **Monitor the network connection**

1. Log on to **nwtraders** as *Computer*User using your password.

2. Open the Performance console by using the Performance shortcut or by using **Run As**.

3. Click **System Monitor**, and then add the following counters:

   a. Network Interface\Bytes Sent/sec

   b. Network Interface\Bytes Total/sec

   c. Server\Bytes Received/sec

4. Record the information for the following counters:

   a. Network Interface\Bytes Sent/sec _____

   b. Network Interface\Bytes Total/sec _____

   c. Server\Bytes Received/sec _____

5. Start Task Manager, and then click the **Networking** tab.

6. Record the Network Utilization: _____

7. Open a command prompt, and then type the following commands:

   CD \Moc\2275\Practices\Mod03

   Connect *PartnerComputer*

   (where *PartnerComputer* is the name of your partner's computer)

8. Switch to report view, and then record the information for the following counters:

   a. Network Interface\Bytes Sent/sec _____

   b. Network Interface\Bytes Total/sec_____

   c. Server\Bytes Received/sec_____

9. In Task Manager, record the Network Utilization: _____

10. Do any of these counters indicate the presence of a bottleneck? If so, which counter?

    _____

11. Close all windows.

Guidelines for Using Counters and Thresholds

Subsystem	Counter	Threshold
	• Monitor page faults • Monitor available RAM • Monitor committed bytes	• Over 5 per second • Less than 5% of total • More than physical RAM
	• % Processor time, % Privileged Time, % User Time • System: Processor Queue Length • Server Work Queues: Queue Length	• Above 85% • Above 2 • Above 2
	• % Disk Time • Current Disk Queue Length	• If more than 50%, check for excessive paging • Greater than 2
	• Server: Bytes Total/sec, Network Interface: Bytes Total/sec	• Higher than the baseline number

Introduction

Deviations from your baseline provide the best indicator of performance problems. You can also check for various types of bottlenecks by monitoring the counters for each subsystem and checking them against the recommended thresholds.

Memory bottlenecks

Check for memory bottlenecks by monitoring the following counters:

Counter	Threshold	Action
Page faults	Sustained page fault rates over 5 per second	Add more memory to the server
Available RAM	Less than 5% of total memory	Add more memory to the server
Committed bytes	Less than physical RAM	Add more memory to the server

Processor bottlenecks

Check for processor bottlenecks by monitoring the following counters:

Counter	Threshold	Action
% Processor time, % Privileged Time, % User Time	Consistently above 85%	Upgrade your current processor or add another processor
System: Processor Queue Length, Server Work Queues: Queue Length	Above 2	Upgrade your current processor or add another processor

Disk bottlenecks

Check for disk bottlenecks by monitoring the following counters:

Counter	Threshold	Action
% Disk Time	More than 50%,	Check for excessive paging (memory bottleneck). If excessive paging is not the problem, replace the disk with a faster unit
Current Disk Queue Length	Greater than 2	Upgrade the hard disk

Network bottlenecks

Check for network bottlenecks by monitoring the following counters:

Counter	Threshold	Action
Server: Bytes Total/Sec, Network Interface: Bytes Total/sec	Higher than the baseline numbers	Upgrade the network adapters or the physical network

Best Practices for Monitoring Server Performance

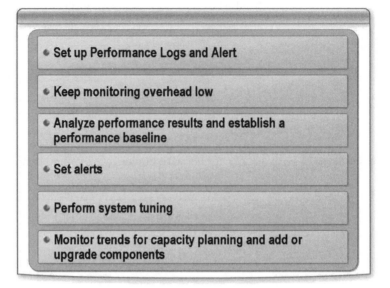

Introduction

Use the following best practices when you monitor the performance of a server.

Performance Logs and Alerts

- Set up Performance Logs and Alerts to monitor your server.

  Set up Performance Logs and Alerts to report data for the recommended counters at regular intervals, such as every 10 to 15 minutes. Retain logs over extended periods of time, store data in a database, and query the data to report on and analyze the data as needed for overall performance assessment, trend analysis, and capacity planning.

  For best results, perform the following tasks before starting System Monitor or Performance Logs and Alerts on the computer that you want to monitor for diagnostic purposes:

  - Stop screen-saver programs.

  - Turn off services that are not essential or relevant to monitoring.

  - Increase the paging file to physical memory size plus 100 MB.

Low overhead

- Keep monitoring overhead low.

  In general, the performance tools are designed for minimal overhead. However, you may find that the overhead increases under each of the following conditions:

  - You are running System Monitor in graph view.

  - You selected an option other than the default, current value, for a report view.

  - You are sampling at very frequent intervals, less than three seconds apart.

  - Many objects and counters are selected.

  Other aspects of performance tool operation that affect performance include file size and disk space that is used by log files. To reduce file size and related disk space usage, extend the update interval. Also, log on to a disk other than the one you are monitoring. Frequent logging also adds demand on disk input and output (I/O).

  If monitoring overhead is a concern, run only the Performance Logs and Alerts service; do not monitor by using a System Monitor graph.

  During remote logging, frequent updating can slow performance due to network transport. In this case, it is recommended that you log continuously on remote computers but upload logs infrequently, for example, once a day.

Performance baseline

- Analyze performance results and establish a performance baseline.

  Review logged data by using the System Monitor graph or by exporting it for printing. Compare the values against the counter thresholds to verify that resource usage or other activity is within acceptable limits. Set your baseline according to the level of performance that you consider satisfactory for your typical workload.

Alerts

- Set alerts.

  Set alerts according to the counter values that you consider unacceptable, as defined by baseline evaluation.

System tuning

- Perform system tuning.

  Tune system settings and workload to improve performance, and repeat monitoring to examine tuning results.

Trends

- Monitor trends for capacity planning, and add or upgrade components.

  Maintain logged data in a database, and observe changes to identify changes in resource requirements. After you observe changes in activity or resource demand, you can identify where you may require additional resources.

Note Use Microsoft Operations Manager for enterprise organization. Microsoft Operations Manager is designed to monitor multiple servers simultaneously. Microsoft Operations Manager provides comprehensive event management, proactive monitoring and alerting, reporting, and trend analysis in a large-scale organization.

Lab A: Monitoring Server Performance

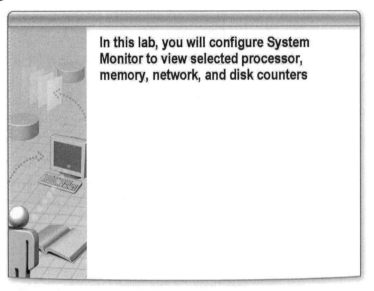

In this lab, you will configure System Monitor to view selected processor, memory, network, and disk counters

Objectives

After completing this lab, you will be able to:

- Configure System Monitor to track CPU usage.
- Create an alert.
- Configure a high CPU usage alert.
- Configure the messaging service.
- Test the alert.

Scenario

You are the systems administrator for an organizational unit on a large network. Recently, users have been complaining that access to the department server is slow. After doing some initial research, you believe that CPU usage is too high. You fix the problem, but you want to be warned before it happens again. You need to configure Performance so that you receive both a visual and an audible alert when CPU usage is running high.

Estimated time to complete this lab: 20 minutes

Exercise 1
Starting Performance with Administrative Credentials

In this exercise, you will log on as a user and then use the **Run as** command to open the Performance Monitor with administrative credentials.

Tasks	Specific instructions
1. Log on to your computer.	▪ Log on to the computer using your domain user account.
2. Start Performance.	▪ Use the **Run as** command to start Performance with administrative credentials.

Exercise 2
Configuring System Monitor to Track High CPU Usage

In this exercise, you will configure System Monitor to track high CPU usage.

Tasks	Specific instructions
▪ Delete the default counters from System Monitor.	▪ In the System Monitor pane, delete the Memory\Pages/sec counter and the PhysicalDisk\Avg. Disk QueueLength counter.

Exercise 3
Creating and Configuring an Alert in Performance Logs and Alerts to Track High CPU Usage

In this exercise, you will create and configure an alert in Performance Logs and Alerts to track the high CPU usage on your server.

Tasks	Specific instructions
1. Create an alert named CPU Alert 2.	▪ Expand **Performance Logs and Alerts,** and then click **Alerts**. ▪ Right-click **Alerts,** click **New Alert Settings,** and then type **CPU Alert 2**
2. Configure an alert so that it triggers when CPU usage is less than 1 gigabytes (GB).	▪ In the **CPU Usage** dialog box, under **Comment,** type **Monitors CPU usage** ▪ Open the **Add Counters** dialog box. ▪ Add the **Processor\% Processor Time** Counter. ▪ Configure the alert to trigger when the value is over **50%.**
3. Send a network message to the console when the alert is triggered.	▪ On the **Action** tab, type the name of your computer in the **Send a network message to** box, and then press ENTER.

Exercise 4
Enabling the Messenger Service

In this exercise, you will enable the messenger service.

Tasks	Specific instructions
1. Start Computer Management with administrative credentials.	▪ Use the **Run as** command to start Computer Management with administrative credentials.
2. Enable the messenger service.	▪ Expand **Services and Applications**, and then click **Services**. ▪ In the details pane, open the properties for **Messenger**. ▪ Change the **Startup type** to **Manual**, and then press ENTER. ▪ Right-click **Messenger**, and then click **Start**.
3. Close Computer Management.	▪ Close Computer Management.

Exercise 5
Testing the High CPU Usage Alert

In this exercise, you will test the high CPU usage alert.

Tasks	Specific instructions
1. Test the high CPU usage alert.	■ Start the following program: C:\MOC\2275\Labfiles\Lab03\cpustres.exe ■ In Performance, view System Monitor. ■ In the **CPU Stress** dialog box, change the activity for **Thread 1** to **Maximum**. ■ When the CPU usage exceeds 50%, the alert will trigger a message every 5 seconds. ■ Close **CPU Stress** to stop the messages.
2. Close all windows and log off.	■ Close all windows and log off.

Microsoft®
Training &
    Certification

Module 4: Maintaining Device Drivers

Contents

Overview	1
Lesson: Configuring Device Driver Signing Options	2
Lesson: Using Device Driver Rollback	17
Lab A: Maintaining Device Drivers	25

Microsoft®

Overview

- Configuring Device Driver Signing Options
- Using Device Driver Rollback

Introduction

To function properly, each device that is attached to a computer requires software, known as a device driver, to be installed on the computer. Every device requires a device driver to communicate with the operating system. Device drivers that are used with the Microsoft® Windows® operating systems are typically provided by Microsoft and the device manufacturer.

This module introduces you to concepts and procedures that will help you maintain device drivers.

Objectives

After completing this module, you will be able to:

- Configure device driver signing.
- Restore the previous version of a device driver.

Lesson: Configuring Device Driver Signing Options

- What Is a Device?
- What Is a Device Driver?
- What Are Device Driver Properties?
- What Is a Signed Device Driver?
- Group Policy Setting for Unsigned Device Drivers
- What Is Group Policy Management Console?
- How to Configure Device Driver Signing Options Using Group Policy
- How to Configure Device Driver Signing Options Manually

Introduction

This lesson introduces devices, device drivers, device driver signing, and Group Policy driver signing settings. This lesson also describes how to configure device driver signing manually and by using Group Policy objects.

Lesson objectives

After completing this lesson, you will be able to:

- Explain devices and types of devices.
- Explain the purpose of a device driver.
- Determine device driver properties.
- Explain signed device drivers.
- Explain the Group Policy setting for unsigned device drivers.
- Explain the Group Policy Management console.
- Configure device driver signing options by using Group Policy.
- Configure device driver signing options manually.

What Is a Device?

* A device is any piece of equipment that can be attached to a computer

* Examples: Video card, printer, joystick, network adapter, modem card

* Devices can be divided into two groups:

  * Plug and Play

    A combination of hardware and software support that enables a computer system to recognize and the device

  * Non-Plug and Play

    Not supported in Windows Server 2003 products

Definition

A device is any piece of equipment that can be attached to a computer.

Examples of devices

Some examples of devices are a video card, a printer, a joystick, a network adapter, a modem card, or any other peripheral equipment.

Types of devices

Devices can be divided into two groups:

■ Plug and Play

Plug and Play is a combination of hardware and software support that enables a computer system to recognize and adapt to hardware configuration changes with little or no user intervention.

You can add or remove Plug and Play devices dynamically, without manually changing the configuration. With Plug and Play, you can be confident that all devices will work together and that the computer will restart correctly after you add or remove the device.

You can install some Plug and Play devices by simply plugging in the device. For other devices, such as Plug and Play Industry Standard Architecture (ISA) cards, you must turn off the computer to install the device, and then restart the computer to initialize the device. Most devices manufactured since 1995 are Plug and Play.

Note For more information about Plug and Play, see the white paper, *Plug and Play*, under **Additional Reading** on the Web page on the Student Materials compact disc.

■ Non–Plug and Play

Plug and Play support depends on both the hardware device and the device driver. If the device driver does not support Plug and Play, its devices behave as non–Plug and Play devices, regardless of any Plug and Play support provided by the hardware.

Non–Plug and Play devices are not supported by products in the Windows Server 2003 family.

What Is a Device Driver?

> - **A device driver:**
>   - Is a program that allows a specific device to communicate with the operating system
>   - Is loaded automatically when a computer is started
> - **Before Windows can use an attached device, the appropriate device driver must be installed**
> - **Use Device Manager to:**
>   - Identify, install, and update device drivers
>   - Roll back to the previous version of a device driver
>   - Disable, enable, and uninstall devices

Definition

A device driver is a software program that allows a specific device, such as a modem, network adapter, or printer, to communicate with the operating system.

Scenario

For example, you are a systems administrator for a department in a large organization. The department recently acquired three new color printers. Users are complaining that all three color printers produce prints that are blurred and grainy. You suspect that the printer device driver is at fault. To solve the problem, you visit the Web site of the printer manufacturer, download the latest device driver for the printer, and then install it on the printer server.

Key concepts

The following key concepts describe device drivers:

- A device driver is loaded automatically when a computer is started.

- Before Windows can use a device that is attached to your system, the appropriate device driver must be installed.

- If a device is listed in the Hardware Compatibility List (HCL), a device driver for that device is usually included with Windows.

  The HCL is a list of hardware that Microsoft compiles for specific products, including Windows Server 2003 and earlier versions of Windows. The HCL for a specific product, such as Windows Server 2003, includes the hardware devices and computer systems that are compatible with that version of the product.

  Note The HCL is updated as new hardware becomes available, so always check the Microsoft Web site at http://www.microsoft.com/hwdq/hcl/ for the latest HCL. When a device is on the HCL but the driver is not included with Windows or available from the Web site, you must obtain the device driver from the device manufacturer.

■ You can use Device Manager, the administrative tool, to:

- Identify the device drivers that are loaded for each device, and obtain information about each device driver.

- Install updated device drivers.

- Roll back to the previous version of a device driver.

- Determine whether the hardware on your computer is working properly.

- Disable, enable, and uninstall devices.

- Print a summary of the devices that are installed on your computer.

Note   After you load the device driver onto your system, Windows configures the properties and settings for the device. Although you can manually configure device properties and settings, you should let Windows do it. When you manually configure properties and settings, the settings become fixed, which means that Windows cannot modify them in the future if a problem arises or there is a conflict with another device.

What Are Device Driver Properties?

Device driver property	Description
Driver Name	Name of the driver file and its location, such as **C:\Windows\System32\drivers\e100b325.sys**
Driver Provider	Name of the company that provided the driver to Microsoft, such as **Intel**
Driver Date	Date that the driver was written, such as **7/1/2001**
Driver Version	Version number of the driver, such as **5.41.22.0**
Digital Signer	Name of the entity that tested and verified the driver to be working properly, such as **Microsoft Windows XP Publisher**

Introduction

One of your duties as a systems administrator may be to monitor the Web sites of hardware vendors to look for updated device drivers and then install them on your server computer. Before installing an updated device driver, you must document the properties of the device driver, such as name, date, and version.

Device driver properties

The following five properties are associated with every device driver:

- *Driver Name.* The physical name of the driver file and its location.
- *Driver Provider.* The name of the company that provided the driver to Microsoft.
- *Driver Date.* The date that the driver was written.
- *Driver Version.* The version number of the driver. The first version is typically named 1.0.
- *Digital Signer.* The name of the entity that tested and verified that the driver works properly.

Example

The properties of a driver for a system device named Intel Pro/100+ Management Adapter with Alert On LAN are shown in the following table.

Property	Description
Driver Name	C:\Windows\System32\drivers\e100b325.sys
Driver Provider	Intel
Driver Date	7/1/2001
Driver Version	5.41.22.0
Digital Signer	Microsoft Windows XP Publisher

Note To view information about a device driver, open Device Manager, double-click the type of device that you want to view, and then on the **Driver** tab, click **Driver Details**.

What Is a Signed Device Driver?

- Digital signature indicates that the device driver meets a certain level of testing and that it has not been altered by another program's installation process

- Use signed device drivers to ensure the performance and stability of your system

- To ensure that device drivers and system files remain in their original, digitally-signed state, Windows provides:

  - Windows File Protection

  - System File Checker

  - File Signature Verification

Introduction

Each device driver and operating system file that is included with Windows has a digital signature. The digital signature indicates that the driver or file meets a certain level of testing and that it was not altered or overwritten by another program's installation process.

An administrator can configure Windows to respond to an unsigned device in one of three ways:

- Ignore device drivers that are not digitally signed

- Display a warning when it detects device drivers that are not digitally signed

- Prevent users from installing device drivers that are not digitally signed

Why use signed device drivers?

Using signed device drivers helps to ensure the performance and stability of your system. Also, it is recommended that you use only signed device drivers for new and updated device drivers.

Note Software for hardware products that display the Designed for Microsoft Windows XP logo or Designed for Microsoft Windows Server 2003 logo has a digital signature from Microsoft. This digital signature indicates that the product was tested for compatibility with Windows and has not been altered since testing.

Tools and components to maintain the digital signature of a device driver

Windows includes the following tools and components to ensure that your device drivers and system files remain in their original, digitally-signed state:

- Windows File Protection

  Windows File Protection prevents the replacement of protected system files, such as .sys, .dll, .ocx, .ttf, .fon, and .exe files. Windows File Protection is a component that runs in the background and protects all files that are installed by the Windows Setup program.

  Windows File Protection checks the file's digital signature to determine whether the new file is the correct version. If the file is not the correct version, Windows File Protection either replaces the file from the backup that is stored in the Dllcache folder or from the Windows Server 2003 compact disc. If Windows File Protection cannot locate the appropriate file, it prompts you for the location.

  By default, Windows File Protection is always enabled and allows digitally signed files to replace existing files. Currently, signed files are distributed through Windows Service Packs, Hotfix distributions, operating system upgrades and Windows Update.

- System File Checker

  System File Checker, **sfc**, is a command-line tool that scans and verifies the versions of all protected system files after you restart your computer. System File Checker replaces overwritten files with the correct system files that are provided by Microsoft. It is part of the Windows File Protection feature of Windows Server 2003. System File Checker also checks and repopulates the Dllcache folder.

  If the Dllcache folder becomes damaged or unusable, use **sfc** with the **/purgecache** switch to repair its contents. Most .sys, .dll, .exe, .ttf, .fon, and .ocx files on the Windows Server 2003 compact disc are protected.

  The following table lists the various **sfc** switches and their descriptions.

Switch	Description
/scannow	Scans all protected system files immediately
/scanonce	Scans all protected system files at the next system start
/scanboot	Scans all protected system files at every start
/cancel	Cancels all pending scans of protected system files
/enable	Enables Windows File Protection for normal operation
/purgecache	Purges the file cache and scans all protected system files immediately
/cachesize=x	Sets the file cache size, in megabytes
/quiet	Replaces incorrect file versions without prompting the user
/?	Displays this list

Note To start a system file check, click **Start**, click **Run**, and then type **sfc /scannow**

- File Signature Verification

  The system files and device driver files that are provided with Windows XP and the Windows Server 2003 family of products have a Microsoft digital signature. The digital signature indicates that the files are original, unaltered system files or that they are approved by Microsoft for use with Windows.

  By using File Signature Verification, you can identify signed and unsigned files on your computer and view the name, location, modification date, type, and version number.

  Note   To start File Signature Verification, click **Start**, click **Run**, type **sigverif** and then click **OK**.

Group Policy Setting for Unsigned Device Drivers

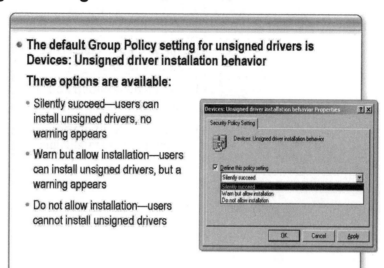

- • **The default Group Policy setting for unsigned drivers is Devices: Unsigned driver installation behavior**

  Three options are available:

  - • Silently succeed—users can install unsigned drivers, no warning appears

  - • Warn but allow installation—users can install unsigned drivers, but a warning appears

  - • Do not allow installation—users cannot install unsigned drivers

---

Introduction

The Group Policy setting for unsigned device drivers is named **Devices: Unsigned driver installation behavior**. You can use it to allow users to install unsigned drivers, to warn users before they install unsigned device drivers, and to prevent users from installing unsigned device drivers.

Example of an unsigned driver

You are a systems administrator for an organization that does not allow users to install unsigned device drivers on their computers. The organization has over 1,000 computers, so enforcing this rule by manually configuring each computer is an impractical solution. The most efficient way to enforce this rule is to automate the setting by configuring Group Policy.

Group Policy options

The **Unsigned driver installation behavior** Group Policy setting has three options:

- ■ *Silently succeed.* Allows the user to install an unsigned device driver without receiving a warning.

- ■ *Warn but allow installation.* Allows the user to install an unsigned device driver, but a warning about installing unsigned device drivers is displayed.

- ■ *Do not allow installation.* Prevents the installation of unsigned device drivers.

What Is Group Policy Management Console?

* An MMC snap-in built on a set of programmable interfaces for managing Group Policy

* Use to manage Group Policy settings across the organization

* Use to simplify automated settings, for example, unsigned driver installation

---

Definition

The Group Policy Management console is a set of programmable interfaces for managing Group Policy, as well as an MMC snap-in that is built on those programmable interfaces. Together, the components of the Group Policy Management console consolidate the management of Group Policy.

The Group Policy Management console lets you manage Group Policy for multiple domains and sites within one or more forests, all in a simplified user interface (UI) with drag-and-drop support.

Manage Group Policy settings for unsigned drivers

You can manage your Group Policy setting for unsigned device drivers for all the users in your organization by using the Group Policy Management console.

How to Configure Device Driver Signing Options by Using Group Policy

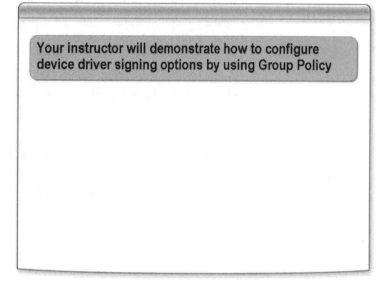

Your instructor will demonstrate how to configure device driver signing options by using Group Policy

Introduction

This topic introduces how to configure device driver signing options by using the Group Policy Management Console.

Procedure

To configure device driver signing options using the Group Policy Management Console:

1. Create a snap-in for Active Directory® Users and Computers.

   a. Log on with your user account.

   b. On the **Start** menu, click **Run**.

   c. In the **Run** dialog box, in the **Open** box, type **runas /user:nwtraders\administrator mmc** and then click **OK**.

   d. When prompted for a password, type **P@ssw0rd** and then press ENTER.

   e. In the **Console1** window, click **File**, and then click **Add/Remove Snap-in**.

   f. In the **Add/Remove Snap-in** dialog box, click **Add**.

   g. In the **Add Standalone Snap-in** dialog box, click **Group Policy Management**, and then click **Add**.

   h. Click **Close**, and then click **OK**.

   Note If you are on a domain controller, click **Start**, point to **Administrative Tools**, and then click **Active Directory Users and Computers**.

2. In the Group Policy Management window, expand **Group Policy Management**, expand **Forest: nwtraders.msft**, expand **Domains**, expand **nwtraders.msft**, expand **Locations**, and then expand your *ComputerName* organizational unit.

3. Right-click your *ComputerName* organizational unit, and then click **Create and Link a GPO Here**.

4. In the **New GPO** dialog box, type *ComputerName* **Unsigned Device Driver Policy** and then click **OK**.

5. Expand *ComputerName*, right-click *ComputerName* **Unsigned Device Driver Policy**, and then click **Edit**.

6. In the console tree of the Group Policy Object Editor window, under **Computer Configuration**, expand **Windows Settings**, expand **Security Settings**, expand **Local Policies**, and then click **Security Options**.

7. In the details pane, double-click **Devices: Unsigned driver installation behavior**.

8. In the **Properties** dialog box for **Devices: Unsigned driver installation behavior**, select the **Define this policy setting** check box.

9. In the drop-down list, click **Do not allow installation**, and then click **OK**.

10. Close all windows.

How to Configure Device Driver Signing Options Manually

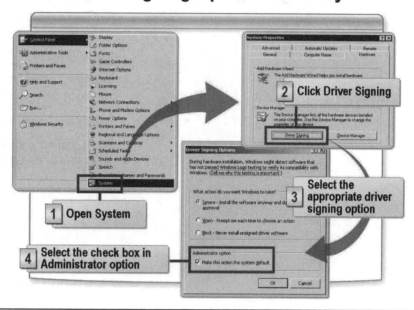

Introduction

Use the following procedure when you must manually configure a computer. For example, you are the systems administrator for the engineering department in a large organization. All the computers in the organization are configured by a policy that blocks the installation of unsigned device drivers. Software developers in your department need to test a new unsigned device driver that they developed. They cannot test the unsigned device driver because of the policy. You must manually configure their computers to allow the installation of unsigned device drivers.

Procedure

To configure device driver signing options manually:

1. Click **Start**, click **Control Panel**, and then double-click **System**.

2. On the **Hardware** tab, click **Driver Signing**.

3. In the **Driver Signing Options** dialog box, in the **What action do you want Windows to take** box, select the appropriate option:

   a. Ignore–Install the software anyway and don't ask for my approval

   b. Warn–Prompt me each time to choose an action

   c. Block–Never install unsigned driver software

4. Under **Administration option**, select the **Make this action the system default** check box, and then click **OK**.

Note   As an administrator, you can select the **Make this action the system default** check box to apply the selected setting as the default for all users who log on to this computer.

Practice: Configuring Device Driver Signing Options

In this practice, you will:

- View the current file signature verification setting by using Control Panel
- Modify the setting using Group Policy
- Verify that the setting has been modified according to Group Policy

Objective

In this practice, you will view the current file signature verification setting by using Control Panel. You will then use Group Policy to modify the setting and verify that the setting was modified.

Scenario

All device drivers must be signed, tested, and approved before users are allowed to install the device drivers on their computers. You will configure Group Policy to enforce the driver signing standards for all computers in the domain.

This practice is a simulation, which you will use as an interactive exercise. To complete this practice, you need the following:

- A computer running Microsoft Windows Server 2003, Windows XP Professional, Windows 2000, Microsoft Windows NT® 4.0, Windows 98, or Windows 95.

- A minimum display resolution of 800 x 600 with 256 colors.

Practice

▶ **To start the simulation**

1. Insert the Student Materials compact disc into your CD-ROM drive.

2. At the root of the compact disc, double-click **Default.htm**.

3. On the Student Materials Web page, click **Multimedia**.

4. Click **Configuring Device Driver Signing Options**.

5. Read the introduction information, and then click the link to start the practice.

Lesson: Using Device Driver Rollback

- **What Is Device Driver Rollback?**
- **How to Restore and Update Device Drivers**
- **Uninstalling Devices and Device Drivers**
- **How to Uninstall a Device Driver**

Introduction

If a device stops functioning after you install an updated device driver for the device, you can use the Roll Back Driver feature to restore the previous version of the driver. By using this feature, you can avoid spending hours searching for a copy of the original driver that was installed. However, you cannot roll back a driver more than once.

This lesson describes how to restore, update, and uninstall device drivers.

Lesson objectives

After completing this lesson, you will be able to:

- Explain device driver rollback.
- Restore a previous version of a device driver and update device driver.
- Describe the effects of uninstalling device drivers and devices.
- Uninstall a device driver.

What Is Device Driver Rollback?

- **After updating device drivers, you might encounter problems such as stop errors or startup problems**
- **If a problem occurs, you can revert to the previous version by using a Device Manager feature called Roll Back Driver**
- **You cannot:**
  - Roll back beyond one driver version
  - Roll back printer drivers
  - Simultaneously roll back drivers for all functions of a multifunction device
- **Why use device driver rollback:**
  - If a problem occurs immediately after you update a device driver, you can restore the previous version by using device driver rollback

Introduction

Updating one or more device drivers can cause problems. For example, a device can stop functioning, a stop error may be displayed, and startup problems can occur. To prevent problems from occurring after you upgrade a device driver, avoid using beta or unsigned device drivers. These device drivers might not be fully tested for compatibility with Windows Server 2003.

Why use device driver rollback?

If a problem occurs immediately after you update a device driver, you can restore the previous version by using the Roll Back Driver feature in Device Manager. If the problem prevents you from starting Windows Server 2003 in normal mode, you can roll back device drivers in safe mode.

Note You must be logged on as an administrator or a member of the Administrators group to roll back a driver, or you must have been delegated this authority.

Driver rollback limitations

When using device driver rollback, be aware of the following limitations:

- You can roll back only one driver version. For example, you cannot restore the second to the last version of a driver.
- You cannot roll back printer drivers because Device Manager does not support or display printer properties.
- You cannot simultaneously roll back device drivers for all functions of a multifunction device. You must roll back each driver separately. For example, for a multifunction device that provides audio and modem functionality, you must roll back the modem driver and the audio driver separately.

How to Restore and Update Device Drivers

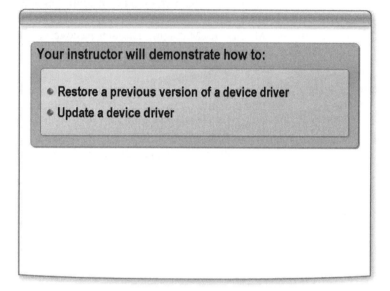

Your instructor will demonstrate how to:

- Restore a previous version of a device driver
- Update a device driver

Introduction

This topic covers the procedures that you use to restore and update device drivers.

Procedure for restoring a device driver

As a systems administrator, you may need to restore a previous version of a driver. For example, a user complains that after he installed a new modem driver on his computer, his connection speed dropped from 56 kilobits per second (Kbps) to 14.4 Kbps. He wants you to restore the previous version of the driver.

To restore the previous version of a device driver:

1. Click **Start**, click **Control Panel**, double-click **System**, click **Hardware**, and then click **Device Manager**.

   > **Note** Another way to open Device Manager is to click **Start**, right-click **My Computer**, click **Manage**, and then click **Device Manager**.

2. In Device Manager, double-click the type of device that you want to restore the device drivers for, right-click the device driver that you want to roll back to, and then click **Properties**.

3. On the **Driver** tab, click **Roll Back Driver**.

4. At the prompt, click **Yes** to confirm that you want to roll back to the previous driver.

   a. If the driver rollback process does not find a previous driver, the following message appears:

   "No driver files have been backed up for this device. If you are having problems with this device you should view the Troubleshooter information. Would you like to launch the Troubleshooter?"

   b. If you answer Yes, the Troubleshooter wizard guides you through a series of steps to help you troubleshoot your device.

Note If rolling back the device driver does not resolve the problem, you can use the Last Known Good Configuration or System Restore. For more information about Last Known Good Configuration and System Restore, see Module 7, "Managing Disaster Recovery," in Course 2275, *Maintaining a Microsoft Windows Server 2003 Environment.*

Procedure for updating device drivers

When hardware vendors develop new devices for computers, the device drivers that are initially included with the product are often rudimentary. A few months later, the hardware vendors often provide newer device drivers that are more stable and offer more features. As a systems administrator, you must visit the Web sites of hardware vendors to download the new device drivers and update your servers.

To update device drivers:

1. Click **Start**, click **Control Panel**, double-click **System**, click **Hardware**, and then click **Device Manager**.

2. In Device Manager, double-click the type of device that you want to update or change.

3. Right-click the specific device driver that you want to update or change, and then click **Update Driver**.

4. The Hardware Update Wizard appears. Follow the instructions.

Note Another way to gain access to the **Update Driver** button is to double-click the type of device driver that you want to update, and then on the **Driver** tab, click **Update Driver**.

Important To perform the preceding two procedures, you must have been delegated the appropriate authority. As a security best practice, consider using **Run as** to perform this procedure.

Uninstalling Devices and Device Drivers

> * If you use Device Manager to uninstall a device driver, the device driver is removed from memory and not from disk
>
> * Uninstall a Plug and Play device by disconnecting or removing the device from your computer
>
> * Disable the Plug and Play device instead of uninstalling a device that you do not want enabled but that should remain attached to the computer, such as a modem

Introduction

When you use Device Manager to uninstall a device driver, the device driver is removed from memory but not from the hard disk. Until you remove the device, Windows automatically reloads the driver the next time the computer is restarted.

Uninstalling a Plug and Play device

You uninstall a Plug and Play device by disconnecting or removing the device from your computer. Some devices, such as cards that plug into the motherboard, require that you turn off the computer first. To ensure that you uninstall a Plug and Play device properly, consult the device manufacturer's installation and removal instructions.

Uninstalling devices vs. disabling devices

If you want a Plug and Play device to remain attached to a computer without being enabled, you can disable the device instead of uninstalling it.

When you disable a device, the device stays physically connected to your computer, but Windows updates the system registry so that the device drivers for the disabled device are no longer loaded when you start your computer. The device drivers are available again when you enable the device.

Disabling devices is useful if you must switch between two hardware devices, such as a networking card and a modem, or if you need to troubleshoot a hardware issue.

Note To enable or disable devices, open Device Manager, double-click the type of device that you want to enable or disable, right-click the specific device you want, and then click **Enable** or **Disable**.

How to Uninstall a Device Driver

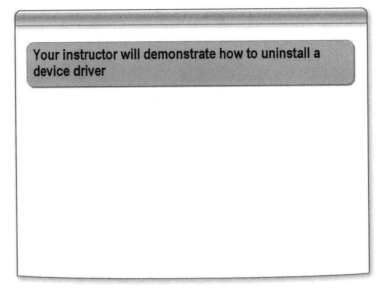

Introduction

As a systems administrator, you may be required to uninstall device drivers. For example, one of the resource servers on the network is scheduled to be upgraded with new hardware devices. You must remove all of the old hardware devices on the server and uninstall the unnecessary device drivers. After removing the devices, you must use Device Manager to verify that all of the unnecessary device drivers are removed. If any unnecessary device drivers remain, you can use the **Uninstall** feature to remove them.

Procedure

To uninstall a device driver:

1. To open Device Manager, click **Start**, click **Control Panel**, double-click **System**, click **Hardware**, and then click **Device Manager**.

2. Double-click the type of device you want to uninstall.

3. Right-click the specific device driver that you want to uninstall, and then click **Uninstall**.

Note Another way to gain access to the **Uninstall** button is to double-click the type of device driver that you want to uninstall, and then, on the **Driver** tab, click **Uninstall**.

---

4. In the **Confirm Device Removal** dialog box, click **OK**.

5. To verify that the devices are removed, open Device Manager, right-click the computer name, and then click **Scan for hardware changes**.

Practice: Using Device Driver Rollback

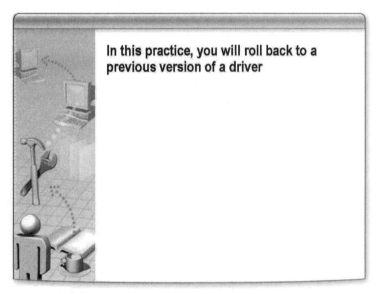

In this practice, you will roll back to a previous version of a driver

Objective

In this practice, you will roll back to a previous version of a device driver.

Scenario

You are the systems administrator for an organizational unit on a large network. A user in the organization downloaded an unsigned driver from the Internet and installed it, which has caused the mouse on the computer to stop working. You must roll back to the previous version of the driver.

Practice

▶ **Install the unsigned mouse driver**

1. Log on to the **nwtraders** domain as *Computer*User with a password of **P@ssw0rd**.

2. Open Control Panel and use **Run As** to open **System** with administrator privileges by holding down the SHIFT key, right-clicking **System**, and then clicking **Run as**.

3. Select **The following user**, type **nwtraders\administrator** and the administrator password in the respective boxes, and then click **OK**.

4. On the **Hardware** tab, click **Driver Signing**, and then set the driver-signing options to **Warn – Prompt me each time to choose an action**.

5. On the **Hardware** tab, click **Device Manager**, expand **Mice and other pointing devices**, right-click the mouse icon, and select **Update Driver**.

6. In the **Hardware Update Wizard**, install the mouse driver using the following parameters.

When prompted	Select
What do you want the wizard to do?	Install from a list or specific location
Please choose your search and installation options	Don't search. I will choose the driver to install.
Select the device driver you want to install for this hardware	Have Disk
Copy manufacturer's files from	Type: **C:\MOC\2275\Practices\Mod04**
Confirm Device Install	Yes
The software has not passed Windows Logo testing	Continue Anyway

7. Restart the computer if prompted.

8. Log on to the **nwtraders** domain as *Computer***User** with a password of **P@ssw0rd**.

9. Open Control Panel, and using Run As, open **System** with administrator privileges.

10. On the **Hardware** tab, click **Device Manager**, open the **Properties** dialog box for the mouse, and then review the driver date and version for the unsigned driver.

11. Roll back to the previous driver, and note the driver date and version.

12. Restart the computer if prompted.

Lab A: Maintaining Device Drivers

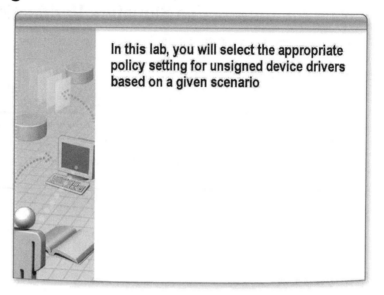

In this lab, you will select the appropriate policy setting for unsigned device drivers based on a given scenario

Objective

In this lab, you will select the appropriate policy setting for unsigned device drivers based on a given scenario.

Scenario

You are the systems administrator for an organizational unit on a network. All 500 users in the organization were issued laptop computers. You are concerned that some users may try to install unsigned device drivers that they find on the Internet. You must change the policy settings so that users are restricted when they try to install unsigned device drivers on their computers.

Estimated time to complete this lab: 15 minutes

Exercise 1
Viewing the Current File Signature Verification Setting

In this exercise, you will view the current file signature verification setting.

Tasks	Specific instructions
■ Log on to the **nwtraders** domain.	a. Log on to the **nwtraders** domain as *Computer*User with a password of **P@ssw0rd**.
	b. In Control Panel, open **System**, click the **Hardware** tab, and then view the default file signature verification setting.

Exercise 2
Modifying the Default Setting

In this exercise, you will modify default settings for all computers by using Group Policy Management Console.

Tasks	Specific instructions
▪ Start the Group Policy Management Console.	a. Use **runas** to start the Group Policy Manager snap-in with administrative privileges: **runas /user:nwtraders\administrator "mmc %windir%\system32\gpmc.msc"**
	b. Expand **Group Policy Management**, expand **Forest:nwtraders.msft**, expand **Domains**, expand **nwtraders.msft**, expand **Locations**, and then click your *ComputerName* organizational unit.
	c. Right-click *ComputerName,* create a new Group Policy object and name it *ComputerName* **Unsigned Device Driver Policy**.
	d. Right-click *ComputerName* **Unsigned Device Driver Policy** to edit the policy.
	e. In the Group Policy Object Editor window, under **Computer Configuration**, expand **Windows Settings**, expand **Security Settings**, expand **Local Policies**, and then click **Security Options**.
	f. Open the **Properties** dialog box for **Devices: Unsigned driver installation behavior**.
	g. Enable the **Define this policy setting**, click **Do not allow installation**, and then click **OK**.
	h. Close all windows.

Exercise 3
Adding a Computer to the Organizational Unit

In this exercise, you will add your computer to the appropriate Nwtraders organizational unit.

Tasks	Specific instructions
▪ Log on to the **nwtraders** domain.	a. Use **runas** to open a command prompt with administrative privileges. b. On the command line, type each of the following commands, and then press ENTER: **cd \MOC\2275\Practices\Mod04** **oumove** c. The computer restarts.

Exercise 4
Verifying the New File Signature Verification Setting

In this exercise, you will verify the new file signature verification setting.

Tasks	Specific instructions
1. Log on to the **nwtraders** domain.	a. Log on to the **nwtraders** domain as *Computer***User** with a password of **P@ssw0rd**. b. In Control Panel, open **System**, and then verify that the default file signature verification setting is set to **Block – Never install unsigned driver software**.
2. Close all windows.	▪ Close all windows and log off.

Microsoft®
Training &
Certification

Module 5: Managing Disks

Contents

Overview	1
Lesson: Preparing Disks	2
Lesson: Managing Disk Properties	17
Lesson: Managing Mounted Drives	24
Lesson: Converting Disks	29
Lesson: Creating Volumes	37
Lesson: Importing a Disk	47
Lab A: Managing Disks	55

Overview

- Preparing Disks
- Managing Disk Properties
- Managing Mounted Drives
- Converting Disks
- Creating Volumes
- Importing a Disk

Introduction

One of the tasks that you perform when administering a server is managing disks. By knowing what tools are available to set up and manage disks and what capabilities are provided by Microsoft® Windows® Server 2003, you can better manage disk drives and use advanced features, such as creating a mounted drive and importing a foreign disk.

This module covers the tasks that you use to manage disks and describes how to use the tools to manage and set up disks.

Objectives

After completing this module, you will be able to:

- Initialize and partition a disk.
- View and update disk properties.
- Manage mounted drives.
- Convert a disk from basic to dynamic and from dynamic to basic.
- Create volumes on a disk.
- Import disks.

Lesson: Preparing Disks

* What Is Disk Management?
* What Is the DiskPart Tool?
* What Is a Partition?
* How to Prepare a Disk
* How to Assign, Change and Remove a Drive Letter
* Multimedia: What Are the Differences Between the FAT, FAT32, and NTFS File Systems?
* How to Convert File Systems
* Best Practices for Preparing Disks

Introduction

When you install a new disk, Windows Server 2003 recognizes it and configures it as a basic disk. A basic disk is the default storage medium and provides limited configuration capabilities.

This lesson describes how to partition a basic disk by using Disk Management and the DiskPart command-line tool. It also explains how file system attributes affect disks and how to use the file systems when you configure disks.

Lesson objectives

After completing this lesson, you will be able to:

* Explain the function of Disk Management.
* Explain the function of DiskPart.
* Explain partitions.
* Initialize, format, and delete a partition by using Disk Management and DiskPart.
* Add, change, and remove a drive letter by using Disk Management and DiskPart.
* Distinguish between FAT (file allocation table), FAT32, and the NTFS file system.
* Convert file systems.
* Explain best practices for preparing disks.

What Is Disk Management?

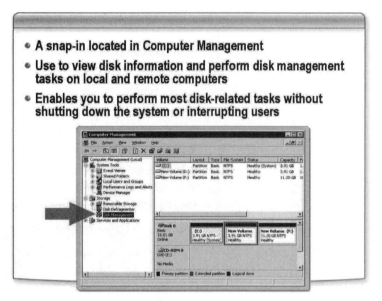

Introduction

Disk Management, a Microsoft Management Console (MMC) snap-in, is a system utility that consolidates all of your disk management tasks for both local and remote administration of Windows Server 2003. Because Disk Management is an MMC snap-in, it uses the interface, menu structure, and shortcut menus that you are accustomed to using. You can gain access to Disk Management in the Computer Management console, or you can create a separate console for it.

Perform disk management tasks

You can use Disk Management to configure and manage your storage space and perform all your disk management tasks. You can also use Disk Management to convert disk storage type, create and extend volumes, and perform other disk management tasks, such as managing drive letters and paths and maintaining Windows Server 2003.

Local and remote administration

When you create a separate console and add the Disk Management snap-in, you can focus the snap-in either on the local computer or on another computer for remote administration of that computer. As a member of the Administrators group or Server Operators group, you can manage disks on a computer running Windows Server 2003 that is a member of the domain, or of a trusted domain, from any other computer running Windows Server 2003 on the network.

For example, you can create a console to which you add multiple Disk Management snap-ins, each focused on a different remote computer. You can then manage the disk storage of all of the computers from that single console.

What Is the DiskPart Tool?

- **You can use the DiskPart command-line tool to manage:**
  - Disks
  - Partitions
  - Volumes
- **Before you can use DiskPart command, you must first list, then select the object to give it focus**
- **When an object has focus, any DiskPart command that you type will act on that object**
- **Use DiskPart to run scripts to do repetitive tasks**

```
Command Prompt - diskpart
DISKPART> _
```

Introduction

By using the DiskPart command-line tool, you can perform many disk management tasks from the command line. Use DiskPart to perform disk-related tasks at the command line as an alternative to using Disk Management.

Use DiskPart to manage objects

DiskPart is a text-mode command interpreter that enables you to manage objects, such as disks, partitions, and volumes, by using scripts or direct input from a command prompt. Administrators often write scripts to perform repetitive tasks.

Give an object focus

Before you can use a DiskPart command, you must first list and then select an object that you want to manage to give it focus. When an object has focus, any DiskPart command that you type acts on that object.

You can list the available objects and determine an object's number or drive letter by using the **list disk**, **list volume**, and **list partition** commands. The **list disk** and **list volume** commands display all the disks and volumes that are on the computer, whereas the **list partition** command displays only those partitions on the disk that have focus. When you use the **list** commands, an asterisk (*) appears next to the object with focus.

You select an object by using its number or drive letter, such as disk 0, partition 1, volume 3, or volume C. When you select an object, the focus remains on that object until you select a different object. For example, if the focus is set on disk 0 and you select volume 8 on disk 2, the focus shifts from disk 0 to disk 2, volume 8.

DiskPart example

The following table shows an example of using the **diskpart** command to focus on a particular disk.

Command	Description	Response
C:\diskpart	Type **diskpart** on the command line.	Microsoft DiskPart version 5.2 Copyright (C) 1999-2001 Microsoft Corporation. On computer: VANCOUVER
DISKPART> list disk	Type **list disk** to request a list of disks on the server. A list of disks, their status, size, and unallocated space appears.	Disk ### Status Size Free Dyn Gpt -------- -------- --------- ------ ---- ---- Disk 0 Online 37 GB 0 B
DISKPART> **select disk 0**	Type **select disk** *n* to focus on the selected disk. Disk 0 is now selected. The object with focus has an asterisk.	DISKPART> list disk Disk ### Status Size Free Dyn Gpt -------- -------- -------- ------ ---- ---- * Disk 0 Online 37 GB 0 B

Partition and volume focus

On a basic disk, the partition focus and volume focus are the same. If you change the focus on one item, you change the focus on the other.

What Is a Partition?

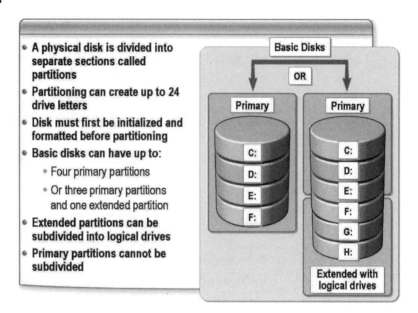

Introduction

Disk partitioning is a way to divide a basic physical disk into sections so that each section, or *partition*, functions as a separate unit. You can use partitioning to divide the hard disk drive into several drive letters so that it is easier to organize data files. Each partition is assigned a different drive letter, such as C or D. After you create a partition, you must format it with a file system before you can store data on the partition.

Partition example

An administrator who wants to keep applications separate from the system files can use partitioning to set up a drive letter for the application files and another drive letter for the system files.

Initialize a disk

When you attach a new disk to your computer, you must first initialize the disk before you can create partitions. When you first start Disk Management after installing a new disk, a wizard appears that provides a list of the new disks that are detected by the operating system. When you complete the wizard, the operating system initializes the disk by writing a disk signature, the end of sector marker (also called a signature word), and a master boot record (MBR). If you cancel the wizard before the disk signature is written, the disk status remains Not Initialized.

Primary partitions

You create primary partitions on a basic disk. A basic disk can have up to four primary partitions or three primary partitions and one extended partition. A primary partition cannot be subdivided. An extended partition can be divided into logical drives.

Note For more information about partitions, see Appendix D, "Partition Styles," on the Student Materials compact disc.

Logical drives

Logical drives are similar to primary partitions, except that you can create up to 24 logical drives per disk but are limited to four primary partitions per disk. You can format a logical drive and assign a drive letter to it.

Extended partitions

You can create an extended partition only on a basic disk. Unlike a primary partition, you do not format an extended partition with a file system. Instead, you create one or more logical drives in the extended partition and then format them with a file system.

Format a disk

You must format a disk before you can use it. Formatting a disk configures the partition with a file allocation table. Formatting prepares the disk for reading and writing. When you format a disk, the operating system erases all the file allocation tables on the disk, tests the disk to verify that the sectors are reliable, marks bad sectors, and creates internal address tables that it later uses to locate information.

Delete a partition

Deleting a partition destroys all of the data in the partition. The partition is then restored to an unallocated space. If you are deleting an extended partition, you must delete all of its logical drives on the disk before deleting the partition.

Assign drive letters

Windows Server 2003 allows the static assignment of drive letters to partitions, volumes, and CD-ROM drives. This means that you assign a drive letter to a specific partition, volume, or CD-ROM drive. It is often convenient to assign drive letters to removable devices in such a way that the devices appear after the permanent partitions and volumes on the computer.

Manage drive letters

You can use up to 24 drive letters, from C through Z. Drive letters A and B are reserved for floppy disk drives. However, if you have only one floppy disk drive, you can use the letter B for a network drive. When you add a new hard disk to an existing computer system, it will not affect previously assigned drive letters.

Important Before you delete or create partitions on a hard disk, be sure to back up the disk contents, because creating and deleting partitions destroys any existing data. As with any major change to disk contents, it is recommended that you back up the entire contents of the hard disk before working with partitions, even if you do not plan to make changes to any of the partitions.

How to Prepare a Disk

Your instructor will demonstrate how to:

- Partition a disk by using Disk Management
- Format a disk by using Disk Management
- Delete a partition by using Disk Management
- Partition a disk by using DiskPart
- Delete a partition by using DiskPart

Introduction

You can use either Disk Management or DiskPart to partition a disk. You can use Disk Management to not only partition the disk, but also to format and assign drive letters at the same time. When you partition an existing disk, you must first delete the partitions. You can use either DiskPart or Disk Management to accomplish this task.

Procedure for partitioning a disk by using Disk Management

To partition a disk by using Disk Management:

1. In Computer Management, open Disk Management.

2. Right-click an unallocated region of a basic disk, and then click **New Partition**, or right-click free space in an extended partition, and then click **New Logical Drive**.

3. In the New Partition Wizard, click **Next**.

4. On the **Select Partition Type** page, click **Primary Partition**, and then click **Next**.

5. On the **Specify Partition Size** page, type *nnn* (where *nnn* is the size in megabytes), and then click **Next**.

6. On the **Assign Drive Letter or Path** page, select the drive letter, and then click **Next**.

7. On the **Format Partition** page:

   a. Select the appropriate file system and allocation unit size.

   b. Type the appropriate volume label.

   c. Select or clear the **Perform a quick format** and **Enable file and folder compression** check boxes.

8. Click **Next**, and then click **Finish**.

Procedure for formatting a disk

To format a disk by using Disk Management:

1. In Computer Management, open Disk Management.

2. Right-click the partition, logical drive, or basic volume that you want to format or reformat, and then click **Format**.

3. Select the options that you want under:

   - **Volume Label**—name the disk.

   - **File System**—select either NTFS or FAT.

   - **Allocation Unit Size**—select the allocated size of the disk that you want to format.

4. If you are sure that the disk is undamaged, select the **Perform a Quick Format** check box.

5. To compress files and folders on the disk, with NTFS volumes only, select **Enable File and Folder Compression**.

Procedure for deleting a partition

To delete a partition by using Disk Management:

1. In Computer Management, open Disk Management.

2. Right-click the partition that you want to delete, and then click **Delete Partition**.

Procedure for partitioning a disk by using DiskPart

To partition a disk by using DiskPart:

1. At the prompt, type **diskpart**

2. At the prompt, type **list disk** and then make a note of the number of the disk on which you want to create a primary or extended partition.

3. At the DISKPART prompt, type **select disk** *n* (where *n* is the disk number of the disk where you want to create the primary or extended partition).

4. At the DISKPART prompt, type one of the following (where *number* is in megabytes):

   - **create partition primary size=***number*

   –Or–

   - **create partition extended size=***number*

   –Or–

   - **create partition logical size=***number*

Procedure for deleting a partition by using DiskPart

To delete a partition by using DiskPart:

1. Open Command Prompt, and then type **diskpart**

2. At the DISKPART prompt, type **list disk**

    Make a note of the disk number of the disk from which you want to delete the partition.

3. At the DISKPART prompt, type **select disk** *n* (where *n* is the disk that you want to delete the partition from).

4. At the DISKPART prompt, type **list partition**

    Make a note of the number of the partition that you want to delete.

5. At the DISKPART prompt, type select partition n, where n is the partition number of the partition that you want to delete.

6. At the DISKPART prompt, type **delete partition**

How to Assign, Change, or Remove a Drive Letter

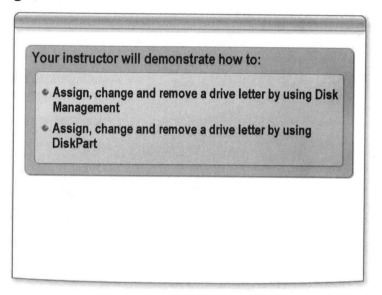

Your instructor will demonstrate how to:

● Assign, change and remove a drive letter by using Disk Management

● Assign, change and remove a drive letter by using DiskPart

Introduction

You can use either Disk Management or DiskPart to assign, change or remove drive letters on partition. As an administrator, you will manage disk drive letters by using these tools.

Procedure using Disk Management

To assign, change, or remove drive letters by using Disk Management:

1. In Computer Management, open Disk Management.

2. Right-click a partition, logical drive, or volume, and then click **Change Drive Letter and Paths**.

3. Do one of the following:

   • To assign a drive letter, click **Add**, and then click the drive letter that you want to use.

   • To modify a drive letter, click it, click **Change**, and then click the drive letter that you want to use.

   • To remove a drive letter, click it, and then click **Remove**.

Procedure using DiskPart

To assign, change, or remove a drive letter by using DiskPart:

1. Open Command prompt, and then type **diskpart**

2. At the DISKPART prompt, type **list volume**. Make note of the number of the volume whose drive letter you want to assign, change, or remove.

3. At the DISKPART prompt, type **select volume** n (where n is the number of the volume whose drive letter you want to assign, change, or remove).

4. At the DISKPART prompt, type one of the following:

   a. **assign letter**=L (where L is the drive letter that you want to assign or change)

   b. **remove letter**=L (where L is the drive letter that you want to remove)

Multimedia: What Are the Differences Between the FAT, FAT32, and NTFS File Systems?

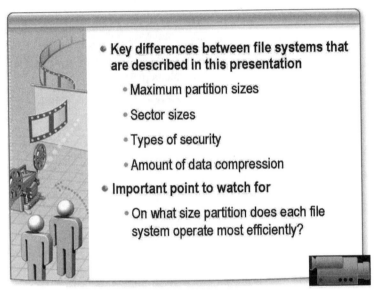

Introduction

Windows supports three main file systems: FAT (file allocation table), FAT32, and NTFS. This presentation describes the main features and uses of each of the file systems.

Key file system features

The following table summarizes the main features of the three file systems.

	FAT	FAT32	NTFS
Max partition size	4 gigabytes (GB)	32 GB	2 terabytes
Sector size	16 kilobytes (KB) to 64 KB	As low as 4 KB	As low as 4 KB
Security	File attributes	File attributes	File, folder, and encryption
Compression	None	None	Files, folders, and drives

How to Convert File Systems

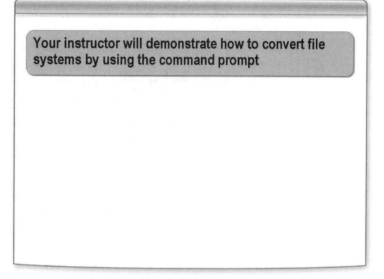

Your instructor will demonstrate how to convert file systems by using the command prompt

Introduction

As a systems administrator, you may be asked to convert an existing volume from FAT32 to NTFS. Use the following steps to perform this task.

Procedure

To convert a volume from a FAT or FAT32 drive to NTFS:

1. In a command prompt, type **convert** *d:* **/fs:ntfs** (where *d:* is the letter of the disk drive).

2. Press ENTER.

Note   If the partition you are converting is the system or boot partition, you must restart the computer running Windows Server 2003.

Best Practices for Preparing Disks

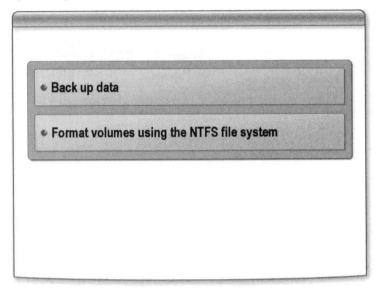

Introduction

When you prepare a disk for partitioning, it is recommended that you back up your data and format your volumes with the NTFS file system.

Back up data

Because deleting or creating partitions or volumes destroys any existing data, be sure to back up the disk contents beforehand. As with any major change to disk contents, it is recommended that you back up the entire contents of the hard disk before working with partitions or volumes, even if you do not plan to make changes to any of the partitions or volumes.

Format volumes using the NTFS file system

Many features in the Windows Server 2003 family of operating systems, such as file and folder permissions, encryption, large volume support, and sparse file management, require the NTFS file system format. Be prepared by formatting your volumes by using the NTFS file system.

Practice: Preparing Disks

In this practice, you will:
- Change the drive letter of a disk
- Delete a partition
- Create an extended partition on a disk
- Configure two logical drives
- Format a logical drive with the NTFS file system
- Format a logical drive with the FAT32 file system

Objective

In this practice, you will:

- Change the drive letter of a disk.
- Delete a partition.
- Create an extended partition on a disk.
- Configure two logical drives.
- Format a logical drive with the NTFS file system.
- Format a logical drive with the FAT32 file system.

Scenario

You are the systems administrator for an organizational unit on a large network. After arriving at work one morning, you read an e-mail message from your manager that includes the following information:

A new server in the graphics department needs additional configuration. You must complete the following tasks:

- The graphics department manager wants the CD-ROM drives on all the departmental servers to use the letter Z.
- The D drive must be deleted, and the 4-GB extended partition must be increased to 6 GB and then divided into two equal parts. One of the graphic artists wants to temporarily use 3 GB of this space for a graphics program based on Windows 95. The D partition should be NTFS and the E partition should be FAT32.

Practice

▶ **Change the drive letter of the CD-ROM drive**

1. Log on to the domain as *Computer***User** with a password of **P@ssw0rd**.

2. Using **Run as** open Computer Management with administrative privileges.

3. Open Disk Management and change the drive letter of the CD-ROM drive to Z.

▶ **Delete the D drive and create a 6-GB extended partition**

1. Using Disk Management, delete the **D** drive.

2. Delete the free space.

3. Create a 6-GB extended partition.

▶ **Create logical drive D and logical drive E**

1. Using Disk Management, create a 3-GB drive named D formatted with NTFS.

2. Create a 3-GB drive named E formatted with FAT 32.

3. Convert E to NTFS.

4. Close all windows and log off.

Lesson: Managing Disk Properties

- What Are Disk Properties?
- How to View Disk Properties
- How to Rescan Disk Properties

Introduction

This lesson explains disk properties. Systems administrators use the information in disk properties when they replace the hard disk in a server. An administrator also must rescan disks when updating disk configurations that have changed.

Lesson objectives

After completing this lesson, you will be able to:

- Explain disk properties.
- View disk properties.
- Rescan disk properties to update disk configuration changes.

What Are Disk Properties?

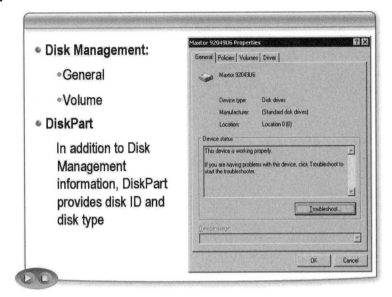

Definition

You can use either Disk Management or DiskPart to view disk properties, which contain information about the physical disk and the volumes that it contains.

Use of disk properties information

Use the information in disk properties when you replace a hard disk or to verify that a specific disk is installed on a server.

Latest disk information

Disk properties provide the latest available information about the disk. You can access this information by using DiskPart or by using Disk Management to open the **Properties** dialog box for the disk. The following tabs in the **Properties** dialog box display disk properties:

■ *General.* Provides the model number and the location of the disk.

■ *Volumes.* Provides the disk number, type, status, partition style, capacity, unallocated space, and reserved space of the disk.

In addition to the information in Disk Management, DiskPart provides the Disk ID and the disk type, such as IDE, ATA, or SCSI.

For example, to order a replacement for a failed hard disk, the systems administrator must know the model, type, and capacity of the original disk. After installing the new disk, the administrator configures it with the disk number, partitions, unallocated space, and volume type.

Rescan disks

After you move hard disks between computers, you must rescan the disks. When Disk Management rescans disk properties, it scans all attached disks for changes to the disk configuration. It also updates information about removable media, CD-ROM drives, basic volumes, file systems, and drive letters.

How to View Disk Properties

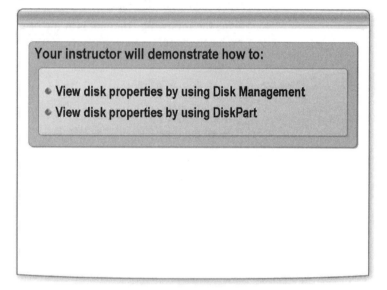

Introduction

Before you replace a hard disk, it is important to know the manufacturer, model number, drive type, and capacity of the drive so that you can find a comparable or exact replacement. After you install the new disk, you must know the disk number, volume type, partition style, and number of partitions or volumes so that you can restore the environment of the previous disk.

Procedure using Disk Management

To view disk properties by using Disk Management:

1. In Computer Management, open Disk Management.

2. In the graphical view or disk list, right-click a disk, and then click **Properties**.

3. Click the **General** tab, and then record the model number.

4. Click the **Volumes** tab, and then record the following values:

   - Disk

   - Type

   - Status

   - Partition style

   - Capacity

Procedure using DiskPart

To view the disk type by using DiskPart:

1. Open Command Prompt.

2. Type the following commands at the prompt, at then press ENTER after each command:

   a. **diskpart**

   b. **select disk 0**

   c. **detail disk**

3. Record the type.

How to Rescan Disk Properties

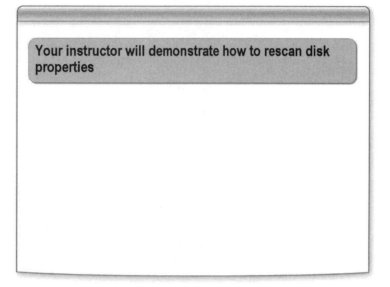

Your instructor will demonstrate how to rescan disk properties

Introduction

When you add a new disk to your computer, if Disk Management does not detect it, you can rescan the disk to update the disk properties.

Procedure

To update disk properties by using Disk Management:

1. In Computer Management, open Disk Management.

2. Click **Action**, and then click **Rescan Disks**.

Practice: Documenting Disk Properties

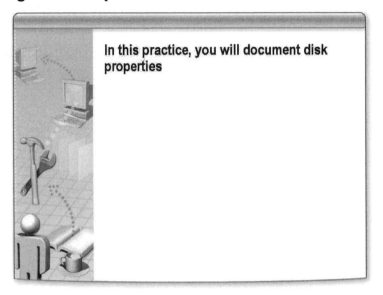

Objective

In this practice, you will document disk properties.

Scenario

You are the systems administrator for an organizational unit on a large network. After arriving at work one morning, you read the following e-mail message from your manager:

> We need to take inventory of all the different disk drives that we have installed on our servers. By doing this, we will be better prepared in an emergency if one of the drives fails. We will be able to order a replacement quickly without having to figure out the model number, capacity, and so on.
>
> Please collect the following information about the disk on the server in the graphics department:
>
> - Manufacturer
>
> - Model
>
> - Disk type
>
> - Drive capacity
>
> You should also collect the volume information so that we do not spend hours trying to remember how the disk was configured in case we need to replace it:
>
> - Disk number
>
> - Partition style
>
> - Number of partitions
>
> - Capacity of each partition
>
> Please write this information in the Systems log book so that we can access the information quickly in case of a disk failure.

Practice

▶ **Examine the properties of a disk**

1. Log on to the domain as *Computer***User** with a password of **P@ssword**.

2. Using **Run as** open Computer Management with administrative privileges, and then open Disk Management.

3. Open the properties for disk 0 and record the following information:

   Model: _____

   Disk number: _____

   Partition style: _____

   Drive capacity: _____

   Number of partitions: _____

   Capacity of C: _____

   Capacity of D: _____

   Capacity of E: _____

4. Open a command prompt with administrator privileges, and then use DiskPart to determine the disk type and record it:

   Disk Type: _____

5. Close all windows and log off.

Lesson: Managing Mounted Drives

- What Is a Mounted Drive?
- What Is the Purpose of a Mounted Drive?
- How to Manage a Mounted Drive

Introduction

Using mounted drives can help you manage and organize data on your server. For example, to provide a more intuitive name for your drive, you can use a mounted drive to add a drive description of an existing partition. Use a mounted drive when you have two drives of related data that logically belong on one drive. Also, mounted drives help you manage the limited number of drive letters that you have to work with on a hard disk.

Lesson objectives

After completing this lesson, you will be able to:

- Explain a mounted drive.
- Explain how to use a mounted drive.
- Create a mounted drive by using Disk Management and DiskPart.
- Delete a mounted drive by using Disk Management.

What Is a Mounted Drive?

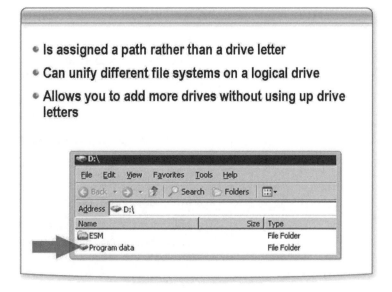

Definition

A mounted drive is a self-contained unit of storage that is administered by an NTFS file system. You can use Disk Management to mount a local drive to any empty folder on a local NTFS volume rather than to a drive letter. This method is similar to creating a shortcut that points to a disk partition or volume. Mounting a drive to a folder allows you to use an intuitive name for the folder, such as Program Data. Users can then save their documents in the Program Data folder rather than to a drive letter.

Assigns drive path not drive letter

When you mount a local drive to an empty folder on an NTFS volume, Disk Management assigns a path rather than a letter to the drive. Mounted drives are not subject to the 26-drive limit that is imposed by drive letters, so you can use mounted drives to access more than 26 drives on your computer. Windows Server 2003 ensures that drive paths retain their association to the drive, so you can add or rearrange storage devices without causing the drive path to fail.

Unifies disparate file systems

By using mounted drives, you can unify into one logical file system disparate file systems such as NTFS 5.0, a 16-bit FAT file system, an ISO-9660 file system on a CD-ROM drive, and so on. Neither users nor applications need information about the volume on which a specific file resides. A complete path provides all the information they need to locate a specified file. You can rearrange volumes, substitute volumes, or subdivide one volume into many volumes without requiring users or applications to change settings.

What Is the Purpose of a Mounted Drive?

- **Adds volumes to systems without adding separate drive letters for each new volume**
  - Disk Management assigns a drive path to the drive rather than a drive letter
    - Drive paths retain their association to the drive
    - Add or rearrange storage devices without the drive path failing
- **Increases number of drives, not storage space**
- **Manages data storage based on work environment and system usage**

Introduction	Using NTFS mounted drives is a convenient way to add volumes to a computer when no drive letters are available. Also, you can add space to a volume by mounting other disks as folders on the volume instead of re-creating the volume on a larger disk.
Add volumes to systems	You can add new volumes to your system without adding separate drive letters for each new volume. Doing this makes it easier to manage your drive letters.
Create multiple mounted drives per volume	You can create multiple mounted drives per volume. For example, you can mount a drive to the C:\Program Files folder. The new drive is logically mounted under C:\, but it does not need its own drive letter.
Manage data storage	Mounted drives help you manage data storage that is based on the work environment and system usage. For example, you can move the My Documents folder to a larger drive when space is low on drive C, and then mount it as C:\My Documents.
Delete a mounted drive	When you delete a mounted drive, all of the files and folders remain on the drive that was mounted. For example, if you mounted drive F as C:\Temp, after you delete it, the files and folders that you copied to C:\Temp are available on drive F.
Examples of using a mounted drive	You can use a mounted drive as a gateway to a volume. When you create a volume as a mounted drive, users and applications can refer to the mounted drive by either the path of the mounted drive, such as C:\mnt\Ddrive, or a drive letter, such as D.
	For example is an application server currently has a drive C that is near its capacity, a drive D that stores data, and an empty drive E. The application uses the C:\Temp folder extensively. You can mount the E drive to C:\Temp to provide additional space for temporary files.

How to Manage a Mounted Drive

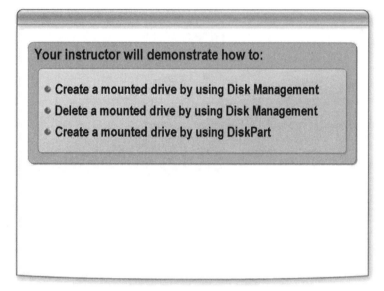

Your instructor will demonstrate how to:

- Create a mounted drive by using Disk Management
- Delete a mounted drive by using Disk Management
- Create a mounted drive by using DiskPart

Introduction

Use a mounted drive to manage server resources more efficiently.

Procedure for creating a mounted drive using Disk Management

To create a mounted drive by using Disk Management:

1. In Computer Management, open Disk Management.

2. Right-click the volume that you want to mount, and then click **Change Drive Letter and Paths**.

3. Click **Add**, browse to **Mount in the following empty NTFS folder**, and then either type the path to an empty folder on an NTFS volume or click **Browse** to locate it.

Procedure for deleting a mounted drive using Disk Management

To delete a mounted drive by using Disk Management:

1. In Computer Management, open Disk Management.

2. Right-click the volume that you want to delete, and then click **Change Drive Letter and Paths**.

3. To delete a volume, click it, and then click **Remove**.

Procedure for creating a mounted drive using DiskPart

To create a mounted drive by using DiskPart:

1. Open Command Prompt.

2. From the NTFS drive or folder that you want to mount elsewhere, type **diskpart**

3. At the DISKPART prompt, type **list volume** and then make note of the number of the volume that you want to mount elsewhere.

4. At the DISKPART prompt, type **select volume** *n* (where *n* is the number of the volume you want to mount elsewhere).

5. At the DISKPART prompt, type **assign mount**=*Path* (where *Path* is the mount drive path that you want to assign to the volume).

Practice: Creating Mounted Drives

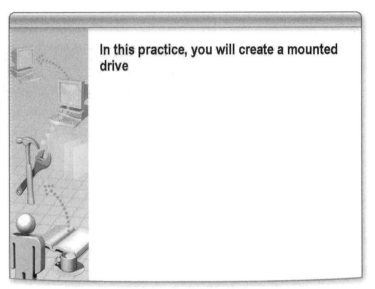

In this practice, you will create a mounted drive

Objective

In this practice, you will create a mounted drive.

Scenario

You are the systems administrator for an organizational unit on a large network. After arriving at work one morning, you read the following e-mail message from your manager:

> The graphics department has a problem. Half of their employees stored their bitmap drawings on the D drive, and the other half of their employees stored their photo work on the E drive. However, the graphics manager, Jeff, wants all the work on one partition. He suggested that we just copy all of the files to the D partition. This is not a solution, because over 65 percent of the D and E drives are full.

> I told Jeff about mounted drives and that you could configure one for him. He wants drive E mounted to the empty D:\Photos folder.

Practice

▶ **To create a mounted drive**

1. Log on to the domain as *Computer*User with a password of **P@ssw0rd**.

2. Create a new folder named **D:\Photos**.

3. Using **Run as** open Computer Management with administrative privileges, and then open Disk Management.

4. Mount drive E to D:\Photos.

5. Close all windows and log off.

Lesson: Converting Disks

- Basic Disks vs. Dynamic Disks
- Results of Dynamic Disk Conversion
- How to Convert Disks

Introduction

When a new disk is installed, it is recognized and configured as a basic disk. To create a dynamic disk, you must convert a basic disk to a dynamic disk. After the conversion is complete, you can create a wide range of dynamic volumes. You can also extend volumes over multiple disks. These capabilities provide you with greater control and helps to prevent data loss due to hardware failure.

Lesson objectives

After completing this lesson, you will be able to:

- Explain the differences between basic and dynamic disks.
- Explain the results of a conversion to a dynamic disk.
- Convert a basic disk to a dynamic disk.

Basic Disks vs. Dynamic Disks

Disk	Benefits
Basic disks	• Use to create segregated space to organize data • Can be divided into up to 4 primary partitions, or up to 3 primary partitions and one extended partition
Dynamic disks	• Use to create volumes that span multiple disks • No limit on the number of volumes per disk • Use to create fault-tolerant disks that ensure data integrity when hardware failures occur

Introduction

A basic disk is the default disk type for Windows Server 2003. A basic disk provides you with limited capabilities for setting up your disks.

Dynamic disks provide you with more flexibility for setting up your hard disk than basic disks provide. For example, you can implement fault tolerance on a dynamic disk but not on a basic disk.

Benefit of basic disks

The benefit of a basic disk is that it provides you with segregated space that you can use to organize your data. You can divide a basic disk into up to four primary partitions or up to three primary partitions and one extended partition that contains one or more logical drives.

Benefits of dynamic disks

The benefits of dynamic disks are:

- A dynamic disk can be used to create volumes that span multiple disks.

- There is no limit on the number of volumes per disk that can be configured on a dynamic disk.

- Dynamic disks are used to create fault-tolerant disks that ensure data integrity when hardware failures occur.

Note For more information about fault-tolerant disks, see Appendix E, "Managing Fault-Tolerant Disks," on the Student Materials compact disc.

Convert basic disks to dynamic disks

Convert basic disks to dynamic disks to:

- Create and delete simple, spanned, striped, mirrored, and RAID-5 volumes.

- Extend a simple or spanned volume.

- Repair mirrored or RAID-5 volumes.

- Reactivate volumes that span more the one disk.

Example of using dynamic disks

Dynamic disks are used in a business environment where the most valuable asset is not the computer, but the data that is stored on the computer. Mission-critical data, that is, data that must be available 24 hours a day, 7 days a week, should be stored on fault-tolerant dynamic volumes.

Note For more information about dynamic disks, see Appendix G, "Using Dynamic Disks," on the Student Materials compact disc.

Note For more information about fault-tolerant disks, such as RAID-5 and mirrored disks, see Appendix E, "Managing Fault-Tolerant Disks," on the Student Materials compact disc.

Results of Dynamic Disk Conversion

- **Can convert a disk from basic to dynamic storage at any time without losing data**
- **Dynamic disks are associated with Disk Groups**
  - Disk Groups help you organize dynamic disks
  - Each disk in a Disk Group stores replicas of the same configuration data
  - Windows initializes the disk with a Disk Group identity and a copy of the current Disk Group configuration
- **Existing partitions on the basic disk become volumes**
- **Dynamic disks can be reverted back to basic disks**
  - Disk structure and data is not maintained
  - Back up data before reverting

Introduction

You can convert a disk from basic to dynamic storage at any time without losing data. When you convert a disk from basic to dynamic, the existing partitions on the basic disk become volumes.

Note   It is recommended that before performing any major configuration of hardware storage devices, you always back up data to another disk.

Disk groups

Dynamic disks are associated with disk groups. A *disk group* is a collection of disks that are managed as a collection. Disk groups help you organize dynamic disks. Each disk in a disk group stores replicas of the same configuration data. This configuration data is stored in a 1-megabyte (MB) region at the end of each dynamic disk.

Disk Group identity

During conversion, Windows initializes the disk with a disk group identity and a copy of the current configuration of the disk group Windows also adds dynamic volumes to the configuration, which represents the old partitions and fault-tolerant structures on the disk. If there are no pre-existing Dynamic/Online disks, you must create a new disk group. If there are existing Dynamic/Online disks, you must add the converted disk to the existing disk group.

Revert to a basic disk

You can revert a dynamic disk to a basic disk, but you lose the data that is on the dynamic disk. To revert a dynamic disk to a basic disk, you delete the data and volumes on the dynamic disk and then re-create a basic partition from the new unallocated space.

How to Convert Disks

> **Your instructor will demonstrate how to:**
>
> - Convert a basic disk to a dynamic disk by using Computer Management
> - Revert a dynamic disk to a basic disk
> - Convert a basic disk to a dynamic disk by using DiskPart

Introduction

Most organizations use dynamic disks in their servers because they provide fault tolerance and because storage space can be extended if needed. The default disk type is basic, so you must convert a disk from basic to dynamic if you plan to use a dynamic disk.

Procedure for converting a basic disk to a dynamic disk using Disk Management

To convert a basic disk to a dynamic disk by using Disk Management:

1. In Computer Management, open Disk Management.

2. Right-click the basic disk that you want to convert, click **Convert to Dynamic Disk**, and then follow the instructions.

Procedure for reverting a dynamic disk to a basic disk using Disk Management

To revert a dynamic disk to a basic disk by using Disk Management:

1. Back up all volumes on the disk that you want to convert from dynamic to basic.

2. In Computer Management, open Disk Management.

3. Right-click each volume on the dynamic disk that you want to revert to a basic disk, and then click **Delete Volume** for each volume on the disk.

4. When all volumes on the disk have been deleted, right-click the disk, and then click **Convert To Basic Disk**.

5. Recreate your partitions, and then restore your data to the basic disk.

Procedure for converting a basic disk using DiskPart

To convert a basic disk to a dynamic disk by using DiskPart:

1. Open Command Prompt, and then type **diskpart**

2. At the DISKPART prompt, type **list disk**

   Make a note of the disk number of the disk that you want to convert to dynamic.

3. At the DISKPART prompt, type **select disk** and then enter the number of the disk you are converting.

4. At the DISKPART prompt, type **convert dynamic**

Note   On dynamic volumes, only the volume focus is important because the previous partition focus is always lost. The disk focus is important only for simple volumes.

Practice: Converting Disks

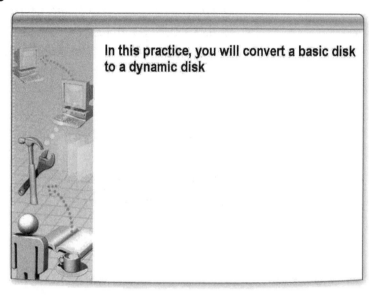

Objective

In this practice, you will convert a basic disk to a dynamic disk.

Scenario

You are the systems administrator for an organizational unit on a large network. After arriving at work one morning, you read the following e-mail message from your manager:

> As you know, the graphics department staff has grown by over 50 percent this year. This growth has caused a problem with their servers because they are running out of storage. However, the manager of the graphics department, Jeff, says that when the disks were originally configured, only 30 percent of the capacity was going to be used, so 50 percent of the disk capacity was unallocated.

> Jeff also may want to make some of the disks in the servers fault-tolerant and wants to know what that entails. He heard that the disks must be dynamic before the partitions can be extended or made fault-tolerant, so he wants to know where he can purchase dynamic disks.

> Would you please go to the graphics department and explain some of these disk concepts to Jeff? Also, convert one of the disks on an existing server to dynamic so that he stops asking me about purchasing dynamic disks.

Practice

▶ **To convert a basic disk to a dynamic disk**

1. Log on to the domain as *Computer***User** with a password of **P@ssw0rd**.

2. Using **Run as** open Computer Management with administrative privileges, and then open Disk Management.

3. Convert disk 0 to a dynamic disk.

4. Restart the computer.

5. Log on to the domain as *Computer***User** with a password of **P@ssw0rd**.

6. Using **Run as** open Computer Management with administrative privileges, and then open Disk Management.

7. Verify that the disk is dynamic.

8. Close all windows and log off.

Lesson: Creating Volumes

- What Is a Simple Volume?
- How to Create a Simple Volume
- What Is an Extended Volume?
- What Is a Spanned Volume?
- How to Create a Simple or Spanned Volume
- What Is a Striped Volume?
- How to Create Striped Volumes

Introduction

Dynamic disks provide features that basic disks do not provide, such as the ability to create volumes, called spanned and striped volumes, that span multiple disks. All volumes on dynamic disks are known as dynamic volumes.

Lesson objectives

After completing this lesson, you will be able to:

- Describe the characteristics of a simple volume.
- Create a simple volume.
- Explain the characteristics of an extended volume.
- Explain the characteristics of a spanned volume.
- Create an extended and spanned volume.
- Explain the characteristics of a striped volume.
- Create a striped volume.

What Is a Simple Volume?

* Contains space on a single disk
* Can be created only on dynamic disks
* Has fewer restrictions than a basic disk partition
* Can use the NTFS, FAT, or FAT32 file systems
* Can be extended if formatted with NTFS

Simple Volume

Definition

A simple volume is a single volume that resides on a dynamic disk. You can create a simple volume from unallocated space on a dynamic disk. A simple volume is similar to a partition, except it does not have the size limits that a partition has, nor is there a restriction on the number of volumes that you can create on a single disk.

Simple volume file formats

A simple volume uses the NTFS, FAT, or FAT32 file system formats. However, you can extend a simple volume only if it is formatted with the version of NTFS that is used in Windows 2000 or the Windows Server 2003 family of operating systems. Also, you can add space to, or extend, a simple volume after you create it.

Use a simple volume for all basic data storage

You can use a simple volume for all data storage until you need more space on your disks. To gain more space, you can create an extended, spanned, or striped volume. For other than a simple volume, though, you need more than one disk.

How to Create a Simple Volume

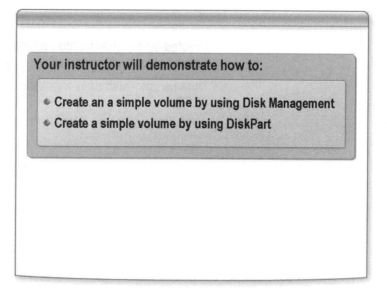

Your instructor will demonstrate how to:

- Create an a simple volume by using Disk Management
- Create a simple volume by using DiskPart

Introduction

Create a single volume on a dynamic disk if you plan to expand the volume in the future.

Procedure for creating a simple volume by using Disk Management

To create a simple volume by using Disk Management:

1. In Computer Management, open Disk Management.

2. Right-click the unallocated space on the dynamic disk on which you want to create the simple volume, and then click **New Volume**.

3. In the New Volume Wizard, click **Simple**, and then follow the instructions.

Procedure for creating a simple volume by using DiskPart

To create a simple volume by using DiskPart:

1. Open Command Prompt, and then type **diskpart**

2. At the DISKPART prompt, type **list disk**

   Make note of the disk number of the disk where you want to create a simple volume.

3. At the DISKPART prompt, type **create volume simple size=**n **disk=**n
   (where **size=**n is the size of the disk in megabytes, and **disk=**n is the number of the disk).

What Is an Extended Volume?

- Created by extending onto unallocated space on the same disk or a different disk
- Must be unformatted or formatted with a version of NTFS

Extended Volume

Definition

You can increase the size of an existing simple volume by extending the volume onto unallocated space on the same disk or a different disk. To extend a simple volume, the volume must be unformatted or formatted with the version of NTFS that is used in Windows 2000 or the Windows Server 2003 family of operating systems.

Additional hard disk space

To make additional space available without reconfiguring your hard disks, you can add space to an existing volume on your hard disk. Exceptions include any volume that contains a system partition, the boot partition, or an active paging file.

Example of using extended volumes

Your organization has increased the number of products it sells and needs additional hard disk space on the D drive to store their new marketing brochures. The current disk space that is used for marketing brochures is 2 GB. The marketing manager predicts that the D drive will run out of space in six months. You look at the D drive in your server and find that the D drive can be extended to include up to 6 GB of unallocated space.

Important   You can extend a volume only if it was originally created on a dynamic disk. A volume that was created first on a basic disk and then converted to a dynamic disk cannot be extended.

What Is a Spanned Volume?

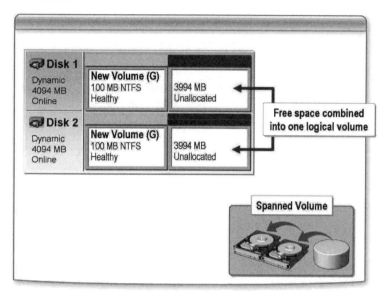

Definition	A spanned volume is a simple volume that allows you to create a single logical volume based on unallocated space that is available on other dynamic disks on the computer. By using spanned volumes, you can use your storage space more efficiently. After a volume is extended, to delete a part of it you must delete the entire spanned volume.
Spanned volume file formats	You can create a spanned volume only by using the NTFS file system. Spanned volumes do not offer fault tolerance. If one of the disks that contains a spanned volume fails, the entire volume fails and all the data is lost.
Increase storage size	You can use spanned volumes to increase storage size when you must create a volume but do not have enough unallocated space for the volume on a single disk. By combining sections of unallocated space from multiple disks, you can create one spanned volume.
Example of a spanned volume	Your organization hires 100 college interns every summer. The interns are provided with an old server to use for their work. The interns estimate they will need 10 GB of storage on their D drive in the next month. You want to add the storage to their assigned drive, but the drive has only 240 MB of unused space. You find that the interns' server has 15 GB of unallocated space on the E drive. You can span the D drive to include 10 GB of storage from the E drive.

How to Create a Simple or Spanned Volume

Your instructor will demonstrate how to:

- Create an extended volume and a spanned volume by using Disk Management
- Create a spanned volume by using DiskPart

Introduction

Increase the storage capacity of a simple volume by extending it to an existing volume that has unallocated space or by creating a spanned volume.

Procedure for creating an extended or spanned volume using Disk Management

To create a spanned volume by using Disk Management:

1. In Computer Management, open Disk Management.
2. Right-click the simple or spanned volume you want to extend, click **Extend Volume**, and then follow the instructions on your screen.

Procedure for extending a simple volume using DiskPart

To create a simple volume by using DiskPart:

1. Open Command Prompt, and then type **diskpart**
2. At the DISKPART prompt, type **list volume**

   Make a note of the number of the basic volume you want to extend.
3. At the DISKPART prompt, type **select volume** n (where n is the basic volume that you want to extend into contiguous, empty space on the same disk).
4. At the DISKPART prompt, type **extend size**=o (where o is the size of the extended partition in megabytes).

What Is a Striped Volume?

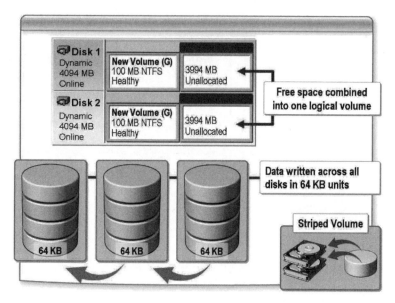

Definition

A striped volume stores data on two or more physical disks by combining areas of free space into one logical volume on a dynamic disk. Striped volumes, also known as RAID 0, contain data that is spread across multiple dynamic disks on separate drives. Spanned volumes cannot be striped.

Blocks of data

Data that is written to the stripe set is divided into blocks that are called *stripes*. These stripes are written simultaneously to all drives in the stripe set. The major advantage of disk striping is speed. Data can be accessed on multiple disks by using multiple drive heads, which improves performance considerably.

Striped volumes performance

Striped volumes offer the best performance of all the disk strategies because data that is written to a striped volume is simultaneously written to all disks at the same time rather than sequentially. Consequently, disk performance is faster on a striped volume than on any other type of disk configuration.

Striped volume uses

Use a striped volume when you:

- Read from or write to large databases.
- Load program images, dynamic-link libraries (DLLs), or run-time libraries.
- Want to provide the best performance for high usage files, for example page files.

Example of striped volumes

Use striped volumes for page files, because striped volumes provide the best performance for high usage files.

How to Create Striped Volumes

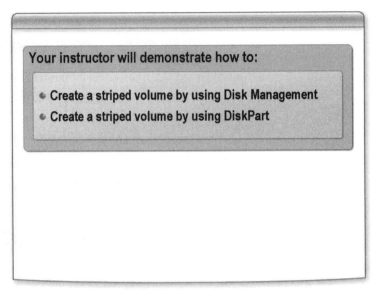

Your instructor will demonstrate how to:

- Create a striped volume by using Disk Management
- Create a striped volume by using DiskPart

Introduction

One way of managing your disks is to use dynamic volumes. To provide the best performance for accessing large databases, for example, configure a dynamic disk as a striped volume.

Procedure for creating a striped volume

To create a striped volume by using Disk Management:

1. In Computer Management, open Disk Management.

2. Right-click the unallocated space on the dynamic disk on which you want to create the striped volume, and then click **New Volume**.

3. In the New Volume Wizard, select **Striped**, and then follow the instructions on your screen.

Procedure for creating a striped volume

To create a striped volume by using DiskPart:

1. Open Command Prompt, and then type **diskpart**

2. At the DISKPART prompt, type **list disk**

   Make a note of the disk number of the disk on which you want to create a striped volume.

3. At the DISKPART prompt, type **create volume stripe size**=n **disk**=n (where **size**=n is the size of the disk in megabytes, and **disk**=n are the numbers of the disks you are striping).

Practice: Creating Volumes

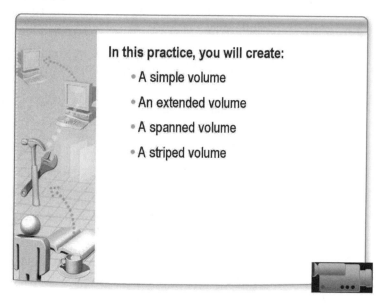

In this practice, you will create:
- A simple volume
- An extended volume
- A spanned volume
- A striped volume

Objective

In this practice, you will create:

- A simple volume
- An extended volume
- A spanned volume
- A striped volume

Scenario

You are the systems administrator for an organizational unit on a large network. After arriving at work one morning, you read the following e-mail message from your manager:

> The graphics department needs your help again. They are pleased with the mount drive solution that you configured earlier, but now they want to enlarge the D volume by another 2 GB. They also want you create another 1-GB volume, named F, on their server.

Practice

▶ **Extend the D volume by 2 GB**

1. Log on to the domain as *Computer*User with a password of **P@ssw0rd**.

2. Using **Run as** open Computer Management with administrative privileges, and then open Disk Management.

3. Extend the D volume by 2 GB.

▶ **Create a 1 GB volume and assign it the letter F**

1. Open the New Volume Wizard, create a 1-GB volume, and then assign it the letter F.

2. Close all windows.

▶ **Create a spanned volume and a striped volume**

Practice setup

This practice is an interactive exercise. To complete this practice, you need the following:

- A computer running Microsoft Windows Server 2003, Windows XP Professional, Windows 2000, Microsoft Windows NT® 4.0, Windows 98, or Windows 95.

- A minimum display resolution of 800 x 600 with 256 colors.

▶ **To start the simulation**

1. Insert the Student Materials compact disc into your CD-ROM drive.

2. At the root of the compact disc, double-click **Default.htm**.

3. On the Student Materials Web page, click **Multimedia**.

4. Click **Creating Volumes**.

5. Read the introduction information, and then click the link to start the simulation.

Lesson: Importing a Disk

- What Is a Foreign Disk?
- What Is an Offline Disk?
- How to Import a Foreign Disk
- How to Reactivate an Offline Disk

Introduction

You can move a disk from another system or within the same system by importing it. After it is imported, Disk Management refers to it as a foreign disk. To manage foreign disks, you must understand the characteristics of a foreign disk, as well as what happens if a foreign disk is not imported properly.

Lesson objectives

After completing this lesson, you will be able to:

- Explain the characteristics of a foreign disk.
- Explain what causes an offline disk.
- Import a foreign disk.
- Reactivate an offline disk.

What Is a Foreign Disk?

* A dynamic disk when moved to a local computer from another computer running:
    * Windows 2000
    * Windows XP Professional
    * Windows XP 64-Bit Edition
    * And Windows Server 2003 family of operating systems
* A disk moved within the same system, in some cases
* A disk moved from a disk group to another computer that contains its own disk group can be displayed as a foreign disk

Introduction

When you move a dynamic disk from one computer to another, Windows Server 2003 automatically considers the disk as a *foreign disk*. When Disk Manager indicates the status of a new disk as foreign, you must import the disk before you can access volumes on the disk.

Dynamic disks moved from one computer to another

You can move dynamic disks to Windows Server 2003 from any computer running Windows 2000, Windows XP Professional, or Windows XP 64-bit Edition, or from another server running Windows Server 2003.

When you move all the disks that contain parts of a volume from one computer to another at the same time, the volume and its data are identical to the original state after the import. All simple volumes on any moved disks are recovered to their original state if the disks have been rescanned.

On a non-redundant volume that spans multiple disks, if you move only some disks from one system to another, the volume is disabled during import. The volume also becomes disabled on the original system. As long as you do not delete the volume on either the original or the target system, you can move the remaining disks later. When all disks are moved over, the volume is recovered to its original state.

Disk failure during a move within the same system

A disk that fails during a move within the same system can appear to be foreign. Configuration data for dynamic disks is stored on all dynamic disks, so the information about which disks are owned by the system is lost when all dynamic disks fail. For example, because volumes can span multiple disks by using simple disk spanning and striping redundancy mechanisms, the display status of a volume in the **Import Foreign Disks** dialog box can become complicated if not all of the disks have been moved.

Another complication can occur when you move a disk and then later move additional disks. For example, if you move one active mirror of a volume from one system to another, and then you move another later, one of the two mirrors appears to be up-to-date on one system, and the other mirror appears up-to-date on the other system. When the two mirrors are put together on the same system, they both appear up-to-date, but they have different contents. For this reason, it is recommended that you move all fault-tolerant and non-fault-tolerant volumes that span disks at the same time.

Note For more information about fault-tolerant disks, such as RAID-5 and mirrored disks, see Appendix E, "Managing Fault-Tolerant Disks," on the Student Materials compact disc.

Groups of disks can be foreign

Groups of disks that you move from one computer to another are grouped according to the computer from which they were moved. Disk Management displays the groups of moved disks as foreign disks. If you move one or more disks from a disk group to another computer that contains its own disk group, the disk group that you move is considered as Foreign until you import it into the existing group.

To import the disks in the foreign disk group, use the **Import Foreign Disks** operation that is associated with one of the disks. The manual operation lists one or more Disk Groups, identified by the name of the computer where they were created.

What Is an Offline Disk?

* Offline disk is a status found in Disk Management
* A dynamic disk can be offline if corrupted or intermittently unavailable
* A foreign disk that fails is always offline
* Reactivate a dynamic or foreign disk to bring it back online

Introduction

Disk Management displays the Offline status when a dynamic disk is not accessible. The inaccessible disk may be corrupted or intermittently unavailable. The Offline status also appears if you attempt to import a foreign dynamic disk, but the operation fails. An error icon appears on the offline disk. The Offline status appears only for dynamic disks.

Remove a disk

When you remove a dynamic disk from a computer, the remaining online dynamic disks retain information about it and its volumes. Disk Management displays the removed disk as a Dynamic/Offline disk named Missing. You can remove this Missing disk entry by removing all volumes on that disk and then using the **Remove Disk** command that is associated with that disk. When you physically remove the last dynamic disk, the Missing entry is no longer displayed in Disk Management.

Foreign disks Reactivate or rescan an offline disk

Reactivating or rescanning an offline disk changes the disk status from **Offline** to **OK**.

Note   For more information about troubleshooting a foreign disk, see Appendix F, "Foreign Disks Volume Status in Disk Management," on the Student Materials compact disc.

How to Import a Foreign Disk

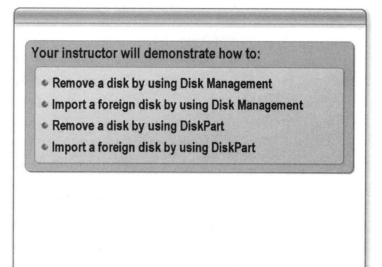

Your instructor will demonstrate how to:

- Remove a disk by using Disk Management
- Import a foreign disk by using Disk Management
- Remove a disk by using DiskPart
- Import a foreign disk by using DiskPart

Introduction

If you must move a disk from one server to another, use the following steps to remove and reconfigure the disk.

Procedure for removing a disk by using Disk Management

To remove a disk by using Disk Management:

1. In Computer Management, open Disk Management.

2. For a dynamic disk, right-click the disk that you want to move, and then click **Remove Disk**. Skip this step for basic disks.

3. If the disk is external, unplug it from the computer. If the disk is internal, turn off the computer, and then physically remove the disk.

Procedure for removing a disk by using DiskPart

To remove a disk by using DiskPart:

1. Open Command Prompt, and then type **diskpart**

2. At the DISKPART prompt, type **remove** [{letter=*D*|mount=*Path*|all}] [dismount] [noerr]

3. If the disk is external, unplug it from the computer.
   If the disk is internal, turn off the computer, and then physically remove the disk.

Procedure for importing a foreign disk

To import a foreign disk by using Disk Management:

1. If the disk is external, plug it into the computer. If the disk is internal, make sure the computer is turned off, and then physically install the disk in that computer.

2. In Computer Management, open Disk Management.

3. Start the computer that contains the disk that you moved.

4. Follow the instructions in the **Found New Hardware** dialog box.

    If the **Found New Hardware** dialog box does not appear, in Control Panel, double-click **Add Hardware** to start the Add Hardware Wizard.

5. Use Disk Management to detect the new disk.

To import a foreign disk by using DiskPart:

1. Open Command Prompt, and then type **diskpart**

2. At the DISKPART prompt, type **list disk**

    Make a note of the disk number of the disk that you want to import.

3. At the DISKPART prompt, type **select disk** *n* (where *n* is the disk number of the disk you are moving).

4. At the DISKPART prompt, type **import [noerr]**

How to Reactivate an Offline Disk

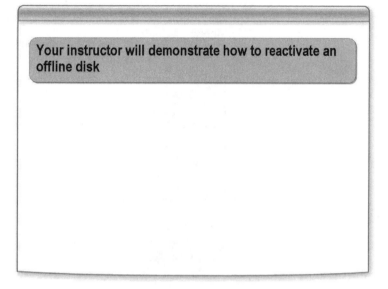

Introduction

Use the following steps when you have moved a disk, but it appears in Disk Management as Missing or Offline. By reactivating the disk, you are changing the disk status to Online.

Procedure

To reactivate an offline disk by using Disk Management:

1. In Computer Management, open Disk Management.

2. Right-click the disk marked **Missing** or **Offline**, and then click **Reactivate Disk**.

Practice: Importing a Foreign Disk

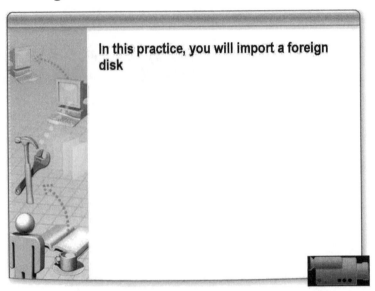

In this practice, you will import a foreign disk

Objective

In this practice, you will import a foreign disk.

Scenario

A hardware failure has occurred on a file server. You must move the disk from the file server to another computer to access the information on that disk while the file server is being repaired. The disk on the file server is configured as dynamic.

Practice setup

This practice is an interactive exercise. To complete this practice, you need the following:

- A computer running Windows Server 2003, Windows XP Professional, Windows 2000, Windows NT 4.0, Windows 98, or Windows 95.

- A minimum display resolution of 800 x 600 with 256 colors.

▶ **To start the simulation**

1. Insert the Student Materials compact disc into your CD-ROM drive.

2. At the root of the compact disc, double-click **Default.htm**.

3. On the Student Materials Web page, click **Multimedia**.

4. Click **Importing a Foreign Disk**.

5. Read the introduction information, and then click the link to start the simulation.

Lab A: Managing Disks

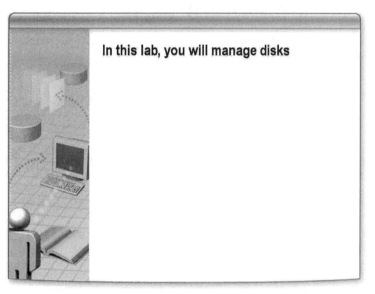

In this lab, you will manage disks

Objectives

After completing this lab, you will be able to:

- Mount a drive.
- Change a drive letter.

Scenario

You are the systems administrator for an organizational unit on a large network. After arriving at work one morning, you read the following e-mail message from your manager:

> The manager of the graphics department called to request some help. The graphic artists are testing some beta software, which requires reconfiguration of the folder structure on their drive D. All their graphics are stored on drive E, but they also want access the graphics from drive D.
>
> I told the manager about mounted drives, and he likes that solution. He wants you to mount drive E to the empty D:\Graphics folder. After that is done, he wants drive D to become drive X. He wants you to begin working on this project as soon as possible.
>
> After the graphics department finishes testing the beta software, remove the mounted drive and rename drive X to D.

Estimated time to complete this lab: 15 minutes

Exercise 1
Mounting Drive E to D:\Graphics

In this exercise, you will mount drive E to D:\Graphics so that there are two paths to the graphics files on drive E.

Tasks	Specific instructions
1. Log on to the network.	▪ Log on with your domain user account.
2. Open Computer Management with administrative credentials.	▪ Using **Run as** open Computer Management with administrative privileges, and then open Disk Management.
3. Mount drive E to D:\Graphics.	a. Create a new folder named **D:\Graphics**. b. In Computer Management, use Disk Management to mount drive E to D:\Graphics.
4. Copy the Labfiles folder to D:\Graphics.	▪ Open Windows Explorer and copy the Labfiles folder to D:\Graphics.

Exercise 2
Changing Drive Letter D to X

In this exercise, you will change drive letter D to X.

Tasks	Specific instructions
1. Change drive letter D to X.	▪ In Computer Management, use Disk Management to change the drive letter from D to X.
2. Verify the existence of the Labfiles folder.	▪ Open Windows Explorer to verify the existence of the Labfiles folder both in X:\Graphics and on drive E.

Exercise 3
Removing Mounted Drive E

In this exercise, you will remove mounted drive E.

Tasks	Specific instructions
1. Remove drive E from the X:\Graphics path.	■ In Computer Management, use Disk Management to remove drive E from the X:\Graphics path.
2. Verify the removal of Labfiles from X:\Graphics.	■ Open Windows Explorer and verify that the Labfiles folder is not listed in the X:\Graphics path.
3. Verify the existence of Labfiles on drive E.	■ In Windows Explorer, verify that the Labfiles folders exists on drive E.

Exercise 4
Changing Drive Letter X to D

In this exercise, you will change drive letter X to D.

Tasks	Specific instructions
▪ Change drive letter X to D.	a. In Computer Management, change drive letter X to D. b. Close all windows and log off.

Microsoft®
Training &
Certification

Module 6: Managing Data Storage

Contents

Overview	1
Lesson: Managing File Compression	2
Lesson: Configuring File Encryption	13
Lesson: Implementing Disk Quotas	21
Lab A: Managing Data Storage	30
Course Evaluation	37

Overview

- Managing File Compression
- Configuring File Encryption
- Implementing Disk Quotas

Introduction

One of your tasks as a systems administrator is to manage the data that you will store on your network storage devices. To manage your data storage, you can compress files and folders to decrease their size and reduce the amount of space that they use on your drives or removable storage devices. In this module, you will learn when and how to compress files and folders.

To manage data, you must also understand encryption. In this module, you will learn about Encrypting File System (EFS), which stores data securely and protects your network.

You will also learn how to administer disk quotas. You use disk quotas to limit the amount of storage space that is available to users.

Objectives

After completing this module, you will be able to:

- Manage NTFS file compression.
- Configure file encryption.
- Implement disk quotas.

Lesson: Managing File Compression

* What Is File Compression?
* What Is the compact Command?
* How to Compress a File or Folder
* What Are the Effects of Moving and Copying Compressed Files and Folders?
* Best Practices for Compressing Files or Folders

Introduction

Compressing files and folders decreases their size and reduces the amount of space they use on your drives and removable storage devices. Microsoft® Windows® Server 2003 supports two types of compression: NTFS compression and compression using the Compressed (zipped) Folders feature.

In this lesson, you will learn about these features and how to use them. You will also learn the best practices that are associated with compressing files and folders.

Lesson objectives

After completing this lesson, you will be able to:

■ Describe file compression.

■ Describe the **compact** command-line tool.

■ Compress a file or folder on an NTFS partition.

■ Explain the effects of moving and copying compressed files and folders.

■ Describe the best practices for compressing files and folders.

What Is File Compression?

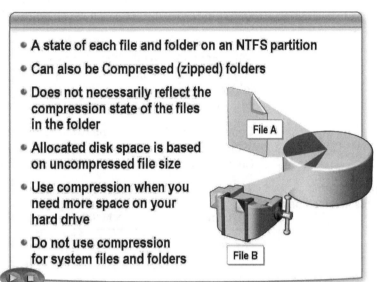

- A state of each file and folder on an NTFS partition
- Can also be Compressed (zipped) folders
- Does not necessarily reflect the compression state of the files in the folder
- Allocated disk space is based on uncompressed file size
- Use compression when you need more space on your hard drive
- Do not use compression for system files and folders

File A

File B

Introduction

Windows supports two types of compression: NTFS file compression and Compressed (zipped) Folders. You use Windows Explorer for both types.

Uses of compression

Use compression when you need more space on your hard disk drive. Compressing files, folders, and programs decreases their size and reduces the amount of space they use on drives or removable storage devices. You can also compress disk drives.

Files that can be compressed the most are text files, bitmap files, spreadsheets, and presentation files. Files that can be compressed the least are compressed graphics files and video files. Avoid compressing system folders and files because this affects the performance of the server.

NTFS file compression

Volumes, folders, and files on an NTFS volume are either compressed or uncompressed. The compression state of a folder does not necessarily reflect the compression state of the files in that folder. For example, you can selectively uncompress some or all of the files in a compressed folder.

When an application or an operating system command requests access to a compressed file, Windows Server 2003 automatically uncompresses the file. When you close or save a file, Windows Server 2003 compresses it again.

Space allocation

NTFS allocates disk space based on the size of the uncompressed file. If you copy a compressed file to an NTFS partition that does not have enough space for the uncompressed file, an error message notifies you that there is not enough disk space for the file.

Compressed (zipped) Folders

Files and folders that are compressed using the Compressed (zipped) Folders feature can be compressed on FAT, FAT32, and NTFS drives. A zipper icon identifies files and folders that are compressed by using this feature.

You can open files directly from these compressed folders, and you can run some programs directly from these compressed folders without uncompressing them. You can also move these compressed files and folders to any drive or folder on your computer, the Internet, or your network, and they are compatible with other file compression programs and files.

Compressing folders by using Compressed (zipped) Folders does not affect the overall performance of your computer. Performance is affected only when Compressed (zipped) Folders is accessed to compress a file.

Comparison of compression methods

The two compression methods are compared in the following table.

Attribute	NTFS file compression	Compressed (zipped) Folders
File system	NTFS	NTFS or FAT, FAT32
Compressible objects	Files, folders, and drives	Files and folders
Performance	Decrease	No decrease
Password protection	No	Yes
Encrypt	No	Yes
Change display color	Yes	No

What Is the compact Command?

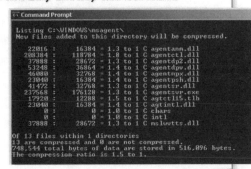

- A command-line tool that you can use to compress files and folders
  - Without parameters, compact displays compression state of current directory and any files it contains
  - You can also use multiple file names and wildcards

Introduction

In addition to using Windows Explorer to compress files and folders, you can use the **compact** command-line tool.

Displays compression state of directory

When used without parameters, **compact** displays the compression state of the current directory and any files that it contains. For example, you can use the following command line to compress all files and folders in the IIS directory:

compact /c c:*IIS**.*

Example using multiple parameters

You can use multiple file names and wildcards with **compact**. You must, however, put spaces between multiple parameters, as shown in the following example:

compact /C | /U] [/S[:_dir_**]] [/A] [/I] [/F] [/Q]** [_filename_ [...]

Each parameter is listed and described in the following table.

Parameter	Description
/C	Compresses the specified files. Directories are marked so that files added afterward are compressed.
/U	Uncompresses the specified files. Directories are marked so that files added afterward are not compressed.
/S	Performs the specified operation on files in the specified directory and all subdirectories. Default value is the current directory.
/A	Displays files with the hidden or system attributes. These files are omitted by default.
/I	Continues performing the specified operation even after errors occur. By default, **compact** stops when an error is encountered.
/F	Forces the compress operation on all specified files, even those that are already compressed. Already-compressed files are skipped by default.
/Q	Reports only the most essential information about the specified pattern, file, or directory. Specifies a pattern, file, or directory.

How to Compress a File or Folder

Your instructor will demonstrate how to:

- Compress a file or folder on an NTFS drive

- Compress a file or folder using Compressed (zipped) Folders

- Compress a file or folder using the command-line tool compact

Introduction

You can use Windows Explorer to compress files and folders by using NTFS file compression or Compressed (zipped) Folders. You can also compress files and folders by using the **compact** command.

Procedure for using NTFS file compression

To use NTFS file compression to compress files or folders on an NTFS drive:

1. In Windows Explorer, right-click the file or folder that you want to compress, and then click **Properties**.

2. In the **Properties** dialog box, on the **General** tab, click **Advanced**, select the **Compress contents to save disk space** check box, and then click **OK**.

3. In the **Properties** dialog box, click **OK**.

4. In the **Confirm Attribute Change** dialog box, click **OK**.

Procedure for using Compressed (zipped) Folders

To compress files or folders by using Compressed (zipped) Folders:

1. In Windows Explorer, in the details pane, right-click any open area, click **New**, and then click **Compressed (zipped) Folder**.

2. Move or copy files to the new folder to compress them.

Procedure for using compact

To compress files, folders, or directories using the **compact** command:

1. Open a command prompt.

2. Type **compact** */c c:***MOC***.* and then press ENTER.

What Are the Effects of Moving and Copying Compressed Files and Folders?

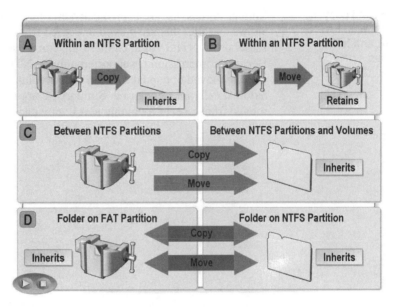

Introduction	Moving and copying files and folders on disk volumes can change their compression state, depending on the compression state of these files and folders and on the file system in which they were created. The compression state of a file or folder created in an NTFS partition is controlled by its compression attribute.
Copy within an NTFS partition	As shown in section A of the illustration, when you copy a file or folder within an NTFS partition, the file or folder inherits the compression state of the target folder. For example, if you copy a compressed file or folder to an uncompressed folder, the file or folder is automatically uncompressed.
Move within an NTFS partition	As shown in section B, when you move a file or folder within an NTFS partition, the file or folder retains its original compression state. For example, if you move a compressed file or folder to an uncompressed folder, the file remains compressed.
Copy between NTFS partitions	As shown in section C, when you copy a file or folder between NTFS partitions, the file or folder inherits the compression state of the target folder.

Section C illustrates copying a file or a folder to a folder. The file or folder takes on the compression attribute of the target folder. For example, if you copy a compressed file to an uncompressed folder, the file is uncompressed when it is copied to the folder. |
| **Move between NTFS partitions** | As shown also in section C, when you move a file or folder between NTFS partitions, the file or folder inherits the compression state of the target folder. Because Windows Server 2003 treats a move between partitions as a copy and then a delete operation, the files inherit the compression state of the target folder. |

Copying files or folders on NTFS volumes

When you copy a file to a folder that already contains a file of the same name, the copied file takes on the compression attribute of the target file, regardless of the compression state of the folder.

Moving and copying files between FAT16, FAT32, and NTFS volumes

Similar to files that are copied between folders on an NTFS volume, section D shows that files that are moved or copied from a folder on a FAT volume to a folder on an NTFS volume inherit the compression attribute of the target folder. Because compression is supported only on NTFS volumes, compressed files that are moved or copied from an NTFS volume to a FAT volume are automatically uncompressed. Similarly, compressed files that are copied or moved from an NTFS volume to a floppy disk are automatically uncompressed.

Practice: Managing File Compression

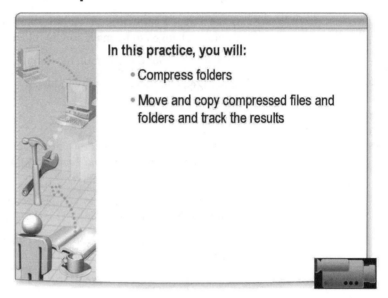

In this practice, you will:
- Compress folders
- Move and copy compressed files and folders and track the results

Objective

In this practice, you will:

- Compress folders.

- Move and copy compressed files and folders, and track the results.

- Identify the effects of moving and copying compressed files and folders.

Scenario

You are the systems administrator for an organizational unit on a large network. The accounting department manager complains to you about the amount of free disk space left on his server's hard disk drive. He wants at least 20 percent more free space without having to move any of the files to tape.

The folder structure of his drive is primarily made up of tax returns from 1997 to 1999. You need to compress the \data\taxes\199*x* folders to create additional free space.

Practice: Compressing the files

▶ **Compress the files**

1. Log on to the domain as *Computer*User with a password of **P@ssw0rd**.

2. Open Windows Explorer.

3. Browse to **C:\MOC\2275\Practices\Mod06\Data\Taxes**.

4. Open the **Properties** dialog box for **Taxes**.

5. Note the Size on disk parameter: _____7.20MB_____

6. Click **Advanced**.

7. Select the **Compress contents to save disk space** check box, and then click **OK**.

8. In the **Taxes Properties** dialog box, click **Apply**, and then confirm that you want the changes to be made to this folder and all subfolders and files.

9. How much room did you gain by compressing the tax folders? _____%.

10. Click **OK**, and then close all windows.

Practice: Moving compressed files and folders (Exercise 1)

▶ **Move the files**

1. On the Student Materials compact disc, under **Multimedia**, open *Managing NTFS File Compression and Encryption*, and then select **Compression Move**.

2. Move the files and folders to various locations on the page, and record the results in the following table.

   The drives in the exercise represent NTFS-formatted drives on the same computer.

Move to:	On same drive		On different drive	
	Compressed folder	**Uncompressed folder**	**Compressed folder**	**Uncompressed folder**
Compressed file				
Compressed folder				
Uncompressed file				
Uncompressed folder				
Use C to indicate compression and U to indicate no compression.				

Practice: Copying compressed files and folders (Exercise 2)

▶ **Copy the files**

1. On the Student Materials compact disc, under **Multimedia**, open *Managing NTFS File Compression and Encryption*, and then select **Compression Copy**.

2. Copy the files and folders to various locations on the page, and record the results in the table below.

   The drives in the exercise represent NTFS-formatted drives on the same computer.

	On same drive		On different drive	
Copy to:	**Compressed folder**	**Uncompressed folder**	**Compressed folder**	**Uncompressed folder**
Compressed file				
Compressed folder				
Uncompressed file				
Uncompressed folder				
Use C to indicate compression and U to indicate no compression.				

Challenge

When you use the **Compression Move**, can you compress all of the files and folders by using the Move operation? Can you uncompress all of the files and folders by using the Move operation?

Best Practices for Compressing Files or Folders

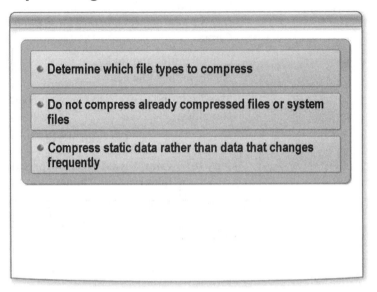

- Determine which file types to compress
- Do not compress already compressed files or system files
- Compress static data rather than data that changes frequently

Introduction

Consider the following best practices for managing compression on NTFS partitions.

Determine which file types to compress

Because some file types can be compressed more than others, determine which file types to compress based on the anticipated size of the compressed file. For example, because Windows bitmap files contain more redundant data than application executable files, this file type can be compressed more than an .exe file. Bitmaps can often be compressed to less than 50 percent of the original file size, whereas an application file can rarely be compressed to less than 75 percent of the original size.

Do not compress already compressed file

Do not compress already compressed files or system files. Windows Server 2003 attempts to compress the file even more, which wastes system time and yields no additional disk space.

Compress static data

Compress static data rather than data that changes frequently. Compressing and uncompressing files incurs some system overhead. By choosing to compress files that are accessed infrequently, you minimize the amount of system time that is dedicated to compression and uncompression activities.

Lesson: Configuring File Encryption

- What Is EFS Encryption?
- How to Encrypt a File or a Folder
- What Are the Effects of Moving and Copying Encrypted Files or Folders?

Introduction

An intruder who has physical access to a computer can easily install a new operating system and bypass the security of the existing operating system. Thus, sensitive data is left exposed. You can add an effective layer of security by encrypting these files with Encrypting File System (EFS). When the files are encrypted, the data is protected even if an intruder has full access to the computer's data storage.

In this lesson, you will learn about encryption, as well as how to manage encryption. You will also learn the effects of moving and copying encrypted files.

Lesson objectives

After completing this lesson, you will be able to:

- Describe EFS file encryption.
- Encrypt a file or a folder.
- Describe the effects of moving and copying encrypted files or folders.

What Is EFS Encryption?

EFS encryption makes data unintelligible without a decryption key

- **EFS encrypts data**
  - Users encrypt a file or folder by setting the encryption property
  - All files and subfolders created in or added to an encrypted folder are automatically encrypted
- **Use EFS to access encrypted data**
  - When accessing an encrypted file, users can read the file normally
  - When users close the file, EFS encrypts it again
- **Use EFS to decrypt data**
  - The file remains decrypted until it is encrypted again
- **Use the cipher command to display or alter encryption of folders and files on NTFS volumes**

Introduction	An attacker can gain access to a shared system by starting a different operating system. An attacker can also steal a computer, remove the hard disk, install the disk in another system, and gain access to the stored files. Files that are encrypted by using Encrypting File System (EFS), however, appear as unintelligible characters when the attacker does not have the decryption key.
EFS provides file level encryption	EFS provides file-level encryption for files created on NTFS volumes. By using EFS, you can ensure that sensitive or confidential data is more secure and cannot be easily read or decrypted by another user.
Use EFS to encrypt data	Encryption and decryption are the primary tasks of EFS. The default configuration of EFS requires no administrative effort—users can begin encrypting files immediately. EFS automatically generates an encryption key pair for a user if one does not exist.
Encryption and decryption options available	Several encryption and decryption options are available to users. Users can encrypt and decrypt files by using Windows Explorer, by using the **cipher** command, or by using the shortcut menu accessed by right-clicking a file or folder.
Encrypted folder contents	Folders that are marked for encryption are not actually encrypted. Only the files in the folder are encrypted, as well as any new files that are created in or moved to the folder.
Use EFS to access encrypted data	Using EFS, users access encrypted files just as they do unencrypted files. Thus, when a user accesses an encrypted file that is stored on disk, the user can read the contents of the file in the normal way. When the user saves the file on disk again, EFS saves the changes as encrypted.

Use EFS to decrypt data

You can decrypt a file by clearing the **Encryption** check box in the **Properties** dialog box for the file. After it is decrypted, the file remains decrypted until you encrypt it again. There is no automatic re-encryption of a file, even if it exists in a directory marked as encrypted.

Users can decrypt a file either by clearing the **Encryption** check box in the **Properties** dialog box for the file, or by using the **cipher** command.

Display or alter encryption on NTFS volumes with cipher

Use the **cipher** command to display or alter the encryption of folders and files on NTFS volumes. Used without parameters, **cipher** displays the encryption state of the current folder and any files it contains.

Parameters of cipher

You can use the **cipher** command with the parameters in the following table to perform the listed tasks.

Parameters	Task description
Use **cipher** with no parameters or with the name of a specific file or folder.	Display the encryption status of files and folders
/e	Set the encryption attribute for folders in the current directory
/e /a	Encrypt files in the current directory
/d	Remove the encryption attribute from folders in the current directory
/d /a	Decrypt files in the current directory
/?	Display all of the options that are available with **cipher**

How to Encrypt a File or Folder

> Your instructor will demonstrate how to:
>
> - Encrypt files or folders by using Windows Explorer
> - Encrypt offline files or folders by using Windows Explorer
> - Encrypt files or folders by using the cipher command

Introduction

Use EFS to encrypt files that must be protected, especially those files that will be shared across the network or over the Internet. Encrypting an offline file helps to ensure that you can protect all of the files on your network.

Procedure for encrypting a file

To encrypt a file or folder by using Windows Explorer:

1. In Windows Explorer, right-click the file or folder you want to encrypt, and then click **Properties**.

2. In the **Properties** dialog box, on the **General** tab, click **Advanced**.

3. In the **Advanced Attributes** dialog box, select the **Encrypt contents to secure data** check box.

4. The encrypted file text within the folder changes color, denoting the encrypted state of the file.

Procedure for encrypting an offline file or folder

Note   Remote Desktop must be disabled for the following procedure to work.

To encrypt an offline file or folder by using Windows Explorer:

1. In Windows Explorer, on the **Tools** menu, click **Folder Options**.

2. On the **Offline Files** tab, select the **Encrypt offline files to secure data** check box.

Procedure for encrypting a file using cipher

To encrypt a file by using **cipher**:

1. Open a command prompt.

2. Type the following command to encrypt a *filename* folder, its subdirectories and its files:

   cipher /e /a /s:\Secret

What Are the Effects of Moving and Copying Encrypted Files and Folders?

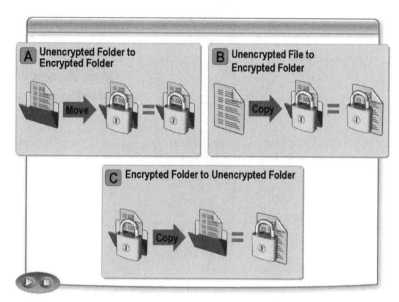

Introduction	All files and folders that are created in a folder marked for encryption are automatically encrypted. Moving and copying encrypted files and folders can change the encryption state of the file or folder, depending upon the situation.
Effect of moving encrypted files	As shown in section A in the illustration, if you move a file from an unencrypted folder to an encrypted folder, the file remains encrypted.
Effect of copying encrypted files	As shown in section B, if you copy an unencrypted file to an encrypted folder, the copied file is encrypted. If you copy an encrypted file from an encrypted folder to an unencrypted folder, the file remains encrypted.

If you copy an encrypted file from an NTFS volume to a FAT or FAT32 volume, the file becomes unencrypted. If you copy a file from a FAT volume to an encrypted folder on an NTFS volume, the file becomes encrypted.

When you encrypt a folder, all files and subfolders that are added to the folder in the future will be encrypted when they are added.

Note For more information about encryption, see the white paper, *EFS*, under **Additional Reading** on the Student Materials compact disc.

Practice: Configuring File Encryption

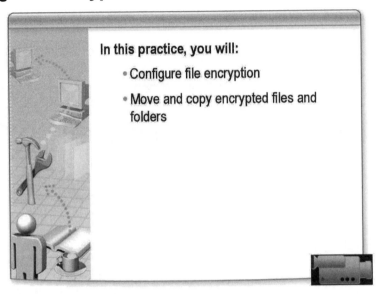

Objective

In this practice, you will:

- Configure file encryption.
- Move and copy encrypted files.
- Identify the effects of moving and copying compressed files and folders.

Scenario

You are the systems administrator for an organizational unit on a large network. The Research and Development (R&D) department has a server that can be accessed by all of the employees in the department. Although the department manager has configured NTFS permissions on most folders to restrict unauthorized users from looking at the files, he wants you to encrypt the R&D folder.

Practice: Encrypting the folder

▶ **Encrypt the R&D folder**

1. Log on to the domain as *Computer*User with a password of **P@ssw0rd**.

2. Open Windows Explorer.

3. Browse to C:\MOC\2275\Practices\Mod06\Data\R&D.

4. Open the **Properties** dialog box for the R&D folder.

5. Click **Advanced**.

6. Select the **Encrypt contents to secure data** check box, and then click **OK**.

7. In the **Confirm Attribute Changes** dialog box, confirm that you want the changes to be made to this folder and all subfolders and files.

8. Close all windows and log off.

9. Log on to the domain as **Administrator** with a password of **P@ssw0rd**.

10. Open Windows Explorer and browse to
    C:\MOC\2275\Practices\Mod06\Data\R&D.

11. Open the file named Tiger Lily. What happens?

12. Close all windows and log off.

**Practice: Moving
encrypted files and
folders (Exercise 1)**

▶ **Move encrypted files and folders**

1. On the Student Materials compact disc, under **Multimedia**, open *Managing NTFS File Compression and Encryption*, and then select **Encryption Move**.

2. Move the files and folders to various locations on the page, and record the results in the table below.

   The drives in the exercise represent NTFS-formatted drives on the same computer.

Move to:	On same drive		On different drive	
	Encrypted folder	**Unencrypted folder**	**Encrypted folder**	**Unencrypted folder**
Encrypted file				
Encrypted folder				
Unencrypted file				
Unencrypted folder				
Use E to indicate encryption and U to indicate no encryption.				

Practice: Copying encrypted files and folders (Exercise 2)

▶ **Copy encrypted files and folders**

1. On the Student Materials compact disc, under **Multimedia**, open *Managing NTFS File Compression and Encryption*, and then select **Encryption Copy**.

2. Copy the files and folders to various locations on the page, and record the results in the table below.

   The drives in the exercise represent NTFS-formatted drives on the same computer.

Copy to:	On same drive		On different drive	
	Encrypted folder	**Unencrypted folder**	**Encrypted folder**	**Unencrypted folder**
Encrypted file				
Encrypted folder				
Unencrypted file				
Unencrypted folder				
Use E to indicate encryption and U to indicate no encryption.				

Lesson: Implementing Disk Quotas

- Multimedia: What Are Disk Quotas?
- What Are Disk Quota Settings?
- How to Enable and Disable Disk Quotas
- How to Add and Remove Disk Quota Entries
- How to Sort Quota Entries
- How to Import and Export Quota Settings to Another Volume

Introduction

Use disk quotas to manage server resources by limiting storage space for users. You can also use disk quotas to track disk usage by users or groups. In this lesson, you will learn how to use disk quotas and how to set up disk entries.

Lesson objectives

After completing this lesson, you will be able to:

- Explain disk quotas.
- Describe disk quota settings.
- Enable and disable disk quotas.
- Add and remove disk quota entries.
- Sort disk quota entries.
- Import and export disk quota settings to another volume.

Multimedia: What Are Disk Quotas?

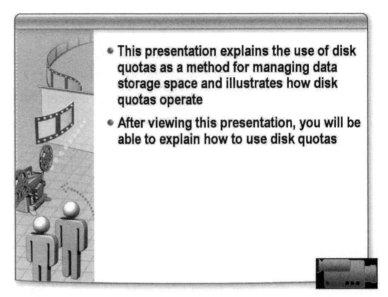

File location

To view the *What Are Disk Quotas?* presentation, open the Web page on the Student Materials compact disc, click **Multimedia**, and then click the title of the presentation.

Do not open this presentation unless the instructor tells you to.

What Are Disk Quota Settings?

- Track and control user's disk space on NTFS volumes
- Prevent users from taking any additional disk space above their quota limit
- Log events when users near and exceed quota limits
- Can be enabled on local volumes, network volumes, and removable drives if they are formatted with NTFS
- Can be enabled on local computers and remote computers
- Cannot use file compression to prevent users from exceeding their limits

Introduction

You can use disk quota settings to prevent users from writing additional data to a disk volume after they exceed their assigned quota limit.

Use disk quotas to track disk space

You can also enable quotas without limiting disk space when you do not want to deny users access to a volume but want to track the disk space use of each user. You can also specify whether to log an event when users exceed either their quota limit or their quota warning level.

Enable quotas on volumes

You can enable quotas on local volumes, network volumes, and removable drives if they are formatted by using NTFS. Also, network volumes must be shared from the volume's root directory, and removable drives must be shared. This is not file sharing, but administrative sharing. When you enable disk quotas for a volume, volume usage is automatically tracked for all users from that point on.

File compression does not prevent exceeding quota limits

You cannot use file compression to prevent users from exceeding their quota limits because compressed files are tracked based on their uncompressed size. For example, for a 50-megabyte (MB) file that is 40 MB after it is compressed, Windows counts the file's original 50-MB size toward the quota limit.

CPU overhead and administration

Enabling disk quotas requires a minimal amount of CPU overhead and no additional administration other than the initial configuration.

Local and remote implementations of disk quotas

You can enable disk quotas on local computers and remote computers. On local computers, use quotas to prevent users from using excessive disk space on a shared folder on your computer, and limit the amount of space that is available to users who log on to the local computer. For remote computers, quotas can ensure that disk space on public servers is not consumed by one or a few users, and that those users are accountable for the use of shared disk space by using public disk space only for necessary files.

Set quotas on remote volumes

You can set quotas on a remote volume by mapping to it by using Windows Explorer or My Computer. You can manage NTFS volumes on remote computers running Windows 2000 and Windows Server 2003. The volumes must be formatted by using NTFS and must be shared from the root folder of the volume.

How to Enable and Disable Disk Quotas

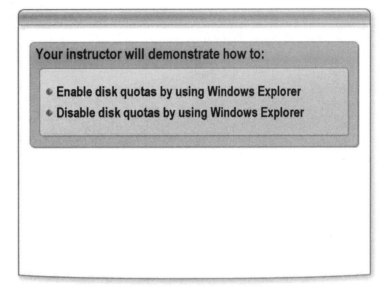

Your instructor will demonstrate how to:

- Enable disk quotas by using Windows Explorer
- Disable disk quotas by using Windows Explorer

Introduction

Use the following procedures to enable and disable disk quotas.

Procedure for enabling disk quotas

To enable disk quotas:

1. In Windows Explorer, right-click the disk volume for which you want to enable disk quotas, and then click **Properties**.

2. In the **Properties** dialog box, on the **Quota** tab, select the **Enable quota management** check box.

3. Select one or more of the following options:

   a. **Deny disk space to users exceeding quota limit**

   b. **Limit disk space to** _____

   c. **Log event when a user exceeds their quota limit**

   d. **Log event when a user exceeds their warning level**

Procedure for disabling disk quotas

To disable disk quotas:

1. In Windows Explorer, right-click the disk volume for which you want to disable disk quotas, and then click **Properties**.

2. In the **Properties** dialog box, on the **Quota** tab, clear the **Enable quota management** check box.

How to Add and Remove Disk Quota Entries

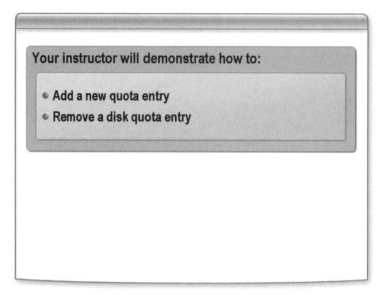

Introduction

Use the following procedures to add and remove disk quota entries. Each new user is considered a quota entry.

Procedure for adding a new disk quota entry

To add a new disk quota entry:

1. In Windows Explorer, right-click the volume for which you want to add a new disk quota entry, and then click **Properties**.

2. In the **Properties** dialog box, on the **Quota** tab, click **Quota Entries**.

3. In the Quota Entries window, on the **Quota** menu, click **New Quota Entry**.

4. In the **Select Users** dialog box, in the **Enter the object names to select** text box, type the domain or workgroup name, followed by a backslash (\) and the username of the user for which you want to impose quotas, and then click **OK**.

5. In the **Add New Quota Entry** dialog box, specify one of the following options:

   a. **Do not limit disk usage**

   b. **Limit disk space to**

Procedure to remove disk quota entries

To remove disk quota entries:

1. In Windows Explorer, right-click the volume for which you want to add new disk quota entries, and then click **Properties**.

2. In the **Properties** dialog box, on the **Quota** tab, click **Quota Entries**.

3. In the Quota Entries window, click the entries for the users you want to delete, and then on the **Quota** menu, click **Delete Quota Entry**.

4. If the **Disk Quota** dialog box appears, click **Yes**, click the files or folders that you want to take action on, and then click one of the following buttons: **Delete**, **Take Ownership**, **Move**.

How to Sort Quota Entries

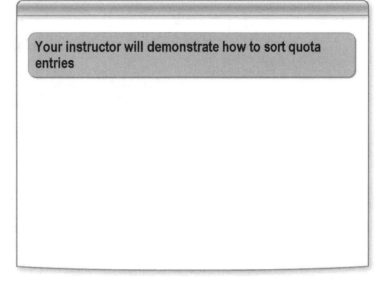

Your instructor will demonstrate how to sort quota entries

Introduction

After setting up the list of users who are using disk quotas, you can use the following steps to sort the results of disk quotas.

Procedure for sorting quota entries

To sort quota entries:

1. In Windows Explorer, right-click the volume for which you want to sort quota entries, and then click **Properties**.

2. In the **Properties** dialog box, on the **Quota** tab, click **Quota Entries**.

3. In the Quota Entries window, on the **View** menu, point to **Arrange Items**, and then click one of the following options:

   a. **By Folder**

   b. **By User Name**

   c. **By Logon Name**

   d. **By Status**

   e. **By Amount Used**

   f. **By Quota Limit**

   g. **By Warning Level**

   h. **By Percent Used**

How to Import and Export Quota Settings to Another Volume

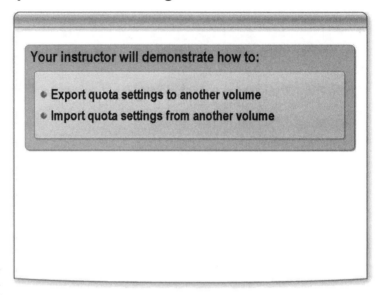

Introduction

By using the list of disk quota users you have set up for one volume, you can save time and effort by importing the settings to other volumes. Use the following steps to export quota settings from one volume and import them to another volume.

Procedure for exporting quota settings

To export quota settings to another volume:

1. In Windows Explorer, right-click the volume to which you want to import quota settings, and then click **Properties**.

2. In the **Properties** dialog box, on the **Quota** tab, make sure the **Enable quota management** check box is selected, and then click **Quota Entries**. Click the user quota settings you want to export.

3. On the **Quota** menu, click **Export**. In the **Export Quota Settings** dialog box, specify a destination folder, type the file name for the saved settings, and then click **Save**.

Procedure for importing quota settings

To import quota settings from another volume:

1. In Windows Explorer, right-click the volume to which you want to import quota settings, and then click **Properties**.

2. In the **Properties** dialog box, on the **Quota** tab, click **Quota Entries**, and then in the Quota Entries window, on the **Quota** menu, click **Import**.

3. In the **Import Quota Settings** dialog box, select the name of the file that contains the quota settings you want to import, and then click **Open**.

4. When you import quota settings a dialog box appears if imported settings will overwrite existing settings for a volume user. Specify whether you want to overwrite the existing user settings.

Practice: Configuring Quota Limits

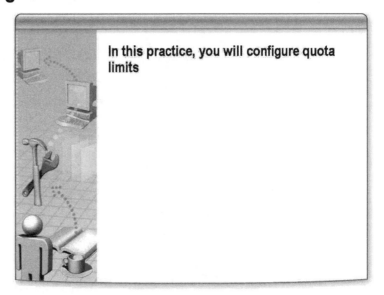

Objective

In this practice, you will configure quota limits.

Scenario

You are the systems administrator for an organizational unit on a large network. The department manager has decided to allocate space on the department server for employees' personal files. However, the manager has asked you to put a 10-MB limit on the amount of personal data that each user is allowed to store on the server. You will need to configure disk quotas to limit the amount of space each user is allowed on the D drive.

Practice

1. Log on to the domain as Administrator with a password of **P@ssw0rd**.

   You must log on as Administrator in this practice, because Windows Explorer cannot be started using the **Run As** command.

2. In Windows Explorer, open the **Properties** dialog box for the D drive.

3. On the **Quota** tab, select the **Enable quota management** check box.

4. Enable the following options:

   a. Deny disk space to users exceeding quota limit

   b. Limit disk space to 10 MB

   c. Set the warning level to 9 MB

   d. Log event when a user exceeds their quota limit

   e. Log event when a user exceeds their warning level

5. Close all windows and log off.

Lab A: Managing Data Storage

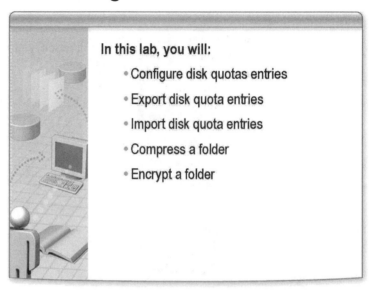

Objectives

After completing this lab, you will be able to:

- Configure disk quotas entries.
- Export disk quota entries.
- Import disk quota entries.
- Compress a folder.
- Encrypt a folder.

Prerequisites

Before working on this lab, you must have:

- Completed the labs and practices from Module 5, "Managing Disks," in Course 2275, *Maintaining a Microsoft Windows Server 2003 Environment.*

  If you have not completed those labs and practices, you must run the following batch file: C:\MOC\2275\Labfiles\Lab06\Mod5.bat.

- Run the setperm script in C:\MOC\2275\Labfiles.

Scenario

You are the systems administrator for an organizational unit on a large network. After arriving at work one morning, you receive the following requests from your manager:

- The organization has decided to implement disk quotas on all of the volumes on its servers. To test this plan, you have been asked to configure disk quota entries on your drive D and then export them to a file. Next, you will import them to your drive E and verify the quota configuration. You will use *Computer*User and GlasgowUser for your testing.

- The marketing department wants you to compress the 5,000 graphics files on its server. The files are in a folder named Graphics.

- The Human Resources department has decided to encrypt all of the personnel files. The HR director wants you to show her how to do this.

Estimated time to complete this lab: 10 minutes

Exercise 1
Configuring Disk Quota Entries

You need to configure disk quota entries for *Computer*User and GlasgowUser for your testing.

Tasks	Specific instructions
1. Log on using the domain user account.	▪ Log on to the domain as *Computer*User with a password of **P@ssw0rd**.
2. Start Computer Management with administrative credentials.	▪ In the **Run** dialog box, use **runas** to start Computer Management: **runas /user:nwtraders\administrator "mmc %windir%\system32\compmgmt.msc"**
3. Configure disk quota entries.	a. In Disk Management, open the **Properties** dialog box for drive D.
	b. On the **Quota** tab, select the following entries: **Enable quota management, Deny disk space to users exceeding quota limit, Log event when a user exceeds their quota limit**, and **Log event when a user exceeds their warning level**.
	c. Configure a quota entry for *Computer*User.
	d. In the **Limit disk space to** box, type **10 MB** and then in the **Set warning level to** box, type **9 MB**
4. Add GlasgowUser quota entries.	▪ Repeat step 3 for GlasgowUser.

Exercise 2
Exporting Disk Quota Entries

In this exercise, you will export the disk quota entries that you created to a binary file.

Tasks	Specific instructions
1. Export disk quota entries to a binary file.	■ In Disk Management, highlight the new quota entries that you created in the previous exercise, and then on the **Quota** menu, click **Export**.
2. Save the quota entries file.	■ Name the quota entries file **export.bin** and then save the file in **C:\MOC\2275\Labfiles**.
3. Close the Quota Entries window.	■ Close the Quota Entries for New Volume (D:) window, close the **New Volume (D:) Properties** dialog box, and then click **OK** to close the remaining dialog boxes.

Exercise 3
Importing Disk Quota Entries

In this exercise, you will import the disk quota entries on drive E.

Tasks	Specific instructions
1. Import disk quota entries to another drive.	a. In Computer Management, open the **Properties** dialog box for New Volume (E:) drive.
	b. On the **Quota** tab, select the **Enable quota management** check box, and then open the Quota Entries window.
	c. Open the **Import Quota Settings** dialog box, and then import the export.bin file.
2. Verify that the three quota entries are displayed.	■ In the Quota Entries for New Volume (E:) window, verify that the three quota entries are displayed in New Volume (E:).
3. Close the windows.	a. Close the Quota Entries for New Volume (E:) window.
	b. Close the dialog box by clicking **OK**.
4. Test the quota entries.	a. In Windows Explorer, browse to C:\Moc\2275\Labfiles\Lab06, and then double-click **diskhog**.
	A command prompt window opens, and the text starts scrolling. Diskhog is a program that creates a small file and then doubles its size repeatedly until there is no more disk space.
	Notice that the text stops scrolling, and the size of the file is displayed.
	b. How big was the junk.txt file before diskhog stopped? _____
	c. Close all windows.

Exercise 4
Compressing a Folder

In this exercise, you will compress the C:\MOC\2275\Labfiles\Lab06\Data\Graphics folder.

Tasks	Specific instructions
1. Select the file to be compressed.	a. In Windows Explorer, browse to C:\MOC\2275\Labfiles\Lab06\Data\Graphics. b. Open the **Properties** dialog box for the Graphics folder, and then click **Advanced**.
2. Compress the folder.	a. Using **Compress or Encrypt attributes**, compress the folder. b. Close all dialog boxes by clicking **OK**.

Exercise 5
Encrypting a Folder

In this exercise, you will encrypt the C:\MOC\2275\Labfiles\Lab06\Data\Personnel folder.

Tasks	Specific instructions
1. Select the file to be encrypted.	a. In Windows Explorer, browse to C:\MOC\2275\Labfiles\Lab06\Data\Personnel. b. Open the **Properties** dialog box for the Personnel folder, and then click **Advanced**.
2. Encrypt the folder.	a. Using Compress or Encrypt attributes, encrypt the folder. b. Close all dialog boxes by clicking **OK**. c. Close all windows and log off.
3. Verify that the contents of the Personnel folder are secure.	a. Log on the domain as Administrator with a password of **P@ssw0rd**. b. Open Windows Explorer, and browse to C:\MOC\2275\Labfiles\Lab06\Data\Personnel. c. Double-click **people**. d. Close all windows and log off.

Course Evaluation

Your evaluation of this course will help Microsoft understand the quality of your learning experience.

At a convenient time before the end of the course, please complete a course evaluation, which is available at http://www.CourseSurvey.com.

Microsoft®
Training &
Certification

Module 7: Managing Disaster Recovery

Contents

Overview	1
Lesson: Preparing for Disaster Recovery	2
Lesson: Backing Up Data	7
Lesson: Scheduling Backup Jobs	25
Lesson: Restoring Data	34
Lesson: Configuring Shadow Copies	44
Lesson: Recovering from Server Failure	60
Lesson: Selecting Disaster Recovery Methods	76
What Are Server Disaster Recovery Tools?	77
Lab A: Managing Disaster Recovery	79

Microsoft®

Overview

- Preparing for Disaster Recovery
- Backing Up Data
- Scheduling Backup Jobs
- Restoring Data
- Configuring Shadow Copies
- Recovering from Server Failure
- Selecting Disaster Recovery Methods

Introduction

This module helps you prepare for a computer disaster by using the features in Microsoft® Windows® Server 2003 to prevent data loss and recover from data losses after they occur. Understanding these features is essential to developing and implementing an effective disaster protection and recovery plan.

Objectives

After completing this module, you will be able to:

- Prepare for disaster recovery.
- Back up data.
- Schedule backup jobs.
- Restore data.
- Configure a shadow copy.
- Recover from server failure.
- Select a disaster recovery method.

Lesson: Preparing for Disaster Recovery

- **What Is Disaster Recovery?**
- **Guidelines for Preparing for Disaster Recovery**

Introduction

This lesson introduces the components of disaster recovery and the methods of recovering data after a disaster occurs. This lesson also provides recommended guidelines that will help you to develop your own disaster recovery plan.

Lesson objectives

After completing this lesson, you will be able to:

- Describe what to include in a recovery plan.
- Explain the guidelines to use when you create a disaster recovery plan.

What Is Disaster Recovery?

- A disaster is a sudden catastrophic loss of data
- Disaster recovery is the process of resuming normal business operations as quickly as possible after the disaster is over
- Disaster recovery process includes:
  - Executing a written disaster recovery plan
  - Replacing any damaged hardware
  - Restoring data
  - Testing all hardware and software before resuming operations

Introduction

A computer disaster is a sudden catastrophic loss of data. The business world depends on mission-critical data more than ever. As a result, organizations are placing a premium on protecting their information technology (IT) assets from data loss and server failure.

Disaster recovery

Disaster recovery is the process of resuming normal business operations as quickly as possible after the disaster ends. Ideally, you can use disaster recovery methods to restore data and services to the state they were in prior to the disaster.

Disaster recovery considerations

For each operating system and application that you introduce to your environment, answer the following questions about disaster recovery:

Disaster recovery method	Considerations
Recovery plan	- What are the possible failure scenarios?
	- What data is critical?
	- How often should you perform backups?
	- How long will you save the backups before reusing the medium?
	- Assuming failure, how much time will it take to restore from the most recent backup? Is that an acceptable amount of downtime?
	- Where will you store the backups, and do the appropriate people have access to them?
	- If the responsible systems administrator is gone, is there someone else who knows the proper passwords and procedures to perform backups and, if necessary, to restore the system?

(continued)

Disaster recovery method	Considerations
Hardware	• How many, what kind, and where are individual computer components, such as hard disks and controllers, processors, and RAM?
	• How many, what kind, and where are external components such as routers, bridges, switches, cables, and connectors?
	• Are the critical hardware and services redundant?
Data restoration	• To what medium, such as tape, compact disc, or disk, will you send the backup?
	• Will you perform backups online, while users are working, or offline?
	• Will you perform the backups manually or schedule them to be performed automatically?
	• How long will you save the backups before reusing the medium?
	• Is the critical data redundant? How often is the critical data updated?
Testing	• If the backup is automated, how will you verify that it successfully occurred?
	• How will you ensure that the backups are usable?

Determine questions based on your situation

This is not a complete list—you must determine other questions based on your particular situation.

Guidelines for Preparing for Disaster Recovery

- Create a disaster recovery plan for performing regular backup operations
- Test your backup files and your backup plan
- Keep two sets of backed-up files: one on-site, for accessibility, and one off-site, for security
- Create a redundant copy of System State data
- Install the Recovery Console as a startup option
- Keep the installation CD where you can easily find it

Introduction

You should develop and thoroughly test a disaster recovery plan. When you test, look for vulnerable areas by simulating as many possible failure scenarios as you can.

Guidelines

Use the following guidelines to prepare for disaster recovery:

- Create a disaster recovery plan for performing regular backup operations.

  Review and incorporate a plan for backing up all of your files on a regular basis. Keep a log of every update in your disaster recovery plan.

- Test your backup files and your backup plan.

  Testing your backup files and recovery plan is an important part of being prepared for disaster recovery. Testing must include the following tasks:

  - Test your uninterruptible power supply (UPS) on the computers running Windows Server 2003 and on hubs, routers, and other network components.

  - Perform full or partial restorations from your daily, weekly, and monthly backup media.

- Keep two sets of backed-up files: one on-site, for accessibility, and one off-site, for security.

  The backup should be accessible, such as on network shared folders or removable media, in case the data must be restored to another computer.

  If possible, make a copy of your backup sets every day and store them at both an on-site and off-site location. That way, if a catastrophic event, such as a fire, destroys all of your computers and on-site backup sets, you can restore all your data later. However, if all of your backups are off-site, every time you need to recover a file, you must get the backup files from the off-site location.

■ Create a backup of the System State data.

Create a backup copy of the System State data in the unlikely event that the hard disk on the server fails and cannot be recovered. This copy can help you restore your operating system to a new hard disk.

■ Install the Recovery Console as a startup option.

Install the Recovery Console on your computer to make it available in case you are unable to restart Windows Server 2003. You can then select the Recovery Console option from the list of available operating systems in safe mode.

■ Keep the installation compact disc where you can easily find it.

Keep the installation compact disc where you can find it easily. You can start the computer from the compact disc and then use the Recovery Console or Automated System Recovery.

Lesson: Backing Up Data

- Overview of Backing Up Data
- Who Can Back Up Data?
- What Is System State Data?
- What Is the Backup Utility?
- Types of Backup
- What Is ntbackup?
- What Is an Automated System Recovery Set?
- How to Back Up Data

Introduction

Backing up your data prevents data loss in case the original files are lost due to hardware or software failure. Windows Server 2003 includes a backup utility, Backup, that backs up data by copying designated files to storage media. You can also use Windows Server 2003 to back up your server by using Automated System Recovery.

Lesson objectives

After completing this lesson, you will be able to:

- Describe the process of backing up data.
- Explain who can back up data.
- Explain the backup of System State data.
- Explain the Backup utility.
- Explain the various types of backup.
- Explain the **ntbackup** command-line tool.
- Explain an Automated System Recovery set.
- Describe guidelines for backup.

Overview of Backing Up Data

> - **Backing up produces copies of data files and folders, stored on alternate media**
> - **Backing up the data on server and client computer hard disks prevents data loss**
> - **Before backing up, decide:**
>   - Which files to back up – if you cannot get along without it, back it up
>   - How frequently to back up
>   - Whether to perform a network backup – weigh the advantages and disadvantages of a network backup

Back Up Data

Introduction

Backup is a single process of copying files and folders from one location to another. Regularly backing up the data on server and client computer hard disks prevents data loss due to disk drive failures, power outages, virus infections, and other such incidents. If a data loss occurs, and you have performed regular backups based on careful planning, you can restore the lost data, whether it is in one file or on an entire hard disk.

There is a general backup rule: if you cannot get along without it, back it up.

When to use a network backup

Perform a network backup when the critical data is on multiple servers or you want to perform a backup over the network. The following table describes the advantages and disadvantages of a network backup.

Advantages	Disadvantages
Backs up the entire network	Users must copy their important files to the servers
Requires fewer tape drives or disks	Cannot back up the registry on remote computers
Less media to manage	Increases network traffic
One user can back up data	Requires greater planning and preparation

How frequently to back up

Backup frequency depends on the following conditions:

- How critical the data is to your organization. You back up critical data more often than data of low importance.

- How frequently the data changes. For example, if users create or modify reports only on Fridays, a weekly backup for the report files is sufficient.

Types of data to back up

System State data is a collection of data that defines the configuration of the operating system on a server. If accidental changes occur or if data is lost in any of the components that make up the System State data, you can restore System State data from a backup. This action restores your computer's configuration to a previously known good state.

Critical data is the data that your organization needs to survive. If you lose this data, which is typically stored on a server, your organization cannot conduct its business. If files are accidentally lost or corrupted, you can use the last known good backup files to restore this data.

Who Can Back Up Data?

- **You must have certain permissions or user rights**
- **Only administrators, backup operators, and server operator groups are allowed to back up data by default on local servers**
  - Or you must be the owner of the files and folders you want to back up
  - Or you must have one or more of these permissions: Read, Read and execute, Modify, or Full Control
- **You cannot back up your files if there are disk quota restrictions**
- **Access to backup files can also be restricted**
- **For security, backup and restore rights can be segregated into two groups**
- **Backup files and directories GPO located in Computer Configuration**

Introduction

You must have certain permissions or user rights to back up and restore files and folders. If you are an administrator a backup operator or server operators in a local group, you can back up and restore any file or folder on the local server to which the local group applies.

Permissions and user rights

To successfully back up and restore data on a computer running Windows Server 2003, you must have the appropriate permissions and user rights, as described in the following list:

- All users can back up their own files and folders. They can also back up files for which they have the Read permission.

- Members of the Administrators, Backup Operators, and Server Operators groups can back up and restore all files, regardless of the assigned permissions. By default, members of these groups have the following user rights: Backup Files and Directories and the Restore Files and Directories as well as Modify and Full Control permissions.

No disk quota restrictions

You must also be certain that there are no disk quota restrictions that may restrict your access to a hard disk, thereby making it impossible for you to back up data. You can check whether there are any disk quota restrictions by right-clicking the disk that you want to save data to, clicking **Properties**, and then clicking the **Quota** tab.

Restrict access

You can also restrict access to a backup file by selecting **Allow only the owner and the Administrator access to the backup data** in the **Backup Job Information** dialog box. If you select this option, only an administrator or the person who created the backup file can restore the files and folders.

Separate backup and restore user rights

For security reasons, many organizations prefer to separate the backup and restore user rights into two groups as follows:

1. Create a Backup group and a Restore group by using Active Directory Users and Computers.

2. Add one set of members to the Backup group and another set of members to the Restore group.

3. Add the Backup group to the **Backup files and directories** Group Policy object (GPO).

4. Add the Restore group to the **Restore files and directories** GPO.

Location of the Backup files and directories GPO

The Backup files and directories GPO and Restore files and directories GPO are located in the following group policy:

Computer Configuration

   Windows Settings

      Security Settings

         Local Policies

            User Rights Assignment

What Is System State Data?

- **The computer uses System State data files to load, configure, and run the operating system**
- **All System State data relevant to your server is backed up**
- **You can back up the following system components:**

Component	When this component is included in System State
Registry	Always
Boot files, including the system files	Always
Certificate Services database	If it is a Certificate Services Server
Active Directory directory service	If it is a Domain
SYSVOL Directory	If it is a Domain Controller
Cluster service information	If it is within a cluster
IIS metadirectory	If it is installed
System files that are under Windows File Protection	Always

Introduction

The System State is the collection of system-specific data maintained by the operating system that must be backed up as a unit. The computer uses these system files to load, configure, and run the operating system.

System State components

Backup refers to the following system files as the System State data.

Component	When included in System State
Registry	Always
Boot files, Com+ Class Registration, including the system files	Always
Certificate Services database	If it is a Certificate Services server
Active Directory® directory service	If it is a domain
SYSVOL directory	If it is a domain controller
Cluster service information	If it is within a cluster
IIS metadirectory	If it is installed
System files that are under Windows File Protection	Always

Back up System State data

When you back up or restore the System State data, all of the System State data that is relevant to your computer is backed up or restored. You cannot back up or restore individual components of the System State data because of dependencies among the System State components. However, you can restore the System State data to an alternate location. If you do this, only the registry files, SYSVOL directory files, Cluster database information files, and system boot files are restored to the alternate location. Active Directory, the Certificate Services database, and the COM+ Class Registration database are not restored if you designate an alternate location when you restore the System State data.

What Is the Backup Utility?

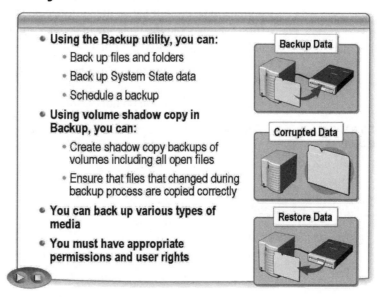

Introduction

The Windows Server 2003 backup utility, Backup, is designed to protect data from accidental loss resulting from the failure of your hardware or storage media. It is the graphical user interface (GUI) version of the Backup utility.

Use to manage backup

You can use Backup to:

- Back up files and folders.
- Back up System State data.
- Schedule a backup job.

You can use the Backup Wizard to back up the entire contents of a server, selected portions of the server contents, or the System State data.

Volume shadow copy

You can use Backup to create shadow copy backups of volumes and exact copies of files, including all open files. For example, databases that are held open exclusively and files that are open due to operator or system activity are backed up during a volume shadow copy backup. In this way, files that changed during the backup process are copied correctly.

Volume shadow copy backups ensure that:

- Applications can continue to write data to the volume during a backup.
- Open files are not omitted during a backup.
- Backups can be performed at any time, without locking out users.

Some applications manage storage consistency differently while files are open, which can affect the consistency of the files in the backup. For critical applications, consult the application documentation or your provider for information about the recommended backup method. When in doubt, quit the application before performing a backup.

Volume shadow copy is enabled by default. If you disable this option, some files that are open or in use during the backup might be skipped. It is recommended that you do not disable this option.

Supports a variety of storage devices

The Backup utility supports a variety of storage devices and media, including tape drives, logical drives, removable disks, and recordable CD-ROM drives.

Types of Backup

- • Backup types define what data is backed up
- • Backup types use archive attributes that show the file has changed since the last backup
- • Select a backup rotation scheme

Type	Actions performed	Clears Archive attribute
Normal or Full	Selected files and folders	Yes
Copy	Selected files and folders	No
Differential	Selected files and folders that changed since the last normal or incremental backup	No
Incremental	Selected files and folders that changed since the last backup	Yes
Daily	Selected files and folders that changed during the day	No

Introduction

The Backup utility provides five backup types that specify what data is backed up, such as only files that have changed since the last backup.

Backup archive attributes

Some backup types use an archive attribute, which indicates that a file was modified since the last backup. When a file is modified, the archive attribute is set, and when you back up the file, the archive attribute is cleared or reset.

Backup types

Backup provides five backup types: normal, copy, differential, incremental, and daily. Each of these backup types targets specific categories of files for backup, such as files that have changed since the last backup or all files in a specific folder.

The following table presents the backup types, the function of each type, whether the backup type clears archive attributes, and tips for using the backup type.

Type	Description
Normal	Backs up all selected files, regardless of the setting of the archive attribute, and clears the archive attribute of all files that are backed up. If the file is modified later, the archive attribute is set, which indicates that the file needs to be backed up.
	Perform a normal backup the first time you create a backup set to set a baseline for future backup jobs.
Copy	Identical to a normal backup except that it does not change the archive attribute, which allows you to perform other types of backups on the files later.
	Use a copy backup to create an additional backup tape or disk without disturbing the archive attributes.

(*continued*)

Type	Description
Differential	Creates backup copies of files that have changed since the last normal backup. The presence of the archive attribute indicates that the file was modified and only files with this attribute are backed up. However, the archive attribute on files is not modified. This allows you to perform other types of backups on the files later.
	Because a differential backup does not clear archive attributes, if you perform two differential backups on a file, the entire file is backed up each time.
	Differential backups use more media than incremental backups, but when you restore the disk, you need only the media that contains the files from the normal backup and the most recent differential backup.
Incremental	Designed to create backups of files that have changed since the most recent normal or incremental backup. The presence of the archive attribute indicates that the file was modified, and only files with this attribute are backed up. When a file is backed up, the archive attribute is cleared.
	Because an incremental backup clears archive attributes, if you perform two incremental backups in a row on a file, the file is not backed up the second time.
	Incremental backups use the minimum amount of media and also save time by not copying all of the files that have changed since the last full backup. However, restoring a disk is inconvenient because you must change the media for each day of the week.
Daily	Backs up files by using the modification date on the file itself, and disregards the current state of the archive attribute. If a file was modified on the same day as the backup, the file is backed up. This type does not change the archive attributes of files.

Important   Your backup plan can combine various backup types. If you combine backup types, archive attributes are critical. Incremental and differential backup types check for and rely on the archive attributes.

Backup scenarios

You perform a normal backup on Monday and incremental backups on Tuesday through Friday. If your disk fails on Saturday, you must restore the hard disk with Monday's tape and then complete the restore process by using the Tuesday-through-Friday tapes in the order that they were written.

You perform a normal backup on Monday and differential backups on Tuesday through Friday. If your disk fails on Saturday, you must restore the hard disk using Monday's tape followed by Friday's tape.

Workers in your organization are required to save their work to a server every hour. Management wants to limit the amount of data that is lost due to a server failure to one hour. To accomplish this, you perform a normal backup on Monday, a differential backup the other four days, and a daily backup every hour.

What Is ntbackup?

- **Use ntbackup command line tool to:**
  - Back up System State data
  - Back up files to a file or a tape
  - Run batch files
- **Important limitations using batch files**
  - You can back up entire folders only
  - You cannot use wildcard characters

Introduction

In addition to Backup, Windows Server 2003 provides a command-line tool, **ntbackup**, that you can use to back up and restore data.

Use the command prompt or batch file

You can perform backup operations from a command prompt or from a batch file by using the **ntbackup** command, followed by various parameters.

There are two important limitations to using batch files to back up your data:

- When you use the **ntbackup** command, you must back up entire folders only. You cannot designate individual files for backup. However, you can designate a backup selection file (.bks file) from the command line, which contains a list of files that you want to back up. You must use the GUI version of the Backup utility to create backup selection files.

- The **ntbackup** command does not support the use of wildcard characters. For example, typing ***.txt** does not back up files with a .txt extension.

What Is Automated System Recovery?

- **A recovery option in the Backup utility that contains two parts: ASR backup and ASR restore**
- **Can back up the operating system**
- **Does not include data files**
- **Creates a floppy disk, which contains information about:**
  - Backup location data
  - Disk configurations (including basic and dynamic volumes)
  - How to accomplish a restore procedure

 Automated System Recovery Wizard
The ASR Preparation wizard helps you create a two-part backup of your system: a floppy disk that has your system settings, and other media that contains a backup of your local system partition.

- **Choose the All information on this computer option, it will back up all data including System State Data**

Introduction

Automated System Recovery (ASR), in the Backup utility, helps you recover a system that does not start. ASR contains two parts: backup and recovery. ASR also creates a floppy disk that is used to store disk configurations during the ASR restore procedure.

ASR restores operating system

Typically, after installing or upgrading to Windows Server 2003, you create a set of ASR disks. The ASR process enables you to restore an installation of Windows Server 2003 to the condition of the operating system at the time that you created the ASR backup set.

ASR Backup Wizard

The ASR Backup Wizard backs up the System State data, system services, and all disks that are associated with the operating system components, but it does not back up data files. The ASR Backup Wizard also creates a floppy disk, which contains information about the backup, the disk configurations, including basic and dynamic volumes, and the restore procedure.

Backup or Restore Wizard

The ASR Backup Wizard provides several backup options. The **All information on this computer** option backs up all data on the computer in addition to the System State data and the operating system components. This option also creates a system recovery disk that you can used to restore Windows in case of a disk failure.

How to Back Up Data

> **Your instructor will demonstrate how to:**
>
> * Back up data files by using the Backup utility
> * Back up System State data by using the Backup utility
> * Back up the operating system and data files by using the Backup utility
> * Back up by using ASR
> * Back up System State data by using ntbackup

Introduction

You can use the Backup utility to make copies of your organization's most important data and your System State data. Use the Backup or Restore Wizard to back up those selected files. You can also use ASR to back up all the files, including program files and System State data files. Use the **ntbackup** command to create a batch file to back up System State data.

Procedure for backing up data files or System State using Backup

To back up files by using the Backup utility:

1. On the **Start** menu, point to **All Programs**, point to **Accessories**, point to **System Tools**, and then click **Backup**.

2. On the **Welcome** page of the Backup or Restore Wizard, click the **Advanced Mode** link.

3. In the **Backup Utility** dialog box, on the **Backup** tab, on the **Job** menu, click **New**.

4. Under **Click to select the check box for any drive, folder or file that you want to back up**, click the box next to each file or folder that you want to back up, or click the box next to **System State**.

5. In the **Backup destination** box, do one of the following:

   * Select **File** if you want to back up files and folders to a file.

   * Select a tape device.

6. In the **Backup media or file name** box, do one of the following:

   * If you are backing up files and folders to a file, type the path and file name for backup (.bkf) file, or click **Browse** to find a file.

   * If you are backing up files and folders to tape, choose the tape you want to use.

7. To select backup options, on the **Tools** menu, click **Options**, and then select the options that you want to use, such as backup type and log file type.

8. Click **Start Backup**, and then make any changes in the **Backup Job Information** dialog box.

Procedure for backing up operating system and data by using Backup

To back up files by using the Backup or Restore Wizard:

1. On the **Start** menu, point to **All Programs**, point to **Accessories**, point to **System Tools**, and then click **Backup**.

2. On the **Welcome** page of the Backup or Restore Wizard, click **Next**.

3. On the **Backup or Restore** page, click **Back up files and settings**, and then click **Next**.

4. On the **What to Back Up** page, click **All information on this computer**, and then click **Next**.

5. On the **Backup Type, Destination, and Name** page, click **Browse**.

6. In the **Save As** dialog box, in the **File name** box, type **D:\Complete.bkf** and then click **Save**.

7. Click **Next**, and then click **Finish**.

Procedure for backing up by using ASR

To store the ASR backup files to the disk:

1. On the **Start** menu, point to **All Programs**, point to **Accessories**, point to **System Tools**, and then click **Backup**.

2. In the Backup or Restore Wizard, click **Advanced Mode**.

3. On the **Welcome** tab, click **Automated System Recovery Wizard**.

4. On the **Welcome to the Automated System Recovery Preparation Wizard** page, click **Next**.

5. On the **Backup Destination** page, select **File** in the **Backup media type** box, type **C:\backup.bkf** in the **Backup media or file name** box, and then click **Next**.

6. Click **Finish** and when prompted, insert a disk into drive A, and then click **OK**.

7. When prompted to remove the disk, click **OK**, and then close all windows.

Procedure for backing up System State data using ntbackup

To back up files by using **ntbackup**:

- At the command line prompt, type:

  ntbackup backup [systemstate] "**@bks** *file name*" **/J** {"*job name*"}
  [**/P** {"*pool name*"}] [**/G** {"*guid name*"}] [**/T** { "*tape name*"}]
  [**/N** {"*media name*"}] [**/F** {"*file name*"}] [**/D** {"*set description*"}]
  [**/DS** {"*server name*"}] [**/IS** {"*server name*"}] [**/A**] [**/V:**{**yes|no**}]
  [**/R:**{**yes|no**}] [**/L:**{**f|s|n**}] [**/M** {*backup type*}] [**/RS:**{**yes|no**}]
  [**/HC:**{**on|off**}] [**/SNAP:**{**on|off**}]

Parameter	Definition
systemstate	Specifies that you want to back up the System State data. When you select this option, the backup type is forced to normal or copy.
@bks *file name*	Specifies the name of the backup selection file (.bks file) to be used for this backup operation. The at (@) character must precede the name of the backup selection file. A backup selection file contains information about the files and folders you have selected for backup. You must create the file by using the graphical user interface (GUI) version of Backup.
/J {"*job name*"}	Specifies the job name to be used in the backup report. The job name usually describes the files and folders you are backing up in the current backup job.
/P {"*pool name*"}	Specifies the media pool from which you want to use media. This is usually a subpool of the Backup media pool, such as 4mm DDS. If you select this parameter, you cannot use the **/A**, **/G**, **/F**, or **/T** command-line options.
/G {"*guid name*"}	Overwrites or appends to this tape. Do not use this switch in conjunction with **/P**.
/T {"*tape name*"}	Overwrites or appends to this tape. Do not use this switch in conjunction with **/P**.
/N {"*media name*"}	Specifies the new tape name. Do not use **/A** with this switch.
/F {"*file name*"}	Logical disk path and file name. Do not use the following switches with this switch: **/P /G /T**.
/D {"*set description*"}	Specifies a label for each backup set.
/DS {"*server name*"}	Backs up the directory service file for the specified Microsoft Exchange server.
/IS {"*server name*"}	Backs up the Information Store file for the specified Microsoft Exchange server.
/A	Performs an append operation. Use either **/G** or **/T** with this switch. Do not use this switch in conjunction with **/P**.
/V:{**yes|no**}	Verifies the data after the backup is complete.
/R:{**yes|no**}	Restricts access to this tape to the owner or members of the Administrators group.
/L:{**f|s|n**}	Specifies the type of log file: **f**=full, **s**=summary, **n**=none (no log file is created).

(*continued*)

Parameter	Definition
/M {*backup type*}	Specifies the backup type. It must be one of the following: normal, copy, differential, incremental, or daily.
/RS:{**yes**|**no**}	Backs up the migrated data files located in Remote Storage. The **/RS** command-line option is not required to back up the local Removable Storage database that contains the Remote Storage placeholder files. When you back up the %systemroot% folder, Backup automatically backs up the Removable Storage database as well.
/HC:{**on**|**off**}	Uses hardware compression, if available, on the tape drive.
/SNAP:{**on**|**off**}	Specifies whether the backup should use a volume shadow copy.

Practice: Backing Up Data

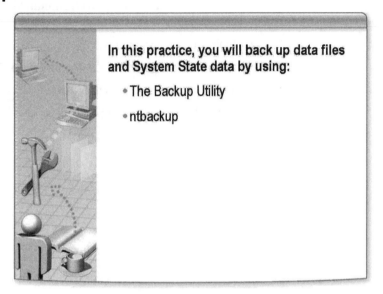

Objective

In this practice, you will back up data files by using:

- The Backup utility
- The **ntbackup** command

Scenario

You are the systems administrator for an organizational unit on a large network. Your department manager is relying on you to be able to quickly restore the C:\MOC folder on the department server in case it is corrupted. The backup must be stored as D:\MOC.bkf.

Practice: Starting the Backup utility using Run as

▶ **Start the Backup utility by using Run as, and back up a folder**

1. Log on to the domain as *Computer*User with a password of **P@ssw0rd** (where *Computer* is the name of your computer).

2. Open Windows Explorer, open the C:\Moc\2275\Practices\Mod03 folder, and then delete all swap.* files.

3. On the **Start** menu, point to **All Programs**, point to **Accessories**, point to **System Tools**, right-click **Backup**, and then click **Run as**.

4. In the **Run as** dialog box, use **nwtraders/administrator** for the account name and **P@ssw0rd** for the password.

5. Click **Advanced Mode**, click the **Backup** tab, expand **Local Disk (C:)**, and then select the **MOC** check box.

6. Back up the C:\MOC folder as **D:\MOC.bkf**.

7. When the backup is complete, close all windows.

Practice: Backing up a folder by using ntbackup

▶ **Back up a folder by using a ntbackup**

1. Open a command prompt with administrator credentials using the **runas** command.

2. In the command window, type:

   ntbackup backup C:\MOC /j ntbackup /f d:\MOC2.bkf

   This command backs up the C:\MOC folder as **D:\MOC2.bkf**.

3. When the backup is complete, close all windows and log off.

Lesson: Scheduling Backup Jobs

- What Is a Scheduled Backup Job?
- What Are Scheduled Backup Options?
- How to Schedule a Backup Job
- Best Practices for Backup

Introduction

In addition to backing up files and folders, the responsibility of a systems administrator includes scheduling backups. Using your organization's backup plan, schedule your backups so that they contain the most complete and up-to-date set of files by using the least time-consuming method.

Lesson objectives

After completing this lesson, you will be able to:

- Explain a scheduled backup job.
- Describe backup schedule options.
- Schedule a backup job by using Backup.

What Is a Scheduled Backup Job?

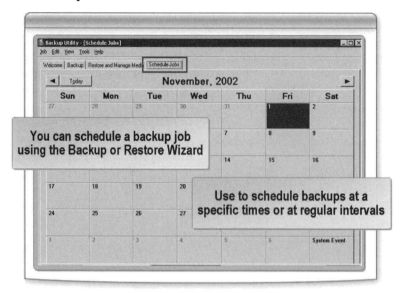

Introduction

To keep backup files up-to-date without having to remember to back them up, you can schedule backup jobs. When you schedule a backup, you can always be sure that the backup copy is available for restoring the data if the original data is lost. You can set up a schedule when you create a backup job or you can create a schedule for an existing backup job.

Two ways to schedule a backup job

Try to schedule a backup job to occur at regular intervals or during periods of relative inactivity on a network.

You can schedule a backup job two ways:

- When you create a new backup job in Backup.

- By using the **Scheduled Jobs** tab in Backup to schedule an existing backup job.

What Are Scheduled Backup Options?

Schedule options	Executes the job:
Once	Once, at a specific time on a specific date
Daily	At the specified time each day
Weekly	At the specified time on each of the specified days of the week
Monthly	At the specified time once a month
At system startup	The next time the system is started
At logon	The next time the job owner logs on
When idle	When the system has been idle for a specified number of minutes

Introduction

Windows Server 2003 provides several options to help you schedule your backup job.

Backup options

The following table describes the options that are available for scheduling backup jobs.

Schedule options	Executes the job:
Once	Once at a specific time on a specific date
Daily	At the specified time each day
Weekly	At the specified time on each of the specified days of the week
Monthly	At the specified time once a month
At system startup	The next time the system is started
At logon	The next time the job owner logs on
When idle	When the system has been idle for a specified number of minutes

How to Schedule a Backup Job

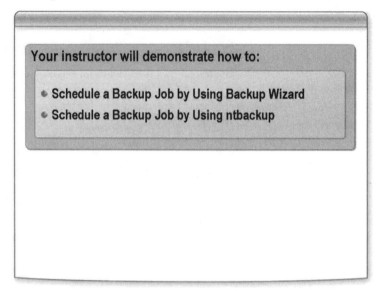

Your instructor will demonstrate how to:

• Schedule a Backup Job by Using Backup Wizard

• Schedule a Backup Job by Using ntbackup

Introduction

You can schedule regular backups by using the Backup or Restore Wizard to keep your archived data up-to-date. You must be logged on as an administrator or a backup operator to schedule a backup job.

Procedure for scheduling a backup job using Backup or Restore Wizard

To schedule a backup job by using the Backup or Restore Wizard:

1. Open Backup, and then on the **Welcome** page of the Backup or Restore Wizard, click the **Advanced Mode** link.

2. In the **Backup Utility** dialog box, on the **Backup** tab, on the **Job** menu, click **New**.

3. Under **Click to select the check box for any drive, folder or file that you want to back up**, click the box next to each file or folder that you want to back up.

4. In the **Backup** destination box, do one of the following:

   a. Select **File** if you want to back up files and folders to a file.

   b. Select a tape device.

5. To select backup options, on the **Tools** menu, click **Options**, and then select the options that you want to use, such as backup type and log file type.

6. On the **Job** menu, click **Save Selections** to save your selections as a backup job file.

7. Click **Start Backup**, make any changes you want in the **Backup Job** Information dialog box, and then click **Schedule**.

8. In the **Set Account Information** dialog box, enter the user name and password that you want the scheduled backup to run under.

9. In the **Scheduled Job Options** dialog box, in the **Job name** box, type a name for scheduled backup job, and then, on the **Schedule data** tab, click **Properties** to set the date, time, and frequency parameters for the scheduled backup.

Procedure for scheduling a backup job by using ntbackup

To schedule a backup by using **ntbackup**:

1. Open Notepad.

2. Type the following command:

   ntbackup backup "C:" /j "Command line backup 1"/f "d:\full.bkf"

3. Save the file as **backup.bat**.

4. Close Notepad.

5. Open a command prompt, and then type the following command:

   at 18:00 /every:M,T,W,TH,F backup.bat

   This command causes drive C to be backed up to D:\full.bkf on the server at 6:00 P.M. every Monday through Friday.

Practice: Scheduling a Backup Job

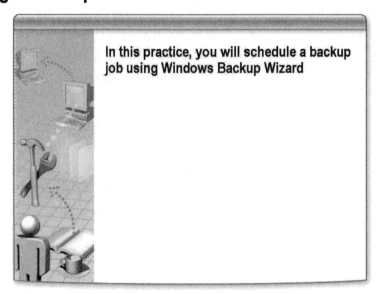

In this practice, you will schedule a backup job using Windows Backup Wizard

Objective

In this practice, you will schedule a backup job by using the Backup or Restore Wizard.

Scenario

You are the systems administrator for an organizational unit on a large network. Your manager wants you to schedule a backup of the C:\MOC folder every night at 11:30 P.M. You want to perform a test run during the day so that you can familiarize yourself with scheduling backups.

Practice

▶ **Schedule a backup job by using the Backup Wizard**

1. Log on to the domain as Administrator with a password of **P@ssw0rd**.

2. Start the Backup utility.

3. Click **Advanced Mode**, and then click **Backup Wizard**.

4. Use the following table to select the appropriate responses.

On the Backup Wizard page	Select
What to Back Up	**Back up selected files, drives, or network data**
Items to Back Up	Expand **My Computer**, expand **Local Disk (C:)**, and then select **MOC**
Backup Type, Destination, and Name	**Browse**
Save As	**Save in:** New Volume (D:)
	File name: MOC3.bkf
Completing the Backup Wizard	Click **Advanced**
Type of Backup	**Normal**
How to Back Up	**Verify data after backup**
Backup Options	**Replace the existing backups**
When to back up	When do you want to run the back up? **Later**
	Job name: **MOC3**
	Click **Set Schedule**
Schedule	Set the start time to begin 5 minutes from now
Set account information	Run as: nwtraders\administrator
	Password: **P@ssw0rd**
	Confirm password: **P@ssw0rd**
Completing the Backup Wizard	**Finish**

5. Use Microsoft Windows Explorer to verify that D:\MOC3.bkf is created.

6. Close all windows and log off.

Best Practices for Backup

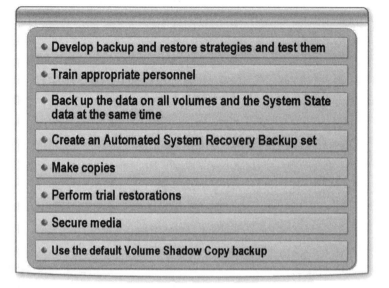

- ● Develop backup and restore strategies and test them
- ● Train appropriate personnel
- ● Back up the data on all volumes and the System State data at the same time
- ● Create an Automated System Recovery Backup set
- ● Make copies
- ● Perform trial restorations
- ● Secure media
- ● Use the default Volume Shadow Copy backup

Introduction

You can protect your organization from data loss by using a set of best practices when you develop your backup plan.

Best practices

Apply the following best practices when you develop your backup plan:

- Develop backup strategies and test them.

   A good plan ensures that you can quickly recover your data if it is lost.

- Train appropriate personnel.

   On minimum-security and medium-security networks, assign backup rights to one user, by using Group Policy, and assign restore rights to a different user. Train personnel with restore rights to perform all of the restore tasks if the administrator is unavailable.

   On a high-security network, only administrators should restore files.

- Back up the data on all volumes and the System State data at the same time. This action allows you to be prepared in the unlikely event of a disk failure.

- Create an Automated System Recovery backup set.

   Always create an Automated System Restore (ASR) backup set when the operating system changes, for example, whenever you install new hardware and drivers or apply a service pack. An ASR backup set can help you to recover from a server failure. ASR protects only the System State files; you must back up data volumes separately.

- Create a backup log.

   Always create a backup log for each backup, and then print the logs for reference. Keep a book of logs to help you locate specific files. The backup log is helpful when you restore data; you can print it or read it from any text editor. Also, if the media containing the backup set catalog is corrupted, the printed log can help you locate a file.

- Make copies.

  Keep at least three copies of the media. Keep at least one copy off-site in a properly controlled environment.

- Perform trial restorations.

  Perform a trial restoration periodically to verify that your files are properly backed up. A trial restoration can uncover hardware or media corruption problems that do not show up when you verify software.

- Secure media.

  Secure the media. It is possible for someone to access the data from a stolen medium by restoring the data to another server for which they are an administrator.

- Use the default Volume Shadow Copy backup.

  Do not disable the default Volume Shadow Copy backup method. If you disable this method, open files that are being used by the system during the backup process will be skipped during the backup.

Lesson: Restoring Data

- What Is Restoring Data?
- How to Restore Files or Folders by Using Backup
- How to Recover from a Server Failure by Using ASR
- How to Restore System State Data
- Checklist for Restoring Data

Introduction

The second part of the disaster recovery process involves restoring the data that you backed up during the first part of the process.

Lesson objectives

After completing this lesson, you will be able to:

- Explain how to restore data.
- Restore System State data.
- Restore files and folders by using Backup.
- Restore data by using ASR.
- Explain guidelines for restoring data.

What Is Restoring Data?

* **Backup Restore feature**
  * Restore files and folders
  * Restore FAT or NTFS files
  * Restore the System State data

* **ASR Restore**
  * Reads the disk configurations from the floppy disk
  * Restores the entire disk signatures, volumes and partitions on the disks required to boot up at a minimum
  * Installs a simple installation of Windows
  * Starts to restore from backup

Restore Data

Introduction

When you use Backup to create a duplicate copy of the data on your hard disk and then archive the data on another storage device, such as a hard disk or a tape, you can use the Restore feature in Backup to easily restore the data.

Restore files and folders

Using Backup, you can restore the archived files and folders to your hard disk or any other disk that you can access.

Back up and restore data on FAT or NTFS

You can use Backup to back up and restore data on either FAT (file allocation table) or NTFS file system volumes. However, if you backed up data from an NTFS volume that is used in Windows Server 2003, it is recommended that you restore the data to an NTFS volume used in Windows Server 2003. If you do not, you may lose data and some file and folder features, such as permissions, Encrypting File System (EFS) settings, disk quota information, mounted drive information, and Remote Storage information.

Restore System State data

You can use Backup to restore the System State data. If the System State data was backed up on a computer and that computer system fails, you can rebuild the computer with the original Windows Server 2003 compact disc and the System State data.

ASR Restore

You can access the restore part of ASR by pressing F2 when prompted in the text mode portion of Windows setup. ASR reads the disk configurations from the floppy disk and restores the entire disk signatures, volumes, and partitions on the disks that are required to start the computer. ASR then installs a simple installation of Windows and automatically starts to restore from backup by using the ASR backup set that you created by using the ASR wizard.

How to Restore Files or Folders by Using Backup

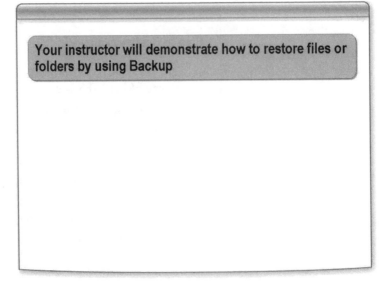

Your instructor will demonstrate how to restore files or folders by using Backup

Introduction

In Backup, when you click the **Restore and Manage Media** tab, the tapes, files, and backup sets from which you can restore data are displayed in a tree view. You can restore complete sets of folders and files or individual files and folders.

Procedure

To restore files or folders by using Backup:

1. Open Backup, and then on the **Welcome** page of the Backup or Restore Wizard, click the **Advanced Mode** link.

2. In the Backup Utility–[Untitled] window, click the **Restore and Manage Media** tab.

3. In the left pane, expand **File**, expand the desired media item, and then select the check box for the items to be restored.

4. In the **Restore files to** box, do one of the following:

   a. Click **Original location** if you want the backed up files and folders to be restored to the folder or folders they were in when they were backed up.

   b. Click **Alternate location** if you want the backed up files and folders to be restored to a folder that you designate. This option preserves the folder structure of the backed up data; all folders and subfolders appear in the alternate folder that you designate.

   c. Click **Single folder** if you want the backed up files and folders to be restored to a folder that you designate. This option does not preserve the folder structure of the backed up data; the files appear only in the folder that you designate.

5. If you selected **Alternate location** or **Single folder**, type a path for the folder under **Alternate location**, or click **Browse** to find folder.

6. On the **Tools** menu, click **Options**, and then on the **Restore** tab, do one of the following:

   - Click **Do not replace the file on my computer**.

   - Click **Replace the file on disk only if the file on disk is older**.

   - Click **Always replace the file on my computer**.

7. Click **OK** to accept the restore options that you have set.

How to Recover from a Server Failure by Using ASR

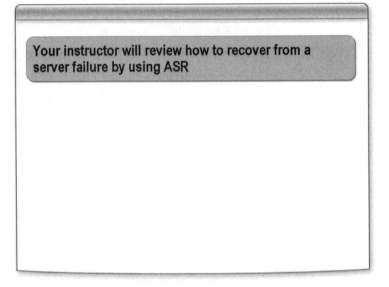

Your instructor will review how to recover from a server failure by using ASR

Introduction

During backup, ASR creates a floppy disk that you can use to restore disk signatures, volumes, and partitions on the disks that are required to start the computer. By using the ASR floppy disk, you can install a simple installation of Windows. Backup automatically begins to restore your operating system by using the ASR wizard after the simple Windows installation is complete.

Remember that ASR does not include data files. After you restore your operating system, you can restore data files by using the backup files that you created during your scheduled backups.

Procedure

To recover from a server failure by using ASR:

1. Make sure the following items are available before you begin the recovery procedure:

   • Previously created ASR floppy disk.

   • Previously created backup media.

   • Original installation compact disc for the operating system.

   • If you have a mass storage controller and an updated driver (different from the driver on the Setup compact disc) is available from the manufacturer, before you begin this procedure, obtain the updated driver on a floppy disk.

2. Insert the original installation compact disc for the operating system into your CD-ROM drive.

3. Restart your computer. If prompted to press a key to start the computer from the compact disc, press the appropriate key.

4. If you have a separate driver file as described in step 1, use the driver as part of Setup by pressing F6 when prompted.

5. At the beginning of the text-only mode section of Setup, press F2 when prompted.

    You are prompted to insert the ASR floppy disk that you previously created.

6. Follow the directions on the screen.

7. If you have a separate driver file as described in step 1, press F6 a second time when prompted after the system restarts.

8. Follow the directions on the screen.

How to Restore System State Data

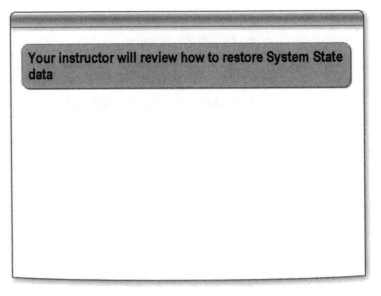

Your instructor will review how to restore System State data

Introduction

When you restore System State data, the current version of your System State data is replaced with your restored version. Also, you cannot choose where to restore the System State data. Backup determines the appropriate location for restoring the System State data based on the location of your current systemroot directory.

Procedure

To restore System State data by using Backup:

1. Open Backup, and then on the **Welcome** page of the Backup or Restore Wizard, click the **Advanced Mode** link.

2. On the **Restore and Manage Media** tab, expand the desired media item, and then click the box next to **System State**.

Practice: Restoring Data

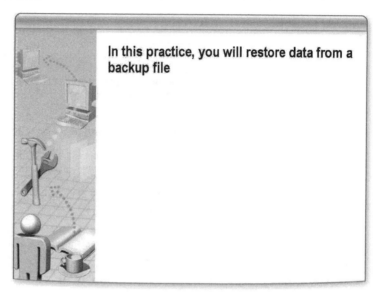

In this practice, you will restore data from a backup file

Objective

In this practice, you will restore data from a backup file.

Scenario

You are the systems administrator for an organizational unit on a large network. You receive an emergency call from a manager, because one of his users accidentally deleted most of the files in a database folder named VSS. You must restore the deleted files as soon as possible.

Practice

▶ **Restore the data from the backup file**

1. Log on to the domain as *Computer*User with a password of **P@ssw0rd**.

2. Open Windows Explorer, and then delete the C:\MOC folder.

3. Start Backup by using **Run as**, and then click **Advanced Mode**.

4. On the **Restore and Manage Media** tab, expand **File**, expand **MOC.bkf**, select the **C:** check box, and then click **Start Restore**.

5. When "Restore is complete" appears in the **Restore Progress** dialog box, click **Close**, and then close the Backup utility.

6. In Windows Explorer, press F5 to refresh the screen, and then verify that the MOC folder appears under **Local Disk (C:)**.

7. Close all windows and log off.

Checklist for Restoring Data

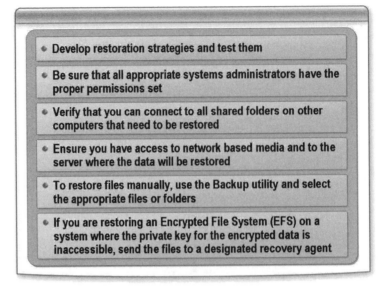

Introduction

After you back up your files to the storage media and follow the best practices for developing a backup plan, you must create a restoration plan. It is recommended that you use the following checklist when you create your organization's restoration plan.

Checklist for restoring data

Apply the following best practices when you create a restoration plan:

- Develop restoration strategies and test them.

  Remember to keep a record of your backup and restoration plans to refer to in the event of data loss.

- Be sure that all appropriate systems administrators have the proper permissions set.

- Verify that you can connect to all shared folders on other computers that must be restored.

  You can use the default user rights of the Backup Operators group to restore your organization's data and system files, or you can segregate backup and restore permissions by individuals.

- Test all shared folders on all servers for which you are responsible to make sure that you can restore data contained in them.

- Ensure that you have access to network-based media and to the server where the data will be restored.

  As part of your restoration plan, be sure that you test your access to the storage media where you backed up your files.

- To restore files manually, use the Backup utility and select the appropriate files or folders.

  Because you may need to restore only certain files, test the procedure that you will use to select and restore only those files, using the Backup utility.

- If you are restoring EFS files on a system where the private key for the encrypted data is inaccessible, send the files to a designated recovery agent.

  For files that are encrypted for security and are therefore inaccessible, perform a test by sending the files to a designated recovery agent. Ensure that you can copy and open all files.

Lesson: Configuring Shadow Copies

- What Are Shadow Copies?
- How to Configure Shadow Copies on the Server
- Previous Versions Client Software for Shadow Copies
- How to View Previous Versions of Client Software
- Shadow Copy Scheduling
- How to Schedule Shadow Copies
- What Is Restoring Shadow Copies?
- How to Restore a Previous Version
- Best Practices for Using Shadow Copies

Introduction

In Windows Server 2003, you can use Shadow Copies of Shared Folders as a data recovery tool. You can use shadow copies to view and restore shared files and folders as they existed at previous points in time.

Lesson objectives

After completing this lesson, you will be able to:

- Explain shadow copies.
- Configure a shadow copy.
- Describe the Previous Versions client software for shadow copies.
- View previous versions of client software.
- Explain scheduling shadow copies.
- Create a shadow copy schedule.
- Explain restoring shadow copies.
- Restore a previous version.
- Explain best practices for using shadow copies.

What Are Shadow Copies?

- **Views the read-only contents of network folders as they existed at various points of time**
- **Use shadow copies to:**
  - Recover files that were accidentally deleted
  - Recover files that were accidentally overwritten
  - Allow version-checking while working on documents
- **Is enabled on a per volume basis, not on specific shares**
- **Is not a replacement for regular backups**
- **When storage limits are reached, the oldest shadow copy is deleted and cannot be retrieved**
- **To change the storage volume, delete the shadow copies first**

Definition

A shadow copy is a feature of the Windows Server 2003 family that provides point-in-time, read-only copies of files on network shares. With Shadow Copies of Shared Folders, you can view the contents of network folders as they existed at various points in time. To view Shadow Copies of Shared Folders, you must install the client software.

Shadow copy scenarios

You can use shadow copies in the following three scenarios:

- Recover files that were accidentally deleted.

  This scenario is the network equivalent of a short-term local backup and restore. If a user accidentally deletes a file, the user can open a previous version of the file and copy it to a safe location.

- Recover files that were accidentally overwritten.

  Shadow Copies of Shared Folders can be very useful in environments where new files are commonly created by opening an existing file, making modifications, and then saving the file with a new name. For example, you might open a financial modeling spreadsheet, make modifications based upon new assumptions, and then save the spreadsheet with a new name to create a new spreadsheet. The problem arises when you forget to save the file by using a new name, thereby erasing the original work. You can use Shadow Copies of Shared Folders to recover the previous version of the file.

- Allow version-checking while working on documents.

  You can use Shadow Copies of Shared Folders during the normal work cycle to check the differences between two versions of a file. For example, you might want to know "What did this paragraph say this morning before I started to rewrite it?"

Shadow copy characteristics

The following characteristics apply to shadow copies:

- Configuring shadow copies is not a replacement for creating regular backups.

- Shadow copies are read-only. You cannot edit the contents of a shadow copy.

- Shadow copies are enabled on a per volume basis. You cannot enable shadow copies on specific shared resources.

- After shadow copies are enabled on a volume, shadow copies are enabled for all shared folders on that volume.

Shadow copies storage

The minimum amount of storage space for shadow copies is 100 megabytes (MB). The default maximum storage size is 10 percent of the source volume or the volume being copied, but you can change the maximum size at any time. When the storage limit is reached, the oldest versions of the shadow copies are deleted and cannot be restored.

Allocate storage space

When determining the amount of space to allocate for storing shadow copies, you must consider both the number and size of files that are being copied, as well as the number of times that the shadow copies are to be copied to the disk.

Store shadow copies on a different volume

You can also store shadow copies on a different storage volume. However, changing the storage volume deletes the shadow copies. To avoid this problem, verify that the storage volume that you initially select is large enough to handle your growing business needs.

Note For more information about shadow copies, go to the Microsoft Technet Services Web site at http://www.microsoft.com/windowsserver2003/docs /VolumeShadowCopyService.swf.

How to Configure Shadow Copies on the Server

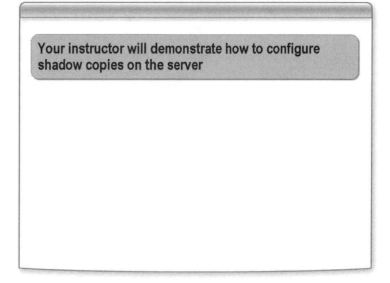

Your instructor will demonstrate how to configure
shadow copies on the server

Introduction

By default, shadow copies are disabled. You can enable shadow copies on the server by completing the following steps, but shadow copies is not enabled on the client computer until the client software for shadow copies is installed on the client computer.

Before you deploy Shadow Copies of Shared Folders, it is recommended that you create a plan that specifies the location and storage limits of the shadow copies. The default storage size is 10 percent of the source volume.

Procedure

To configure shadow copies:

1. In Computer Management (Local), in the console tree, right-click **Shared Folders**, point to **All Tasks**, and then click **Configure Shadow Copies**.

2. Select the volume where you want to enable Shadow Copies of Shared Folders, click **Enable**, and then click **Yes** when prompted to enable shadow copies.

Previous Versions Client Software for Shadow Copies

---

* **Previous Versions client software for Shadow Copies of Shared Folders is installed on the server**
  * %systemroot%\system32\clients\twclient\x86 directory
  * Place the client software on a shared resource and send an e-mail with instructions on how to download and use
* **Client view of shadow copies**
  * Use if users work with files that are located in shared folders on your network
  * Use to access previous versions of files

Introduction

Before users can use and access shadow copies, they must install the client software for shadow copies. The client software allows users to access previous versions of their files and folders from a shared folder.

Previous versions on client computers

Shadow copies are copies of files that are located on the server and appear as previous versions on the client computers. Shadow copies can be used on both servers and clients to view and locate previous versions of files. Both views are created by the systems administrator.

Locations of shadow copy views

The locations of the shadow copies for both views are as follows:

- The server portion of Shadow Copies of Shared Folders is located on the **Shadow Copies** tab of the **Local Disk Properties** dialog box.

- The client view of the shadow copies is referred to as **Previous Versions** and is located in the **Properties** dialog box of the shared folder.

Client software for shadow copies

The client software for shadow copies is installed on the server in the %systemroot%\system32\clients\twclient\x86 directory. You can distribute the client software in a variety of ways; consider the various options before deployment. Windows Server 2003 provides several tools, such as Group Policy, that can make deploying and maintaining the client software easier.

Alert users

It is recommended that you place the client software on a shared resource and then send an e-mail message to users that describes the function of the software and how to install it.

For example, you may want to inform users that:

- A new feature, Previous Versions, is enabled on the following file server: *server\sharedresource*.

- Files are scheduled to be copied at 7:00 A.M. and noon, Monday through Friday. Remember that these are copies of the files as they exist at these times and do not reflect any changes that are made to the files after these times.

- Saving your work frequently is still the best way to ensure that your work is not lost.

- To install the software, go to *server\sharedresource* and double-click **twclient.msi**.

Helps recover files for users

Accessing previous versions of files is useful because you can:

- Recover files that were accidentally deleted. If you accidentally delete a file, you can open a previous version and copy it to a safe location.

- Recover files that were accidentally overwritten. If you accidentally overwrite a file, you can recover a previous version of the file.

- Compare versions of file while working. You can use previous versions when you want to check what has changed between two versions of a file.

Other distribution methods

You can use Group Policy to install the client software for shadow copies.

Note　For more information about installing software using Group Policy, see Course 2279, *Planning, Implementing, and Maintaining a Microsoft Windows Server 2003 Active Directory Infrastructure*.

How to View Previous Versions of Client Software

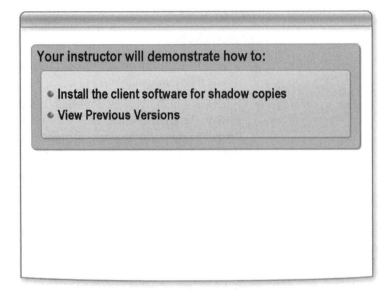

Your instructor will demonstrate how to:

- Install the client software for shadow copies
- View Previous Versions

Introduction

Before a user can view a previous version of a file or folder, you must install the client software for shadow copies on the user's computer. Use the following procedures to install the client software and view the previous versions.

Procedure for installing Previous Versions client software

To install client software for shadow copies on a client computer:

1. On the command line, type **\windows\system32\clients\twclient\x86\twcli32.msi** and then press ENTER.

2. In the Previous Versions Client Setup Wizard, click **Finish**.

Procedure for viewing previous versions

To view the previous version of a file or folder:

1. On the **Start** menu, click **Run**.

2. In the **Run** dialog box, type *Computername***Share** (where *Computername* is the name of the server hosting shadow copies).

3. Right-click any file or folder, and then click **Properties**.

4. Click the **Previous Versions** tab.

Shadow Copy Scheduling

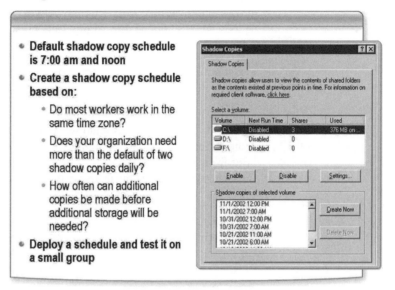

- **Default shadow copy schedule is 7:00 am and noon**
- **Create a shadow copy schedule based on:**
  - Do most workers work in the same time zone?
  - Does your organization need more than the default of two shadow copies daily?
  - How often can additional copies be made before additional storage will be needed?
- **Deploy a schedule and test it on a small group**

Introduction

When you enable Shadow Copies of Shared Folders, a default schedule is also created. Although this schedule may work for your organization, evaluate the work habits of your users before you use the default schedule.

Create a shadow copy schedule

When you create a shadow copy schedule, consider the location of your users. The default schedule is 7:00 A.M. and noon, daily. If users are located across multiple time zones, you probably need to create more than the default of two shadow copies per day.

If you increase the number of scheduled shadow copies, consider how often copies can be added without requiring additional storage. Before deploying Shadow Copies of Shared Folders, it is recommended that you create a plan that specifies where to store the shadow copies and what the storage limits are. You can store up to 64 shadow copies per volume. When this limit is reached, the oldest shadow copy is deleted and cannot be retrieved.

Deploy a small test group

You may want to create an initial schedule and deploy it for a small group to test whether your schedule creates enough shadow copies while staying within your storage limits. Also, consider asking your users about their work habits and when they think that a shadow copy would be beneficial. For example, knowing that they make most of their errors in the late afternoon or first thing in the morning can help you determine the best schedule for your specific users.

Scenario

You have enabled Shadow Copies for Shared Folders on all file servers and are using the default schedule. Your organization has a flexible schedule that allows employees to work any time between 8:00 A.M. and 6:00 P.M., as long as they work 8 hours a day. Many users create files between noon and 6:00 P.M.

Question: Are these files protected by shadow copies if users save them every hour?

Answer: The files of users who modify and save their files between noon and 6:00 P.M. are not saved by shadow copies until 7:00 A.M. the next day. To protect their files, set up a schedule to create shadow copies of their files every hour from 8:00 A.M. to 6:00 P.M. every weekday. Depending on storage limits, this schedule provides the users with up to five days of shadow copies.

How to Schedule Shadow Copies

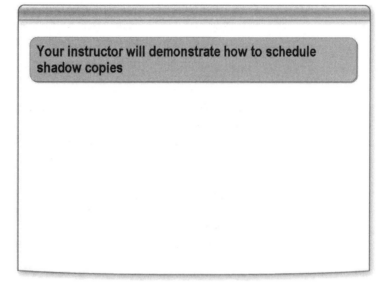

Your instructor will demonstrate how to schedule shadow copies

Introduction

You can create a shadow copy schedule to automatically provide copies of files as they appear at various points of time. You can use shadow copies as another option for providing a backup of files that you can to recover from data loss.

Procedure

To create a shadow copy schedule:

1. In Computer Management, in the console tree, right-click **Shared Folders**, point to **All Tasks**, and then click **Configure Shadow Copies**.

2. Under **Select a volume**, click the volume for which you want to create a schedule, and then click **Settings**.

3. In the **Settings** dialog box, click **Schedule**, and then change the settings as appropriate.

What Is Restoring Shadow Copies?

- Shadow copies are restored using previous versions of files and folders

If...	Then
No previous versions are listed	The file has not changed since the oldest copy was made
Restoring a previous version of a folder	Shadow copies deletes the current version
Restoring a file	File permissions are not changed
The Previous Versions tab does not appear in Properties	Shadow copies may not be enabled
Copying a file	File permissions are set to default

Introduction

After you create a shadow copy, you can use it to restore shared files and folders to a previous version.

Note You can only restore a shadow copy from a client.

Restored files and folders using previous versions

If no previous versions are listed on the Previous Versions tab, the file has not changed since the oldest copy was made.

When you restore a previous version of a folder, files in the current folder that were not in the previous version of the folder are overwritten. If you do not want to delete the current version, use **Copy** to copy the previous version to a different location.

Example of a previous version folder

For example, the current version of a folder contains files A, B, and C. The previous version of the folder contained only files A and B. After you restore the previous version, the folder contains the previous version of file A, the previous version of file B, and the current version of file C.

File permissions are not changed

When you restore a file, the file permissions are not changed. Permissions remain the same as they were before you restored the file. When you copy a previous version of a file, the permissions are set to the default permissions for the directory where the copy of the file is placed.

Restoring overwrites the current version

Restoring a previous version overwrites the current version. If you restore a previous version of a folder, the folder is restored to its state at the date and time that you selected. Any changes that you made to files in the folder before that time are lost.

How to Restore a Previous Version

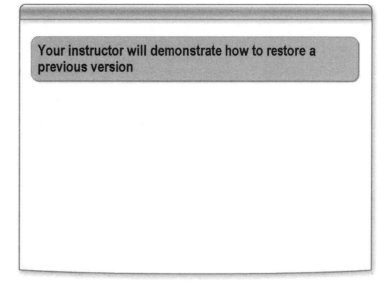

Your instructor will demonstrate how to restore a previous version

Introduction

You can restore data from previous versions of files and folders, assuming that the client software is installed on a computer running Windows XP (client) or Windows Server 2003, and you configured the volumes for which you want to create shadow copies.

Procedure

To restore shadow copies:

1. In Windows Explorer, locate the file or folder that you want to restore, right-click the icon, and then click **Properties**.

2. In the **Properties** dialog box, on the **Previous Versions** tab, select the version that you want to restore, and then click **Restore**.

Practice: Configuring Shadow Copies

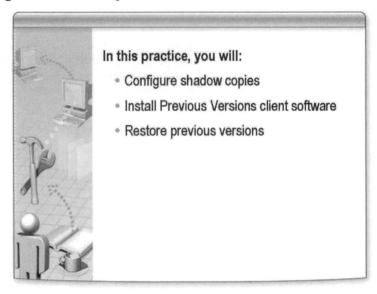

Objective

In this practice, you will:

- Configure shadow copies
- Install Previous Versions client software
- Restore previous versions

Scenario

You are the systems administrator for an organizational unit on a large network. Users who work with shared folders on the department server frequently complain about file corruption caused by other users.

For example, a user who is working on a Microsoft PowerPoint® presentation asks a colleague to review the presentation. After the colleague reviews the presentation, the user reopens the file and finds that some of the slides are corrupted or missing. The IT department cannot restore the file, so the user must re-create the missing slides. To provide users a way to recover previous versions of their work, you decide to configure a shadow copy of the shared folder to solve the problem.

Practice: Configuring shadow copies

▶ **Configure shadow copies on drive C**

1. Log on to the domain as *Computer*User with a password of **P@ssw0rd**.

2. In the **Run** dialog box, use the **runas** command to start Computer Management with administrator privileges by typing:

   runas /user:nwtraders\administrator "mmc %windir%\system32\compmgmt.msc"

3. Expand **Computer Management**, expand **System Tools**, right-click **Shared Folders**, point to **All Tasks**, and then click **Configure Shadow Copies**.

4. Enable shadow copies for the C:\ volume.

5. Click **Settings**, click **Schedule**, click **Advanced**, schedule shadow copies to made every minute of every day, and then save your changes.

6. In Computer Management, expand **Shared Folders**, right-click **Shares**, and then click **New Share**.

7. Share the C:\MOC\2275\Practices\Mod07 folder as **Mod07**.

8. In Computer Management, click **Shares**, right-click **Mod07**, and then click **Properties**.

9. Allow *Computer***User** to have full control on the Mod07 folder for both share permissions and NTFS permissions.

Practice: Installing Previous Versions client software

▶ **Install Previous Versions client software**

1. Using **runas**, start a command prompt with administrator privileges.

2. Install the Previous Versions client software, located at windows\system32\clients\twclient\x86\twcli32.msi.

Practice: Restoring a previous version

▶ **Restore a previous version**

1. Open the **Run** dialog box.

2. Open Mod07 by using the Universal Naming Convention (UNC) for your computer, by typing *Computer***Mod07** and then pressing ENTER.

3. Open the Test folder, and then open Shadow.txt.

4. On the first line, replace "Best practices" with "changed text".

5. Save your work, and then close Shadow.txt.

6. Open the **Properties** dialog box for Shadow.txt.

7. On the **Previous Versions** tab, restore the previous version of the file and then close the dialog box.

8. Open Shadow.txt and verify that "Best practices" appears in the first line of the restored version of the file.

9. Close all windows and log off.

Best Practices for Using Shadow Copies

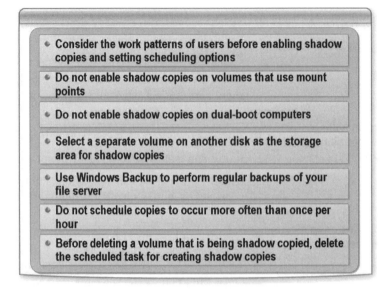

- Consider the work patterns of users before enabling shadow copies and setting scheduling options
- Do not enable shadow copies on volumes that use mount points
- Do not enable shadow copies on dual-boot computers
- Select a separate volume on another disk as the storage area for shadow copies
- Use Windows Backup to perform regular backups of your file server
- Do not schedule copies to occur more often than once per hour
- Before deleting a volume that is being shadow copied, delete the scheduled task for creating shadow copies

Introduction

Shadow copies can help you restore lost or corrupted data files. It is still a good idea, however, to maintain your regular backup file schedules.

Best practices

Consider the following best practices when you configure shadow copies and create a shadow copy schedule:

- Adjust the shadow copy schedule to fit the work patterns of your users.

- Do not enable shadow copies on volumes that use mounted drives.

  The mounted drives are not included when shadow copies are made. Enable shadow copies only on volumes without mount points or when you do not want to make shadow copies of the shares on the mounted volume.

- Do not enable shadow copies on computers with a dual-boot configuration.

  If you have enabled a dual-boot configuration on a computer running an earlier operating systems (such as Microsoft Windows NT® 4.0) the shadow copies that persist during the reboot may be corrupted and unusable when the computer is started in Windows Server 2003.

- Select a separate volume on another disk as the storage area for shadow copies.

  Using a separate volume on another disk provides better performance and is recommended for heavily used file servers.

- Creating shadow copies does not replace performing regular backups.

  Use Backup in coordination with shadow copies to provide your best restoration scenario.

- Do not schedule copies to occur more often than once per hour. The default schedule is set for 7:00 A.M. and noon. If you decide that you need copies to be made more often, make sure you allot enough storage space and that you do not schedule copies to be made so often that server performance is degraded.

- If you delete the volume but not the shadow copy task, the scheduled task fails and an Event ID: 7001 error is written to the event log. Delete the shadow copy task before deleting the volume to avoid filling the event log with these errors.

Lesson: Recovering from Server Failure

- What Is Safe Mode?
- What Are Safe Mode Options?
- What Is Last Known Good Configuration?
- How to Start a System Using Safe Mode and Last Known Good Configuration
- What Is Recovery Console?
- How to Use the Recovery Console
- What Is a Windows Startup Disk?
- How Startup Files Function
- How to Create a Windows Startup Disk

Introduction

If a server fails, Windows Server 2003 provides several options that you can use to restore the computer. Understanding these options and their functions can help you to restore a server to working condition.

Lesson objectives

After completing this lesson, you will be able to:

- Explain safe mode and when to use it.
- Describe safe mode options.
- Explain Last Known Good Configuration and when to use it.
- Start a computer by using safe mode and Last Known Good Configuration.
- Explain the Recovery Console and when to use it.
- Use the Recovery Console.
- Describe the Windows startup disk.
- Describe how startup files function.
- Create a Windows startup disk.

What Is Safe Mode?

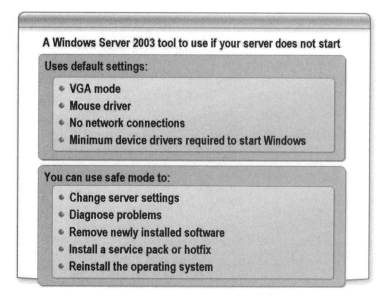

A Windows Server 2003 tool to use if your server does not start

Uses default settings:
- VGA mode
- Mouse driver
- No network connections
- Minimum device drivers required to start Windows

You can use safe mode to:
- Change server settings
- Diagnose problems
- Remove newly installed software
- Install a service pack or hotfix
- Reinstall the operating system

Definition

If your computer does not start, you may be able to start it in safe mode. In safe mode, Windows uses default settings, video graphics adapter (VGA) mode, the mouse driver, no network connections, and the minimum device drivers that are required to start Windows.

There are three safe mode options. You must log on in all modes, either by using the domain administrator account or by using the local Security Accounts Manager administrator account, depending on which safe mode option you select. Network connections are available in safe mode depending on the option that you use.

Start a computer using Safe Mode

If your computer does not start after you install new software, new hardware, or a new driver, you may be able to start it with minimal services in safe mode and then change your computer settings, remove the newly installed software, or remove new hardware that is causing the problem. You can reinstall a service pack or the entire operating system, if necessary.

Use Safe Mode to diagnose problems

Safe mode helps you diagnose problems. If a symptom does not reappear when you start in safe mode, you can eliminate the default settings and minimum device drivers as possible causes. If a newly added device or a changed driver is causing problems, you can use safe mode to remove the device or reverse a change.

What Are Safe Mode Options?

Option	Description	Use
Safe Mode	Starts with only basic files and drivers	When you suspect a recently installed application is causing the problem
Safe Mode with Networking	Starts with only basic files and drivers, plus network connections	When you need to verify that the networking subsystem is operational
Safe Mode with Command Prompt	Starts with only basic files and drivers. After you log on, the command prompt is displayed instead of the Windows desktop, Start menu, and Taskbar	When you need to use command-line troubleshooting tools

Introduction

Windows Server 2003 includes advanced startup options that you can use when you troubleshoot and repair startup problems and when you connect the computer to a debugger. These startup options enhance your ability to diagnose and resolve driver incompatibility and startup problems.

Note   To display the advanced startup options, press F8 during the operating system selections phase of the startup process in Windows Server 2003.

Advanced startup options

The following table describes the Windows Server 2003 advanced startup options.

Option	Description
Safe Mode	Loads only the basic devices and drivers that are required to start the computer, including the mouse, keyboard, mass storage devices, base video, and the standard, default set of system services. This option also creates a log file.
Safe Mode with Networking	Loads only the basic devices and drivers that are required to start the computer and enable networking. This option also creates a log file.
Safe Mode with Command Prompt	Same as safe mode but starts a command prompt instead of the graphical user interface. This option also creates a log file.

Safe Mode examples

The following examples describe when to use the Safe Mode options.

- *Safe Mode*. Use this mode when you suspect that a recently installed application is causing the problem.

- *Safe Mode with Networking*. Use this mode when you must verify that the networking subsystem is operational and when you need access to the network to obtain the files.

- *Safe Mode with Command Prompt*. Use this mode when you must use command-line troubleshooting tools. You can use this mode when the other modes fail to start the computer.

What Is Last Known Good Configuration?

- Starts the computer using the registry information and drivers that Windows saved at the last successful logon

- Removes any device drivers or systems settings changed since since the last successful logon

- Provides a way to recover from problems such as a newly configured driver that may be incorrect for your hardware

- Does not solve problems caused by corrupted or missing drivers or files

- Use only in cases of incorrect configuration

Definition

The Last Known Good Configuration startup option uses the registry information and drivers that Windows saved at the last successful logon. When you use this option to start a server, any changes made to driver settings or other system settings since the last successful logon are lost. Use this option only in cases of incorrect configuration.

Recover from newly added incorrect drivers

You can use the Last Known Good Configuration startup option to recover from a problem by reversing driver and registry changes that you made since you last started Windows Server 2003. Windows Server 2003 does not update Last Known Good Configuration information in the registry until the operating system successfully restarts in normal mode and a user logs on and is authenticated.

Restores information for the registry

Using Last Known Good Configuration restores information for the registry subkey HKEY_LOCAL_MACHINE\SYSTEM\CurrentControlSet. Also, if you updated any device drivers, using Last Known Good Configuration restores the previous drivers.

Resolves startup or stability problems

Using Last Known Good Configuration can help you resolve startup or stability problems. For example, if a Stop error occurs immediately after you install a new application or device driver, you can restart the computer and use Last Known Good Configuration to recover from the problem.

Using Last Known Good Configuration can help you recover from problems such as a newly added driver that may be incorrect for your hardware. It does not solve problems that are caused by corrupted or missing drivers or files.

Use with Safe Mode

When you suspect that a change you made to your computer is causing a problem, it is recommended that you use Last Known Good Configuration before you try other options, such as safe mode. However, even if you decide to use safe mode first, logging on to the computer in safe mode does not update the Last Known Good Configuration. Therefore, using Last Known Good Configuration remains an option if you cannot resolve your problem by using safe mode.

How to Start a System Using Safe Mode and Last Known Good Configuration

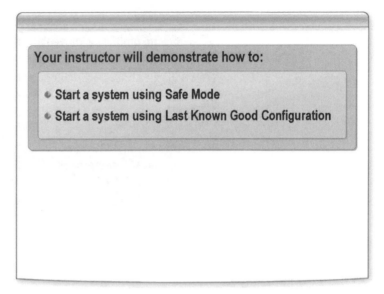

Your instructor will demonstrate how to:

- Start a system using Safe Mode
- Start a system using Last Known Good Configuration

Objective

Safe Mode and Last Known Good Configuration options load a minimal set of drivers. You can use these options to start Windows so that you can modify the registry or load or remove drivers.

Procedure for starting a system using Safe Mode

To start your system by using Safe Mode:

1. Restart your computer.

2. When you see the message "Please select the operating system to start," press F8.

3. Use the arrow keys to highlight the appropriate Safe Mode option, and then press ENTER.

4. Use the arrow keys to highlight an operating system, and then press ENTER.

Procedure for starting a system using Last Known Good Configuration

To start your system using Last Known Good Configuration:

1. Restart your computer.

2. When you see the message "Please select the operating system to start," press F8.

3. Use the arrow keys to highlight **Last Known Good Configuration**, and then press ENTER.

4. Use the arrow keys to highlight an operating system, and then press ENTER.

What Is the Recovery Console?

- Starts a command-line console on a system in which a software problem is preventing the system from starting
- Accesses drives on your computer

With Recovery Console, you can:

- Enable or disable device drivers or services
- Copy files from the installation CD for the operating system, or copy files from other removable media
- Create a new boot sector and new master boot record (MBR)

Definition

The Recovery Console in Windows Server 2003 is a command-line console that you can start from the Windows Server 2003 Setup program. The Recovery Console is particularly useful if you must repair a system by copying a file from a disk or compact disc to the hard disk, or if you must reconfigure a service that is preventing a computer from starting properly.

Specify which installation of Windows

When you start the Recovery Console, you must specify the installation of Windows Server 2003 to log on to, even on a server with a single-boot configuration. You then must log on using the local Administrator account.

Minimal version of Windows Server 2003 operating system

The Recovery Console is a minimal version of the Windows Server 2003 operating system that you can use to start Windows Server 2003 when all other startup options fail. By using the minimal set of commands in the Recovery Console, you can repair damaged system components, such as a damaged boot sector, that prevent you from starting the computer any other way.

Use to perform repair tasks

You use the Recovery Console to perform the following repair tasks:

- Enable and disable services that prevent Windows Server 2003 from starting.

- Read and write files on a local drive, including drives that are formatted with the NTFS file system. The Recovery Console recognizes and enforces NTFS permissions.

- Format hard disks.

- Repair a boot sector.

- Copy files and system files from a floppy disk or compact disc.

To use the Recovery Console

When using the Recovery Console, you must log on by using the local built-in Administrator account that resides in the local security database. On a domain controller, this is a minimal database that Windows Server 2003 creates when you install Active Directory. This database contains only the Administrator user account that you use to perform repair tasks on a domain controller when Active Directory is not available, such as when you run the Recovery Console.

> **Note** If you choose not to install the Recovery Console, or if it does not start because the partition on which you installed it is inaccessible, you can start the Recovery Console from the Windows Server 2003 compact disc. Start the computer by using the Windows Server 2003 compact disc or Setup boot disks. When prompted to choose whether to set up Windows Server 2003 or repair an existing installation, select the repair option..

Recovery Console commands

When you run the Recovery Console, you can get help on the available commands by typing **help** at the command prompt and then pressing ENTER.

The following table describes the commands available in the Recovery Console.

Command	Description
attrib	Displays the attributes of the files in the current folder
batch	Executes commands specified in a text file
bootcfg	Repairs boot configuration and recovery
chdir (cd)	Displays the name of the current folder or changes the current folder
chkdsk	Checks a disk and displays a status report
cls	Clears the screen
copy	Copies a single file to another location
delete (del)	Deletes one or more files
dir	Displays a list of files and subfolders in a folder
disable	Disables a system service or a device driver
diskpart	Manages partitions on your hard disks
enable	Starts or enables a system service or a device driver
exit	Exits the Recovery Console and restarts your computer
expand	Expands a compressed file
fixboot	Writes a new partition boot sector onto the system partition
fixmbr	Repairs the master boot record of the partition boot sector
format	Formats a disk
help	Displays a list of the commands that you use in the Recovery Console
listsvc	Lists all available services and drivers on the computer
logon	Logs on to a Windows Server 2003 installation
map	Displays the drive letter mappings
mkdir (Md)	Creates a folder
more	Displays a text file
rmdir (rd)	Deletes a folder
rename (ren)	Renames a single file
systemroot	Sets the current folder to the systemroot folder of the system that you are currently logged on to
type	Displays a text file

How to Use the Recovery Console

> **Your instructor will demonstrate how to:**
>
> - **Install the Recovery Console**
> - **Start and use the Recovery Console from the Windows Server 2003 Setup CD**
> - **Start and use the Recovery Console from the boot loader menu on the server**

Introduction

You should install the Recovery Console before you need to use it so that it is on the hard disk when you do need it. You install the Recovery Console from a Windows Server 2003 compact disc.

Procedure for installing the Recovery Console

To install the Recovery Console:

1. In a command prompt, change to the I386 folder on the Windows Server 2003 compact disc.

2. At the command prompt, type **winnt32 /cmdcons** and then press ENTER.

3. Click **Yes**, and then click **OK**.

Procedure for starting and using the Recovery Console from the Setup compact disc

To start and use the Recovery Console from the Windows Server 2003 Setup compact disc:

1. Insert the Setup compact disc and then restart the computer from the CD-ROM drive.

2. When prompted for the Windows installation, type **1** and then press ENTER.

3. When the text-based part of Setup begins, follow the prompts; select the repair or recover option by pressing R.

4. When prompted, type the Administrator password.

5. At the system prompt, type the appropriate Recovery Console commands.

   For information about commands, type **help** for a list of commands, or type **help** *commandname* for help on a specific command.

6. To exit the Recovery Console and restart the computer, type **exit**

Procedure for starting and using the Recovery Console from the server

To start and use the Recovery Console from the operating system boot menu on the server:

1. Start the computer, on the boot loader menu select **Microsoft Windows Recovery Console**, and then press ENTER.

2. When prompted for the Windows installation, type **1** and then press ENTER.

3. Type the password for the local Administrator account, and then press ENTER.

4. At the command line, type **help** to display all of the available commands. You can use these commands to repair the server.

   For instructions on how to use a specific command, at the command line, type **help** *commandname*.

What Is a Windows Startup Disk?

* **Allows you to access a disk drive with a faulty boot sequence, for example:**
  * Damaged boot sector
  * Damaged master boot record (MBR)
  * Virus infections
  * Missing or damaged Ntldr or Ntdetect.com files
  * Incorrect Ntbootdd.sys driver
  * To boot from the shadow of a broken mirror
* **Windows Startup disk must include**
  * Ntldr
  * Ntdetect.com
  * Boot.ini

Definition

A Windows startup disk allows you to access a disk drive that has a faulty boot sequence. You may also be able to use a Windows startup disk to start the operating system on a computer running Windows Server 2003.

Use a Windows startup disk to work around the following startup problems:

- Damaged boot sector
- Damaged master boot record (MBR)
- Virus infections
- Missing or damaged Ntldr or Ntdetect.com files
- Incorrect Ntbootdd.sys driver

The Windows startup disk must include the Ntldr, Ntdetect.com, and Boot.ini files, and may require ntbootdd.sys, which is the device driver for your hard disk controller renamed to ntbootdd.sys.

Note   The attributes of the Ntldr, Ntdetect.com, and Boot.ini files are typically set to system, hidden, and read-only. You do not have to reset these attributes for the startup disk to work, but you must reset them if you copy these files to the hard disk.

Using the Windows startup disk

If you must replace a corrupted boot file on drive C, start the Recovery Console. At the Recovery Console command prompt, insert the Windows startup disk and copy the appropriate boot file to the root directory on drive C.

How Startup Files Function

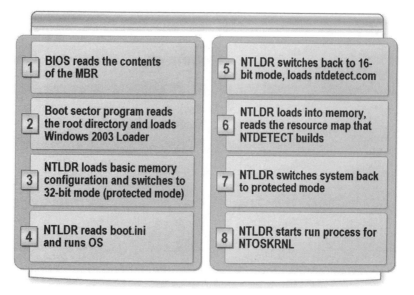

1 BIOS reads the contents of the MBR	**5** NTLDR switches back to 16-bit mode, loads ntdetect.com
2 Boot sector program reads the root directory and loads Windows 2003 Loader	**6** NTLDR loads into memory, reads the resource map that NTDETECT builds
3 NTLDR loads basic memory configuration and switches to 32-bit mode (protected mode)	**7** NTLDR switches system back to protected mode
4 NTLDR reads boot.ini and runs OS	**8** NTLDR starts run process for NTOSKRNL

Introduction

If your server fails to start, and you must start the computer temporarily, start it by using the Windows startup disk. If the problem is caused by one of the three boot files, you will be able to run the server normally.

Function of the boot files

The boot files function as follows.

1. After the power-on self test (POST) loads the system BIOS into memory, the BIOS reads the contents of the Master Boot Record (MBR). The MBR takes control and reads the contents of each partition's various boot sectors to find a bootable sector.

2. The bootsector program reads the root directory and loads Windows Server 2003 Loader (NTLDR).

3. NTLDR loads the basic memory configuration and switches to 32-bit mode (protected mode). NTLDR then places itself into high memory to free up as much memory space as possible.

4. NTLDR reads boot.ini and runs the operating system. If boot.ini is not present, NTLDR assumes that Windows Server 2003 is in the \Windows directory on the C drive.

5. NTLDR switches back to 16-bit mode and loads ntdetect.com, which is a 16-bit application. NTDETECT determines the computer's physical environment. This determination occurs every time Windows Server 2003 starts, so the environment can change for each boot.

6. NTLDR loads into memory and reads the resource map that NTDETECT builds.

7. NTLDR switches the system back to protected mode. NTLDR then sets up the ring 0 mode for the kernel and loads the proper kernel (NTOSKRNL) for the computer. NTLDR pulls in the proper Hardware Abstraction Layer (HAL) and all boot drivers. Everything that NTDETECT collects becomes the HKEY_LOCAL_MACHINE/HARDWARE Registry key.

8. NTLDR starts the run process for NTOSKRNL.

How to Create a Windows Startup Disk

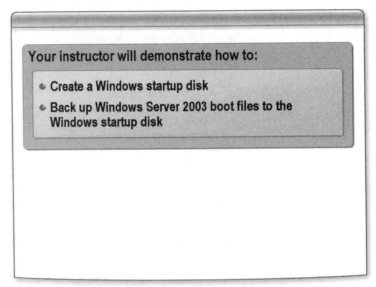

Introduction

You may encounter a situation when it is not possible to start Windows or any other operating system on your computer. This situation can occur when Windows is installed on a computer that has an Intel x86-based processor, and the boot record for the active partition or files that are required to start Windows becomes corrupted.

Use the following procedures to create and use a Windows startup disk. A Windows startup disk contains only the files that are necessary to start the operating system with the remainder of the Windows system files installed on the hard disk drive.

Procedure for creating a Windows startup disk

To create a Window startup disk:

1. Place a blank floppy disk in drive A.
2. On the **Start** menu, click **Windows Explorer**.
3. In Windows Explorer, expand **My Computer**.
4. Right-click **3½ Floppy (A:)** and then click **Format**.
5. In the **Format 3 ½ Floppy (A:)** dialog box, click **Quick Format**, click **Start**, and then click **OK**.
6. In the **Formatting 3 ½ Floppy (A:)** dialog box, click **OK**, and then click **Close**.

Procedure for backing up boot files

To back up Windows Server 2003 boot files to the Windows startup disk:

1. In Windows Explorer, click **Local Disk (C:)**.

2. On the **Tools** menu, click **Folder Options**.

3. On the **View** tab, clear the **Hide protected operating system files (Recommended)** check box.

4. In the **Warning** box, click **Yes**, and then click **OK**.

5. Copy the following files to drive A:

   - Boot.ini

   - Ntdetect.com

   - Ntldr

   If either the Bootsect.dos or the Ntbootdd.sys file resides in the system partition, also copy these files to the boot disk.

6. Open a command prompt, type **attrib –h –s –r a:*.*** and then press ENTER.

7. On the **Tools** menu, click **Folder Options**.

8. On the **View** tab, select the **Hide protected operating system files (Recommended)** check box, and then click **OK**.

9. Remove the disk from the drive, and label it **Windows startup disk**.

Practice: Recovering from Server Failure

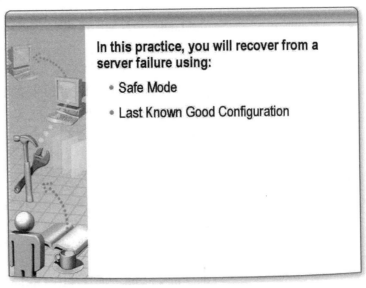

Objective

In this practice, you will recover from a server problem by using:

- Safe Mode
- Last Known Good Configuration

Scenario

You are the systems administrator for an organizational unit on a large network. You install a new software package on a server. After installation is complete, you restart the computer. After you log on, the computer malfunctions. You will fix this problem by using Last Known Good Configuration and Safe Mode.

Practice

▶ **To start your computer using Last Known Good Configuration and Safe Mode**

1. Log on as Administrator with a password of **P@ssw0rd**.

2. Open the **Run** dialog box, type **\MOC\2275\Practices\Mod07\install.bat** and then click **OK**.

3. After the computer restarts, log on as Administrator.

4. Note the unusual behavior. What does the computer do?

   _____

5. When the computer restarts, use Last Known Good Configuration to start Windows Server 2003.

6. Log on as administrator.

7. Did this work? Why or why not?

   _____

8. When the computer restarts, use Safe Mode to start Windows Server 2003.

9. Log on as administrator.

10. Did this work? Why or why not?

    _____

11. On the **Start** menu, click **Search**.

12. In the **Search Results** dialog box, search for all bootme files. Delete any bootme files in the Windows folder.

13. Restart your computer, and then log on as Administrator. What happens?

    _____

14. Log off, and then log on again. Does the problem appear to be solved?

    _____

Lesson: Selecting Disaster Recovery Methods

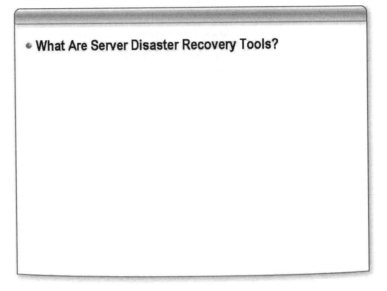

Introduction

By using the system recovery tools, backup, and restore, you can implement a disaster recovery method for most common data losses.

Lesson objective

After completing this lesson, you will be able to determine which disaster recovery solutions to use to recover data during a server failure.

What Are Server Disaster Recovery Tools?

Disaster Recovery Tool	Function
Safe Mode	Use when a problem prevents starting Windows Server 2003 normally
Last Known Good	Use only in cases of incorrect configuration
Backup	Use to create a duplicate copy of data on your hard drive and then archive the data on another storage device
Recovery Console	Use if you cannot fix the problems by using one of the startup methods
Automated System Recovery (ASR)	Use when restoring data from backup

Introduction

To recover your system, you can use Safe Mode, Last Known Good Configuration, Backup, Recovery Console, ASR, or some combination of these tools, as well as others such as shadow copies. Follow the recommended best practices when you use these disaster recovery solutions.

Disaster recovery tools

The following table lists disaster recovery tools in the preferred order of use, from tools that present little or no risk to data, to those that might cause data loss. Safe Mode and Backup are available in both safe and normal startup modes.

Disaster recovery tool	Function
Safe Mode	Use when a problem prevents Window Server 2003 from starting normally.
	Safe mode is a startup option that disables startup programs and nonessential services to create an environment that is useful for troubleshooting and diagnosing problems.
Last Known Good Configuration	Use only in cases of incorrect configuration. By using Last Known Good Configuration, you can recover by reversing the most recent driver and registry changes made since the last time you logged on to Windows Server 2003.
Backup	Use to create a duplicate copy of data on your hard drive and then archive the data on another storage device.
	Backup is a tool for saving data, such as System State data. Before you troubleshoot problems, attempt workarounds or apply updates.

(continued)

Disaster recovery tool	Function
Recovery Console	Use if you cannot fix the problems by using one of the startup methods.
	In addition to Last Known Good Configuration and safe mode, users can use Recovery Console to attempt manual recovery operations.
Automated System Recovery (ASR)	Use when restoring data from backup.
	Use this option instead of reinstalling Windows because ASR restores system settings and critical files on the system and boot partitions.
	Because the ASR process formats disks, consider this a last resort when using Last Known Good Configuration, Backup, restoring system state data, or Recovery Console does not solve the problem.

Note For more information about how to select the correct recovery tool or combination of tools to correct the specific disaster you encounter, see Appendix H, "Which Recovery Tool Do I Use?"

Lab A: Managing Disaster Recovery

In this lab, you will:
- Install the Recovery Console
- Back up System State data
- Create a Windows startup disk
- Recover from a corrupt registry by using Last Known Good
- Recover from a corrupt registry by restoring System State data
- Recover from a corrupt boot file by using the Windows startup disk

Objectives

After completing this lab, you will be able to:

- Install the Recovery Console.
- Back up System State data.
- Create a Windows startup disk.
- Recover from a corrupt registry by using Last Known Good.
- Recover from a corrupt registry by restoring System State data.
- Recover from a corrupt boot file by using the Windows startup disk.

Estimated time to complete this lab: 45 minutes

Exercise 1
Installing the Recovery Console

In this exercise, you will install the Recovery Console.

Tasks	Specific instructions
1. Log on to your computer.	■ Log on to the domain using the administrator account.
2. Install the Recovery Console.	a. Insert the Windows Server 2003 compact disc into the CD-ROM drive.
	b. Close the Welcome screen.
	c. Open a command prompt and change to the I386 folder on the Windows Server 2003 compact disc.
	d. At the command prompt, type **winnt32 /cmdcons** and then press ENTER.
	e. Follow the on-screen directions for installing the Recovery Console.
	f. Remove the Windows Server 2003 compact disc from the CD-ROM drive.

Exercise 2
Backing Up the System State Data

In this exercise, you will use the Backup Wizard to back up the System State data for your computer on your drive C.

Tasks	Specific instructions
■ Start the Backup Wizard and back up the System State data.	**a.** In the **Run** dialog box, type **ntbackup** **b.** Click **Advanced Mode** and then start the Backup Wizard. **c.** Select the following option: Only back up the System State data. **d.** On the **Backup Type, Destination and Name** page, browse to C:\MOC\2275\Labfiles\Lab07. **e.** Use **SysState** as the filename. **f.** Close all windows when the backup is completed.

Exercise 3
Creating a Windows Startup Disk

In this exercise, you will create a Windows startup disk.

Tasks	Specific instructions
1. Format a disk.	a. Insert a floppy disk into the drive.
	b. Using Windows Explorer, format the disk.
2. Copy Windows Server 2003 boot files to the disk.	a. In Windows Explorer, expand **Local Disk (C:)**.
	b. On the **Tools** menu, click **Folder Options**.
	c. On the **View** tab, clear the **Hide protected operating system files (Recommended)** check box.
	d. Use Windows Explorer to copy the following files to the disk:
	• Boot.ini
	• Ntdetect.com
	• Ntldr
	• If either the Bootsect.dos or the Ntbootdd.sys file resides in the system partition, also copy these files to the disk.
	• Open a command prompt and type **Attrib –h –s –r a:*.***
	e. On the **Tools** menu, click **Folder Options**.
	f. On the **View** tab, select the **Hide protected operating system files (Recommended)** check box.
	g. Remove the disk and label it "Windows startup disk."

Exercise 4
Recovering from a Corrupt Registry (Part One)

In this exercise, you will recover from a non-responsive computer. The cause of this problem was the installation of a software package that modified the registry. (The source for this exercise is the Microsoft Knowledge Base article at http://support.microsoft.com/kbid=317246.)

Tasks	Specific instructions
1. Install the software.	▪ Using Windows Explorer, browse to **C:\MOC\2275\Labfiles\Lab07** and then double-click **inst_01.bat**.
❓ What happens when the computer restarts?	
❓ What do you need to do to recover from this disaster?	
2. Recover from a corrupt registry.	**a.** Restart your computer, and then press F8 to open the Windows **Advanced Options** menu. **b.** Select the option that you can use to recover from a corrupt registry.

Exercise 5
Recovering from a Corrupt Registry (Part Two)

In this exercise, you will recover from a non-responsive mouse. The cause of this problem was the installation of a software package that modified the registry. (The source for this exercise is the Microsoft Knowledge Base article at http://support.microsoft.com/kbid=317246.)

Tasks	Specific instructions
1. Log on to your computer.	■ Log on to the domain using the administrator account.
2. Install the software.	a. Open Windows Explorer, browse to C:\MOC\2275\Labfiles\Lab07, and then double-click **inst_04.bat**.
	b. When the computer restarts, log on to the domain as an administrator.
❓ What do you need to do to recover from this disaster?	
	_____
3. Recover from a corrupt registry using Last Known Good Configuration.	a. Shut down, and then restart the computer.
	b. Press F8 go open the Windows **Advanced Options** menu.
	c. Select **Last Known Good Configuration** to resolve this problem.
	d. Log on to the domain using the administrator account. Did this resolve the problem? _____
4. Recover from a corrupt registry by restoring System State data using the keyboard. Use the following keys to navigate in the Backup program: ALT + TAB CTRL + ESC TAB ENTER CTRL + TAB SPACEBAR Up arrow Down arrow Right arrow Left arrow	a. Log on to the domain using the administrator account.
	b. Open the **Start** menu by pressing the _____ + _____ keys.
	c. Use the arrow keys to select **Run**, and then open the **Run** dialog box by pressing _____.
	d. In the **Run** dialog box, type **ntbackup** and then press _____.
	e. In the **Backup or Restore Wizard** dialog box, use the _____ key to select **Advanced Mode** and then press _____.
	f. In the Backup Utility – [Untitled] window, use the _____ + _____ keys to select **Restore and Manage Media**.
	g. In the **Restore and Manage Media** page, use the _____ key to highlight **File** in the tree view pane, and then use the _____ key to open the tree.
	h. When the tree is open, use the _____ key to traverse the tree until you get to the **Systate.bkf** entry, and then use the _____ key to view the **System State** check box.
	i. When the System State check box is displayed, use the _____ key to highlight it, and then use the _____ key to select **the System State** check box.
	j. Start the system restore process by pressing the _____ key, and then press the _____ key twice to confirm your choice.
	k. When the restore process is complete, close the **Restore Progress** dialog box by pressing the _____ key, and then restart the computer.

Exercise 6
Recovering from a Corrupt Boot File

In this exercise, you will recover from a corrupt boot.ini file.

Tasks	Specific instructions
1. Log on to your computer.	▪ Log on to the domain using the administrator account.
2. Install the software.	▪ Using Windows Explorer, browse to C:\MOC\2275\Labfiles\Lab07, and then double-click **inst_03.bat**.
❓ What do you need to do to recover from this disaster?	
3. Recover from a corrupt boot file.	a. Insert the Windows startup disk in drive A, and then restart the computer. b. Log on to the domain using the administrator account. c. Use Windows Explorer to copy the a:\boot.ini file to C:\. d. Remove the Windows startup disk. e. Shut down, and then restart the computer.

Microsoft®
Training &
Certification

Module 8: Maintaining Software by Using Software Update Services

Contents

Overview	1
Lesson: Introduction to Software Update Services	2
Lesson: Installing and Configuring Software Update Services	13
Lesson: Managing a Software Update Services Infrastructure	24
Lab A: Maintaining Software by Using Software Update Services	36
Course Evaluation	41

Overview

- Introduction to Software Update Services
- Installing and Configuring Software Update Services
- Managing a Software Update Services Infrastructure

Introduction

This module introduces Microsoft® Software Update Services, a tool for managing and distributing software updates that resolve known security vulnerabilities and other stability issues in Microsoft Windows® 2000, Windows XP, and Windows Server 2003 operating systems. This module also describes how to install the client and server components of Software Update Services. It also provides necessary information about managing the Software Update Services infrastructure.

Objectives

After completing this module, you will be able to:

- Explain Microsoft Software Update Services.
- Install and configure client computers to use Software Update Services.
- Install and configure servers to use Software Update Services.
- Manage the Software Update Services infrastructure.

Lesson: Introduction to Software Update Services

- Multimedia: Software Update Services
- What Is Windows Update?
- What Is Automatic Updates?
- Comparison of Windows Update and Automatic Updates
- What Is Software Update Services?
- Software Update Services Process

Introduction

Traditionally, systems administrators keep systems up-to-date by frequently checking the Windows Update Web site or the Microsoft Security Web site for software updates. Administrators manually download available updates, test the updates in their environment, and then distribute the updates manually or by using their traditional software-distribution tools.

By using Software Update Services, administrators can perform these tasks automatically.

This lesson describes Software Update Services and explains how it works with Windows Update and Automatic Updates.

Lesson objectives

After completing this lesson, you will be able to:

- Describe Software Update Services.
- Describe Windows Update.
- Describe Automatic Updates.
- Compare Windows Update and Automatic Updates.
- Describe how Software Update Services is used.
- Explain the Software Update Services process.

Multimedia: Software Update Services

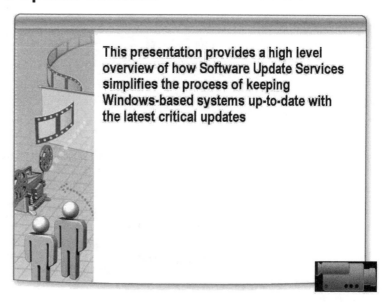

This presentation provides a high level overview of how Software Update Services simplifies the process of keeping Windows-based systems up-to-date with the latest critical updates

File location

To view the *Software Update Services* presentation, open the Web page on the Student Materials compact disc, click **Multimedia**, and then click the title of the presentation.

What Is Windows Update?

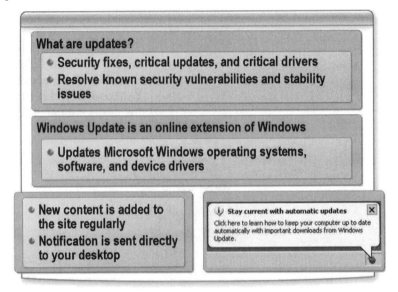

Introduction

Windows Update is the online extension of Windows that helps keep your systems up-to-date. Use Windows Update to select updates for the operating systems, software, and device drivers on your network. New content is added to the site regularly, so you can always get the most recent updates to help protect your server and the client computers on your network.

What are updates?

Updates can include security fixes, critical updates, and critical drivers. These updates resolve known security vulnerabilities and stability issues in Microsoft Windows 2000, Windows XP, and Windows Server 2003 operating systems.

Update categories

The categories for the Windows operating system updates are:

- *Critical updates*. Security fixes and other important updates to keep computers current and networks secure.

- *Recommended downloads*. Latest Windows and Microsoft Internet Explorer service packs and other important updates.

- *Windows tools*. Utilities and other tools that are provided to enhance performance, facilitate upgrades, and ease the burden on systems administrators.

- *Internet and multimedia updates*. Latest Internet Explorer releases, upgrades to Microsoft Windows Media® player, and more.

- *Additional Windows downloads*. Updates for desktop settings and other Windows features.

- *Multilanguage features*. Menus and dialog boxes, language support, and Input Method Editors for a variety of languages.

- Deployment guides and other software-related documents are also available.

Notification is sent to your desktop

When an update is available for your computer, Windows Update notifies you by displaying a balloon in the lower right corner of your screen when you first log on. You can then download the update, postpone updating your computer, or go to the Windows Update Web site to read about the available update.

Software Licensing

The update method that you use for your network depends on the size of your network, number of users, and computer locations. Before you determine which option to use, however, you are required to license the Microsoft software that you are using. Microsoft has volume software product licenses that grant you the legal right to run or access a software program.

Note   To learn more about Microsoft Volume Licensing agreements, go to the Microsoft Licensing Web site at http://www.microsoft.com/licensing.

What Is Automatic Updates?

Automatic Updates client software can download packages from the public Windows Update site or a server running Software Update Services

- Enables you to specify how and when you want to update Windows
- After download is complete, an icon appears with a message, updates are ready to be installed
    - Administrator can choose to install or not

Introduction

By using Automatic Updates, you can specify how and when you want to update Windows. These updates include everything from critical updates to enhancements.

Includes a range of options

Automatic Updates includes a range of options for downloading updates. For example, you can set up Windows to automatically download and install updates on a schedule that you specify. Or you can choose to be notified when updates are available for your computer and then download the updates in the background so that you can continue to work uninterrupted.

Notification of available updates

After the download is complete, an icon appears in the notification area with a message that the updates are ready to be installed. When you click the icon or message, Automatic Updates quickly guides you through the installation process.

If you choose not to install a specific update that has been downloaded, Windows deletes its files from your computer. If you change your mind later, you can download it again by opening the **System Properties** dialog box, clicking the **Automatic Updates** tab, and then clicking **Declined Updates**. If any of the updates that you previously declined still apply to your computer, they appear the next time that Windows notifies you of available updates.

Exercise caution

Exercise caution whenever you download programs from the Internet. Some attackers disguise attacks as harmless programs to compromise security on your computer. To assure you that the programs you download from Windows Update are from Microsoft, all files are digitally signed. The purpose of digital signatures is to ensure the authenticity and integrity of the signed files. Automatic Updates installs a file only if it contains this digital signature.

Automatic Updates client deployment

You can install the updated Automatic Updates client on your client computers by using one of the following methods:

- Install Automatic Updates client by using the Windows Installer package (.msi file).

- Install Windows 2000 Service Pack 3 (SP3).

- Install Windows XP SP1.

- Install Windows Server 2003.

Note For more information about deploying Software Update Services, see the white paper, *Deploying Software Update Services*, under **Additional Reading** on the Web page on the Student Materials compact disc.

Comparison of Windows Update and Automatic Updates

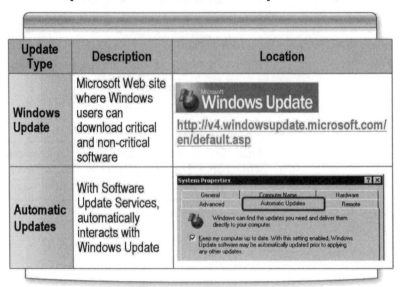

Update Type	Description	Location
Windows Update	Microsoft Web site where Windows users can download critical and non-critical software	**Windows Update** http://v4.windowsupdate.microsoft.com/en/default.asp
Automatic Updates	With Software Update Services, automatically interacts with Windows Update	*System Properties dialog box*

Introduction

Keeping Windows-based systems current with the latest updates can be a complicated task for systems administrators. Using Windows Update or Automatic Updates can make this task easier to perform.

Service packs

Windows Update and Automatic Updates send notices to Windows users about available service packs. Service packs are the means by which product updates are distributed. Service packs may contain updates for system reliability, program compatibility, security, and more.

Windows Update and Automatic Updates

Windows Update and Automatic Updates are two separate components that are designed to work together to keep Windows operating systems secure.

- Windows Update is a Microsoft Web site from which Windows users can download critical and non-critical software.

- Automatic Updates enables you to automatically interact with the Windows Update Web site to obtain the critical software updates. As a systems administrator, you have full control over the level of this interaction with Automatic Updates by using Software Update Services.

What Is Software Update Services?

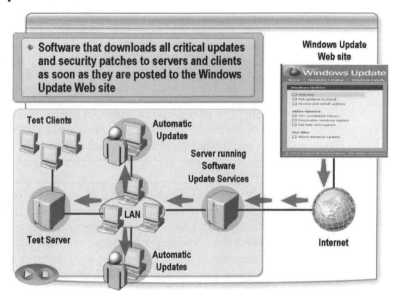

| **Definition** | You can use Software Update Services to download all critical updates to servers and clients as soon as they are posted to the Windows Update Web site. |

Server component

You install the server component of Software Update Services on a server running Windows 2000 Server, Windows XP, or Windows Server 2003 inside your corporate firewall. A corporate service allows your internal server to synchronize content with the Windows Update Web site whenever critical updates for Windows are available. The synchronization can be automatic or the administrator can perform it manually.

By synchronizing with the Windows Update Web site, your internal server that is running Software Update Services can pull the update packages and store them until an administrator decides which ones to publish. Then, all the clients that are configured to use the server running Software Update Services will install those updates.

Client component

You can control which server each client computer connects to and then schedule when the client performs all installations of critical updates either manually by means of the registry or by using Group Policy from the Active Directory® directory service.

Synchronizes content from Windows Update

You can configure servers running Software Update Services to synchronize content from the Windows Update Web site. You can also configure these servers to download content from a content distribution point that you create manually. Second-tier servers running Software Update Services can synchronize both content and the list of approved packages. By using this method, you can simplify the update management process by managing updates from a central location.

Deployment of staged updates

You can stage update deployment by using multiple servers running Software Update Services. You can set up one server in your test lab to publish the updates to lab client computers first. If these updates are installed correctly on these computers, you can then configure your other servers running Software Update Services to publish their updates to the rest of your organization. By using this method, you can ensure that these changes do not harm your standard desktop operating environment.

Note   For more information about Microsoft Software Update Services, see the white paper, *Software Update Services Overview*, under **Additional Reading** on the Student Materials compact disc.

Note   Software Update Services is not intended to serve as a replacement for your enterprise software-distribution solution, such as Microsoft Systems Management Server (SMS) or Microsoft Group Policy-based software distribution. Many customers use solutions such as SMS for complete software management, including responding to security and virus issues, and these customers should continue using these solutions. Advanced solutions such as SMS provide the ability to deploy all software throughout an enterprise, in addition to providing administrative controls that are critical for medium and large organizations.

Software Update Services Process

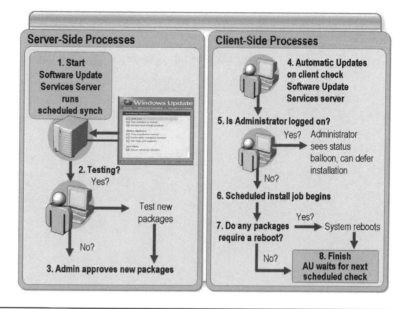

Introduction

The process for using Software Update Services involves both the server running Software Update Services and the client computers on a network. If both are configured, the administrator can review the update packages and approve them for installation.

Server-side processes

1. The server running Software Update Services runs a scheduled synchronization with Windows Update and receives new packages of updates.

2. The systems administrator reviews the new packages and determines whether testing is required.

   a. If testing is required, the administrator sends the new packages to be tested.

   b. If testing is not required, the administrator proceeds to step 3.

3. Administrator approves the new packages of updates.

Client-side processes

1. Automatic Updates on client computers check the server running Software Update Services server daily and download new approved updates packages from either the server running Software Update Services or the Windows Update Web site.

2. At the scheduled update time, Software Update Services checks whether the administrator is logged on.

   a. If logged on, the administrator sees a status balloon on the desktop and decides whether to defer or run the installation.

   b. If the administrator is not logged on, step 6 is performed.

3. The scheduled installation job begins, and Automatic Updates installs new or changed packages.

4. Automatic Updates checks whether the new packages require a restart of the server or client.

   a. If a restart is required, the system restarts after all the packages are installed.

   b. If no restart is required, the installation is completed.

5. Automatic Updates waits for the next scheduled check.

Lesson: Installing and Configuring Software Update Services

- **What Are Software Update Services Server Distribution Points?**
- **Server Requirements for Software Update Services**
- **How to Install and Configure Software Update Services**
- **Automatic Updates Configuration**
- **How to Configure Automatic Updates**
- **Guidelines for Testing Content for a Software Update Services Environment**

Introduction

Software Update Services consists of both client-side and server-side components to provide a basic solution to critical patch management.

This lesson explains how to install and configure the client-side and server-side components of Software Update Services.

Lesson objectives

After completing this lesson, you will be able to:

- Explain server distribution points for Software Update Services.

- Describe server hardware and software requirements for Software Update Services.

- Install and configure Software Update Services on the server.

- Explain Automatic Updates configuration.

- Configure Automatic Updates.

What Are Software Update Services Server Distribution Points?

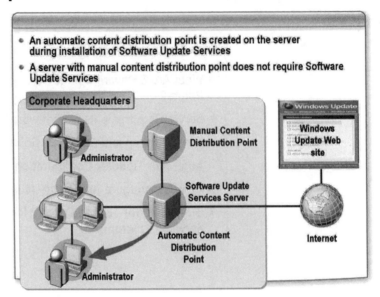

Introduction

The server that is running Software Update Services controls content distribution. That server can distribute the updates automatically, or the administrator can overrule the default and manually distribute the updates by using a content distribution point.

Content distribution points

There are two ways to create a content distribution point:

- *Automatic.* When you install Software Update Services on a server, an automatic content distribution point is created on that server. When the server is synchronized, its content is updated from the Windows Update Web site.

  The content distribution point is located on the Web site in a virtual root (v-root) named /Content on the server running Internet Information Services (IIS). If you choose to maintain content on Microsoft.com, this automatic content distribution point is empty.

- *Manual.* You can also manually create a content distribution point on a server running IIS version 5.0 or later. The server with the manual content distribution point does not require Software Update Services.

Why set up a manual content distribution point?

You may want to set up a manually configured content distribution point in any of the following situations:

- Multiple servers in your organization are running Software Update Services and you do not want all of the servers to access the Internet to synchronize content.

- Some sites on your network do not have Internet access.

- You want to test content in a test environment and then push the tested content to your production environment.

Note To set up and configure a manual content distribution server, see the white paper, *Deploying Software Update Services*, under **Additional Reading** on the Student Materials compact disc.

Server Requirements for Software Update Services

* **Hardware requirements**
  * Pentium III 700 MHz or higher
  * 512 MB of RAM
  * 6 GB of hard disk space for setup and security packages
* **Software requirements**
  * Windows 2000 Server with Service Pack 2 or higher or Windows Server 2003
  * IIS 5.0 or higher
  * Internet Explorer 6.0 or later
* **Server requirements**
  * Software Update Services software must be installed on an NTFS partition

---

Introduction

You install the server component of Software Update Services by using a Windows Installer package that installs the necessary server files and configures Internet Information Services. To ensure that your server can support Software Update Services, check the hardware and software capabilities of your server. Setup will not allow you to install the software if your computer does not meet the following requirements.

Hardware server requirements

A server running Software Update Services requires the following hardware:

- Pentium III 700 megahertz (MHz) or later
- 512 megabytes (MB) of RAM
- 6 gigabytes (GB) of hard disk space for setup and security packages

A server with the preceding hardware running Software Update Services can support approximately 15,000 clients.

Software server requirements

Each server running Software Update Services requires the following software:

- Windows 2000 Server with Service Pack 2 or later, or Windows Server 2003
- IIS 5.0 or later
- Internet Explorer 6.0 or later

Disk requirements

In addition to the preceding hardware and software requirements, the Software Update Services software must be installed on an NTFS partition on the server. The system partition on your server must also use NTFS, because FAT32 does not offer security.

Note   For more information about server requirements for Software Update Services, see the white paper, *Deploying Software Update Services*, under **Additional Reading** on the Web page on the Student Materials compact disc.

How to Install and Configure Software Update Services

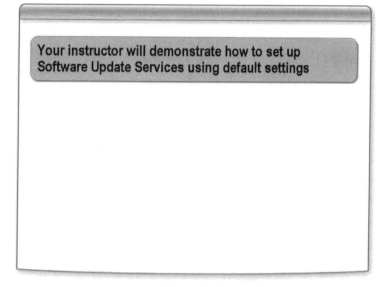

Introduction

A systems administrator is responsible for installing and setting up Software Update Services. You can install the software using the default configuration by downloading the software from the Microsoft Software Update Services Web site.

Procedure for setting up Software Update Services using default settings

To set up Software Update Services:

1. Download Software Update Services from http://www.microsoft.com/windows2000/windowsupdate/sus/default.asp.

2. Double-click the **SUS101SP1.exe** file to begin the installation process.

3. In the Setup Wizard, on the **Welcome** page, click **Next**.

4. Read and accept the **End User License Agreement**.

5. Select the **Typical** check box.

6. Click **Install**, and then click **Finish** in the Setup Wizard to open the Software Update Services administration Web site in Internet Explorer.

Automatic Updates Configuration

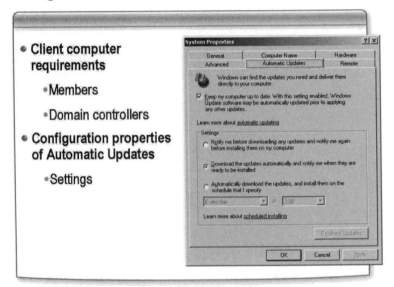

* **Client computer requirements**
  * Members
  * Domain controllers
* **Configuration properties of Automatic Updates**
  * Settings

Introduction

You can choose from several options in Automatic Updates to control how to update clients. Choose the option that provides most appropriate update method for your organization.

Automatic Updates settings

By using the following settings, the local administrator can control how updates are downloaded and installed:

- The administrator is notified before updates are downloaded and before the downloaded updates are installed.

- Updates are automatically downloaded, and an administrator is notified before updates are installed.

- Updates are automatically downloaded and installed based upon a specified schedule.

The administrator is notified by means of an icon and a balloon in the notification area to the right of the taskbar buttons. The download notification is similar to the installation notification. All notification events are logged in the system event log.

Automatic Updates setting configurations

The Group Policy object (GPO) that is located in the Computer Configuration\ Administrative Templates\Windows Components\Windows Update folder specifies whether the computer receives security updates and other important downloads through Automatic Updates. When enabled, it also specifies the download and installation behavior.

Administrator control using policies

You can control the behavior of Automatic Updates by configuring Group Policy objects in an Active Directory environment. Administrator-defined configuration options that are driven by Group Policy always take precedence over user-defined options. Also, Automatic Updates Control Panel options are disabled on the target computer when administrative policies are set.

Requirements for the client computer

Client computers must be running the updated Automatic Updates client and Windows 2000 (Service Pack 3), Windows XP (Service Pack 1), or Window Server 2003.

How to Configure Automatic Updates

Your instructor will demonstrate how to configure Automatic Updates by creating an Automatic Updates GPO for your organizational unit

Introduction

Use the following procedure to configure client-side Automatic Updates by using Group Policy. Using Group Policy to configure Automatic Updates for your client computers saves time. After you configure your client computers, specify from which server each client will receive its updates.

Procedure

To create an Automatic Updates Group Policy object for an organizational unit, using the name of your classroom computer as an example:

1. On the **Start** menu, point to **Administrative Tools**, and then click **Group Policy Management**.

2. In the Group Policy Management window, expand **Group Policy Management**, expand **Forest: nwtraders.msft**, expand **Domains**, expand **nwtraders.msft**, expand **Locations**, and then click **London**.

3. Right-click **London**, and then click **Create and Link a GPO Here**.

4. In the **New GPO** dialog box, type **London SUS Automatic Updates** and then click **OK**.

5. Right-click **London SUS Automatic Updates**, and then click **Edit**.

6. Under **Computer Configuration**, expand **Administrative Templates**, expand **Windows Components**, and then click **Windows Update**.

7. In the details pane, double-click **Configure Automatic Updates**.

8. In the **Configure Automatic Updates Properties** dialog box, click **Enabled**, and then click **Next Setting**.

9. In the **Specify intranet Microsoft update service location Properties** dialog box, click **Enabled**.

10. In the **Set the intranet update service for detecting updates** box, type **http://***ComputerName* (where *ComputerName* is the name of your computer).

11. In the **Set the intranet statistics server** box, type **http://***ComputerName* (where *ComputerName* is the name of your computer) and then click **OK**.

12. Close the **Group Policy Object Editor** dialog box, and then close the Group Policy Management window.

Practice: Installing and Configuring Software Update Services

In this practice, you will:

- Install and configure Software Update Services
- Set Group Policy to configure Automatic Updates for the client computers

Objective

In this practice, you will install and configure Software Update Services, and you will set Group Policy to configure Automatic Updates for the client computers.

Scenario

You are the systems administrator for an organizational unit on a large network. The network environment includes computers based on Windows 2000, Windows Server 2003, and Windows XP. You must ensure that the latest service packs and critical updates are installed on all the computers. You also need to automate the updates by installing Software Update Services and setting Group Policy to configure the Automatic Updates client software on all computers. Because this practice requires you to do extensive work as an administrator, you will log on as an administrator for efficiency reasons.

Practice: Installing Internet Information Services

▶ **Install Internet Information Services**

1. Log on to the domain as Administrator with a password of **P@ssw0rd**.

2. Insert the Microsoft Windows Server 2003, Enterprise Edition compact disc into the CD-ROM drive.

3. When the Microsoft Windows Server 2003 Family window appears, click **Exit**.

4. In Control Panel, open **Add or Remove Programs**, and then open **Add/Remove Windows Components**.

5. In the Windows Components Wizard, select the **Application Server** check box, and then follow the on-screen directions to install it.

6. Close all windows.

Practice: Installing Microsoft Software Update Services

▶ **Install Microsoft Software Update Services**

1. Open Windows Explorer.

2. Browse to C:\MOC\2275\Practices\Mod08.

3. Open SUS10SP1.exe.

4. Follow the on-screen directions to perform a custom installation with the following parameters.

    a. Save the Microsoft Software Update Services Web site files to D:\SUS\Content.

    b. Support English language.

    c. Manually approve new versions of approved updates.

5. Notice that the Software Update Services administration Web site is located at http://*ComputerName*/SUSAdmin.

6. Close all windows and log off.

Guidelines for Testing Content for a Software Update Services Environment

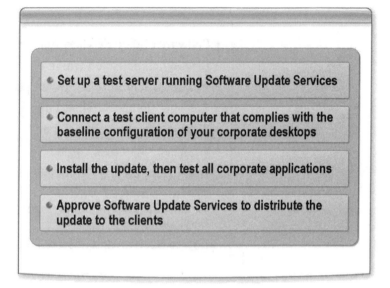

Introduction

Although Software Update Services does not include a specific test option, you can perform some basic testing before you approve installation of the update.

Guidelines for testing content

Use the following test plan to install updates on the client computers on your network:

- In a test lab, set up a test server running Software Update Services.

  Use the server running Software Update Services to download the new updates. During testing, you can read the details about the new updates and decide which ones to accept.

- On a test client computer running your standard operating environment, download the Automatic Updates client component, and then install the packages that you want to test.

  Connect the test client computer to the Windows Update site on the Internet by using your browser and the following URL: http://windowsupdate.microsoft.com.

- Install the update, and then test all corporate applications.

  You can apply the packages that you want to test on that client. Remember that you will see only the updates that are applicable to the test computer.

- Approve the updates from Software Update Services to distribute the updates to the clients.

  Approval is the final step in completing the updates from Software Update Services. Systems administrators can schedule the update to begin after hours, if Automatic Updates for the client computers is configured to do so.

Lesson: Managing a Software Update Services Infrastructure

- Software Update Services Administration Web Site
- How Synchronization Works
- How to Synchronize Software Update Services Content
- Software Update Services Logs
- What Is a Synchronization Log?
- What Is an Approval Log?
- How to Review and Approve Software Update Services Logs
- What to Back Up and Restore for Software Update Services
- How to Back Up and Restore Software Update Services

Introduction

As an administrator, you decide whether to install updates immediately after they are downloaded, or to test the updates first. This lesson discusses how to view the synchronized content, as well as how to approve and install the updates.

It is important to have your Software Update Services configuration backed up and ready to restore in the event of a disaster. This lesson also describes how to be ready to update your network even in the case of a network disaster.

Lesson objectives

After completing this lesson, you will be able to:

- Explain the features and function of the Software Update Services Web site.
- Describe how synchronization works.
- Synchronize Software Update Services content.
- Describe Software Update Services logs.
- Explain the synchronization log.
- Explain the approval log.
- Review and approve Software Update Services logs.
- Describe what to back up and restore for Software Update Services.
- Back up and restore Software Update Services.

Software Update Services Administration Web Site

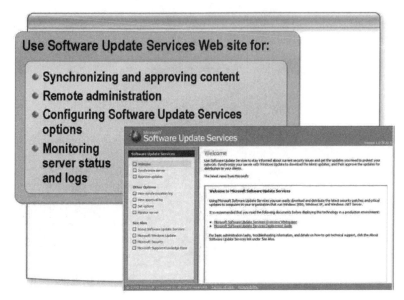

Introduction

To manage Software Update Services, you perform the following four main administrative tasks:

- Configure the server after initial installation.

- Manually or automatically synchronize content between the Windows Update Web site and the server running Software Update Services.

- Select and approve synchronized content to be published to computers running the Automatic Updates client.

- Monitor server status and logs.

Administrative tasks

You perform these administrative tasks by using Web pages that are hosted on the server running Software Update Services.

You can access these pages on a corporate intranet by using Internet Explorer 5.5 or later. If you try to connect to the administration Web site with a version of Internet Explorer earlier than version 5.5, an error page appears, reminding you to upgrade Internet Explorer.

Note You must be a local administrator on the computer running Software Update Services to view this Web site.

Note If you try to browse to the administration Web site and "http 500-12: Application Restarting Error" appears, press F5 to refresh your browser.

How Synchronization Works

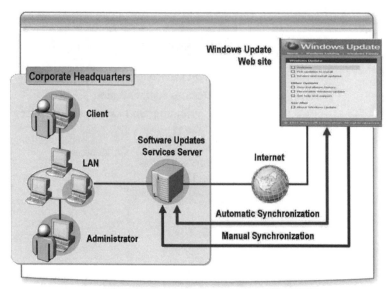

Introduction

Synchronization is the method by which updates are pulled from the Windows Update Web site and are then sent to the network server running Software Update Services. As an administrator, you synchronize updates either manually or automatically.

Automatic synchronization

If a Software Update Services server is configured to accept updates automatically, the systems administrator can review the updates on the Software Update Services Web site before the updates are downloaded. After reviewing the updates, the systems administrator can decide whether to approve the updates. After the updates are approved, they are updated at the next scheduled time for clients using Automatic Updates.

Manual synchronization

If a server is configured for Software Update Services, but requires a systems administrator to manually synchronize the updates, the updates remain on the Windows Update Web site until the administrator reviews and approve them.

Select your content source

You can synchronize content on your server running Software Update Services from the Internet-based Windows Update Web site from another installation of Software Update Services, or from a manually configured content distribution point.

You can configure your content source on the **Set options** page under **Select which server to synchronize content from**.

To synchronize content from the servers using Windows Update on Microsoft.com, click **Synchronize directly from the Microsoft Windows Update servers**.

To synchronize content from another server running Software Update Services or a manually configured content distribution point, click **Synchronize from a local Software Update Services server**. In the text box, enter the name of the server from which to synchronize.

Handling updated content

As new updates are released, they are posted to the servers that are using Windows Update so that you can download them and host them locally on your server running Software Update Services.

During synchronization, updated content is marked on the Approve updates page as "Updated."

The administrator can customize the behavior for updates that are approved by the administrator, but whose content is updated during synchronization:

- *Option 1.* An approved item continues to be approved even if it is updated during synchronization.

  To select this option for handling updated content, on the **Set options** page, click **Automatically approve new versions of previously approved updates**.

- *Option 2.* An approved item is automatically unapproved if it is updated during synchronization.

  To select this option for handling updated content, on the **Set Options** page, click **Do not automatically approve new versions of previously approved updates. I will manually approve these later**.

  Select this second option if you want to test the updates package before your client computers download and install it.

How to Synchronize Software Update Services Content

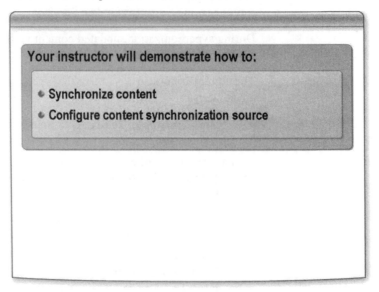

Your instructor will demonstrate how to:

- Synchronize content
- Configure content synchronization source

Introduction

You can configure your content source for updates from the Software Update Services Web site. By using this method, you can synchronize content directly from the Windows Update Web site or synchronize content from another server running Software Update Services.

After viewing the synchronized updates, you can approve the update. Go to the Software Update Services Web site to view the updates that have been synchronized from the Software Update Services server.

Procedure for synchronizing Software Update Services content

To synchronize Software Update Services content:

1. On the Software Update Services administration Web site, in the navigation bar, click **Synchronize server**.

2. Click **Synchronize Now**.

3. You are notified when the synchronization is complete.

Procedure for configuring content source

To configure the content synchronization source:

- On the Software Update Services Web site, click **Set options page**.

    a. To synchronize content from servers using Windows Update Web site, under **Select which server to synchronize content from**, click **Synchronize directly from the Microsoft Windows Update servers**.

    b. To synchronize content from another server running Software Update Services or a manually configured content distribution point, under **Select which server to synchronize content from**, click **Synchronize from a local Software Update Services server**. In the text box, enter the name of the server from which to synchronize.

Software Update Services Logs

> **The synchronization and approval logs are two logs that the administrator uses to approve updates**
>
> - Located in an administrator-accessible folder on the server
> - A Web page is provided to view status of updates
> - Automatic Updates client polls the server running Software Update Services for new approved updates to install
>   - If approved, client computers will begin to download these new items

Introduction

Every 22 hours, minus a random offset, your Automatic Updates client computers poll the server running Software Update Services for approved updates to install. If there are new updates to be installed, the client computers begin to download these new approved updates.

Note   After an approved update is installed, Software Update Services does not uninstall it if it becomes unapproved.

Synchronization and approval of updates

Because most Software Update Services tasks involve the synchronization and approval of updates, a synchronization log and an approval log are provided to the administrator. These logs are stored as XML files in an administrator-accessible folder on the server.

A server-monitoring Web page is provided so you can view the status of updates for target computers, because these are stored in the server's memory and might occasionally need to be refreshed.

What Is a Synchronization Log?

- **Keeps track of content synchronizations that have been performed**
- **Contains the following information:**
  - Time of last synchronization
  - Success and Failure notification information
  - Time of the next synchronization if scheduled
  - Update packages that have been downloaded and/or updated since the last synchronization
  - Failed update packages
  - Manual or Automatic synchronization
- **Log can be accessed from the navigation pane in the administrative user interface**

Introduction

During synchronization, all content from the Windows Update Web site is sent to the servers running Software Update Services that you have configured on your network. As an administrator, you can view the synchronization information on the administration Web site.

Synchronization log

To keep track of the content synchronizations that it performs, each server running Software Update Services maintains a synchronization log that contains the following information:

- Time that the last synchronization was performed.
- Success and failure notification information for the overall synchronization operation.
- Time of the next synchronization, if scheduled synchronization is enabled.
- The update packages that have been downloaded and/or updated since the last synchronization.
- The update packages that failed synchronization.
- The type of synchronization that was performed (Manual or Automatic).

How to access the log

You can open the log from the navigation pane of the Software Update Services administration Web site. You can also access this file by using a text editor. The log file, History-Sync.xml, is located in the \AutoUpdate\Administration subfolder in the folder that contains the Software Update Services Web site.

What Is an Approval Log?

- **Keeps track of the content that has been approved or not approved**
- **Contains the following information:**
  - Record of each time the list of approved packages was changed
  - List of changed items
  - New list of approved items
  - Record of who made the change: server administrator or the synchronization service
- **Log can be accessed from the navigation pane in the administrative user interface**

Introduction

An approval log is maintained on each server running Software Update Services to keep track of the content that has been approved or not approved.

Approval log information

An approval log contains the following information:

- A record of each time the list of approved packages was changed.
- The list of items that changed.
- The new list of approved items.
- A record of who made this change: the server administrator or the synchronization service.

How to access the log

You can open the log from the navigation pane of the Software Update Services administration Web site. You can also access this file by using a text editor. The log file, History_Approve.xml, is stored in the \AutoUpdate\Administration subfolder in the folder that contains the Software Update Services Web site.

Note   If you do not want any packages to be available to your client computers, clear all check boxes, and then click **Approve**.

For more information about which updates you have approved, click **View approval log** in the navigation bar.

Note   The updates that you approved are downloaded only by client computers that have the updated Automatic Updates client installed and configured.

How to Review and Approve Software Update Services Logs

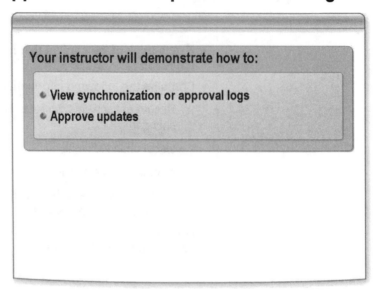

Introduction

As an administrator, you are responsible for managing and installing the updates that you configure for your network. Use the following steps to view the synchronization log and approve the updates, so they can be installed.

Procedure for viewing logs

To view the synchronization or approval logs:

■   On the **Software Update Services Administrator** page, click **View Synchronization Log** or **View Approval Log**.

Procedure for approving updates

To approve updates:

1.   On the **Software Update Services Administrator** page, click **Approve Updates**.

2.   If approved, the updates are installed.

What to Back Up and Restore for Software Update Services

- **Web site directory where the administration site was created**

- **Software Update Services directory that contains content**

- **IIS metabase that stores all of the configuration settings for IIS**

  - Similar to the registry which stores all of the configuration settings for Windows Server 2003

Introduction

If the server running Software Update Services encounters a startup failure, or any other situation that requires reinstallation of the operating system and/or the Software Update Services, it is a good idea to have a recovery plan in place.

Back up Web site, directory, IIS metabase

To have a fully functional server running Software Update Services after a disaster, you must back up the Web site directory that the administration site was created in, the Software Update Services directory that contains the content, and the IIS metabase.

IIS metabase stores configuration settings

The IIS metabase is a database that stores all of the configuration settings for IIS. The metabase is similar to the registry that stores all of the configuration settings for Windows 2003.

How to Back Up and Restore Software Update Services

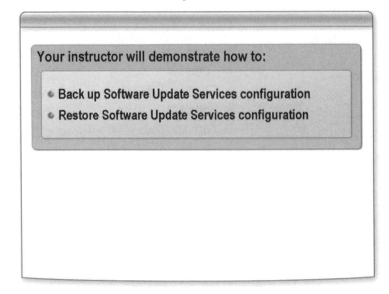

Introduction	Back up Software Update Services by using the **ntbackup** command.
Procedure for backing up Software Update Services	To back up Software Update Services using **ntbackup**:

1. In the **Run** dialog box, type **ntbackup** and then click **OK**.

2. On the **Welcome to the Backup or Restore Wizard** page, click **Advanced Mode**.

3. In the Backup Utility – [Untitled] window, click the **Backup** tab.

4. Expand **Local Disk (C:)**, and then select the **Inetpub** check box.

5. Expand **Windows**, expand **system32**, expand **inetsrv**, and then select the **MetaBack** check box.

6. In the **Backup media or file name** box, specify the name of the backup file, and then click **Start Backup**.

7. In the **Backup Job Information** dialog box, click **Start Backup**.

8. When the backup is complete, click **Close**.

Procedure for restoring Software Update Services

To restore Software Update Services after a failure:

1. Uninstall Software Update Services and IIS.

2. Physically disconnect the server from the network.

3. Reinstall Software Update Services and IIS.

4. Restore the backup file by using **ntbackup**.

5. Reconnect the server to the network.

Practice: Managing Software Update Services

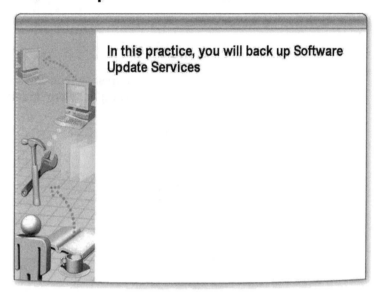

In this practice, you will back up Software Update Services

Objective

In this practice, you will back up Software Update Services.

Scenario

You are the systems administrator for a large network that is using Software Update Services. You need to back up your Software Update Services installation.

Practice

▶ **Back up Microsoft Software Update Services, the Administration site, and the IIS metabase**

1. Log on to the domain as *Computer*User with a password of **P@ssw0rd**.

2. In the **Run** dialog box, type **runas /user:nwtraders\administrator ntbackup**

3. When prompted for the password, type **P@ssw0rd**

4. On the **Welcome to the Backup or Restore Wizard** page, click **Advanced Mode**.

5. On the **Backup** tab, expand **Local Disk (C:)**, and then select the **Inetpub** check box.

6. Expand **Windows**, expand **system32**, expand **inetsrv**, and then select the **MetaBack** check box.

7. Save the backup file in C:\MOC\2275\Practices\Mod08\MSUS01.bkf.

8. Start the back up.

9. When back up is complete, close all windows, and then log off.

Lab A: Maintaining Software by Using Software Update Services

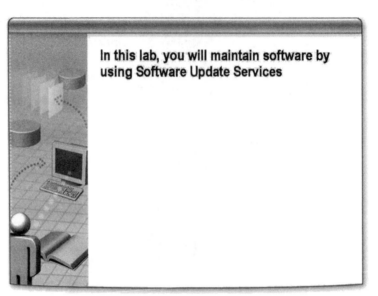

Objectives

After completing this lab, you will be able to:

- Create a Group Policy object to configure Automatic Updates.

- Use Software Update Services to distribute software update packages.

Estimated time to complete this lab: 30 minutes

Exercise 0
Install Sample Test Packs

In this exercise, you will install sample test packs for the lab.

Tasks	Specific instructions
1. Prepare to install sample test packs.	▪ Log on to the domain as administrator.
2. Install sample test packs.	a. Open Windows Explorer. b. Browse to C:\MOC\2275\Labfiles\Lab08. c. Run the installation file.

Exercise 1
Create a Group Policy Object to Configure Automatic Updates

In this exercise, you will use Group Policy Management to create a Group Policy object to configure automatic updates for the client.

Tasks	Specific instructions
▪ Create an Automatic Updates GPO for your organizational unit.	**a.** Open Administrative Tools and start Group Policy Management.
	b. In Group Policy Management, expand **Forest: nwtraders.msft**, expand **Domains**, expand **nwtraders.msft**, expand **Locations**, and then expand *ComputerName* (where *ComputerName* is the name of your computer).
	c. Right-click *ComputerName*, select the option to create a new GPO link, and name it *ComputerName* **SUS Automatic Updates**.
	d. Right-click *ComputerName* **SUS Automatic Updates**, and then click **Edit**.
	e. Under **Computer Configuration**, expand **Administrative Templates**, expand **Windows Components**, and then open Windows Update.
	f. Open Configure Automatic Updates.
	g. Enable **Configure Automatic Updates**, and then go to the next setting.
	h. Enable the intranet Microsoft update service location.
	i. Set the intranet update service for detecting updates by typing **http://***ComputerName* (where *ComputerName* is the name of your computer).
	j. In the **Set the intranet statistics server** box, type **http://***ComputerName* (where *ComputerName* is the name of your computer).
	k. Apply the settings and then close all windows.

Exercise 2
Prepare Sample Software Update Packages for Your Clients

In this exercise, you will prepare sample software update packages for your clients.

Tasks	Specific instructions
▪ Prepare sample software update packages for your clients.	a. Open a **Run** dialog box, and type **http://localhost/SUSAdmin**
	b. On the Microsoft Software Update Services Web page, click **Set options**.
	c. Under **Select which server to synchronize content from**, select **Synchronize from a local Software Update Services server**.
	d. In the **Synchronize from a local Software Update Services server** box, type **http://**_ComputerName_**/TestContents** as the Software Update Services server.
	e. Click **Apply**, and then click **OK**.
	f. Click **Synchronize server**, and then click **Synchronize now**.
	g. Click **OK** to close the message box.
	h. Select and approve the first two updates.
	i. Accept the License Agreement.
	j. A message box appears informing you that the updates are available for distribution to your clients.

Exercise 3
Verify the Updates are Available to the Clients

In this exercise, you will verify that the updates are available for the clients.

Tasks	Specific instructions
■ Verify that the updates are available for the clients.	a. Wait for five minutes, and then click the new updates icon in the lower right hand corner.
	b. In the **Automatic Updates** dialog box, click **Details**.
	c. Read the detail information, close all windows, and then log off.

Course Evaluation

Your evaluation of this course will help Microsoft understand the quality of your learning experience.

To complete a course evaluation, go to http://www.CourseSurvey.com.

Microsoft will keep your evaluation strictly confidential and will use your responses to improve your future learning experience.

Microsoft Windows Server 2003
Enterprise Edition 180-Day Evaluation

The software included in this kit is intended for evaluation and deployment planning purposes only. If you plan to install the software on your primary machine, it is recommended that you back up your existing data prior to installation.

System requirements

To use Microsoft Windows Server 2003 Enterprise Edition, you need:

- Computer with 550 MHz or higher processor clock speed recommended; 133 MHz minimum required; Intel Pentium/Celeron family, or AMD K6/Athlon/Duron family, or compatible processor (Windows Server 2003 Enterprise Edition supports up to eight CPUs on one server)

- 256 MB of RAM or higher recommended; 128 MB minimum required (maximum 32 GB of RAM)

- 1.25 to 2 GB of available hard-disk space*

- CD-ROM or DVD-ROM drive

- Super VGA (800 · 600) or higher-resolution monitor recommended; VGA or hardware that supports console redirection required

- Keyboard and Microsoft Mouse or compatible pointing device, or hardware that supports console redirection

Additional items or services required to use certain Windows Server 2003 Enterprise Edition features:

- For Internet access:
  - Some Internet functionality may require Internet access, a Microsoft Passport account, and payment of a separate fee to a service provider; local and/or long-distance telephone toll charges may apply
  - High-speed modem or broadband Internet connection

- For networking:
  - Network adapter appropriate for the type of local-area, wide-area, wireless, or home network to which you wish to connect, and access to an appropriate network infrastructure; access to third-party networks may require additional charges

Note: To ensure that your applications and hardware are Windows Server 2003–ready, be sure to visit **www.microsoft.com/windowsserver2003**.

* Actual requirements will vary based on your system configuration and the applications and features you choose to install. Additional available hard-disk space may be required if you are installing over a network. For more information, please see **www.microsoft.com/windowsserver2003**.

Uninstall instructions

This time-limited release of Microsoft Windows Server 2003 Enterprise Edition will expire 180 days after installation. If you decide to discontinue the use of this software, you will need to reinstall your original operating system. You may need to reformat your drive.

Notes

Notes

Notes

Notes

Notes

Notes

MSM2273ACP/C90-02045